LIBERTY OR DEATH

Patrick French is a writer and historian, born in England in 1966. He is the author of *Younghusband: The Last Great Imperial Adventurer* ('Beautifully written, wise, balanced, fair, funny and above all extremely original' William Dalrymple), which won the Somerset Maugham Award and the Royal Society of Literature W. H. Heinemann Prize, *Liberty or Death: India's Journey to Independence and Division* ('French is the most impressive Western historian of modern India currently at work' *Herald*), which won the *Sunday Times* Young Writer of the Year Award, *Tibet, Tibet: A Personal History of a Lost Land* ('Compassionate . . . compelling and brilliant . . . far and away the best book on Tibet I have read' *Daily Telegraph*) and, *The World Is What It Is: The Authorized Biography of V. S. Naipaul* ('One of the most gripping biographies I've ever read' Hilary Spurling), which won the National Book Critics Circle Award and the Hawthornden Prize. His most recent book is *India: A Portrait* (Allen Lane, 2011).

Books by Patrick French

Younghusband: The Last Great Imperial Adventurer

The Life of Henry Norman

Liberty or Death: India's Journey to Independence and Division

Tibet, Tibet: A Personal History of a Lost Land

The World Is What It Is: The Authorized Biography of V. S. Naipaul

India: A Portrait

PATRICK FRENCH

Liberty or Death

India's Journey
to Independence and Division

PENGUIN BOOKS

PENGUIN BOOKS

Published by the Penguin Group
Penguin Books Ltd, 80 Strand, London WC2R ORL, England
Penguin Group (USA) Inc., 375 Hudson Street, New York, New York 10014, USA
Penguin Group (Canada), 90 Eglinton Avenue East, Suite 700, Toronto, Ontario, Canada M4P 2Y3
(a division of Pearson Penguin Canada Inc.)
Penguin Ireland, 25 St Stephen's Green, Dublin 2, Ireland (a division of Penguin Books Ltd)
Penguin Group (Australia), 250 Camberwell Road, Camberwell, Victoria 3124, Australia
(a division of Pearson Australia Group Pty Ltd)
Penguin Books India Pvt Ltd, 11 Community Centre, Panchsheel Park, New Delhi – 110 017, India
Penguin Group (NZ), 67 Apollo Drive, Rosedale, North Shore 0632, New Zealand
(a division of Pearson New Zealand Ltd)
Penguin Books (South Africa) (Pty) Ltd, 24 Sturdee Avenue, Rosebank, Johannesburg 2196, South Africa
Penguin Books Ltd, Registered Offices: 80 Strand, London WC2R ORL, England

www.penguin.com

First published in Great Britain by HarperCollins Publishers 1997
Published in Penguin Books 2011

002

Copyright © Patrick French, 1997
Maps by John Gilkes
Artwork by Abigail Ashton-Johnson

Printed in England by Clays Ltd, St Ives plc

978-0-241-95040-1

www.greenpenguin.co.uk

Penguin Books is committed to a sustainable
future for our business, our readers and our planet.
This book is made from Forest Stewardship
Council™ certified paper.

ALWAYS LEARNING   **PEARSON**

This book is dedicated to the memory of my mother
Lavinia French

CONTENTS

PART III The Beginning of History

ILLUSTRATIONS

The spy chief Philip Vickery as a young police officer at the Delhi *durbar* of
1911. (*Oriental and India Office Collections of the British Library*)

The Mahatma strides out: Mohandas Gandhi and his entourage on the epic
salt march of 1930. (*Gandhi Smarak Sangrahalaya*)

'Hopie' and Doreen. Their Excellencies the Marquess and Marchioness of
Linlithgow during a garden party at Viceroy's House in New Delhi.
(*John Glendevon,* The Viceroy at Bay)

Subhas Chandra Bose after being elected as President of Congress at
Haripura in 1938. (*Sunil Janah*)

Stafford Cripps, Abul Kalam Azad and Jawaharlal Nehru outside the
Secretariat of the Government of India in New Delhi in 1942.
(*R.R. Bharadwaj*)

'An Indian maid with bangles on . . .': Leo Amery, Ramaswami Mudaliar,
the Jam Saheb and Winston Churchill in the garden at 10 Downing
Street. (*Topix*)

Quit India! A photograph taken for the Communist Party newspaper
People's War of burning police vehicles in a Calcutta street. (*Sunil Janah*)

'Two obstinate old men': M.A. Jinnah and M.K. Gandhi feign friendship
after their abortive talks in Bombay in 1944. (*Sunil Janah*)

Simla, 1945. The Viceroy Lord Wavell greets Sir Khizar Hyat Khan Tiwana,
watched by Dr Khan Sahib. (*Penderel Moon (ed.),* Wavell: The Viceroy's
Journal)

Simla, 1945. A newly released Pant, a nervous Jinnah, an inscrutable
Rajagopalachari, the Assamese leader Mohammad Saadulla, and a tense
Azad. (*Penderel Moon (ed.),* Wavell: The Viceroy's Journal)

Simla, 1945. The Sikh leader Master Tara Singh on his way to the
conference. (*Penderel Moon (ed.),* Wavell: The Viceroy's Journal)

'Other Men's Flowers': Archie Wavell after being garlanded at the Lingaraj
Mandir in Bhubaneswar, Orissa. (*Penderel Moon (ed.),* Wavell: The
Viceroy's Journal)

Jawaharlal Nehru addressing a meeting of the All-India Congress
Committee. (*Sunil Janah*)

Mohandas Gandhi. (*Gandhi Smarak Sangrahalaya*)

A rare photograph showing Chakravarti Rajagopalachari's eyes. (*Sunil Janah*)

The Congress politician Sarojini Naidu. (*Sunil Janah*)

Organizers of political rallies such as this one in Bengal were required to
  provide a table and chair for the ubiquitous Special Branch shorthand
  reporter. (*Sunil Janah*)
The dapper Muslim League leaders Liaquat Ali Khan and Mohammad Ali
  Jinnah during emergency talks at Downing Street in December 1946.
  (*Penderel Moon (ed.)*, Wavell: The Viceroy's Journal)
The end-game: Archie Wavell and Freddie Pethick-Lawrence on their way to
  see the Prime Minister in December 1946. (Illustrated London News
  Picture Library)
Street painting of Netaji Subhas Chandra Bose dressed as the Supreme
  Commander of the Indian National Army.
Calcutta, 1946. A temporary moment of Hindu–Muslim unity. (*Sunil Janah*)
Vallabhbhai Patel. (*B. Krishna/Gandhi Memorial, Rajghat*)
'The momentum of our previous prestige': Mountbatten takes over the
  remains of British power from Wavell in March 1947. (Illustrated
  London News *Picture Library*)
Dickie Mountbatten and Mohandas Gandhi at their first meeting, 1 April
  1947. (*Associated Press*)
The founder of Pakistan, the Quaid-i-Azam Mohammad Ali Jinnah,
  portrayed as an Islamic hero by a street artist.
Street painting of Pakistan's first Prime Minister, Liaquat Ali Khan.
The back-seat driver: Sardar Patel and Pandit Nehru. (*B. Krishna/Homai
  Vyarawalla*)
V.P. Menon, the civil servant who formulated the plan under which British
  rule in India came to an end. (*PIB, New Delhi*)
The Prime Minister Pandit Jawaharlal Nehru with Lord and Lady
  Mountbatten on the day of India's independence. (*Associated Press*)
Muslim families from east Punjab in a refugee camp in Lahore. (*Charles Still
  Collection*)
Hindu families from east Bengal fleeing their village by boat. (*Sunil Janah*)
'The light has gone out': a man shields himself from the Calcutta sun on the
  morning after Mahatma Gandhi's murder. (*Sunil Janah*)
Looking 'inexpressibly sad and careworn', and surrounded by a crowd of
  nearly a million people, Pandit Nehru accompanies his mentor's corpse
  to its cremation. (*Gandhi Smarak Sangrahalaya*)

MAPS

GLOSSARY

badmash – a villain

bania – a Hindu from the shopkeeper or merchant caste

bhajan – a Hindu holy song

Bharat – the official Indian name for India, sometimes used with Hindu nationalist overtones

brahmacharya – celibacy

brahmin – a Hindu from the highest, originally priestly, caste

chappal – a sandal

chowkidar – a guard or watchman

chunni – a scarf worn by a woman

churidar – wrinkled pajama trousers worn by men, baggy at the top and tight at the ankle

dacoit – a bandit

dalit – a Hindu outside the caste system, sometimes referred to as an untouchable

dhaba – a roadside eating place

dharma – religious duty

dhoti – a loincloth worn by men

durbar – a ceremonial court assembly

fatwa – a decree issued by a Muslim religious leader

ghazal – an Urdu poem, usually with romantic overtones

goonda – a potentially violent criminal hooligan

gurdwara – a Sikh temple

harijan – Mohandas Gandhi's term for a *dalit*, literally meaning a child of god

hartal – a total strike, involving closure of shops

iftar – the meal eaten at sunset during *Ramazan*, and the gifts given to poor Muslims at such a time

jatha – an organized band or squad

ji – a suffix added to names to indicate reverence and affection

jihad – a Muslim religious struggle or crusade

khadi – hand-woven cloth

kurta – a loose, long shirt

lathi – a sturdy stick, usually made of bamboo

lungi – a cloth coming down to the knees, usually worn only by Muslim men

maharajah – a Hindu or Sikh princely ruler

Marwari – a member of a prosperous merchant community originating in Marwar in Rajputana, but now spread throughout India

masjid – a mosque

millat – the Muslim religious community, occasionally used to denote Muslims in general

mohajir – a migrating Muslim, usually used to denote an Urdu-speaker who moved to Pakistan in 1947

mohalla – the residential parts of a town or city

mullah – a Muslim teacher or reader of the Quran, and traditionally an expert in Islamic law

Mussulman – a Muslim

namaz – Muslim prayers

nawab – the Muslim equivalent of a *maharajah*, originally used to denote a senior official in the Mughal Empire

nawabzada – the son of a *nawab*

Parsi – a member of a prosperous Zoroastrian community, originating in Persia, whose members are often found on India's west coast

patel – a farmer

pir – a Muslim spiritual guide

puja – a Hindu ceremony

qaum – an Islamic term meaning people, nation or community

Ramazan – the Muslim month of fasting or purification

sadhu – a Hindu holy man

sanyasi – a Hindu who has renounced everyday life to follow a religious vocation

satyagraha – the force of truth, meaning non-violent resistance

sharia – Islamic law

sherwani – a long, formal coat

swadeshi – the use of indigenously-made materials, especially *khadi*

swaraj – self-rule

taluqdar – a landlord in the United Provinces

tonga – a horse-drawn cart

zamindar – a landlord

ACKNOWLEDGEMENTS

I would like to thank the following people for their help. In Bangladesh: Parveen Ahmed, Syed Hessamuddin Ahmed, Madhab Chandra Banik, Uday Hassan, Addu Karim, Iskander Karim, Sharjeel Karim, Nasim Khan of the SPGRC, Rebecca Ladbury, K.G. Mustafa, Ataus Samad, Mir Shawkat Ali and Valerie Taylor. In India: Javed Abdulla, Ameena Ahuja, Ratan Bhandari, Jonathon Bond, Urvashi Butalia, Manorma Dewan, Rajmohan Gandhi, Mushirul Hasan, Rosey Hurst, Ashok Row Kavi, Raj Khanna, Rani Khanna, Pradip Krishen, Sanjana Malhotra, Nirmal Mangat Rai, K.B. Mehta, Pankaj Mishra, Kabir Nath, the Nawab of Palanpur, Prabubhai Patel, Indrasingh Rawat, Arundhati Roy, Nayantara Sahgal, Robinder Sarin, Karan Singh, Marn Singh, Patwant Singh, Phul Singh, Narinder Singh Soch, Jigme Tashi, Tarun Tejpal, D.R. Trivedi of the Gandhi Smarak Sangrahalaya, Madhukar Upadhayay, Nirmal Verma and Mohammed Yunus. In Pakistan: Zafar Abbas, Mumtaz Ahmed Khan, Tahira Mazhar Ali, Karamat Ali Khan of the Tahrike Karkanan Pakistan, Ejaz Azim, Tazeen Faridi, Phil Goodwin, Tahirah Hamid, Anwar Ahmed Hanafi, Faez Isa, Saida Isa, I.A. Rahman, Ahmed Rashid, Piari Rashid, Hashim Raza, and Z.H. Zaidi of the Quaid-i-Azam Papers Project.

Elsewhere: Akbar Ahmed, Alan Campbell-Johnson, Willy Dalrymple, Roger Ellis, Aileen Fisher Rowe, Katherine Frank, Hugh French, Maurice French, Francis Harrison, Lady Pamela Hicks, H.V. Hodson, Peter Hopkirk, Christopher Hurst, Sunil Janah, Alastair Lamb, Dick Lamb, Tessa Lambourne, Sir Ronald Lindsay, Sam Miller, Diana Newman, Francesca Orsini, Sophia Plowden, Emma Reeves, Sir Robert Rhodes James, Ritu Sarin, Rosemary Satterthwaite, Sir Ian Scott, James Symington, Charles Vyvyan, Liz Vyvyan and Willa Walker. I would also like to thank David Blake, Tony Farrington and Jill Geber of the Oriental and India Office Collections of the British Library, Chris Carnaghan of the Indian Police Retired Association, Billy Dove of the Attlee Foundation, Helen Ellis, Caroline Hotblack and Annie Robertson of HarperCollins, Brenda Levenson of Foreign Office Declassification Services, the staffs of the British Library, the National Archives of India, the School of Oriental and African Studies Library, the Wavell Estate and Wiltshire Library Services. My most fervent thanks are reserved for Michael Fishwick, David Godwin and Robert Lacey, for their support and tolerance throughout the creation of *Liberty or Death*.

There is a character in Barbara Trapido's novel *Brother of the More Famous Jack* who observes that other men begin their books by thanking their wives for acting as 'high-grade editorial assistants'. His, on the other hand, rarely reads books, and when she does they are not written by him. I am in the same position, so instead I will thank Abigail Ashton-Johnson for her originality, her love and her certainty, none of which I would change for the world.

PATRICK FRENCH

Wiltshire, April 1997

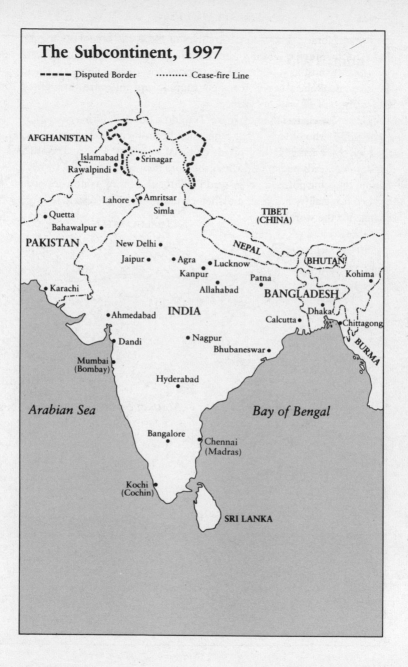

The Subcontinent, 1997

----- Disputed Border .... Cease-fire Line

AFGHANISTAN

Islamabad • Srinagar
Rawalpindi •

Lahore • • Amritsar
Simla

• Quetta
Bahawalpur •

TIBET
(CHINA)

PAKISTAN

New Delhi •

NEPAL

Jaipur • • Agra
Kanpur • Lucknow

BHUTAN

Patna

Kohima

• Karachi

Allahabad

BANGLADESH

INDIA

• Ahmedabad

Dhaka

Calcutta •

Chittagong

• Dandi

• Nagpur

BURMA

Mumbai
(Bombay)

Bhubaneswar •

Hyderabad
•

Arabian Sea

Bay of Bengal

Bangalore
•

Chennai
(Madras)

Kochi
(Cochin) •

SRI LANKA

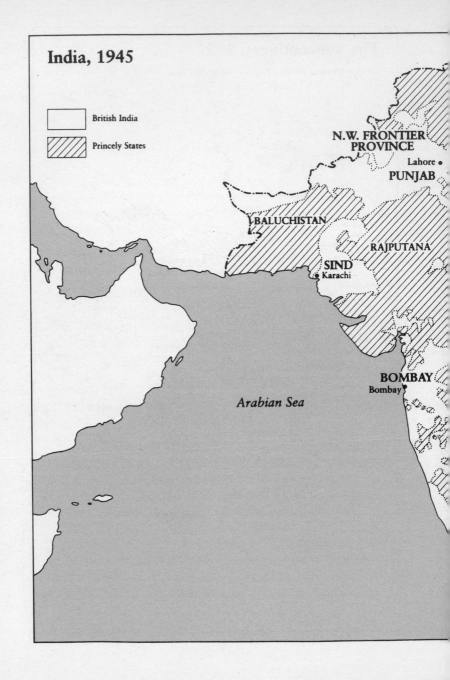

India, 1945

British India

Princely States

N.W. FRONTIER PROVINCE

Lahore •

PUNJAB

BALUCHISTAN

RAJPUTANA

SIND

Karachi •

BOMBAY

Bombay •

Arabian Sea

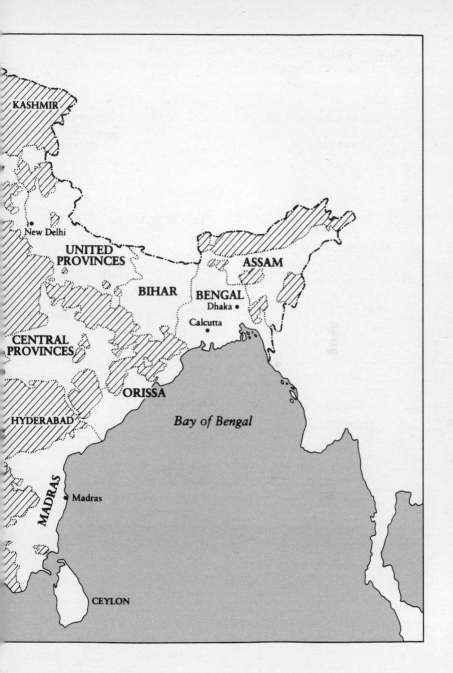

INTRODUCTION

In March 1966, a couple of months before I was born, the Prime Minister Harold Wilson announced plans to publish sets of official documents from important periods in Britain's foreign relations. This led to the arrival of the twelve, magisterial volumes of *Constitutional Relations Between Britain and India: The Transfer of Power 1942–7*, the final one appearing in 1983. Trawling through literally millions of pieces of paper, a group of historians built up a remarkably detailed documentary collage of the last six years of British rule in India, showing the way in which policy was conceived, formulated and implemented. An Indian newspaper described these books as 'a kind of interpretive gospel, a sutra series', while one reader made the fair observation that they had 'a coherence so effective that the volumes afford probably the most complete evidence published for the decision-making process in government anywhere'.[1]

As I worked my way through *The Transfer of Power* while researching this book, it became clear that one class of document had been excluded: intelligence. This was an important omission, since like all unelected regimes, the British-controlled Government of India was forced to rely heavily on surveillance and covertly obtained information in order to retain supremacy. When I examined the archives of the India Office (the British government department which gave the Viceroy his orders), I found that certain important categories of 'Public and Judicial' documents had been judiciously withheld from the public. I asked the declassification unit of the Foreign Office to review the status of these files, and after more than a year of prodding, they finally agreed to release all but a handful of them.

The consequence appeared in ninety-two battered, bottle-green boxes, with brass catches and flaking cream labels marked 'Note by Security Service 1943: Communist Survey of India', or 'S.C. Bose', or 'Censorship: H.H. The Pope and Apostolic Delegates'. These were the archives of Indian Political Intelligence, or IPI, which was founded shortly before the outbreak of the First World War and survived until independence in 1947. Its existence had been mentioned to me by various elderly members of the Indian Civil Service, usually in hushed tones, but I had never realized how significant and wide-ranging an operation it had been. Although it was always a fairly small organization, it was apparent that IPI had played a central role in the attempted maintenance of British dominion over the Indian Empire.

After a few hours in the company of the ninety-two boxes, I gave them my own collective name. It was *The Loss of Control*, the correlative to *The Transfer of Power*. From the mid-1930s onwards, they evoked a consistent theme of fragility, as if successive administrations had been surprised at having been able to bluff their way through another few years. *The Transfer of Power* and *The Loss of Control* altered my view of the lead-up to Indian independence considerably, as I came to realize that the British decision to quit had been based on neither altruism nor strategic planning. It was not the logical culmination of a policy of benign imperial stewardship, like a kindly parent allowing a child to ride its bicycle unassisted from the moment it learned to pedal. Nor was it the inevitable consequence of unquenchable socio-political forces, with the people of India rising up as one to drive the invaders into the sea. For many Indians, especially in the south, the deals sewn up by English-speakers in New Delhi in the 1940s were of distant importance.

Rather, the British left India because they lost control over crucial areas of the administration, and lacked the will and the financial or military ability to recover that control. The documentation of the last years of the Indian Empire provided an unexpected tale of confusion, human frailty and neglect, moving from the florid incompetence of Churchill's wartime India policy to the feeble indecision of Attlee's post-war government. Many of the key events of the 1940s were the result of chance, or even of error, and some of the most important decisions of the period were made on an almost random basis. Nor was there any inevitability about the fact that the Indian Empire was dissected and partitioned, leaving a pair of accidental wings called East and West Pakistan sprouting from a truncated India's shoulders.

Yet few moments in modern history have had a more lasting impact on so many people. As the writer and politician André Malraux suggested, Britain's decision to get out of India was 'the most significant fact of the century'.[2] It removed three-quarters of King George VI's subjects overnight, reduced Britain to a 'third rate power', and proved that the practice of European imperialism was no longer sustainable.

The nature of the political settlement in 1947 had a calamitous impact on the subcontinent, leading to the reciprocal genocide and displacement of millions of Hindus, Muslims and Sikhs, three Indo–Pakistan wars, the blood-drenched creation of Bangladesh, and the long-term limitation of the region's global influence. Although more than a fifth of the world's population presently lives in the territory of Britain's former Indian Empire, continued internal conflict has left South Asia with little cohesiveness and minimal international clout. Nearly half of all Pakistani government expenditure still goes on the cold war with India, focused on the running sore of Kashmir.

In order to explain how the present situation came about, I have concentrated on the developing conflict between Congress, the Government of India and the Muslim League, which led to the transfer of power on the night of 14–15 August 1947. Inevitably for a book on this subject, the story converges on Nehru's 'midnight hour', and passes through it before refracting out towards the present. I have in many cases excluded events, ideas and structures (Maulana Maudoodi's Jamaat-i-Islami, for instance, or Lord Linlithgow's plans for princely federation) which at the time looked significant, but which ultimately proved irrelevant. Instead I have mainly tended to emphasize specific and symbolic aspects of the history which may have seemed unimportant at the time, but which came to have a marked bearing on the final settlement. I have also concentrated on the character and personality of certain essential individuals – namely Mohandas Gandhi, Mohammad Ali Jinnah, Vallabhbhai Patel, Winston Churchill and Lords Wavell and Mountbatten – who through the interplay of events were propelled into vital roles, and so were able to remould Asia and change the lives of millions.

I was conscious, however, that by approaching the past through documents and dignitaries, I risked writing bureaucrat's history rather than living, human history. So I have included accounts of my own encounters, travels and interviews with people in India, Pakistan and Bangladesh, not because they were the makers of political history, but because it is individuals and families who are affected by the choices that politicians make. They are the ones who win, or lose.

In his autobiography, Jawaharlal Nehru wrote: 'Nurtured from childhood in the widespread belief that the East is a mysterious place, and in its bazaars and narrow lanes secret conspiracies are being continually hatched, the Englishman can seldom think straight on matters relating to these lands of supposed mystery. He never makes an attempt to understand that somewhat obvious and very unmysterious person the Easterner.'[3] As the most gracefully bi-cultural of India's leaders, Nehru was certainly in a position to know. Although in communal terms I probably count as Irish rather than English, I have taken notice of his point, and tried to unwrap the relevant Eastern heroes from the cotton wool in which they have been swaddled for so long. My ambition was to deal with them and their conduct as frankly and directly as I could.

While the substantial humiliation and cultural trauma experienced by the recipients of colonialism should not be discounted – as one person put it to me: 'How would you behave if a whole lot of Indians took over your country and forced you to wear *dhoti-kurta* and speak Hindi and eat with your hands?' – it is true that there has been a failure to 'think straight' about the reasons behind the actions of the protagonists of Indian independence. Although the subcontinent may at first sight seem a haphazard and incomprehensible place to an outsider, after a time it reveals itself to be a complex and highly structured society. The leading Indian politicians of the 1940s knew exactly what they were doing, and in general showed greater competence than their opponents in London.

For many years, British books on India formed a small but precise genre of their own, involving the use of phrases like 'the heady smell of spices and woodsmoke', and descriptive evocations of cruel maharajahs, sly holymen, rebellious tribesmen and the heat of the Deccan, together with occasional appearances by tigers, missionaries, memsahibs, gymkhanas, Kipling and tiffin. This extended into histories of the edifice lately termed 'the Raj', and although it is now rare to find imperial dogma articulated so openly, a nostalgic subtext still hovers beneath the pages of many books, like a loyal native bearer lurking discreetly under the verandah of one of M.M. Kaye's bungalows.

The subcontinental response to this British-imagined India has been richly impressive in the realms of fiction, but generally flimsy when it comes to historical or biographical writing. Too often, a narrow, obfuscatory nationalism has been the only way of facing the region's history, enabling the father of the nation – be he Jinnah or Gandhi – to emerge dressed in a spotless suit, *sherwani* or *dhoti*. There has been a consistent failure to recognize or acknowledge the real role of Indian politicians in what happened in the 1930s and forties. Although personally I believe that British rule in India had a primarily destructive effect, it does not follow that the ousters of the imperialists were therefore blameless, or that they do not share responsibility for what took place. Even at its height, the European presence in the subcontinent never amounted to more than 0.05 per cent of the total population. British rule in India was always a joint venture, which depended heavily on collaboration.

While it lasted, it was an effective but shallow way of governing, which may explain why all that remains of the Indian Empire half a century on is a handful of fine buildings, a stagnant legal system and bureaucracy, and a mutated language. Even in 1964, V.S. Naipaul could write: 'They left no noble monuments behind and no religion save a concept of Englishness as a desirable code of behaviour – of chivalry, it might be described, tempered by legalism'.[4]

The British did not, as is often claimed, give India democracy, except in a primitive form at the level of provincial government. The decision to grant a universal franchise to the people of India (and from time to time to the people of Bangladesh and Pakistan) was made by the relevant elites after independence. The most durable legacy of the Indo–British encounter can be found in the British Isles, in the form of two million citizens of subcontinental descent – 'the Asian community', as politicians say, although whether a Bengali Muslim and a Gujarati Hindu really belong to the same community must be open to question.

The story of India's journey to independence and division remains a contentious and hugely sensitive area of history. In Britain it is viewed as an embarrassment, in Bangladesh as a betrayal, in India as a mixed blessing, and in Pakistan as a matter too tender even to be seriously discussed. Its ambiguity is summed up in Patrick Henry's phrase from the American War of Independence, 'Give me liberty, or give me death,' which was borrowed and reworked by Indian freedom fighters. As a slogan, 'Liberty or death' had infinite possibilities. I found it was used to promote entirely contradictory concepts: wartime civil disobedience during the Quit India movement; fighting on the side of the British against the Germans; and fighting on the side of the Japanese against the British.[5] It was later appropriated by the Muslim League politician Liaquat Ali Khan, who proclaimed: 'Pakistan or death.'[6] In 1947, the people of Britain's Indian Empire were left with both liberty and death, in an enduring and tragic combination.

PART I

The Quest for Freedom

'I was born to destroy this evil government'

MOHANDAS GANDHI, 1930

ONE

Spies and Bomb-Throwers

In May 1910, the stout, bronchial, philandering Edward VII died of pneumonia. His unspectacular reign had only begun in his sixtieth year when, as a result of the death of his mother Queen Victoria, he had been drawn from among the ranks of the unemployed to become King. During his nine years on the throne he had snorted at Lloyd George's budget proposals, made substantial amounts of money with the assistance of the financier Sir Ernest Cassel, and sought succour and comfort from his mistress, Alice Keppel. The bluff monarch used her as a tactful and effective conduit to his ministers, some of whom he found 'deplorably common'. After his death, Edward was replaced as King Emperor by his rather straitlaced son George, a stiff, dull, unimaginative character with a tobacco-stained beard and a sober approach to public duties.

King George V's coronation in 1911 was a spectacular propaganda coup, a myriad of Indian princes and imperial prime ministers filling Westminster Abbey for the seven-hour ceremony. His role as ruler of the British Empire was re-emphasized later that year, when he and Queen Mary sailed across the Arabian Sea and he became the first reigning British monarch to visit India. This was the age of high imperialism, when brute force was to an extent forsaken in favour of pomp as a means of asserting authority. The strategy succeeded in a limited way, although the British were perhaps more impressed by it than their subjects.

Huge celebrations and parades were arranged for the royal visit. In an amazing feat of organization, a giant *durbar* (see glossary) was held in Delhi, involving officials and potentates from all over India, numerous tented camps and even the laying of a light railway system with sixteen stations. Security was tight, and a twenty-one-year-old Irish Protestant called Philip Vickery, freshly commissioned into the Indian Police, was given the awesome job of guarding the King Emperor's cream 'bedroom tent' every night.

New tables of precedence were printed, cinematographic photographers appointed, maps of the various miniature tented cities prepared, a polo ground dusted down, crowds brought in by train from the Punjab to cheer, and a photograph of the new ruler distributed to every village in India. Elaborate processions took place, the five-year-old Nawab of Bahawalpur riding past on a camel, saluting the monarch with a short sword. A problem arose when the Maharajah Gaekwar of Baroda arrived at a presentation wearing full court dress and priceless jewels, and then proceeded to strip down until he wore only 'the ordinary white linen everyday dress of a Mahratta'. At this point, he was observed to make 'a very inadequate obeisance' to the King.

As for His Majesty, he mounted a white horse and rode out to meet the people, followed by the Viceroy, Lord Hardinge. George V had refused to sit on an elephant, and chosen to wear an unremarkable grey-banded 'Curzon' topee rather than a crown, so few people realized who he was. He tried making 'salaams' at the crowd, which helped a little. 'H.M. told me,' wrote Hardinge, 'that he was disappointed at his non-recognition by the people.'[1] Hardinge, who had been a friend of the rumbustious Edward VII and thought Mrs Keppel an 'excellent influence' on him, seems from his memoirs to have been unimpressed by his new sovereign.

Matters improved a little the following day when the King and Queen went to the Red Fort, Delhi's most significant edifice. There they donned their jewels, including a new crown, which had been conveyed to India specially for the occasion, and 'kindly consented to show themselves to the thousands of natives', presumably in imitation of Shah Jehan.[2] King George's ADCs, trussed up in their regimentals, must have looked a little less exciting than the half-naked eunuchs who used to accompany the Mughal emperor to his public audiences at the same venue three centuries earlier. Still, George V made an announcement which may have been remarkable enough for the comparison to be ignored. It was sufficiently important that not even Queen Mary had been told of it in advance: the Government of India was to be shifted from Calcutta to Delhi, where a magnificent new city would be built.

'Does India exist?' wondered Salman Rushdie in 1987. 'If it doesn't, what's keeping Pakistan and Bangladesh apart?'[3]

The idea of India, or at least of *Bharat* or *Mahabharat* (the Sanskrit term for India, or Great India), has always been locked into the cultural identity and oral history of its inhabitants. For four millennia its boundaries have altered and mutated. From the inside, or from a distance, India appears sprawling, inclusive and plural, a land of infinite variety: how, ask the insiders, could the people of its border regions wish to be attached to anybody else? From its frontiers, it looks hulking, monolithic and over-assertive: how, ask the outsiders, can its brutalities and contradictions be so readily ignored by its own people? Like China and the United States, India seems the centre of the universe when you are there, and a monolith when you are not.

The shape of Britain's Indian Empire can be loosely linked to ancient times. The concept of India stretches out from the Harappa civilization, centred around the Indus river in the Punjab, which existed over two thousand years before the birth of Jesus Christ, and passes through the Mauryan Empire under King Ashoka in the third century BC, which covered the whole subcontinent except the southern tip. In 997 AD, Indian society – or Hindu society as it would come to be seen by some in retrospect – was tempered dramatically for 950 years by successive invasions and occupations. The territory that academics now call 'South Asia' was given a name by Arab and Persian outsiders: Hind, or Hindustan, the land beyond the Indus river.

997 was the year in which Mahmud of Ghazni swept down from Afghanistan, being the first of the Islamic invaders of Bharat who now inhabit the demonology of Hindu nationalism. However, as Jawaharlal Nehru pointed out to his more communally-minded colleagues, Mahmud of Ghazni was a warrior first, and a Muslim second. The sultans of Delhi established themselves, quelling the indigenous Rajputs and maintaining power across northern and parts of southern India with some degree of constancy until the final collapse of Mughal rule in 1856. Tamburlaine entered Delhi at the end of the fourteenth century, and his descendant Babur founded the Mughal dynasty with the aid of matchlock guns and the legendary blood-curdling horsemen of Central Asia. The Great Mughals enjoyed varying levels of popularity among their subjects. Akbar was revered in the late sixteenth century for the abolition of both cow slaughter and the *jizya* – the poll tax on non-

Muslims; Aurangzeb, who took the throne in 1658, expanded his empire ruthlessly.

Portuguese, French and Dutch merchants established their toehold on the coast of India during the sixteenth century. The British at first moved more slowly than their rivals, although once they got started their success was impressive. One of the earliest arrivals, Ralph Fitch, wrote a letter home in the 1580s which was to be echoed by many other young English travellers over the coming centuries. 'They have a very strange order among them – ' he reported, 'they worship a cow and esteem much of the cow's dung to paint the walls of their houses . . . They eat no flesh, but live by roots and rice and milk.'[4]

In the year 1600 these adventurers were granted a royal charter by Queen Elizabeth I, and began trading as best they could, the only difficulty being that they had few goods which appealed to the inhabitants of the Mughal Empire. During the next two centuries they developed their commercial power along the coast of India and into Bengal, and as the Mughal Empire crumbled, secured their own position, beating off French rivalry. Guided by Robert Clive, the gangsters of the East India Company began to expand under the cover of indigenous local rulers, to whom they offered 'protection' in exchange for revenue. This privatized imperialism during the period of 'Company Raj' represents European incursion into India at its most rapacious. In 1770, bled of its wealth by merchants and their agents, Bengal declined into a disastrous famine.

Three years later, Lord North's British government regulated the Company, bringing the major 'presidencies' of Bengal, Madras and Bombay under the authority of Bengal, whose governor now became Governor General. Twenty years later the *zamindari* system was brought in, whereby tax collectors in Bengal were given title to the land they administered, thus changing India's concept of land possession for ever. It meant that as debts developed, the ownership of land shifted to absentee landlords and urban bankers. Instead of a fluid, fluctuating system based on the power and patronage of a given ruler, the British brought India new institutions predicated on precise boundaries, laws and regulations. British control became impersonal, using local intermediaries as the link between its own authoritarian bureaucracy and the Indian people.

A new class of English-speaking Indians emerged, with at least a pragmatic degree of loyalty towards the dominant power. Their rulers derided them as '*babus*', or clerks, yet many of them came to use their knowledge of the British system as a means to undermine its authority. During the first part of the nineteenth century, the British territorial hold expanded through military conquest, extending into the Punjab and Sind. Land was also scooped up under the new 'heirs natural' law, whereby only a verifiable royal son could inherit a local ruler's kingdom.

In the 1850s telegraph wires were put up and railway tracks laid down, improving communications and strengthening the capacity for coast-to-coast administration substantially. In 1857 there was a widespread uprising against British rule, referred to generally as a 'mutiny', but caused by many factors other than the matter of the greasing of the cartridges for Hindu sepoys' guns with beef fat. The illegal annexation the previous year of the territory of the Nawab of Oudh – the area that became the main part of the United Provinces – was extremely damaging, especially to the Muslim perception of the British. The introduction of the Enlistment Act, under which Indian soldiers could be sent anywhere, even overseas (destroying their caste status if they were Hindus), also helped provoke the revolt. The uprising induced rapacious violence on all sides, while the vengeful reprisals that came in its aftermath destroyed whatever shallow mutual trust existed.

In 1858 the British government introduced major reforms, transferring the rights of the East India Company to Queen Victoria's headgear, the Crown. The responsibility of the Governor General was expanded, although his autonomy was restricted by the appointment of a Secretary of State for India in London, who retained ultimate power. The chain of command stretching from the House of Commons to an Indian village was complex, and varied hugely according to time and circumstance. The Viceroy not only represented the monarch, but also as Governor General was the head of the Government of India, which had demands and views of its own. Racial segregation grew, Europeans confining themselves to clubs and cantonments, and the army was strengthened with British troops. Efforts were made to ensure that Indian soldiers did not come from the part of the country in which they were serving – a tradition that continues to this day. The theory of 'martial races' was developed, the principle being that certain groups within India would naturally make loyal mercenaries, while others would not.[5]

A variation of the *zamindari* system was extended into some other parts of India, so that the *taluqdars*, or administrators, of Oudh could now become hereditary rulers of the lands where they collected taxes.

The Indian Civil Service or ICS was expanded. In 1854 recruitment had started through open public examination in London, although it was not until fifteen years later that the first Indian applicant succeeded, and he was soon disqualified on a technicality. There was however no legal colour bar in the ICS; it was simply that the system was skewed radically against Indians at every level.

The nature of British administration in India was formalized, and the annexation of territory ended. Small but important enclaves along the coast remained under Portuguese and French colonial rule. Existing indigenous potentates, whose kingdoms made up around a third of the land mass of the Indian subcontinent, were now cultivated as bulwarks against any future uprising, and their loyalty was secured through confirming or renegotiating their treaties with the East India Company.

Several of India's hereditary princes controlled thousands of square miles of land, while others only ruled a few hundred acres. Their lands were incorporated as 'Native States' within the British Indian Empire, and the rulers were left free to practise whatever form of autocracy they chose, providing they remained loyal to Queen Victoria, the fount from whom all power within the Empire theoretically flowed. The remaining two-thirds of the subcontinent, which became known as 'British India', was divided up into administrative provinces. Although the British government now had dominion over an Indian Empire, its powers of direct control were limited.

Lord Hardinge, despite his starchy appearance, was a rather liberal viceroy. His reversal of Lord Curzon's unpopular administrative partition of Bengal, which was announced at the Delhi *durbar* by King George V at the same time as the shift of India's capital, alienated British business interests. Hardinge also infuriated them by joining Mohandas Gandhi in protesting against the treatment of Indians in South Africa, and by overruling the hard-line Governor of the Punjab, Sir Michael O'Dwyer, by quashing the death sentence on twenty-four men who had been convicted of dacoity without the production of any hard evidence. This is not to suggest that Charlie Hardinge was entirely progressive. His opinion on the Maharajah of Idar ran as follows: 'He excelled as the best pig-sticker in India, but he had been trained to fight a boar on foot with only a knife in his hand, and when the boar charged he would jump aside, catch the boar by a hind leg as it passed and kill it with one blow of the knife ... He was truly "a white man" among Indians.'

Two days before Christmas 1912, a year after the King's visit to India, Hardinge alighted at Delhi railway station and clambered aboard an enormous elephant. Sitting in an elaborate silver howdah, he advanced slowly down Chandni Chowk, a thoroughfare of great symbolic significance. It had once been the finest boulevard and market of the Mughal Empire, only to be turned into a charnel ground in the aftermath of the 1857 revolt, when the victorious British hanged countless nawabs, rebels and rajas down the middle of it. Now it had been chosen as the processional route for the Viceroy, who had come to inaugurate the construction of Edwin Lutyens and Herbert Baker's new Delhi.

His Excellency had not got far when his helmet shot into the air, a bang was heard six miles away, and the servant holding the State Umbrella was blown to pieces. Hardinge subsequently remembered noticing some yellow powder on his elephant, and feeling 'as though somebody had hit me very hard in the back and poured boiling water over me'.[6] An unknown Indian had hurled a bomb at the living symbol of imperial power. One of the Viceregal eardrums burst, and it was to take many years for all the nails, screws and gramophone needles to work their way out of his body. An ADC quickly climbed up onto some wooden cases, and carried the Viceroy down from the howdah like a baby. He was taken to Viceregal Lodge, unconscious. The unsuccessful assassin was never caught, but afterwards a maharajah told Lord Hardinge that he was amazed the accompanying troops had not massacred the crowd in Chandni Chowk, as the Mughals would have done in their day.[7]

The beginning of the twentieth century had seen an upsurge in the use of strategic killing as a political tool. The President of the United States was murdered in 1901 by an anarchist, the Russian premier assassinated in 1911, and, crucially, the Archduke Franz Ferdinand shot dead in Sarajevo in 1914. The attack on the Viceroy Lord Hardinge was the high point of revolutionary terrorism by Indian nationalists. Within political circles there was considerable disagreement over the virtues of the use of violence, some people feeling that the destabilization of imperial structures was the surest route to liberty, others that the crassness of bomb-throwing provided the British with a good justification for using repressive measures. In the end, violence came to be rejected by most nationalists in favour of Gandhian passive resistance.

Most of the plots laid by Indian revolutionaries, both within India and abroad, were notoriously incompetent and poorly planned. There are many stories of explosions occurring too early or late, or of terrorists being arrested as a result of bragging about their crimes before committing them. Ultimately bomb-throwing proved notably less effective than non-violence in ridding India of British rule, so its perpetrators have tended to be ignored. However, the historian of imperial intelligence Richard Popplewell makes the point that the British authorities were able to defeat them 'only by developing a complex intelligence network on a global scale . . . it is misleading to regard the Indian revolutionary movement as powerless simply because it failed so completely in the end'.[8]

The notion that violent actions should be used as a means of ending British rule had flourished sporadically since 1857, and gained serious support around the turn of the century. In 1897, following celebrations in honour of the birth of the seventeenth-century Maratha warlord Shivaji, a British official was killed in Poona. In 1905 a group of Indian students had set up house in Highgate in London and began to publish a magazine called *The Indian Sociologist*, which preached a romanticized version of India's history and called on all patriots to rise against their oppressors. One of its founders was a brother of the poet and Congress activist Sarojini Naidu. The *Sociologist*'s line was that loyalty to Britain assumed disloyalty to India. The magazine was promptly banned, but copies made their way into India through French and Portuguese territories such as Pondicherry and Goa. Explosives and revolvers also arrived by this route, apparently dispatched from Paris, and some of the Highgate students took up military training.

India House, as the Highgate headquarters was named, soon became a centre for subversive activity, and links were established with Irish and Egyptian activists. Travelling fellowships were set up for Indians to come to London and 'study'. The director was Vinayak Savarkar, a fiery twenty-five-year-old man from Maharashtra who was later known as 'Veer', or 'warrior'. While in India he had studied Sanskrit and launched campaigns against the British. He set off for London to qualify as a barrister, fell in love with an English woman called Margaret Lawrence, and wrote a passionate, Hinducentric account of the events of 1857 under the title *The Indian War of Independence*. This was soon added to the viceregal equivalent of the Vatican's *Index Librorum Prohibitorum*, and it remained banned until 1947. When Mohandas Gandhi spent two nights at India House on a visit to Britain, and attended a subscription dinner of Indian militants as the guest of honour, the other speaker was Savarkar. Accounts of the event note that it was the revolutionary who attracted greater interest and enthusiasm than the conciliator.

As various violent outrages took place in India, the British authorities decided, probably incorrectly, that many of them were emanating from India House. Hearing that the police were onto him, Savarkar did a flit to Paris, only to be lured back to Victoria station, where he was promptly arrested and charged with the quaint crime of 'conspiring to deprive His Majesty the King of the Sovereignty of British India'. He avoided execution, but was sentenced to fifty years on the Andaman Islands below the Bay of Bengal, which were India's answer to Alcatraz. Savarkar jumped overboard at Marseilles and ran around the docks barefoot in striped pyjamas seeking asylum before being captured by his police escort and transported into exile. He became a national hero in India, and on his early release founded the hard-line Hindu Mahasabha, which was to be implicated in Gandhi's murder in 1948. Today he is an icon of India's Hindu nationalists.

In 1907, in response to plans to dissect Bengal and in recognition of the fiftieth anniversary of the 1857 revolt, an attempt was made to blow up the province's governor, Sir Andrew Fraser. It failed, but the explosion blew a huge crater in the track behind his train. The unremarkable Viceroy Lord Minto introduced repressive measures across India, and promulgated the Police Act in the Punjab. Two years later an explosive device was lobbed into his carriage, but both he and his wife survived. In the same year two attacks took place in London, their proximity to the heart of imperial power having an important psychological effect on the British government.

First, a pair of young Bengali radicals secured a meeting at the India Office with a senior official, only to slap him, rather flamboyantly, full in the face. Then Sir William Curzon Wyllie, the Political ADC to the Secretary of State for India Lord Morley, was shot dead on the steps of the Imperial Institute. During the subsequent trial, his Punjabi assassin pleaded a political defence on the grounds that he was a patriot and the British were occupying his country. He was hanged at Pentonville prison.

The Government of India's reaction to the killing of the Secretary of

State's closest adviser was sharp. As Morley himself suggested to the Viceroy, 'the ordinary square-toed English constable, even in the detective branch, would be rather clumsy in tracing your wily Asiatics'.[9] Superintendent John Wallinger, who was renowned as one of the most effective detectives in the Indian Police, was seconded to the India Office in London and made responsible for the personal security of top officials. 'W' as he was termed was 'charged to cooperate with the Home Security organizations here in detecting subversive activities among Indians' in the United Kingdom.[10]

Before 1904 the British authorities had no proper police intelligence system in India. To an extent this stemmed from complacency about the stability of their rule, but it was also the result of the lack of any comparable operations in London. The scale of the covert security and intelligence services in Britain today would have been unthinkable a hundred years ago, since during the nineteenth century the British had shown a temperamental aversion to professional intelligence-gathering. For instance, the Governor of the United Provinces was nervous that the Viceroy Lord Curzon's attempt to create a limited all-India police intelligence service might 'develop into a centralized secret Police Bureau such as exists in the Russian Empire'.[11] It was not until the First World War that information obtained by secretive means began to play an integral part in the formulation of British government policy.

Curzon was responsible for making substantial reforms to the Indian Police. In 1904 he created a Criminal Investigation Department or CID in each of the provinces of British India, and a central Department of Criminal Intelligence. The latter organization was based in Simla, the summer capital of British India. Initially it had only a small staff, including a fingerprint bureau, a photographic section and a graphologist, and was not permitted to establish a proper secret service, but only to employ informants on a casual basis. The Department of Criminal Intelligence was assisted where necessary by Special Branch and Military Intelligence, and most of its personnel were either British or Anglo-Indian, although a Muslim detective, Munshi Aziz-ud-Din, was made Assistant Deputy Director in 1906.

In 1911 the Director of Criminal Intelligence Sir Charles Cleveland made a bid to raise the prestige of his department by predicting that a 'hidden fire' of violent nationalism was set to sweep across India. He was to be proved right the following year, when Lord Hardinge was blown off his elephant. Ironically, Cleveland himself had to shoulder the blame, and his reputation within the Indian administration never recovered. Responsibility for investigating the attack was handed over to another eminent police officer, David Petrie, who later became the chief of MI5.

It was the Department of Criminal Intelligence that sent John Wallinger to London to set up a fledgling intelligence section within the India Office, with most of its practical surveillance work being done by British police officers. At first Scotland Yard objected to the presence of 'W' on their patch, and it took him some time to establish a secure position. In the years leading up to the First World War his organization was developed and expanded, and given the name of 'Indian Political Intelligence', or IPI. Wallinger, who was able to speak Marathi, Gujarati and Hindustani, proved so effective at infiltrating Indian groups in Britain and in Paris that his detractors soon fell silent.

In 1915 he was joined by a second high-flying Indian Police officer, who spoke French and German and was charged with expanding and developing the network. He was Philip Vickery, the young Irish man who had guarded the King Emperor's tent at the Delhi *durbar*. They were both given commissions in the British Army – Vickery as a lieutenant and Wallinger as a colonel – so that officially they could work as employees of Military Intelligence. Together they spread their operations across Europe into Italy and Switzerland, and Wallinger even managed to recruit the writer Somerset Maugham as a spy; he subsequently used his controller as the ineffectual 'R' in several short stories. Another of Wallinger's star agents was a Dr Condom, who had to flee Lake Geneva by motorboat when his cover was blown by the Germans. According to Popplewell, the covert battle for India was 'the only area of the intelligence history of the First World War in which human intelligence played a decisive and exclusive role'.[12]

Earlier in the same year a special committee had been set up in Whitehall to tackle the problem of Indian subversion, with representatives from the India Office, the Admiralty, MI5 (which at that time was still known as Section MO5g of the War Office), the Foreign Office and the Colonial Office. It was particularly concerned about covert German backing for Indian revolutionaries, as well as the risk of mutiny among the many Indian soldiers fighting in France. A special security and counter-espionage unit called MI5(g) was set up to focus on India, and by February 1917 it employed twenty-seven officers, of whom eight were Indian

Policemen. Given that MI5 had an entire staff of nineteen people at the outbreak of war, this was a considerable deployment, and one which reflects the paramount importance given to the maintenance of the security of the Indian Empire as part of the overall war effort.

The India-related work of the British security service was to be an incidental cause of its rapid growth, and many of the staff of both MI5 and Special Branch during the decades following the war were recruited from either the Indian Police or other colonial police forces. To the annoyance of the Government of India, London rather than Calcutta, Simla or Delhi was to remain the clearing-house for all intelligence relating to India right up until independence. This could create serious complications, with the Indian authorities at times being unaware of the ulterior motives of the geographers, journalists and plant hunters travelling along their northern borders.

It was not only in Europe that serious wartime challenges arose to British rule in India. Curzon's failed attempt to split Bengal had provoked an upsurge of nationalist protest, and the province had become the focus of both the constitutional and revolutionary faces of the freedom movement. As a baffled King George V once asked a new governor of the province, 'What is *wrong* with Bengal?'[13] Agitation became so intense that by late 1915 Sir Charles Cleveland felt he was 'losing ground week by week'. At one point there was a serious risk that the province would become ungovernable. A Defence of India Act was passed in 1915 which made repression easier, since it suspended legal remedies by permitting the authorities to arrest, detain and expel suspects without trial or stated cause. When the crackdown came it was swift and savage, coordinated by Charles Tegart, who ran the intelligence branch of the Bengal Police. Like many of the leading policemen in India, Tegart was an Irish Protestant with firm opinions on how to handle native disorder.

According to Sir Percival Griffiths's history of the British Indian Police, which goes by the curious title *To Guard My People*, Tegart was revered among British residents as a fearless genius. He had survived several assassination attempts, was rumoured to disguise himself as an old Bengali woman or a Sikh taxi-driver when visiting unlikely locations, and was said to have informers and secretive shadows all over Calcutta.

Indian accounts of the Bengali revolutionary movement record that he was ruthless in his methods, and renowned for using torture – ice, needles and beating – to obtain information. One Bengali politician remembers that Tegart 'went out of his way to try out methods of torture on the revolutionaries. He was very efficient, and it was reputed that he was trained at Scotland Yard and specially deputed for repressing the revolutionary movement.'[14] In his working notes for his book on the Indian Police, Griffiths has an admiring recollection from a colleague of the police chief, which never made it as far the published edition. It recalls that Tegart's favoured method of interrogation involved discharging a revolver several times over a suspect's head, and then pointing the gun into the man's face and asking the key question. As his entry in the *Dictionary of National Biography* decorously puts it: 'Even some who had sought his life became, after passing through his hands, his allies and helpers.'[15]

Further violent activity was sparked by the Easter Rising in Dublin in 1916, when armed Irish Republicans rose in revolt against the British, and revolutionaries in Bengal took up the slogan 'England's difficulty is Ireland's opportunity', applying it to their own situation. When a Bengali political prisoner died as a result of a hunger strike, a telegram arrived from the widow of a Sinn Fein 'martyr' saying that Ireland joined India in its grief, and adding, 'Freedom shall come.' Jawaharlal Nehru made the point in his autobiography that even among Congress moderates there was 'little sympathy with the British in spite of loud professions of loyalty . . . There was no love for Germany of course, only the desire to see our own rulers humbled. It was the weak and helpless man's idea of vicarious revenge.'[16]

A simultaneous serious threat was arising in Canada and North America. Veer Savarkar's role as public enemy number one had been taken by Lala Har Dayal, an Oxford-educated anarcho-syndicalist who operated out of California. At first he had taken little interest in Indian politics, preferring to foment world revolution, but after the attack on Lord Hardinge's elephant he became fired with nationalist zeal. He established links with Indians in Portland, Oregon, and gained the support of immigrant Punjabi labourers on the west coast of the United States. The group invented patriotic songs with lines like, 'People say the Singhs are no good/Cry aloud, let's kill the whites,' and started a free newspaper called *Ghadr*, or 'Revolt', exhorting their countrymen to revive their 'manliness'. They made much of the fact that a hundred thousand British soldiers could be knocked into the sea in a moment if India's three hundred million people rose against them.

The popular movement spread quickly, and Har Dayal was arrested, only to skip bail and escape. The Indian nationalist threat in North

America was initially tackled by an immigration official in Vancouver called William Hopkinson, but his career as a spy-master ended in 1914 when he was shot dead in the street by a Sikh revolutionary. The police back in India believed that Har Dayal had recruited thousands of overseas revolutionaries who were now ready, with the outbreak of war with Germany, to return home and overthrow British rule. During the course of 1914 a substantial number of Punjabis returning from Europe and the USA were either put under surveillance or arrested pre-emptively.

Despite this, some managed to form an alliance with Bengali revolutionaries, and made plans for an uprising, only to be betrayed by a police informer and arrested before the date of the proposed attack. Eighteen of the accused plotters were hanged, and over a hundred transported for life. This action caused grave resentment within the Punjab, which bubbled with vengeance over the coming years. In addition, German intelligence agents operating in the USA purchased a substantial volume of arms and ammunition, including several thousand rifles. The weapons were loaded on to a schooner called the *Annie Larsen*, which set off for a rendezvous with a larger boat that would deliver the cargo to Calcutta in time for Christmas 1915. There were various errors, and the weapons never reached their destination.[17]

After the assassination of Hopkinson, a more elaborate British spying operation known as MI1c was established in North America. It operated without the knowledge of the federal government, although it cooperated with the US law enforcement agencies. After the war it was closed down by the American government. This was a serious blow to the British intelligence community, but IPI were one step ahead, having already secretly recruited their own permanent 'contact' in the USA. In 1919 the contact was joined by his handler Philip Vickery, who remained in Canada and the USA for three years running an undeclared operation.[18]

Thus, on three fronts – Europe, North America and India itself – British rule over its Indian Empire suffered a severe test in the period 1907 to 1918. It was not a mass internal uprising or a fatal destabilization, but it was enough to offer a more serious challenge to the long-term maintenance of authority than at any time since 1857. The end of the First World War offered a fresh opportunity for British and Indians alike, with many people, including Gandhi, believing that political liberalization and conciliation was now a serious prospect. Instead, 1919 brought the Amritsar massacre.

Two Men from Gujarat

Mohandas Gandhi ('Mahatma' being an honorific title meaning 'great soul' which has supplanted his given name in many minds) was the most famous Indian since the Buddha, and the most influential political campaigner of the twentieth century. His message of truth, tolerance and peaceful resistance against injustice has been hailed as an inspiration by people ranging from Albert Einstein to the Dalai Lama. Perhaps the best-known image of Gandhi is the slight figure who attended a reception held by George V at Buckingham Palace, clad symbolically only in a shawl and *khadi dhoti*. When asked by reporters whether he had been appropriately dressed, he replied that His Majesty had been wearing enough for both of them.[1]

If Gandhi is your hero, it can be a deflating experience to read what he actually did and said at crucial points in India's political history. The authorized version of the Mahatma is very different from the real one. Far from being a wise and balanced saint, Gandhi was an emotionally troubled social activist and a ruthlessly sharp political negotiator. As India's Transport Minister Dr John Matthai said in 1947, the final failure to reach a satisfactory settlement with the Muslim League stemmed in part from the 'Gujarati mentality' of the Congress leadership – 'i.e. that of a trader driving a hard bargain'.[2]

The plaster Mahatma encapsulated in Richard Attenborough's 1982 film *Gandhi* is plainly inaccurate. As Salman Rushdie has written: 'To make *Gandhi* appeal to the Western market, he had to be sanctified and turned into Christ – an odd fate for a crafty Gujarati lawyer – and the history of one of the century's greatest revolutions had to be mangled.' The film leaves us with the message 'that the best way to gain your freedom is to line up, unarmed, and march towards your oppressors and permit them to club you to the ground; if you do this for long enough, you will embarrass them into going away.'[3] There were innumerable reasons for the British quitting India, but embarrassment was not one of them. This version of events, though, appeals not only to the Western market, but also within India, where the Congress hold on power during the decades succeeding independence has made the portrayal of a blameless and beatific father of the nation politically useful.

Gandhi remains the most baffling and inconsistent figure in the Indian freedom movement, a man who worshipped truth yet often had trouble identifying it, who shunned adulation yet seemed to do all he could to encourage it. Although he is perhaps the most documented person in human history, it is at times hard to establish his motivation, his thinking, or even his opinions. For instance, his launching of the Quit India movement in 1942, which can be seen as the single most important action of his life, remains shrouded in such mystery that even the most astute of his many biographers, Judith Brown, writes that it is 'almost impossible at this distance of time to understand how Gandhi's mind was working'.[4]

A close reading of his statements on a particular subject usually results not in a sense of illumination, but of obfuscation. He often changed his mind, and many of his pronouncements amount to mental springcleaning rather than an exposition of ideology. His opponents during his lifetime portrayed this as hypocrisy, but in fact there always seems to have been a sincerity to his actions. To British officials he was 'a twister', and his methods were simply devious: one provincial governor described him as being as 'cunning as a cartload of monkeys'. The befuddlement about his aims and motives, however, extended beyond Whitehall and New Delhi and into his own head. If in doubt about a suitable course of action, Gandhi would resort to tuning in to his often arbitrary 'inner voice', and expect others to listen to its dictates.

Although he never wrote a full-length book, Mohandas Gandhi's published sayings, speeches, articles and letters run to around thirty million words, and represent the work of an entire department of the Government of India. At present there are about five thousand works of what the writer Ved Mehta has termed 'Gandhiana', including nearly a thousand books published in Britain alone. They range from the voluminous *Collected Works* to wonders like *Inter-War Scandinavian Responses to the Mahatma*. Most of these follow the standard tenets of 'Gandhian hagiology', which Mehta observes 'is noted for its ornate redundancy, its petrified Victorian Indian-English, its grandiloquent claims, and its reverent lore'.[5]

Gandhi's famous *Autobiography*, which was first published as a series of articles in the 1920s, is indicative of his singularity. The book's themes are apparent from the chapter titles, which include 'The Canker of Untruth', 'A Sacrifice to Vegetarianism' and 'More Experiments in Dietetics'. It is an elusive book, and readers in search of an exposition of India's freedom movement will be disappointed. The *Autobiography* is a work of Victorian moral sermonizing, linked to the author's experiences of wrestling with his conscience. Its subtitle – *The Story of my Experiments with Truth* – is itself an example of his approach. For Gandhi, truth was never a static reality, but always a fluid concept that adjusted according to his personal whim. This was to cause him considerable problems as a political negotiator, since his own recollections of discussions rarely tallied with those of other participants.

One of the results of Gandhi's experimentation with truth was that he was apt to move rapidly between different aspects of human life, and try to unite them within a unified theory. He intertwined religion, politics and philosophy with personal health, sexual relations and dietary fads. For him there was no distinction between the public, the private and the political. As his children found to their cost, it was not possible to have a one-to-one relationship with Gandhi. In an effort to avoid deceit, he tried to be open about all his doings. Thus, when it became known that he was sleeping with his great-niece Manu, he announced at a prayer meeting that 'he did not want his most innocent acts to be misunderstood and misrepresented. He had his granddaughter [sic] with him. She shared the same bed with him. The Prophet had discounted eunuchs who became such by an operation . . . It was in the spirit of God's eunuch that he had approached what he considered his duty.'[6]

The day-by-day diaries of Gandhi's long-term secretary Mahadev Desai ('M.D.') are instructive in their confusion, since they show the way in which Gandhi's thoughts and interests leapt backwards and forwards. According to the publisher's blurb, the two men had 'such an inseparable relation that they were like two bodies with one soul', and the only comparable work of literature was 'that of Bosswel [sic], the learned English writer, who has noted the events of Dr. Johnson's life in his dairy [sic]'.[7]

On one page, Gandhi will be instructing a follower to add turmeric to her diet; on the next he will be promoting the need for cow protection, absolute punctuality and the use of Hindi; then he will begin attacking 'the drink evil' and the smoking of cigarettes; next he will condemn inter-caste liaisons and the remarriage of widows, only to change his mind a few pages later and vigorously promote it. The logic of some of his pronouncements is hard to follow. After the massacre at Jallianwala Bagh in Amritsar in 1919, he complained that the dead 'were definitely not heroic martyrs. Were they heroes they would have unsheathed the sword, or used at least their sticks or they would have bared their breast to Dyer and died bravely when he came there in all insolence. They would never have taken to their heels.'[8]

There were many contradictions in Gandhi's way of living. He deified poverty and condemned modern industrialism, yet relied on lavish donations from the Birla, Sarabhai and Bajaj families, whose fortunes came from just such sources. He always travelled with a giant entourage of disciples, many of whom were renowned for their cold hauteur towards outsiders, yet he claimed to dislike special treatment. He wished to live like India's rural peasantry, but wherever he went herbs, vegetables and chaste goats would be garnered, buildings scrubbed, whitewashed and decorated in an appropriate style, and mud refrigerated for him to smear on his stomach as one of his many 'nature cures'. His opponent Mohammad Ali Jinnah made the point that he spent less than Gandhi on train fares despite travelling first class, since he only had to buy one ticket.

A remarkable amount of Gandhi's time and energy was taken up not with the fight against British rule, but with the promotion of social change. He was a great believer in the increment of human excrement, which he referred to as 'black gold'. He had elaborate theories about its management and its use in the cultivation of crops, a passion that must have been aided by his having no sense of smell. His biographers tend to steer clear of his bodily preoccupations, but they form a substantial chunk of his *Collected Works*, and it is hard not to see them as critical to an understanding of his personality. He had an obsessive interest in other people's diets and internal health, and his cure for almost any ailment was a saline enema, which he liked to administer to his acquaintances himself. His letters to his followers are full of instructions on matters such as the use of hip baths as a cure for vaginal discharge, and his opening question each day to his female disciples was: 'Did you have a good bowel movement this morning, sisters?'[9]

In recent years Gandhi's personal quirks have received a wider airing in India, and his practice of sleeping with naked girls has been ridiculed by the Shiv Sena leader Bal Thackeray. This has provoked a furious response, including street demonstrations, from Congress loyalists. The most controversial jibes have come from Ashok Row Kavi, an outspoken journalist and homosexual rights campaigner. His fifteen minutes of fame came in April 1995 on Rupert Murdoch's Star TV Channel, when he appeared as a guest on a chat show called *Nikki Tonight*. Kavi told his flaxen-haired interviewer that Gandhi was a 'bastard *bania*' – simultaneously bringing in both caste and parentage. His words resulted in a debate in the Indian parliament, the Lok Sabha, the axing of *Nikki Tonight*, cringing apologies from the executives of Star TV, and a prosecution against Kavi by Gandhi's grandson Tushar Gandhi which is still being heard in the Bombay courts.

Ashok Row Kavi is deliberately provocative; his mission is to cause outrage in pursuit of a serious agenda. He is not repentant, insisting that 'the so-called Mahatma came from the *bania* caste, and was born before his father's marriage to his mother – so I could hardly say he was *not* a bastard *bania*.' He maintains that he has a serious point to make about Gandhi, whom he describes as a 'Hindu extremist' and an 'anal fetishist'. 'How on earth can we take him seriously?' he wondered. 'People want to put him on a pedestal and call him a saint, when really he was just a crazy fanatic. I say that putting M.K. Gandhi in charge of India's independence movement was like appointing Jesus Christ as Israel's foreign minister – a big mistake.'[10]

After he took his vow of *brahmacharya* or sexual abstinence in 1906, Gandhi seems to have adopted massage and purgation as a substitute for other intimate contact. In his book *Gandhi and his Apostles*, which explores some of the more baffling aspects of the Mahatma's teachings, Ved Mehta makes the interesting point that despite his detailed reading of contemporary ethical and social writers, Gandhi was unaware of the emotional or psychological implications of his 'experiments'. There are numerous reports of the distress caused to members of his entourage by being separated from him, and of the 'hysterical' reactions of his bed-sharers when he showed the slightest sign of rejecting them.

When Gandhi's Bengali interpreter Nirmal Kumar Bose told him his sexual experiments were unwise, and that according to Sigmund Freud people 'are often motivated and carried away by unconscious desires in directions other than those to which we consciously subscribe', Gandhi replied that he had only once heard mention of Freud's name and knew

nothing about his writings.[11] This gap in Gandhi's understanding is not
to suggest that a Freudian or even a psycho-biographical analysis is the
only way to understand him, but it is ironic that the man whom many
regard as the embodiment of human wisdom should have shown such
naivety about his own motivation.

Mohandas Karamchand Gandhi was the sixth and youngest child of an
elderly father, Kaba, and a pious mother, Putlibai. He was born in October
1869 in the fishing town of Porbandar in Gujarat, which was part of the
Bombay Presidency. There is a story that as a small boy, Mohan took
down a household deity from its pillar and perched briefly in its place,
which seems a suitable apprenticeship for his later vocation. The family
were vegetarian, and followed a strand of Hinduism that held various
tenets of the rigorously non-violent Jain religion. They were from the
modh bania or grocers' caste; in India the term '*bania*' is often used in
a pejorative sense to indicate a shrewd and greedy bargainer, a trait that
Gandhi kept throughout his life.

Kaba Gandhi was the Chief Minister of the local Princely State, acting
on behalf of the ruler or Thakur Saheb. This implies that he was a figure
of considerable status, but in fact his role was similar to that of the agent
or factor of a large estate. When Mohan was thirteen, his father arranged
his marriage to Kasturba, the daughter of a local merchant. The child
bridegroom treated his wife strictly, and their relationship remained spiky:
their early life was spent bickering, and in old age they rarely spoke to
each other. When Mohan was seventeen he made his first train journey
to the largest local city, Ahmedabad, and took an academic examination
which he narrowly passed. On the advice of a family friend he sailed to
Britain for his further education, although local community leaders had
declared he would be stripped of his caste if he left India.

In his *Autobiography*, Gandhi presents himself as a shy, inward, ner-
vous boy who sipped cocoa alone in his London bedsit for three years.
In fact he made many contacts when he was in the city, meeting among
others Cardinal Manning, the Theosophists Madame Blavatsky and Annie
Besant, the Parsi politician Dadabhoy Naoroji and the cricketing prince
Ranjitsinhji. He enrolled at the Inner Temple and moved to Bayswater,

took lessons in elocution, the violin and ballroom dancing, put on a silk top hat, stiff collar, patent leather boots and spats, and carried a silver-topped cane. Rather than concentrating on work like most other Indian students in London, he consorted with a host of cranks, moralists, high-fibreists, Darwinians and utopian communitarianists. Before long he was preaching vegetarianism and pacifism house to house, and writing articles for a paper called *The Vegetarian Messenger*. His dietary obsessions were already apparent, as he progressed from bread, oatmeal and cocoa to milk, cheese and eggs, and then to fruit alone before reverting to vegetables and nuts.

Gandhi passed his Bar exams and returned to Gujarat at the age of twenty-one. His mother, to whom he was devoted, had died while he was away. He went to Bombay, but found himself unable to master his nervousness sufficiently to appear in a courtroom, and for nearly two years he did clerical work. When he was offered a job in South Africa working for a law firm with Porbandar connections, he accepted out of desperation. Leaving his wife and three young sons in India, he sailed to Natal in 1893.

Gandhi's time in Africa represents the most influential period of his life, as it was there that he formulated the moral strategies for which he later became famous. He reached Natal at the age of twenty-four, and finally left when he was forty-five. He practised as a lawyer, although never with great success, and realized that his real skill lay in political organization. When he discovered that the authorities in Natal were planning to deprive Indians of the right to vote, he launched a popular campaign. His political activities were matched by the role of moral crusader, since he was living in a society of gold mines and profiteering, with an imbalanced population full of rapacious men, and many European and Indian women working as prosti-tutes. By 1896, when he returned to India to collect his wife and children, he was the focus of vicious hostility from white South Africans who por-trayed him as a promoter of Indian immigration.

Gandhi was fighting for the rights of Indians, whom he saw as a distinct community, with Muslims, Hindus and Parsis being welded together fairly easily since they were abroad. He objected to being classed with Africa's black majority, whom he refers to as '*kaffirs*' on the rare occasions that they are mentioned in his writings. His most famous campaign was over the Transvaal government's Asiatic Registration Bill. His refusal in 1906 to register under the new pass laws can be seen as the beginning of *satyagraha*, which literally means 'truth force' but is usually translated as 'non-violent resistance'. Two years later he promoted the public burning of registration certificates, and was sentenced to imprisonment with hard labour. His marches, displays of protest and the subsequent negotiated settlement with the Minister of the Interior J.C. Smuts are precursors of his methods in India in the 1920s and thirties.

Gandhi's spiritual and social ideas were also being developed during this time, and he set up successive idealistic communities called Phoenix Farm and Tolstoy Farm. He was strongly influenced by weighty nine-teenth-century works including Tolstoy's *The Kingdom of God is Within You* and Ruskin's *Unto This Last*, which he read on a train journey to Durban and claimed was 'impossible to lay aside', an odd assertion to make about such an impenetrable book. Gandhi later asserted that *Unto This Last* had provoked an 'instantaneous' transformation in his life. He began to preach his new morality to those around him; when he thought a friend was too emotionally attached to an expensive pair of binoculars, he threw them into the sea. His aim was to live as wholesome and simple a life as possible, regardless of the wishes of his wife and children.

Kasturba Gandhi was small, strong-willed, and conventional. She remained orthodox in her religion, disliked hearing the *Gita* except from the lips of a Brahmin, and at first objected to wearing hand-spun cloth. She rebelled quietly against her husband, insisting on having private sleeping quarters and her own spending money although it was against his regulations. She emerges as an insubstantial figure in most accounts of Gandhi's life. In his *Autobiography*, he wrote that 'Kasturba herself does not perhaps know whether she had any ideals independently of me ... We never discuss them, I see no good in discussing them.'[12]

Kasturba did not share her husband's political and social ideals. One of her rare known pronouncements was, 'Men are not blessed with the kind of common sense that women have, for we understand the language of sorrow better than they do.' It is apparent that they disagreed over the upbringing of their four sons, who were denied any formal education because of their father's theories. In later life they had continual worries over their son Harilal, who drank and gambled and briefly converted to Islam. Gandhi felt this was the result of his having led a 'carnal and luxurious life' while the boy was a child, but Kasturba thought there might have been a more prosaic explanation.

In 1906 Gandhi told his wife that he was taking a vow of *brahmacharya*, believing it would help to conserve his 'vital fluids' and raise him to a higher spiritual plane. His decision is said to have stemmed from the fact that he had been having sex with Kasturba while his father lay dying, and in his *Autobiography* he describes this as 'a blot I have never been able to efface or forget'.[13] Whether or not it was the deciding factor, Gandhi's attitude towards sexuality remained troubled throughout his life. He saw it not as a creative result of human desires and emotions, but as a repellent bodily function through which men became 'emasculated and cowardly' and women were defiled. His ambition was that sexual intercourse should be eradicated from human relationships altogether, except for the specific purpose of reproduction. Although there were elements of Hindu mythology in all this, there was also a good chunk of the prudish Victorian schoolmaster.

In January 1915 Gandhi and his family returned to Bombay, and he was awarded the prestigious Kaiser-i-Hind gold medal in the New Year's Honours List. His achievements on behalf of Indians in South Africa had given him a considerable reputation, but on the advice of his political mentor, the respected Congress traditionalist G.K. Gokhale, he avoided open politics. Instead he travelled all over India, being shocked and worried both by the poor and dirty conditions in which many Indians seemed content to live, and by the contempt with which they were treated by officials. He set about translating his experiences into action, and the death of Gokhale later that year helped him to develop a new ideology, unfettered by the liberal, parliamentary line of the older generation.

Gandhi believed that India was in need of total moral and spiritual regeneration. His theory of Indian self-rule (*Hind Swaraj*) was that his people had fallen victim to Western ideology, and needed to return to simple village life. His interest in spinning-wheels, religion and sanitation were viewed as ridiculous by most established Indian politicians, and at first he was written off as a crank. With funds from some Gujarati mill-owners, he set up a community or *ashram* on the banks of the Sabarmati river near Ahmedabad. He began to develop a reputation as a *rishi* or holy man, and pilgrims came to demand *darshan* or 'seeing' of him, in the belief that it would bring them spiritual benefit.

At Sabarmati Ashram Gandhi attempted to concentrate on establishing a perfect community, but was continually distracted by outside events. He had to deal with dozens of daily visitors, write for various publications, and give daily public discourses on the *Gita*. He once said that running the ashram was more exhausting than being Viceroy of India. As '*Bapu*' or father to the community, he was continually taken up by squabbles between the inmates over spinning, stealing, seductions, food, and worries when practitioners of *brahmacharya* began to engage in sexual experimentation. Adolescent groping among boys in the ashram school resulted in the already skinny Gandhi going on a week-long fast, a traditional form of Indian protest.

At this time he still believed in the benign nature of the British Empire. At the outbreak of the First World War he had raised an ambulance corps staffed by Indians in Britain. When the Theosophist Annie Besant founded a 'Home Rule League' he refused to support any agitation, since he believed the British Empire was the best framework for India and that self-rule within the Empire was bound to be granted once the war was over. 'Mrs Besant,' he said, 'you are distrustful of the British; I am not, and I will not help in any agitation against them during the war.'[14]

In 1917 he travelled to Bihar to investigate complaints that British landowners were swindling their tenant farmers over the growing of indigo, which had become worthless owing to the invention of a new synthetic blue dye. He took detailed testimony from farmers, and provoked a partial climbdown by the authorities. This gave him a reputation as a man who won practical victories, rather than just talking about them.

At a crucial Delhi war conference in 1918, Gandhi supported a resolution proposed by the Viceroy Lord Chelmsford encouraging Indians to join the army – an action that he subsequently tried to wriggle out of in his *Autobiography*. Shortly afterwards he asked the Congress politician Mohammad Ali Jinnah to join the recruitment drive, on the bizarre grounds that it would encourage Indian nationalism. Even by the strange logic of Gandhi, his letter to Jinnah was peculiar: 'Seek ye first the Recruiting Office and everything will be added unto you.'[15] The war ended soon afterwards and the recruiting sergeant's problem was solved – although he was so disturbed by what he had done that he had an emotional collapse.

Mohammad Ali Jinnah, the man who altered India's history by cracking the edges off the diamond and creating what was then the fifth largest sovereign state in the world, is the forgotten player in the story of India's independence and division. Neither side seems especially keen to claim him as a real human being, the Pakistanis restricting him to an appearance on the banknotes in demure Islamic costume. Generally he emerges late in the plot as a shadowy villain whose urge to create a Muslim homeland was motivated more by malice, spite and personal vanity than by statesmanship or a wish to protect the rights of a religious minority. In Lord Mountbatten's phrase, which would probably have been endorsed by most of the Congress leadership in 1947, Jinnah was 'absolutely, completely impossible'.[16] Even the apotropaic national hero Mohandas Gandhi described him as a 'maniac' and 'evil genius'.[17] Richard Attenborough's *Gandhi* (banned in Pakistan, which makes it all the more alluring) has Jinnah as a demented trickster, blundering about and muttering unsourced lines such as, 'I will have India divided or I will have India destroyed.'

The truth about Jinnah is that his political ideology developed and matured in a gradual and complex way over fifty years, and that the founder of the homeland for Indian Muslims remained a secularist of sorts to the end. In Pakistan itself he has been an uncomfortable father of the nation, and it was not until 1993 that the first volume of his papers was published. (The collected works of Gandhi, by comparison, run to ninety lovingly prepared volumes.) Yet his achievement, however flawed it may be, was phenomenal. As his biographer Stanley Wolpert has written: 'Few individuals significantly alter the course of history. Fewer still modify the map of the world. Hardly anyone can be credited with creating a nation-state. Mohammad Ali Jinnah did all three ... Jinnah virtually conjured that country into statehood by the force of his indomitable will.'[18]

Jinnah was one of seven children, born around 1876 to a Muslim family from Gujarat who were living in Karachi. In later life he would claim to have been born, like Christ, on 25 December, but there is no evidence for this. Although Indian Muslims are predominantly Sunni, the Jinnah family were Shia Khojas, making them a minority within a minority. He can first be found as Mahomedali Jinnahbhai – the ending *'bhai'*, meaning brother, is attached to many Gujarati names. Like many coastal Muslims, the family worked as traders and merchants, migrating easily between the interlinked economies of Bombay, Surat, Jamnagar and Karachi. They had the advantage over local Hindu *banias*, with whom they had much in common, of not having a cultural or religious prohibition on crossing the sea.

Jinnahbhai's father was a dealer in cotton, grain, seed, sugar and manufactured goods, and later a successful banker and money-lender. Young Jinnahbhai, who remained a very sharp businessman throughout his life, was packed off to England by his father in January 1893 to work as an apprentice book-keeper in the offices of Douglas Graham and Co., a leading managing agency. It was an unusual and ambitious step for a family in their position, and they took the precaution of marrying the boy to a Muslim girl called Emibhai a few weeks before he sailed.

Jinnahbhai soon abandoned account books in favour of study at Lincoln's Inn, despite his father's opposition to his becoming a barrister. He enjoyed strolling around the streets of London, visiting the British Museum, and developed an interest in politics, going to the House of Commons to listen to the maiden speech by Britain's first Asian Member of Parliament, Dadabhoy Naoroji. He had been elected as the Liberal Member for Central Finsbury, despite being vilified as a 'black man' during his election campaign by the outgoing Tory Prime Minister Lord Salisbury.

Unlike Gandhi, who undertook a remarkably similar voyage into London life, Jinnahbhai does not seem subsequently to have been troubled by shedding the outward trappings of his cultural heritage. Before long he had adjusted his name to the lifelong M.A. Jinnah, and forsaken his Sindhi tunic and turban for smart hand-tailored suits, starched collars, two-tone shoes, spats and a monocle, apparently in emulation of Joseph Chamberlain. In later life he owned over three hundred exquisite suits, and was said never to wear the same silk tie twice to court.

He left London in the summer of 1895, independent, eligible, arrogant, self-contained and extremely strong-willed. He had come close to staying in England and taking up a career on the stage, only being dissuaded by strong pressure from his father. He remained an actor of sorts for life, using the props of dapper suits and co-respondent shoes as a fastidious counterbalance to those of another eminent Gujarati, who favoured a photogenic *khadi dhoti* and shawl. Jinnah does not seem to have been close to his family, with the exception of his younger sister Fatima, who shared his life in his later years. He called in briefly to see them at Karachi – both his mother and his child bride had died while he was away – and then set off for Bombay to make his name as a barrister.

Success came quickly, one colleague remembering him as 'omnipotent' as soon as he came into a courtroom, partially because people were afraid of his precise, powerful, aloof manner. He combed his jet-black hair, grew a tentative moustache, and was said to scrub his hands scrupulously throughout the day. Jinnah attended a meeting of the political campaigning organization the Indian National Congress in Bombay in 1904, and was immediately marked out as a promising newcomer. Two years later he travelled to a Congress session in Calcutta, acting as secretary to the ageing and respected Dadabhoy Naoroji. Before long he gained a reputation as an uncompromising but resolutely non-communal politician. He must have realized that if he were to succeed in Congress like Naoroji and G.K. Gokhale (a mentor whom he shared with Gandhi), it would not be by virtue of his Muslim origins, but through a secular appeal.

Under the reforms introduced by the Liberal Secretary of State for India Lord Morley in 1909–10, 'the honourable Mr M.A. Jinnah, Muslim member from Bombay' became one of the first Muslim members of the new Central Legislative Council. The first time he rose to speak, Jinnah clashed with the flabbergasted Viceroy Lord Minto by denouncing the 'cruel treatment' of indentured Indian labourers in South Africa. When the Viceroy remonstrated, Jinnah answered: 'My Lord! I should feel much inclined to use much stronger language.'[19] An open rebuttal of this kind from an Indian member was not something the Lat Sahib was used to, and he did not reply. Like Gandhi, Jinnah had no interest in seeking promotion through deference to his rulers.

In 1913 he decided to join another political organization, the Muslim League, while insisting that such action did not 'imply even the shadow of disloyalty to the larger national cause'. As the Congress activist Motilal Nehru told his friends, 'unlike most Muslims [Jinnah is] as keen a nationalist as any of us. He is showing the community the way to Hindu–Muslim unity.'[20] Jinnah became well known in the years leading up to the First World War as a promoter of religious unity, insisting that Hindus and Muslims should battle together for an end to colonial rule.

He remained a Congress stalwart, and in 1913 sailed to Liverpool with Gokhale for an official meeting with Lord Islington, the Under-Secretary of State for India. On return, he put forward a sensible proposal that the India Office should be funded by the British exchequer, rather than from India. He was also adamant that Indians should be allowed to become officers in the Indian army – after all, they were 'good enough to fight as sepoys and privates'. His political method was to campaign on small but important constitutional issues of this kind. The notions of revolutionary terrorism or a mass popular uprising were anathema to him.

At the winter session of the Legislative Council in 1916, Jinnah persuaded eighteen other elected members to sign a memorandum supporting constitutional change. It was a reasonable and carefully argued document, leaving the indigenous princely rulers intact but proposing that a 'full measure' of self-government should be introduced in British India's eleven provinces, and that the country as a whole should attain a similar status to other dominions within the British Empire. It was a fair, if conservative, proposal for moves towards greater autonomy, not far from the solution that finally came into law in 1935 under the Government of India Act. The British War Cabinet rejected the idea outright.

Although the families of Jinnah and Gandhi had at one point lived little more than thirty miles apart in Gujarat, the similarities in their origins did nothing to unite the two men. The fatally antagonistic tenor of their relationship was set at their very first meeting. It took place in January 1915 at a garden party organized by the Gurjar Sabha (Gujarat Society) of Bombay to celebrate Gandhi's return from South Africa. Jinnah was the chairman of the society, and in response to his speech of welcome, Gandhi said he was 'glad to find a Mahomedan not only belonging to his own region's Sabha, but chairing it'.

This would be a little like a British politician commenting publicly on a colleague's foreign racial origins, in a situation where such matters were entirely incidental. As Wolpert writes: 'Had he meant to be malicious rather than his usual ingenuous self, Gandhi could not have contrived a more cleverly patronizing barb, for he was not actually insulting Jinnah, after all, just informing everyone of his minority religious identity. What an odd fact to single out for comment about this multifaceted man, whose dress, behaviour, speech, and manner totally belied any resemblance to his religious affiliation!'[21]

THREE

The Force of Truth

The slaughter by troops under the command of General Reginald Dyer of an estimated 379 civilians at Jallianwala Bagh at Amritsar on 13 April 1919 represents one of the most enduring and harrowing images of twentieth-century British rule in India.

Its horror obscures its singularity: it was not representative of the official imperial response to disorder, but an aberration that had a devastating effect on the Government of India's claim to operate under the rule of law. This is not to suggest that the British regime in India was innately benign, but simply that it was dependent on the ultimate democratic sanction of the House of Commons, many of whose members would not countenance the use of excessive force in the maintenance of law and order. As one fictional character has put it, 'there has always been something perversely precise about British oppression; the legal edifice of the Raj was built on the premise that anything resulting from the filling of forms in quadruplicate could not possibly be an injustice.'[1]

At the end of the First World War, the Indian Empire was suffering from acute inflation and an influenza epidemic. The government had to tread a difficult path between control and conciliation, and the comparative insecurity of its position made it veer in favour of repression. This came in the form of the infamous Rowlatt Act, or 'Black Act', which extended the wartime sanctions of the Defence of India Act, enabling suspected subversives to be arrested or deported without trial. Sir Sidney Rowlatt is one of the forgotten anti-heroes of India's struggle for freedom. He was a comparatively insignificant judge with a fiscal bent, and the *Dictionary of National Biography* reveals that his 'classical scholarship, although restrained by an essentially modest nature, could, when the occasion demanded, produce elegant, impromptu Latin verse'.

He was appointed by chance to chair a committee on revolutionary activity in India, and his eponymous report proved to be one of the key stimulants in mobilizing mass opposition to colonial rule. It was an outrageously repressive measure, under which nationalist campaigners could for instance be imprisoned without trial for up to two years for crimes such as the possession of seditious newspapers. The Rowlatt Act was a fatal mistake, for as the Liberal Secretary of State for India Edwin Montagu wrote, governing by means of one's police force was a 'convenient, but very dangerous' tactic.

The measures were pushed through India's Central Legislative Council by the Viceroy, Lord Chelmsford, despite the opposition of all twenty-two elected Indian members, since there were another thirty-four official nominees who could ensure that whatever London said, happened. During the debate Jinnah observed that there was 'no precedent or parallel in the legal history of any civilized country to the enactment of such laws', and when the Bill was passed into law in March 1919 he resigned from the Council on the grounds that 'the constitutional rights of the people have been violated', and that the legislation 'ruthlessly trampled upon the principles for which Great Britain avowedly fought the war'.[2]

According to recent research, the repressive terms of the Rowlatt Act stemmed from senior figures in the Indian Police, 'who, for the first time, were able to influence a political decision of wide importance'. The Department of Criminal Intelligence played a 'very considerable' role in formulating the Act, and Rowlatt himself believed that the forces of law and order as they stood were 'beaten'. Thus the legislation was 'not so much an arrogant act by a victorious imperial power, as a recognition by the Indian Police of their own weakness'.[3] The irony is that it was the introduction of the Rowlatt Act itself that provoked unrest on an unparalleled scale.

Nationalists such as Gandhi saw the new law as an insulting betrayal of the support they had given to the British during the war – a war in which over a million Indians had fought, and sixty-two thousand had died. Agitation and strikes were especially strong in the Sikh heartland of the Punjab, and when a pair of nationalist leaders were arrested in Amritsar on 10 April, there were public demonstrations, and posters were exhibited of 'English monkeys'. Three Europeans were killed in the rioting that followed. The provincial Governor Sir Michael O'Dwyer responded with what was in effect martial law, giving General Dyer control over the city. When thousands of people assembled illegally for a public meeting in Jallianwala Bagh, a large walled garden in the heart of the city, the troops were given free rein.

Dyer ordered his soldiers to pour hundreds of rounds of ammunition into the crowd. The shooters were not, as Salman Rushdie suggests in *Midnight's Children*, 'fifty white troops' (although they do metamorphose into 'fifty crack troops' in later editions of the novel), but rather, as was usual in such cases, Gurkha and Indian mercenaries. Afterwards Indians were made to crawl on their bellies down a street in which an English woman had been attacked, and to salute if they saw a European. Dyer said subsequently that the firing was intended not merely to disperse the crowd, but to generate 'the necessary moral and widespread effect'.

Old Mrs Bhandari came from a Parsi business family that had once owned all the ice-houses in the Punjab. Her father had liked Art Deco, and built himself a house in Amritsar from pictures in *Country Life*, filling it with clean, angular furniture, Kishco knives and Meakin china. Now it was covered by creepers and bougainvillaea, although its contents were unchanged. I sat in the jasmine-laden garden with Mrs Bhandari while she reminisced about the days when you could drive from Amritsar to Lahore in a morning. The previous day I had been up to the Pakistan border, and watched the rival border guards stamping and strutting at Wagah, the subcontinental equivalent of Checkpoint Charlie.

'I was thirteen years old when we had the trouble in the Jallianwala garden,' she said, pointing imperiously at one of her Sikh staff, who was attempting to drag a buffalo out of a flowerbed. 'My father took the view that the protesters should never have been there in the first place. They had been told not to go, but they took no notice and so they were shot. That is what happened. They've always been headstrong, these Sikhs.'

Mrs Bhandari clapped her hands and ordered the *chowkidar* to summon a *tonga* to take me to Jallianwala Bagh. We trotted through the streets of Amritsar, past a row of bicycling men in neat orange turbans, and a painted poster advertising aerobics classes. I reached the site of the massacre by walking down a narrow lane, about six feet wide, which was and is the only entrance or exit to the garden. It was very calm and quiet, full of birds and flowers, with a few people walking slowly around the wall. The bulletholes were still there, ringed with metal plates, as was the large open well into which terrified people had jumped to escape the firing. Sikh boys, their hair scraped into cloth-wrapped balls, were playing on the lawn.

A prominent painted notice said the ground was 'hallowed with the mingled blood of about 2,000 innocent Hindus, Sikhs, and Mussulmans who were shot by British bullets', and added that under Section 2B of the 1951 National Memorial Act: 'Cigar, paan, tobacco, narcotics, and any sort of eatable and drinkable thing are not allowed inside the memorial complex . . . No person shall wash or bleach any cloth or spread them for the purpose of drying.'

In the aftermath of the killing Sir Michael O'Dwyer defended Dyer's actions, but the Secretary of State for India insisted he be relieved of his command, and referred to his conduct as 'racial humiliation'. Montagu's refusal to tolerate a return to the barbarous methods of the nineteenth century was itself perceived as treachery by many in the military, whose idea of fair play had been conditioned by five years of fighting in the most gruesome war in modern history. Dyer returned to Britain to a reward of £26,000 from readers of the *Morning Post*, a jewelled sword inscribed 'Saviour of the Punjab', and a vote of support in the House of Lords.

It was this reaction to Jallianwala Bagh that led many previously moderate Indians to lose faith in the British. The House of Lords may have seen the massacre as acceptable, but in India it was perceived as grisly mass murder. The forces of pragmatic conservatism were swept aside, and a new radicalism entered Indian nationalist politics.

Sir Michael O'Dwyer, who already had a reputation for ruthlessness, became a focus of hatred among Punjabis. Their revenge came in 1940, when he was shot dead in London by a film extra and former Sikh Ghadr activist from Patiala called Udham Singh, who had been under IPI surveillance for some years. Using the alias Frank Brazil, he had previously been caught smuggling revolvers into India, dealing in obscene postcards, and 'living with a white woman' – although this was not in itself enough to provoke a pre-emptive arrest. During his trial he would only answer to the name 'Mohamed Singh Azad' – a Muslim name, a Sikh name, and '*azad*', meaning 'free' – to symbolize the fact that he was acting on behalf of all the communities of India. Udham Singh was sentenced to death, and has subsequently gained a reputation as one of

India's heroic martyrs.[4] His ashes were repatriated in the 1970s on the orders of the Prime Minister Indira Gandhi, who was herself assassinated a few years later by two Sikh bodyguards in a revenge attack for her conduct in Amritsar.

In 1917 the thirty-eight-year-old Edwin Montagu (derided by his Tory opponents as 'Monty Jew') had introduced the first significant attempt to answer the aspirations of Indian nationalism. He told the House of Commons on 20 August – almost thirty years to the day before the eventual departure of the British from India – that the government intended 'the increasing association of Indians in every branch of the administration and the gradual development of self-governing institutions with a view to the progressive realization of responsible government in India as an integral part of the British Empire'.[5] It was a tiny, cautious step, but it was a start. Unfortunately, many of his initiatives were to be undermined by the powerful War Cabinet.

Montagu's constitutional changes had to be developed in cooperation with the Viceroy, who was noticeably less liberal in his opinions than his ostensible superior in London. The 'Montagu–Chelmsford' reforms were put into effect six months after the Jallianwala Bagh massacre, and George V announced an amnesty for political prisoners. The 1919 legislation transferred a measure of executive responsibility to the provinces of British India. It was presented as 'half-in-half rule', or 'dyarchy' (although few Indians shared Sir Sidney Rowlatt's knowledge of the Classics), but in practice it was closer to 'nine-tenths to one-tenth' rule, since true control remained in British hands.

There were small but important practical changes. Examinations for the Indian Civil Service were now held in Delhi as well as London; as Jinnah had suggested, the India Office was funded out of the London exchequer (a significant financial saving for India); the Legislative Council was enlarged and democratized and its new Indian ministers given 'safe' portfolios like education, health and agriculture; most importantly, it was agreed that a ten-year statutory inquiry would be held to investigate 'whether and to what extent it is desirable to establish the principle of responsible government' in India. Had these reforms come a year or two earlier, there might have been an enthusiastic reaction from Indian politicians, but as it was they were greeted with a lukewarm response.

The 1919 legislation had another far-reaching effect. Money now had to be diverted to the new provincial authorities to enable them to operate, which put a fresh strain on the central budget. Forty per cent of the expenditure of the Government of India went on military costs, so it was resolved that the Indian Army should not be deployed abroad except in emergency. This plan was approved, unwillingly, by London, and it was agreed that in future the part of the British Empire that needed the Indian troops would have to bear the cost. As the historian John Gallagher put it: 'Now the Indian Army was a fire-service which worked on contract, which turned out only in emergency, and which was bound first to its own ratepayers.'[6] This creation of an internal market within the Empire was to have crucial material repercussions during the Second World War.

The Indian National Congress had been founded in December 1885 under the auspices of Allan Octavian Hume, a retired ICS official who believed he was guided by astral correspondence from 'mahatmas' and 'gurus' around the world.[7] The inaugural meeting was attended by seventy-three people, of whom two were Muslim. Most of the early Congress luminaries were lawyers, businessmen, merchants and doctors from the Hindu and Parsi upper-middle class, who resented their lack of political representation despite having done well financially under British rule. Under the guidance of figures such as G.K. Gokhale, Dadabhoy Naoroji and Pherozeshah Mehta, Congress developed along respectable lines for three decades, needling the Government of India with detailed critiques of its economic, social and fiscal policies, while playing no official role in the adminstration.

Congress nearly turned radical in 1907, when it split between Bal Gangadhur Tilak and Bipin Chandra Pal's 'New Party', which favoured direct confrontation with the British and the boycott of imperial institutions, and conservative constitutionalists like Gokhale who thought it better to cooperate with progressive forces in the British government. The traditionalists won, and it was not until the appearance of Mohandas Gandhi at the end of the First World War that Congress developed into a genuine populist movement.

Gandhi diverted Congress away from its upper-class Brahmin base, and from the use of English, a language understood by only a tiny minority of the population. As this took place, traditionalist Congress figures departed to form the National Liberal Party. Sabarmati Ashram was Gandhi's political base, and he won support from figures such as Motilal Nehru and his son Jawaharlal, the Ahmedabad barrister Vallabhbhai Patel, and Chakravarti Rajagopalachari, a lawyer from Madras sometimes described as Gandhi's 'conscience'.

Gandhi's acuity lay in confronting the British on their own territory, a skill that he had developed in his challenges to the British Empire in South Africa. The mass mobilization of thousands of people was a tricky problem for any government. Gandhi was clearly not a revolutionary terrorist, and since the British prided themselves on the judicial basis of their rule, he could not be treated like one. They ruled through legal authoritarianism rather than arbitrary totalitarianism, and thus there was little they could do beyond imprisoning him and his followers on a temporary basis. While Stalin would have rounded up the Congress leadership and quietly executed them, successive Viceroys were to send them back and forth to and from prison with baffling regularity for almost three decades.

Far from 1919 being the year in which India's freedom movement was quelled by the gentle concessions of the British Parliament, it marked the start of serious agitation. The outspoken tactics of Gandhi appealed to an entirely fresh audience, and Congress was now transformed from the club of India's civilized elite into a populist political organization. It gained the financial backing of Marwari and Gujarati *bania* merchants and industrialists, and Gandhi set up an efficient central organization to run it. If 1919 was the year of the boycott of British-made goods and institutions, 1920 marked the moment of quiet revolution. That December, at Nagpur, Gandhi launched nationwide *satyagraha* – the notion that freedom could be obtained through 'the force of truth', or non-violent resistance. Shops, schools and colleges were boycotted, and bonfires were made of imported foreign cloth. Jail-going became a symbol of pride rather than of shame.

His stand was uncompromising, and brave. Rather than proposing negotiations and conferences with the British, he wanted *swaraj* (self-rule) within one year. It was an extraordinarily ambitious concept, and its radicalism attracted followers in their tens of thousands. The voices of gradualism were ignored. Within a remarkably short time Gandhi had become the undisputed king of Congress, having generated a mass popular following and sidelined more traditional politicians like Motilal Nehru and the influential Bengali Chittaranjan Das.

After the Jallianwala Bagh massacre, Gandhi's conception of the freedom movement offered a new path to many of India's previously constitutionally-minded politicians. His method was not aggressively destructive, but rather a simple refusal to operate within the confines of British structures. He was not a violent maniac lobbing bombs at imperial officials, nor was he a stiff-collared neo-Britisher who saw Westminster as the fount of all authority. The cry of '*swaraj* within one year' persuaded many Indians that it might genuinely be possible to provoke an end to British rule. What Gandhi promoted was a vision of India as a free nation, and a return to a mythical golden age of '*Ram Rajya*', when the Kingdom of God, as represented by the deity Lord Ram, ruled on earth.

Although his idea of *satyagraha* had originally come from the Sermon on the Mount, Gandhi was offering a largely Hindu agenda. It was one that had an incalculable resonance in a country where religious belief was inextricably bound into the fabric of everyday living, and a belief in sanctity and sacrifice was embedded in popular thought. Although the categorization of Indian society into distinct groups can be portrayed as a strategy of colonial control, and few 'Hindus' would have perceived themselves as such before the late nineteenth century, Gandhi was tapping into a supremely influential reservoir of common identity that united almost three-quarters of the population of the Indian Empire.

By his use of Hinduism as a political tool, Gandhi unwittingly opened a Pandora's Box that has yet to be closed. He mobilized an entirely new non-English-speaking section of Indian society that had not previously been involved in politics. The difficulty was that by invoking a dream of '*Ram Rajya*', Gandhi alienated many Muslims, and ultimately helped to bring about the rise in the fortunes of the Muslim League. His hope was that he could maintain a strong religious message but at the same time avoid offending Muslims. As he once said: 'So far as I am concerned, my heart owes allegiance to only one religion – the Hindu Dharma. I am proud to call myself a Hindu, but I am not at all a Hindu Pharisee.'[8]

In practice this could not work, and by Gandhi's own admission Muslims found it hard to empathize with his ideas. As he told his confidant Mahadev Desai privately in 1918: 'Though we do say that Hindus and Muslims are brothers, I cannot conceive of their being brothers right today ... Not all religious distinctions will be wiped out in future, but Hinduism will captivate Muslims by the power of its compassion.'[9]

The idea of being captivated by Hindu compassion was not one that appealed to many Indian Muslims, who valued their religious faith as an essential part of their own identity. Nor were they lured by Gandhi's favourite ashram song: 'Raghupati Raghava Raja Ram,/Patita pavana Sita Ram,/Ishwara Allah tere nam,/Sabko Sanmati de Bhagavan' ('Ram the King of Raghu clan, you and [your consort] Sita are the purifiers of sinners, Ishawar and Allah are your names, give us wisdom, Lord'). Chants such as 'Jai Krishna, Hare Krishna' and 'Samb Sadishav, Samb Shiva' were equally exclusionary, as was Gandhi's fondness for 'Bande Mataram', a song that was considered offensive to non-Hindus. As the Muslim League leader Syed Ali Imam had said as early as 1908 with reference to Congress leaders: 'I ask the architects of Indian nationalism, both in Calcutta and Poona, do they expect the Musalmans of India to accept ... the sectarian cry of "Bande Mataram" ... and the Sivaji Celebration?'[10]

Although Gandhi made a point of including readings from the Quran in his prayer sessions, this did not amount to a genuine tolerance for an alternative way of thinking and being, as embodied in Islam. When his son Manilal planned to marry a Muslim woman, Gandhi opposed it vigorously on the grounds that it would be contrary to dharma. India's Muslims found it hard to accept Gandhian statements such as his speech when visiting a goshala or sacred cowshed in Bihar in December 1920: 'I would not regard him a Hindu, who is not prepared to give his life to save a cow. Cow-protection is dearer to me than life itself. Were it the duty of a Muslim to kill a cow, as it is his to do his namaz, I would have told him, "I should have to fight with you also." But cow-killing is not his religious duty. It is our inimical behaviour towards the Muslim that has driven him to cow-slaughter.'[11]

Gandhi's Muslim detractors started to present him simply as a front-man for Hindu revivalism, but in fact his hope of captivating Islam with compassion seems to have been genuine, if dangerous. He was a Gujarati Hindu to his core, who lived at a pitch of overblown idealism that came to alienate other groups in Indian society. His was not a cynical choice, yet he was taking a significant risk, like a person who lights a match to inspect a firework.

His initial method of uniting Hindus and Muslims politically was through endorsing the leaders of the Khilafat movement, which was to be crucial in generating Muslim support. The Khilafat movement consisted of those who backed the Sultan of Turkey (the Ottoman Caliph or Khalifah), whose empire was about to be divided up by the victors of the Great War. It was an ancient institution, and its dismemberment appeared to represent an attack on the heart of the world's Islamic tradition. Many of India's Sunni Muslims looked to the Caliph as the fount of their faith. They wanted him to retain sufficient political power to defend Islam, and to continue as the guardian of the Holy Places.

The leading figures behind the Khilafat movement, whom Gandhi described as his closest friends, were two burly brothers, Shaukat Ali and Mahomed Ali. They were born in the 1870s into a land-owning Muslim family in Rampur and educated at Aligarh, and were founding figures in the Muslim League before becoming radicalized and forming the Central Khilafat Committee and what became known as the 'Young Party'. They were a strident and aggressive pair, who had spent the war interned in prison on account of their pro-Turkish sympathies. The younger brother, Mahomed, was the predominant player, a diabetic with a degree from Oxford University. His response to the Anglo–Afghan war of 1919 was to call for a *jihad* in support of the Amir of Afghanistan, which got him thrown into prison and unsettled some of his supporters. By associating with the Ali brothers, Gandhi seemed to be encouraging a hard-line brand of Islam, and it looked to many as if he was hitching the cause of the Ottoman emperor onto his agitational chariot out of expediency rather than a genuine devotion to Hindu–Muslim unity.

When the Khilafat movement faded in the mid-1920s, Mahomed Ali described his alliance with Gandhi as having been a marriage of convenience, and made the troubling assertion that political constitutions 'like pretty women are meant to be violated'. Many Hindus thought he was a fanatic, and were disturbed by Gandhi's espousal of his cause. The pugnacious Bengali writer Nirad Chaudhuri remembered the Khilafat volunteers as rank extremists: 'They were recruited from the lowest Muslim riffraff of Calcutta and looked more repulsive still in their shabby uniforms of a military type. They were particularly aggressive and were brandishing their whips at people.'[12]

Gandhi's nationwide *satyagraha* of 1920–21 generated a substantial degree of unrest and disruption across north India, but was not enough to unseat the British rulers. In April 1921 Lord Reading took over as Viceroy from Lord Chelmsford, and proposed 'full provincial autonomy' and an extension of dyarchy in exchange for a suspension of *satyagraha*. Gandhi turned him down, believing that the offer was not sincere and that the proposals would soon be diluted by the government in London. Lord Reading was an interesting choice as Viceroy. He was the first and only Jewish holder of the post, and his father was a London fruit trader. Despite joining the Merchant Navy as a ship's boy at the age of fifteen, he ended up as a Liberal MP, Attorney General and Lord Chief Justice of England. He had some doubts about accepting the position of Viceroy of India, being especially nervous about the heat in Delhi. Consultations were held with a former imperial grandee: 'Climate?' barked Lord Curzon. 'The Viceroy has not to concern himself with climate. He goes wherever he wishes.'[13]

1921 passed, and Gandhi's sanguine slogan of '*swaraj* within one year' had not been realized. Thousands of people, including Gandhi himself and many of his Congress colleagues, were thrown into prison by Reading in a swift and ruthless crackdown. Non-violent resistance was clearly not achieving what had been intended. Then, in February 1922, Gandhi abruptly resolved to suspend civil disobedience altogether, following the burning to death of twenty-two Indian policemen in Chauri Chaura by a mob of supposed *satyagrahis*. For many Muslims, the future of the Khilafat was a heartfelt issue, and they felt abandoned and betrayed by Gandhi's precipitate decision. For more radical Hindus, this baffling move to end *satyagraha* over a single incident of isolated violence was a plain capitulation to the British. Nor were matters helped when nineteen members of the Chauri Chaura mob were executed by the authorities, and another two hundred transported.

Gandhi's panicky reversal induced no British response, with Lord Reading being unwilling to renew the offer he had made a few months before. When Gandhi eventually emerged from prison in February 1924, his interest in the Khilafat movement had evaporated. He stepped back from politics and concentrated on village health and sanitation, education, the eradication of 'untouchability', and the production of hand-spun *khadi* cloth, which he saw as essential to the rebuilding of India's village economies and national self-respect. The final nail in the coffin of the

Khilafat came not from the victors of the Great War, but from the Turkish leader Kemal Ataturk, who thought the power of the Caliph was, like the wearing of the fez, an anachronism in the modern country he was trying to build, and abolished it.

Although Reading was tough, pragmatic and unsentimental, he was not rigid in all respects. Unlike some of his contemporaries, he could see that any use of a 'divide-and-rule' policy would be extremely dangerous in the longer term. In 1924 he told the Secretary of State for India that Hindu–Muslim conflict was 'a menace to the peace of the country. Some, doubtless, think that this is to our advantage, but, if so, they fail to realize how grave the situation might become if the feeling between the two communities continues to grow more antagonistic and fails to be alleviated by some compromise.'[14] During the first part of the 1920s, communal relations worsened considerably. Activists of the right-wing Hindu-nationalist Mahasabha took to using water-tanks to 'purify', and in some cases drown, Muslims whose forebears had converted from Hinduism, and there were repeated religious riots in Lucknow and Allahabad in the United Provinces. Mohandas Gandhi's political techniques had mobilized Indian society in an unprecedented way, but they had also stimulated antagonistic forces that had previously lain dormant.

In October 1906, thirty-five members of the Muslim nobility had come to Simla to petition the then Viceroy Lord Minto for the protection of the rights of their community. The growth in the importance of Dhaka as a provincial capital following the temporary division of Bengal by Lord Curzon had provoked Muslim leaders into making political representations at the highest level. Lord Minto assured the delegation that Muslim rights would be safeguarded, and subsequently endorsed the principle of separate electorates, which were brought in three years later, whereby Muslims voted for representatives from their own community. Separate electorates gave legal protection to the rights of the minority, who were in general less prosperous than Hindus, but they also exacerbated religious divisions.

The Simla meeting is generally presented within the Congress demonology of the Muslim League as a key moment in the evolution of modern

India, when perfidious Mussulmans and scheming Britishers joined hands to assure the ultimate break-up of united Mother India. One of the crucial pieces of evidence is a much-quoted entry that Lady Minto made in her diary that night, claiming that her husband's actions had prevented 'sixty-two million people from joining the ranks of the seditious opposition'. In fact, it would seem that Minto's actions were pragmatic and even incidental, and that he was simply taking the chance to gain support from a small bunch of land-owning loyalists.

A few months later the Muslim League was founded under the auspices of Salimullah Khan, the Nawab of Dhaka. It was a select club with no popular mandate or membership, which hoped through allegiance to the British Crown to protect its own members' position. As the League's first president, Nawab Viqar-ul-Mulk, Mushtaq Hussain, said at the opening meeting, 'the political rights of a subject race thrive best in the soil of loyalty, and consequently the Mussalmans should prove themselves loyal to their Government before they can ask for any of their rights.' Viqar-ul-Mulk was a strong-willed feudal baron from Aligarh with a powerfully traditional view of society. He spoke, he said, for the rights of the '*qaum*' – an untranslatable Islamic term usually rendered as race, group, community or nation, which even today is redolent with meaning and implication for politicians in India, Pakistan and Bangladesh.

The President's speech continued, in Urdu: 'The Mussalmans are only a fifth in number as compared with the total population of the country, and it is manifest that if at any remote period the British Government ceases to exist in India, then the rule of India would pass into the hands of that community which is nearly four times as large as ourselves ... Then, our life, our property, our honour, and our faith will all be in great danger ... woe betide the time when we become the subjects of our neighbours, and answer to them for the sins, real or imaginary, of Aurangzeb, who lived and died two centuries ago, and other Mussalman conquerors and rulers who went before him.' In his opinion, Muslims should help to stamp out sedition, 'side by side with the British Government'.[15]

The creation of separate Muslim electorates in 1909 caused immediate problems, the Viceroy's private secretary pointing out that various other minorities were now starting to ask for 'separate courts of justice, separate schools etc.' Many Hindus thought Muslims were being unfairly favoured, and there were instances of Muslim tenants being evicted, Muslim merchants being refused credit, and, in Agra, Muslim prostitutes being boycotted.[16] Although it may have been the comparative poverty of many Muslims, and the need to protect the *qaum*, that led the League to support the creation of separate Muslim electorates, its impact went much deeper than anticipated.

To many Indian nationalists (and their ranks at this stage included a considerable number of Muslims) the creation of these new electorates was simply a Machiavellian move designed to spread discord and division among different groups in Indian society, a classic use of a 'divide-and-rule' strategy, whereby one community was set against another in order to buoy up the position of the imperial power. In the view of many Indians today, the creation of divided electorates was a deliberate strategy to provoke the demand for a Muslim homeland, and thereby destroy the coherence and unity of India.

A belief that the British used a deliberate policy of divide-and-rule in India from 1857 onwards has been an essential component of Indian nationalist thinking throughout this century. Put simply, the claim is that before colonial control began, religious harmony spread through the Indian subcontinent from Cape Comorin to Chitral. In the words of one historian: 'Before British rule there were no tensions between people along communal lines. Hindus and Muslims lived together in peace.'[17] The idea that London ran an elaborate and protracted conspiracy can be borne out by selective quotation from British officials, ranging from the words of a Colonel Coke in 1860, who stated that '*divide et impera* should be our principal aim,' down to a comment in a 1946 Intelligence Bureau report that 'communal disorder must not disturb us into action which would reintroduce anti-British agitation,' and stressing the advantages of keeping disorder on 'the appropriate plane of communalism'.[18]

According to popular belief in India, divide-and-rule was a deliberate, centrally orchestrated strategy. It is summed up well in the version found in *Tamas*, or 'Darkness', a popular television mini-series broadcast in India during the late 1980s. In the novel on which *Tamas* was based, Richard, a British Deputy Commissioner, spends much of his time provoking conflict between Hindus, Sikhs and Muslims (rather in the way that Marlowe's Jew of Malta would 'go about and poison wells'), and refers privately to such actions as 'government policy'. At the end of the book, a local Muslim leader sees that 'it was the Englishman who had again masterminded the whole game'.[19]

One problem with the conspiratorial version of divide-and-rule is that it presupposes an extraordinary degree of foolishness among India's politicians. It suggests that figures such as Gandhi and Jinnah were content simply to be passive tools, and allow themselves to be manipulated and divided by a large spider in a bowler hat sitting at the centre of a web in Whitehall. Nor is there any evidence in the voluminous private papers and diaries of British representatives in India that they relished communal violence; if anything, they were terrified of the destabilization that resulted from it. Moreover, if communal antagonism was simply a colonial creation, it might have been expected to evaporate soon after the transfer of power in 1947.

Most importantly of all, this version of divide-and-rule implies a remarkable degree of coherence in British policy, by successive governments, Tory, Liberal and Labour, over nine decades. There are certainly specific instances when British politicians and officials used Hindu–Muslim antagonism as a strategic tool. It was encouraged for instance by the Secretary of State for India Lord Birkenhead in the 1920s and by the Viceroy Lord Linlithgow in the 1940s, with the support of the Prime Minister Winston Churchill. When a colleague expressed 'anxiety about the growing cleavage between Moslem and Hindu', Churchill 'at once said: "Oh, but that is all to the good." '[20]

However, what the British did not do was follow a coherent doctrine which promoted communal hatred as a matter of official policy; they were pragmatists, and it would not have been in their interests to do so. As one politician wrote, Hindu–Muslim hatred did 'not make either of them more friendly to us or make India easier to govern'. In the words of V.P. Menon, who had an insider's view from the late 1930s onwards, 'the policy of the British Government in India was evolved more by the exigencies of time and circumstance than as the result of deliberate planning.'[21]

For a brief moment during the First World War, Mohammad Ali Jinnah had offered a bridge between the Indian National Congress and the Muslim League. His proposals, usually known as the Lucknow Pact, were for Indian self-government within the British Empire, with 'weightage'

in favour of minorities. In December 1916 he told the Muslim League in a passionate speech that his solution, and the guarantees it offered Muslims, could decide 'the fate of India's future, India's unity, and of our common ideals and aspirations for constitutional freedom'. He added (to the embarrassment of later generations of Pakistani historians) that India was experiencing 'a new-born movement in the direction of national unity which has brought Hindus and Muslims together involving brotherly service for the common cause'.[22] Earlier that year, Jinnah had been shouted at by the League's *mullahs* for his Western clothes and his use of English rather than Urdu, but now he won their support.

The Lucknow Pact was a carefully framed legal document which guaranteed percentages of Muslims on each provincial council. Tilak, the Congress firebrand who had now turned into a more mellow and pragmatic politician, gave the plan his support and ensured the organization's acceptance. It was the high point of Jinnah's career as a nationalist politician, and at the time it was seen as a historic achievement. However, the Lucknow Pact was soon to be overtaken by events.

By 1918 the Muslim League had become noticeably more radical, although it was still run by Muslim landlords. The days of unequivocal loyalty to the British Crown were over. Jinnah remained an Indian nationalist, alternating between Congress and the League. The subsequent suggestion that he was a closet Muslim separatist all along is belied by a comment he made in August 1919 in response to the protracted questioning of a British Parliamentary Committee on India's future. When asked whether he wished 'to do away in political life with any distinction between Mohammedans and Hindoos', Jinnah replied: 'Yes. Nothing will please me more than when that day comes.'[23] Asked by Sir John Rees, a Tory MP and former government official: 'Do you seriously suggest that a useful comparison can be made between the electorate . . . of an Oriental Empire and the existing electorates in Europe?' Jinnah's reply was typically sharp: 'I suggest this, that the sooner you give up your ideas of differentiating Oriental people from European people the better.'[24]

By now Jinnah was married. During the First World War he had begun wooing Ratanbai, or 'Ruttie', Petit, the young daughter of one of Bombay's richest Parsi merchants. They courted in Darjeeling, and Jinnah was soon pursuing Ruttie, although her father, Sir Dinshaw Petit, was adamantly opposed to the marriage, even taking out lawsuits against his former friend and barrister. Mohammad Ali Jinnah, characteristically, would not let go, and he and Ruttie married when she was just eighteen at his luxurious house on Malabar Hill in Bombay. She had converted to Islam a few days before, and taken the name of Mariam, which is what Jinnah's more orthodox Muslim colleagues now called her. All links with her family were severed until her separation from Jinnah less than a decade later. Their first and only child, a daughter called Dina, was born on the night of 14 August 1919.

Jinnah was now in his early forties, and Ruttie had a flamboyance to her character that, initially at least, inspired and stimulated him. His wife was beautiful, shocking, with long hair, bejewelled headbands, and she smoked cigarettes in an ivory and silver holder. She was intelligent but unhappy, taking refuge in a rather dippy kind of mysticism of the type that was fashionable at the time. At a dinner given by the Governor of Bombay, Lord Willingdon, Ruttie wore a low-cut Parisian evening dress, and Lady Willingdon promptly ordered a servant to bring her a 'wrap' on the grounds that she might feel cold. Jinnah was so insulted that the couple left at once, and never saw the Willingdons again socially.

When a public leaving party was held for Willingdon by some eminent Bombay Parsis, Jinnah organized a disruptive boycott, shouting down a speech by the esteemed money-lender and opium trader Sir Jamsetjee Jeejeebhoy. Jinnah and his supporters were hustled out by the police, and he became, rather to his surprise, a hero on the streets of Bombay. A memorial hall was built in his honour following spontaneous fund-raising, and named People's Jinnah Hall. Now, with the founder of Pakistan effaced from the history of Indian nationalism, it is referred to anonymously as 'P.J. Hall'. This was the only time that Jinnah ever became physically involved in direct action to make a political point.

When Gandhi had first proposed the concept of *satyagraha*, Jinnah was doubtful. He abhorred the notion of abandoning his elegant legal chambers and European clothes. Despite the similarity of their social origins, the two men offered diametrically opposed prototypes of leadership. Jinnah was a constitutionalist and a social elitist, who did not wish to soil his carefully scrubbed hands by consorting with the masses. As he told Gandhi, a non-cooperative strategy would in his view appeal mainly to the young, the ignorant and the illiterate. He was right of course, but it was precisely this spread of the freedom movement to new levels of Indian society that was to put the British authorities on the back foot.

At Christmas 1920, with Gandhi's radical tactics in the ascendant, there was a meeting of Congress at Nagpur. Membership was rising fast, and a new type of activist was emerging. Not only was Gandhi generating huge excitement among Hindus, but he was also gaining Muslim support through his backing of the Khilafat movement. For the first time, a nationalist leader had successfully appealed to workers and peasants from both communities. A resolution at Nagpur endorsing Gandhi's strategy was greeted by 'deafening, prolonged cheers and applause', and seconded by the once-deported Congress hero Lala Lajpat Rai. Jinnah, resolute as ever in his opinions, opposed the mood of the meeting, determined to state that he believed such radicalism would be counterproductive. His feelings towards the new hero of Congress had never been warm, but the fanaticism with which Gandhi was now being hailed must have made things worse. Earlier that year Gandhi had irritated Jinnah by writing a letter to Ruttie, making a dig at his European appearance and saying, 'Do coax him to learn Hindustani or Gujarati.'[25]

Jinnah thought Gandhi's tactics were turning a political campaign into 'an essentially spiritual movement'. As he stalked up to the platform he was howled down with cries of 'Shame, shame,' and berated for referring to his opponent as 'Mr Gandhi'. 'No,' howled the audience, 'MAHATMA Gandhi.' It is notable that there is no report of the Mahatma rebuking his disciples. So it was that the proponement of Hindu–Muslim unity and author of the Lucknow Pact was hounded from the Congress meeting. As his biographer has written: 'He left Central India with Ruttie by the next train, the searing memory of his defeat at Nagpur permanently emblazoned on his brain.'[26]

FOUR

Routes to Freedom

During the 1920s India's freedom movement veered in several different directions. Elements within Congress, headed by the Bengali leader Chittaranjan Das and the Allahabad lawyer Motilal Nehru, favoured entry into the administrative councils of British India, in particular the Legislative Council in New Delhi and the various councils in the provinces, as a means of undermining British rule from the inside. This move was agreed while Gandhi was absent in prison, despite the opposition of his followers such as the Bihari Rajendra Prasad and the Tamil Chakravarti Rajagopalachari. The Viceroy Lord Reading played the Congress division for all it was worth, coaxing cooperators into positions of responsibility and trying to regain the support of India's professional classes.

The appointment of a hard-line Tory Secretary of State for India in 1924 ensured that any thoughts of a liberalization in policy were abandoned. The new India Secretary was 'F.E.', Lord Birkenhead, a notorious bigot who 'felt a profound mistrust of the Montagu–Chelmsford policy and a belief that India would not be capable of supporting Dominion Status for centuries'. Like most formulators of Indian policy in Whitehall, his views were based on a profound simplification of the subcontinent's life and society: his son, who doubled as his biographer, made the laughable suggestion that Birkenhead 'had the "feel" of the country in a manner unusual in one who had never visited it, and he attributed this to an intensive reading of Kipling's Indian books'.[1]

In October 1925 a replacement for Reading was chosen, his appointment being inspired by the imperial stickler, the King Emperor George V. He was the forty-four-year-old Edward Wood, Lord Irwin, who turned out to be a conciliatory and perceptive Viceroy, and an awkward match for the crusted Birkenhead in the India Office. Irwin was a high Tory, Anglican and human being, standing six foot five in his stockinged feet, with no great achievements to his name but a good reputation. He was missing a left hand, but was otherwise conventional: wealthy, landed, Eton and Oxford, with historical family links to the Indian Empire. When he arrived in New Delhi in the spring of 1926 he had no particular line on India, but his propitiatory policy was soon to be dubbed 'Irwinism' by angry opponents, especially in the Tory-dominated India Defence League.

British supremacy in India was looking comparatively secure at this time, owing to Reading's skilful use of concession and repression, and the fragmentation of the forces of nationalism. Things soon fell apart when Lord Birkenhead decided to appoint the promised statutory inquiry into India's constitutional future in advance of the expiry of the ten-year limit laid down by Montagu in 1919, since he 'recoiled' from the prospect of a possible future Labour government being able to do so. He chose to pack the commission with his own nominees, the chairman, his ignorance about India apparently giving him a degree of neutrality, being Sir John Simon, a rich, competent, ambitious and theoretically Liberal politician. He sat with six other British Parliamentarians, including Viscount Burnham, Colonel Lane-Fox and Major Clement Attlee, with the remit of encouraging political stagnation. Birkenhead's failure to appoint a single Indian member did what Gandhi had failed to do – namely to unite the disparate strands of Indian nationalism.

During the course of the 1920s the Indian National Congress had suffered not only from internal splits between the 'Swarajists' who favoured council entry rather than Gandhian marching, spinning and non-cooperation, but also from the rise of a radical left-wing element. Although the personal ascendancy of Mohandas Gandhi was intact, his campaigns had wrung no definite concessions from the British government. One of the few really effective *satyagraha* campaigns was in Bardoli in Gujarat in 1927–28, over levels of taxation. Its success showed that when protest was run on a small scale on a specific issue, it could force the authorities to react.

The Bardoli campaign was organized by Vallabhbhai Patel, a Gujarati lawyer in whom Gandhi had placed great trust. He had slightly hooded eyes, a wide nose, a big moustache and a face that could change from granite to sweetness and back again in a moment. As one observer wrote later, Patel displayed 'a certain serenity which invariably accompanies real strength of character'.[2]

In Bardoli he ran a campaign against the payment of land tax, in response to the government's decision to increase revenues after a poor harvest. He divided the region into sectors, with each sector having a commander with *sainaks*, or soldiers, under him. Every day fifteen thousand copies of a news-sheet would be circulated by horsemen, and drums would be beaten whenever bailiffs came to a village with the intention of impounding property. The authorities were disturbed by civil disobedience on such a wide scale, and the *Times of India* wrote: 'Iron discipline prevails in Bardoli. Mr Patel had instituted there a Bolshevik regime in which he plays the role of Lenin ... The women of Bardoli have been taught amazingly seditious songs with which they incite their men to hate the Government.'³

The *satyagraha* succeeded, with the old revenue assessments being restored. The campaign had an important psychological effect on all sides, since it challenged the idea that the colonial power was unassailable. Patel became known as Gandhi's 'Deputy Commander', and later as Sardar or Sirdar, a title meaning chief, and one that he shared with Kitchener of Khartoum. Grassroots campaigning gave him a good understanding of the exercise of power, and of the strengths and weaknesses of the British administration.

All his life he retained an earthy, rural perspective, often using metaphors about buffaloes, fields and wells while others talked in high-flown poetic language. He had been born in October 1875 in a village near Nadiad, about fifty miles south of Ahmedabad. His family were *patidars*, or small landowners with significant influence in the local community. During his schooldays he was known for being blunt and uncompromising. Unwilling to be restricted to his village, he became a pleader in criminal cases in the district courts in Borsad, and gained a reputation for his mastery of the facts and his powers of cross-examination, as well as his fearlessness in challenging police officials and the local British collector. One day in court he was handed an urgent telegram informing him that his young wife had died. He glanced at it, put it in his pocket, and continued with the case.

The next year, having spent nearly a decade saving money, Vallabhbhai Patel sailed for England. Although his background was uncannily similar to that of two other Gujaratis, Mohammad Ali Jinnah and Mohandas Gandhi, he lacked even their limited social connections. Taking lodgings in Bayswater, he put on a European starched collar, tie and suit for the first time, and worked with unremitting zeal until he passed his Bar exams. With various certificates of distinction and a fistful of recommendations, he returned to Ahmedabad in 1913. It was a considerable achievement for a Gujarati district pleader in his late thirties.

Patel set up a successful law practice, and became involved in municipal affairs under the influence of his elder brother Vithalbhai, who was politically active. He attended a large political meeting of the Gurjar Sabha in 1917 at which both Jinnah and Gandhi were present. At first he had been cynically sceptical of the tactics of this *sanyasi* from South Africa, but after the success of Gandhi's campaign against the indigo planters of Bihar, and his refusal to obey the orders of local magistrates, Patel was converted to the cause. He realized that breaking the law in a deliberate and structured way could be an extremely effective tool against the British, since their system of control was based on legalism. He adopted Gandhi as his guru, gave up bridge, cigarettes, smart suits and velvet hats, and put on a *dhoti*. For a man of Patel's character, it was a remarkable reversal.

In 1921 he organized the annual meeting of Congress at Ahmedabad, at which the party consolidated its transformation into a popular movement after the session at Nagpur the previous year. All 'European' chairs were removed from the huge pavilion in which the conference was held, and Indian self-respect became its theme. As Jawaharlal Nehru wrote, Congress changed from being 'an English-knowing upper class affair where morning coats and well-pressed trousers were greatly in evidence' into a mass movement.[4] A saffron, white and green tricolour was proclaimed as the national flag, *khadi* as the national dress, Hindi as the national language, and Mahatma Gandhi as the national leader. It was an explosive moment for Congress, and one that represented a genuine upsurge in popular support while at the same time alienating numbers of Muslims, Bengalis, Dravidians and political gradualists.

Vallabhbhai Patel played an important role in Gandhi's own understanding of rural Gujarati life, since despite appearances, Gandhi was in many respects an outsider when he returned from South Africa. As a former local pleader whose father had been a peasant proprietor, Patel knew rural society with an intimacy that was denied to Gandhi. They were an effective combination. According to his biographer, Patel 'acted as his master's interpreter to the villagers ... If Gandhi had a *bania*'s suave, courteous veneer hiding his firmness and determination, Patel had the bluntness of a soldier and the astuteness of an organizer.'[5]

During the 1920s Patel abandoned his career as a barrister and concen-

trated on working as a freedom fighter. Most of the major civil disobedience campaigns of the decade were influenced by him, from the tax
boycott at Kaira to a *satyagraha* at Nagpur over the right to display the
Congress flag in public. Gandhi, who was always a good talent-spotter,
recognized his skills and entrusted many decisions to him, knowing that
despite his radical rhetoric, he was a cautious and pragmatic man who
would never allow a campaign to get out of control – except on purpose.

1928 marked a significant upsurge in nationalist agitation. That year the
Simon Commission set off for India on a fact-finding mission, only to
be greeted by boycotts and placards reading 'Simon, Go Home!' The
'Jinnah Group' within the Muslim League refused to meet the members
of the Commission, and the Indian National Congress organized mass
demonstrations wherever Simon and his entourage travelled. Birkenhead
tried to play on India's internal divisions, writing privately to the Viceroy
Lord Irwin that: 'We have always relied on the non-boycotting Moslems;
on the depressed community; on the business interests; and on many
others, to break down the attitude of boycott.' In a clear strategic use of
'divide and rule' he issued orders that all meetings between Sir John
Simon and 'representative Moslems' should be widely publicized, so that
they might 'terrify the immense Hindu population by the apprehension
that the Commission is being got hold of by the Moslems and may
present a report altogether destructive of the Hindu position'.

After the return of the Commission to England, Birkenhead wrote to
Irwin that Simon had 'conceived a deep resentment at the antics and
demeanour of the Swarajists, and an absolute contempt for their political
capacities', adding a few days later that 'it does not do to take these
people too seriously; indeed I find it increasingly difficult to take any
Indian politicians very seriously.' Birkenhead's stand was summed up
when he wrote that 'the phrase "Dominion Status" should not be used
to describe the ultimate goal' of Britain's India policy, since it had 'been
laid down that Dominion Status means "the right to decide their own
destinies", and this right we were not prepared to accord India at present,
or in any way prejudge the question whether it should ever be accorded'.[6]
The fact that in April 1928 the Secretary of State for India doubted whether

India 'should ever be accorded' self-rule within the British Empire shows just how immense a task Congress faced.

Birkenhead's stand was by now entirely at odds with that of Irwin. In June 1929, the Labour Party leader Ramsay MacDonald arrived at Downing Street with a narrow majority. His new India Secretary was William Wedgwood Benn, a former Liberal with reasonably progressive views on India – or radically progressive ones, if you compared him to his predecessor. Significantly, the defeated Conservative Prime Minister Stanley Baldwin agreed to give bipartisan support to MacDonald's new India policy. This was that there would be a 'declaration' by the Viceroy in support of eventual dominion status for India, which had been defined by Lord Balfour at the 1926 Imperial Conference as meaning an 'autonomous community within the British Empire, equal in status'. Overseas policy was now shared between the Foreign Office, the India Office, the Colonial Office and a new Dominions Office. Under MacDonald's proposal, British control would in the short term be restricted to viceregal and military power, and provincial government within British India would pass into Indian hands. It was this concession that launched Winston Churchill on his vehement and destructive Parliamentary opposition to India's freedom movement, which was to have such significant repercussions in the 1940s.

Lord Irwin was summoned home, and authorized to announce in New Delhi that His Majesty's Government saw 'the attainment of Dominion Status' as the logical outcome of Montagu's declaration of 1917. This was progress, but it was slow; as before, it had come too late to temper the radicalism of a new generation of Indians. Birkenhead was outraged by the declaration, since it effectively prejudged and wrote off any report that the Simon Commission might produce.

As before, London's politicians were lagging far behind Indian public opinion. A young Bengali Congress activist, Subhas Chandra Bose, now called for 'complete independence' and an end to 'this slave mentality'. Like Motilal Nehru's son Jawaharlal, he offered a powerful left-wing agenda instead of the gradualism of council entry or the spinning of *khadi* cloth. Moreover, the influence of the Communist Party of India was growing, particularly within the All-India Trade Union Council, despite intense surveillance and interference from the authorities. The party's executive was arrested in 1929, and kept under detention for four years without ever being convicted.

Aware that new forces were at work in Congress which challenged his own position, Mohandas Gandhi decided to defuse them by putting a supposed radical into a position of power. He chose Jawaharlal Nehru, who although not yet forty, was suddenly catapulted into a central role in the organization. Gandhi described him as a man 'truthful beyond suspicion . . . a knight *sans peur et sans reproche*'.[7]

At the annual session of Congress at Lahore that year Nehru arrived on a white horse to proclaim the message of '*purna swaraj*' or total independence, and told the massed crowds: 'I am a socialist and a republican, and am no believer in kings and princes, or in the order that produces the modern kings of industry, who have greater powers over the lives and fortunes of men than even the kings of old, and whose methods are as predatory as those of the old feudal aristocracy.'[8] It was a position that was distinctly at odds with that of many right-wing Congress traditionalists.

Although his family were Kashmiri Brahmins, Jawaharlal 'Joe' Nehru had been born in the United Provinces in November 1889. It was a progressive household, influenced by what Hindu hardliners liked to denounce as 'Persian' culture, meaning that the Nehrus were happier speaking Urdu or Arabic than Hindi. Jawaharlal's father Motilal was a strong-tempered, hard-working and successful barrister, who lived the life of India's anglicized elite in a house called Anand Bhawan in Allahabad. It had electric lights, a tennis court, a swimming pool and swarms of servants. Motilal dutifully attended meetings of the Indian National Congress, but did not initially allow politics to interfere with his way of life.

His only son was given a British tutor, and at the age of fifteen was packed off to school at Harrow to become an English gentleman. Jawaharlal did not enjoy himself, although when he left to go to Trinity College Cambridge, his headmaster recorded that he was 'a thoroughly good fellow, and ought to have a very bright future before him'.[9] At Cambridge he read Nietzsche, Shaw, Wilde and Havelock Ellis, and led a dreamy, rich, sybaritic, angst-ridden life, knowing he was unfulfilled but lacking the impetus to do something about it. He drifted through Bar School in a similar mood, before returning to Allahabad to work with his father in a desultory fashion. In 1916 he underwent a grandiose arranged marriage to another Kashmiri Brahmin, Kamala Kaul, who was just seventeen years old. They were to have one child, Indira, born the following year.

Towards the end of the First World War Jawaharlal began to take a mildly active role in politics, stimulated initially by the arrest of the British-born campaigner for Indian freedom Annie Besant, who had set up a comparatively innocuous organization called the Home Rule League. His father Motilal was also becoming more politically involved, and in 1919 was elected for a year as President of Congress.

It was the massacre at Amritsar that year which marked a turning point for both Nehrus. Previously they had taken a moderate view of British rule, seeing it as essentially benign despite its injustices. Amritsar, and perhaps more importantly the dismissive British reaction to it, roused a new radicalism among India's Westernized elite. Although Motilal at first favoured participation in the councils of British India, Jawaharlal followed Gandhi and embraced total non-cooperation.

In the 1920s Jawaharlal became involved in grassroots rural agitation across the United Provinces. Under Gandhi's guidance he began to gain an entirely new perception of Indian life. For the first time he saw the degree of deprivation, hunger and exploitation that was suffered by many of his fellow people, and his political opinions shifted to the left. As he said in retrospect, 'I was totally ignorant of labour conditions in factories or fields, and my political outlook was entirely bourgeois.'[10] The father followed the son's lead, and Motilal burnt all his exotic foreign clothes, put on *swadeshi* and gave up his impressive wine cellar. In 1921 both Nehrus found themselves in prison.

The early 1920s were years of personal fulfilment for Jawaharlal. He had found a purpose to his life, and wrote later that he had at that time been 'full of excitement and optimism . . . untroubled by doubts'. However, within a short time he began to question many aspects of Gandhi's message, in particular his emphasis on purity and sacrifice, his praise of poverty and the Hindu-revivalist talk of a return to '*Ram Rajya*'. He also made the point in his autobiography that Gandhi was 'delightfully vague' about what he actually meant by *swaraj*, and noted, 'he always spoke, vaguely but definitely, in terms of the underdog, and this brought great comfort to many of us, although, at the same time, he was full of assurances to the top-dog also. Gandhi's stress was never on the intellectual approach to a problem but on character and piety . . . Often we discussed his fads and peculiarities among ourselves and said, half-humorously, that when *swaraj* came these fads must not be encouraged.'[11]

In 1926 Jawaharlal and his wife Kamala sailed to Europe to seek treatment for her tuberculosis, accompanied by his sister and brother-in-law Vijaya Lakshmi Pandit and Ranjit Pandit. He took part in an inter-national conference against imperialism in Brussels, read a good deal about European socialist and communist theory, and travelled with wide eyes to the Soviet Union. His political ideology again shifted significantly, and he came to see India's problems as being as much about social injustice as about colonial rule. He decided that the answer was centralized state planning and rapid industrialization.

When he arrived back in India his opinions had diverged significantly from those of Gandhi, who still wanted a return to a medieval world of wholesome and self-sufficient village communities. Gandhi was un-daunted by their differences, and installed him as Congress President for the forthcoming year. This was partly the result of personal instinct and favour, assisted by his accurate belief that Jawaharlal could act as a bridge between a new generation of Congress radicals and his own tra-ditional supporters. The younger Nehru would be a bulwark against his less malleable contemporaries.

Under his presidency, Congress proclaimed 26 January 1930 as Inde-pendence Day, and a fresh round of *satyagraha* became inevitable. Jinnah saw such an approach as a dangerous threat to India's security, and proposed instead that the government of Ramsay MacDonald should announce an immediate plan to introduce dominion status. As the tri-colour was unfurled to the cry of '*Inquilab Zindabad,*' or 'Long Live Revolution,' the freedom movement entered a new stage. The campaign for *purna swaraj* as opposed to cooperation with a fairly progressive new Labour government was geared as much to uniting the disparate elements in Congress as it was to fighting British rule. As a police intelligence report noted, it was Gandhi the *bania* rather than Gandhi the idealist who had won the day. The creation of Jawaharlal Nehru as President, and the exclusion of the Calcutta radical Subhas Chandra Bose even from the Congress Working Committee, had been entirely the result of Gandhi's influence within the organization. Nehru was attracting a more outspoken membership, yet, like Lord Irwin, he had a plausible and aristocratic bearing which helped to diffuse criticism.

An indication of the surging radicalism of the movement can be gained from the fact that a resolution deploring a recent bomb attack on the viceregal train and 'congratulating the Viceroy and Lady Irwin and their party, including the poor servants' on their lucky escape, was only passed by a doubtful show of hands against a background of 'indignant cries'. Even after the independence resolution had been passed, Gandhi felt uncertainty about how to proceed. He wrote in his magazine *Young India* in January 1930 that it was 'difficult to discover an effective and innocent formula' with which to oppose British rule, and that it might even be 'impossible to offer civil disobedience at this stage in the name of the Congress'.[12] He realized a new initiative was needed, and that the boycotting of foreign cloth shops and liquor stores – two of his favourite tactical obsessions – would not be enough to generate mass activism.

In the middle of February 1930, a secret meeting of the Congress Working Committee was held at Sabarmati Ashram in Ahmedabad, with Gandhi himself being given powers to launch civil disobedience at his own discretion. He got round the 'Chauri Chaura' problem by insisting that only those who believed in non-violence as an article of faith, rather than as a political expedient, should be responsible for organizing the *satyagraha*. This meant that if violence did break out, it could not be blamed on the Congress hierarchy. All those who thought that Gandhi's position as a serious political force had been eclipsed in the 1920s were about to be surprised. He had a most effective scheme up his sleeve.

His latest method of confrontation with the British Empire was intended to be inclusive of all religious communities, neutral in its effect on Indian vested business interests, and insignificant to the internal workings of the British regime. It was also beautifully symbolic – that the government tax on salt should be boycotted, since it was a restriction, by an alien regime, on a basic necessity of life. A long walk would take place, a kind of mass pilgrimage, beginning at Sabarmati Ashram and ending on a beach at Dandi, 240 miles away. There the seventy-eight marchers, hand-picked by Gandhi, would collect handfuls of muddy salt, and boil and purify it to make it palatable.

The *satyagrahis* were all male, and about half of them came from Gujarat or Maharashtra, including Gandhi's son Manilal and his secretary Pyarelal. The rest were from all over India, including one from Bengal, one from Sind, one from Bihar, and even one from Nepal. Each marcher was required to spin some *khadi*, exude peacefulness, engage in group prayers and keep a diary before he settled down for the night. Despite Gandhi's superficially impeccable non-sectarian credentials, it is noticeable that only two of the seventy-eight marchers were Muslim.

The salt *satyagraha* turned out to be the most famous of Gandhi's many campaigns; its greatest strength was its simplicity. It combined the essentials of Gandhi's ideology, linking political action with religious mortification, while symbolically challenging the heart of imperial authority. For as Nirad Chaudhuri observed, Gandhi was never simply a politician: 'It is thought that he brought religion into politics in order to raise it to a higher plane. On the contrary, the truth was that Mahatma Gandhi took politics into religion in order to become a new kind of religious prophet.'[13] Here he could become Moses leading his people through the desert, or the Lord Buddha on his Mahabhinishkraman, or Ramchandra advancing to Lanka.

Gandhi's first recorded opposition to the salt tax had been when he was a student in London. Ever since his childhood in Porbandar, with the Arabian Sea 'almost within a stone's throw', lapping at the town's walls, he had felt an affinity to the sea and to water.[14] He had grown up in a society where people made their living from the sea, from fishing and trading, and despite his aversion to cars and aeroplanes, he always loved sailing. (*Hind Swaraj* was written on board ship, as he sailed from London to Durban.) So where better to challenge the King Emperor than on the coast of his native Gujarat, by scooping up a handful of salt, a commodity given freely to the Indian people by the ocean, and now taxed by the imperial power?

Before setting off he wrote a long letter to Lord Irwin, beginning 'Dear Friend,' and saying he had 'hugged the fond hope' that a solution might be found to India's problems, but the Viceroy's failure to give an assurance that the British government would 'support a scheme of [immediate] full dominion status' meant he had no choice but to protest, 'For my ambition is no less than to convert the British people through non-violence and thus make them see the wrong they have done to India.'[15] The letter was delivered to Viceregal Lodge, again with careful symbolism, by an English hand, which belonged to one of Gandhi's ashram acolytes, Reginald Reynolds. Irwin's response, as was to be expected, was a formal and unequivocal letter refusing to back down. The authorities in New Delhi proclaimed themselves to be unmoved, the Revenue official in charge of the salt tax calling the march a 'somewhat fantastic project', while Irwin himself dismissed it as a 'silly salt stunt'.

The days before the march were very tense, Sardar Vallabhbhai Patel being arrested in Borsad as he made preparations for the arrival of the pilgrims. Jinnah stated in the Central Legislative Assembly that Patel's arrest 'cut at the roots of the principle of freedom of speech'.[16] A meeting was held on the banks of the Sabarmati, just upriver from the ashram, attended by at least seventy-five thousand people. Letters of support arrived in their hundreds from all over the world, and Gandhi gave numerous press interviews. The cartoonists enjoyed themselves, one depicting Gandhi pouring salt onto the tail of the British Lion, while another showed Churchill making saltpetre (a component of gunpowder) as his opponent made salt. On the evening of 11 March Gandhi made a speech to the ten thousand people attending his prayer meeting, saying he did not know what the future held for him, and that he thought this might be the last time he spoke to them at Sabarmati.

His prediction proved correct. The sixty-one-year-old Mohandas Gandhi, frail, stiff and cold, wearing his usual *khadi dhoti* and shawl and carrying a long staff in his right hand, set off at first light the next morning, pursued by his seventy-eight *satyagrahis*, all busily reciting *bhajans* and sacred chants. He would never return to Sabarmati Ashram.

Mohammad Ali Jinnah had faded from Indian politics by 1930. There had been a brief triumph in 1924 when he united with Motilal Nehru to form a political group in New Delhi's Legislative Assembly, which passed a resolution to allow 'rupee tenders' in India for Government of India purchases, rather than only allowing sterling tenders which were made in London. This was typical of Jinnah, spotting a subtle but important opportunity to benefit Indian interests. He remained an adamantly optimistic supporter of communal unity: '*Swaraj*,' he told the Muslim League at a meeting in Lahore in 1924, 'is an almost interchangeable term with Hindu–Muslim unity . . . the advent of foreign rule, and its continuance in India, is primarily due to the fact that the people of India, particularly the Hindus and Mohammedans, are not united and do not sufficiently trust each other.'[17]

There were various attempts by the British to use Jinnah's rupture with Gandhi at Nagpur to their advantage, hoping that he might join the ranks of the Indian 'toadies' who helped to prop up imperial rule. When Lord Reading offered him a knighthood he refused, saying he hoped to die as 'plain Mr Jinnah'. In that Jinnah believed in participating in the political structures of British India, he was suspect in the eyes of the more radical nationalists, yet he was always careful how far he went in his support. When the Simon Commission visited India he opposed those Muslim Leaguers who were willing to meet its members, and boycotted the delegation, both officially and socially.

In January 1928 he told the Muslim League during a speech in Calcutta: 'Jallianwala Bagh was a physical butchery, the Simon Commission is a butchery of our souls. By appointing an exclusively white Commission, Lord Birkenhead has declared our unfitness for self-government ... I welcome the hand of fellowship extended to us by Hindu leaders from the platform of the Congress and the Hindu Mahasabha. For, to me, this offer is more valuable than any concession which the British Government can make.'[18] British insensitivity, and the usual flip-flop in policy between compromise and oppression, had succeeded in temporarily uniting many different shades of Indian opinion.

Later that year Jinnah took a Muslim League delegation to Congress in an attempt to create a new version of his Lucknow Pact of 1916. It included the Bombay barrister M.C. Chagla and the Oxford-returned Liaquat Ali Khan, a young politician from the United Provinces whom Jinnah thought showed great ability. As a counterblast to the Simon Commission, Motilal and Jawaharlal Nehru had been deputed to form their own commission, and devise a constitution that would satisfy all communities. Their report was an optimistic document, full of talk about communal harmony, but the small print – and Jinnah was only ever interested in the small print – effectively did away with the constitutional guarantees for Muslims embodied in the Lucknow Pact. Jinnah dismissed it privately as simply a 'Hindu position'. To him, it was a betrayal, and he wanted to make sure it was amended.

Jinnah's point was that Muslims could not simply rely on promises of Hindu goodwill in a free India: they needed legal protection written into law – a third of the seats in a central legislature, for instance – in order to avoid the risk of dictatorship by the majority. Otherwise, the claims of areas such as the Punjab and Bengal, where Muslims were in a majority, might be overruled by a Hindu-dominated central parliament. In a telling phrase, he told the delegates to the Indian National Congress convention that it was up to the Hindus to be generous, since a minority 'cannot give anything to the majority'.

Some Congress leaders were inclined to support him, and continue with the comparative generosity that Tilak had shown twelve years before at Lucknow. But opinion was hardening. A speaker for the Hindu Mahasabha explicitly rejected the Muslim League case. Why make concessions? Surely the freedom of India from British rule was more important than minority rights? Knowing that support for Jinnah within the League was fluid, and that eminent Congress Muslims such as Abul Kalam Azad were willing to accept the Nehru report, the meeting rejected Jinnah's claim to special treatment. This was in effect the end of Jinnah's career as an Indian nationalist politician. From now on he came to believe, quietly at first, in separation, either in the form of powerful, autonomous provinces within a federal system, or ultimately in an independent state.

Up until 1928, many activists in India had shifted cheerfully between different wings of Congress and the Muslim League, or into regional political organizations, without membership of one assuming rejection of another. The freedom movement was broad and diverse, but now things were changing. Determined that Muslim India should speak with a united voice, and knowing his own position within the League was tenuous, in March 1929 Jinnah proposed a new common agenda. It included a federal Indian constitution with various safeguards for Muslim culture and religion, which has become known in Pakistani folklore as 'Jinnah's Fourteen Points', evoking Woodrow Wilson's declaration of 1918. (There were in fact fifteen or twenty-one points, depending on which draft of Jinnah's document you read.) However, the meeting of the Muslim League was in no mood to support this strategy, and Jinnah was thrust into the wilderness.

He returned to his legal practice with vigour, remaining as meticulously dressed as ever. Unlike many rich Indians, he had never been plump, but now he became as lean as a whippet, chain-smoking Craven A cigarettes. One of the few portraits of him at this stage in his life can be found in the autobiography of M.C. Chagla, *Roses in December*. Chagla was a political admirer and assistant to Jinnah, who worked as a junior in his chambers. He seems to have had a grudge against his former mentor, partially on the grounds that Jinnah was unhelpful during the early stages of his career as a barrister.

Chagla later became India's High Commissioner in London, and as a nationalist Muslim was bitterly opposed to the creation of Pakistan. Although he is a biased source, he has some interesting insights, observing that 'Jinnah was a poor lawyer, but a superb advocate. He had a very striking personality, and the presentation of a case as he handled it was a piece of art.'[19] Chagla admired his tenacity, but found him 'cold and unemotional', and noted he had no interests outside law and politics. Intriguingly, Chagla wrote that for him 'it was inconceivable that Jinnah should ever have come to be the main architect of Pakistan.'[20]

One anecdote is revealing. When Jinnah was campaigning among the Muslims of Bombay, his wife Ruttie appeared in her usual glamorous clothing carrying a tiffin basket. She clambered down from a stately limousine and said: ' "J!" – that is how she called him – "guess what I have brought you for lunch." Jinnah answered: "How should I know?" and she replied: "I have brought you some lovely ham sandwiches." '[21] Angry and embarrassed, the aspiring Muslim leader sent her away.

By the mid-1920s, Jinnah seems to have been interested in little outside his work. Ruttie took to spending much of her time with one of her husband's political supporters, Kanji Dwarkadas. Still in her twenties, and unable to gain her husband's attention, she tried to communicate with spirits, and may have developed a drug dependency. Her energy was devoted to their daughter Dina and a collection of cats, dogs and other pets. Her protracted correspondence with Dwarkadas is full of references to séances, psychic powers and possible remedies for her 'clogged soul'.

By the late 1920s, he and Ruttie had become almost estranged, and were spending little time with each other. Jinnah seemed increasingly haughty and dispassionate. He was ageing rapidly, and suffered from bronchial infections. Ruttie moved out of their house and rented a suite at the luxurious Taj Mahal Hotel in Bombay. Then she sailed to Paris with her mother, where she became deliriously ill, and returned to India virtually bedridden. Jinnah spent February 1929, the month between his rejection by Congress and his rejection by the Muslim League, in a flat in New Delhi. On 20 February, on his young wife's twenty-ninth birthday, he received a telephone call saying that she had died. Although Dwarkadas insisted that, as a quasi-Theosophist, Ruttie would have wished to be cremated, Jinnah had her buried in Bombay's Muslim cemetery. At the end of the ceremony he broke down and wept like a child. Chagla observes that this was the only occasion he ever saw Jinnah show 'some shadow of human weakness'.

By 1929, Jinnah's disillusion with the Congress version of Hindu–Muslim unity was complete, and his political and personal optimism had been badly eroded. While Congress passed the 'purna swaraj' resolution and Gandhi set off on his celebrated march to Dandi to scoop salt off the seashore, Jinnah withdrew into the luxurious seclusion of his house on Malabar Hill. Having no taste for mass agitation, he departed for England in October 1930, resolved to establish his legal practice in London. He turned in on himself, showing a formal, brittle surface to the outside world. His was not a brusque, careless coldness, but rather a form of self-protection, a deliberate closing of the shutters by a sensitive man who had been badly scalded.

FIVE

The March to the Sea

One night I walked through a Muslim *mohalla*, past hens crammed into wire baskets, and chickens which hung fluttering in bunches, tied together by their feet. I was in Gujarat, the aquifer of India's freedom movement, and the pre-First World War stamping ground of Gandhi, Patel and Jinnah. Lamb kebabs were roasting, fanned with strips of cardboard by small, leaping, white-lace-topi-topped boys. Inside a café were huge vats of bubbling, greasy mutton, and thick round wads of dough frying on a giant metal circle. A man with big glasses and oiled hair flicked the food artfully, dabbing salt and chopped herbs and onions onto bowls and plates and dishes. On a shiny wooden table stood a stack of sticky sweets, red circles swirling through the centre.

I was a few miles from Sabarmati Ashram, where Gandhi began his salt march in 1930, in the choking, metallic sprawl of Ahmedabad, the textile metropolis of Gujarat. There had been persistent communal riots here for decades. The city's fifteenth-century Jama Masjid was supposedly made of slabs and stones gathered from smashed Hindu temples. Just below the ubiquitous MG Road, the name being Mahatma Gandhi's enduring gift to urban India, lay the Muslim Quarter. It was exclusive, its own place, full of stares and self-protection, which turned to inclusion after a few days.

Outside Al-Din Tailors a man with a grey moustache was separating huge blocks of dates, piled up onto a stall constructed from bicycle wheels and a slice of metal. Beside him, by a pile of rubble, sat a very old, blind woman with a nodding hand and a lap full of coins. A group of thin, ragged men lined the pavement, expectant and orderly, waiting for their *iftar* food. It was *Ramazan*, the Muslim month of fasting. One shop was selling *bidis*, boiled sweets, *paan* and cigarettes, overlooked by a torn poster titled 'Top Officials of the World', showing Margaret Thatcher in a Bee Gees jacket and Ronald Reagan with smears of bad stubble. The shop was being tended by two men in their fifties, Iqbal Khan, a tailor, and his friend Yusuf Khan, 'expert in sight testing, eyewear and goggles'.

They talked about the days of independence and *satyagraha* and the emptiness of political promises. Here in Ahmedabad, they saw Muslims as a persecuted minority. They were loyal to India, *Bharat*, they said, again and again, and rejected Pakistan. For them, it was certainly not the land of the Prophet, peace be upon his name. Jinnah was a decoy who had led the Muslims into the wilderness. I had encountered the same line all over the country; a person's identity as an Indian Muslim seemed to be predicated on a vehement denunciation of Pakistan and all it represented.

'Mr Jinnah wanted to make a home for Muslims, but most of us didn't go,' said Yusuf Khan, rubbing his hands on his long white shirt. 'My mother and father didn't want to go to Punjab – the language and food is different there, they didn't even think of going. My family came from this place only.'

'So who did go to Pakistan?'

'The rich families went, who were able to travel, except those near the border where . . .' his voice was lowered, '. . . where they were all made to go, driven from their homes by the Sikhs and Hindus, and their fields and bullocks were taken.'

'Pakistan-Akistan has no meaning for us here,' said Iqbal Khan, the tailor. 'It was just political talking. Things are happy in Ahmedabad. You see, there are more Muslims in India than there are in Pakistan. We do business with Hindus and things are happy. Only sometimes people come from outside, and create problems.'

When I asked him his opinion of Gandhi he shrugged, looked quizzically at Yusuf Khan and then laughed. 'I believe these words,' he answered, 'God is good, man is bad.'

One evening later in the week I climbed into a stinking auto-rickshaw, driven by a wild, slightly disturbed man called Mohammad Rafiq, and went to Sabarmati Ashram to watch an elaborate *son-et-lumière* about the life of Mohandas Gandhi. The driver and I were the only members of the audience, sitting, waiting beneath a crescent moon in the cold on uncomfortable metal chairs. The show finally began with a long cadence of Gujarati music, and the smooth-voiced narrator told us the Mahatma had cared greatly for punctuality. Then he narrated the story of the great man's exploits in South Africa, his salt march, and the various struggles against the rule of despotic imperialists. Above us flew thousands of crows, and fruitbats which swooped low, skimming your face.

On the way back I asked Mohammad Rafiq what he thought of Gandhi, and he replied with a shout: 'Hindu, Hindu, only Hindu – what is he for Ahmedabad? What did that man care for Muslims? What did he know? Nothing.' As we drove back into town Mohammad Rafiq flourished a long, hand-held hooter, waving and squeezing it viciously at his fellow rickshaw drivers as if it were a small, rabid dog.

To get to Sabarmati Ashram, you sit in a traffic jam for an hour or more. I had fondly imagined it would still be in the middle of nowhere, flanked by leafy forests and green fields. In fact it is surrounded by the mean urban sprawl of the city of Ahmedabad, which is huge, and spreading, and has the worst pollution in India. In the middle of the city there is no wind or air – just a choking, floating bundle of harsh, foul, black, metallic fumes.

Inside the ashram were some willow trees and palm trees, flocks of whirling, chirping birds, a strong smell of insanitation, and endless parties of schoolgirls with pigtails who sat cross-legged in the 'Prayer Area' singing the national anthem. By the main gate was an admiring plaque commemorating Sardar Vallabhbhai Patel as 'The Ironman who integrated all the Princely State'. The ground was covered by a layer of brown sand, while the buildings were low, square and airy, with red-tiled roofs. Like Tolstoy and Phoenix ashrams in South Africa, this place had once been a centre of vigorous social and political activity.

I went into a room full of dark-green filing cabinets, and after some time was summoned into an office with pink walls, a bed in the corner, and a wall covered in photographs of Nehru. Behind a desk sat the ashram secretary, Mr Amrut Modi. He was squat and grumpy, bored rather than hostile, and it was impossible to hold his attention for more than a few seconds. He told me he had once worked for the revered land reformer Vinoba Bhave, who was depicted on the door of the office wearing Ray-Bans, and that he was now responsible for preserving Gandhi's legacy. Mr Modi had the air of a government functionary, and a look of deep, almost existential boredom. His idealism appeared to have evaporated half a century ago.

I spent some days working in the ashram archives. A broken air-conditioning unit had been hacked aggressively into a wall, leaving gaps of visible daylight; facing it was a clock, two hours slow. Each morning I was required to complete a long and complex admissions form, full of headings and sub-sections, despite being the only researcher in the building. The archives contained a seven-hundred-page book by an Australian who had walked the route of the salt march in 1983. It was very earnest, and packed with details about rickshaw drivers who had overcharged him by a couple of rupees, that perennial worry of the foreign tourist in India. There was one notable discovery in the book: a *satyagrahi* on the march had in later life been indicted for murder.

As I wandered about in the morning sun one day, and scrambled along the banks of the wide, stagnant Sabarmati river, I met Laxmi Kant, who invited me back to his office to take tea. He was the ashram's accountant, lacked teeth, and had been there for thirty-odd years. On his desk sat a grey telephone inside a wooden box, a typewriter swathed in plastic, and stacks of brown paper tied up with rope. He wore slip-on plastic shoes, and had a concerned air. Above him was a big picture of the Mahatma, and a cage containing a pair of tiny munias. People came and went, and a sweeper moved between our feet like a crab, which I tried not to find disconcerting.

Laxmi Kant explained: 'When I first came here to the ashram there were many Gandhi followers, weaving *khadi*, supporting ourselves. In those days politicians were helping the masses, but now they are helping their mouths. Poor people, village people follow Gandhi-ji, but the power at the top does not. That is our trouble.'

'Have people forgotten Gandhi-ji?' I asked him.

'Look at the salt march,' he answered, 'now the State Government takes a sales tax on everything, so you see salt tax can vary between 5 per cent and 15 per cent. Salt with iodide – let's say plastic-pouch-packaged – can be even more expensive. It is becoming big business. Fishermen have the same problem. Big ships are coming with nets. Gujarati fishermen cannot even have proper fishing harbours – their demands are hanging afire – while the big industries have all facilities handed to them on a silver platter.'

Mr Kant sent me off to see Vijaybhai Atodaria, an elderly former teacher who had been at the ashram since the age of eleven. He was standing outside Hridaya Kunj ('Heart of the Garden'), which was Gandhi's own hut, and wore a waistcoat with three clutches of brown buttons down the front. He had bare feet, white trousers, the usual *khadi kurta*, a pepper-and-salt moustache and white hair. Mr Atodaria was the keeper of Hridaya Kunj, and enormously proud.

He showed me a book containing the signatures of eminent visitors he had welcomed. They included the former Indian Prime Minister and auto-urine therapist Morarji Desai, America's first lady and first child Hillary and Chelsea Clinton, the revered Nelson Mandela, India's pouting premier Narasimha Rao (who was about to be put on trial for corruption), and even Britain's very own Uncle Jim Callaghan. Mandela's note in the book read: 'Feelings of joy and happiness filled our hearts as we went in and out of the Ashram, feeling the heavy and pervading presence of the Mahatma.'

Mr Atodaria told me that a variety of politicians had set off on the march. The former Prime Minister Rajiv Gandhi, aided by a fleet of support vehicles, a gigantic entourage of Congress sycophants and a specially laid tarmac road, had managed about ten miles before returning to New Delhi.

In the Mahatma's own room there were three grass mats, two cotton-clad cushions, and a low desk with a statue of the three wise monkeys and an old watch. I felt elated to be there, to think of him sitting on that very cushion, planning the dissolution of the British Empire in a pan of seawater. My reverie was disturbed when a group of trainee tax inspectors appeared. One of them showed me a photograph of Gandhi in South Africa in 1906, captioned: 'Red Cross service in Zoolu Revolt, he was Sergeant-Major'. The leader of the group ('Commissioner of Income Tax, Ahmedabad') announced to the party, so that I could hear: 'Ability to survive tough times and purity of his soul is what makes Gandhi important today. Go to look at the masses if you wish to see Gandhian ideas. It is the dignity of toil in action.' A month or two later I read in a newspaper report that most of Ahmedabad's tax officials had just been arrested on charges of fraud.

Even by the standards of rural India, the latrines at Sabarmati Ashram were sinks of iniquity. There was the sour-sweet stench of bubbling urinals that splashed over your feet, excrement-smeared holes in the ground, redundant tins full of ash and *bidi* stubs, a bank of dead light-switches and countless smears of vivid, expectorated orange-red betel juice.

Now, Mahatma Gandhi had strong things to say on the subject of sanitation, and he is known to have angrily reprimanded any of his followers who failed to engage in regular toilet cleaning. In the list of daily 'sayings' in his *Collected Works* you can find such useful apophthegms as: 'The first service is latrine-cleaning.' I thought I had better go and consult the ashram's stumpy-toothed director.

'Mr Modi,' I asked, 'who cleans the toilets at the ashram?'

'One sweeper woman comes,' he answered, squinting, pulling a toothpick out of his mouth, leaning back on his chair, 'but she always leaves after an hour, so it becomes dirty.'

'But don't you – as a Gandhian – clean the toilets yourself, in accordance with his teachings?'

He looked up at the ceiling, where a lizard could be seen scurrying. 'We all clean the toilets together, on Gandhi-ji's birthday,' came his answer, gradually, 'as a symbol to show that we understand his message.'

An hour or so later I went off to meet the founder of the Environmental Sanitation Institute, which was affiliated to the ashram. As I approached the entrance, I noticed I was in a strange sculpture park. Sprouting out of a concrete lawn, like giant mushrooms or small shrubs, were perhaps a hundred toilets of every size, shape and variety. There were long drops and short drops, and ones where you stand with your feet on little platforms, ones where you sit, or stand, or crouch, or squat.

I was ushered into a sort of office, and directed up onto a raised dais. A plump, rather handsome man, dressed in the now familiar *khadi* outfit, turned to me after a few moments with the unbeatable opening line: 'Welcome. My name is Mr Toilet.' He then introduced me to two colleagues, Mr Mankad ('superintending engineer, Gujarat Water Supply and Sewerage Board') and Professor Pathak ('respected scholar, ecologist also'). The engineer was young, round and jolly, while the professor wore tweeds and looked rather distinguished, like a stately tortoise.

Mr Toilet gave a command, and a smiling man, who turned out to be his son and co-worker, handed me an envelope marked 'Mr Toilet (Ishwarbhai Patel) – At A Glance Biodata'. Out popped a concertinaed printed document, full of photographs and a section titled 'Abound in Awards', detailing Mr Toilet's myriad achievements. It explained that as a schoolboy, 'once he used the stick and basket of a toilet scavenger, the community people immediately blamed him for touching scavenger as a sin. He was sprinkled with water to make him touchable. After this incident a thought of devotion to cleanliness born in his tender mind, leading him with full vigour, enthusiasm for nearly four decades as a low cost sanitation technologist – Mr Toilet ... His mission is for uplift of downtrodden sweepers and scavengers and eradication of evil of sociocultural inequalities, the second independence, remaining work of M.K. Gandhi.'

Mr Toilet's story was a remarkable one. He had been born into a prosperous farming family in northern Gujarat in the 1930s, but after his youthful encounter with the scavenger's stick and basket, he had literally devoted his life to sanitary matters. As an example to others he had refused an arranged marriage into a landowning farming family. 'No, I took as my own wife a *dalit*, a downtrodden girl, to help with the upliftment of grassroots people.'

His institute had trained thousands of village health workers and engineers, built many wells and 'bathing platforms', inaugurated countless toilet exhibitions and soak-away pits, and constructed, he said, over a quarter of a million rural latrines. Now he sat on a national commission on sanitary workers in New Delhi, and was a recipient of the coveted Padma Shri. He told me that his whole life's activities had been based on his devotion to the memory and the message of Mahatma Gandhi.

'I have a precept,' he whispered confidentially, 'which I should like you to remember. It is this: "WATER IS LIFE". '

When I thought about Mr Toilet some months later, I decided he was one of the most impressive people I had met in Gujarat.

I noticed an ancient man in a *khadi dhoti*, spectacles and wooden-pegged *chappals* like the ones Gandhi had worn. His feet were badly cracked. It was difficult to get him to talk, but with encouragement from a Parsi woman called Babsy, he told me his name was Mangaldas Kuberbhai, and that he had been at the ashram since he was a child. He was carrying a wooden suitcase (I was permitted a quick peep inside) which contained a spinning wheel, and he said he spent several hours each day spinning cotton, as Gandhi himself had taught him. He refused to say anything about his personal memories of the great man.

'But what do you think were Gandhi-ji's most important teachings?' I asked, in desperation.

He thought for a long time before answering: 'That humanity should have love, and there should be social uplift for ladies.' He paused, and then continued with a wave of his hand, 'And, of course, that there should be prohibition of wine.'

I set off from Sabarmati Ashram to Dandi on 30 January. It was forty-eight years to the day since Gandhi's assassination. That morning the air was hot and clear, and the staff of the ashram had organized a ceremony in honour of the Mahatma's martyrdom. At the gate were lines of police, soldiers, press photographers and gleaming white Ambassador cars with red flashing lights. This signified the presence of politicians. With the Indian gift of conjuring a spectacle out of nowhere, a huge platform had been built outside Gandhi's own room, and covered with long mattresses and bolsters. Above it was a huge, brightly coloured cloth awning, and all around were flags and banners, and bunches of leaves tied onto bamboo poles. Opposite the platform sat about two thousand schoolchildren and devotees. Behind them stood a line of beefy men in white shorts and t-shirts, like something out of the 1936 Berlin Olympics.

To my surprise, I was summoned up onto the platform to sit with the guests of honour, who included Mr Modi, Mr Toilet, Professor Pathak, some important local religious leaders and various Congress politicians. Lots of songs were sung, and speeches uttered into a large microphone. There was a lull, and then Mr Modi, to loud murmuring approval, introduced me to the crowd as a young American who was about to follow Gandhi's salt march. This was embarrassing, but no speech was required. I enjoyed my adjusted nationality, which seemed typical of Mr Modi's lax approach to life. Then we had a two-hour harangue from a visiting speaker about Ruskin, Tolstoy and the perils of air travel.

When Gandhi marched to the sea he walked down tracks strewn with flower petals and green leaves, and he gave speeches to huge public gatherings. He exhorted the people to boycott foreign cloth, renounce any official posts, and to resist the lure of alcohol and cigarettes. Despite his age, he walked strongly and at great speed. As Lord Irwin wrote with some disappointment, Gandhi was 'regrettably hale and hearty'. This must have been the result, thought the Viceroy, of his lacking vices, 'such as drink or anything else'.

It was now approaching midday. I was feeling reasonably hale and

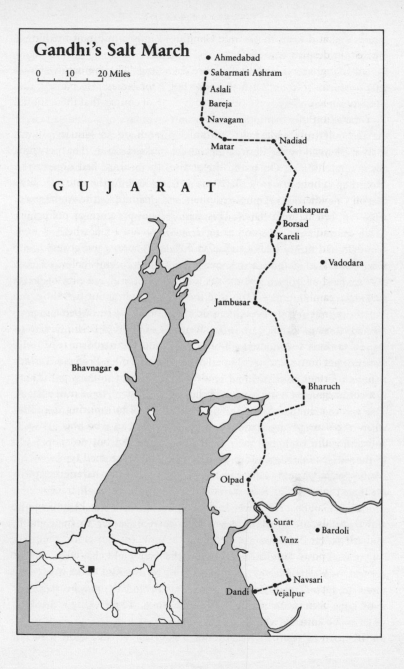

Gandhi's Salt March

0   10   20 Miles

GUJARAT

Ahmedabad
Sabarmati Ashram
Aslali
Bareja
Navagam
Matar
Nadiad
Kankapura
Borsad
Kareli
Vadodara
Jambusar
Bhavnagar
Bharuch
Olpad
Surat
Bardoli
Vanz
Navsari
Dandi
Vejalpur

hearty, and was keen to get my feet into Gandhi's footsteps. The road out of Ahmedabad was crowded and dusty as I set off past Videocom Bazooka Store and Jayalaxmi Tyre Service. Lorries whipped past me, and after a couple of hours I felt like quitting, it was so hot and dusty, and so desperately polluted.

Gandhi and his entourage took twenty-two days of walking to cover the 240 miles to Dandi; I was to do it in ten days, for my plans were soon accelerated by the desiccating suburban degradation that had over-taken rural Gujarat. On parts of the journey the road was simply too choked and congested to walk. I was to travel variously by bicycle, foot, Maruti One microbus, Limca delivery truck, dust-choked auto-rickshaw, and even, briefly, on a flat wooden cart drawn by a leathery old camel, which sprayed lightly scented green urine on both me and its driver with some glee. I quickly realized that Mohandas Gandhi's world had gone. Since he walked to the sea to subvert the King Emperor, the population of India has quadrupled and the fields of Gujarat have been overwhelmed by industrial pollution.

It was a depressing experience as I made my way through Navagam, Nadiad, Borsad, Kareli, Jambusar, Bharuch and Navsari on my way to Dandi. At times I wondered whether these semi-industrial parts of India were not just some vast, terrible mistake. This was the face of the country that, as a foreign tourist, I had never seen. I was not in the giant shanty towns and slums of Bombay, or the alluring poverty of Himalayan villages. This was the comparative grinding deprivation of farming communities where the younger generation have gone to the cities, of blocked wells and unfinished buildings with protruding metal rods waving hopelessly in the wind, of day labourers who are not paid what they are promised by the *patels*, of politicians and local officials who have better things to do than their job, of aspiration and dislocation, of satellite television promising a life that will never come, of a world where old village customs and traditions are breaking down with no replacement but alienation, the seed ground of extremist politics.

Aslali, where Gandhi and I spent the first night, has now almost merged into Ahmedabad. It looked fairly prosperous, with two- and three-storey buildings facing a pond, but behind them were banks of mud huts, their walls painted with cow dung. There was no drinking water piped into the village, and a woman said they had to walk up to the big road to fetch it. Nearby was a huge lorry park, filled with red and orange 'private carrier' trucks, stacked with lethal steel girders. They were painted with the usual Indian bumper slogans, varying from the obvious 'All India Permit, Blow Horn, Dipper Please', to the inexplicable (if frequent) 'Wait for Side', and the invaluable 'Careful. Use Diper at Night'. The ground in the lorry park was drenched with oil and discharged diesel.

At Bareja, home to two squalid *dhabas*, the population had risen from 2,400 in Gandhi's time to twenty-five thousand today. Many people here were still farmers, and some of the richer ones used harvesting machines. A few miles further on at Navagam, there were fields of wheat surrounded by bushy trees. Old men with blackened, creased faces and bright white turbans sat by the roadside, guarding camel carts filled with straw. They told me the water they got from the river was polluted with chemicals from the textile mills of Ahmedabad, and they all had stories of rashes and skin disease experienced by their families. When I asked about Gandhi, they shrugged their shoulders and were vaguely complimentary. One man said, 'Once this was called Dandi Marg, but now he is forgotten here.'

The fields beside the winding track down to Nadiad and Kankapura were very lush, with tobacco plants growing in them. I was now close to the place where Vallabhbhai Patel had launched his campaign against the payment of taxes in 1928. A shopkeeper told me that local children were employed to roll tendu leaves into *bidis*, for which they were paid a minimal amount. For the first time I was feeling that I was in real, remote, rural India, with big leaping monkeys, screeching parrots and crowds of startled children. In Kankapura itself there were tiny huts, and no electricity or telephones, just wild pigs and dogs and miniature ponies that looked like goats. I felt an authenticity, that what I was seeing was close to what was here in 1930. People were very friendly, if astonished by my presence, and old men in *dhotis* with brown stumps for teeth showed me the place where Gandhi-ji forded the Mahi river to reach Kareli. It was clear they revered his memory, and were honoured he had crossed their river at this spot on his epic march.

While Gandhi was here, on the eighth day of his journey, he complained about his followers using labourers to carry their kerosene Kitson lamps and provisions. By this stage his hand-picked pilgrims had been joined by several hundred other marchers. They were exhorted to remember the religious as well as the political purpose of the excursion, and

Gandhi read them extracts from the Bible as well as from the *Gita*. That evening he was visited by Jawaharlal Nehru, who had travelled down to support the pilgrimage and, arriving as night was falling, been forced to wade through the river to reach the *satyagrahis'* camp.

In later life, Nehru would write that the sight of Gandhi on his way to Dandi, 'marching, staff in hand . . . the pilgrim on his quest for truth, quiet, peaceful, determined and fearless', was his most enduring mental image of the old man.[1] The next morning they discussed the virtues of sacrifice, and a few days later his father Motilal Nehru decided to donate the family's ancestral home, Anand Bhawan in Allahabad, to the nation. From 22 March 1930 it was renamed 'Swaraj Bhawan', and became a centre of Congress activism.

Heading south again I passed lakes and rivers. The soil was turning red. On one track I met cattle herders in red outfits, with topknots and big earrings. The region looked poor, and women were carrying water on their heads in big tins. A round man called Hockey ('an English name, like the sport') said the big factories towards Bharuch were getting all the good water; here it was saline. He added, flashing jewelled fingers, that much of the wealth in the area came from overseas, in the form of pounds and dollars, and that each village had 'foreigner houses', owned by those who were working in Europe, America and the Gulf.

Bharuch, or Broach, turned out to be huge; it took nearly two hours to get to the centre by auto-rickshaw. It was here that Gandhi proclaimed 'the duty of disloyalty' – the idea that loyalty to an oppressive government was itself a crime. It is recorded that he addressed a crowd of fifteen thousand people, two hundred of whom were Muslim. This, notably, was the largest group of Muslims known to have listened to him during the march.[2] Bharuch was a factory port during the time of the East India Company, and has been a trading place for more than two thousand years. Like much of urban Gujarat, it was fairly evenly divided between Hindus and Muslims. At a business level there is a symbiotic relationship, Muslims for example running the taxi services and Hindus controlling the petrol distribution.

Bitten by too many nights in roadside guest-houses, I decided to stay in a supposedly fancy hotel. I waited while a feral character in overalls rewired the bathroom and pretended to change the sheets. Drinking strong tea, I spoke to Anil Narayan Naik, a thin waiter in slippery brown trousers who said he was a Christian. He disapproved strongly of the decadence caused by satellite-beamed foreign television, but was proud of the fact that his manager had installed it in every room. He said Mahatma Gandhi was responsible for the division of India and the creation of Pakistan.

As I was ushered into my room, the man in overalls proudly flicked a single switch which simultaneously activated a row of neon striplights and a loud television. 'Star Plus TV is the best channel for you,' he announced, pressing one of the buttons below the blaring screen. Slumped on the bed in a stupor, I found I was facing *Baywatch*, followed by *BBC Food and Drink*. This was the new India.

Over the sixty miles between Bharuch and the next big city, Surat, I walked through beautiful villages where little stalls sold sugarcane, purple carrots, red onions, peas in their pods, sweet potatoes and tiny pale aubergines. Yet much of the time I noticed nothing but the severity of the chemical pollution, and the fatalism with which it was accepted. Again and again people told me there were regulations, and inspections, and even occasional fines, but that nothing ever changed. I passed a biogas plant with a sign outside reading 'Affluence Through Effluent' – a Gandhian slogan if ever there was one.

In Olpad, a lonely town just north of Surat, I met G.R. Patel, a talkative old shopkeeper who sold 'dry goods' and was an ardent anglophile. He had two cousins who worked in a valve factory in Walsall. We were brought glasses of water by his rather taciturn son, Giris, who seemed less keen on the British connection. When pressed, Giris told me he was a market trader specializing in electrical goods.

'Is your stall here in Olpad?' I asked him, nodding towards the shops across the road.

'No,' he replied, deadpan. 'It's in West Bromwich.'

When Giris had departed, G.R. said, 'My son lives in your country but he is still a Gujarati.' There was a pause, and I could see him pondering before he spoke again. 'He tells me that in England they call him a Paki. Why do they do this? My boy has never been to Pakistan. Why would he want to go there? The place is full of Mussulmans.'

On the far side of Surat, where bubonic plague had struck the previous year, I disembarked from the bus and walked along the road until I reached the village of Dhaman, where the fields were yellow and wreathed with dust.

Ranchod Patel was sleek and strong in a *dhoti* and cotton vest. He was seventy-seven years old and could remember the salt march. Gandhi had made a speech by the lake, and all the children had climbed up trees to see him. 'We listened to him talk,' said Ranchod Patel, as we sat on a swinging wooden seat outside his house, 'and then we walked along with him towards the sea. But Gandhi-ji said to us, "Go home, I don't want you to walk with me because I walk too fast." He was having a joke. We were just young children, you see. He was a good man, but he was too worried about the British rule.'

'Weren't you glad when independence came?' I asked.

'The British never came into my village, and I don't like to travel to the city. The government makes the rules and I live my life. It makes no difference. Same to same.'

'So how old were you when you first saw a European?'

'Around thirty years old,' came the inevitable answer, 'when a man like you came here following the salt march of Gandhi-ji, and asked me the same question.'

When I reached Navsari it was getting dark and I felt tired out from talking and travelling. I walked up the main street, past a statue of the mutual hero of Gandhi and Jinnah, Dadabhoy Naoroji MP, the 'Daboo Parsee General Tailors' and a cinema where *Bandit Queen* was showing. It was getting dark when I went into the Gupta Dining Hall. Before serving me, the proprietor performed a brief *puja*. Turning on the fans and lights in the long room was integrated carefully into a chanting and incense-wafting routine. Then he declared his restaurant open for the evening, and ordered me a de-luxe *thali*. It was the only dish on the menu.

On the morning of 6 April 1930, Mohandas 'Mahatma' Gandhi took a ceremonial bath in the sea. The previous evening he had issued a brief statement saying: 'I want world sympathy in this battle of Right against Might.' During the journey, a third of all Indian officials along the route of the march had resigned their posts in protest against British rule.

To the intense irritation of the *satyagrahis*, the local magistrate had ordered the police to stir up the salt deposits on the nearby mud flats, which rather limited the photographic possibilities. Undaunted, Gandhi marched to the shore at Dandi and picked up a lump of salty mud. He was met by a shout of 'Hail, law breaker!' from the Congress activist Sarojini Naidu, a graduate of Girton College, Cambridge. A striking, outspoken woman, she was rumoured to have had an affair with Jinnah, whom she later praised for his 'tender intuition' and 'virile patriotism'. All over the beach, marchers, freedom fighters and local onlookers began to collect salt and purify it. Later that day Gandhi auctioned a lump of salt for the impressive sum of sixteen hundred rupees.

The salt *satyagraha* spread far beyond the coast of Gujarat.[3] In southern India, Rajagopalachari led a march from Trichinopoly to Vedaranniyam, overlooking the Palk Strait towards Ceylon, and was arrested with his band of followers. Up on the North-West Frontier, many miles from the sea, there was a large popular demonstration at Peshawar by Khan Abdul Ghaffar Khan's pro-Congress group known as the 'Red Shirts'. Unrest spread to Bombay and Karnataka. These demonstrations were followed by the rather more aggressive Chittagong armoury raid, when a group calling itself the 'Indian Republican Army' seized a large number of weapons from a local armoury and issued an independence proclamation. The historian Sumit Sarkar has called the Chittagong raid 'the most spectacular coup in the entire history of terrorism'.[4]

To everybody's surprise, Gandhi was not arrested on the seashore at Dandi. Instead he returned a few miles inland, where he stayed in a specially built palm-leaf hut, and wondered what to do next. He knew that Irwin and his advisers were in a quandary: 'The government's plight is that of the serpent which has swallowed a rat,' he said. 'It would find it hard to resort to either course of action – allowing me to remain out or putting me behind the bars.'[5]

Over the next few weeks there were various salt-related demonstrations, which culminated in an assault on an officially run salt-production plant at Dharasana. Nearly two thousand marchers including the Mahatma's son Manilal and Sarojini Naidu attempted to storm the building. Using steel-tipped *lathis*, police beat back the advancing army of non-violent resisters. Two people were killed and 320 injured.

It was this overreaction by the forces of law and order – descriptions of which were publicized throughout Europe and the United States by reporters who had witnessed it – that turned the salt tax campaign into a propaganda coup for Congress and put the British back on the defensive. The Viceroy Lord Irwin responded by imprisoning almost twenty thousand protesters, and Gandhi was arrested at his hut in the middle of the night and taken to Bombay by train. From there he was driven to Yeravda Jail in a large yellow Studebaker, and on arrival was greeted by handshakes and tipped hats from prison officials. With the Congress Working Committee and tens of thousands of demonstrators in the cells, Irwin could do little but sit tight while back in London the India Office tried to invent a new policy.

As Congress activists languished in prisons around the country, the British government went ahead and convened a 'Round Table' Conference in London. Although in the eyes of many Tories this was a dangerously progressive move, as far as Congress was concerned it was an empty gesture. Gandhi announced that he was interested in 'complete freedom', not in procrastination by Whitehall, and refused to attend. Subhas Bose suggested that the aim of the conference was to bring 'a large number of nondescript Indians nominated by the alien Government . . . to England and make them fight amongst themselves for the amusement of the British people'.[6] Jawaharlal Nehru dismissed the delegates as an 'assembly of vested interests', with the British offering 'seats for the Hindus, for the Muslims, for the Sikhs, for the Anglo-Indians . . . Opportunism was rampant, and different groups seemed to prowl about like hungry wolves waiting for their prey – the spoils under the new constitution'.[7]

The Conference began in November 1930, the delegates consisting principally of princes, *taluqdars*, members of the loyalist National Liberal Federation and various leaders of minority groups. Platitudes were spoken, but little of substance was achieved.

I left my room in the Hotel Gupta at 5 a.m., wearing a white *khadi kurta* and Gandhian sandals made of 'naturally dead cow hide', determined to reach the coast that day. It was bitingly cold. I walked fast past shapes huddled in blankets by the roadside, hunched figures pushed to the side of the pavement.

When I reached Vejalpur, a stallholder had started a fire out of twigs, and we drank hot gingery *chai*. I was off quickly, past the 'Navsari Agricultural Project (Paddy Testing) Centre' and spiked bushes. Tall badh trees stood at the roadside with long aerial roots hanging down from them. As the sun came up I was joined by giant 'SCHOOLAUTO' rickshaws packed with children, waterbottles and school bags strung over the back of the rickshaw like webbing. I watched water buffalo stampede in a field of sugarcane stubble, running wild while two boys tried to control them. The light was thin. An old man in a Gandhi cap was piling cow-dung patties into a stockade.

Towards midday I got to the Gandhi Smriti Mandir (Sacred Gandhi Memorial Site) and met Indrasingh Rawat, to whom I had been given an introduction by Mr Modi from Sabarmati Ashram. He was smiling and sixty-odd, dressed as expected in *khadi*, and I liked him at once. There was a lounging son called Rakesh in a black shellsuit with pink fluorescent stripes on the legs, who said he was a farming expert, and looked like a Samoan wrestler. 'I have respect for Gandhi-ji,' said Rakesh, chewing gum and slicking back long black hair, 'but I am not a follower.' Inside the house was his young wife of two days, called Laxmi, the henna patterns from the wedding ceremony still visible on her hands and feet.

'I do not call myself a traditionalist,' said Mr Rawat, 'so I did not force my daughter-in-law to live in our house. However she chooses to do so.'

Laxmi smiled coyly, happily, then disappeared out into the yard.

'Other foreigners have followed the salt march,' said Mr Rawat. 'There was one from the United States of America and also an English man called Paul Satya, who had a ponytail in his hair.' *Satya* means truth, so this may not have been his given name.

He took me up a row of steps into a large white bunker, suspended in mid-air on four long concrete stilts. It was intended as a sort of museum to Gandhi. There were some good photographs of the Mahatma, including one with a goat and one with Jinnah. There was also a picture of the opening session of the 1931 Round Table Conference. The delegates were sitting at an E-shaped construction, like the conjoined tables at a wedding party. This solved a question on which I had been pondering for some time.

I noticed that the building dipped down in the middle, which made me feel rather queasy as I climbed up the floor to look at the photographs on the walls. 'Is there a structural problem here, Mr Rawat-ji?' I asked. I knew that he used to be a civil engineer before abandoning everyday living in 1965 in favour of Vinoba Bhave's Bhoodan movement, which aimed to acquire land for the landless. 'Oh, no!' he replied. 'It is deliberate. We constructed our building in the shape of a Gandhi cap, combined with a boat since we are near the sea. That is why our floor may make you seasick.' Only in India, I thought.

We walked back to Mr Rawat's house and sat on chairs by the front door, drinking hot water. The house overlooked a shallow lake. He said to me, 'I believe in world peace, that Almighty Godfather is one, irrespective of religions or of your country. When one *crore* [ten million] people came to Calcutta from Bangladesh in 1971, I went with 185 peace workers and helpers to stop the conflict and rioting. Gandhi's message is truth and non-violence. I believe that as it diminishes in India, so it is growing in the West. Gandhi's other message, maybe his most important teaching, was the importance of celibacy. For fourteen years my wife and I, by mutual consent, have had celibacy within marriage.' At this point he turned to his wife, who nodded convincingly. 'It is as Gandhi-ji and Kasturba had. By practising yoga, I am able to direct my energy in a spiritual direction. My slogan is "*Om Shanti*" – Peace. I own no insurance and no property.'

He took me to see the hut where Gandhi had stayed. A wooden sign read: 'This is the place from where Mahatma Gandhi was arrested by the British Government after midnight on May 4 1930, under Bombay Regulation XXV of 1827, which provided for detention without trial.' The walls were made of palm leaves, or *khajoori*, woven into split bamboo, and the floor was spread with soft, dry earth. I was tired from walking, and Mr Rawat suggested I might rest there for a while. I lay under a cotton blanket. It was a beautiful place to sleep, cool and breezy under the shade of a mango tree, and it was exhilarating to know that Gandhi had lain there before he was taken by the police late one night.

At three o'clock in the afternoon I started off out of the village, my feet and my calves throbbing. The road to the sea was dead straight. I walked across the hard stones, and the sun hit me and hit me and hit me again. Around me nothing was happening, continuously. Each day I had been amazed by the sheer physical stamina of Gandhi, walking along these tracks at sixty-one, ever resilient. As I reached Dandi I was feeling sick, watching a man round-net fishing in a little inlet. At the coast there were two small semi-circles of huts, four stalls and a noisy sugarcane-crushing machine which whirred, empty. The people there were indifferent, even hostile. The beach was grey and flat. A few long wooden boats rocked out at sea in the distance.

I reached the shore, but the salt was little more than a thin, crumbly, grey-brown crust which lay on top of the sand. I picked up a handful and watched it crumble away through my fingers. I was in Dandi. The salt march had ended, and I knew that Gandhi's dreams for Gujarat – and for India – had not been realized. I reached the shallow water, dipped in my hand, made the sign of the cross, involuntarily, and kept on walking while my knees buckled.

SIX

A Half Nude Gent

In late January 1931, Gandhi was released by Lord Irwin. The Viceroy now tried the dramatic tactic of attempting to solve India's political crisis through open negotiation. With Gandhi's disciple Mirabehn (an admiral's daughter formerly called Madeleine Slade) in attendance, preparing dates and milk for her master on the marble floor outside Irwin's study, the two men held talks. On 5 March they announced an agreement. Gandhi would end civil disobedience of all kinds, including the boycott of British goods, and attend the next Round Table Conference in London. In return Irwin would recognize the virtues of the *swadeshi* movement, and release the thousands of imprisoned freedom fighters.

The Gandhi–Irwin Pact was a triumph for both men. Sarojini Naidu referred to them as 'the two mahatmas'. The Congress leader was for the first time treated as an equal, while the Viceroy restored peace with no further bloodshed. Although it was a mutually beneficial agreement, inevitably it was denounced on both sides. More radical elements within Congress saw it as a capitulation by Gandhi in exchange for the vaguest of British promises, while right-wing Tories thought it a disgraceful surrender to the forces of disorder.

Throughout his viceroyalty, Irwin showed a degree of foresight, realizing that suppression could only succeed in the short term. Unlike many British ICS officials at this time, who in Nehru's words 'judged Indians from the sycophants and office-seekers who surrounded them and dismissed others as agitators and knaves', the Viceroy understood that mass civil disobedience was the result of more than the seditious agitation of a handful of troublemakers.[1]

However, Lord Irwin gave way to Jinnah's old enemy Lord Willingdon in the summer of 1931, just as construction of the magnificent new Viceroy's House in New Delhi was completed. Willingdon was a standard-issue top-ranking bureaucrat who had served in senior positions around the Empire, despite being poor at day-to-day administration. On arrival in India he wrote to tell his son how daunted he felt: 'But the atmosphere is really getting better and Gandhi is losing some of his influence, though of course with the masses this half nude gent will always be looked upon as a god. I'm seriously thinking of trying the same stunt to see what they would think of me as a Mahatma.'[2]

Willingdon's difficulty was that it made little difference whether he was nude, half nude or fully dressed. As he wrote to his son a few weeks later: 'The real trouble is that Gandhi looks upon himself as equal and parallel with me in working the administration of the country and not without some reason. You see, the negotiations for this settlement were carried out by the then Viceroy and Gandhi on absolute terms of equality and the conditions for Gandhi calling off his civil disobedience campaign were agreed upon as between two opposing generals.' He knew that the best he could hope for during his tenure of office was to hold the line. 'I have told you what I think of the settlement, and must own I rather wish Irwin had been here to sweep up the mess he left behind him!'[3]

The second Round Table Conference, which was held in London in autumn 1931, achieved little more than the first. There was the usual selection of Sikh activists, Muslim Leaguers, British officials and princely spokesmen. Gandhi came as the sole representative of Congress, accompanied by an entourage consisting of his secretaries Pyarelal and Mahadev Desai, his financier G.D. Birla, the faithful Mirabehn and various other admirers. His potential as a negotiator was limited by the tight remit he had been given by the Congress Working Committee before his departure, which still insisted on the demand for *purna swaraj*.

Dr Bhimrao Ramji Ambedkar attended the Conference in order to speak for the 'depressed' or 'downtrodden' castes. Ambedkar was angered when Gandhi maintained that he represented all the castes of Hinduism 'in his own person'. A protracted battle ensued over whether a special 'award' of reserved seats should be allocated to the depressed castes, Gandhi vigorously opposing the proposal, which he saw as an example of 'divide-and-rule' which would destroy Congress's ability to speak for the whole Indian nation. In Ambedkar's view, Gandhi's practice of calling the casteless '*Harijans*' or 'Children of God' was little more than political posturing. It should also be noted that every other delegate, and in particular the three Muslim League representatives, vehemently objected to Gandhi's assertion that he, as the voice of Congress, spoke for the entire Indian people.

The new Secretary of State for India, Sir Samuel Hoare, had been given a warning by Willingdon of what to expect: 'He may be a saint, he may be a holy man; he is I believe quite sincere in his principles; but of this I am perfectly certain, that he is one of the most astute politically-minded and bargaining little gentlemen I ever came across.'[4] The discussions soon foundered on the divisions within the different sections of Indian society that were represented by the various delegates. In most meetings Gandhi was in a minority of one, since the other special-interest groups could only benefit from specific political concessions, while Congress rejected any move that limited its own claim to be the one true representative of the Indian nation.

Gandhi returned to Bombay in December, with his political reputation diminished among his supporters. A week later, owing to a revival of rent strikes and civil disobedience in the United Provinces, he was returned to prison. Willingdon was inclined towards repression rather than negotiation, so with the aid of various legal ordinances, the working structures of Congress were outlawed and its activists arrested once more.

Shortly before this took place, Sardar Patel was elected President of Congress. The right-wing 'Old Guard' of India's west coast, epitomized by Patel and Gandhi, reasserted itself against younger and more radical elements. The two men spent 1932 and much of 1933 together in Yeravda Jail. Patel ministered to the Mahatma, making him a special beverage each morning of baking soda, lime, honey and warm water. At Gandhi's instigation, he began to learn Sanskrit.

Although they had a number of disputes, Patel believing that Gandhi tried too hard to accommodate minorities, it was perhaps the high point of their relationship. Patel had found during his *satyagraha* campaigns that Muslims and Parsis were apt to cooperate with the authorities too readily, which was his official excuse for holding them in low esteem. Although he was a confirmed follower of Gandhi, he felt able to tease him, for instance over his dietary obsessions, and was a good antidote to the boot-faced disciples who began to cluster around the Mahatma in his later years. When Gandhi received a letter in his capacity as India's agony aunt from a man who was worried his wife was too ugly, Patel suggested he write back and tell him to have his eyes put out.

During Lord Willingdon's unimaginative viceroyalty, control was retained by activating obscure laws and ancient ordinances. Jawaharlal Nehru noted in August 1933 – his father Motilal having died a fortnight after being released from prison in 1931 – that 'India was the ideal police state, and the police mentality pervaded all spheres of government. Outwardly all non-conformity was suppressed, and a vast army of spies and secret agents covered the land.'[5] The phrase 'a vast army' was an exaggeration, but it is true that the activities of intelligence operatives had now begun to extend into many areas of daily life. The politician Rafi Ahmad Kidwai was irritated by the interceptors of his mail delaying its arrival, and after some thought he sent a letter of complaint to himself, which solved the problem.

In November 1930, Jinnah had attended the first Round Table Conference in London, at which he stated that four main parties were involved in the negotiations – the British, the princely rulers, the Hindus and the Muslims. This was a new departure in his political strategy, presenting the Muslims of India not as people with special interests and wishes, but as a distinct group in their own right. The Government of India's senior consultative official at the Conference, Sir Malcolm Hailey, reported back privately to Irwin, with the combination of racial and social snobbery at which the British excel: 'Jinnah is of course a good deal mistrusted . . . But then Jinnah of course was always the perfect little bounder and as slippery as the eels which his forefathers purveyed in the Bombay market.'[6]

Jinnah was now living in London, having summoned his faithful sister Fatima and his daughter Dina. They ensconced themselves in a large house with eight acres of garden in Hampstead. Breakfast was served at nine o'clock sharp, and he was then driven in his Bentley to his chambers in King's Bench Walk by his chauffeur, Bradbury. Lunch was generally taken at Simpson's, and was sometimes followed by dealings in stocks and shares. Dina was sent to boarding school, and the sombre Fatima, who had hated the late Ruttie and refused to have her name mentioned, guarded her brother ferociously. She controlled the household, and they dined together most evenings, alone, in silence. As Jinnah's biographer Stanley Wolpert wrote, Fatima became 'his sister-confidante, nursemaid, sounding board, and defender-against-the-outside-world'.[7]

Jinnah's legal practice prospered, perhaps not quite to the degree he might have hoped, but enough to earn him £25,000 a year. While Gandhi and Nehru divested themselves of their worldly possessions and languished in squalid British prisons, Jinnah developed a variety of financial interests, and bought several flats in Mayfair. Soon he was juggling a substantial portfolio of properties in different parts of the world. He had thoughts of trying to enter the British Parliament as a Labour MP, but no offers of seats were forthcoming. It is claimed that a Labour Party activist from Yorkshire opposed his selection on the grounds that he would not wish to be represented by 'a toff like that'.

It was during this period that the idea of a homeland for Indian Muslims came to be seriously considered. The original invention of 'Pakistan' can be traced back to a variety of locations. Purists usually begin with the suggestion by the radical British MP John Bright in 1858 that the Indian Empire might be broken up into several smaller states; then proceed erroneously to the intellectual influence of the college at Aligarh founded by the nineteenth-century Mughal grandee Sir Syed Ahmed Khan; and stop off at a meeting in Allahabad in 1930 at which the Punjabi barrister and Urdu poet Muhammad Iqbal proposed the 'two-nation theory' – that India was fundamentally divided between Hindus and Muslims. Iqbal was, like Jinnah, a barrister from Lincoln's Inn, and he was also a respected Islamic scholar and philosopher. At this meeting he proposed that irreconcilable differences between Hindus and Muslims meant separation was the only way forward. He did not yet envisage an independent state, but rather 'the creation of a Muslim India within India'.

The next, defining step came from one Choudhry Rahmat Ali. It was on the upper deck of a London bus that the name 'Pakstan' or 'Pakastan' first flashed before his eyes. He finally settled for 'Pakistan', which meant 'land of the pure' and doubled as an acronym of Punjab, Afghan (meaning the people of the North-West Frontier Province), Kashmir, Sind and Baluchistan. These were the areas of north-west India where Muslims were in a majority; Bengal, in the east, did not come into the equation at this point. In 1933 Rahmat Ali published a pamphlet under the title 'Now or Never'. Although its proposals grew out of Iqbal's speech, it was the first conception of total national separation. The new nation, he wrote, symbolized 'the proclamation of our freedom from British–Bania domination; the release of our nation from the bonds of Minorityism'.[8]

Little is known about Rahmat Ali, who vigorously pursued his 'Pakstanian' campaign from a bedsit in Cambridge, bombarding politicians and dignitaries with pamphlets. Some reports say he was a Bengali, others that he came from the North-West Frontier. In fact he was a Punjabi, from a poor background, born in 1897 and educated at Islamia College, Lahore. He became tutor to the Nawab of Bahawalpur (who at the age of five had saluted King George V at his Delhi *durbar*), and secured a place at Cambridge in 1931 owing to the recommendations of his teachers. The uncertainty about his life even extends to the question of his facial hair: when he was in his twenties living in Lahore, 'some say he was clean shaven, and some report that he had big moustaches which curled at the extremities, some adding that he sported a short, elegant beard'.[9]

Rahmat Ali was intense and deeply religious, a confirmed bachelor, and, according to his biographer, 'a Cambridge man par excellence', with gravitas and a strong sense of 'mission'. Like Jinnah he smoked Craven A cigarettes and was immensely fastidious, even making his landlady in Cambridge leave his dishes to drip dry, as he thought tea towels were unclean. This devotion to hygiene was not enough to secure a meeting with Jinnah: in 1934 he made efforts to see him for discussions, but the great man was too busy. In later years, as their aims diverged, Rahmat Ali launched aggressive attacks on Jinnah. His own ideas became progressively more eccentric, and by the time of his death from a chill in 1951, he was proposing a total of ten Muslim 'stans' across 'Pakasia', ranging from 'Maplistan' in southern India, through 'Siddiqistan' and 'Haideristan', to a union of Bengal and Assam with the wondrous name of 'Bang-i-Islam'. They would form part of a series of homelands for the world's Muslim community, or *millat*.

It is clear from contemporary documents that Rahmat Ali's scheme for a Muslim homeland gave form and a name to an existing sentiment. His 'Pakistan National Movement' is even mentioned in a German book on Islam, published in 1933 in Berlin. In 1940 he was to return to Karachi, but his apparent extremism led to hounding by the authorities. Rejected, as prophets are meant to be in their own lands, he was later refused a Pakistan passport, and he began to suspect he was being poisoned. Desperate, rejected, and slightly deranged, he disappeared into exile in October 1948 and was buried in an unmarked grave in Cambridge, leaving substantial debts.

Although the notion of Pakistan was memorably dismissed by a British Parliamentary Committee in 1933 as 'only a students' scheme . . . chimerical and impracticable', fewer than ten years later it was being taken seriously by most Indian Muslim leaders. The demand for a separate homeland was a radical bargaining position in fraught times, and

presented a direct challenge to the Indian National Congress. The underlying flaw, which was bypassed in the heady rush for power, was that
Islam was not in itself enough to bind people together.

Many rural Muslims had more in common with neighbouring
Hindus, sharing bridal songs and death rites, than with their co-
religionists at the other end of the subcontinent who spoke a different
language. An Urdu-speaker from the United Provinces might have the
same god as a Sindhi, but that did not mean they could communicate
with each other. The generic term 'Mussulman' concealed Sunnis and
Shias, rich and poor, Sufis and orthodox, Mughal descendants and converted Sudras, northerners and southerners, women and men, Bengalis
and Punjabis. As the historian Francis Robinson has pointed out in the
context of the United Provinces Muslims: 'They had no racial homogen-
eity, little common history and many conflicting interests. Some were
descended from converts, others from Arabs, Turks, Persians, Afghans
and Central Asians. Some spoke Urdu, others the various dialects of the
province – Braj, Bhojpuri and Awadhi.'[10]

Most important of all, nearly half the potential citizens of Pakistan,
whatever its precise boundaries, would be left behind. Muslims made up
just under a quarter of the total population of Britain's Indian Empire,
and although the majority of them were concentrated in the north-east
and north-west of the subcontinent, others were scattered throughout
the country. In the Madras Presidency in the south, for instance, Muslims
made up less than 5 per cent of the population. The apparent solution
to this quandary was the 'hostage theory', which maintained there would
be enough Hindus and Muslims remaining on either side of the border
to ensure reciprocal good treatment of minorities. It was a hopeful dream.

Through the 1930s, Mohammad Ali Jinnah travelled back and forth
between Britain and India. In early 1935 he attempted to secure a new
Hindu–Muslim agreement with Dr Rajendra Prasad, the president of
Congress, but his demands for the protection of the rights of Muslims
were rejected, and no progress was made. The Communal Award that had
followed the Second Round Table Conference put Bengali and Punjabi
Muslims in a strong position – they retained their separate electorates,
and were given more seats than any other community in the provincial
assemblies. Jinnah could see that new forces were at work among India's
Muslims, and that the time was coming when an inspirational new
Muslim League leader might be needed. He decided to move back to

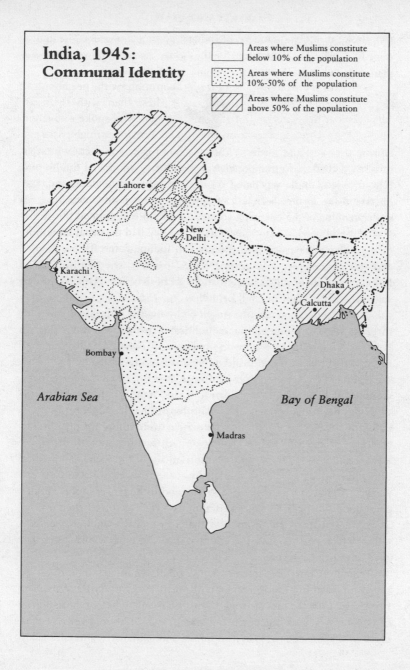

India, 1945:
Communal Identity

Areas where Muslims constitute
below 10% of the population

Areas where Muslims constitute
10%-50% of the population

Areas where Muslims constitute
above 50% of the population

Lahore

New Delhi

Karachi

Dhaka

Calcutta

Bombay

Arabian Sea

Bay of Bengal

Madras

India, while maintaining his house in Hampstead. It looked as if destiny was calling, but, being Jinnah, he preferred not to commit himself sooner than was necessary.

During the 1930s and forties, Winston Churchill was the leading Parliamentary defender of a traditionalist approach towards the British Empire. His attitude to India was based on instinct rather than on reason. Like his friend the former Secretary of State for India Lord Birkenhead, his understanding of the country's social and religious structures was superficial. He had a broad, emotional, Edwardian belief in the racial superiority of the pinkish-grey races and the need to maintain the British Empire, and was not interested in hearing logical reasons why his dismissal of Indian nationalism might be outdated and destructive. Lord Irwin once suggested that since Churchill held views on India similar to those of 'a subaltern a generation ago', he might be interested in updating them by meeting some prominent Indian political activists who were then in London. 'I am quite satisfied with my views of India,' came the bulldog's reply. 'I don't want them disturbed by any bloody Indian.'[11]

Churchill's champion and entomber, Martin Gilbert, asserts in his volumes of biography that the great man's stand on India during the 1930s has been misrepresented as plain blimpishness, when really it was based on a belief in 'vigorous social reform and a more liberal administration . . . Churchill was in fact concerned throughout with the future welfare and unity of India, and was worried about the social and political difficulties which would be created by the dominance of the Congress party.'[12] Although Churchill's prophecies about the power of the 'Hindoo priesthood' – by which he meant Brahmins – were to some extent realized after independence, the irony was that it was his own wartime India policy which was to push the country into the crisis which ultimately gave power to Congress.

Whether Churchill's interest in the plight of India's minorities was based on anything more than opportunism looks doubtful. As was to happen again in the case of Hong Kong, the moment before the handover of a colony was an unconvincing one at which to suddenly become concerned about the rights of its oppressed inhabitants. Churchill's fellow

Tory MP Eddie Winterton once said during a House of Commons debate on India that Churchill's trouble was that he could not 'shovel enough earth over his past to obliterate it from human view'.[13] His contemporaries noted that he had a curious obsession with India, as if its size and voluptuousness was integrally bound up with his own vision of Britain's place in the world. During a Parliamentary debate he was described as being 'demented with fury' over the whole subject. His prejudices were reinforced by letters from imperial stalwarts and officers in the Indian Cavalry, and by sources such as Katherine Mayo's book *Mother India*, a hugely popular 1920s compendium of bigotry and prejudice about the failings of Indians.

As a member of Lloyd George's government, Churchill had reluctantly accepted Montagu's moves in 1917 and 1919 towards Indian involvement in Indian affairs. It was in 1929 that he made his first serious stand. When Stanley Baldwin backed Ramsay MacDonald's policy under which the Indian Empire would eventually become a 'full self-governing dominion' like Canada or Australia, Churchill denounced the notion as 'criminally mischievous'. Baldwin had pragmatically agreed to give bipartisan support, knowing that the strength of nationalist agitation in India could not be kept under control indefinitely. He took a similar view to Lord Irwin, who wrote: 'The whole of history seems to teach me that, once separatist ideas take firm hold in the heart of an emotional people, they are pretty difficult to eradicate ... what is important is to make perfectly plain to India that the ultimate purpose for her is not one of perpetual subordination in a white Empire.'[14]

Churchill joined a newly formed Indian Empire Society, which opposed Indian self-rule, and the strongly pro-Empire 'Die-hards' in his own party who had previously distrusted him began to view him as a supporter. In January 1931 he resigned from the Opposition front bench, and paraded around the country, giving speeches and writing newspaper articles in an attempt to drum up support against concessions to Congress. His 'wilderness years' had begun. When the Gandhi–Irwin pact was agreed two months later, Churchill was outraged, and made his memorable assertion that it was 'alarming and also nauseating to see Mr Gandhi, a seditious Middle Temple lawyer, now posing as a fakir of a type well-known in the East, striding half-naked up the steps of the Vice-regal palace, while he is still organizing and conducting a defiant campaign of civil disobedience, to parley on equal terms with the representative of

93

the King-Emperor. Such a spectacle can only increase the unrest in India and the danger to which white people there are exposed.'[15]

Around this time Churchill widened his approach, and moved from a purely anglocentric line of attack based on the theory of imperial stewardship, to an argument which included the injustices of Indian society. As an unreconstructed upper-class Edwardian, he was an unlikely champion of the rights of the depressed castes, but he claimed that without the 'guiding and protecting hand' of the British, India's Muslims and lower castes would be 'bled and exploited' by a high-caste Hindu government. His battle continued through the early 1930s, with the Conservative Party whips using every means to undermine him and his supporters. Baldwin made the point that the greatest risk to a peaceful settlement in the subcontinent was posed by 'extremists in India and at home'.

Yet the 'extremists' had substantial popular support across Britain. There was strong backing from old ICS and Indian Army officers, the Lancashire cotton industry, retired missionaries, armchair imperialists and India hands of all sorts. The India Defence League, with Rudyard Kipling as one of its vice-presidents, generated a huge following among Tory Party activists. It gained the support of over fifty MPs and numerous constituency associations, and its success has been described as 'the nearest thing the Conservative Party has had to a genuine grass-roots revolt than at any time since the 1840s'.[16]

As with current debates over the appropriate degree of British integration within the European Union, there was a powerful popular movement among the patriotically correct that on principle opposed concessions to foreigners. Churchill's claim that democracy was 'totally unsuited' to Indians gained him strong support among rank-and-file Tories. The other chief proponents of this line were General Sir Henry Page Croft, Lord Carson, the Duchess of Atholl and the former Governor of Bombay Lord Lloyd. Their stand got the backing of the Junior Imperial League, the Grand Council of the Primrose League and the League of Conservative Women, who did not wish to see the British Empire dismantled on the orders of a seditious fakir who failed to wear trousers when meeting the monarch.

The movement against reform had a fervent edge to it. Many of the 'Die-hards' were Christian imperialists, who saw the British as having a quasi-religious 'providential mission' to care for India. Page Croft asserted in a speech that their 'ideal of government' was 'the nearest approach to Christianity'. He believed that the exchange of British rule for 'the ideals of the worship of Shiva or Kali' would constitute a 'spiritual abdication'.[17]

Despite the strength of their following, and support from the anti-Baldwin 'insolent plutocracy' of the press barons Beaverbrook and Rothermere, the 'Die-hards' could not translate their movement into Parliamentary votes. An attempt in 1931 to overturn a government Bill giving the dominions control over their own foreign policy was defeated by 369 votes to 43, while a similar division in 1933 regarding the Simon Commission produced a result of 297 to 42. To his opponents Churchill began to look like a purely destructive force, out to wreck the government. His continuing campaign and his more general attacks on Baldwin cemented his isolation from mainstream politics.

The future of India had become one of Churchill's guiding political interests, despite the fact that his ideas were outdated even by the standards of the time. A combination of tactical misjudgements and the caustic propaganda against him by the party machine during the 1930s damaged his political reputation. When he discovered in early 1934 that the Secretary of State for India, Sir Samuel Hoare, had manipulated evidence to a Select Committee, he failed to use his revelations effectively. A Parliamentary report exonerated Hoare, and Churchill's bitter response in the House of Commons lacked the detailed factual information that would have enabled him to gain a victory. His low standing in the party was not helped when his boorish son Randolph stood as an independent on an India ticket at a by-election in January 1935. Churchill supported the campaign reluctantly; Randolph lost and let in a Labour candidate.

When the Government of India Bill came before Parliament in early 1935, Churchill denounced it as a 'gigantic quilt of jumble crochet work . . . built by the pygmies'. Through his fervent opposition to each clause, he debased the coinage of his own rhetoric, which was one of the reasons why many politicians were to suspect him of crying wolf over German rearmament. Lord Linlithgow, a reactionary Tory stalwart, told him he was 'hairy, hanging from a branch' in his attitudes on India. Churchill denounced the Bill in the strongest terms, claiming it would create 'inefficiency, nepotism and corruption', and leave far too much responsibility in the hands of provincial governments. He thought the 'Section 93' powers, under which the British governors of the provinces could rule by proclaiming a state of emergency, meant little and could never be used since, like the powers of the British monarch, they only existed 'in theory'. He was to prove entirely mistaken on this point.

The Bill's essential provisions recognized and gave significant administrative power to the provincial governments of British India, expanded the electorate, and provided for a federation between British India and the Princely States, as the autonomous Native States were now called. This plan for federation, which at the time was thought to be one of the most important components of the Bill, was never realized owing to the princely order's obstinacy over relinquishing any of its privileges, and the acceleration of British decline caused by the Second World War. Burma was hived off from India and given its own governor, who was accountable to London rather than to the Viceroy. The Bill did not make any concessions at the centre, and postponed dominion status indefinitely.

The arguments and debates filled over four thousand pages of *Hansard*. What is extraordinary in retrospect is that so tame and limited a political measure could ever have caused such excitement, with Churchill and his supporters convinced that its limited concessions were extremely dangerous. Today the proposals and counter-proposals over the status of each strand of India's internal administration seem arcane.

In June 1935 the Government of India Act emerged battered and bruised from five years of conferences, debates and discussion. Sam Hoare gave way to the surprisingly conciliatory former Governor of Bengal Lord Zetland as Secretary of State for India. The Bill had been passed by 382 votes to 122, with 38 of the 122 voting against it because they thought it too conservative. The prolonged and ferocious battle over the legislation meant that by the time it was implemented, Indian sentiment had been severely alienated and the Act had little genuine support. As Nanda Saheb wrote in his biography of Gandhi, the moves of successive British governments towards Indian self-rule were invariably reluctant and cumbersome, so that 'each instalment tended to become out of date by the time it was actually granted. The reforms of 1919 might well have appeased political India in 1909; the reforms of 1935 would have evoked enthusiasm in 1919, and an equivalent of the Cripps offer in 1940 could have opened a new chapter in Indo–British relations.'[18]

Within the context of local government in British India, Indians were now able to play a part at all levels of decision-making. In addition, the franchise was extended to around thirty-five million people – which still left over 90 per cent of the population without even the smallest democratic political voice. Most of the Princely States continued to be run as dictatorships, where dissent was usually repressed with even more vigour than in British India. By dispersing nationalist politicians to the provincial level, and bolstering the position of the princes, the British were able to consolidate their own power in New Delhi. Control over defence and foreign affairs was kept, crucially, in the Viceroy's hands. On top of Section 93, another clause allowed him to order the federal legislature to pass laws superseding the decisions of the provinces in the event of internal disturbance. The Act of 1935 was not a way of cutting loose from India, but of reinforcing British control.

During the course of the 1920s and 1930s, Indian Political Intelligence (IPI) in London and the Intelligence Bureau (the IB, which had formerly been called the Department of Criminal Intelligence) in New Delhi kept a close watch on freedom fighters of all types. IPI's information supplemented the weekly reports put out by the IB, which carried a notice from the Government of India's Home Department saying the document had to be 'kept under lock and key in personal custody', and then 'burnt after perusal by recipients'.[19] Serious political organizations such as Congress and the Muslim League were submitted to detailed research and analysis, while violent revolutionaries and smaller groups were trailed, watched and infiltrated.

From around the time of the First World War until the transfer of power in 1947, the British authorities in India operated a surveillance and intelligence operation of great skill against the forces of nationalism. This was done on a limited budget, and with a small number of highly effective officers and their contacts. Freedom fighters were aware that this was happening, although not of its extent. Jawaharlal Nehru wrote after a visit to Europe in the 1920s that he had met Indians who were 'talking a revolutionary language, making daring and fantastic suggestions. They seemed to have the impress of the British Secret Service upon them.'[20]

For practical reasons a large number of Indians were themselves involved in surveillance and infiltration. By the 1920s, the British were thinking increasingly in terms of integrating Indians into the police and the military as a means of binding them to the imperial power. This was seen as a long-term aim. In 1924 a Royal Commission issued a report which stated that the ICS should aim to become half-Indian by 1939. The police would have until 1949 to achieve this gentle target, and the army until 1952.

As it became apparent during the early non-cooperation movement that Indian nationalism was a growing rather than a waning force, the position of IPI was formalized and expanded. Although it remained under the official supervision of the Secretary of State for India, in 1923 it stopped operating through the India Office and was linked for working purposes to the Security Service, or MI5, which was responsible for imperial counter-intelligence as well as internal security in Britain. The thinking behind this was that stability in India was a 'home' matter, rather than a 'foreign' one, which would have come within the remit of the Secret Intelligence Service (SIS, or MI6). Given that almost three-quarters of the citizens of the British Empire were Indian, IPI was of central importance.

Three years after the link was established with MI5, John Wallinger or 'W' retired as the organization's director. Philip Vickery was appointed in his place, having returned from running IPI's operation in North America. Although he was only thirty-six, Vickery had been an integral part of IPI's development for more than ten years, and had been awarded an OBE for his work in undermining the Ghadr or 'Revolt' movement. Around fifteen to twenty people worked under him in the central adminis-tration of Indian Political Intelligence in London, and he had an unknown number of agents and contacts in the field. Most surveillance work within Britain was done by police officers on secondment.

When it was founded, IPI had concentrated on violent activists, especially those linked to German attempts at destabilization or connected with the Ghadr movement. It has been assumed until now that imperial intelligence operations were confined to the perpetrators of assassinations or explosions. According to the historian Richard Popplewell, 'the intelli-gence agencies of the British Empire were not concerned with spying on non-violent nationalists'.[21]

Although this statement may have been true up until the First World War, it is clear from the volume of material in the recently released IPI archives that the policy did not last beyond 1914. As political terrorism declined, IPI's remit was widened, and by the 1930s it was pursuing all manner of people. For the last three decades of British rule in India, intelligence-gathering was extended massively, since with the rapid rise of Congress it was seen as the only way of retaining the upper hand. Covertly obtained information began to take on an increasing importance in the formulation of policy and decision-making, for as H.V. Hodson, who himself had substantial knowledge of the workings of the British administration in India, wrote in *The Great Divide*: 'A regime such as that which ruled India depends more upon secret intelligence than does one rooted in popular support and national patriotism.'[22]

Many of the IPI files on individual suspects are stunningly innocuous. Students, businessmen, writers and scientists were all watched, often for the most trivial of reasons. Any Indian travelling to Europe without a clear motive was suspect. If they remained in Britain for any length of time they were investigated, usually with the help of Scotland Yard detectives. To take a random selection, there were files on Gurdit Singh Dara, a Rawalpindi barrister who published an occasional magazine called *Hind* and sold sweets to other Indians in London; the author Clemens Palme Dutt, who had an 'active Communist background'; Sasadhar Sinha, a Bengali who had a bookshop in Great Russell Street and was known to consort with other Indians – an informer had even seen him in conversation with other Indians of 'revolutionary views' in the Reading Room of the British Museum; and 'Raja' Mahendra Pratap, a crackpot who had plans for establishing world government, but who was described in the records of IPI as an 'Indo-Afghan seditionist'.

A substantial file was kept on Krishna Menon, a prominent activist who ran the India League in London and acted as a roving ambassador for Congress in Europe. He was a controversial man, despised by many within the Congress hierarchy both as a playboy and as a left-wing extremist. However, his position was secured by his close links with Jawaharlal Nehru. IPI kept him under continual surveillance, and Vickery and his officers must have been relieved by one report which stated that Menon was disliked by Indians in London on account of his 'careerist schemings'.

The wealth of detail about Menon's daily activities, engagements and conversation makes it clear that one of his immediate entourage must have been an IPI informer. His file contains intercepts of many letters and telegrams, including some from British politicians such as the Labour MP Reg Sorenson. All his outings and speeches at venues like the Conway Hall were recorded, as were his meetings with foreign ambassadors, since he was suspected of Communist leanings. There is also intercepted correspondence from Congress leaders. One letter from Nehru in 1940 advises Menon to beware of promises from Labour politicians – Attlee in particular – and reminds him: 'Remember always that the language Congress uses, at Gandhiji's instance, is peculiarly mild and inoffensive when it is thinking of action.'[23]

IPI was also responsible under the 'Sea Customs Act' for making decisions relating to the censorship of material entering India. Thousands of books were put on a proscribed list, some on the grounds that they were political and others because they could promote violence. Thus restricted publications ranged from works on Stalin, fascism, political philosophy and employment, to such relics of the Great War as *Explosives for Home Guards* and *The Manual of Grenades* by Major J.I. Cowan. IPI's definition of subversive material was surprisingly broad, so that many unremarkable works of literature could only enter India by being smuggled through French or Portuguese coastal territories.

Indian Political Intelligence occupied the unique position of operating from London, a privilege denied to any other imperial or dominion intelligence agency. Its financial resources were supplied 'from secret service funds appropriated for that purpose from Indian revenues', which meant that Indian taxpayers paid for their own surveillance. Although after 1923 its offices were in the same London building as MI5, it retained its autonomy and was allowed access to information and records collected by Security Service agents. In return it took over responsibility for MI5's work within the Indian subcontinent, so that it 'served not only the Government of India ... but also the Security Service, acting in the capacity of the latter's India/Burma section'. IPI was a far more important organization than has previously been realized, since it was always described simply as the 'London liaison office' of the Intelligence Bureau.[24]

Notwithstanding the usual inter-service rivalry, IPI also worked 'in close touch with the Intelligence Service (SIS)'. This was despite collecting 'information in the UK and in certain foreign countries independently of the Security and Intelligence Services', and maintaining 'organizations of its own' in Britain, Europe and the USA. In communications with other departments within the Whitehall machine Vickery is never named, but always referred to as 'IPI' or 'the IPI'. He signed his correspondence with the initials 'IPI', in the same way that the head of MI6 uses the letter 'C', and the head of MI5 used to use the letter 'K'.

Vickery's network was highly secret. Its existence was never acknowledged officially, and its contact with the outside world was always through indirect channels. All dealings with India went via the Director of the Intelligence Bureau in New Delhi, and IPI's communication with the India Office was routed through a single senior civil servant, usually one of the two assistant under-secretaries of state. This meant that even in the upper echelons of the Government of India, only a handful of people were aware of IPI's function or the real nature of its operations. For most officials it was simply an acronym for an anonymous organization about which they knew little.

In a note written by Vickery himself, he reveals that IPI was responsible for any 'matters calculated to affect the security of India', and in particular 'the detection of subversive movements of any description aimed at British rule'. This very broad function meant that over the years IPI concentrated on subjects as diverse as 'Russian, German and Japanese penetration, Communist underground subversive activity, the Khilafat movement, the Sikh Ghadr conspiracy, and Congress anti-British propaganda, whether from the orthodox Congress standpoint or in the form of Congress left-wing socialism or of the Forward Bloc connected with the Bose family'.[25]

It was a wide remit, and it gave IPI a crucial significance within the British Indian Empire.

The exceedingly tall Victor 'Hopie' Hope, Second Marquess of Linlithgow and Knight of the Thistle, was a Scottish landowner, born to power and status, his father having died young after serving as Lord Chamberlain and Governor General of Australia. He took over from Lord Willingdon as Viceroy and Governor General of India in April 1936. The forty-nine-year-old peer, formerly of Eton College and the Royal Scots, had no strong qualifications for the job, apart from having chaired a Royal Commission on Indian agriculture and the Parliamentary Committee on Indian constitutional reform in 1933–34. Yet he was to spend longer in office than anybody since Lord Dalhousie, ninety years earlier.

Lord Linlithgow's policy during his term as Viceroy was one of caution and unimaginative stagnation, tempered by repression, a deep political cynicism and occasional cunning. He was no romantic imperialist, writing that India and Burma were only part of the British Empire because they were 'conquered countries which have been brought there by force, kept there by our control, and which hitherto it has suited to remain under our protection'.[26]

Linlithgow pursued a strategy that led in the end to disaster, as a lack of initiative tends to when exhibited by a politician in a crisis. Nehru described him as 'slow of mind, solid as a rock and with almost a rock's lack of awareness'. His final year as Viceroy was one of great repression; he left India with blood on his hands. An unmitigated old-school administrator of his kind might have been some use in India as a ceremonial figurehead towards the end of the nineteenth century, but by the time of the fall of Singapore and Burma in 1942, he was a disaster. His colleague Leo Amery wrote in his diary that Linlithgow was 'quite incapable of saying anything simply and clearly', adding, 'I am not surprised his negotiations with Indians come to nothing.'[27]

Linlithgow's Reforms Commissioner H.V. Hodson thought him 'a big man, in character as well as stature. In his presence you were aware of heavy weight behind his thoughts and actions.' Many people found him forbidding and stern, a problem exacerbated by a lugubrious physiognomy caused by childhood polio. Linlithgow was married to the 'gay and delightful', and similarly tall, Doreen, and the family went in to dinner every evening to the strains of the Viceroy's band playing 'The Roast Beef of Old England' – an odd choice of tune in a predominantly Hindu country. Like King George V, who had died in January and been replaced – briefly – by his son Edward VIII, Linlithgow was a stickler for protocol. He once wrote a four-page letter to the Secretary of State for India complaining that the Maharajah of Patiala had arrived at a Delhi princely function wearing 'the broad riband of a Rumanian order' and 'the Greek Order of the Redeemer', and asking what punitive action was recommended. The Linlithgows relaxed by chasing butterflies in the hills above Simla, staff being issued with butterfly nets. One such safari was interrupted when a bearer, rather optimistically, attempted the seduction of the Vicereine.

Linlithgow was the first Viceroy to broadcast to the Indian nation over the wireless after his investiture. Patronizingly, he told his listeners that just as he did not favour any one of his five children, so he would not favour any one religious community over another. He also made it plain that if in doubt, he would prefer suppression to dialogue: 'Amongst the manifold duties of the Viceroy, none is more vital than that of the maintenance of peace and good order throughout India. Believe me, my friends, that I can do you no greater service than by the vigilant and effective discharge of this duty.'[28] He was soon well into his stride, having a whole battalion barred from serving at Viceroy's House when he saw a night sentry commit the crime of flicking a lighted cigarette butt.

He found Gandhi at their first meeting to be 'shrewd' and 'courteous', although 'implacable in his hostility to British rule in India, to the destruction of which he has dedicated every fibre of his mind'. As for Jinnah, he did not 'frankly feel any deep confidence in him'.[29] Linlithgow exhibited an immediate distaste for the Indian National Congress, believing that 'the ultimate purpose of Nehru and Gandhi is to make for the overthrow of the government by organization of agrarian mischief on a grand scale'.[30]

By now Congress was having to reassess its political tactics. During the 1930s its constitution was changed so that the Congress Working Committee was chosen by the President. This made the annual presidential election a crucial matter. Gandhi played an important part in manipulating the choice or President, and when the candidate was not to his liking, he responded with passive resistance. The Mahatma's calculated resignation from Congress in 1934 to pursue social reform did not alter this situation, and he continued to wield monumental authority through a small group of loyalists known as the Old Guard, including Patel, Prasad, Kripalani and Rajagopalachari.

They were not disciples in a religious sense, and often had strong doubts about Gandhi's faddism, but they were convinced that he was the symbol through which political campaigns should be conducted, and independence ultimately attained. The breadth of Gandhi's appeal was essential to their approach, as was his ability to quench Nehru, who was believed to have influence over younger activists who were liable to leave Congress altogether and turn to either bomb-throwing or Communism. In 1936 Gandhi cleverly defused Nehru by proposing him for a second time as Congress President. Nehru's wife had just died of tuberculosis in Lausanne, and he agreed reluctantly, under pressure from the increasingly powerful left-wing factions in the freedom movement, who had now organized themselves within the structures of Congress as a separate group called the Congress Socialists. This was despite his disagreement with operating under the terms of the 1935 Government of India Act, which he believed was simply a way of reinforcing British rule and reactionary Indian interests.

In 1936 Gandhi established a new community in central India called Sevagram, where he was joined by distant family members and various disciples. They included his Secretary Mahadev Desai, a vague, chunky Punjabi assistant called Pyarelal, a leper, a Pole, a Japanese monk, Pyarelal's doctor sister Sushila Nayar, and the unpopular, ubiquitous Mirabehn, whose brother-in-law was an official in the Madras Presidency. Initially Sevagram was intended to be a working village rather than an ashram, but it soon attracted even more outlandish figures than Sabarmati in Ahmedabad. The inmates included an Indian academic who roamed the forests naked with sealed lips, having taken an indefinite vow of silence. Sardar Patel called the place a 'menagerie', and relations between its members were often fraught. At times there was so much bickering that the Mahatma considered disbanding it.

Gandhi concentrated increasingly on social affairs in the 1930s, identifying himself with India's landless peasantry, a group that had grown rapidly during the past three decades. He preached and wrote on matters such as village sanitation, nutrition and health, the correct maintenance of cleanliness in a kitchen, and the appropriate way to clean your teeth with a twig. His biographer Judith Brown makes the point that the picture of the determined and passionate campaigner traipsing the muddy tracks of rural India lecturing on village hygiene gives 'a truer impression of the deepest in Gandhi than the political campaigns or the negotiations with those in power which generated the bulk of the written historical records of his life'.[31]

By now Gandhi's global fame was such that he received letters from all over the world, enclosing what Pyarelal described as 'personal problems, metaphysical riddles, moral conundrums, advice, blame, threats, abuse and what not'. Although he considered himself the 'mother' of his followers, Gandhi was lonely and had failed to achieve the detachment and inner calm towards which he had been striving for his entire life. He was now in his sixties, and had become increasingly erratic and autocratic in his assertions, and suffered occasional physical and emotional collapses. As India's tensions grew worse, he took the failings of society upon himself. Far from relapsing into stately, saintly, wise old age, he blamed himself for the nation's violence and antagonism. As Brown writes: 'Although the ageing Mahatma seemed to the public a tranquil spirit, he was often moody and experienced a turbulent anger with himself, his family and his close colleagues.'[32]

During the 1920s he had even tried self-flagellation as a means of expunging his anger, although later he abandoned this method. On one occasion he wrote that he was so 'aflame with anger' at his own sins that he 'rose and struck myself hard blows and only then did I have peace'.[33] Gandhi was at war with himself, unable to resolve his own drives and desires. His regular days of silence were largely an attempt to contain his anger. He was a man with strong passions, who never found celibacy or the renunciation of material pleasures an easy burden.

The climax came one morning in April 1938, when the sixty-eight-year-old Mohandas Gandhi had an involuntary orgasm. Feeling that this challenged his spiritual integrity, the Mahatma was cast into a state of gloom and what he called a 'well of despair'. He made a public declaration that his own impurity was a major cause of the problems in Indian society – a statement that shows how he had come to confuse internal and external matters, as did his assertion that the 1934 earthquake in Bihar had been sent as a punishment for the sin of untouchability. It was as a result of this ejaculation that Gandhi took up the practice of sharing his bed with young women, in an attempt to test his vows of *brahmacharya*. He believed that the pursuit of genuine non-violence was impossible without physical purity.

From the late 1930s onwards, Gandhi was a liability to the freedom movement, pursuing an eccentric agenda that created as many problems as it solved. V.S. Naipaul has put it more bluntly: 'Gandhi lived too long.'[34] With the exception of a few people such as Patel and Rajagopala-chari, whom he treated as equals, the Mahatma was surrounded by syco-phants and oddballs. When his friend, adviser and doctor M.A. Ansari died in 1936, Gandhi lost an important link to India's Muslims. His attempt two years later at a personal rapprochement with Jinnah was doomed on account of their prolonged mutual antagonism. He had called Ansari his 'infallible guide' on Muslim matters, and now he had to cast around for a replacement.

The man eventually chosen was Maulana Abul Kalam Azad, a figure of superficial gravitas with no real popular power base, whom Gandhi began to mistrust as time passed. Azad became a central figure in Indian politics, more for what he represented than for what he achieved. His frank autobiographical memoir *India Wins Freedom* is an important work about the attainment of independence, since many of its claims have become accepted wisdom. After independence Azad was made India's education minister, and he is still promoted within the country's schools as the perfect exemplar of the communally all-embracing nature of the forefathers of the modern Indian state.

Azad looked the part: wise, elegant and distinguished, with his facial hair clipped neatly in an Islamic style. Sarojini Naidu and Jawaharlal Nehru liked to suggest that he must have been fifty years old at birth, such was the gravity of his manner. He was a great orator and a learned scholar, but he was also arrogant, elitist and self-important. The trouble with Azad was that he never lived up to the heavy weight of expectation that was placed on his shoulders, and his disdain for the unwashed masses prevented him from ever gaining a popular following: he was respected, but he was never loved.

Reputed to have been a childhood genius who published perfect Urdu *ghazals* at the age of eleven, Azad also had a reputation as a theologian, gaining the name of 'Maulana', a title conferred on Muslims of great learning. He came from a family of Islamic scholars and administrators, and was born in Mecca in 1888 as Firoz Bakht, later changing his name to Abul Kalam Azad – '*azad*' meaning free. To the disapproval of his family he took an active role in politics, and started a weekly paper called *Al Hilal*. His initial public role was within the Khilafat movement, and unlike many other eminent Muslims he did not believe in supporting the British in exchange for protection. He was originally a believer in pan-Islamism, and unlike Jinnah joined Congress as a Muslim leader rather than as a secular politician. By the 1930s their roles had reversed, and Azad became a determined secularist.

In 1940 he was to be made Congress President as an antidote to the rise of the Muslim League, and gave a moving speech in which he opposed Jinnah's 'two-nation' theory: 'I am proud of being an Indian,' he asserted. 'I am indispensable to this noble edifice and without me this splendid structure of India is incomplete ... I can never surrender this claim.'[35] The problem for Azad by the mid-1940s was that the Muslim League jibes of his being a compliant Muslim 'show-boy' inside Congress gave every impression of being true: it was apparent that he would not have occupied such an important position within the party if he had not been a Muslim.

Maulana Azad did not live up to the myth he allowed to be created around himself. The irony is that without him, the last ten years of British rule in India lack a single Congress Muslim of national stature. This fact has persuaded many people to take him more seriously than he deserves. In 1989 the historian Rajmohan Gandhi published a devastating line-by-line analysis of Azad's celebrated book *India Wins Freedom*, under the title *India Wins Errors*, showing that it is riddled with astounding lies and misrepresentations. As the grandson of both Mohandas Gandhi and Chakravarti Rajagopalachari, Rajmohan Gandhi knew and venerated Azad during his childhood. His book is filled with a profound sense of disillusion as he makes the icon crumble.

India Wins Freedom traduces the role of Nehru, Patel and Prasad in particular, and allows Azad to emerge as the only politician with clear foresight or clean hands. All major achievements are described as if he was personally responsible for them, and failures are blamed on others. His accounts of the negotiations of the 1940s are plainly inaccurate, and he claims responsibility for everything from quelling the Royal Indian Navy mutiny to installing an interim Congress government in 1946. According to the recollections of Nehru's Secretary M.O. Mathai, who is himself admittedly a less than watertight source, the celebrated Maulana had a weakness for whisky and champagne, and 'dictated the book in the evenings . . . when he was inebriated'.[36]

As the most prominent Congress Muslim following the death of Dr Ansari, Azad was crucial to the image of the movement, and he allowed himself to be used as a puppet of the Old Guard, acquiescing to decisions that he personally opposed. He accepted the orders of the high command, but in retrospect claimed his role had been entirely different, and that he had fought his corner bravely to the end. Rajmohan Gandhi writes in his conclusion that Azad felt compelled 'to suppress his failures and exaggerate his colleagues' mistakes. *India Wins Freedom* is evidence not of courage but of its lack; it is a story not of how India won her freedom but of how Azad lost his spine.'[37]

SEVEN

The Limits of Government

During 1937, while the Viceroy Lord Linlithgow was meant to be coaxing Congress into backing the implementation of the Government of India Act, unrest grew as railwaymen and jute workers went on strike over low wages. There were communal disturbances in Bombay, with rioters being punished by whipping. In the provincial elections of the same year Congress won a stunning victory over the disparate regional and religious parties, gaining the largest share of the vote in nine of the eleven provinces of British India, and an absolute majority in six of them. There was no voting in the Princely States. However, Congress refused to cooperate until the Viceroy gave an indication that he would not interfere with provincial governments by ordering governors to exert their emergency powers. It was a reasonable demand, although perhaps not one that was worth making a great fuss about at such an early stage.

Linlithgow refused to budge. Despite pressure from figures such as his predecessor Lord Irwin, now reincarnated as Lord Halifax, he would not give Congress even the most basic assurance. Political progress in such a tense atmosphere required occasional risks, but Linlithgow was temperamentally unsuited to making a leap for peace. Finally, on the orders of the Cabinet, he gave a little ground. More radical elements within the All-India Congress Committee, led by Jai Prakash Narayan, opposed joining the ministries on principle, since it implied an endorsement of British colonial rule, but they were defeated by 135 votes to 78.

Congress took office in the late summer of 1937 in Bihar, Bombay, Madras, the United Provinces and the Central Provinces. Linlithgow remained taciturn, and little mutual trust developed. Yet the very fact that provincial governments did remain in place for nearly two years, although in partial and strained cooperation with New Delhi, is an achievement for which the Viceroy deserves some credit. Congress rule in British India was now beginning, and the rupture with the Muslim League came out into the open.

Sardar Patel's position as a pivotal force in the movement was ensured when he was made Chairman of a new Congress Parliamentary Board, formed in response to the introduction of provincial autonomy. Although left-wing elements within the party opposed the creation of the board, they were overruled. Under Nehru's presidency in 1937, resolutions were put forward to affiliate trades unions and peasant groups to Congress, and to boycott the government. The Old Guard allowed the proposals to be accepted, but then ensured they were defeated by the larger All India Congress Committee. Nehru protested bitterly about this 'authoritarianism', but he and his supporters did not have the capacity to break the power of Gandhi and Patel. There is no reason to doubt the conclusions of a secret Intelligence Bureau report which stated in 1937 that 'Nehru's part is incidental: he is the high-grade tool . . . in the hands of the skilled craftsman.'[1]

With grave doubts, Congress accepted provincial power on British terms. As one nationalist historian has written: 'The formation of the Ministries by the Congress changed the entire psychological atmosphere in the country. People felt as if they were breathing the very air of victory and people's power, for was it not a great achievement that khadi-clad men and women who had been in prison until just the other day were now ruling in the secretariat and the officials who were used to putting Congressmen in jail would now be taking orders from them?'[2]

Using the provincial legislatures, the Congress chief ministers reformed tenancy laws, regulated moneylenders, expanded education and introduced public health measures. At the same time they fought ideological battles among themselves, alienated many Muslims, and in some cases developed disturbingly autocratic tendencies. As Chairman of the Parliamentary Board, Patel ruled the ministries with an iron rod. He welded together opposing forces, removed anybody who refused to submit to his will, influenced the selection of candidates, smothered revolts, disciplined backsliders and sacked the incompetent. By 1937 he was in control of the mechanics of the party, using the experience in mass organization he had gained in the 1920s. Some Congress Socialists were sidelined and even expelled, since he considered them to be 'sappers and miners' of the Communist Party. In response to Nehru's talk of 'the inevitability of class war', Patel declared that he was more interested in practical matters: 'Being a farmer myself, and having identified myself with the peasantry for years, I know where the shoe pinches.'[3] As members of the Indian Civil Service used to say, if the dead body of the Sardar were stuffed and placed on a chair, he would still rule over them.

The degree of nepotism and jobbery horrified the still idealistic Gandhi, who said he would 'go to the length of giving the whole Congress organization a decent burial, rather than put up with the corruption that is rampant'.[4] The British authorities assessed accurately that Gandhi would not tolerate an internal dissipation of the forces of nationalism. An Intelligence Bureau report stated in October 1938 that he was worried that 'the holding of office was weakening Congress as a national and anti-British movement in a variety of ways. We also know that Mr Gandhi has made statements more than once to the general effect that he expected that he might have to lead once more before he died a widespread unconstitutional movement.'[5] The IB was right.

Back in India after his sojourn in London, Mohammad Ali Jinnah knew his only chance of securing serious national influence was by unifying the nation's plethora of tiny Muslim groups behind the common banner of the Muslim League. He had managed to secure a merger in 1936 between the League and a United Muslim Party run by the hereditary Nawab of Dhaka, which gave a new unity in Bengal, the only group still left out being the Krishak Praja, or Peasants and Workers Party, run by the mercurial Bengali Fazlul Huq. Jinnah also made concessions during the 1930s to regional magnates, and to specifically theocratic Islamic interests such as the Jamiat-ul-Ulema and the Mujtahids. However, in the same year, under the influence of Maulana Azad, the Jamiat-ul-Ulema switched their support to Congress in exchange for provincial cabinet office.

This defection earned Jinnah's undying hatred for Azad, whom he now took every chance to denounce as a traitor to his people. When Azad sent Jinnah an enquiry about a specific aspect of League policy, he received a vitriolic telegram in response: 'I refuse to discuss with you, by correspondence or otherwise, as you have completely forfeited the confidence of Muslim India. Can't you realize you are made a Muslim show-boy Congress president to give it colour that is national and to deceive foreign countries . . . The Congress is a Hindu body. If you have self-respect resign at once.'[6]

Jinnah's strategy was severely undermined in the provincial elections of 1937, when Congress scored their resounding win. Although the League did well in some key places, such as the United Provinces, where it gained twenty-nine of the thirty-five reserved Muslim seats it contended, Congress won almost all the non-Muslim seats. A situation had developed whereby Congress had gained a phenomenal popular mandate across the Indian subcontinent, but, crucially, without securing Muslim votes. For all its theoretical non-sectarianism, Congress was simply not attracting Muslim voters in large numbers.

Nor was the League doing so, despite Jinnah's efforts at internal reform and progress, and his assertion that he was still standing 'shoulder to shoulder' with Congress in its opposition to British rule. The League won only 109 of the 482 seats reserved for Muslims, and Congress appeared to be justified in viewing it as little more than an irritant. This was a mistake, for during the late 1930s Jinnah was able to turn it into a serious political force. He was extremely effective in attracting, recruiting and motivating wealthy, bright, well-educated younger Muslims such as Liaquat Ali Khan from the United Provinces, the Raja of Mahmudabad, whose family were the largest landlords in Lucknow, and Mirza Abol Hassan Ispahani of the financial family of Calcutta. None of these men was a religious communalist, yet all were in favour of using religious nationalism as a means of safeguarding the Muslim position.

Mahmudabad's father had been close friends with Motilal Nehru in the early years of the century, and the change in family loyalty is indicative of the Congress–League split that occurred during the late 1930s and early 1940s. The young Raja remembered in old age that Jawaharlal Nehru had shown 'nothing but contempt for the Muslim League', which alienated many otherwise moderate younger Muslims. 'The more Nehru spoke contemptuously and violently about the League and Jinnah, the more I disliked the Congress. This feeling was shared by a large number of the Muslims I knew who, but for this, would have shown less antipathy to the Congress.'[7]

While Congress was securing its own position in the provinces, Muslim Leaguers began to portray the larger party as an arrogant monolith which ignored Muslim interests. As one fictional political campaigner said in a speech, 'There are eighty million Mussalmans in this country, who are invisible! . . . It is Congress which can't see us. It is the party of the Nation that is blind. It first bleaches us with its secularism till we are transparent and then walks through us, as you and I would walk through *jinns* and ghosts. For Nehru's Congress, we are permanently invisible.'[8]

For many Muslims, the social radicalism of a figure such as Nehru or Bose was a challenge to the security and the sanctity of their Islamic faith. The promise of secularism was no more alluring to a hard-line Muslim than it was to a fiercely communalist Hindu Mahasabhite. In the 1937 elections Congress only managed to return a total of twenty-six Muslim representatives in the open, unreserved seats, out of more than 1,500 contested constituencies. This represented under 2 per cent of the total, although Muslims made up 22 per cent of India's population. For many in the Congress leadership, the temptation was obvious: blame the British policy of separate electorates for this debacle, ignore it, and push ahead with the battle for freedom. If Congress could win power without the Muslims, there seemed little reason to make concessions to them.

At the same time, the Muslim League became more outspoken. Jinnah made a a militant speech at Lucknow in October 1937, leading to the passing of a resolution demanding, for the first time, 'the establishment in India of full independence in the form of a federation of free democratic States in which the rights and interests of the Musulmans' were paramount. He told the audience that Muslims could not 'expect any justice or fair play' from the 'exclusively Hindu' Congress. The *Pioneer* newspaper noted that Jinnah was dressed in a long *sherwani* rather than his usual London pinstripes, and that the vote had been carried unanimously, with nearly five thousand delegates 'standing amidst shouts of *Hindustan Azad* [Free India], *Islam Zindabad* [Long Live Islam] and *Allah-ho-Akbar* [God is Great]'.[9]

Rather than seeing this new Islamic radicalism as a warning, Nehru continued to discount the communal problem, cooing that such 'opponents of Congress ... have nothing to do with the masses'. It was true that the League was not a mass party, yet many poor Muslims looked to their local landlords rather than to Congress, and many landlords in turn looked to the leadership of the League for security. Flushed with pride and self-assurance at its victory, Congress believed it could do without a minor and discredited figure such as Jinnah and the political grouping that he represented.

After all, Nehru knew that in the Muslim-majority provinces of Punjab, Sind and the NWFP, only one Muslim Leaguer had been elected. It looked as if Congress, on its own, was now powerful enough to make a serious bid for power in New Delhi. From the figures, it seemed that at best the League would control around 15 per cent of the seats in the legislatures of British India, and could therefore be bypassed. As the historian Ayesha Jalal has written, this 'was to prove to be one of the gravest miscalculations by the Congress leadership in its long history'.[10]

Jawaharlal Nehru proceeded to claim publicly that the Muslim League 'represents a group of Muslims, no doubt highly estimable persons . . . functioning in the higher regions of the upper middle classes and having no contact with the Muslim masses'. He went on, impulsively and pro-vocatively: 'May I suggest to Mr Jinnah that I come into greater touch with the Muslim masses than most of the members of the Muslim League.'[11] Nehru's approach looks unwise, in retrospect. He was stretching a point, and failing to grasp the strength of Muslim unity when provoked by an outside threat. The cry of *jihad*, of holy war and 'Islam in danger', was a uniquely potent force.

The insults of Congress stirred Jinnah into action. The logical, perhaps the only, way of bonding all Muslims together was through an appeal to their religious roots. As Nehru ordered Congress recruitment among the 'Muslim masses' to be stepped up, so the antagonism between the two sides grew, each party manipulating the frustration and anger of its sup-porters in the political contest. By the end of the 1930s, the struggle for liberty was coming to be supplanted by the battle between the politicians who claimed to represent Hindus and Muslims.

The Muslim League benefited from the public image that Congress was assuming at this time, which was far from attractive to many Muslims. To Jinnah, with his substantial portfolio of property, Nehru's espousal of land distribution and socialist thinking as a way of dealing with India's poverty was anathema. For the rich and influential Muslim landowners of the United Provinces, the typical Congress worker was not an alluring prospect: 'with their homespun clothes, Gandhi caps, aggressive vegetari-anism and Hindi speech they reminded the Muslim with any pretensions to gentility . . . of all the values that he did not share with the humbler Hindu.'[12]

During 1937–39 Jinnah set out to follow the lead of Gandhi and create a mass party. From 1937 until his death in 1948, he was to remain President of the Muslim League. The price of membership of the League was dropped to a tiny but symbolic two annas – half the fee for joining Congress. The structure of the organization was reformed, mirroring that of their opponents, and a working committee was created. Urdu rather than Hindi was promoted as the new national language. An All-India

Muslim Students' Federation came into being, and Islamic history and culture was promoted at universities such as Aligarh. Although the League was still controlled and bankrolled by the rich, there were efforts to introduce policies of social protection. Vague proposals were put forward for a minimum wage, an improvement in hygiene and sanitation, and the abolition of usury, although Jinnah himself continued to play the financial markets.

There was a radical new edge to Jinnah, as he realized he was gaining serious popular support among Muslims across northern India. He knew that he needed to be ruthless in securing his own internal power within the League. Overtures from Congress were now rejected, and his party thrived on its perceived isolation, maintaining that no dialogue was possible until it was recognized as the 'one authoritative' body representing India's Muslims. Jinnah's most crucial achievement during this period was to persuade regional leaders such as Sir Sikander Hayat Khan, the powerful Unionist Party Chief Minister of the Punjab, and Fazlul Huq of Bengal, to ally their forces to the League. This was done for expediency, and amounted to a sacrifice of the League's internal coherence in exchange for possible future influence. Grassroots support for Rahmat Ali's independent 'Pakistan' was still minimal.

Between 1937 and 1939, the League made much of alleged discrimination against Muslims by Congress provincial ministries, both by the civil administration and by the police. There were cases, for instance, of Muslim butchers being beaten for selling beef. Yet the League's case was not especially strong. As one commentator on the period points out, almost half of the civil and police services at this point were British, and many of them were considered to be pro-Muslim: 'While isolated cases of petty tyranny by local officials may have occurred in remote villages and towns in the Congress-controlled provinces, the theory of a concerted tyranny directed against the Muslim community would be difficult to sustain.'[13]

One particular grievance was over the use of the song 'Bande Mataram' ('Hail to the Motherland') as the new anthem of all Congress ministries. It was deemed to be offensive to Muslims, and remains a source of conflict in India to this day. The song was taken from a late-nineteenth-century novel called Anandamath by the famous Bengali writer Bankim Chandra Chatterji, in which a group of Hindu ascetics who follow the goddess Kali fight vigorously against their Muslim and British rulers. It is a provocative song, praising all India's communities while pointedly excluding the Muslims, but it was far too popular for Congress to consider abandoning it. The impression was now taking root in Muslim communities that Islam was under attack. Each incident could be whispered, adapted, retold and exaggerated; grievances began to fester which would finally erupt into the communal violence of 1947.

Subhas Chandra Bose was a big, pale, moon-faced Bengali with a broad forehead and a fondness for fried fish cutlets. Unlike his colleague Jawaharlal Nehru, to whom he bears a superficial similarity, he felt a strong loathing for most things British. He was born in 1897 into a family of Bengali Hindus who were proud of their heritage, but sufficiently anglicized for his lawyer father to be a keen reader of John Milton and William Cowper, and to have been awarded the official title of Rai Bahadur in recognition of his services on the Bengal Legislative Council. His mother was strict and religious, with a strong colour prejudice, being inordinately proud of her own family's fair skin.

Bose and his brothers were educated among the elite at Presidency College in Calcutta. He picked up the Bengali tradition of revolutionary rebelliousness, and embraced romantic authoritarianism, writing as a teenager on a visit to Darjeeling that there was 'no better way of reviving our Aryan blood than to consume meat and scale mountains'.[14] When a British teacher at his college treated some students in a disparaging fashion, he was *gheraoed*, or surrounded, by a mob and beaten with slippers. The eighteen-year-old Subhas Bose was deemed to be a ringleader, and expelled. In 1919 he sailed to England, and enrolled as a student at Cambridge. Although he felt strong animosity towards his hosts ('Nothing makes me happier than to be served by the whites and to watch them clean my shoes'), he admired their energetic discipline, and attempted unsuccessfully to join the Officer Training Corps.[15]

Throughout his life he had a weakness for men in uniform, and he was always touchy about any challenge to his own position or status. Nirad Chaudhuri, who knew him and who worked for some time as Secretary to his brother Sarat, found Subhas 'emotionally tense and unstable beneath a cold mask', and thought he suffered from 'turbulence in his personality' which provoked 'fits of rage like a caged beast of prey'.[16] While at university Subhas was troubled by strong sexual desires, which he tried hard to overcome and suppress; many of his friends thought this had a damaging effect on him.

He passed the entrance examination into the Indian Civil Service at the age of twenty-four, only to refuse to join. After wrestling with his conscience, he had decided his mission was to fight for his country's freedom, by whatever means necessary. He visited Ireland, and for the rest of his life felt a strong sense of identification with the nationalist activists Michael Collins and Sir Roger Casement. On his return to India in 1921 he met Mohandas Gandhi for the first time, and from the outset thought he showed a 'deplorable lack of clarity' in his political aims. Bose also disliked Gandhi's paternalistic views on the role of women in society, and disagreed with his belief in non-violence.

The powerful regional leader 'Deshbandhu' Chittaranjan Das of east Bengal became his political guru. During the 1920s Bose worked with Das, who was Mayor of Calcutta, and was put in charge of the city corporation. He ensured that all corporate purchases of fabric and lightbulbs were of local provenance, and treated British officials with condescension. In 1924 he was arrested and deported to an insanitary prison in Mandalay in Burma on suspicion of supporting violent revolutionaries. No charges were ever brought, and he was held without trial for three years.

By the late 1920s, Subhas Chandra Bose had emerged as a national figure within Congress, with a reputation as a young radical. At the 1928 annual meeting of the party in Calcutta, he recruited a squad of supple young men and women in khaki. They carried *lathis*, and became known as the Congress Volunteer Force, with Bicycle, Cavalry and Coded Messages divisions. The troops paraded on the Calcutta Maidan early each morning under the eye of General Officer Commanding Bose, who dressed himself in breeches, aiguilettes and long leather boots. Gandhi disliked the Force's paramilitary overtones, and complained about the saluting, strutting and clicking of heels. The British authorities did not take it too seriously.

At the conference Bose put forward a resolution supporting full independence for India rather than dominion status. Gandhi opposed it strongly, saying it was a 'hollow phrase', and he won the vote by 1,350 to 973, although interestingly two-thirds of the Bengali delegates voted with Bose. The battle with the Mahatma was to be continued over the coming decade.

During the 1930s, like most Indian politicians, Bose spent a good deal of time in prison on fatuous charges under the Willingdon crackdown. During this period he suffered from serious health problems, including gallstones and digestive trouble. While he was free he served as Mayor of Calcutta, and proved effective at disrupting the wishes of the British Governor of Bengal. In 1933 he was released from jail, on the condition that he left India. From a base in Vienna he travelled to Italy, Poland, Bulgaria, Yugoslavia and Switzerland, acting as what he called 'the Ambassador of India in Bondage'. He met de Valera in Ireland, Mussolini in Italy, and Gide and Malraux in France. Although he was prevented from entering Britain, he was kept under continual surveillance by IPI agents.[17]

Bose followed developments in India closely. He read a good deal, studied religion and started to take an increasingly theoretical and ideological approach to politics. His experience widened, and he formed a working alliance with Vallabhbhai Patel's brother Vithalbhai, who was also working as a roving freedom fighter and who ran an organization called the Indo-Irish League. When Bose returned to Bombay in 1936 he was at once arrested, but on his release the following year he set about rebuilding his power base within Congress. His status grew, especially in Bengal, and he gained the backing of the influential Nobel Prize-winning Bengali poet and artist Rabindranath Tagore.

Despite having publicly attacked Congress activists for their blind loyalty to Gandhi, Bose was elected President of the party in 1938 on Gandhi's orders. He arrived at the annual meeting at Haripura in Gujarat on a chariot pulled by fifty-one bulls, and made a speech promoting socialist ideology, despite knowing his position was weakened by the Old Guard's control over both the Congress Working Committee and the party's structures. The reactionary Gandhian J.B. Kripalani was serving as Party Secretary, and Bose and his leftist supporters could achieve little. During the course of the year there were disputes with Gandhi and Patel over their interference with Congress in Bengal.

At the end of 1938 Gandhi decided Bose should be replaced as the party's President, and in the absence of a more inspiring candidate nominated Dr Pattabhi Sitaramayya, a faithful nonentity from south India.

Bose was asked to stand down, but refused. To everybody's surprise he was re-elected for 1939 by a narrow majority. This was a major challenge to Gandhi's power, and the Mahatma responded with a subtle statement congratulating the victor, adding that 'Subhas Babu, instead of being President on the sufferance of those whom he calls rightists, is now President elected in a contested election. This enables him to choose a homogeneous cabinet and enforce his programme without let or hindrance . . . After all Subhas Babu is not an enemy of his country.'[18]

Naively, Bose assumed he would be able to bring in the programme on which he had campaigned. Gandhi however instituted a programme of non-cooperation against the usurper, withdrawing all support for him within the party organization. The membership of the Congress Working Committee resigned, leaving only Subhas and his brother Sarat to do their worst. Sarat was an influential politician in his own right, but was always unpopular with the British, the Viceroy Lord Wavell later dismissing him as 'a stupid man, with an egg-shaped head'.[19] They attempted to put together an alliance of left-wing activists, but were hampered by Subhas's failing health.

The next annual meeting was held at Tripuri in central India in March 1939, with Gandhi declining an invitation to attend. His supporters, though, were out in force, and an iron-fisted combination of Pandit Pant and Sardar Patel soon destroyed Bose's position through a series of technical manoeuvres. As one left-wing activist put it, 'the Sardar sat on the dais – a figure of granite, confident of strangling the ambitious upstart.'[20] After rowdy scenes, the Tripuri session ended with Bose's presidency in tatters. He had been forced to attend many meetings on a stretcher, and there were rumours that his opponents were willing sickness upon him through the practice of black magic.

Afterwards he pleaded in desperation with Gandhi for support, but the wily Mahatma stood firm. Bose crumbled and resigned, and Rajendra Prasad was installed in his place. Although there were powerful left-wing elements in Congress, they were not united, and the consolidated strength of the Gandhian right wing that had been built up during the 1930s could not easily be broken. Bose now formed a new group within Congress called the 'Forward Bloc', which he hoped would serve as a flag around which the party's radical activists would rally. His success was limited, with Nehru complaining that the Forward Bloc stood for little more than 'an anti-programme'. Although Bose had been squashed by the Old

Guard, he was still only in his early forties, and continued to enjoy strong popular support across the subcontinent.

In April 1938, Gandhi had made a special trip to Jinnah's house on Malabar Hill in Bombay. The meeting was inconclusive, and was followed a few weeks later by negotiations between Jinnah and Bose, as Congress President. These too went nowhere, and confirmed the growing antipathy between the rival movements. At the same time, Nehru's outspoken attacks on Chamberlain's policy of appeasing Hitler were causing further ruptures with the British. That August Jinnah took his chance and travelled to Simla, where, together with Sir Sikander Hayat Khan, he indicated to the Viceroy that the League would be willing to offer support to the British in return for a postponement of 'federation', which was seen as acting against Muslim interests. This was later matched by Jinnah's assurance of martial loyalty during any forthcoming war, which was important given the high proportion of Muslim soldiers in the Indian army.

Jinnah was now enjoying a new degree of reverence from his supporters. By now he had another house in Aurangzeb Road in New Delhi, as well as a smart ivory-coloured Packard Eight car with a cigar lighter and rear curtain. At a meeting in Patna in December 1938, the League decided to organize a women's central committee, headed by Jinnah's devoted sister Fatima, which gave a new momentum to the campaign, despite the reservations of Islamic traditionalists about female politicians. Jinnah told the meeting that Congress wanted Muslims to be 'mere footpages', and expected them to accept whatever they were offered by the Hindu majority 'as from a mighty sovereign'. He said he wanted rights, not favours, and that Congress did not speak for Christians, scheduled castes or 'untouchables', non-Brahmins, Muslims and many others. He made his most aggressive attack yet on Gandhi, painting him as a Hindu extremist. It was a fitting revenge for the years of perceived slights: 'I have no hesitation in saying that it is Mr Gandhi who is destroying the ideal with which the Congress was started. He is the one man responsible for turning the Congress into an instrument for the revival of Hinduism. His ideal is to revive the Hindu religion and establish Hindu Raj in this country, and he is utilizing the Congress to further this object.'[21]

At first, Jinnah had looked like too lightweight a politician to be of much importance to the British, but as a global war loomed, his stature grew accordingly. In April 1939 the British Parliament passed an amendment to the Government of India Act, giving the Viceroy full executive power over the provinces in an emergency. On 3 September Lord Linlith-gow announced that India was at war with Germany, and only sub-sequently deigned to hold talks on the subject with Indian political leaders. While permissible in strictly legal terms, this was a destructive move. When he unilaterally declared war on India's behalf, Lord Linlithgow observed that: 'Confronted with the demand that she should accept the dictation of a foreign power in relation to her own subjects, India has decided to stand firm.' The irony of this observation was probably lost on him. He maintained that Britain, and hence India, were standing up for ideals of morality and international justice: 'Nowhere do these great principles mean more than in India.'[22]

When Linlithgow saw Gandhi the day after declaring war, in order to see whether he could gain his support, he told him that plans for 'federation' with the Princely States had been 'suspended for the present'. Gandhi was in a fearful pickle, torn as he had been in 1914 between supporting the British war effort and making a bid for India's freedom. In a letter back to London, Lord Linlithgow reported that Gandhi had 'told me that the idea of any enemy defacing or damaging Westminster Abbey or Westminster Hall or any of the other monuments of our civiliz-ation was intolerable to him . . . and he contemplated the present struggle "with an English heart". I was greatly struck with the depth of real feeling which, so far as I could estimate, Mr Gandhi showed during this part of our conversation, his emotion at times being so marked as to make it impossible for him to continue with what he was saying.'[23]

On the same day he saw Jinnah, and wrote: 'I have the strong impres-sion that Mr Jinnah had come with the object of offering me his party's support in return for the abandonment of Federation,' which was in accordance with League intimations the previous year.[24] It is clear from Linlithgow's correspondence with the India Office throughout 1939 that he was acutely aware of the benefits of having Muslim backing during any conflict.

Since 1936, Nehru had given innumerable speeches in condemnation of Hitler, and was as strong a critic of Chamberlain's policy of appease-ment as any of Churchill's friends in the House of Commons. Congress had resolutely opposed the rise of fascism, and with more preparatory tact and thought by Linlithgow, might well have backed his declaration of war. However, the method of the announcement caused great resent-ment, and the ministries, after considerable internal debate, finally resigned in eight of the eleven provincial assemblies they controlled. This honest but miscalculated move by Congress curtailed their influence, left the British infuriated, and gave the Muslim League a new lease of life.

The declaration of war increased the degree of police repression and surveillance across India. The authorities were determined that the war effort would not be harmed by any political subversion or revolutionary outbreaks, and Germans, Austrians and Italians working in India were rounded up in their hundreds and interned. Bengal's fledgling Nazi Party was broken up by the police, and the German Consul in Calcutta, who was known to be a senior SS official, was arrested in an early-morning raid, his codebooks being seized as he attempted to destroy them. The Intelligence Bureau had been intercepting his mail for some time, using an Indian jeweller to forge replacement seals.

There were also worries over external activists using the war as an opportunity to subvert the Government of India. In mainland Europe, IPI agents began to keep even closer tabs on Indian subjects, and trailed them wherever they went. A booklet entitled 'Suspect Civilian Indians on the Continent of Europe' was issued every two months. It contained hundreds of names, giving physical descriptions, passport and visa details, aliases, accounts of recent movements and summaries of political views. In many cases these were entirely innocuous, being confined to a general wish that Indians might have a little more say in the running of their country, or perhaps a vague sympathy for Congress. But there were more serious instances: Indians who had previously been connected with the revolutionary Ghadr movement and were now living in Vienna or Berlin were found to have established links with the Nazis. These activists later operated through a 'Free India Centre' in Berlin.[25]

The Intelligence Bureau was also concerned about 'the political perversion of Indian students during their time in British universities', and deputed 'Indians of good standing' to quell any nascent perversity among their compatriots.[26] In 1941, two thousand trainee Indian engineers were sent to Letchworth in Hertfordshire as 'Bevin Boys' to do industrial work. When the Congress envoy Krishna Menon went to visit them, a plainclothes police constable (number 318E) was sent in pursuit. His report was fairly innocuous, and no action was taken.[27] Another target was the Indian Workers' Union, which represented Indians working in Britain. Its leaders were kept under constant surveillance by Special Branch, and plans were made to intern them after India Office lawyers ruled that there was 'no provision by which an Indian can be removed from the UK'.[28] A close watch was kept on British Communists who supported the cause of Indian nationalism.[29] Working on the 'careless talk costs lives' principle, the Intelligence Bureau was especially worried about information of any kind leaking out through foreign territories on India's coast. One of the worst offenders turned out to be the Vatican's Ambassador to India, which led to IPI opening a large file entitled 'Censorship: H.H. The Pope and Apostolic Delegates'. An undercover agent discovered that the Most Revd. Leo Kierkels was using his diplomatic bag to communicate 'anti-British matter' to the Pope, including classified information on Maltese and Italian POWs and internees in India. As a result his diplomatic immunity was suspended, his mail was intercepted, his cyphers were banned and he was kept under surveillance.[30]

Congress was in a tricky situation at this time, making plans for individual acts of civil disobedience, but divided as to what they might do on a national basis. The problem, as so often, was that giant swathes of the public had little serious interest in politics. Over two million Indians were to enlist voluntarily in the armed forces during the course of the war, and many millions more profited from defence contracts and other wartime jobs. Gandhi himself offered in 1940 to go to see the Nazis and make peace, on the grounds that 'Herr Hitler' could not be 'as bad as he is portrayed'. This was followed by a statement of extreme pacifism, in which he told the British people to lay down their arms, and if necessary give up their property to the Axis invaders: 'If these gentlemen choose to occupy your homes,' he suggested, 'you will vacate them.' It was a strategy that was unlikely to gain him much support in Britain.

The League were now leaning towards the British, and Linlithgow noted that Jinnah 'was seen to blush' when he made this point to him. As Linlithgow wrote to the Secretary of State for India Lord Zetland, he had 'a vested interest' in Jinnah's position. In public, of course, the Viceroy pretended he was doing his utmost to bring Indian leaders to reach agreement, which was clearly not the case. His support for Jinnah was never motivated by anything more than pragmatic political cynicism; he was happy to make use of the Muslim leader despite believing he was cursed by 'personal vanity' and 'would be quite as bad a master as Gandhi'. Moreover, 'he represents a minority, and a minority that can only effectively hold its own with our assistance.'[31]

Just as Congress was making overtures to the League about issuing a joint demand for a British declaration of war aims, Jinnah disrupted any potential unity by insisting that Congress should first stop its 'mass contact' recruitment campaign among Muslims. To nobody's surprise, Nehru refused. When the Congress provincial ministries resigned, Jinnah announced a 'Day of Deliverance', and became more virulent in his statements, accusing Congress of destroying Islamic culture and of interfering with Muslims' political rights. Jinnah did not have a strong hand, and knew he needed to play it carefully. As Linlithgow's successor Lord Wavell wrote as late as January 1944, 'Jinnah is not going to sell out on a rising market,' and would be unlikely to temper his demands 'until he feels that his influence has reached its peak'.[32]

As the political power of the Muslim League increased, Jinnah made his demands more explicit. In a magazine article in January 1940, he wrote that the British needed to put together a new constitution which recognized 'that there are in India two nations who both must share the governance of their common motherland'.[33] Two months later the moment of truth came, and a specific claim was made for the first time for the creation of a separate 'Pakistan'.

The crucial meeting of the Muslim League took place in Minto Park in Lahore, the capital of the Punjab. It has since been renamed Iqbal Park, although it is invariably referred to by its original name, and a tall, spiky and very ugly minaret has been placed at its centre in honour of the meeting. Around sixty thousand people were present, sitting on the floor in a giant tent. Jinnah sat on a throne, clad in *churidar* and a traditional Muslim *achkan* coat, and a little below him sat his sister Fatima, wearing a sari of ivory silk. It was the biggest meeting the League had yet held, and Jinnah's personality was growing with the adulation he received. The Quaid-i-Azam or 'Great Leader', as he had now been dubbed, lit a Craven A and addressed the rapt crowd for two hours in English, a language which very few of the thousands of listeners can have understood.

'Brother Gandhi,' he told them, 'has three votes, and I have only one vote.'[34] He compared the unhappy union of Britain and Ireland to the yoking together of Hindus and Muslims. The needs of the *qaum* had to be protected, for: 'The Musalmans are not a minority. The Musalmans are a nation by any definition.'[35] This two-nation strategy would have many advantages, not least that arithmetic could be thrown out of the window. As a *qaum*, or 'nation', the status of Muslims would be guaranteed throughout India, regardless of those areas where they were in a minority.

The statement that has become known as the 'Lahore Resolution' was passed on 23 March 1940. It demanded that 'geographically contiguous units are demarcated into regions which should be so constituted, with such territorial adjustments as may be necessary, that the areas in which the Muslims are numerically in a majority as in the North-Western and Eastern zones of India, should be grouped to constitute "Independent States" in which the constituent units shall be autonomous and sovereign.' The reference to 'territorial adjustments' apparently suggested the prospect of gaining some extra territory and better lines of communication, rather than the idea of partitioning Bengal and the Punjab.

This crucial resolution implied through the deliberate ambiguity of the phrase 'independent states' that more than one new independent Muslim state might be created. In other words, there could possibly be an East Pakistan and a West Pakistan without a single central government. Fazlul Huq of Bengal, who helped to draft the resolution, clearly thought that it signified an independent Bengal.

However, as such an outcome would have meant a major loss of bargaining power for Jinnah, he later indicated that he envisaged one Pakistan, with two 'wings' to it. This issue was finally clarified only by the Delhi Resolution of April 1946, which proposed that: 'Pakistan Zones, where the Muslims are in a dominant majority, be constituted into a sovereign independent state.'[36] This meant that the administration of East Pakistan would be controlled from West Pakistan, a disastrous proposition which was to lead in the end to the bloodshed of 1970–71, and the creation of Bangladesh.

Astoundingly, the Muslim League at no point between 1940 and 1946 clarified precisely what they meant by the Lahore Resolution. It was not a detailed or coherent statement of Muslim demands, and Jinnah was careful to maintain the uncertainty. Questions of boundaries, population shifts, methods of administration, rights of minorities, and, most crucially of all, whether the Pakistan zones and the rest of India would share some kind of central federal authority, were simply not resolved. There is a reasonable case for arguing that Jinnah never really believed in a totally independent Pakistan, and that he used the Lahore Resolution merely as a bargaining counter. The big regional leaders, especially in the Punjab and Bengal, backed Jinnah because they thought his demands would boost their own provincial status. They ignored the risk of communal disorder that his separatist approach was liable to bring.

So it was that the man whom Motilal Nehru had once said was 'showing the way to Hindu–Muslim unity' became the prophet and founder of an Indian Muslim homeland. The 'two-nation' theory embodied in the Pakistan demand was a clever idea, in that it enabled Jinnah to promote himself as the voice of all the Muslims of India. As Ayesha Jalal has written in her carefully argued book *The Sole Spokesman: Jinnah, the Muslim League and the Demand for Pakistan*, 'Jinnah's appeal to religion was always ambiguous . . . and evidence suggests that his use of the communal factor was a political tactic, not an ideological commitment . . . Asserting that Muslims were a nation avoided the logic of numbers.'[37] The Muslim League was never a truly religious party. Theocratic elements within the *millat* in several instances denounced the League as ungodly and Jinnah as an unbeliever, and few of its prime activists were obvious religious communalists – a figure such as Jinnah or Liaquat Ali Khan could hardly be represented as a 'mad *mullah*'.

The obvious and ultimately insoluble problem with the Lahore Resolution was that it effectively ignored the fate of Muslims living outside the north-east and north-west of India. There were huge swathes of the country – in Rajputana, the Central Provinces and the whole of southern India – where Muslims amounted to less than 10 per cent of the population. Were they to migrate to the Pakistan zones, or stay put and hope for the best? Jinnah's answer, when pressed, was the 'hostage theory': namely that the presence of a Hindu minority in Muslim areas, and vice-versa, would secure the mutual good treatment of each minority community.

Even prominent Muslims, such as Sir Sikander Hayat Khan, realized that their own vision of Hindu–Muslim–Sikh amity was doomed if the League's ambitions were to be fulfilled. But there was a huge groundswell of support for the Resolution. It was radical, and the kind of answer that people wanted in these dangerous and uncertain times. Congress was uncertain how to react, preferring to laugh off the demand for Pakistan. Nehru dismissed it as 'fantastic', Gandhi called it 'baffling', and Rajagopalachari condemned it as the product of a 'diseased mentality'. As Nehru's niece said, the Nehru family regarded the very idea of Pakistan as 'a joke – it seemed absurd to imagine that such a thing could ever happen to India'.[38]

The British reaction to the Lahore Resolution is instructive. There was an important exchange of telegrams between London and New Delhi in April 1940. The Secretary of State for India Lord Zetland told Linlithgow that in a forthcoming Parliamentary speech he intended 'pouring cold water on the Muslim idea of partition formally advocated in the Lahore resolution, though not necessarily at this stage conclusively rejecting it. I should emphasize that this would be a counsel of despair and wholly at variance with the policy of a united India which British rule has achieved and which it is our aim to perpetuate after British rule ceases.'[39]

Linlithgow's reaction was that the Pakistan demand might give the British some useful leverage, and so separation should not be condemned outright. Although he thought Jinnah's idea was 'very largely in the nature of bargaining', they should not speak against it since 'any overemphasis on unacceptability and faults of Muslim scheme would be politically unfortunate ... and I think you will probably feel with me that wise tactics would be to keep our hands free until critical moment is reached in future constitutional discussions.'[40] By using the Muslim League's demands in this way, the Viceroy was playing a complex game of political brinkmanship, which was to have lasting consequences for the future of Asia.

PART II

The Struggle for Power

'His Majesty's Government has no longer the power
to take effective action'

Letter to Winston Churchill from the Viceroy Lord Wavell, 1944

EIGHT

Outside India

By the late 1930s Winston Churchill was depressed and taciturn, and getting on badly with his wife Clemmie. He spent much of his time down in the country at Chartwell, drinking to excess and pontificating to his entourage. The outbreak of war in September 1939 changed everything. His dire prophecies about Germany's intentions had proved correct, and he joined the War Cabinet, returning to the Admiralty which he had run a quarter of a century earlier.

Winston Churchill had had an extraordinary career. Born in 1874, he was a neglected child, abandoned by his dysfunctional parents into the care of his nurse. When the social reformer Beatrice Webb met him in 1903, she thought him 'egotistical, bumptious, shallow-minded and reactionary, but with a certain personal magnetism'.[1] Debacles such as the 1911 Sidney Street siege, his conduct as First Lord of the Admiralty during the 1914–18 war, which led to him being described as 'a public danger to the Empire' by no less a figure than Admiral Jellicoe, and most particularly his defiant line over Baldwin's India policy, had dented his reputation among his colleagues. They feared him as a maverick, but in 1940 they turned to him to save their skins.

The ever-perceptive Anthony Storr classifies Churchill as an 'extroverted intuitive' – somebody who seeks action rather than contemplation, is inconsiderate and selfish in their treatment of others, yet at the same time has a marked ability to catch the moment, and 'a keen nose for things in the bud pregnant with future promise'.[2] In May 1940 Churchill replaced Neville Chamberlain as Prime Minister, offering himself as the saviour of his nation, the man who would battle on against the odds even when the invader was at the gates. It was Churchill's keen nose and his capacity to seize the day that made him so effective and inspirational as a war leader. The people of Britain came to love his hunched shoulders, his gravelly voice, his V-for-Victory sign, his romper suits, his peculiar pronunciation of foreign words, the omnipresent cigar, and his baroque, bombastic, florid, nostalgic speeches – speeches which would have seemed a little absurd in more regular circumstances.

His intransigent dynamism made him less good as a peacetime strategist, and explains the peculiarity of some of his opinions. As Storr writes, 'Churchill was a poor judge of character. The sober, steadfast, and reliable seldom appealed to him. What he wanted were people who would stimulate, amuse and arouse him.'[3] Temperamentally, by upbringing and by instinct, he was a a believer in a racially-based imperialism. He could not countenance the possibility of presiding over the break-up of the British Empire, and most especially he could not accept the loss of its heart, the sprawling Indian subcontinent. However great Winston Churchill may have been as Britain's wartime leader, he was to prove a disaster for India.

One of the movers in the destruction of the discredited man with the furled umbrella had been Leo Amery, who quoted Cromwell's famous words, 'In the name of God, go!' at Chamberlain on the floor in the House of Commons in May 1940. It was obvious that in Churchill's new administration a tough India policy would be maintained, so the comparatively liberal Minister Lord Zetland resigned as Secretary of State for India. He had proposed that India should be given dominion status after the war, with built-in safeguards for the British position, but Churchill opposed such a move. This job was offered to Amery, a former Colonial Secretary who had hoped to take a crucial economic or defence post in the War Cabinet, and was most disappointed at the idea of being India Secretary. With no enthusiasm, he accepted the post.

Amery was an interesting choice, in that he had strongly opposed Churchill's line on India during the great debates of the early 1930s. Yet, as so often with British politicians, his views were liberal only in comparison to those of hidebound reactionaries, as represented by Churchill and his entourage. Now that he was Prime Minister, Churchill was able to reassert the views that he had promoted so powerfully but unsuccessfully during his wilderness years. His policy became one of minimum concession in order to retain control. As the historian John Charmley put it, 'he became a sort of one-man India Defence League in his own Cabinet'.[4]

During his time as India Secretary, Amery was to have little success in running his tentatively progressive policy proposals past the Cabinet, most of whom had no interest in the Indian subcontinent and lived in mortal terror of challenging the cigar-puffing old growler who had appointed them to office. Amery had to contend with the likes of the ICS grandee-turned Colonial Secretary Lord Lloyd, who thought that 'any and every sort of self-government for Indians is a mistake.'[5] Even Clement Attlee rarely opposed Churchill in Cabinet over India, leaving Amery to characterize the Labour ministers in his diary as 'mice' and 'incredibly feeble creatures'.

Leopold Amery was a curious politician, with complex, detailed but generally impractical ideas, and a degree of theoretical political belief that is generally rare in the Tory mind. He was, incidentally, no fewer than seventeen inches shorter than the Viceroy, Lord Linlithgow. Born in India in 1873, where his father was an official in the Indian Forest Department, Amery was intelligent, pugnacious, deaf and athletic, a long-winded public speaker, keen traveller and fellow of All Souls. Like Jawaharlal Nehru and Winston Churchill, he had been to school at Harrow, and this gave him a special rapport with the Prime Minister.

Although Amery was in awe of his old schoolfriend, he felt confident standing up to him during discussions, knowing that Churchill was liable to change his tune as a result of an angry exchange, and adopt as his own a policy that a few moments earlier he had been busily denouncing. Amery was one of a handful of associates, along with Lord Beaverbrook and Brendan Bracken, who was permitted to progress past the silk dressing-gowns in the Prime Ministerial bedroom and become a 'Companion of the Bath'. Thus the question of a replacement for Linlithgow was pondered amid pomades and quivering pink flesh, Amery noting in his diary that 'we discoursed while he was drying himself down.'[6]

In his younger days, Amery had sided with the Conservative 'Die-hards' and, according to the *Dictionary of National Biography*, became known as a 'passionate advocate of British imperialism', and was 'drawn into extreme right-wing politics'. As Colonial Secretary in the 1920s, he had set up the Empire Marketing Board and done his best to implement the 'Anglo-Saxonist' imperial vision of his heroes Joseph Chamberlain and Lord Milner, of a group of 'partner states' thriving in unity around the world, all linked to the British Crown.

In a briefing to Amery in June, Linlithgow acknowledged the strength of Jinnah's position. It was a fair assessment, although it would have infuriated the likes of Nehru, Gandhi and Azad had they read it. In the Viceroy's opinion: 'Congress is essentially a Hindu party, though it contains Muslim elements . . . there is no justification on a broad view for

Linlithgow disliked the Cripps Mission and all it stood for, and hid Sir Stafford in quarantine in Karachi for twenty-four hours before allowing him to reach Delhi. Behind his back he referred to his visitor as 'Sir Stifford Crapps'. Moreover, Cripps and his entourage – which was collectively known as 'the Crippery' – were very conscious that their political standing had been staked on the success of these negotiations. With Jinnah and the Muslim League celebrating the anniversary of the Lahore Resolution, Cripps arrived in India with a reputation for being pro-Congress.

Unlike Linlithgow, who preferred to stay tucked away in imperial splendour at Viceroy's House, Cripps made a point of trying to get some sense of the atmosphere on the streets. The news was bleak, and he was seriously worried by the situation he found, reporting to Churchill on 1 April that the country was heading for chaos: 'Unrest is growing amongst the population . . . The food situation is causing disquiet . . . The outlook so far as the internal situation goes is exceedingly bad.' It is perhaps an indication of the general mood following the fall of Burma and Singapore that when his telegram to Churchill was being deciphered, 'available military' came out as 'frail military', while 'Britisher' emerged as 'appeaser'.[3]

Amery and Linlithgow thought Cripps's analysis of the dangers in India was alarmist, and that the collapse of his Mission might be no bad thing. The Viceroy thought it would weaken the position of the Congress leadership until after the war, for in his view, 'if Congress fails this time it may be the end, for many long years, of any constitutional progress in India' – which would, apparently, 'leave a great many people relieved at heart'.[4]

The US newspapers were however most enthusiastic about the Cripps Mission, seeing it as the panacea for India's troubles. On 10 March 1942, just before the Mission set off, Roosevelt sent Churchill a letter in which he set out his personal views. He hoped that 'the injection of a new thought' on the subject might be useful. His suggestion was that 'a temporary Dominion Government' might be set up: 'Such a move is strictly in line with the world changes of the past half century and with the democratic processes of all who are fighting Nazism.'

In an earlier draft of the letter he admitted to his ally that his opinions were 'based on very little firsthand knowledge on my part', but felt there was 'real danger in India now that there is too much suspicion and

regarding [the Muslims within Congress] as of any very decisive importance ... at the present time the only organization which can speak on
behalf of the Muslims of India as a whole is the Muslim League under
Jinnah.' He continued: 'There are from time to time signs of considerable
internal tension in the League [but Jinnah] remains in complete control
and is the person to be negotiated with, and the only person in a position
to deliver the goods.'[7]

Although Jinnah's political position was strengthening, there was still
no very clear understanding of what his new 'Pakistan' might be. If he
knew the answer himself, he was keeping quiet in public. In February 1941
a secret memorandum was prepared for him called 'What is Pakistan?' It
carved up the parts of India where no one religious group was in a clear
majority, which shows that even at this stage the Muslim League realized
that individual provinces might have to be bisected in order to satisfy
other political parties. Under the proposals in 'What is Pakistan?', places
such as Ambala in the Punjab, which was poor and full of Sikhs and
Hindus, were lopped off from Pakistan, while prosperous areas such as
Assam, where Muslims represented around a third of the population,
were retained. The document also noted that the Princely State of Hyderabad was large enough to become fully independent.

Amery's line in the House of Commons was that Indian constitutional
reform could be re-examined at the end of the war. There were attempts
among ministers to agree a 'statement' which would develop this position
further, and in July 1940 Linlithgow made his final concession, proposing
to London that they should guarantee moves towards dominion status a
year after the war ended. However the War Cabinet vetoed the idea,
suggesting instead that after the war ended a representative body might
be convened with a view to determining a new constitution for India.
Dominion status would be on offer at some unspecified date in the future,
but it would depend on agreement among the Indian parties involved –
implying a possible Muslim veto.

Churchill himself was strongly against a declaration of any kind on
India, both temperamentally and on account of more pressing military
concerns. He interfered in Amery's discussions with Linlithgow by
insisting on seeing all the telegrams that had passed between them. This
was against precedent: as Amery said, it was 'absurd that what are in
effect private conversations' should be seen by the Prime Minister. Churchill objected to the telegrams' tone, and told Amery he would 'sooner

give up political life at once, or rather go out into the wilderness and fight, than to admit a revolution which meant the end of the Imperial Crown in India'.[8] Amery decided against resignation only because of the fraught wartime situation.

Eventually agreement was reached, and in August 1940 Linlithgow formally put forward the idea of a post-war settlement. It was vague, and it was not much of an offer, and Congress (which had an obsessive and unnecessary dislike of the phrase 'dominion status' – after all, Ireland, which was a dominion, remained neutral during the war) rejected it. This appears to have been what Linlithgow wanted, and he immediately wrote a memorandum to his provincial governors that he was prepared 'to crush the organization as a whole' if Congress launched civil disobedience – as he knew full well it would.[9] Congress promoted individual *satyagraha* in an effort to save face, and by June of the following year twenty thousand activists had been arrested without dislodging the British. At this point the campaign petered out, and British opinion hardened. Congress were now in a very weak position, having resigned from office in the provinces and launched a *satyagraha* campaign, yet with no discernible effect.

In his attempt to inflict a fatal blow on the freedom movement, Linlithgow made a request to London to be allowed to implement a 'Revolutionary Movement Ordinance'. This would enable him to arrest Congress leaders whenever he wanted, and would proclaim the whole of Congress an illegal organization. However Amery thought this was too strong, and instead gave him the option of banning specific bodies such as the Congress Working Committee.

Linlithgow was now uninterested in any kind of cooperation; he regarded the Congress leaders as traitors for behaving in such a way while the British Empire was fighting for survival. He saw that India was of strategic importance in the war, and that agitation would have to be suppressed if control was to be retained. India's defence production – Bihari saltpetre was essential for bomb-making, for instance – was crucial to Allied plans. Presuming that there were enemy intentions of an invasion of India, possibly by a joint German–Japanese pincer movement through the North-West Frontier and Burma, Linlithgow clamped down on anything that could disrupt the war effort. He saw himself, in the words of one historian, as 'the Churchill of the East, standing at the head of the Indian Empire, the sole obstacle preventing a juncture of the Japanese and the German forces in India or the Middle East'.[10]

In October 1941 the Prime Minister sent a telegram to his Viceroy asking him to stay on until the spring of 1942: 'I have the greatest confidence that you will hold the position firm on the lines that we have agreed,' wrote Churchill. 'It is most necessary that those with whom you have to deal should realize ... the support which you receive from His Majesty's Government.'[11] The following year the request was renewed, and Linlithgow agreed to remain in India until April 1943 to hold the line.

The Muslim League was still rising. Its 1941 annual session was held in Madras, and attended by over a hundred thousand activists. Behind the skeletal Jinnah on the platform sat 'Periyar' E.V. Ramaswami Naicker, whose Dravidistan Justice Party was campaigning against the imposition of north Indian culture and the Hindi language. The union of the Muslim League and the Justice Party was another political marriage of convenience that had begun at the outbreak of war, for it was in the interests of both groups to link up and denounce Congress and all its works. Jinnah was flanked by fearsome Muslim League Guards, who wore grey uniforms and liked escorting him to public events with their swords drawn. In his speech, Jinnah appealed to the British to stop their 'policy of appeasement' towards those who were frustrating the war effort – namely the Congress *satyagrahis.*

In July his flirtation with Linlithgow turned sour, when the Viceroy asked the Muslim provincial chief ministers to sit on a National Defence Council, but did not invite Jinnah to join them. As a result Jinnah ordered the chief ministers (who had a nominal attachment to the Muslim League) to boycott the Council. They complied, with the exception of Fazlul Huq of Bengal, who resigned from the League, denouncing Jinnah, in what can now be seen as part of the nascent movement that finally led to the creation of Bangladesh, as 'a single individual who seeks to rule as an omnipotent authority even over the destiny of thirty-three millions of Muslims in the province of Bengal'.[12] Huq was soon joined by the Nawab of Dhaka, and they were both attacked publicly by the increasingly autocratic Jinnah as being 'guilty of the grossest treachery'. The Pakistan movement's political support in Bengal was eroded further, which was to have grave consequences in the future.

Around this time the Intelligence Bureau realized that Jinnah held the key to future political developments, and commissioned a detailed report entitled 'Congress and the Muslim League: A Study in Conflict', based on 'highly secret sources'. It stated that the Punjabi leader Sir Sikander Hayat Khan had 'made it absolutely clear that he would on no account tolerate Jinnah's interference in the internal affairs of his Province', and that political progress was therefore dependent on Sir Sikander's future policy. The main conclusion of the report was that 'the present direction of Indian political thought lies largely in the hands of the two great adversaries, Gandhi and Jinnah: vainglorious, determined, domineering men, impatient of opposition, clever in their various ways but completely obsessed with conflicting ideals which they are pursuing with almost appalling relentlessness.'

The IB believed, however, that once the war came to an end, 'a consideration of all available material suggests that they will probably not hesitate to abandon their present entrenched positions and to enter the field of negotiation and adjustment immediately the contest for power starts. Whether Gandhi or Jinnah will come out on top in the ensuing fight for political ascendancy depends on circumstances which cannot at present be foreseen.'[13]

Events in East Asia during the early months of 1942 changed the complexion of Indian politics for good. In February the imperial fortress of Singapore surrendered to the Japanese after a week's fighting, through a combination of incompetence and poor planning, and the competing military demands of the war in Europe. 62,000 British and Commonwealth troops were captured, and were to be treated with vicious contempt by the Japanese. Singapore's collapse was soon followed by the fall of Malaya and Burma.

It was a monumental blow to Britain's prestige in Asia, and led to the development of a popular feeling in India that their British rulers were no longer invincible. During the months leading to the fall of Burma, the British had been suppressing information about bombing and casualties, with the effect that there was considerable public unrest when news leaked out into India. The authorities in New Delhi were nervous that Hindus had a 'brotherly feeling' for the Japanese.

In January 1942 Churchill was as resolute as ever about India, optimistically telling Attlee: 'The Indian troops are fighting splendidly, but it must be remembered that their allegiance is to the King Emperor, and that the rule of the Congress and Hindoo Priesthood machine would never be tolerated by a fighting race.'[14] Attlee was in turn becoming worried that Linlithgow was 'defeatist' in his approach towards Indian politicians, and suggested to Amery in the same month that it might be 'worth considering whether someone should not be charged with a mission to try to bring the political leaders together'.[15]

When Generalissimo and Madame Chiang Kai-shek decided to visit India in 1942, Churchill became greatly excited, trying to cajole the Chinese leader into making speeches which favoured the British line. Chiang Kai-shek was not at all cooperative, announcing plans to visit Gandhi at his ashram and implying that he might make comments of encouragement towards Indian nationalism. Linlithgow sneakily undermined his ability to do so, noting in an internal document: 'I have taken steps to prevent the Generalissimo from obtaining transport to Wardha whether by train, air or road.' The Chinese suspected that something of this kind was going on, but two weeks later Linlithgow cheerfully lied that 'no attempt was made to restrict his movements.'[16]

Linlithgow ordered all provincial governors to launch a 'hearts and minds' campaign to improve the British position in India, through appealing to such virtues as 'national pride, honour and self-respect' in the hearts of their Indian subjects. New Delhi would provide 'a continuous stream of propaganda material' for this purpose.[17] He was finding his position a considerable strain, and asked Amery to 'cushion' him from 'explosions in the Prime Minister's mind'. He also thought Churchill's plan to make some kind of broadcast or statement on India was 'dangerous and amateurish to a degree ... I am carrying here, almost single-handed, an immense responsibility. Indeed I do not think it is to exaggerate to affirm that the key to success in this war is now very largely in my hands.'[18] In March 1942 the Cabinet put together a new declaration on India which offered the possibility that moves might be made towards granting it dominion status.

In the period before the Americans joined the war, President Roosevelt sent a personal envoy to London to liaise with Churchill. He was Averell Harriman, a stodgy character with an acute attraction to power who soon began having an affair with the glamorous Pamela Churchill, who was then married to Winston's son Randolph. She was later to marry Harriman and become a substantial political power-broker in her own right in Washington, and US Ambassador to France. In the curious system of power alliances under which the British Establishment operated, this was no disadvantage in Harriman's dealings with the Prime Minister, since Churchill was extremely anxious to, in his own word, 'drag' the Americans into the war by whatever means possible. Lord Beaverbrook, for one, was delighted by the news of the liaison: 'To have FDR's personal representative, the man charged with keeping Britain safe, sleeping with the prime minister's daughter-in-law was a wonderful stroke of luck.'[19]

In early 1942 Churchill was in an unhappy position. His government was becoming unpopular, and blackouts, ration books and military defeats in the Far East all conspired against him. He was also bedevilled by US pressure over India. Against all his instincts, he had to at least consider some form of liberalization in exchange for American financial and potential military support for the war. At the Newfoundland Conference in August 1941, Churchill and FDR had agreed a statement of common war and peace aims known as the Atlantic Charter. With the bombing of Pearl Harbor in December of the same year, and the arrival of America in the war, it became imperative for Britain to remain on good terms with its paymaster in the USA. There was a high initial degree of cooperation between Churchill and Roosevelt, Churchill even informing the US President that the British had cracked American codes, but there were also underlying tensions.

The Atlantic Charter contained a clause supporting 'sovereign rights and self-government'. Roosevelt assumed this applied universally; Churchill that it only referred to countries under occupation by his enemies. It became the cause of a substantial dispute between them. Although the Allies were supposedly fighting for the cause of liberty, the man with the big cigar was convinced that liberty should not be granted to those he considered his racial inferiors. When the Governor of Burma, Sir Reginald Dorman-Smith, suggested to him a few years later that a transfer of power in Burma would have to take place before too long, Churchill sent him packing. In his opinion, nationalist agitators throughout the Empire should be neither listened to nor encouraged: rather, 'What those people need is the sjambok.'[20]

Roosevelt was adamant about the need for British concessions, especially in India. In February 1942 he told Harriman to deliver 'a highly sensitive personal message' to Churchill, asking what action was going to be taken. Harriman later described this as 'one of the most difficult assignments he handled for Roosevelt', knowing that Churchill was a heartfelt imperialist who thought the future of India was Britain's business alone.[21] Harriman conveyed Roosevelt's views on India without espousing them himself.

There was never likely to be a meeting of minds between the two leaders over this question, and Harriman knew he had to tread carefully. The disastrous collapse in the Far East had tightened America's grip on Britain. As Harriman wrote in a letter to Roosevelt on 6 March, 'Unfortunately Singapore shook the Prime Minister himself to such an extent that he has not been able to stand up to this adversity with his old vigor.'[22] Everything in Churchill's temperament, inheritance and ideology militated against conceding power to Indian politicians, but his position was extremely weak, and he was pragmatic enough to know he had no choice but to cooperate with the United States.

FDR had never been to the subcontinent, and even Harriman thought that 'Stalin showed rather more sophistication than Roosevelt in the discussion of India' during a meeting between the Soviet and American leaders, since Stalin appreciated the complexities of Indian religion and caste, in a way that the President did not.[23] Under the influence of Chiang Kai-shek, Roosevelt came to think that Churchill would have to make urgent concessions in India if the risk of an uprising or a Japanese invasion were to be curtailed.

Even supporters of FDR thought his position on India was inconsistent and poorly informed. His view was based partially on instinctive American opposition to European colonialism, and also to a dislike of the British Empire's role as a commercial closed shop. The United States made vigorous attempts to alter British policy in India, yet Roosevelt, for all his New Deals and talk of freedom for India, had some worrying ideas of his own.

In an extraordinary letter to the Foreign Office in August 1942, an official at the British Embassy in Washington reported that 'amongst many other thoughts thrown out by the President' was a plan to try to cross-breed and develop 'an Indo-Asian or Eurasian or (better) Euroindasian race' as a counterbalance to the 'nefarious' Japanese. Roosevelt's ideas came from a Professor Hrdlicka of the Smithsonian Institution, who was studying, on the President's orders, 'the effect of racial crossing'. The idea was that certain 'racial crossings' were good, while others were dangerous. The President and the Professor were reported to have had

NINE

Do or Die

Although few members of the Cabinet had grasped the fact, the British in India by now faced an impossible situation. The moral argument had clearly been won by their opponents, and the political tide of the moment was running against them. As a prominent Bombay missionary wrote in a private report for the Viceroy at the end of 1941 on the general situation in India: 'At almost any gathering of students a speaker has only to quote from the latest speech of Mr Amery or any other British statesman regarding India to evoke roars of laughter . . . All this shows that the problem which we have to face is more a psychological than a political one.'[1]

Amery's instinct was that Congress would not accept the Cripps Mission because they would be 'shocked by the idea that India may be divided if they are not prepared to make terms with the Muslims', but that the whole exercise would therefore benefit the British position. He wrote: 'My impression is that the most likely result will be a grudging admission that some advance has been made by us, but that it is not sufficient to warrant Congress taking a part in the government of the country beyond helping with ARP [Air Raid Precautions], &c. locally. I am not sure that that would not be the best solution.'[2] The fact that the Secretary of State for India was still thinking in terms of ARP is an indication of the limitations of the British government's policy.

Both Amery and Linlithgow had failed to grasp – in the way that Wavell and Mountbatten would – the broader theme. The key problem was in the end, like many things in politics, quite simple: the British claimed to be fighting a war in support of freedom and democracy, yet India was under foreign occupation. Amery was unable to see that the issue was not the nature of British rule, or the degree of Indian participation in it, but rather one of nationalism. Indians wanted to be free, as Gandhi once said, to make their own mistakes.

dissatisfaction in too many places'. The President even quoted the slogan that Churchill so disliked: 'Asia for the Asiatics'.[5] The Prime Minister's private response to all this was 'contemptuous', but he knew he could not bite the hand that fed him. Rattled not only by American words but also by the pro-Congress intervention of the Canadian Prime Minister, William Mackenzie King, Churchill restated his government's position in the House of Commons, saying that Cripps sought 'assent not only from the Hindu majority but also from those great minorities amongst which the Muslims are the most important ... India has a great part to play in the world struggle for freedom.'[6]

The talks that Cripps now embarked upon were complicated by the presence in New Delhi of a representative of FDR, Colonel Louis Johnson, who was ostensibly charged with discussing military matters, but in fact had a much wider brief. A prosperous lawyer from West Virginia with no previous experience of India, he was renowned among US diplomats for being 'coarse, bombastic and ignorant', and was an altogether inappropriate choice for such a delicate task as encouraging a happy outcome to tricky negotiations. Linlithgow was extremely wary of any American intervention. As he wrote to Churchill in August regarding the proposed visit of another US politician: 'My experience of peripatetic Americans which is now extensive is that their zeal in teaching us our business is in inverse ratio to their understanding of even the most elementary of the problems with which we have to deal.'[7]

'In the recent history of India,' Nehru told Louis Johnson, 'there has not been such a combination of fiercely anti-Indian freedom elements in the British government as we have had during the past two years and still have today.'[8] Johnson drank this in; he took the view that Cripps and Nehru could reach a solution 'in five minutes' if both parties were free to negotiate. This was probably true, in that all Churchill really wanted from the Mission was a decline in pro-Indian feeling among the higher reaches of the American political machine. Amery later denounced Johnson to Linlithgow as 'a real mischief-maker', and Johnson did not help his own position when he said, in the presence of a British army officer in civilian clothes, that he was 'fed up with the complacency' of the British authorities in India.

Stafford Cripps chose the tactics of consultations, soundings, midnight meetings, qualified assurances and detailed negotiation with a wide variety of players, including the more radical nationalists whom Linlithgow disdained. He went to the Nehru family home, Anand Bhawan, and attended the marriage of Nehru's daughter Indira to a Parsi insurance salesman called Feroze Gandhi, who at least had the distinction of supplying his wife with a politically useful surname. Indira embarrassed herself by offering the distinguished visitor some 'potato cripps'. The Crippery hoped that with sufficient wheeling and dealing, an agreement would somehow be struck. Had Cripps succeeded there is little doubt that it would have secured his place in history as a diplomatic negotiator of great skill. He failed, and in retrospect it is apparent that he never had much chance of success. Most of the British government disapproved of his Mission, and many within the ranks of Indian nationalism saw him as little more than a Churchillian decoy.

Nehru had himself met Cripps in June 1938 while on a trip to Europe, and stayed at his country house in order to meet Attlee, Nye Bevan and Harold Laski. He disliked the way Cripps expected Congress to accept whatever was on offer: 'He was a lawyer who stated his case powerfully and expected it to prevail . . . Both his technique and his brief left him no room for manoeuvre.'[9] Nehru and the Congress President Azad took the view that the British were in a very weak position, and that the solution Cripps was proposing would depend heavily on cooperation from the incumbent Viceroy, which was unlikely to be forthcoming.

Lord Linlithgow soon became angry at Cripps's failure to consult him during the negotiations, and wheedled Amery into giving him permission to telegraph his views direct to Churchill. Once this Churchill–Linlithgow axis was established, the Cripps Mission was doomed, as each move that he made had been pre-empted. Amery was foolish to allow this to happen, forgetting the way Linlithgow had used a similar tactic to undermine his own position at the India Office when he first took office. The Prime Minister jumped at the idea, telling Linlithgow to 'telegraph personal to me . . . exactly what you think'.[10] Churchill also had Cripps's growing personal popularity in Britain to contend with, an additional reason for hoping his Mission might fail. As Amery wrote privately, the Prime Minister had been shrewd to 'send off this dangerous young rival on the errand of squaring the circle in India'.[11]

The Churchill–Linlithgow axis gave them the opportunity to manipulate Cripps to great effect. Thus when Linlithgow telegraphed to London to suggest that an Indian might have a nominal 'defence coordination portfolio' on the Viceroy's Council, with all power being retained with the Commander-in-Chief and the Viceroy, he knew perfectly well in advance that Congress would reject the deal. Before long Cripps was getting brisk 'What does this mean?' telegrams from Churchill over each point he was attempting to negotiate.

Linlithgow's crucial coup came on 8 April, when he learned that Congress and Louis Johnson had been told of a possible 'formula' to solve the impasse in advance of the Viceroy's private office. Downing Street was notified of this, and Cripps soon received a 'MOST IMMEDIATE – CLEAR THE LINE' telegram from the Prime Minister. Churchill insisted that Johnson was 'not President Roosevelt's personal representative in any matter outside the specific mission dealing with Indian munitions', and that Roosevelt was 'entirely opposed to anything like US intervention or mediation', which was not true.[12] The following day Churchill was assuring Cripps, 'there can be no question of want of confidence' in him, but the Mission had by now reached the end of its useful life.

When Congress turned down the British proposals, Winston Churchill sent Roosevelt a copy of Cripps's letter outlining the failure of the negotiations. The Prime Minister was delighted, as the last thing he wanted was to become bogged down in constitutional details relating to India. 'I feel absolutely satisfied we have done our utmost,' he told FDR. But the President was still not satisfied. With the advice of Louis Johnson ringing in his ears, he telegraphed back at once asking for further negotiations, adding that in the eyes of the American people it was British unwillingness 'to concede to the Indians the right of self-government' that had been at the root of the breakdown. Churchill was so furious at this that 'the string of cuss words lasted for two hours in the middle of the night'. In a draft cable, which was later toned down, he responded that he would certainly not countenance any concessions to the nationalists: 'I am sure that I could not be responsible for a policy which would throw the whole sub-continent of India into utter confusion while the Japanese invader is at its gates.'[13]

Three months later, Chiang Kai-shek sent a letter to Roosevelt, pointing out that the war effort would be hindered both in India and elsewhere if there was any kind of uprising against British rule: 'Should however the situation be allowed to drift until an anti-British movement breaks out in India, any attempt on the part of the British to cope with the crisis by enforcing existing colonial laws or by resorting to military and police force, will only help to spread disturbances and turmoil.'

Roosevelt tried once more to put pressure on Churchill, with no success. Churchill responded with the usual anti-Congress propaganda, claiming that the freedom movement lacked the support of the bulk of the population, since 'Congress represents ... non-fighting Hindu elements, and can neither defend India nor raise revolt.'[14] As a result FDR announced that the thousands of American troops in India were there only to help the Chinese and to liberate Burma, and not to uphold Britain's Indian Empire. This strong moral position was slightly undermined by reports that American soldiers, together with their British and Australian counterparts, were engaging in the molestation and even rape of Indian women.

The background to the USA's diplomatic pressure over India is worth examining. In an opinion poll in 1942, between 70 and 80 per cent of Americans said they were aware of British negotiations. This was a very high proportion for a foreign policy issue, and of those polled, only 2 per cent definitely opposed Indian independence. A poll conducted a year later showed that while most of the American population favoured Indian independence, only 20 per cent thought it should be granted immediately.[15] Yet by 1945, fewer than half of those polled said they were aware of what was happening in India, showing that US interest in India was essentially a news-led blip which reached its high point during 1942.

The Cripps Mission was a distraction. Sir Stafford had been sent to New Delhi to give India's politicians a promise of jam tomorrow in exchange for cooperation today. However, the quality and quantity of the jam was not specified. As Amery admitted in his diary, all Cripps really had to offer was 'what is essentially a pro-Moslem and reasonably Conservative policy'.[16] India would retain its existing constitution until the end of the war, with a slight increase in indigenous representation, and a vague promise of constitutional discussions after the war had ended.

The crucial point about the Mission is that Cripps negotiated well beyond his remit, going much further over the matter of Indian participation within the Government of India than had been agreed. His final offer to Congress included an Indian-staffed administration, with only home affairs and defence remaining in British hands, although such a concession had never been authorized by London. It is certain that this proposal would not have got past Churchill or his Cabinet. Similarly, London never accepted his assurance that there would be 'cabinet government' in New Delhi, with the majority view being accepted by the Viceroy. The draft Cripps offer that was turned down by Congress in 1942 was substantially more generous than Churchill had ever intended.[17]

When Congress issued their rejection, they put it down to not wishing to be 'fettered and circumscribed' by conditional promises, and also mentioned, quite reasonably, the voiceless inhabitants of the Princely States who were not being helped by the proposals. The problem with the British overture was that there was little incentive for Congress to accept it. As Gandhi suggested, Cripps was offering little more than a post-dated cheque on a failing bank. He knew that Britain was on the run, that the Empire had been badly if not fatally damaged by the fall of Burma, Malaya and Singapore, and that if Congress was to wait until the war was over, the balance of power might have shifted even further in their favour.

Although they had every reason for holding out, by rejecting the British offer Congress missed a chance to strengthen their own position. In the words of one historian, the Cripps Mission 'was crushed by the monolithic millstones of Churchillian Conservatism and Congress nationalism'.[18] What they failed to take into account was the way in which Muslim bargaining power was likely to increase as the impasse with London grew. As in the aftermath of the 1937 provincial elections, Congress discounted the potential clout of the Muslim League.

Although Jinnah still lacked genuine support in the provinces where Muslims formed a majority, the Cripps Mission increased the chances of the creation of Pakistan. At a press conference in New Delhi on 29 March, in answer to a question as to whether there was anything to stop two provinces from different parts of India 'trying to club together and to form a separate union', Cripps replied: 'That would be impracticable. Two contiguous provinces may form a separate union.' At the same time he stated that it would not be impossible to have 'a rearrangement of boundaries as between the two unions, and exchange of populations to get the larger majority in each'.[19]

This was the first time that the prospect of autonomous provinces staying outside India had been publicly discussed by the British. It is apparent that Cripps suspected many big Muslim landlords and politicians were really more interested in the future of Punjab and Bengal than in any pan-Indian Muslim unity. He believed that Jinnah might be challenged if the League's feeble grip on its alleged followers was tested.

As Jalal argues, had Congress taken up the Cripps offer, 'Jinnah would have been in danger of being dumped unceremoniously into a wilderness from which this time there would be no return'.[20]

The Congress suggestion that their own response to Cripps could be 'considered to be the unanimous demand of the Indian people' was soon repudiated by Jinnah, who asserted that Congress did not represent Muslims, or even all of India's Hindus. The period following the Cripps Mission marked a fatal split between the Viceroy and Congress, and between Congress and the Muslim League. The British response to the failure of the Mission was to try a head-in-the-sand policy. 'You are absolutely right,' wrote Linlithgow to Amery on 7 May, 'in thinking that the less interested we now appear to be in Indian politics the better.'[21] 1942 was the moment of political and mental alienation on all sides.

The Marquess of Linlithgow noted laconically at the end of one document, 'Goodbye Mr Cripps,' and made a significant marginal note: 'I am myself now quite sure that self-government is incompatible with unity.'[22] Linlithgow's personal view of Cripps was summed up by one of his gamekeepers back on his estates in Scotland, who declared: 'The cheek of the man, to think that he could do in a fortnight what His Lordship hasn't been able to do in six years.'[23] Linlithgow was soon advising Amery not to let Cripps broadcast about India on the wireless, and was full of spurious indignation when Cripps implied that he had been to blame for undermining the negotiations – the claim was 'wholly without foundation and most damaging and embarrassing'.

The Viceroy and the Secretary of State now decided that India's predicament might be solved by some bureaucratic wrangling and an extension of the Viceroy's Executive Council. As usual, they failed to see the broader picture. Huge attention was paid to Indian 'politicians' – pragmatists at best, and traitors in the eyes of many Indian nationalists – who could be given formal positions. Most of these figures, as so often in post-colonial situations, faded from the scene within minutes of the departure of the imperial power. Back and forth between London and New Delhi went countless discussion documents. How about the appointment of 'old Jogi', Sirdar Sir Jogendra Singh, 'a Punjab Taluqdar, served on Indian Sugar Committee, Indian Taxation Enquiry, Indian Sandhurst Committee' as Minister for Education, Health and Lands; or perhaps Sir Mahomed Usman 'knighted 1928, K.C.I.E. 1933' (who had a reputation as a notorious reactionary who hoped the sun would never set on the British Empire) to oversee Posts and Air?

Leo Amery even made the bizarre suggestion that the lack of senior British figures at the head of the Indian Civil Service might be solved by sending out 'a rising young man' or two from the House of Commons to act as a provincial governor. The Viceregal response to the notion of wet-eared types from the Home Counties trying to sort out Congress was predictable. 'Good God!' he minuted on Amery's letter.[24] Another of the Secretary of State's pet theories was that India's problems might be solved by 'an increasing infusion of stronger Nordic blood'. He even seemed to think that his own speeches on India, which he had turned into a book and sent around the globe, might be the answer. Soon he was telling Linlithgow that since 'Nehru and Co.' were embarking on 'a policy of real mischief', their support was bound to crumble. In the meantime he hoped 'very much that the Duke of Gloucester's visit [to India] will be a real tonic to the loyal elements'.[25]

The trouble with Amery was that he approached the whole question of India's future from an intellectual rather than a human perspective. He was a preachy sort of statesman, his diaries and correspondence being full of false modesty about his own status. He was endlessly taken up with constitutional schemes proposed by his academic friends, and seemed to think that with enough minutely analysed discussion documents and position papers, Congress might somehow be coaxed or even bored into submission. His approach to imperial propaganda can be gleaned from a private letter he sent to the Viceroy recommending that 'all reasonable facilities and guidance' be given to 'a considerable literary figure' who was on his way out to India to write a book about the virtues of British rule. The considerable figure was none other than the lightweight journalist Beverley Nichols.[26]

The leaders of Congress faced a dilemma. Should they launch a revolt against British rule, taking the opportunity presented by the current weakness of their oppressor, or should they sit tight for fear of encouraging the Germans and the Japanese? Nehru's schoolgirl niece Nayantara Pandit had summed up the quandary in a letter to her father, a prominent

Congress activist, at the outbreak of war. 'Do you think that India should help England?' she asked. 'If she did, then Germany would be squashed, which would be one good thing. If she didn't, England might be beaten, and then Germany and Japan together would march into India . . . What do you think about it?' Nayantara herself favoured action: 'I think we jolly well ought to fight, like Patrick Henry, "Give me liberty or give me death."'[27]

As Indian unrest grew in the aftermath of Cripps's failure, press censorship was extended and Lord Linlithgow denounced the pronationalist 'tripe' that was being written in the leader columns of the *Manchester Guardian* and the *News Chronicle*. His conduct spurred many nationalists into a more extreme position. Seeing no future in political negotiation, Linlithgow set about making plans for repression. With the war now entering a crucial phase, he felt that nothing could be permitted which might disrupt either defence production or troop movements. He launched a smear campaign against Congress, claiming they were pro-Nazi for not supporting his declaration of war. This was despite the fact that he knew perfectly well that they had passed three separate resolutions during 1942 reiterating sympathy for the Allies.

Thanks to the work of British police officers and their network of Indian informers, Linlithgow was able to keep a close eye on the activities of the Congress Working Committee. In liaison with Philip Vickery back at IPI in London, the Intelligence Bureau tried to ascertain the strength of any possible rebellion against British rule. The Director of the Intelligence Bureau (DIB) was now Denys Pilditch, who had taken over from Sir John Ewart in 1939. Pilditch was a police officer in his early fifties who had joined the Indian Police three years after Vickery, and had worked in surveillance and intelligence since the 1920s.

The introduction of provincial autonomy under the 1935 Government of India Act had threatened the British surveillance machine. The police in each province now came under the local Home Ministry, which meant that information on subversion of any kind had to be reported to a non-British Home Minister who had political affiliations. This potential breakdown in British control was circumvented by the appointment of a highly influential Central Intelligence Officer in each province, who reported directly to the DIB in Delhi. At the same time the Intelligence Bureau became an offshoot of the Home Department of the central government, which meant that the DIB reported to a boss who was invariably a British official, as there was no intention of allowing such a crucial department to pass to one of the Indian members of the Viceroy's Executive Council. In most cases the DIB went straight to the Viceroy, who had special responsibility for the IB in his capacity as India's Governor General.[28]

An intercepted letter was shown to Linlithgow on 10 May containing drafts of a Congress resolution outlining their future policy. Scientific analysis showed that the draft resolution had been written on Gandhi's own typewriter, and amended by Rajendra Prasad and later by Nehru. It showed, according to an accompanying letter from the notoriously hard-line Governor of the United Provinces, Sir Maurice Hallet, that Gandhi was 'a fifth columnist or a Quisling and we must be very watchful of his activities'.[29] The official position was hardening, another provincial governor calling Gandhi 'the Hitler of Indian politics' and saying he and his followers were in need of 'a cold douche'.[30]

Gandhi now claimed that Britain was incapable of defending India, and stated that a free nation's first step would be to negotiate with Japan. This strange statement caused consternation, as almost all of the Congress Working Committee disagreed with him. A secret report for the Intelligence Bureau revealed that, 'Nehru disapproved strongly because it meant India's becoming a passive partner of the Axis Powers. He declared that Gandhi's decision was governed by his belief that the Axis would win the war.'[31] Nehru was adamant that British troops would be needed in the event of a Japanese attack on India. Gandhi's ideas were eccentric, in that India would clearly have been a more tempting target for the Japanese if British troops had been withdrawn. Non-violent resistance would be less effective in the face of an invading foreign army than it was against an entrenched colonial ruler. *Satyagraha* was a protest tactic, which Gandhi was trying to elevate into a defence strategy.

Another intercepted Congress letter contained a draft of what later became known as the 'Quit India Resolution'. It called for a mass campaign of peaceful non-cooperation, and stated that 'Japan's quarrel is not with India. She is warring against the British Empire.'[32] After discussion, these controversial lines were in fact deleted from the final version of the resolution, but Linlithgow leaked the draft text to the *Hindu* newspaper as part of his war against Gandhi. The veteran nationalist Rajagopalachari described this as 'a sad abuse of the proprieties', although personally he was strongly opposed to any kind of mass civil unrest, realizing that it would only lead to bloodshed. In a speech in June he said that escape into a British prison by the Congress leadership represented neither 'fulfilment of duty nor heroism'. But Rajaji was a lone voice.

There is a strong case for seeing Gandhi's actions at this time as the last, desperate throw of an old man, a principally anarchic move, calculated to provoke a breakdown of government, social revolution and a return to his mythical *Ram Rajya* and wholesome village life. It was apparent that the British would not voluntarily abandon India in wartime, so Gandhi must have realized that a revolution was the probable result of successful mass disorder. His stand, which was accepted rather feebly by most of his colleagues although they disagreed with it, unleashed wild forces and set a dangerous precedent for the post-war period.

Pilditch of the IB learned through an intercepted letter that Gandhi was 'hatching plans for some kind of popular movement'. He noted in his weekly report that Gandhi had told a secret Congress meeting: 'My self-esteem will not allow me to help in strangling my strangler. No, I cannot help the Japanese. Having earned my freedom I remain neutral.'[33] Each one of Gandhi's bizarre and often contradictory statements was scrutinized, as the British authorities tried to decide whether his comments were genuinely seditious. There was particular concern over a demand he made in his newspaper, *Harijan*: 'Leave India to God. If that is too much, then leave her to anarchy.'[34]

As always with Gandhi, his political statements were mixed in with his dietary, religious and bovine opinions. He wrote a letter to Linlithgow deploring the fact that American and British troops in Bihar were eating 'milch cows and plough cattle'. Anxious that this should not become a pretext for a non-cooperation campaign, the Viceroy intervened and the steak-chompers were curbed. There was also official concern over a letter from Mirabehn saying, 'I am that daughter of the late Admiral Sir Edmond Slade, who came to Gandhiji seventeen years ago,' and requesting to meet Linlithgow. This was refused, but she was allowed to see his Private Secretary, whom she informed that the Mahatma was motivated by 'pure friendship' for the British, yet wanted immediate independence. To nobody's surprise, this did not provoke a change in government policy.

In consultation with London, Linlithgow began to make plans for the wholesale arrest of the Congress leadership. He feared they might be planning to use the tactics of Irish Republicans in the period following the 1916 Easter Rising, and set up a parallel alternative government. Leo

Amery sent several letters to 'Bobbety' Cranborne, the new Secretary of State for the Colonies, enquiring about the best destination for these troublesome nationalists. The legal position was clear: people lawfully detained in India could equally be detained in a British colony. It was decided that the Congress Working Committee should be deported to Uganda, and Gandhi himself to Aden or the Sudan. Then up popped a lawyer in the India Office in London, pointing out that the relevant ordinance did not extend to 'detention while in transit', which meant that if the seventy-three-year-old Mahatma wished to jump ship as he drifted up the Gulf of Aden, nobody would be allowed to stop him.

A further problem soon emerged. The Governor of Aden, Sir Hathorn Hall, a functionary who wore the First Class Order of the Brilliant Star of Zanzibar on his bosom, sent a worried telegram to Lord Cranborne saying: 'In view of acute shortage of suitable accommodation in Aden, I should be grateful for some indication of the total number of the party and racial composition.'[35] This presumably meant that suitable accommodation would be offered only to those who were wearing pale skin. Heads were scratched, and it was finally decided that deportation would cause too many problems, so plans were made for Gandhi's internment within India.

On 4 August, Mr Parkin of the Special Branch in Lucknow issued a report based on intelligence information received from a spy within Congress in the United Provinces: 'The movement is to start,' he believed, 'with a general strike of schools, colleges, Govt. offices, mills, workshops, aerodromes and markets ... The cutting of telegraph wires, removal of railway line, occupation of police stations and Government Offices.' In order to continue the agitation once the leadership had been arrested, district 'dictators' would be chosen, 'each dictator nominating his successor. Name to be kept secret. A central committee in the province will direct. Couriers where possible to be women.' Parkin concluded with the claim that 'a direct incentive has been and is being given to all subversive elements to join with the Congress in doing their utmost to paralyse the Government in the shortest possible time.'[36] The War Cabinet in London now gave Linlithgow the authority to initiate full-scale repression.

On 8 August 1942 the famous 'Quit India' resolution was accepted by the All-India Congress Committee despite the reservations of Nehru, Azad, Rajagopalachari and many other senior figures. The meeting took place at Gowalia Tank in Bombay. While the representatives deliberated, a crowd of many thousands gathered in the heat, in an atmosphere of electrified expectation. The key phrases of the resolution stated, after a long preamble about the war, that Congress resolved 'to sanction, for the vindication of India's inalienable right to freedom and independence, the starting of a mass struggle on non-violent lines on the widest possible scale'. It also contained the proviso, written in inclusive language, that if the leadership were to be arrested, 'every man and woman who is participating in the movement must function for himself or herself within the four corners of the general instructions issued'.[37]

That afternoon the resolution was passed, and India's future was determined. Jinnah was later to refer to the launch of the Quit India movement as 'the Mahatma's "Himalayan blunder"'.[38] '*Karenge ya Marenge,*' proclaimed Gandhi in a speech at the tank, 'Do or Die.' The Viceroy might try to strike a bargain, he warned, 'But I will say: "Nothing less than freedom" . . . Here is a mantra, a short one, that I give you. You may imprint it on your hearts and let every breath of yours give expression to it. The mantra is: "Do or Die." We shall either free India or die in the attempt; we shall not live to see the perpetuation of our slavery.'[39]

TEN

Blackmail and Terror

Using a prearranged codeword that was flashed to all of India's provincial governors on the night of the Gowalia Tank meeting, the Bombay government moved swiftly to arrest the Congress leadership early the following morning. Linlithgow had given the command, although his Executive Council (consisting largely of previously cooperative Indian functionaries) had strongly opposed the move. The arrests all went smoothly, except for that of Govind Vallabh Pant, 'who appears to have been angry at being woke up so early and gave some trouble, with the result that he did not get to the station in time to catch the special train'.[1]

Nehru, who was arrested at a family flat in Bombay, later described the start of the Quit India movement as 'the zero hour of the world'. According to one of his biographers: 'The household staff were hardly unfamiliar with arrests. They quickly laid out a breakfast which Jawaharlal loved: a bowl of cornflakes, eggs, bacon, toast, coffee. The inspector saw the spread and said there was no time for breakfast. "Shut up!" said Nehru. "I intend having breakfast before I go."'[2] India's future Prime Minister was to be kept in prison for 1,040 days.

On departure from Queen Victoria Terminus in Bombay, which has since been renamed in honour of the Maratha warlord Shivaji, crowds had gathered to see the celebrities being carted off to jail. The unfortunate Deputy Inspector-General Sharp got off to a bad start when a protester occupied his seat. As the train reached Poona, instead of being whistled through as planned, the stationmaster had arranged for some urgent shunting to take place, and the train had to stop. Seeing a crowd of Congress supporters on the platform being charged by *lathi*-wielding police, Nehru jumped out of the corridor window 'with remarkable agility', closely followed by Sharp, who tried to coax him back onto the train.

Nehru 'struggled violently', insisting that the beating of his comrades should cease, and shouting 'I don't care for your bloody orders' at the

Inspector. 'He is a big man,' wrote Sharp in his police report, 'and was having a fair share of the struggle with me.' With the aid of two constables and a sub-inspector, the eminent nationalist was dragged back on board the train. One policeman 'as proof of the violence' suffered a kick in the leg and a small scratch on the wrist. As for Sharp, 'I myself am feeling the effects of a sprained finger.'[3]

For several months Nehru's family had no idea where he had been taken. His sister Vijaya Lakshmi Pandit was arrested in the middle of the night by seven truckloads of armed policemen. 'Such was the power of non-violence!' wrote her daughter. 'We waved goodbye to her as she drove away looking more petite and helpless than ever in the midst of that formidable escort.'[4]

The Working Committee was imprisoned in Ahmednagar Fort, having been received in some style by their jailers. Once he was safely locked up, Nehru slept, kept fit, took up gardening, played cards, had his letters intercepted, became ever more strongly anti-British, and was kept company by a cat named Chando, who died during the sojourn. Joining him in the fort were eleven other eminent politicians, including Abul Kalam Azad, Pandit Pant, Asaf Ali, J.B. Kripalani, Pattabhi Sitaramayya and the sixty-seven-year-old Vallabhbhai Patel. It was an impressive combination, and as they were not held in solitary confinement, the prisoners were able to formulate party policy as best they could with a lack of outside news. As Congress President, Azad insisted on being treated with special respect.

Mohandas Gandhi and his immediate entourage – his secretary Mahadev Desai, his wife Kasturba, the devoted Mirabehn and his doctor Sushila Nayar – were taken to a different location on their own train and given special treatment. The Aga Khan's palace in Poona was their rather luxurious prison. Linlithgow had been nervous about how Gandhi would take to this treatment, and was worried that most provincial governors had said he should be released back to his ashram if he went on a hunger strike. At the palace, having been given a good breakfast on the train from Bombay, 'with waiters, menus, and all the rest – all the rest except freedom!', things proved very comfortable for the prisoners. On arrival Mirabehn became concerned about the Mahatma's diet, and went to see the head jailer, a tall Parsi called Mr Kateley. 'What about goat's milk?' she asked. 'Bapu has had hardly anything to eat.' 'Goats are kept ready,' he replied.[5] Three goats were tethered in the yard, waiting to be milked.

Following the arrests, the situation in Delhi became 'extremely serious'. There was a *hartal*, or strike, by Hindu shopkeepers, although most Muslims refused to close their shops. The city's income tax office and a branch railway station were burnt down, as well as several other buildings. The police opened fire, killing fourteen people. It was reported from Delhi that: 'The firing by British soldiers and the acts of Anglo-Indian Sergeants of forcibly removing Gandhi caps and burning them have fanned this hatred to a boiling point.'[6] In Bombay the republican Congress tricolour was raised in public places, and police opened fire on chanting, stone-throwing crowds in six places in the city.

The Communist Party were in a difficult position, vehemently opposing British rule, but not wanting to give succour to the Axis powers. They continued to assert that mass agitation would be fatal to the war effort, and said that the defeat of Nazism should be the overriding aim of the Indian people, in accordance with their orders from Moscow. One intelligence officer noted: 'As was to be expected the communists' attempt to run with the hare and hunt with the hounds led to some minor defections from their own party and also to the unpopularity of their present policy among Congress sympathizers. The communists as a party count for little at the moment.'[7]

The authorities were still uncertain precisely what course of action the Congress leadership had planned. On 4 September they intercepted a letter written by one of Nehru's young nieces in Allahabad to a friend who was studying in Lucknow. Part of it ran: 'You asked about the non-violence question. Gandhiji's instructions are to completely paralyse the Government in any way possible, short of murder ... It is also important to work up wives and kids of Government officials and show them that their men folk are utter pansies. No one should attack and bodily injure anyone else, but short of that you can do anything.'[8] As a CID officer noted, 'the writer is in a position to know'. Sir Maurice Hallet took immediate action, informing New Delhi: 'I have directed the search of Anand Bhawan and her arrest for clearly it is a centre for distribution of plans.'[9]

As an avowedly constitutionalist politician, Jinnah avoided becoming entangled in the agitation. Realizing that the Congress uprising reinforced the importance of the Muslim League, he was content to stand aloof from the Quit India movement. This exacerbated the communal divide, Hindus claiming that Muslims were not true nationalists since they refused to join the mass action. A British report from Bengal in late September noted that agitation had been restricted to the Hindus around Calcutta: 'There have been no violent demonstrations by mobs of peasants in eastern Bengal where the population is predominantly Moslem.'[10]

The police were doing their best to identify the source of the agitation, as it spread and continued. They believed that various wealthy backers of Congress were encouraging disruption. Special Branch claimed that an agent of the industrialist G.D. Birla had offered twenty-five thousand rupees to the General Secretary of the Calcutta Tramway Workers' Union if he would foment a tram strike throughout Calcutta: 'Birla Brothers and the Marwari community are financing the acts of sabotage and strikes in furtherance of the Gandhi movement so as to hit the British Capitalists hard.'[11] Meanwhile Deputy Inspector General Murray of the Bihar CID reported that 'rural areas especially North Bihar are in an extremely disturbed condition ... crowds armed with *lathis*, spears, swords and daggers are constantly on the move looking for opportunities to loot and sabotage.'[12]

Most of the Quit India agitation was concentrated in Bihar, the United Provinces, Bengal, Bombay, Delhi and Rajputana. There was little action in the south of India, and many people in rural areas were completely unaware of the huge disturbances that were taking place. In some towns shops selling alcohol were picketed in accordance with Gandhi's teetotalitarianism, while elsewhere 'rowdy urchins' stopped passers-by who were wearing European clothes and ripped off their jackets, collars and ties. They also engaged in 'petty acts of mischief, like the burning of hats', Gandhi caps being issued as a replacement. Europeans were greeted in the streets with spittle and the catcall '*Bharat Choro!*', 'Quit India!' In Bombay a pirate radio station was established to broadcast propaganda against the 'foreign monkeys'.

Jai Prakash Narayan, the General Secretary of the Congress Socialist Party, went as far as making plans to occupy Delhi. He was soon arrested, but escaped rather daringly from Hazaribagh Central Prison. Narayan asked for all US troops stationed in India to support the Indian freedom movement, and favoured 'the formation of guerrilla fighting bands in India to do sabotage work', hoping that elements within the Indian army would turn out to be loyal to Congress rather than to the King Emperor, and join the movement.

According to Congress documentation, there were numerous

instances of police brutality. A senior official of the government of the Central Provinces was said to have ordered the shooting of curfew-breakers in Nagpur, and 'boasted at the club in the evening that he had jolly good fun having shot down twenty-four niggers himself'.[13] It was reported that, 'In Saeedpur, Commissioner Nethersole greeted the Tehsil-dar [a local official] with a couple of kicks. He also laid waste the market and had several persons whipped publicly. A patriot was stripped naked and tied to a tree and they started beating him with thorny bamboo sticks. He was asked to repent for being a Congressman and to promise that he would never put on *khadi* again . . . When he fell unconscious they applied salt over his wounds and sent him to prison.'[14]

One activist, Usha Mehta, remembered: 'The police were absolutely brutal in their attitude towards women, and even pregnant women were not spared. Women were victims of brutal *lathi*-charges . . . One of them in Bombay, I know, was raped not by one officer but by officer after officer, including the British officers . . . she wanted to commit suicide.'[15] The authorities in Cawnpore had tried to recruit women to deal with female demonstrators at public events, but a forlorn police report noted: 'Experiment was not a success. Only prostitutes volunteered.'[16]

Resistance grew as public buildings were torched and railway lines torn up. A group of policemen were doused in kerosene and burnt to death. For six weeks much of the country came close to revolution. The authorities responded with public floggings, the burning of villages and collective fines. When the administration lost control in Bihar, Lord Linlithgow ordered the machine-gunning of rioting crowds from the air in Patna. In some areas (to the embarrassment of later generations of Congress historians) activists were joined by criminals, bandits and *dacoits*, and even by anti-Brahmin activists who set up 'people's courts' in a forerunner of the Naxalite movement.

As the revolt grew, arrests took place across the subcontinent in their thousands. On the orders of the Viceroy, the treatment of Quit India or 'Q' prisoners was heavy-handed: they were not brought to trial, or per-mitted to receive visitors. One well-known activist in Lahore, Sita Devi, was dragged to prison despite being seriously ill. Her daughter remembered shouting at the arresting police officers that they were 'rocks on the road to freedom and suckers of our blood. After that we children used to go out and throw date seeds covered in dried mud at British soldiers when we saw them in the street. We were fearless.'[17]

Within a month of the Quit India resolution, even the official figures showed that several hundred people had been killed. Fifty-seven battalions of regular British soldiers were now tied up in India, many of them fighting civilians and trying to prevent the insurrection from spreading. New Delhi implemented the Revolutionary Movement Ordinance, which toughened state control further. Whipping was revived as a punishment, and five thousand people were detained without trial.

Interestingly, the courts stood out against much of the repression. For example, a twenty-two-year-old vegetable hawker in Bombay was shot and killed by a pair of British sub-inspectors for shouting a nationalist slogan as their police lorry drove past. In the subsequent court case, the jury found there had been 'no cause to open fire'. However, the Commissioner of Police refused to take any action. Both the provincial high courts and the Federal Court overturned government decisions, and even the legality of some ordinances.

New Delhi responded by overruling legal decisions, and 'displayed an unrepentant indifference to the efforts by Indian courts to hinder their freedom of action'. They 're-issued Ordinances – with slight revisions – as soon as laborious court proceedings had declared them invalid'. As one historian of the subject has written: 'In this, as in other ways, the Government were acting consciously in a reckless fashion, attempting to hold the line.' It was a desperate expedient, and one that could only last for a limited time. Ever since the outcry over the Jallianwala Bagh massacre of 1919, the Government of India had always been careful to operate within the rule of law in their treatment of rebellious nationalists. Now they were using draconian tactics, which rebounded on them once the immediate crisis had passed. Before long they were left 'standing alone amidst the shambles of their former legitimacy'.[18]

Linlithgow himself had no great concern about civil liberties, feeling that they were of less importance than holding the line against internal and external agitation. He was irritated by the degree of opposition to Section 3 of the Bombay (Emergency Powers) Whipping Act exhibited by Labour backbenchers in the House of Commons. The Governor of Bombay assured him that whipping was 'exceedingly useful', and that magistrates usually ordered 'ten to twelve stripes against a maximum of thirty' on 'the tough, sturdy, bullying type of offender'.[19] The Viceroy himself noted that 'students and riff-raff' were behind most of the trouble. He thought 'spankings', as he called them, were no bad thing, but that they should be restricted to 'hooligans, looters and dangerous characters of low status', and not used on those in a position to complain.

Although in general the Indian members of the Indian Police remained solidly behind their imperial paymasters, Linlithgow was concerned that some of them did not have 'their hearts in the job'. There was however no serious breakdown in the internal discipline of the police. In a letter to Amery answering a query about their brutality, Linlithgow said the only example he could think of was in Multan, 'when some boys who had been throwing stones at the police took refuge in a pond, got out of their depth and were drowned'. This was untrue; the Viceroy knew from an internal document sent to him by the Governor of the Punjab that the stoned policemen had in fact 'ducked some of them in a pond', drowning three in the process.[20]

Although Linlithgow held firm, he knew he was paying a heavy price in terms of future Congress cooperation. Churchill rejoiced that he had 'got them on the run', but by the end of 1942 sixty thousand people had been arrested. On 31 August, the Viceroy admitted in a cipher telegram to Churchill: 'I am engaged here in meeting by far the most serious rebellion since that of 1857, the gravity and extent of which we have so far concealed from the world for reasons of military security. Mob violence remains rampant over large tracts of the countryside.'[21] India was spiralling out of control.

Aware that the British were losing the propaganda war, especially in the United States, Linlithgow and Churchill were anxious to find evidence that Congress and the Nazis were in some kind of secret alliance. Agents were despatched to make investigations around India's northern borders. They were disappointed, the CID eventually reporting that 'there is no evidence to prove directly controlled enemy activity in India ... the activities of Axis powers in connection with the recent disturbances have been almost entirely confined to propaganda on the wireless.'[22] This did not stop Churchill and his ministers from regarding Congress as traitors for what they were doing.

The claim that the Quit India movement was pro-Nazi was clearly inaccurate. Nehru in particular was resolutely anti-fascist, but, as he had reasonably pointed out, it was hard for the people of India to fight for the freedom of Poland when they were themselves under foreign occupation: 'If Britain fought for democracy, she should necessarily end imperialism in her own possessions and establish full democracy in India. A free democratic India would gladly associate herself with other free nations for mutual defence against aggression.'[23]

Leo Amery, cerebral as ever, took the view on the very day that the Quit India resolution was passed that the 'really interesting thing, as it may prove in historical retrospect, is the extent to which in fact the Government of India has been expanded and modified within the last two years'.[24] Even in November 1942, with the rebellion well under way and tens of thousands of people imprisoned, he tried to think up worthy new schemes, writing to the Viceroy: 'I still think that there is great advantage in making the Indian members of your Executive responsible, through whatever sub-Committee they may appoint, not for framing a constitution, but for setting in motion some of the processes required before any constitution-making body can come into being.' Linlithgow, who was a realist if nothing else, made the simple note in the margin: 'I despair!'[25]

Churchill remained detached from political realities in India, declaring in the same month in a memorable speech at the Lord Mayor's banquet: 'I have not become the King's First Minister in order to preside over the liquidation of the British Empire.'[26] When Roosevelt made a reference to the arbitrary arrest of nationalist leaders, Churchill was sent into a rage, claiming that if Gandhi had not been interned, the Japanese would probably now be marching into India. 'Personally,' he wrote, 'I have no doubts that in addition there would have been an understanding that the congress [he did not dignify it with a capital letter] would have the use of sufficient Japanese troops to keep down the composite majority of ninety million Moslems, forty million Untouchables and ninety million in the princes states.'[27]

At the higher echelons of government, Anglo–American relations worsened as the war proceeded. Roosevelt became ever more unsympathetic towards British imperial policy, and the allies began to diverge over the conduct of the war in the Far East. The US came to see Britain as being primarily concerned with maintaining its power in India, rather than fighting the Japanese in China as the Americans were doing. Perceived British intransigence over decolonization made the State Department keener than it might have been on the importance of China as a global power in a post-war world.

Roosevelt made a renewed effort in early 1943 when he sent his friend William Phillips, a distinguished East Coast diplomat, to India as his personal representative, with the rank of ambassador. This was done with British support, through gritted teeth. Although he was a fairly conservative figure, Phillips took a strong stand against British policy. He was not impressed by the intransigence of Linlithgow, who cheerfully told him he was in India as 'a war Viceroy'.[28] Phillips believed that New Delhi's policy was dangerously stagnant and outdated, and proposed a meeting of imprisoned Indian leaders, presided over by an American mediator. FDR was too cautious even to suggest this to Churchill.

The only coup Phillips managed was to get a formal intelligence toehold in New Delhi, in the form of a six-person 'special SSO mission' which would work with British spies – 'our people here', as the Viceroy called them.[29] The SSO (normally known as the OSS, or Office of Strategic Services) had been set up by Roosevelt the previous summer to coordinate all US intelligence gathering. At the end of the war it was dismantled, and reconstituted as the CIA. Churchill disliked the efforts Phillips had made to encourage mediation, and the next time they met, he 'waved his finger' at him. An IPI agent reported that once he had returned to the USA, Phillips was heard at a private meeting speaking in 'very critical terms on the subject of British administration in India'.[30]

As the repression of the Quit India movement continued, Churchill shocked even a pair of tame, plump, visiting Indian dignitaries by saying to them, as they stood in the garden at 10 Downing Street: 'What have we to be ashamed of in our government of India? Why should we be apologetic or say that we are prepared to go out at the instance of some jackanapes? ... Look at the condition even now. An Indian maid with bangles on can travel from Travancore to Punjab all alone without fear of molestations. That is more than can be said in this country today, where our Wrens and Waafs cannot go two miles with the same feeling of safety ... I am not going to be a party to a policy of scuttle.'[31]

The visitors were His Highness the Maharajah Jam Saheb of Nawana-gar and Sir Ramaswami Mudaliar, who had been given seats in the War Cabinet in what Churchill called 'a generous gesture to loyal Indians'. However, a day or two before their arrival in London, in a typically subtle piece of British diplomatic duplicity, the Prime Minister's Office had sent a note to the relevant departments ordering that any copies of the War Cabinet papers that were given to the pair should first be doctored so as to remove anything of substance.[32] This was not an unusual decision; many India-related documents produced in Whitehall carried the code-word 'GUARD', which meant they were not to be sent to India. Within days of the Jam Saheb's arrival, the India Office had arranged for him to give an interview to the *Sunday Express*. Amery described it happily as being 'of first-rate propaganda value'.[33]

Ensconced securely in the Aga Khan's palace, Gandhi continued in his role as the indefatigable correspondent of imperial collapse. Numerous letters covering a variety of bizarre topics were despatched to the Viceroy under the handwritten address 'DETENTION CAMP, POONA'. Linlithgow (who was tempted to reply on paper headed 'DETENTION CAMP, NEW DELHI') often had to refer back to Whitehall for guidance on precise points that his detainee raised. When Gandhi heard of the death of a former viceroy's son, he wrote to say: 'I have just read about the sad but heroic death of Hon'ble Peter Wood in action. Will you please convey to Lord Halifax my congratulations as well as condolences on the sad bereavement?'[34]

Another letter said that he wanted to be joined in prison by his secretary Pyarelal and 'Sardar Vallabhbhai Patel, who was under my care for the control of his intestinal trouble'.[35] This was too much for Linlithgow, who activated his Secraphone – a sort of primitive scrambling device – and told the Governor of Bombay to refuse the request. This refusal was not to be given in writing; instead a British official should convey the message verbally. The Marquess's instructions were precise: 'The Collector should be on his dignity, refuse to allow himself to be won over by Gandhi's charm, and carefully avoid any undue geniality.'[36]

The Viceroy and the Mahatma had a protracted correspondence on the subject of the Quit India movement. Gandhi maintained that the outbreaks of violence had been caused by the savagery of British repression, while Linlithgow argued that responsibility lay with Gandhi and Congress for initiating the initial disruption. Gandhi, who was already depressed by the sudden death of his lifelong companion Mahadev Desai in captivity, took Linlithgow's words as an attack on his personal integrity, and announced plans to go on a three-week fast from 9 February 1943.

His followers and his opponents were baffled by this, and uncertain precisely what he hoped to achieve by it. Once plans for the fast were announced, letter after letter and telegram after telegram passed between the India Office, New Delhi and provincial officials. Gandhi's optional fast certainly seemed to cause the War Cabinet more worry than the looming famine in Bengal. Secret memoranda were circulated as they tried to decide what they should do, and no fewer than nine doctors were sent off to the Aga Khan's palace. The redoubtable Sarojini Naidu was moved there, where she adopted the role of 'matron-in-chief', and plans were made for Gandhi's son Devadas to go and supervise the fast. The Secretary to the Governor of Bombay went to ask Gandhi if he would like to be released from prison for the actual period he was fasting. Gandhi wrote a note, since he was having a day of silence, telling the man to come back at 9 p.m. (which meant 10 p.m., as Gandhi was observing his preferred chronological system, which he called 'old time'), and then refused his offer. Each word of each proposal that Linlithgow made on the subject was first referred back to Amery, who passed it to a war-weary Cabinet, Churchill often 'sailing in with a monologue' just as a decision was being taken.

The fast began with Gandhi taking water tempered by 'juices of citrus fruit' to make it palatable. As the days passed, Linlithgow showed 'unflinching steadfastness', in accordance with London's orders. In his view it was Gandhi's own decision if he chose to starve himself to death. He told Amery that if Gandhi died, it 'may have considerable emotional reaction, and give us a good deal of trouble', but the Government of India would not give in to 'a wicked system of blackmail and terror'.[37] Amery, typically, ordered Linlithgow to refer in public not to Gandhi's 'fast' but to his 'restricted diet'.

The Viceroy did all he could to keep the subject out of the press, and when the news broke he tried his best to manipulate it. He wrote to Churchill on 26 February that Gandhi was 'the world's most successful humbug . . . The degree of nervous tension and hysteria engendered by all this Hindu hocus pocus is beyond belief. I am suggesting slyly to certain American correspondents here that it has not been so much a matter of having their heart-strings plucked as of their legs being pulled.'[38]

When Churchill sent an aggressive telegram to Roosevelt on the subject, Linlithgow praised it as 'first-class stuff'.

Gandhi's health declined rapidly. Already skeletal, he lost over a stone, and became drowsy and listless. Before long the nine Indian members of the Viceroy's Executive Council were buckling. After 'tense discussions' Sir Homi Mody, Madhao Aney and Nalini Sarkar decided they preferred patriotism to position, and quit. Four others were left undecided, and only two Indians remained on board. An indication of Linlithgow's true view of the importance of this much-vaunted body can be gained from the fact that he left the three empty departments (one of which was Commerce) to be run by civil servants for four months before filling the vacancies. Although the British pretended that the council was a valued advisory cabinet, it was powerless in regard to any serious issue, since even a vote of censure by the Legislative Assembly could not overturn the decision of the Viceroy.

Churchill's personal reaction to the fast was vigorous and unsympathetic. 'I have heard,' he told Linlithgow in a secret telegram, 'that Gandhi usually has glucose in his water when doing his various fasting antics. Would it be possible to verify this?'[39] To the Prime Minister's disappointment, the Viceroy replied that the Mahatma was being encouraged to take glucose, but 'refused absolutely'. As the fast progressed, and it seemed that Gandhi was on the verge of lapsing into a coma, Churchill began denouncing him as an 'old humbug' and a 'rascal'. He would not be swayed into ordering his release, and told Field Marshal Smuts, 'I do not think Gandhi has the slightest intention of dying, and I imagine he has been eating better meals than I have for the last week' – given the Prime Minister's gluttonous eating and drinking habits, this is somewhat doubtful – 'What fools we should have been to flinch before all this bluff and sob-stuff.'[40] His hostility to the Mahatma was becoming pathological, and even slightly deranged. Gandhi was now deemed 'a thoroughly evil force, hostile to us in every fibre'.[41]

Enquiries were made all over India as to likely reactions to the death of the father of the nation. General Wavell, the Commander-in-Chief in India, thought there would be little reaction from Indian troops, as Gandhi opposed 'the vested interests of the "Martial" classes'. Linlithgow, after much consideration, decided that in the event of Gandhi's death, 'the wise course would be in no circumstances to half-mast flags', but all offices would be closed upon request to a provincial governor.[42] If Gandhi

Previous page The spy chief Philip Vickery as a young police officer at the Delhi *durbar* of 1911.

Above The Mahatma strides out: Mohandas Gandhi and his entourage on the epic salt march of 1930.

Right 'Hopie' and Doreen. Their Excellencies the Marquess and Marchioness of Linlithgow during a garden party at Viceroy's House in New Delhi.

Left Subhas Chandra Bose after being elected as President of Congress at Haripura in 1938.

Below Stafford Cripps, Abul Kalam Azad and Jawaharlal Nehru outside the Secretariat of the Government of India in New Delhi in 1942.

'An Indian maid with bangles on . . .' Leo Amery, Ramaswami Mudaliar, the Jam Saheb and Winston Churchill in the garden at 10 Downing Street.

Right Quit India! A photograph taken for the Communist Party newspaper *People's War* of burning police vehicles in a Calcutta street.

'Two obstinate old men': M. A. Jinnah and M. K. Gandhi feign friendship after their abortive talks in Bombay in 1944.

Simla, 1945. The Viceroy Lord Wavell greets Sir Khizar Hyat Khan Tiwana of the
Punjab, watched by Dr Khan Sahib of the North-West Frontier Province.

Above Simla, 1945.
A newly released Pant,
a nervous Jinnah,
an inscrutable
Rajagopalachari, the
Assamese leader
Mohammad Saadulla,
and a tense Azad.

Right Simla, 1945. The
Sikh leader Master Tara
Singh on his way to the
conference.

Left 'Other Men's Flowers': Archie Wavell after being garlanded at the Lingaraj Mandir in Bhubaneswar, Orissa.

Below Jawaharlal Nehru addressing a meeting of the All-India Congress Committee.

were to die, the Governor of Bombay was to telegraph the codeword EXTRA to Amery, which would result in the release of the statement: 'The Government of India regret to announce that Mr Gandhi died while in detention at Poona at — hours on — from collapse/heart failure following a self-imposed fast.'[43]

Finally, on 3 March 1943, to everyone's relief, the fast ended, with Gandhi very much alive. He took a little fruit pulp mixed with goat's milk and had an enema. Amery wrote smugly to Linlithgow: 'I think we – and by that I mean specially you – have come remarkably well out of the whole affair'; a statement which seems little short of ludicrous in retrospect, with Amery and Linlithgow long forgotten and Gandhi deified around the world.[44]

Through all this, Amery had continued, in his usual vein, to propose complex constitutional solutions. He told the Viceroy that various academics believed the example of the Swiss Constitution might be the way to solve the Indian dilemma, as it would encourage regional and minority representation. 'The Swiss system works so well on the whole, and gives so much greater stability, that there is much to be said for it in Indian conditions,' he told a sceptical Linlithgow.[45] The Viceroy was not impressed, and wrote that he was 'quite certain that no oriental will accept defeat in a ballot as final: rather he will start at once to recover by intrigue, blackmail and corruption, that which he has lost in fair fight!'[46] With Linlithgow's head buried firmly in the sand and Amery's waving about in the clouds, there was little chance of political progress.

Jinnah, meanwhile, continued to shore up his own position. Throughout the Second World War, it was crucial for him to retain the backing of the leading Muslim politicians of the Muslim-majority provinces. Without it, his credibility in any post-war negotiations would be severely limited. In order to secure the support of the key regional political leaders from Bengal and the Punjab, and to maintain his influence in New Delhi, he attacked Congress and its supposed plans for dictatorship, while being careful to provide no clear definition of the Pakistan demand.

The other provinces of the putative Pakistan were also wooed sporadically during the war years. In Sind there were protracted factional squabbles, and Jinnah was generally derided, while in the North-West Frontier Province, politics were chaotic. When Congress resigned from the provincial ministries, tribal divisions in the NWFP came to the fore. One politician, Aurangzeb Khan, became chief minister and developed a nominal attachment to the Muslim League, but it was widely believed that the British Governor was his true backer. There was certainly no Muslim League infrastructure at all out on the frontier, and public campaigning was restricted to Leaguers dressing up an ancient stork in a white *dhoti*, placing a large pair of spectacles on its beak, and parading it through the streets of Peshawar, 'in a procession with a ticket marked "Mahatma Gandhi"'.[47]

Crucially, Jinnah sought Punjabi endorsement. Without the Punjab, Pakistan would lack its first and most important letter, and its viability as a country would be non-existent. The province's Chief Minister Sir Sikander Hayat Khan's alliance with Jinnah was shaky, and in 1941 he was even considering a rapprochement with Congress. His death in December 1942 put paid to this idea. Sir Sikander's successor was Khizar Hyat Khan Tiwana, another Punjabi Unionist Party Muslim grandee, but one who lacked his political skills. Khizar gave the nominal support of his party to Jinnah, and several years of horse-trading ensued as Khizar tried to cope with the machinations of provincial rivals such as the family of the Nawab of Mamdot, the Daultanas of Multan and Sikander's son Shaukat Hayat Khan. Khizar was sincere but inexperienced, and it did not take Jinnah long to undermine him.

It is not an exaggeration to say that the untimely death of Sir Sikander Hayat Khan was one of the most important factors in the ultimate creation of Pakistan. He had been a highly influential political figure, and he might easily have swung against Jinnah and the League had he lived longer. His influence had kept the Punjab comparatively calm during the war, and his support for the British had been essential in the supply of troops. His death represented a crucial moment in Jinnah's career, for without it he would have had great trouble in tightening the League's grip on the Muslims of India.

As a British agent who attended a closed session of the Muslim League in April 1943 in Delhi reported of Jinnah: 'He has become more aggressive, more challenging and more authoritative . . . It cannot be denied that he is today more powerful than he has ever been. Sir Sikander's death and the consequential disappearance of the fear of a strong rival Muslim organization being created . . . constitute a set of circumstances which have lent an unusual lustre to Jinnah's leadership and augmented his strength and striking power to a degree never before attained.'[48]

Although he had linked the powerful local Unionist Party with the

League, Sikander was never a believer in the version of the Muslim homeland that finally emerged. After the Lahore Resolution was passed, he made several public statements against it. Privately he referred to Pakistan as 'Jinnistan', and told the Secretary to the Governor of the Punjab Penderel Moon that he believed Jinnah's 'hostage theory' was ludicrous. In his opinion, 'Pakistan would mean a massacre,' since Muslims in west Punjab would soon 'cut the throat of every Hindu *bania*'.[49] It was an accurate prediction.

By the end of 1942, the Quit India movement had been suppressed. Although isolated acts of sabotage continued, such a large number of key activists had been detained that it had lost its momentum. India was calm, if only on the surface. An underlying worry at this time was the country's financial situation. Since early 1940, the Indian government had paid its ordinary defence expenditure, plus a contribution towards those Indian troops fighting in the Middle East and elsewhere. London was responsible for the rest of the cost. As Britain was obliged to repay India in sterling for this rupee expenditure, a huge sterling asset had been created, on paper, for the Government of India.

The Chancellor of the Exchequer, Sir Kingsley Wood, hoped that much of this debt might be scaled down or written off, as it was damaging Britain's economic position. The matter came to a head at the end of 1942, when the Viceroy, aware of the grave political dangers of a change in the system of calculating payments, made an 'earnest appeal' to the War Cabinet not to raise the matter. Churchill agreed, reluctantly, to let the matter drop for the moment.

Amery took the odd line that the sterling balances should neither be adjusted nor seen as a debt, since a credit note at the Bank of England was as good as cash. Instead, holders of sterling needed to be persuaded that it was not in their interest to depreciate the value of their assets by rushing to spend them, or by converting them to dollars. In his view, any tampering with the sterling balances would destroy confidence in the pound. He even thought, rather optimistically, that the debt was 'a most powerful instrument of Empire unity', since it increased the significance of the global bloc known as the 'sterling area' where the British currency was used.[50] By mid-1943, Britain's sterling war debt to India reached £800 million. This was to create significant problems over the coming years.

Lord Linlithgow was meanwhile on his way out, returning to his estates in Scotland having served a long and exhausting seven-year term in office. From the Churchillian perspective, Linlithgow's most impressive achievement was to have established stronger military links with the Princely States, supplied troops, and to have maintained Indian defence production despite widespread insurgence. Gandhi sent him a letter of farewell, telling the King Emperor's retiring representative that: 'Of all the high functionaries I have had the honour of knowing, none has been the cause of such deep sorrow to me as you have been. It has cut me to the quick to think of you as having countenanced untruth.' Yet, Gandhian as ever, 'I still remain your friend.'[51]

The question of Linlithgow's successor caused Churchill great worry. In late 1942 he told Amery it was 'occupying his mind from morning to night'. India was a continual, obsessive irritation to Churchill: 'I hate Indians,' he announced. 'They are a beastly people with a beastly religion.'[52] At times the War Cabinet would have to sit through tirades such as: 'Are we to incur hundreds of millions of debts for defending India in order to be kicked out by the Indians afterwards?' As Amery noted in his diary, the fact that 'we are getting out of India far more than was ever thought possible and that India herself is paying far more than was ever contemplated . . . just doesn't enter his head.'

Leo Amery often found himself alone when trying to defend a policy initiative, since none of the Labour ministers such as Attlee or Cripps 'ever really have the courage to stand up to Winston and tell him when he is making a fool of himself'.[53] A number of Labour politicians were themselves imperialists, of varying and at times naive kinds. The President of the Board of Trade Hugh Dalton, for instance, thought that everything might be solved in India if the British were to 'organize, indirectly and discreetly, some alternative political party to the Congress, and prevent the latter from winning so many elections'. He put the plan to a former India Office Minister, Eddie Devonshire, who did 'not seem to think this feasible'.[54]

Attlee was instinctively conservative over India. As the Labour peer Lord Listowel remembered in a lecture he gave in 1980: 'My youthful illusions were soon shattered when I found that the representatives of the Labour Party on the India Committee were no more radical than their Conservative colleagues, and that Attlee as Chairman was a muted echo of his master's voice.'[55] Having been educated at the Empire's forcing-house, Haileybury, Attlee was a quiet believer in the white man's burden, claiming that Indians objected to British rule 'not by the measure of Indian ethical conceptions but by our own, which we have taught them to accept'.[56] Amery repeatedly complained in his diary that Attlee's line on India was too cautious.

Regarding Linlithgow's replacement, Amery plumped for Attlee, and Attlee proposed Rab Butler, while everybody else suggested Sam Hoare, and Hoare canvassed Bobbety Cranborne – but it was reported that Cranborne was too ill, his father was too old and his wife was too rude. Harold Macmillan was considered, but rejected as 'unstable'. Anthony Eden was almost given the job, then Churchill decided he needed him at home. The Warden of All Souls proposed an Indian viceroy: 'But a Hindu, or Moslem, or Maharajah?' wrote Amery in his diary. 'I thought of the Jam Sahib.'[57] Typically, Amery suggested himself, but even Churchill, he wrote, 'thought this very sporting but that it would be objected to both on the score of age and of my being a Diehard!!'[58]

The Prime Minister was loath to lose any of his ministers, given the demands of the war. In June 1943, when it was clear that the exhausted Linlithgow was reaching the end of his tether, Churchill had a brainwave. The eminent but cussed Commander-in Chief in India, Field Marshal Sir Archibald Wavell, who had lately accompanied him on a trip to Washington, had been a source of perpetual annoyance. Churchill thought him defeatist and cautious, while Wavell in turn maintained that Churchill was always expecting 'rabbits to come out of empty hats'. The Prime Minister wished to remove Wavell from military command, and had even tried to persuade the Australians to appoint him as their Governor General. Why not send him back to India, but this time as Viceroy? Leo Amery thought it a fair if entirely unexpected idea, and 'as good a solution as any, quite apart from the fact that it fits in with the reorganization of the Eastern Command and brings Auchinleck back as Commander-in-Chief India'.

A few days later, on reading Wavell's biography of the soldier and administrator Lord Allenby, Amery discovered that the Viceroy-designate had forward-looking political views. He noted presciently in his diary that it would not surprise him if Wavell proved to be 'more radical before long than most politicians'.[59] The Secretary of State was quite right, for far from being a crusty old militarist, Wavell turned out to be a progress-ive, creative and fearless realist with an unquenchable determination to do something about the crisis in India. Although he had been chosen by default, Wavell was to prove the most significant and outspoken viceroy of the century, and would introduce the framework for India's indepen-dence. After all his worry over the appointment, the unsuspecting Prime Minister had recruited a quiet revolutionary.

ELEVEN

Living in a Golden Age

Archie Wavell was an unusual and complex person, whose thickset appearance and gruff military exterior concealed considerable insight and an enigmatic, romantic sensibility. He loved the theatre, and was the compiler of an anthology of poetry called *Other Men's Flowers*, the contents of which he knew by heart. Wavell was renowned for being profoundly shy and awkward in social situations, and for lapsing into protracted, ambiguous, impenetrable silences. His ability to communicate was hampered by his having only one eye, and by being almost totally deaf in one ear. King George VI described him as 'an oyster', Attlee said he was inflexible, while Churchill thought he ought to be running a provincial golf club.

Wavell's wistful humility inspired an extraordinary devotion, particularly within the armed forces, and he was regarded by many soldiers as a great general, who was only betrayed by the folly of politicians. The wife of his last Comptroller at Viceroy's House remembered that she always felt at ease in his presence, whereas whenever she sat next to his successor Lord Mountbatten at dinner, 'he would be charming for a few seconds and then spend the rest of the meal looking around and giving orders. Lord Wavell was so sweet that you always felt a sense of security . . . He would sit there in silence for ages with his battered, noble face and his bad ear. My late husband and I were both absolutely devoted to him.'[1]

Wavell had been a scholar at Winchester, and unlike most viceroys he did not come from an aristocratic or a political background. His indolent and portly wife Eugenie was known as 'Queenie', and they had three daughters and a son. Although he had only joined the army under pressure from his father, in the summer of 1939 he was appointed Commander-in-Chief of British forces in the Middle East, and his Army of the Nile was responsible for the spectacular victories over Italian forces in 1940–41 which did much to boost morale back in Britain. At the start of 1942 he was posted to South-East Asia as Supreme Commander, just as the devastating Japanese onslaught on Malaya, Singapore and Burma began, but he was quickly replaced by the American General Douglas MacArthur. Wavell went to India as Commander-in-Chief, where he had to defend a difficult strategic position with minimal support, as well as coping with the considerable internal unrest created by the Quit India movement.

At the time of his unexpected appointment as Viceroy and Governor General of India, Wavell was staying in London at a sumptuous house in Belgrave Square, described by the diplomatist Harold Nicolson as 'baroque and rococo and what-ho and oh-no-no'. It belonged to his friend Henry 'Chips' Channon, a wealthy Conservative MP in his early forties.

Channon had married Lady Honor Guinness in 1933, and become an integral cog in London's high society, combining political machination with social intrigue. Despite his prominent position, he was in fact an outsider, the son of a prosperous Chicago businessman. His flamboyant aestheticism and fluid sexuality made him the focus of much hostility and disapproval among sections of the British Establishment, and his reputation today rests not on any political achievement, but on his celebrated diaries. Despite the removal of some of the more compromising passages, the published extracts show him to have been by turns intuitive, vain and astute, and one of the most interesting characters to emerge from their pages is, surprisingly enough, Archibald Wavell.

Channon paints a vivid portrait of Wavell's understated and continually unexpected personality. The Field Marshal tended to grunt, murmur and bump into things, caught off-balance by his bad eyesight and poor hearing. He was usually hopelessly lost in a social situation until somebody gave him a conversational lead, and he was quite unaware of the reverence in which he was held by the public. If he found somebody boring or unsympathetic he would lapse into one of his famous awkward silences, yet if he liked them he would suddenly thaw, and a torrent of anecdotes, descriptions and verses from Keats or Shakespeare would gush forth. Wavell's commonplace book is as illuminating as Channon's diary. A quotation from Eric Linklater – 'The rebel, the striker and the heretic are nearly always right' – is not one which would be included by many commanders-in-chief in any generation.

Chips Channon and Wavell first met in 1941 in Cairo, when Channon was on a visit to his boyfriend Major Peter Coats. 'Master Coats' as he was known to his intimates, was Wavell's ADC and 'Lord Chamberlain'. Channon found Lady Wavell vague and amusing, 'a large, lazy woman with wonderful turquoise eyes', and he developed an immediate rapport with her husband. He thought him 'rare, gentle, detached', and was fascinated by his laconic air. After they had spent some time together, Channon wrote in his diary, 'I cannot get over Wavell's modesty, his lack of surface brilliance, his intellectual detachment and seeming boredom with military matters. He is on a grand scale and as great as he is charming.'[2]

In April 1943 Wavell and Peter Coats arrived in London, and stayed at Channon's house in Belgrave Square. Wavell had recently been presented with his Field Marshal's baton, and Channon enjoyed being at the height of the social whirl, running the war hero about town and holding cocktail parties in his honour. Wavell then went to Washington with the Prime Minister, returning to stay with Channon for another few weeks. The day after Churchill offered Wavell the viceroyalty they lunched at the Athenaeum, and Channon advised him to swallow his misgivings and 'rejoice' at the appointment: 'Delhi and Vice-regal trappings, rather than Cheltenham and the simple life: it is not given to every soldier to have so brilliant a retirement.'

Chips Channon revelled in the social cachet of having the Viceroy-designate of India as his house-guest, taking him to lunches and dinners all over London. 'P[eter],' he wrote in excitement, 'says that I am the FM's best, and perhaps only, friend. I must say that his own are a mummified lot who have failed to keep pace with life, and "Archie" likes life, and youth.'[3] Wavell was strangely childlike in his response to his host's devotion, borrowing Channon's clothes and allowing him to dress him, 'putting in his links (mine)', wrote Chips, 'and tying his tie'.

An unexpected triangular friendship grew up between Coats, Wavell and Channon. According to speculation in wartime Cairo, 'Wavell was himself homosexual – although almost certainly an inactive one.'[4] The Field Marshal remained in Channon's words 'soldierly withal', and his precise sexual orientation is unknown, as his private papers have never been released. Still, he clearly enjoyed the ambience of homosexual society, the parallel world that existed alongside the conventional version, and was tolerated providing discretion was maintained.

Rumours began to circulate in London that Channon had 'rigged'

Wavell's appointment as Viceroy, although there is no evidence to support this. Channon was good at political intrigue and kept a close ear to gossip, but he had no interest in Indian politics – indeed he had no particular ideological views, being interested mainly in politicians as personalities. There were also rumours, which reached the War Cabinet, about the inappropriate circles in which Wavell was moving. As Ronald Lewin quaintly put it in his biography *The Chief*, Wavell behaved 'like a man who had lost his bearings' when confronted with the 'less acceptable qualities' of Chips Channon. It was considered improper for a man in Wavell's position to consort so brazenly not only with indiscreet socialites such as Emerald Cunard, but with acknowledged homosexuals. 'I have surrounded this poor lonely man with affection,' wrote the scalded Channon in his diary, 'and now people gossip.'[5]

Churchill's Chief-of-Staff General Hastings 'Pug' Ismay was ordered to fix the situation. He sent Wavell's son, Archie John, to have a word with his father and advise him to quit Channon's milieu, but Wavell was unmoved and unmoving, clearly relishing his ride on the roundabout of exuberant gay high society. Channon was his loyal, fastidious, romantic and amusing friend, and he had no intention of abandoning him. Only in mid-July, when Queenie arrived from India, did the Viceroy-designate depart Belgrave Square and move into a suite at the Dorchester Hotel.

Although Wavell has often been depicted as a war-scarred soldier in the thrall of ICS officials, and in particular his 'first class' Private Secretary Evan Jenkins, he in fact started his term as Viceroy with a greater working knowledge of Indian internal politics than either his predecessor or his successor. He made substantial efforts, for instance, to persuade provincial governments and princely rulers to implement economic and agricultural development projects, some of which were eventually incorporated into Nehru's first five-year plan. The writer and politician Sirdar Pannikar has even suggested that 'there were only two Englishmen in two hundred years who really penetrated into the soul of India, and they were both soldiers.'[6] One was Archie Wavell; the other, incidentally, was the explorer and mystic Sir Francis Younghusband.

In the months before Lord Linlithgow's retirement, Wavell would spend time each morning reading documents at the India Office and holding discussions with officials and Leo Amery. He was unwilling to let the political situation stagnate. Waking at 3 o'clock one morning, he put together an idealistic if naive proposal, which he himself described as 'fantastical', that he should hold a secret conference of India's imprisoned leaders. It was actions such as this that led to many India hands doubting his credentials for the job of Viceroy. In the opinion of H.V. Hodson, the Reforms Commissioner-turned journalist who later became one of the chief promoters of the Mountbatten line, Wavell made 'no impression of being the strong ruler which a great soldier might be expected to be'.[7]

Wavell planned that on his arrival in New Delhi he would summon Gandhi and Nehru, as well as other politicians such as Ambedkar, Rajago-palachari and Jinnah. He would suggest to them that they needed to take decisions which would lead to a swift solution, and would assure them that the British wanted self-government for India as early as possible. They would then be put into a room, with access to a secretariat of experts on matters such as constitutions, international law and so forth, and be left there until they reached a solution. Wavell's reason for this approach, he told Evan Jenkins, was that he had always believed that when orthodox methods have failed, you should try unorthodox ones. His proposal was tidied up and watered down, and presented to Winston Churchill and his ministers. They were not amused; the last thing they wanted was a Viceroy who showed initiative.

During his months in London, Wavell attended a number of Cabinet meetings, which gave him some idea of the Prime Minister's approach to Britain's most important colony. Despite knowing Churchill and his opinions fairly well, the Field Marshal was surprised. 'He hates India,' wrote Wavell in his diary, 'and everything to do with it, and as Amery said in a note he pushed across to me "knows as much of the Indian problem as George III did of the American colonies" . . . He was in his most intractable form.' Later Wavell was to note: 'What I want is some definite policy, and not to go on making promises to India with no really sincere intention of trying to fulfil them.'[8]

Wavell realized early on that he was in for a difficult ride. Unlike most members of the Cabinet, he was never willing to bow to Churchill's tirades, which was one of the reasons why he had been sent off to a distant civilian post in the first place. After another meeting at Downing Street, Wavell saw that his working relationship with the Prime Minister was not going to be a happy one. Churchill had been 'menacing and unpleasant . . . he fears a split in the Conservative Party and trouble in Parliament over any fresh political advance in India, so is determined to block it as long as he is in power . . . I have discovered that the Cabinet is not honest in its expressed desire to make progress in India; and that very few of them have any foresight or political courage.'[9]

The letters and reports of Archie Wavell stand out among the thousands of official British documents preceding the transfer of power in India. He dealt in realities. If the British were going to quit India, how in practice would they do it? If the Pakistan demand was conceded, what would be the boundaries of the new state? It was this same bluntness that in the end provoked his downfall, for he was oblivious to the diplomatic, smooth-tongued nuances and compromises that are necessary to get a policy adopted by democratic politicians. Having expressed his views rather dogmatically to the Cabinet or to the India Committee, he would usually sink into grim silence, ignoring anyone who brought up what he saw as petty or irrelevant objections. This endeared him to neither Churchill nor Attlee.

On 6 October 1943, a farewell dinner was held for the recently ennobled Viscount Wavell at Claridge's. 'P.M. very angry about the paper on Indian policy,' wrote Wavell, '(I believe he almost refused to come to the dinner) and told me he could not possibly accept it.'[10] Fired up by anger and alcohol, Churchill gave a characteristic speech, full of ludicrous exhortations such as: 'Famines have passed away . . . pestilence has gone . . . If the day should come, as I pray it may not, when we cast down for ever our responsibilities there, and vanish from the scene, this episode in Indian history will surely become the Golden Age as time passes, when the British gave them peace and order, and there was justice for the poor, and all men were shielded from outside dangers.'[11]

This speech caused grave worry to officials at the India Office, who felt that certain phrases undermined the guarantees given by Cripps, and that it was extremely tactless given the growing famine in Bengal and the number of people in prison. Eventually Downing Street was persuaded that it should not be published. Poor Amery, meanwhile, said he felt like a medieval criminal who had been tied between 'two wild horses galloping in different directions'.[12] Churchill's only consolation on the question of India came in letters from friends such as his old ally Page Croft, who was now a peer. A few days after Wavell's departure, he wrote to say: 'The failure of Gandhi to rouse India against the King-Emperor is one of the happiest events of the war.'[13] The Prime Minister loved statements of this kind, and had Page Croft's letter printed up and distributed to the Cabinet and beyond.

On arrival in New Delhi later in October, Wavell had a brief meeting with his departing and demoralized predecessor, who told him, 'we shall have to continue responsibility for India for at least another thirty years.'[14] There is little to be said in favour of His Excellency the Marquess of Linlithgow's viceroyalty. He was notoriously stiff and ponderous, insisting that members of his Council, including the Indian representatives, wore tailcoats whatever the weather. All his secret documents were kept in a locked black box which would accompany him, it is believed, even on visits to the lavatory. Even Amery, whose own pronouncements were hardly monuments to clarity, wrote of Linlithgow: 'If ever a man was incapable of stating a case simply in private or public it is he.'[15]

During this crucial period of change and crisis, it must be doubted whether a lantern-jawed Elder of the Church of Scotland was the best person to have held power in New Delhi. 'Hopie' Linlithgow had no understanding or even comprehension of Indian nationalism, and his favoured combination of stagnation and oppression brought about a dangerous hardening of attitude on both sides. As Attlee once wrote, he showed a 'crude imperialism' which was 'fatally short-sighted'.[16]

On his arrival at Victoria Station, the retiring plenipotentiary was greeted not only by the customary delegation of government ministers, but by a demonstration of about twenty Indians. An IPI report reveals that 'Rafique ANWAR unfurled a black paper placard, attached to two pieces of wood, measuring about two feet by one foot, upon which was painted in white letters the words: "BUTCHER OF INDIAN MASSES RETURNS HOME".' The placard was promptly seized by police, provoking other activists to produce banners painted with slogans such as 'LINLITHGOW BROUGHT DEATH, FAMINE, PESTI-LENCE' and 'NAZIS STARVE EUROPE, BRITISH IMPERIAL-ISTS STARVE INDIA'.[17] Lord Linlithgow died, of natural causes, while shooting pheasants in the winter of 1952.

The new Viceroy took an immediate grasp on his post, and began by sending a copy of his anthology *Other Men's Flowers* to the imprisoned Jawaharlal Nehru, having heard that he was keen on poetry. His wife Queenie took up Red Cross work. Wavell was supported by an impressive pair of Indian Civil Servants, Evan Jenkins as his Private Secretary and George Abell as his Deputy Private Secretary. The ubiquitous Major Peter Coats was reincarnated as Comptroller – a sort of all-purpose hotel manager and major domo at Viceroy's House. When an eminent Indian visitor complained that there was a rat in his room, Coats replied: 'Ah, a rat, sir. Those are for our most distinguished guests, the others only get mice.'

Another new appointee who arrived in New Delhi at this time was Lord Louis Mountbatten, who had been put in charge of South-East Asia Command (SEAC). It was a remarkable promotion for a forty-three-year-old naval officer, which occurred as in Wavell's case because all the most suitable candidates were unavailable. Churchill thought Mountbatten's appointment would 'command public interest and approval, and show that youth is no barrier to merit'.[18] As Supreme Allied Commander, Mountbatten was elevated – in theory at least – to a position on a par with MacArthur in the Pacific and Eisenhower in the Mediterranean. He commanded all Allied forces in Burma, Ceylon, Siam, the Malay Peninsula and Sumatra, although most of this territory was in enemy hands.

Wavell had supported Mountbatten's appointment from the outset, thinking it bold and innovative at a time when the Allies were in a disastrous position in Asia. The new Commander-in-Chief in India, Claude Auchinleck, was less enthusiastic. 'The Auck' retained command in India itself, but did not enjoy having a young whippersnapper treading on his toes by operating out of the same city. Although his relations with Auchinleck thawed slightly, in mid-1944 Mountbatten transferred his headquarters from New Delhi to Kandy in Ceylon. His greatest problems arose with his American deputy, General 'Vinegar Joe' Stilwell, who thought Mountbatten 'publicity crazy' and a 'pisspot', and the British in general 'bastardly hypocrites' and 'pig-fuckers'.[19]

One of Wavell's first actions as Viceroy was to travel around the country, inspecting the situation in troubled areas such as the Punjab, the United Provinces and Bengal, trying to boost morale. In the opening months of his viceroyalty he travelled almost a thousand miles a week by DC3 aeroplane, jeep, car and train. He made an important decision to reinstate regular meetings of the eleven governors of the provinces of British India; Linlithgow had not deigned to hold a single one. This move enabled the Government of India to present London with coherent advice and a more unified point of view.

Wavell's immediate worry was the developing famine in Bengal, which had been allowed to spiral out of control. He visited Dhaka and Calcutta, ordered increased military assistance in food distribution, and sent an urgent telegram to Amery demanding the appointment of a new Governor of Bengal, as the present one, who was up for retirement, had become listless and exhausted. Although Wavell berated the 'inefficiency' of the administration of Bengal's Chief Minister Khwaja Nazimuddin, whom he thought 'straight but incapable', he knew that urgent outside assistance was needed.

Wavell began a running battle with London, trying to buy more grain for India. Churchill was not inclined to be helpful, since he followed the advice of his crony Professor Lindemann (now Lord Cherwell, and nicknamed 'Baron Berlin'), who claimed the Bengal famine was a statistical invention. Cherwell, an established bigot who apparently felt 'physical repulsion' when non-whites were in his presence, took the line that the famine was a figment of the Bengali imagination, and could be solved by better food distribution. Wavell thought him an 'old fraud and menace'. The Viceroy's request for a guarantee of a million tons of grain during the course of 1944 was answered with an offer of a quarter of that amount, and a reciprocal demand from London for Indian rice. Before long Wavell was writing, 'I expect the P.M. is regretting that he ever appointed me,' but by late June 1944 he had extracted 450,000 tons from the War Cabinet.[20]

The Bengal famine was, like most famines, caused by a multiplicity of factors, including poor distribution and lack of imports, as well as food shortages. Statistically the crop yield in 1943 was the worst that century, but it was not substantially lower than it had been in 1942. The recorded annual death rate in Bengal rose from an average of 1.2 million to 1.9 million in 1943. Many of the deaths were from malaria, cholera, pneumonia and the diseases which accompany malnutrition. Some of the blame fell on Nazimuddin and on the failings and apparent corruption of Suhrawardy, his Minister for Civil Supplies. Congress accused the Muslim League of profiting financially from the famine, and Jinnah promptly distanced himself by decreeing that League officials should not hold posts in the Bengal government.

Churchill's decision to restrict grain imports to India in order to save ships for the war effort was deliberate, and to that extent the famine was man-made. Congress claimed that the diversion of food to British troops was causing the crisis. Although the military purchase of food stocks in Bengal was in fact minimal, there was a lot of panic buying caused by communal tensions and genuine fear of Japanese invasion. By May 1943, rice prices had risen tenfold. The British response to this was dilatory, and Wavell was the first person to take serious action to coordinate rationing and curtail profiteering.

It is estimated that between one and three million people died over the three years of the Bengal famine, and in some areas whole villages perished. Jinnah stated in the Legislative Assembly in New Delhi that the British were 'irresponsible' and 'incompetent' to have allowed the famine to develop, and pointed out that Churchill's administration would not have remained in office for twenty-four hours if people had been dying of starvation in their thousands every week on the streets of Britain. Wavell's initial grasp of Jinnah's position was shallow; he saw the dandy clothes and the cosmopolitan manners, and was surprised that 'these big Punjab landlords should be so dominated by a down-country lawyer', but in time he came to understand his political methods.[21]

With Wavell installed in place of Linlithgow, Leo Amery felt able to take a much firmer line over the famine. The unsympathetic Minister for War Transport, Viscount Leathers, wished to cut back the limited grain shipments that already existed, but Amery insisted that if anything they ought to be increased. Wavell's telegrams to the India Office on the subject were brief and very firm, and must have been a welcome relief after the loquacious obfuscation of Linlithgow.

Wavell wrote that he considered the Cabinet's stand over food imports to Bengal to be nothing short of 'scandalous', and threatened resignation if nothing was done to halt the deaths from starvation. Amery can be commended for the force with which he backed up Wavell on this point. He was frequently infuriated by his encounters with the Food Grains Committee, writing after one meeting that: 'Grigg [the Secretary of State for War] and Cherwell spent all the time pointing out India ought not to be what it is, both suggesting that a certain number of wealthy Indians should be hanged.'[22]

Under pressure from Wavell and Amery, Churchill asked Roosevelt if he could borrow US ships to bring wheat from Australia. 'Last year we had a grievous famine in Bengal through which at least 700,000 people died,' he wrote at the beginning of 1944. At least a million tons of rice and grain would be needed if Wavell was 'to hold the situation, and so meet the needs of the United States and British and Indian troops and of the civil population especially in the great cities'.[23] The Americans refused to assist, for fear of damaging their own war effort.

An interesting conclusion to the protracted battle with the United States can be found in a letter from Churchill to the former Viceroy Lord Halifax, who was now Ambassador to the United States. The Prime Minister clearly felt he had done well, writing: 'The President has been very good to me about India throughout these years and has respected my clearly expressed resolve not to admit external interference in our affairs.'[24] By the end of the war, India was out of the headlines altogether in the USA, and American deeds were quieter than their words. A bill in 1945 to allow a mere hundred Indians a year to migrate to the United States, supported by both the President and the State Department, was defeated in Congress, and only passed in 1946.

In February 1944, when the worst of the crisis had passed, Wavell sent a telegram to Amery which read: 'Bengal famine was one of the greatest disasters that has befallen any people under British rule and damage to our reputation here . . . is incalculable. Attempt by His Majesty's Government to prove on the basis of admittedly defective statistics that we can do without help demanded would be regarded here by all opinion British and Indian as utterly indefensible . . . They must either trust the opinion of the man they have appointed to advise them on Indian affairs or replace him.'[25]

Wavell was comparatively progressive on Indian representation, wanting to have Indian secretaries in his private office and an Indian Finance Member for his Executive Council, now that it was becoming 'much more like a Cabinet'. This would have been a dramatic step, and the first time that an Indian had ever been in charge of a genuinely important department of state within the Government of India. He also wanted the role of the Government of India's Agent-General in Washington to be strengthened by becoming independent of the British Embassy. Both these suggestions were vetoed by the War Cabinet.

Each small move that Wavell tried to make was stifled by the lack of imagination or interest back in London. If he wanted to write a letter to the imprisoned Gandhi, it had first to be referred to Amery, who would stiffen it and put up a draft to the Cabinet. Each word would then be picked over by ministers with little knowledge or understanding of the situation in India. Often the Prime Minister would order some irrelevant amendment, or command for instance that the missive 'should be stiffer and less forthcoming in tone'.[26]

Wavell's proposed reply to some fairly innocuous remarks from Gandhi was overturned in favour of 'either the longer draft approved by the War Cabinet (telegram No. 17258) subject to the amendment proposed above, or the shorter draft (No. 17797)'.[27] Wavell knew that the hostile tone he was compelled to adopt in these letters was reducing his potential usefulness as a political negotiator, but thought this may have been deliberate on Churchill's part. He made a characteristically quirky diary entry, writing that if Gandhi were to die in prison, 'I might go down to the readers of two thousand years hence with the same reputation as Pontius Pilate; my Council would play the part of the Sanhedrin; and perhaps one of the Princes could be cast for Herod.'[28]

In early May 1944, Wavell was told by the Bombay government that their eminent prisoner in the Aga Khan's palace was in seriously bad health, and that it would seem prudent to discharge him. The recent death of Gandhi's wife Kasturba had sent him into a state of deep distress. A few days later another report came saying that Gandhi was 'really ill ... and that his memory and headpiece may be affected'. In mid-May, after a flurry of telegrams to London, Wavell ordered his release. Churchill was 'very annoyed', and at once regretted having authorized it. His anger increased when Gandhi managed a swift recovery, and began to despatch messages to his latest adversary in Viceroy's House. In Churchill's view Gandhi was 'officially dead', and had no business to be writing letters.

After a short break in Simla, where he entertained his friends Noël Coward and Cecil Beaton, Lord Wavell made a fresh political move. In late August 1944 he convened a conference of the eleven governors of the provinces of British India, several of whom were using Section 93 to retain control of their territory. He believed the war was coming to an end, and thought a political initiative would have more chance of success the earlier it came. He also wrote privately: 'I wonder if we shall ever have any chance of a solution till the three intransigent, obstinate, uncompromising principals are out of the way: Gandhi (just on 75), Jinnah (68), Winston (nearing 70).'[29]

Wavell told the governors that the British were 'sitting pretty' in the short term, but that as soon as the war ended, 'His Majesty's Government's cheque would be presented and have to be honoured'. He pointed out that the Indian Civil Service would be 'tired and weak', British soldiers would be thinking only of demobilization, and there would be many demobbed Indian troops, 'some of them discontented'.[30] He restated these views to Amery, and asked for swift action: 'India is quiet now, and can be kept quiet until the Japanese war ends, though there is much bitterness among political Indians, who have no confidence in the intentions of HMG to secure political progress.'[31]

In Wavell's view it was up to London to take the initiative, and fast. One of the eleven provincial governors said that 'general mistrust' and 'increasing hostility' had developed towards British people in India, while the retiring Governor of Bengal, Richard Casey, went as far as to say that they should 'announce not only their willingness but their determination to get out', and 'publish a time-schedule of the stages by which they will get out'.[32] Interestingly, all the provincial governors were 'emphatically of the opinion' that 'a positive move must be made before the end of the war with Japan'. These ICS stalwarts are usually presented – in Attenborough's film *Gandhi*, for example – as ancient, bigoted, port-swilling buffoons. In fact at the time of the handover of power most of them were in their early fifties and, compared to the War Cabinet's India Committee, decidedly progressive in their political opinions.

By this time, Mohandas Gandhi's approach to India's future was becoming almost as bizarre as that of his adversary in Downing Street. He sent Churchill a letter, which he claimed was 'of a sacred character', answering the 'half-naked fakir' jibe of more than a decade before. 'I have been long trying to be a *faqir* and that naked – a more difficult task. I therefore regard the expression as a compliment, though unintended.'[33] Wavell was not amused ('I cannot imagine anyone with Gandhi's reputation writing so stupid a letter'), and hoped it would not irritate Churchill into vetoing proposals for political negotiation. The Indophobe's reply was unusually calm, brief and measured. 'Pray send the following telegram,' he told Amery. '(Quote) The Prime Minister desires me to acknowledge with thanks the receipt of your letter of July 17 to him (Unquote).'[34]

Amery himself, perhaps unnerved by Wavell's tendency to take the initiative, continued to turn out hopeless, scholarly proposals. Might 'the Russian village system' provide the best way of running Indian local government, he wondered? 'I am increasingly coming to the view,' he told the Viceroy in October 1944, 'that India's main grievance and source of bitterness is not the existing Government of India but Downing Street and the House of Commons.' Rather than having an interim government leading to a transfer of control as Wavell suggested, Amery wanted to use India's Defence Council ('adding to it some of the leading service men') as a sort of unelected, unaccountable, free-floating Cabinet. The British government would 'declare here and now that we recognize India as enjoying the full freedom and status enjoyed by the Dominions', and Westminster would give up 'any power to legislate for Indian affairs from here except at the request of an Indian Government'.[35]

In effect, under this scheme Wavell would become the dictator of India, with no legislative checks on his power. Backing him as 'ministers' would have been a tiny clique of princes, placemen and army officers. No representation of India's imprisoned nationalist leaders was envisaged. It is hard to think of any constitutional proposal in India's history that was quite as crazy as this one, or one more likely to have provoked a Congress-backed revolution. As Wavell wrote shrewdly, the Secretary of State for India had 'a curious capacity for getting hold of the right stick but practically always the wrong end of it'.[36]

In 1944 there were several attempts to bridge the divide between Congress and the Muslim League. The Tamil Congress politician Chakravarti Raja-gopalachari put together a formula whereby a referendum would be held in Muslim-majority areas to decide whether the inhabitants wished to separate from India. This was something close to Pakistan, and Veer Savarkar, the former revolutionary terrorist who was now President of the Hindu Mahasabha, spoke out strongly against it, telegraphing to Amery: 'Hindusabhites can never tolerate breaking up of union of India their fatherland and holyland.'[37]

Since 1932 the Hindu extremist group the Rashtriya Swayamsewak Sangh (RSS) had been affiliated to the Mahasabha, and the two groups had been operating in concert. By the time that a keen fan of Adolf Hitler called Madhav Golwalkar took over the RSS in 1940, 'it numbered 100,000 trained and highly disciplined cadres pledged to an ideology of uncompromising communalism'.[38] It was primarily a Brahminical, urban, north Indian and Maharashtran phenomenon, whose members paraded in khaki shorts and played team games, regarding themselves not so much as a proto-fascist army, but as a patriotic community organization which defended the position of Hindus.

There was an attempt in September 1944 by Gandhi to resolve the rift with Jinnah, which Patel considered an unwise move. Gandhi wrote Jinnah a letter in Gujarati, and they met at Jinnah's house in Bombay in September 1944. Both sides were wary, and no agreement was reached. Although Gandhi intimated that the Rajagopalachari formula could break the impasse, a few days later he was attacking the principle of Pakistan. Using the offensive language that would be taken up by the BJP half a century later, he wrote: 'I find no parallel in history for a body of converts and their descendants claiming to be a nation apart from the parent stock. If India was one nation before the advent of Islam, it must remain one in spite of the change of faith of a very large body of her children.'[39]

Gandhi irritated Jinnah by asking to address a meeting of the Muslim League, and made apparent concessions which he then overturned and reworded. There was no settlement, as a result of Gandhi's imprecision and Jinnah's intransigence. Jinnah preferred to continue building up his power base, knowing that his case thrived from being in opposition. At the end of their dialogue, Gandhi told the press that Jinnah was 'suffering from hallucination when he imagines that an unnatural division of India could bring either happiness or prosperity to the people concerned'.[40] One British official wrote that the negotiations had reached a 'pitiful conclusion', and that the arguments 'between these two obstinate old men show that the spirit of accommodation was entirely lacking, and that each was determined to give nothing away'.[41] Lord Wavell's diary entry ran: 'The two great mountains have met and not even a ridiculous mouse has emerged.'[42]

In October, the Viceroy's new Reforms Commissioner, V.P. Menon, stepped in and presented a short, cogent proposal as to how the situation might be moved forward. Owing to his inexperience Menon had been appointed on an 'officiating basis' only, but as little reform was expected in the short term a better-qualified commissioner was not sought. Menon stated that the collapse of the Bombay talks between Jinnah and Gandhi had 'revealed an irreconcilable difference of opinion between the Muslim League and the Congress . . . My suggestion is to summon a Conference of representative leaders of political parties and interests not exceeding twenty-five in number . . . under His Excellency's auspices.' The hope would be that 'the duel between the Congress and the Muslim League' would thereby be curtailed.[43]

Jinnah was in the ascendant, but only because provincial Muslim politicians were prepared to offer him conditional backing. They retained total control over their local affairs, and the League's writ did not run in their territories; there was only a cursory grassroots Muslim League organization in Bengal and the Punjab. Yet since there was no serious rival for the post of all-India Muslim spokesman, Jinnah could afford to bide his time, playing a long game.

When Lord Louis Mountbatten came to see Wavell in September 1944 following a trip to London, he told him that Churchill had been 'as intractable as ever about India, seemed to regard sending of food to India merely as "appeasement" of Congress; and it was only the efforts of the Chiefs of Staff, who realized the necessity for feeding India if it was to be a stable base for operations, which produced any food at all . . . P.M. was quite furious about Gandhi's release and subsequent activities, and in fact quite impossible about India. Leo Amery, who does stand up to him, had accused P.M. of a "Hitler-like attitude" to India, and had got a first-class rocket.'[44]

The picture of Churchill that emerges from the diaries of his wartime colleagues is certainly disturbing. His senior foreign policy adviser Sir Alec Cadogan records him 'simply drivelling' at meetings, spewing forth 'irrelevant, redundant talk'. Hugh Dalton complains of 'an infinitely rambling discussion' of the War Cabinet over the wording of a telegram to Gandhi, while Field Marshal Alan Brooke noted that Churchill seemed content to let India starve, while still wanting to use it as a base for military operations.

As if his troublesome gallstones were not enough to contend with, Leo Amery had to endure discussions in Cabinet which consisted of 'a long grumbling monologue by Winston, talking into his cigar' on subjects such as the need to recapture the Andaman Islands from the Japanese, and the evils of the Mahatma ('a traitor who ought to be put back in prison'). By now, Churchill's opinions about India were becoming more extreme by the day. In August 1944, Amery wrote that a 'long tirade on the worthlessness of the Indian army was too much for me and I went for him hammer and tongs pointing out what India had done ever since it saved the Middle East'. It was Churchill's ignorance over India that seems to have irritated Amery more than anything else, and he even accused the Prime Minister, in Cabinet, of talking 'damned nonsense'.

Amery noted that meetings were apt to be taken up by the Prime Minister 'shouting' about India, and complaining that its inhabitants were 'breeding like rabbits'. He wrote after one such encounter that his leader was 'not quite normal on the subject of India ... He seems quite incapable of listening or taking in even the simplest point but goes off at a tangent on a word and then rambles on inconsecutively ... Certainly a complete outsider coming to that meeting and knowing nothing of his reputation would have thought him a rather amusing but quite gaga old gentleman who could not understand what people were talking about.'[45]

Churchill told Amery that once the war was over, he would feel 'no obligation to honour promises made at a time of difficulty', and hoped instead to inspire 'a great regeneration of India'. This would be achieved by an entirely impractical scheme of 'extinguishing landlords and oppressive industrialists', promoting 'collectivization on Russian lines', and replacing 'wretched sentimentalists like Wavell' with 'new men'. Amery was left wondering 'whether on this subject of India he is really quite sane – there is no relation between his manner, physical and intellectual, on this theme and the equability and dominant good sense he displays on issues directly affecting the conduct of the war'.[46]

It might be argued that Churchill had better things to do than worry about India: after all, he had a war to run. His problem was that as an imperialist, he had a duty to maintain his Empire. It was clearly unreasonable to expect India to provide nearly two million soldiers to fight on behalf of the Allies, yet to take little serious interest in feeding its people. The irony is that the maintenance of good relations with India's nationalist politicians would have helped the Allied war effort.

Churchill became unbalanced whenever the subject of India was raised, owing to his instinctive conviction that Britain's status as a world power rested on its imperial possessions. Rather than countenance a constructive withdrawal, he preferred a scorched-earth policy. It was obvious, given the degree of popular unrest in India, that British rule could not continue for much longer, unless military deployment on a gargantuan scale were to be sanctioned by Parliament. But there was no enthusiasm within any party, or any money in the Exchequer, to support such a course of action. Churchill himself had no real answer, and after the failure of the Cripps Mission he never progressed beyond an undefined and emotional urge to make sure that India remained within the British Empire.

Most importantly, Churchill devoted a surprising amount of his time and energy to India, although almost always in a destructive rather than a constructive way. As Wavell noted in May 1945, a crucial Cabinet meeting on India was held up by the Prime Minister giving a protracted and irrelevant discourse on 'the methods of officering the Indian army'. Amery's diaries are full of Churchill's tirades and claims about the situation in Bengal or the Punjab, but they rarely record any positive actions or general policy decisions. In one entry Amery complains that throughout his time as India Secretary, he had not succeeded in holding a single serious discussion about India with Churchill, but had only dealt with emergencies as they arose.

On 24 October 1944, following the completion of his first year as Viceroy, Lord Wavell dispatched a cogent, forthright and well-turned letter to the Prime Minister. He compared himself to Oliver Twist, always asking for more. 'I know you have often found me a difficult and troublesome subordinate,' he began, but 'I have not always found you an easy master to serve ... I have always told you the truth as I saw it without fear of consequences ... I feel very strongly that the future of India is the problem on which the British Commonwealth and the British reputation will stand or fall in the post-war period.' If instead of 'a friendly partner' India became 'lost and hostile', the British were 'likely to be reduced in the East to the position of commercial bag-men ... I feel that the vital problems of India are being treated by HMG with neglect, even sometimes with hostility and contempt.'

For instance, Whitehall had decided to raise the wages of Indian soldiers, without even consulting New Delhi in advance. The cost to the taxpayer, at a time of rampant inflation in India, would be £50 million a year. Wavell was a pragmatic strategist, not an idealistic decolonizer, believing that although 'in an entirely misplaced sentimental liberalism we took the wrong turn with India twenty-five or thirty years ago', he had no choice but to deal with the situation as it stood. 'What I have in mind is a provisional political Government, of the type suggested in the Cripps declaration,' linked to a serious and genuine attempt 'to reach a constitutional settlement'.[47] He knew that the present position could not be sustained much longer. As Francis Younghusband had written as early as 1930 in his book *Dawn in India*, the British had little choice but to concede power to Indian nationalists, since the only alternative was to 'regard our army as a garrison, increase it, and rule by force', which was anathema to imperial paternalists.[48]

'The present Government of India cannot continue indefinitely, or even for long,' wrote Wavell, hoping that his strong words might move Churchill into thinking about the matter seriously. Throughout the course of 1943 and 1944, law and order within India had been deteriorating severely. Large numbers of political activists and leaders were still imprisoned, but a new, younger and more dangerous type of nationalist was emerging. The regular reports from the Intelligence Bureau were becoming more worrying by the week. 'Though ultimate responsibility still rests with HMG,' wrote the Viceroy, 'HMG has no longer the power to take effective action . . . we must make some imaginative and constructive move without delay.'[49]

Churchill took a month to reply to this letter, and when he did, his answer was dismissive. The time to consider such matters, he suggested, was 'at leisure and best of all in victorious peace', and with that he wished the Viceroy a Happy New Year. The Prime Minister was determined to ignore any such proposals, telling Amery that Wavell was merely 'cringing to the Hindus'. Hindus, in this context, seems to have been an all-purpose word for the inhabitants of Britain's Indian Empire.

Wavell recorded in his diary that the government's attitude to India was 'negligent, hostile and contemptuous to a degree I had not anticipated', and sent a telegram to Amery on 1 December to say that a decision was needed urgently: 'I am quite sure that present time is most favourable opportunity we have had for some years to make progress with Indian problem, but that it must be taken at once.' He then repeated an earlier request he had made to fly back to London at once, 'and state case personally'.[50]

Amery, frightened of further antagonizing Churchill, pushed Wavell's proposals about and then wrote a politician's letter to Attlee asking him to intervene, since 'we cannot possibly put ourselves in the position to have it come out in the future that we refused even to consider his proposals'.[51] Eventually matters were referred by the War Cabinet to the India Committee, which was run by Attlee. After rambling, dull discussions, they finally rejected Wavell's plans. Stafford Cripps was the only member to dissent, saying he first wished to hear what the Viceroy had to say in person. The general feeling was that the proposals were 'substantially identical' to those Wavell had submitted on his arrival in India in October 1943, and they knew of 'no change since then in the Indian situation which would render these proposals acceptable'.

Why not procrastinate, since 'Sir Tej Sapru has convoked a conference of prominent political personages in India' who might come up with something 'to merit consideration'?[52] Sir Tej Bahadur Sapru was a Kashmiri Brahmin whose National Liberal Federation had split off from Congress after the First World War, but by now he had little political clout, and was concentrating on running India's Boy Scouts. His 'Non-Party Conference' was an irrelevant sideshow. At Westminster he was known as 'the postman', since his principal role was as a point of contact between Congress and British politicians. As Wavell had informed London several weeks earlier, Sapru's deliberations were 'going to fail and need not detain us'. Wavell believed Sapru 'talked platitudes with the air of wisdom of an Elder Statesman which he fancies himself to be; I have always thought him rather an old fraud'.[53]

With India sliding towards internal chaos, Amery managed to postpone any trip to London by Wavell, thanks to the connivance of Attlee, who ruled privately that 'the right time for a visit would be the beginning of June'. Wavell responded angrily with a telegram protesting 'in the strongest possible terms' against this decision, and adding: 'India is quiet on the surface but political situation is deteriorating rapidly ... I feel HMG *must* face the Indian problem without further delay.'[54] Eventually the India Committee gave in, and Wavell flew to London on 21 March 1945, accompanied by Queenie, Evan Jenkins and V.P. Menon. This was a full five months after his original 'move without delay' letter to Churchill.

TWELVE

Dilli Chalo

The Prime Minister was thoroughly grumpy over Wavell's attempt to offer the Indian people something more than further repression, and refused Amery's suggestion that he hold a private dinner at Downing Street to enable the Viceroy to meet members of the government. 'I consider my meeting with him had better be purely official,' he decided.[1] Wavell was fobbed off with the India Committee, which was controlled by the Deputy Prime Minister, Clement Attlee.

Still trapped in its old way of thinking, the government was anxious that, before anything else happened, Congress should be made to issue a formal withdrawal of the Quit India Resolution. Wavell told them the subject was dead, 'but that to try and bury the corpse might revive it'.[2] What he wanted was a quick political decision about how to proceed. Instead of action, he had to endure protracted debates with Attlee's committee, and was then ignored by them for weeks at a time. Attlee was almost as unhelpful as Churchill, motivated by an innate conservatism and caution over India. Wavell's response to the political peregrinations of the India Committee was to make sharp statements of his own position, and then lapse into silence. He felt he was being treated like an 'Untouchable in the presence of Brahmins', and wrote in his diary: 'What a crew they are for a perilous voyage!'[3]

He also had to endure the chilling ignorance of the Cabinet Food Committee. Lord Leathers refused to make any ships available to deliver grain to India, and was apparently 'indifferent to the possibility of famine in India', while full of 'smooth evasions and false promises' over the future availability of transport. Lord Cherwell was wheeled out to produce 'fatuous calculations' about harvests and yields in the manner of a Stalinist statistician. After one meeting of the Cabinet the Viceroy wrote in his diary that although nothing was going to India, food and shipping had been sent to Holland, and noted 'the very different attitude towards feeding a starving population when the starvation is in Europe'.[4]

Leo Amery's support for a request by Wavell to see a summary of the India Committee's discussions, in order to gain 'some indication of how our minds are working', was rejected by Attlee. The Labour leader thought the very fact that Wavell had made such a suggestion showed 'the disadvantage of having a Viceroy with no political experience'.[5] Yet all Wavell wanted, after a year and a half as Viceroy and Governor General of India, was something resembling a government policy, or at least an indication of the direction in which future policy might be heading. Instead he was left loitering in London, while Churchill pondered other matters.

In the opening days of 1945, Amery raised an issue with Wavell which was to have serious implications for the retention of British power. He asked what should be done about the Intelligence Bureau (which was technically under the control of the Home Department of the Government of India) in the event of genuine nationalist politicians coming into power in New Delhi. What would happen to the IB if its key targets, namely the Congress leadership, suddenly became its masters? The matter was complicated by the future fate of Indian Political Intelligence in London. As Paul Patrick, the senior civil servant who provided the link between IPI and the India Office, wrote in a 'note', 'I gather from IPI that SIS under the wing of the Foreign Office has been trying to obtain a greater measure of control over MI5.'[6] It was thought that this control might in practice extend to IPI.

Denys Pilditch, the Director of the Intelligence Bureau, believed the answer would be to introduce 'a convention – backed by the Governor General's over-riding powers – conferring on DIB immunity from curiosity or inquisitiveness about his records and sources of information'.[7] However, figures within the intelligence community in Whitehall were concerned that this protection would be too vague, and that such a 'convention' would be hard to enforce. As Wavell's pressure on the Cabinet for some political action in India intensified, the Whitehall establishment closed ranks and made certain that its intelligence-gathering operation would not be compromised.

On 27 April, while he was in London, Wavell was informed that the British government would shortly activate 'Section (40)2 of the Ninth Schedule to the Government of India Act (1935)' – one of the obscure 'over-ride' clauses which enabled real power to remain in British hands, while pretending that Indians were in control. This enabled the Viceroy, in his capacity as Governor General, to 'authorize the DIB . . . to withhold from any department any information under his control and to decide the form in which any information is imparted'.[8] In practice this meant that the intelligence agencies would no longer be answerable to the executive of the Government of India.

There was some precedent for this, in that throughout the war IPI had withheld information from India Office ministers in order to protect the source of intercepted 'Enigma' radio traffic. Sir Stewart Menzies, the head of SIS who also ran the code-breaking centre at Bletchley Park, had ordered Philip Vickery to make sure that nothing obtained from 'ULTRA' sources was disclosed 'in any form to any non-service minister or official without [SIS's] prior concurrence'.[9] This secrecy over ULTRA was however accepted practice throughout Whitehall, since some ministers did not have full security clearance, and was rather different from the DIB's broad permission to keep back 'any information under his control'.

Vickery himself had been given the rank of colonel at the outbreak of war in order to facilitate his access to restricted secret intelligence. After VJ Day he asked Cecil Silver, a civil servant who had been his right-hand man at IPI since the summer of 1937, to draft a letter to the 'Security/Intelligence organizations with which I am most closely concerned in the UK', namely 'MI5 and SIS'. The letter should thank them for their help to India and Burma during wartime, and stress 'our indebtedness to them for placing their most secret information at my disposal whenever it was considered to be of use to the Government of India'.[10] This shows that IPI was able to operate right across the board within the British secret services, and had access to material that was usually restricted within the service that had created it.

In mid-1945 Pilditch was told by London to sift all IB records 'immediately' and divide them into internal and external sections. This was because the Intelligence Bureau had carried out some of its own surveillance in foreign countries, and also possessed a substantial volume of IPI material that had been sent out to India over the years. The authorities in Whitehall wanted to make certain that in the event of a 'political' Indian taking charge of the Home Department, IB and IPI operatives and informers would be protected, and any compromising documents destroyed or sent to England.

Pilditch was told to mention as few facts as possible to putative Indian ministers, supposedly to prevent a 'deterioration in security'. Restricted information included the names of the various intelligence agencies in London, since 'it is the accepted practice here to conceal their existence so far as is possible.'[11] Vickery even wondered whether it might be possible not to mention IPI at all to any new honourable Home Member, who would theoretically be controlling it and providing its budget. Like the other British security and intelligence agencies at this time, IPI was an organization which officially did not exist.

In April 1945 the economist John Maynard Keynes prepared a paper for the War Cabinet on Britain's 'overseas financial policy for the period of transition following the defeat of Japan'. It was a document of substantial historical importance, since it identified and summed up the economic bind in which successive British governments were to find themselves over the next ten years. He pointed out that 'by cunning and kindness', Britain had managed to keep most of its wartime debts in sterling rather than in foreign currency or gold, and that it was therefore in the debtors' interest not to disrupt the British economy. However, the debt had now reached the 'prodigious total' of £3,000 million, which made British post-war financial independence from the United States impossible without substantial cuts in public spending.

Keynes took the view that imperial profligacy was the obvious target, since Britain's 'financial embarassments' were 'mainly the result of cash expenditure' in Africa, the Middle East and India, 'without the Treasury knowing either beforehand or afterwards, what it has been spent upon'. Between 1942 and 1944, the British government had spent £2,000 million on policing and administering the Empire: 'Thus it is this expenditure which is *wholly* responsible for our financial difficulties.' Keynes asserted that from the date of a ceasefire in Asia, Britain would be running an overseas deficit of around £1,400 million a year, and that unless such spending was brought 'under drastic control at an early date ... our ability to pursue an independent financial policy in the early post-war years will be fatally impaired'.[12]

Sadly, this advice was ignored both by the Prime Minister Winston

Churchill and his successor Clement Attlee, although it was a problem that had been deepening for the previous two decades. Churchill hoped the Empire might somehow be conjured into continuity, while Attlee deluded himself into thinking all former imperial subjects would unite for evermore in a gooey bond of brotherhood called the Commonwealth. The Empire was no longer turning a profit, or even paying its way. Between 1924 and 1937 Britain's trade surplus with India had fallen from £75 million to £23 million, yet few politicians had been willing to accept the advantages of British withdrawal. The result was what the historian Correlli Barnett has called 'one of the most outstanding examples of strategic over-extension in history'.[13]

Even at its zenith, the coherence of the British Empire depended on self-confidence. It was never the unified pink swathe of territory seen in old atlases, but a collection of dominions, protectorates, crown colonies and dependencies held together with the aid of propaganda and the Royal Navy. In retrospect it is surprising it lasted as long as it did, since, with the exception of Malaya, all the imperial colonies were losing money from the 1920s onwards. The Suez crisis of 1956, which is often depicted as the moment of Britain's final imperial collapse, was in fact little more than the spasmodic twitching of a phantom limb.

After Indian independence, Britain continued to play at being a major world power, maintaining a large standing army in the Middle East, acting as banker to the sterling area with the aid of American cash, and investing millions of pounds in East African groundnuts. The result was systemic economic and political decline, encouraged on all sides of the House of Commons, which was to have a destructive lasting effect on Britain. By 1950 the Colonial Office was to have tripled its pre-war size, and Britain would be spending between 3 and 4 per cent of its gross national product on Commonwealth defence. The belief in Empire remained long after its practical uses had evaporated, but rather than accept the fact and cut loose from old ties, successive governments preferred to concentrate on the management of decline.

As the war in Europe approached its end, Wavell was still hanging about in Whitehall waiting for some decision from the Cabinet. He went to see Linlithgow, whom he liked, but found 'dry and cynical'. MPs of all parties were far more concerned about the possibility of a general election than about any problem east of Suez. Yet tension was mounting in India, with daily telegrams arriving from officials in New Delhi containing details of unrest. It was clear that Wavell's own standing was being damaged by the length of time he was being kept waiting for an answer. As he had predicted, the looming end of hostilities was making Congress far less accommodating. He was to observe on 8 June, VE-Day, that 'HMG has been so slow that the opportunity has been missed.'

Churchill was, perhaps understandably, more concerned with the recent death of Roosevelt and Lloyd George, victory parades, church services, a general election and an end to the blackout than with any possible uprising in India. Chips Channon, who dined with the Wavells every few days while they were in London, reported that the Viceroy was 'gentle, loving and lovable', but had 'made an unfavourable impression in high political circles, who consider him a great man, an angel and a gentleman, but a very unastute politician'.[14] Finally, on 31 May, Churchill acquiesced and agreed to a conference of Indian nationalist leaders. The Viceroy left for New Delhi early the following morning.

This attempt to head off growing unrest infuriated the members of the Viceroy's Executive Council, who knew that any rapprochement with Congress would undermine and even destroy their own standing. The poor be-knighted *taluqdars* turned on Wavell and condemned his actions, briefing the press with secret information he had given on his discussions in London. The manner of their opposition probably did Wavell no harm, since, in his words, it 'exposed them to further ridicule as a collection of irresponsible placemen'.[15] The British now began to turn their backs on the Indian toadies who had loyally supported them during the Quit India movement, for they realized that however much they disliked it, the real power lay with the likes of Nehru and Gandhi – and Jinnah. Jinnah was the complication, the grit in the nationalist oyster. He had backed the British during the war, but only as far as it suited him, always maintaining his essential opposition to their rule. Unlike the Indians on the Executive Council, he supported the imperial power as a tactic rather than as a way of life.

The Congress Working Committee was released from prison, and a conference began in the ballroom of Viceregal Lodge in Simla on 25 June 1945. The delegates included figures from Congress, the Muslim League and several smaller regional political parties. Maulana Abul Kalam Azad was still in post as Congress President from 1940, owing to the impossibility of holding internal elections during the Quit India crackdown. They were conveyed to and from meetings in hand-pulled rickshaws, and in several instances found themselves having to encounter their political rivals face to face for the first time. The delegates made a strange combination: the pro-British Punjabi leader Khizar Hyat Khan Tiwana in an elaborate white turban, Azad in an *achkan* and slippers, Jinnah in a pale double-breasted suit, Gandhi in a *dhoti* and shawl. Some were nationalists and revolutionaries, freshly released from jail and blinking in the sunlight, while others were allies of the British for whom government-sponsored events were familiar occasions. In all, there were twenty-two delegates, ranging from the Congressmen Rajagopalachari and Pant, to the Muslim League's Liaquat Ali Khan, and the Sikh leader Tara Singh.

Gandhi was not quite sure whether he was there or not, telling Wavell at a preliminary meeting that 'he represented nobody except himself', and might not attend the actual conference. Wavell recorded that the interview constituted 'mainly a discursive monologue by Mr Gandhi, interspersed by numerous digressions, such as a most graphic description of the death of his Private Secretary, and a relation of his carrying down of the wounded General Woodgate from Spion Kop in 1899'. Jinnah was scathing about Gandhi's tactic of claiming to take no part in negotiations, saying he 'pretended not to belong to the Congress when it suited his book', but was in reality 'the Dictator of Congress'.[16]

The Simla Conference was soon scuppered by Jinnah's refusal to allow any Muslims who were not members of the League to serve on a new Viceroy's Council. It was obvious that Wavell could not accept this, for as he wrote in a telegram to Amery: 'Muslim League does not repeat not represent all Muslims in India and considerable section of Muslims not only in Punjab but elsewhere would be outraged by admission that it does.'[17] Many years later Amery made a brief but interesting handwritten note regarding the Simla Conference. 'The immediate wrecker was Jinnah,' he suggested, 'but the real wrecker perhaps the long delay before Archie was allowed to try, and so Winston.'[18]

The Viceroy thought Jinnah was behaving with 'arrogance and intransigence'. As a new tack, Wavell tried producing a list of his own nominees for the Viceroy's Council, which contained five Muslim members, consisting of four from the League and one from the Punjab's Unionist Party. Jinnah would not accept this. When the conference failed, Congress suggested that Wavell should have proceeded regardless without Jinnah, but in practice that was clearly impossible, as he was the only politician with a halfway convincing claim to speak for India's Muslims. The Simla Conference was the first move in the final stage of British rule, and confirmed the hostility between Congress and the Muslim League.

In his report on the conference, Wavell concluded: 'Jinnah is narrow and arrogant, and is actuated mainly by fear and distrust of the Congress. Like Gandhi he is constitutionally incapable of friendly cooperation with the other party. Azad is an old-fashioned scholar with pleasant manners . . . His main object is to get even with Jinnah and the League Muslims who despise him as a paid servant of the Congress. Nehru is an idealist, and I should say straight and honest.' He added that although Simla had failed over 'Jinnah's intransigence about Muslim representation', the 'deeper cause' was genuine Muslim distrust of Hindus. 'Their fear that the Congress, by parading its national character and using Muslim dummies will permeate the entire administration of any united India is real, and cannot be dismissed as an obsession of Jinnah and his immediate entourage.'[19]

An underlying reason for the breakdown of the talks, Wavell believed, was the previous British policy of excluding nationalists from central government: 'One of the troubles is that none of the principal leaders – Gandhi, Jinnah, Nehru, Liaquat, Patel – have any administrative experience; and they do not understand how the machinery of Government works in practice; and think entirely on the lines of all questions being decided by party votes.'[20]

The Simla Conference failed to expose the real nature of Jinnah's position. As the governors of Bengal and the Punjab had predicted, Jinnah's conduct during the talks inflated his credibility, while failing to reveal the fact that he had little serious backing in the two main Muslim-majority provinces. The governors of both provinces wanted Wavell to 'expose' the possible consequences of the creation of Pakistan, rather than trying to break the Indo–British deadlock through the creation of an interim government. Although Wavell took no immediate action, he saw the validity of their argument, and raised the matter with London.

One dark night in January 1941, having grown a beard and disguised himself as a 'Muslim up-country gent' with the name of Mohammad Ziauddin, a plump Bengali in his early forties was smuggled out of his house in Elgin Road in Calcutta by his nephew. The man had recently been released from prison, and was presently under strict house arrest. He was driven south in a Wanderer car for some time to confuse his pursuers, then headed west. Wearing a fez, he took a train to a station on the edge of Delhi, where he boarded the Frontier Mail to Peshawar. From there, assisted by political associates and disguised as a mute Pathan pilgrim, he rode a mule across the Afghan border, clambered onto a truck, and was driven to Kabul. After a brief delay, secret agents spirited him to Germany, where he had plans to recruit an army and march to Delhi to drive out the British imperialists. His passport said he was an Italian named Orlando Mazzotta. In fact he was none other than the former Congress President, Subhas Chandra Bose.

Back in Calcutta, wild rumours were circulating – Subhas Babu had gone to Russia, or to Hong Kong, or had become a *sanyasi*. His remarkable feat was marred only by the recollections of Nirad Chaudhuri, who was working for Subhas's brother Sarat at the time: 'The so-called escape has been represented as a clever feat of outwitting the British administration in India by adroit planning and daring execution, somewhat similar to the rescue of Mussolini by Hitler. Certainly, it would have been clever if Subhas Bose had been under house arrest and surveillance. But he was not.'

Chaudhuri described the dash to Berlin as an act of 'deplorable futility', and later suggested that the subsequent 'glorifying myth' of Bose had its origin 'in the emotional compulsion for the Bengali middle class to believe that through Subhas Bose they played a decisive role in gaining political independence for India, and to deprecate Gandhi's role as far as possible'.[21] During the first thirty years of its existence Congress had been dominated by Bengalis, but after the rise of Gandhi they were sidelined. From 1917 until independence, Chittaranjan Das and Subhas Bose were the only Bengalis to serve as Congress President.

Nirad Chaudhuri's view of Bose is shared by few Indians today. His reputation as a national hero stands at a high, even if this has been achieved by adjusting the historical facts to suit prevailing political and cultural demands. Bose has somehow been appropriated by Communists, Congress and Hindu nationalists, all of whom are certain he was their champion and supporter. He is seen as the one leader of India's freedom movement who dared to fight the British with the sword, and who was not implicated in the creation of Pakistan.

Some present-day Indian street paintings depict Subhas Bose as Kalki, the final manifestation of the god Vishnu who rides on a white horse to save the world from destruction, while others show him as Shivaji, whose escape from the clutches of Aurangzeb mirrors that of Bose from the perfidious Britishers. Some more extreme Indian politicians are currently calling for the erection of a statue of Adolf Hitler, using the inverse logic that since Hitler was a supporter of Bose, he must have been a great man. Meanwhile newspaper columnists assert with total conviction that had he lived, Bose would have prevented both the horrors of 1947 and the war with China in 1962.

Calcutta's Dum Dum Airport and Bombay's Marine Drive have long been renamed in his favour, as have thousands of roads and buildings across the country. In 1997, the centenary of Bose's birth, there were exhibitions and parades, drawings of him in the artist's blood, a specially minted two-rupee coin, huge posters of his face all over Delhi, and even, for the first time, a decision to incorporate him into India's Republic Day celebrations. Despite the wartime conduct of Bose's Indian National Army, whose soldiers Chaudhuri described as 'the most contemptible and dishonourable seen in any country or age', an army band played 'Kadam kadam badhaye jaa', an INA marching song purportedly based on 'The animals went in two by two', in state celebrations in January 1997.[22] It was greeted by louder roars from the crowd than any other tune.

A campaign has been started to rename the Andaman Islands after Bose, his birthday has been proclaimed a national holiday, the central government has set aside hundreds of thousands of rupees for 'research' into his life, and MPs have made requests in the Lok Sabha for a fresh inquiry into his present whereabouts.

For many people believe Bose did not die in an air crash in 1945, but is alive and well and waiting for an appropriate moment to reappear, like Elvis Presley and Lord Lucan. According to a report in the *Times of India* in January 1996, when a government minister referred to Bose's death at a public meeting, 'about 150 people, waving large bamboo sticks with a tricolour and imprint of a leaping tiger, first shouted him down. Thereafter, about fifty of them ran towards the dais to attack the minister leaving many persons, including foreign delegates, aghast.' The attackers claimed that since Bose was 'still very much alive and in India, the minister had no business to say, "Till the end of his life . . ." '.[23]

When I was in Bombay, I attended an exhibition about Bose's life, with films, photographs, and giant plaster relief paintings of his greatest exploits. Several of the people there seriously believed that his Indian National Army had marched to Delhi in 1947 and swept the British from power. Afterwards, as I walked up Netaji Subhas Chandra Bose Road, I passed a building marked 'Beachview, Proprietor Vinay B. Wagh, Sculptor'. Inside were hundreds of clay, bronze and plaster figures. Workers were making models and measuring elbows.

I sat and had a cup of tea with Vinay B. Wagh, a jittery man with heavy black spectacles and a short-sleeved electric blue shirt. It turned out that this was a family firm which had made sculptures of India's national heroes for three generations, and that their bronzes stood in state on plinths all over the subcontinent. Mr Wagh was a barometer for Indian perceptions of the past, since his life had been spent watching history shift as the present changed.

He told me that the market for national heroes had changed a good deal over the years, and that in the old days the King Emperor and the big Parsi business leaders had always been the most popular. At one time there was a lot of demand for Gandhi and Nehru, but now everybody wanted Bose, or else a figure from ancient times. The big corporations still commissioned statues of the present Mr Birla or Mr Tata, but otherwise 'Man-Leader Bose', as he called him, was winning. The Gandhi market in particular was tailing off, as a result of earlier over-production.

When we went on a tour of his workshop, I asked Mr Wagh why his statues were so tall, rather than life-size. He picked up a bronze arm belonging to Sardar Patel, stroked it, and answered with great seriousness that an increase of 20 per cent on real height ensured popular respect for the subject. 'Otherwise people might mock and make fun, as if he was a doll. A national hero should always be larger than life.'

When Subhas Chandra Bose arrived in Germany in the spring of 1941, his aim was to secure a 'declaration' on India by the Axis Powers in support of a free India. The request was considered, but no definite action was taken. Bose had meetings with officials, and proposed to the Foreign Minister, Ribbentrop, that a 'Free Indian Government' should be established. Aided by a loan, Bose hoped to raise a military force consisting largely of Indian prisoners-of-war, march them into India and sweep away the British Empire. Although such a course of action naturally appealed to the Nazis, they were astute enough to realize that it was impractical. Bose's contention that the Indian people were on the verge of a united uprising against their rulers was clearly wishful thinking.

For the next two years Bose was kept waiting. He was given a luxurious house in Charlottenburg in Berlin, with quasi-diplomatic status, a car, driver, cook and live-in lover. While the rest of Germany survived on rations, he took up alcohol, cigarettes and beef for the first time. The lover was an Austrian woman named Emilie Schenkel, with whom he had a daughter in late 1942. They had met in Vienna during the 1930s and, according to some reports, had secretly married. Bose persuaded various Indian activists from across Europe to join him in Germany, apparently unaware that their movements were being monitored by IPI agents. He travelled to Italy for a meeting with Mussolini, but the Duce was no more forthcoming than his German allies; the Foreign Minister Count Ciano wrote in his diary that 'the value of this upstart is not clear.'[24]

Bose and his colleagues were permitted to establish an 'Indian Legion', but to their disappointment only a few thousand Indians agreed to join, out of a total of nearly seventeen thousand held in German prisoner-of-war camps. The greeting '*Jai Hind*', 'Hail India', was adopted as their salutation, a springing tiger as their emblem, and the title 'Netaji' was given to Subhas Bose. At the time 'Netaji' was generally interpreted either as Führer or Great Leader, although today a more favourable gloss is put on it as simply being a respectful honorific. The factory of Rudolf Souval of Vienna provided '*Azad Hind*' ('Free India') stars, medals, swords and metal tiger heads for Bose's new army. They received little support from their German military trainers, most of whom exhibited stronger racial prejudice towards the recruits than their British counterparts had ever done. Some of the Indian Legion was sent to the Italian front, and proved to be of minimal military value.[25]

The Axis Powers were primarily interested in Subhas Bose for his propaganda value. He was allowed to start a 'Free India Centre' in Berlin, staffed by Indians, which published anti-British material and made regular radio broadcasts to the subcontinent in various Indian languages. After the Cripps Mission in 1942, Bose said in a broadcast: 'I can tell you with all seriousness that these three Powers [Japan, Germany and Italy] want to set India free and independent,' a statement that was clearly untrue.[26]

The precise nature of Bose's collaboration with Hitler's regime continues to be debated, with his supporters claiming it was an entirely pragmatic alliance. He was certainly more than the jackbooted fascist puppet depicted by the British press at the time, and he made it clear to German officials he was opposed to the racialism underlying Nazi ideology. However, the discipline of the Reich certainly appealed to him, and he said openly that his political philosophy amounted to 'a synthesis between National Socialism and Communism'.[27]

It was apparent to Netaji Bose that he would not get the backing he wanted in Germany, and after a private meeting with Adolf Hitler he was taken by submarine to Japan in early 1943. General Tojo proved more forthcoming, and Bose was given support in recruiting an Indian National Army from prisoners-of-war in the Far East. This had already been tried after the fall of Singapore and Malaya, when a fledgling force was set up by an Indian Army officer called Mohan Singh, aided by Rash Behari Bose, the revolutionary who was said to have thrown a bomb at Lord Hardinge's elephant in 1912. They had soon fallen out with each other, and the army collapsed.

The arrival from Europe of a politician of Bose's calibre was enough to generate considerable support among the two million Indians in the region. Huge rallies were held in Singapore pledging support and money, with crowds waving 'Liberty or Death' banners. Bose told them he wanted recruits for 'the liberation of India . . . I am confident that with the help of my countrymen in east Asia, I shall be able to organize such a gigantic force as will be able to sweep away the British power from India, in conjunction with those who have already been fighting at home . . . *Inquilab Zindabad, Azad Hind Zindabad*! [Long Live Revolution, Long Live Free India!]' They would march to the Red Fort in Delhi, he told them, and their war cry would be '*Dilli Chalo!*' (On to Delhi!), like the Meerut mutineers of 1857. He gave radio broadcasts in English and Bengali, telling his listeners in Churchillian tones that all he had to offer them was 'hunger, thirst, forced marches and death'.[28]

The support Bose managed to generate for his new Azad Hind Fauj (Free Indian Army, but usually known as the Indian National Army, or INA) was powerful and genuine. Although some captured Indian Army officers were tortured in an effort to make them join up, around ten thousand prisoners made a voluntary decision to back Bose. News of the Bengal famine was supposedly a significant factor in alienating men who had once sworn their loyalty to the King Emperor.

Bose was brutal and resolute in the pursuit of his goal, forcing rich Indians to contribute money to the cause, and sending the feared Japanese Security Police to visit defaulters. He sanctioned the use of 'finger pressers' and 'water treatment' on a suspected fifth columnist. Yet much of his backing was genuine. The Allied defeat in Asia in 1942 had caused grave damage to the standing of the British Empire, and many Indians living in Japanese-controlled territory assumed it was only a matter of months before it was swept away for good. For them Bose was not a fascist fellow-traveller but a hero, fighting for Indian independence on 'the second front'. The lack of effective IPI or Military Intelligence agents in the Far East at the time prevented the British authorities from realizing the strength of Bose's support, and they dismissed his army as Japanese-inspired fifth columnists, or 'JIFs'.

Soldiers were recruited into the INA from among the Indian civilian population of the Far East as well as from prisoner-of-war camps. The precise size of the INA varies widely depending on whose account you are reading: Military Intelligence in Delhi after the war believed it was about sixteen thousand strong, although its veterans claim a figure closer to fifty thousand, which includes many soldiers who were not properly armed. A 'Rani of Jhansi' regiment for women was formed, named after the warrior queen who had fought against the British in 1857. Subhas Bose asked a young doctor called Lakshmi Swaminathan to cut her hair, remove her sari and put on a khaki bush shirt. She agreed, having been an admirer of the radical Bengali politician since childhood, and became the regiment's commanding officer.[29]

Netaji Bose appointed himself Supreme Commander of the Indian National Army, as well as being Head of State, Prime Minister and War Minister of a Provisional Government of Azad Hind. Earlier in the war the Japanese had captured the Andaman and Nicobar Islands, so they were put under his theoretical control and renamed 'Shaheed' (martyr) and 'Swaraj' (self-rule). Eight countries around the world recognized

Bose's government, and he received a personal message of congratulations from the Irish Prime Minister Eamon de Valera. In October 1943 he declared war on Britain and the USA, despite lacking any military hardware. Within months he had moved his headquarters to Rangoon in Japanese-occupied Burma, where he had been imprisoned by the British in the 1920s. His government began to print its own currency, and Bose made fruitless attempts to obtain proper equipment for his soldiers from the Japanese.

It was agreed that the INA would accompany Japan's Imperial Army on their advance against the Allies at Arakan in Burma and Imphal in India. With his lack of military experience, Bose assumed this would be a fairly straightforward operation, and was under the impression that as soon as his forces reached Assam there would be a mass uprising by the Indian people against the British. However, the Allied army under General Slim were in a strong defensive position, and the Japanese were soon forced to retreat. The campaign was a disaster for both the Japanese and the INA, and more than half the total force died, many of them from disease.

It was a savage confrontation. In the summer of 1944 Lord Wavell received a letter from the Governor of Assam, Sir Andrew Clow, describing a tour of the battlefields in the Naga Hills. At Kohima, the site of the deepest Japanese advance into Indian territory, the land was 'scarcely recognizable', and covered in 'evidence of the grim fighting for the various hills. The whole scene is one of desolation which Stopford [the General commanding the 33rd Indian Corps] said reminded him of the Somme. The pleasant woods all along the skyline are reduced to shivered tree trunks with scraps of parachutes for foliage and all the open spaces are thick in mud and littered with bunkers and all the debris of war ... The Deputy Commissioner's compound seemed to be a graveyard of the men of the Dorsets, with a very few of his flowers growing amid the mounds.'[30]

According to Colonel Shah Nawaz Khan, who commanded an INA regiment, his troops were abandoned and left without supplies by the Japanese during the assault on Imphal. Although they engaged in some fighting, they occupied primarily defensive positions as they were not properly equipped. Many of them starved, and thousands of enfeebled INA soldiers were captured by the British. In desperation, Netaji Bose told members of his army to arrest any fellow soldier 'if he behaves in a cowardly manner or to shoot him if he acts in a treacherous manner'. When some soldiers deserted, Bose ordered the fashioning of effigies of them 'in cardboard or straw or clay ... either in human or in animal form', so that 'every member of the camp should give full vent to his disgust and hatred against the traitors'. This was to be followed by 'the singing of the National Anthem and collective shouting of slogans'.[31]

In May 1945 the INA surrendered in Rangoon, except for Bose and a handful of his soldiers who escaped. His retreating force suffered severe casualties, being bombed and strafed from the air. From the accounts of survivors it appears that Bose now became entirely fearless, having decided to die fighting. On several occasions he came within inches of death, which led his soldiers to believe he was charmed and invincible. After a six-week march they reached an area of Burma which was outside Allied control, and Bose fled first to Bangkok and then to the island of Formosa.

Back in India, captured INA soldiers were questioned. Those of high rank and 'more than ordinary security interest' were taken to the Combined Interrogation Centre at Delhi, which was controlled by the Director of Military Intelligence.[32] It soon became apparent to the debriefers that they were dealing not with press-ganged victims, but with devoted followers of Netaji Bose. They reported to Lord Wavell that captured INA troops were adamant that their march to Delhi ('*Dilli Chalo*') was not yet over. An interrogated INA officer believed that they failed 'solely owing to lack of equipment'. Up until now, the British had believed the INA consisted simply of conscripts and a handful of fanatical neo-fascists. Now all the information they were picking up showed this was inaccurate. Reports from the Intelligence Bureau stated that there was substantial popular support from the Indian public for the INA prisoners, and that it was too late for British counter-propaganda.

An officer in the Indian Army who had spent time with captured INA soldiers reported through SEAC's Military Intelligence system that they had been 'deeply affected by Subhas Bose's inspiring leadership and clever propaganda', and regarded themselves as 'the liberators of their motherland ... The personal influence of Subhas Bose on all ranks of the INA is tremendous and undeniable.' They continued to address each other by their INA ranks, so that a theoretically mutinous captain from the Indian Army was called 'Colonel Saheb'. The report concluded that the prisoners were 'thoroughly imbued with Bose's ideas', and that it was 'doubtful if they can be rehabilitated as soldiers again'.[33]

As popular unrest spread across India with the release of the Congress Working Committee and many other political activists, the fate of the captured soldiers of the INA became critical. It was apparent from the nationalist press that many Indians saw them as heroes, who in an act of perhaps misguided bravery had risked their lives to fight for their country's freedom. If the Allies had been willing to forge an alliance with the murderous Stalin in pursuit of a victory over Hitler, they said, why was it wrong for Netaji Bose to have joined hands with the Japanese Emperor?

Luckily for Leo Amery, he never had to deal with the problem, for he had been swept from power with many of his colleagues in the Labour avalanche in the British general election of July 1945. His departure was the cause of some glee in India, newspapers claiming he had been 'one of the main instruments of the British government for emasculating the Indian people'.[34]

Had Amery remained in office, he would have been in an embarrassing position, since his own son John had spent the war doing much the same as Bose – namely making broadcasts for the Germans and recruiting Allied prisoners-of-war, although in his case to fight the Russians rather than the British. His son's actions must have been a great burden, especially since Linlithgow had a son who was a prisoner of the Germans, Vickery's son died of his wounds in Italy a month before VE-Day, and Wavell's only son was severely wounded in a raiding column in Burma. John Amery was hanged as a traitor in Wandsworth Prison in December 1945. His father never returned to Parliament, devoting his final years to vigorous public activity and the writing of a convoluted, self-important autobiography. Leo Amery was not a believer in the virtue of compression: by the time of his death he had written three volumes, but not yet reached the India Office.

Three days after the Allied victory over Japan, Subhas Chandra Bose climbed into an aeroplane that was to take him from Formosa to Manchuria. It crash-landed on take-off, breaking into pieces and bursting into flames. There are various accounts of this event, with minor discrepancies between them which have led to elaborate theories that Bose did not die but escaped to the Soviet Union. As his death had twice been reported erroneously in the past, even Lord Wavell had doubts when he first heard about it.

The recently released archives of Indian Political Intelligence prove conclusively that Bose was killed in 1945. Since rumours were circulating that he was still alive, IPI arranged for Military Intelligence in Delhi to investigate the matter. Captain Turner of the War Crimes Liaison Section in Formosa was put on to the case, and he managed to locate the last person to have seen Bose alive. This was Captain (Medical) Taneyoshi Yoshimi, who was under arrest in Stanley Gaol. He gave a statement that resolved the matter: 'I personally cleaned his injuries with oils and dressed them. He was suffering from extensive burns over the whole of his body, though the most serious were those on his head, chest and thighs ... During the first four hours he was semi-conscious ... He murmured, and muttered in his state of coma, but never regained consciousness. At about 2300 hrs he died ... I injected Formalin into the body, and also had the coffin partly filled with lime.'[35] The coffin was then taken away and Bose's body was cremated.

In September 1945 the All-India Congress Committee passed a resolution on the INA saying: 'it would be a tragedy if these officers, men and women were punished for the offence of having laboured, however mistakenly, for the freedom of India,' and calling for their release.[36] Despite the warning signs, the Commander-in-Chief Field Marshal Auchinleck decided with Wavell's blessing to hold a court martial in the symbolic public setting of Delhi's famous Red Fort in November. Three senior INA officers, one Muslim, one Hindu and one Sikh, were put on trial and charged among other things with 'waging war against the King'. It was an immense political miscalculation; had the court martial taken place with a little more speed and discretion, it might well have passed unnoticed.

Politicians who had previously condemned the Indian National Army rushed to support the three officers, saying they were simply patriots who had been caught on the losing side. Jawaharlal Nehru, who had at one point said he would fight against the INA, and even Sir Tej Bahadur Sapru, joined the defence team, which argued that the three had been fighting on the orders of Bose's legally constituted Government of Azad Hind, and so were not mutineers. They were convicted and sentenced to transportation for life all the same, but Auchinleck was so overwhelmed by the public outcry that he cashiered and released them soon afterwards. With India already on the verge of breakdown, he could not do anything that might provoke a collapse in the loyalty of the Indian Army. The Intelligence Bureau submitted a report which stated that 'there has seldom been a matter which has attracted so much Indian public interest', and that any punishment of INA soldiers would result in 'racial bitterness which will last down through the ages'.[37]

Wavell himself was adamant in his condemnation of the INA, regarding them as 'cowards and softlings'. This was occasioned by his instinctive soldierly dislike of deserters, as well as by the experience of meeting Gurkha soldiers who described torture by Bose's followers. Having had his son's hand blown off by a grenade while leading an attack against the Japanese at Mogaung, Wavell's personal aversion to the INA was strong. In his view, they had sworn an oath to the King Emperor of their own free will, and their actions were contrary to all principles of military discipline.

His anger extended to their Congress supporters, whom he accused of having encouraged unrest while he was defending their country from invasion. As he told the King in 1946: 'I can never entirely rid my mind of the recollection that in 1942, at almost the most critical period of the war for India, when I was endeavouring as Commander-in-Chief to secure India with very inadequate resources against Japanese invasion, the supporters of Congresss made a deliberate effort to paralyse my communications to the Eastern front by widespread sabotage and rioting.'[38]

Although Wavell's colleague General Tuker thought the best destination for the heroes of the Indian National Army was 'the wall and the firing squad', it was finally agreed only to charge those soldiers who were known to have committed 'acts of gross brutality, resulting in some cases in death, upon their fellow countrymen'.[39] Even this was not a success, and the first trial provoked a fresh outcry. Throughout 1946 there were continual demonstrations calling for the release of the remaining INA detainees, and severe riots in Calcutta which showed Wavell how serious the possibility was of greater unrest. He postponed a final decision on the INA soldiers' fate, and a small number of them remained in custody.

The adulation of Bose in India today is enormous. He fulfils an important psychological role as the patriot who stood up to the British, despite the fact that in strategic terms his Indian National Army was an irrelevance. It did nothing to drive the British from India, although the INA trials did help to destabilize imperial authority. Bose was motivated by a conviction that the elimination of British rule was a moral duty that had to be achieved, at any price. This blinded him to the conduct of his German and Japanese allies, and to the military practicalities of what he was hoping to do. The last word goes to a Dhaka newspaper editor: 'Subhas Babu may have been a patriot, but he was foolish and short-sighted. I spent my youth fighting the British Empire, but I have to tell you this – if I was given a choice between Japan, Germany or Britain as my master, I would choose the British every time.'[40]

THIRTEEN

A Mass Battle for Freedom

The Labour victory of July 1945 increased the vigour of Indian nationalism, and was welcomed by many in Congress, who thought it 'a spur to quick action'.[1] The appointment of the seventy-four-year-old Freddie Pethick-Lawrence as Secretary of State for India, however, was not a cause for much rejoicing. A warm, friendly, waffling man with cordial aims for India, he had a dangerously loose grasp on the complexities of his new job. An old Etonian socialist with a substantial private income, Pethick-Lawrence was remembered by one fellow Labour MP as 'a foolish old dodderer [who had] graduated out of the trendy Left of his youth'.[2]

In his younger days, he and his wife had been vigorous campaigners for women's suffrage, even enduring prison and force-feeding in pursuit of the cause. During the war, Mrs Pethick-Lawrence had infuriated Churchill by making public appeals for the release of prominent female Quit India prisoners. Like his predecessor, Pethick-Lawrence had an academic approach towards Indian politics, and loved detailed and irresolute discussion. Unlike Amery, he had a strong bias in favour of Congress.

Pethick-Lawrence was quickly packed off to the House of Lords by Attlee, which stopped him from being able to make statements on India to the House of Commons. He was a poor public speaker, and was referred to by ill-mannered lobby journalists as 'Pathetic' Lawrence. The junior minister who spoke on his behalf in the Commons was Arthur Henderson, a stolid and unremarkable politician, which enabled Attlee and Stafford Cripps to take Parliamentary command on matters relating to India. Official policy now migrated from the sullen, bigoted intransigence of Churchill's wartime administration to a breathless, poorly informed and irrelevantly theoretical approach under Attlee's new model army.

Pethick-Lawrence's opening letter to Wavell set the tone for the rest of his tenure as India Secretary. 'I have only been in office a week and I have not had time yet to do more than begin to find my bearings,' he wrote.[3] In one of his first public statements on taking office, he proclaimed: 'All through my life I have been greatly attracted to the Asiatic attitude towards fundamental issues' – whatever that might mean. 'Although I lay no claim whatever to be an Orientalist ... I can say that I am acquainted with the elementary conceptions which form the basis of Indian thought and that they have exercised a profound influence on my life.'[4]

Joined by the dispassionate Clem Attlee, the cadaverous Stafford Cripps, the impish Education Minister Ellen Wilkinson, Viscount Stansgate (the former India Secretary William Wedgwood Benn) and the young Earl of Listowel (who had briefly been a junior minister at the India Office during the war), Pethick-Lawrence formed a new India Committee. Its remit was extended to cover Burma as well.

In August, a few days after the defeat of Japan, Attlee's new government summoned Wavell home for talks. The Reforms Commissioner V.P. Menon and George Abell accompanied him. Wavell found the new Secretary of State for India to be 'a most charming old gentleman', but loquacious and politically vague. Labour MPs were concerned that detained political activists should be released, and wanted the Congress Socialist Party to be unbanned, but otherwise daily worries over fuel and rationing at home left little time for Parliamentary interest in India.

In his spare time, the Viceroy went to see Winston Churchill, who told him in a typically grandiloquent simile that 'the anchor' (meaning himself) had gone and that Wavell was now 'on a lee shore with rash pilots'. The former Prime Minister's legacy had already been severely undermined, despite his wartime victories. As the historian John Charmley has written, 'Churchill stood for the British Empire, for British independence and for an "anti-Socialist" vision of Britain. By July 1945 the first of these was on the skids, the second was dependent solely upon America and the third had just vanished in a Labour election victory.'[5]

The new Labour Government's India policy was to create a 'constitution-making body' of unelected Indians, to attempt to put together a politicized Viceroy's Council, and to resurrect the Cripps offer of 1942, although it should have been apparent that it had little life left in it. Their most important decision was to hold fresh elections to the assemblies of the eleven provinces of British India, and to the central assemblies in New Delhi.

The Governor of the Punjab, Sir Bertrand Glancy, thought an election would be a mistake. He pointed out that Jinnah would be 'hailed as the champion of Islam' for entirely the wrong reasons: 'I am gravely perturbed about the situation, because there is a very serious danger of the elections being fought, so far as Muslims are concerned, on an entirely false issue . . . The uninformed Muslim will be told that the question he is called on to answer at the polls is – Are you a true believer or an infidel and a traitor?'

Glancy believed that an undivided Punjab being shoehorned into a Muslim Pakistan would lead to rebellion by Hindus and Sikhs: 'the consensus of opinion is that, if Pakistan becomes an imminent reality, we shall be heading straight for bloodshed on a wide scale; non-Muslims, especially Sikhs, are not bluffing, they will not submit peacefully to a Government that is labelled "Muhammadan Raj". Hence it appears to me to be of vital importance to take action, before it is too late, to deflate the theory of Pakistan.'[6] Glancy was right about the risks of the League fighting the campaign on a false platform, but he was perhaps ignoring the likely political fall-out of a failure to hold an election of any kind. Congress was seriously restless, and had the power to provoke a mass uprising if it chose.

The problem for Wavell was that nobody in Whitehall seemed to have realized that monumental changes had taken place in the Indian political consciousness during the war years. They did not take up his suggestion that the demand for Pakistan should be faced squarely, and before long Wavell gained the impression that the Labour Government were 'obviously bent on handing over India to their Congress friends as soon as possible'.[7] Still, at least Attlee only kept his envoy waiting for just over a fortnight, rather than the five months Churchill had allowed to pass, before giving him something that resembled a policy.

Light relief was provided by Chips Channon, who had retained his Parliamentary seat while Tories all around were losing theirs. Channon reported in his diary that the Viceroy was 'fatter and browner' than before, and wished him to come out to India on holiday. Wavell even intervened with Pethick-Lawrence in an attempt to get Channon a seat on an aeroplane, but there were thousands of others with more pressing claims to go east. The pair of diarists had to make do with cocktails with Noël Coward and Lady Diana Cooper, to which Wavell arrived punctually, 'on foot, followed by a detective'. The next night they dined alone at Claridge's, and a few days later Channon scampered down to the BOAC station to watch 'the luxurious Vice-regal train pull out' and have 'an affectionate conversation' with his friend. 'The Viceroy is really an old sweetie,' he wrote, 'but very cautious in his dealings with Government officials.'[8]

Back in New Delhi, there were internal changes at Viceroy's House, the faithful Peter Coats leaving after six years' service as, successively, Wavell's ADC, Secretary and Comptroller. Evan Jenkins departed to take over from Glancy as Governor of the Punjab, a crucial position, and his job as Private Secretary to the Viceroy was taken by the young but formidable George Abell. Abell was to become perhaps the most important ICS official in the years leading up to independence, with the possible exception of the Reforms Commissioner V.P. Menon, who consolidated his position significantly during the final year of British rule.

Abell had joined the ICS in 1928, served as a District Officer in the Punjab, and become Deputy Private Secretary to Wavell just before his fortieth birthday. Some Congress officials regarded him as pro-Muslim, but there is no real evidence to support this. One of Abell's friends described him as 'big, genial, good-looking, confident and totally trustworthy. Although he was a triple blue he wasn't smug or pompous, I think because he felt at ease with himself. He was a real Wavell fan. He admired the Viceroy's reticence and his learning, but sometimes had to cool him down in his dealings with London. George was always very discreet about his time as Private Secretary – "private means private", he would say – but he did indicate that Wavell had used him as an intermediary with Gandhi, whom he found difficult.'[9]

In November 1945 Nehru told Wavell he 'could make no terms whatever with the Muslim League under its present leadership and policy', since it was 'a reactionary body with entirely unacceptable ideas'.[10] Wavell was coming to believe that any Congress-backed outbreak of mass popular unrest would be almost impossible to quell, since the police and the army were so demoralized. India was becoming frenzied, with Congress calling for immediate independence under a government of their choosing, and Jinnah announcing that 'Pakistan is a question of life and death for us.'

Wavell was clear that firm action of some kind had to be taken at once, whether it was conciliatory or repressive. At the same time as worrying about politics, he was having to deal with issues such as substantial labour unrest, serious food shortages in southern India, the decimalization of India's coinage, and a lack of coal.

Wavell sent a secret memorandum to London in early November saying: 'We are now faced in India with a situation of great difficulty and danger ... Congress leaders everywhere, but particularly Vallabhbhai Patel in Bombay and Nehru and Pant in the United Provinces, have been making statements and speeches which can only be intended to provoke or pave the way for mass disorder ... I must accordingly, with the utmost gravity, warn HMG to be prepared for a serious attempt by the Congress, probably next spring, but quite possibly earlier, to subvert by force the present administration in India. Half measures will be of no use in dealing with a movement of this kind, and the choice will lie between capitulating to Congress and accepting their demands – whatever they may be – and using all our resources to suppress the movement.'[11]

Around this time, Nehru declared in a public speech: 'India must not wait for the next move of the Labour Government,' but should 'prepare herself for a mass battle for freedom'.[12] Wavell heard echoes of 1942, when Congress had succeeded in provoking what Linlithgow called 'the most serious rebellion since that of 1857', with a minimal amount of planning or preparation. He knew that this time an uprising would be hard to withstand.

The Viceroy assessed that there were eleven British and forty-four Indian infantry battalions (a little under fifty thousand soldiers) available for the maintenance of internal security, with a variety of infantry brigades, armoured regiments, and one airborne division potentially available from GHQ Reserve.[13] In addition, the army had its usual back-up: logistics staff, transport personnel, signallers, doctors, engineers, military police and the Service Corps or 'Jam Stealers'. Yet each soldier was theoretically charged with the control of ten thousand Indian civilians. If suppression was to be the British government's chosen course in response to a widespread uprising, Wavell would need reinforcements. The War Office quickly decided that there were no more British troops available to be sent to India.

The Commander-in-Chief in India, Auchinleck, reported on 1 December that conflict was looming: 'Congress will have learned from the 1942 disturbances how easily rail, road and telephone communications can be disrupted and the paralysing effect of such disruption ... There are now large quantities of unlicensed arms throughout India and there will be many ex INA men to use them, if they feel so inclined.'[14] Things could only be worse the second time round. As one of his military advisers wrote, they would be 'extremely lucky to get through till June next without serious trouble'.

As 1945 came to an end, Wavell felt able to write in his diary that despite the limitations in the approach adopted by Attlee and Cripps, 'a Labour Government has on the whole made things easier, since rather more attention is paid to India and the outlook is rather more sympathetic'. However, 'I shall consider myself very fortunate if I am writing with any cause for satisfaction at the end of 1946.'[15]

The next proposal put up by London was that a cross-party delegation of a dozen political shakers should go out to India, to try to get some grasp on what was happening. As Freddie Pethick-Lawrence told Attlee, perhaps thinking of himself, 'There are a good many Members of the Party who take a keen interest in India but lack real knowledge about it.'[16] The group arrived on 5 January 1946, 'many hours late and rather weary', reported Wavell, but 'I like what I have seen of them.'[17]

Gandhi's treatment of the Parliamentary Delegation was disturbing. For some time he refused to see them, and when he did, he would not take part in any serious discussion. When they tried to get down to policy, he would just repeat mantras such as 'Get off our backs' and 'The slave clings to his chains,' as if that would solve matters. He was busy 'testing' the British MPs in his usual fashion; as one member of the Delegation wrote, 'Gandhi was always testing other people's sincerity but keenly resented anyone trying to test his.'[18]

The problem with Gandhi at this stage in his life was that he lacked a willingness to make the necessary adjustments in his outlook now that the British were clearly making plans to leave India. Instead, he followed his old patterns of behaviour, as if he were still fighting the battles of the 1920s and thirties. The Governor of Bengal told Wavell in December 1945 that during a private interview with him, Gandhi had insisted 'that all recent violent Congress speeches were outcome of failure at Simla ... His political reasoning lacked realism and balance.'[19]

On their return to Britain after a month, the Parliamentary Delegation trooped off to Downing Street to report to Attlee. None of them came up with anything very useful, although Muriel Nichol and Reg Sorensen (one of Churchill's wartime *bêtes noires* over British oppression in India) thought that whatever their personal inclinations, the principle of Pakistan needed to be conceded as soon as possible. One delegate seriously 'emphasized the urgency of the issue', and stated presciently that if 'the Muslim League were bypassed in relation to constitution making, there would be widespread violence. Therefore, it is necessary to offer Jinnah Pakistan on the basis of the Muslim Majority Areas.'[20]

The author of this statement was Major Woodrow Wyatt, who had just been elected to Parliament as a youthful Labour MP. Although in later years Wyatt was to gain a reputation as a right-winger, largely owing to his tabloid commentary under the amusingly inaccurate headline 'The Voice of Reason', in 1946 he was one of Labour's rising stars. The future of India had become a topic of great concern to him, and unlike most of his colleagues, he had actually troubled to go there and find out what was happening before forming a fixed opinion. Wyatt realized that Pakistan was more than a fantasy in Jinnah's mind; it was a serious proposition with support from many Indian Muslims.

Three days after Christmas 1945, Wavell sent the India Office a study of the political situation, developing his claim that the objective of Congress was to seize power for itself, since the leadership was not in a mood for compromise. If they chose to, they could launch a revolt against British rule along the lines of the Quit India movement. Wavell therefore drew up a top secret emergency plan to be used 'if, as is quite likely, the Congress and the Muslim League are unable to come to any agreement on the Pakistan issue . . . It is of course essential that knowledge of this breakdown plan should be restricted to the smallest number of people and that there should be no disclosure.'[21]

This document laid down various observations, the essential one being that the British might be forced into the position of having to impose a unilateral settlement if Congress and the League would not cooperate with each other. If this were to happen, Wavell thought they should concede 'Pakistan' only in those areas where Muslims were in a defined majority. It would not be fair to Sikhs or Hindus to hand over to the Muslim League the whole of a province such as the Punjab or Bengal, since each side of the territory had a different communal composition. Wavell pointed out the obvious but apparently previously unnoticed fact that Jinnah would want an exact statement of the boundaries of the proposed Muslim areas: 'To meet such a request we should, I think, be ready with a detailed demarcation ... I will put forward proposals shortly.'[22]

The proposals were despatched to the India Office by Wavell on 7 February 1946, in the form of a telegram. It suggested possible boundaries for Pakistan, covering those areas where Muslims 'can advance a reasonable claim; modifications in boundary might be negotiated and no doubt the interests of Sikhs in particular would be carefully considered [as a way of] preventing immediate violence by Sikhs'.[23] It seems likely that the Viceroy was following the guidance of his Private Secretary George Abell, who knew from his service in the Punjab the importance of land settlements, rivers and district boundaries, and would have been well aware of the implications of what was being suggested.

Wavell's telegram represents one of the most important documents in the history of the transfer of power in India, since it was the first serious official attempt to show what the Muslim League's 'Pakistan' might mean in practice. He wrote that 'if compelled' to demarcate those areas in the north-east of India where Muslims were in a genuine majority, he would recommend the Chittagong and Dacca (Dhaka) divisions, the Rajshahi division excluding Jalpaiguri and Darjeeling, the Sylhet district of Assam, and the three eastern districts of the Bengal Presidency. On no account could Calcutta be included, as it had a Hindu majority. However, it was possible that it could become a 'free port' in exchange for some concessions over the central government by the League. The boundaries that Wavell's telegram gave to the eastern wing of 'Pakistan' correspond closely to the borders of East Pakistan that would be drawn in August 1947.

More importantly, in the case of the north-west of India, Wavell faced up to the insoluble complication of having over five million members of the Sikh minority scattered through the Punjab. Although most of them were in the east of the province, there were over half a million Sikhs in the west Punjab districts of Rawalpindi, Lyallpur and Montgomery. So, as potential 'Pakistan' territory, Wavell recommended Sind, the North-West Frontier Province, British Baluchistan (the rest of Baluchistan consisted of Princely States), and the main administrative divisions of western Punjab – namely Rawalpindi, Multan and Lahore, but 'less Amritsar and Gurdaspur districts'. As Kashmir was a Princely State, it was not mentioned.

Although this definition of the western wing of Pakistan lost the natural border imposed by the Beas and Sutlej rivers (the boundary of the great nineteenth-century Sikh ruler Ranjit Singh), Wavell stated: 'Gurdaspur must go with Amritsar for geographical reasons and Amritsar being sacred city of Sikhs must stay out of Pakistan.'[24] This was a simple point, and had it been agreed at once by the India Office as a matter of policy, much bloodshed might have been averted. In essence, Wavell was asserting that since the city of Amritsar and its surrounding district constituted the heart of Sikhdom, it would clearly be impossible to place it within a Muslim homeland.

Given that Amritsar could not become part of Pakistan, the adjoining district of Gurdaspur (which was only 51 per cent Muslim) should also stay out of Pakistan so as to give Amritsar some geographical protection. If Gurdaspur did go to Pakistan, the thousand square miles of Amritsar district would be cut off and left as a lone Sikh island, floating in a hostile Muslim sea. On all sides Amritsar would be bounded by Pakistani ground, except on its south-eastern flank, where it would border a Princely State called Kapurthala. This small kingdom was inhabited by a Muslim majority, although its ruler was a Sikh, and it would in practice have cut off Amritsar Sikhs from their co-religionists to the east. On paper the question of Gurdaspur and Amritsar looked like a minor point, but it was to prove a focus of the start of the massacres of August 1947. On any neutral assessment, it was clear that Gurdaspur and Amritsar would have to be treated as if they were one unit, whether they became part of India or of Pakistan.

The response of the officials back in London is instructive. Six days after the despatch of Wavell's telegram, a junior clerk at the India Office drew three primitive sketch maps on the basis of the information that the Viceroy had provided. Significantly, Gurdaspur district was marked as being part of the potential Pakistan, although there is no written explanation for this decision, and in all other respects Wavell's advice was followed to the letter. There is however no sign of political motivation, as the main map is simply titled: 'Northern India showing "Pakistan" confined to Moslem-majority districts', and Gurdaspur did on paper have a Muslim majority.[25] It was probably a simple clerical error, even if it was to have far-reaching symbolism.

As Wavell's document revolved around Whitehall, each civil servant made his observations in its margin. There is a sense from their notes that they were rather astounded by what Wavell had written, yet knew they had to take it seriously. As Paul Patrick, the influential Assistant Under-Secretary at the India Office, minuted: 'It is difficult to believe in the viability of this from the financial, economic or defence standpoints.'[26] It is clear from the civil servants' reactions that none of them favoured the dismemberment of Britain's Indian Empire at independence, or thought that the creation of Pakistan would be beneficial. The claim that the British had secret plans all along to partition India (an allegation that is still believed by many Indians of a certain age) cannot be supported from the internal memoranda and documentation of Whitehall officialdom.

At a meeting with the Director of the Intelligence Bureau in mid-January 1946, Wavell heard 'that Congress is in militant mood and out gunning for the Muslims, confident that they can down them. [The DIB] thinks they are prepared to take office in the Provinces . . . and will then secure control of Government servants and make [British] action against Congress impossible.'[27] It was the most serious threat assessment the Intelligence Bureau had made to date.

On 18 February, sections of the Royal Indian Navy mutinied in Bombay for six days, and were backed by some technical units of the army. The original provocation had been the conduct of various British naval officers, in particular Commander King of the frigate *Talwar*, who was prone to address his men as 'black bastards' and 'jungli Indians'. The Bombay mill-workers joined the naval ratings, and a sense of incipient revolution spread across parts of the country. Crowds brought food for the mutineers. At its height the mutiny involved seventy-eight ships and twenty thousand sailors, extending to Calcutta and Karachi.

Congress were disturbed by the actions of the Royal Indian Navy, and fearful of losing control over the freedom movement if they supported the uprising. The Bombay Communist Party launched a general strike, but to Wavell's relief Patel intervened by going to Bombay to persuade the mutineers to surrender. Over two hundred people were killed by troops during the restoration of authority, and hundreds more were injured. Many nationalists saw Congress's failure to support the naval rebellion as a betrayal, feeling that they were now more interested in power than in freedom. One of the mutiny's leaders, B.C. Dutt, claimed later that the cowardice of politicians had encouraged the break-up of India: 'Our struggle was gradually affecting the Indian army ... There would have been a fight; many of us would have died, but there would have been far less bloodshed than in 1947.'[28]

Congress was no more willing than the British government to give an unequivocal statement of its position over the Muslim League's demand for Pakistan. It was nervous of its own unity unravelling if it were to face the issue directly. The handful of nationalist Muslims within Congress, such as Azad, were a vulnerable target, as was the claim that the movement represented all regions, minorities and scheduled castes. Like the British, they hoped that by ignoring Jinnah he would simply go away. They failed to bear in mind that he was a seriously tenacious operator, whose trump card was his claim that the forthcoming provincial elections of late 1945 and early 1946 were in effect to be a referendum on Pakistan.

There was a strong religious edge to the Muslim League's campaign, with students from Aligarh Muslim University parading through rural villages, invoking the martyrdom of Imam Husain, the grandson of the Prophet, and telling the locals that in the new Congress Raj cows would be tethered in their mosques. Urdu poems were written and recited, with verses such as: 'Do you remember the Dilli [Delhi] wallahs [i.e. the Mughal emperors],/They lived in the Red Fort once,/You were kings then, you carrot-eating wretches,/But only those who wield a stick can protect their sisters.'[29]

Congress won a landslide victory in the elections. They formed the government in all the provinces of British India except Bengal and Sind, where the Muslim League took control, and in Punjab, where a Unionist–Congress–Panthic Sikh coalition under Malik Sir Khizar Hyat Khan Tiwana came in despite the League having won the largest share of the vote. This meant that Congress provincial leaders were back in the positions of power they had held before their resignation from office in 1939–40, and this gave a corresponding boost to the status of the Congress leadership in New Delhi. In the provinces of the proposed Pakistan, things were as chaotic as ever: it was only in Muslim minority areas such as the United Provinces that Pakistan seemed unreservedly popular. It was seen as a homeland and a safe haven for Muslims, while its status as a sovereign nation would reinforce the position of those Muslims who remained in Hindustan.

Across the eleven provinces of British India, Congress won around 90 per cent of the seats, while the League gained about the same proportion of the reserved Muslim seats. In the elections for the Central Assembly in New Delhi, the League took all thirty Muslim seats. As Jalal put it: 'Jinnah's success at the polls in 1946 owed a great deal to the reluctance of the British to tell the voters what Pakistan entailed . . . With the British and the Congress sitting on the fence, Muslims, whatever their persuasion, saw the best security in having a strong spokesman in the final negotiations to settle these difficult matters.'[30] Thus the political claims of both Congress and the Muslim League were vindicated by the votes they received in the provincial elections, and communal antagonism was only enhanced.

In the Punjab, Jinnah had hoped to dislodge the Unionists. The province's Governor, Sir Bertrand Glancy, thought a clear statement that Ambala and Jallundur districts would not form part of Pakistan would at least give the Unionists something to campaign about, and would force the true effects of the Pakistan demand to be confronted. As London refused to clarify the borders of any Muslim homeland, and to specify how the province would or would not be partitioned, the election was presented to the voters as a battle between 'Pakistan' (the land of the pure) and 'Kafiristan' (the land of the non-believers). The position was damaged further in December 1945, when the Unionist ministry had to requisition grain, which was a drastic step in the 'breadbasket' of India. Although the Muslim League had few members in the Punjab, it gained seventy-five of the eighty-eight Muslim seats, and would have formed the government had it not been for the curious alliance between Congress, the Unionists and some Sikhs.

In Bengal, the concept of what Pakistan might be was rather different, although the League was hardly any better structured or organized. It seems that most Bengalis were determined to maintain a united Bengal. The local politician H.S. Suhrawardy was now the ostensible Muslim League leader, although he had numerous differences with Jinnah. As elsewhere, Bengali Muslims felt they could best be represented by the League, which looked as if it was championing Muslim interests in dealings with the British. It gained an overwhelming victory, polling almost 90 per cent of the total Muslim vote, and Fazlul Huq was the only candidate to win against a Leaguer. Immediately after the election, Suhrawardy tried to form a coalition with Congress, but this was vetoed by Congress leaders in New Delhi.

The local Sind Muslim League under G.M. Syed was in open revolt, forming a breakaway group known as the 'Syed League', which wanted an autonomous 'Sindhi Pakistan' or 'Azad Sind', with no Punjabi interference. In their elections there was no clear mandate for any one party, and a minority League administration was formed under Ghulam Hussain, at the discretion of the Governor. In the North-West Frontier Province the League took only seventeen of the thirty-six Muslim seats. However, this was simply because Congress, in the form of Khan Abdul Ghaffar Khan and his brother Dr Khan Sahib, had for many years had a power base on the frontier, and most Pathans appeared to vote entirely on local issues.

In the elections for the reserved Muslim seats in the Legislative Assembly in New Delhi, the League won a resounding 87 per cent of the vote, with Congress scraping little more than a token 1 per cent. Across India, the League had polled nearly three-quarters of all Muslim votes – a stunning improvement from its feeble performance a decade earlier. This support was based not on a grassroots movement, but on local politicians jumping on the League's bandwagon, and the use of religious and communal hatred as an electoral tactic. Jinnah had now been pushed forward as the champion of Islam and the public face of the demand for Pakistan. He knew he had to fulfil his mandate, or watch his support disappear as quickly as it had grown.

The rapid electoral success of the Muslim League during 1945–46 was dependent on an exploitation of extended family, kin and spiritual loyalties, especially in the Punjab, the province that was to be the cornerstone of the new state of Pakistan. Muslim leadership in rural Punjab had traditionally been centred on custodians of the shrines of Sufi saints, in the person of the hereditary *pirs* or spiritual guides who controlled them. In the 1937 elections, in which the League had not won a single Muslim seat in either Bengal or the Punjab, the *pirs* had treated the League as urban outsiders, and backed the Unionist Party as representing continuity and tradition. Now in 1945–46, with the collapse of Sir Sikander Hayat Khan's old Unionists, the clergy switched their backing to the League, which they saw as offering greater security and a possible opportunity to establish an Islamic state, based on the *sharia*.

The *pirs* issued religious directives or *fatwas* advising their followers to back the Muslim League at the polls. According to one study, the feudal control that *pirs* and landlords exercised 'was far more important in mobilizing support for the League than the popularity of its demand for Pakistan'.[31]

Jinnah was prepared to exploit this ambiguity in the pursuit of votes. Thus a 'Muslim' political party was brought to power on the back of a wave of vigorous religious nationalism, which misrepresented the aims of the essentially secularist League leadership back in New Delhi. For most voters, the credibility of Jinnah's stated ambitions was of secondary importance. As the historian Anita Inder Singh put it, for 'most Leaguers in 1945–6, Pakistan appears to have stood for some sort of general salvation from Hindu domination and symbolized an Islamic revival in India'.[32]

For Jinnah's opponents the results were shocking, since it was apparent that his rhetoric was based on popular support rather than on his own fantasy or the wishful thinking of a handful of reactionary ICS officials, as Jawaharlal Nehru had always liked to claim. Many leading Congressmen, locked away in prison since 1942, found their theories about the Muslim League tumbling down around their ears. Now they had to deal with Jinnah, whether they liked it or not.

By 1946, both Congress and the League were losing their grip over their followers, since the *goondas* of Bengal and Punjab had an agenda that neither Jinnah nor Gandhi could contain. At the end of March the DIB reported to Wavell that the British authorities were 'living on the edge of a volcano'.[33] Law and order in India was deteriorating fast, with Congress in a confrontational mood thanks to Churchill's culpable lack of policy over the previous three and a half years, and the sudden growth in the political clout of the Muslim League. The Viceroy's mood was only cheered by an intelligence report that the Congress Working Committee was anxious for a settlement, since its members felt that power might be slipping into the hands of a younger, more revolutionary generation.

FOURTEEN

A Large Piece of Green Baize

While Wavell's document about the potential borders of Pakistan was being pondered, Clement Attlee decided to exhume Sir Stafford Cripps and send a new mission to New Delhi. This idea had first been proposed by the rather unlikely figure of Major John McLaughlin 'Billy' Short, formerly of the 5/11th Sikhs, and now a liaison officer at the Ministry of Information. He was one of a crop of 'experts' whose views were sometimes sought and pondered by the India Office. Billy Short's notion was that a trio of ministers should be despatched to India with the 'ostensible purpose' of considering 'the terms of a treaty between Britain and India'; but that its secret purpose would be 'a missionary journey round India to create the right atmosphere'.[1]

It was late in the day to try a strategy of this kind, but Pethick-Lawrence liked the idea, and on 22 January 1946 it was minuted that the Cabinet agreed that 'a Mission of three Ministers of Cabinet rank should be sent to India, to arrive in the middle of March, to conduct the forthcoming negotiations on the constitutional problem'.[2] In mid-March the trio, consisting of Stafford Cripps, Freddie Pethick-Lawrence and the First Lord of the Admiralty, 'A.V.' Alexander, flew to India. It was now almost a year and a half since Wavell's original, urgent letter to Winston Churchill, telling him that His Majesty's Government had 'no longer the power to take effective action' and should 'move without delay'. During the interval India had been lurching out of control without any serious action being taken.

Accompanying this Cabinet Delegation, which was sometimes known as the Cabinet Mission, were eleven civil servants and hangers-on. They included a baffled Deputy Under-Secretary of State from the India Office, Sir William Croft, and the India Office's 'adviser on publicity questions', Alec Joyce. Joyce had worked as an 'officer on special duty' for IPI for two years during the 1930s, being awarded an OBE for his pains, so he may have had other activities to attend to apart from giving briefings to the press. There were also Majors Woodrow Wyatt and Billy Short, as personal assistants to Cripps.

The mission's aim was 'the setting up of machinery whereby the forms under which India can realize her full independent status can be determined by Indians ... with the minimum of disturbance and the maximum of speed.'[3] Its deliberations were assisted by a new-fangled innovation known as a 'Conference Facility': a secure teleprinter, rather like a primitive telex, which could be used for the immediate exchange of messages with London.

The gimlet-eyed Sir Stafford Cripps stepped into the white heat of the Indian summer with an absolute determination to find a resolution to the 'India Question', which was fast becoming an issue of such intense and tangled complexity that most British politicians preferred to steer well clear of it. It was like the Schleswig-Holstein Question, which Lord Palmerston claimed was only ever understood by three people – but the first was dead, the second was mad, and the third had forgotten. The Labour Party liked to think that Stafford Cripps was the only person who understood the India Question. Many Indians disagreed. As Nehru had written to a friend in 1942, Cripps had surprising 'woodenness and insensitiveness, in spite of his public smiles ... Always he seemed to impress upon us that he knew the Indian problem in and out and he had found the only solution for it.'[4]

During the war years, Cripps the scientist had been put in charge of aircraft production by Churchill, and now in Attlee's government he was wearing his economist's hat as President of the Board of Trade, charged with spending American cash in the pursuit of a post-war industrial recovery. Aided by his piercing legal mind and his experiences in 1942, he was confident he could find a settlement in India. It was made clear that he was in control of the mission, and that Alexander and Pethick-Lawrence had only been allowed on the outing to make it look more dignified. Although it was called a Cabinet Delegation, it was in fact a rerun of Cripps's wartime excursion, but this time without a growling Churchill pulling the plug back in Downing Street.

The Delegation's problem was that it was painfully ill-equipped for the task it faced. As Secretary of State for India, Pethick-Lawrence was the official leader of the mission, but he had literally no experience in the art of diplomatic negotiation. Cripps was the only one of the three delegates with any grasp of the intricacies of constitutional settlements or the principles of cutting a deal, but the trouble with him was that he knew his reputation as Labour's Indophilic fixer depended on securing an agreement, and he was willing to pay almost any price to get one. He had great mental ability, but poor judgement, being willing to dodge around in search of agreement. As Sardar Patel told Wavell some months later, Cripps was willing to say different things to different people.

The third member of the Delegation, Alexander, was a working-class Labour stalwart, renowned as a keen Protestant and drinker, but with no previous experience of India. He was a dedicated fan of Chelsea Football Club, staunchly patriotic, and he found politicians who dressed in *dhotis* 'baffling and tricky'. Alexander was in short an old-fashioned right-wing Labour Party imperialist, who had been sent by Attlee to leaven the decolonizing enthusiasm of the two public-school socialists he was accompanying. He tended on instinct to back Wavell's less credulous attitude towards Congress, and over the coming weeks the two men formed a diplomatic alliance, dining together while Cripps and Pethick-Lawrence loitered over *daal* and rice with their Congress contacts.

After one dinner at Viceroy's House, Alexander expressed a wish to play the piano. An instrument was carried in by 'six splendid Pathans in red uniforms', and the First Lord of the Admiralty banged out music-hall songs and even 'The Red Flag', to the horror of Wavell's ADCs. An ICS official was heard to murmur, 'Treachery to the Sovereign,' but the quietly subversive Viceroy found it most amusing.[5]

The Delegation, which had now been joined by Wavell in his capacity as Governor General, had its first meeting with Indian nationalist politicians on April Fool's Day. The encounters began without any coherent agenda, remit or common strategy having been established between the four British negotiators. Nor was there a clear idea about what they hoped to gain from consulting a particular person. Much of their time was spent talking to nonentities who had no real relevance to the transfer of control. Interviewees on the second morning ranged from the Nawab of Bhopal to the Sindhi leader G.M. Syed. That evening Wavell wrote in his diary that Pethick-Lawrence was 'a charming old gentleman but no man to negotiate with these tough Hindu politicians', since he began each meeting 'by giving away independence with both hands, and practically asking Congress to state their highest demands . . . he is no poker player'.[6]

The Pethick-Lawrence technique proved especially useless with

Mohammad Ali Jinnah, whose fondness for woolly idealism had evaporated at Nagpur in 1920. Wavell recorded that the Muslim leader endured 'ten minutes of rambling platitudes' about 'the welfare of the world . . . without any sign of interest', and that at the end of the meeting 'we had made no progress whatsoever'.[7] With Congress sitting tight, Jinnah's own demands became firmer than ever, since he knew the Muslim League's best hope of a favourable deal rested on a British-imposed settlement rather than on any subsequent haggling with a victorious Congress. Alexander, beer sweating out of his pores, observed that Jinnah was 'the only man I know who walks around with a built-in air-cooler'.[8]

Any attempt by the Delegation to argue with the cadaverous chain-smoker over the economic viability of Pakistan, or the practicalities of defending his north-western frontier without a unified military command, went nowhere. Jinnah was ruthlessly tenacious in the defence of his own position, and simply refused to concede any ground. Naturally, this improved his standing as a tough negotiator and fighter among his supporters. Many Muslims saw the machinations of the Cabinet Delegation as a straightforward attempt to deny their political claims, and some even wished to launch an immediate *jihad* to fight for their new nation. Jinnah knew this would be disastrous, and even hinted secretly that the British might retain control of defence and foreign affairs for many more years so as to protect minority interests.

The Quaid-i-Azam's grip on India's Muslims was strengthening perceptibly. One prominent Leaguer told a convention in Delhi in April 1946 that a bullet would have to first travel through the chests of a hundred million Mussulmans before it could touch their leader. Sardar Shaukat Hayat Khan, Sir Sikander's bloodthirsty son, said: 'I represent the martial clans of Pakistan who do not believe in words but in actions . . . I speak for the Punjabi soldier, and I say that three-quarter million demobilized soldiers in the Punjab are pledged to achieve Pakistan . . . we beg of you [Jinnah] to give the word of command.'[9]

Lord Pethick-Lawrence had little idea why he was in New Delhi beyond a vague, guilty desire to transfer power and give India her freedom. The question of who, precisely, was to be the recipient of that power was one which he had never seriously addressed. This was the problem that had to be faced again and again during Europe's mid-twentieth-century retreat from Empire, but Pethick-Lawrence was content to dodge it. In his opinion, the philosophy of the saintly Mahatma Gandhi and Pandit

Nehru seemed much the same as that mysterious 'Asiatic attitude towards fundamental issues' he had mentioned in his first meeting with the press. Pethick-Lawrence was sure that with enough cordial conversation between the parties, a solution could be reached.

Certainly the Indian National Congress was the only political grouping that could lay claim to mass support throughout the subcontinent. It certainly had a better case than anybody sitting in London for being the sole representative of the Indian people. However, its popular mandate rested only on elections within the provinces of British India with (owing to the mean-spirited terms of the 1935 Government of India Act) a severely restricted franchise. The inhabitants of the 561 Princely States had never had a chance to vote at all, while many Muslims, depressed castes, regionalists and hard-line Hindus rejected altogether the claim that Congress spoke on their behalf.

Gandhi and Nehru may have done their utmost to make their party an inclusive, nationwide movement of liberation, but it was hard to refute the charge that in practice it was controlled by northern Brahmins and Banias. Churchill's fears of a Congress takeover were beginning to be realized. The irony was that it had been his own repressive policy in India during the war years that had provoked mass political unrest and made India ungovernable. With British control ebbing away, Congress had stepped into the breach as the most credible alternative to the existing administration in New Delhi.

'I thought the interview with Gandhi, naked except for a *dhoti* and looking remarkably healthy, was rather a deplorable affair,' wrote the troubled Viceroy. Pethick-Lawrence was dribbling 'deference' and 'his usual sloppy benevolence', he wrote, while Gandhi 'began with the demand for the abolition of the salt tax . . . and finished with the meant-to-be plausible proposal that Jinnah should be asked to form a Ministry – the catch being that he would be subject to the Hindu majority in the Central Assembly (I had heard this idea put forward before) . . . G. is a remarkable old man, certainly, and the most formidable of three opponents who have detached portions of the British Empire in recent years: Zaghlul [in Egypt] and de Valera [in Ireland] being the other two. But he is a very tough politician and not a saint.'[10]

If the Field Marshal had an acerbic view of the Mahatma, it was based on direct, first-hand experience. Having been released from prolonged imprisonment during which his wife and secretary had died, and he himself had come close to death, Gandhi was intransigent. He believed control should be handed over to Congress as soon as possible, and that it should be up to them rather than the British how power was devolved to the Indian people. His proposal that Jinnah should form a Muslim League administration was an idea he had been floating for some time, and was clearly destructive since the League could never have carried a majority in the assembly, and would soon have been swept from office. Gandhi's tactic here was identical to the 'Bose Protocol' he had used at Tripuri in 1939, when he responded to Subhas Chandra Bose's unwelcome election as Congress President by inviting him to do his best, while at the same time demolishing the administrative framework that would have enabled him to operate.

As Wavell told Nehru, Congress was in practice asking the Delegation to 'hand over India to a single party' which was 'deeply distrusted' by Muslims, princely rulers and many others.[11] Given the assurances they had gained from the Labour Party in the past, it was understandable that Congress thought the three visiting ministers could be steamrollered.

Within days of the talks beginning, Wavell was in a state of barely suppressed anger and dismay. Freddie Pethick-Lawrence's only achievement was to have increased the political tension by making rash, benevolent promises to anybody he encountered. Wavell characterized the hopeful India Secretary as a 'gushing babbler', who was so full of 'long-winded appeasement speeches' that before long the one-eyed Viceroy was left wanting to grab hold of 'a large piece of green baize, a knobkerry or some other extinguisher'.[12]

There was no serious attempt in the talks to answer Sikh demands for political protection, despite Billy Short's support for their claims. The accepted British view was that other matters had to be dealt with first. 'Master Tara Singh,' wrote Wavell rather cynically one evening, 'came and poured all the sorrows and apprehensions of the Sikhs once more out of the back of his throat through his thick grey beard into my ear where it arrived a bit muffled but I had heard it all so many times before that I could pretty well have said his piece myself.'[13] In Wavell's view the Sikhs lacked 'political sense', and their case seemed to rest on the fact that they had received preferential treatment from the British in the past, and so should continue to have their support. It is clear that India's six million Sikhs were severely hampered by having no credible leader or spokesman in New Delhi during the 1940s.

The fate of the autonomous Princely States was also put to one side, although the British were clear that legally they had no choice but to allow them to retain their independent status once paramountcy (or overall British control) had reverted. In 1942 Cripps had been generous to the Princely States, saying that if they did not join the new Indian Union, they would 'remain in exactly the same situation as they are today', owing to the fact that their relations with the British were 'governed by treaties'.[14] There was even a suggestion that Imperial troops might be retained within their borders. However, within a short time the strong position of the princes was to be weakened by internal disputes. In December 1944 the leaders of their 'trade union', the Chamber of Princes, had resigned over a British proposal to adjust their formal relationship with the Crown Representative.

The princes themselves were operating incoherently by 1946, and their response to the possible end of imperial rule was craven and unrealistic. The Nizam of Hyderabad sent a telegram to Lord Wavell in May which summarized the princely approach. It contained the usual royalist platitudes, namely that India's princes 'boast to enjoy their high position and privileges under the benign rule of His Majesty the King-Emperor and whose untied [sic] voice is Long Live Britannia as presence of British Government is no doubt a sure guarantee of peace and tranquillity in India and a great blessing for Princely Order'.[15] Order, peace, tranquillity and the British government were all, however, on their way out.

Cripps was meanwhile bypassing his fellow delegates and concentrating on secret meetings and discussions, in the hope of securing a back-door agreement. He maintained lines of communication to different political groupings within Congress, while his assistant Woodrow Wyatt kept in touch with Jinnah and the League. At one point Cripps was even stuck with one visitor in a reception room while another hid in a bedroom, 'like a French farce'. Wavell disapproved strongly of this tactic of informal meetings, and was convinced Cripps was making promises which could cause subsequent problems. The complexity of the negotiations was such that Cripps was probably wise to keep all channels open, since informal contacts can often be crucial in resolving disputes of that type. Wavell was however right in objecting to Cripps and Pethick-Lawrence going to Gandhi's far from apolitical morning prayer meetings, since this increased the distrust of the Muslim League significantly.

After a few weeks, the Delegation had made a variety of concessions, but gained no points in return. The 'three Magi', as Wavell called his visitors, had even given ground over the control of any interim administration, which the Viceroy thought was one of the last bits of effective leverage the British had left. Since this would be a Congress–League coalition, he knew that he would only be able to hold it together if he retained his legal powers as Governor General. Nehru intended to call the interim cabinet a 'provisional national government', and insisted that it must have full sovereign powers. 'Congress,' noted the Viceroy, 'so far from giving away anything, have increased their demands, and Jinnah has not conceded an acre of Pakistan.'

Wavell was now pessimistic, writing that 'the frankincense of goodwill, the myrrh of honeyed words, the gold of promises – have produced little. Indian politicians are not babes even if they do wear something like swaddling clothes.'[16] The ill-structured approach of the Delegation had pushed the parties into extreme positions, and during one crucial breakdown in the talks Pethick-Lawrence told Jinnah to write down his demands on paper, which meant he would obviously not be able to rescind them later.

As the Cabinet Delegation went about its business, the imperial management team back in the bowels of Whitehall was getting worried. Since the beginning of the year, Philip Vickery had been coping with cuts in the 'contingencies' budget of Indian Political Intelligence, since the ICS officer who ran the Government of India's Home Department had felt unable to maintain a high level of funding given the political and financial climate in New Delhi. Vickery had pointed out that MI5, 'although considerably reduced in strength is still five times its pre-war size and I am told has no intention of reverting to anything like its pre-war establishment'. But he finally gave in and made cutbacks.

He reduced his personal staff to a superintendent, three 'officers' and ten secretaries, and agreed to 'eliminate two of my organizations, one in Canada and the other in Switzerland – the latter of which is in charge of a Vice-Consul who was nominated as such by the Foreign Office at my request', and who had been in the post for twenty-six years. Vickery was loath to sack any more of the agents and contacts who had been so painstakingly cultivated over the decades. He wrote a letter to the DIB saying he hoped Congress would 'realize the importance of the Intelligence machine' and 'cannot conceive' that they would 'hurriedly scrap that section of your office which collects external information'.[17]

However, it was not until the departure of the three Magi for India that Whitehall's security and intelligence agencies woke up to the gravity of the situation. It was possible that at the drop of a hat, responsibility for IPI and the IB might pass into the hands of their enemies, namely the Congress leadership. Vickery tried to limit the potential for damage by suggesting a transfer of control away from India. After all, 'I am not only acting as the DIB's representative in this country, but also assisting IIMG by functioning as the Indian section of the Security Service.'

He was especially worried by a personal communication he had received via India's Director of Military Intelligence, Major General O'Brien, who was on a visit to London: 'He told me that the DIB was very worried about the future of IPI and had asked him to convey a message to me to the effect that he was wondering if it could be handed over to other control e.g. in London.'[18] The DIB was no longer Sir Denys Pilditch, who had been switched to London in the middle of the previous year to act as an 'adviser to the Secretary of State for India'. The Intelligence Bureau was now run by the fearsome Norman Smith, who had joined the Indian Police in the same intake as Pilditch, and served as Inspector General of Police in Bombay during the Quit India movement.

There were serious legal and constitutional implications in this projected course of action. IPI had been set up at a time when British authority over the Government of India was absolute, so the current problem had never been envisaged. Initially it had been funded and run by the India Office, but after the 1935 Government of India Act came into effect it was reconstituted as an autonomous branch of the Intelligence Bureau and funded by the Home Department in New Delhi. Switching control of IPI and its band of agents to London would in effect constitute the theft of an important Indian asset by what was shortly to become a foreign power.

Throughout March 1946 there were discussions between the India Office and MI5 over the best course of action. They were agreed that 'even if the Commonwealth tie is not broken' it was 'very unlikely that the present system could survive'. Then, on 25 April, as the Commonwealth premiers met in London, Cripps went about his business in India, and

Palestine went up in flames, an extraordinary meeting of the Empire's senior spooks took place at a building a few minutes' walk from Parliament Square.

The participants were 'C' – Sir Stewart Menzies, the urbane former master of the Eton beagles, now master of spies at SIS, who had brought along Colonel Valentine 'Vee Vee' Vivian, a dapper Indian Police officer with a glass eye; 'K' – Sir David Petrie, the dour head of the Security Service who had previously worked in IPI and served as Director of the Intelligence Bureau for much of the 1920s, and still bore scars on his legs from being shot by a Sikh Ghadr revolutionary in 1914, accompanied by Dick White, who was later to successively head both MI5 and MI6; the DIB – the hard-nosed Norman Smith, summoned urgently from New Delhi on a 'flying visit'; the uninspiring Sir David Monteath ('*Recreations*: golf, gardening'), the most senior civil servant in the India Office; and Paul Patrick, the Assistant Under-Secretary of State for India who acted as the nexus between the India Office and the secret services (hence '*Club*: Travellers').

After some consideration it had been decided to exclude Vickery from the discussion, since the meeting's ostensible purpose was to consider 'the future of the Indian Intelligence organization in the United Kingdom', and his presence might have caused embarrassment.[19] He was, however, shown the minutes of the meeting, which were taken by a trusted amanuensis of Paul Patrick called Mr Gibson. Although some details of the encounter are still retained under Section 3/4 of the Public Records Act 1958, that ubiquitous scourge of the researcher into Whitehall's archives, the gist is clear.

The men agreed they 'might be prepared to continue their present degree of cooperation [between the British secret services and the Indian administration] so long as DIB remained a European: but it is very unlikely that they would be prepared to cooperate if DIB as well as the Home Member were to be an Indian – in which event IPI would have to be closed down'. Smith informed them that arrangements had been made 'for the security and destruction if necessary of his records'. One of those present, presumably Petrie of MI5, ordered Smith to maintain his existing network of operatives by supplying the UK intelligence agencies 'with the information enabling them to establish relations with suitable contacts in India'.[20]

This was followed up a few months later at a meeting of the Joint

Intelligence sub-Committee, an offshoot of the Cabinet Committee which oversees Britain's security and intelligence agencies. According to a minute initialed by Paul Patrick (a portion of which is still classified), measures were agreed 'for safeguarding the records in India emanating from the British Security Service and SIS and steps were taken by the India Office and the Foreign Office to ensure that the recommendations were carried out. At the same time the Security Service and SIS were invited to examine the means of obtaining covert intelligence in India and adjacent countries and for this purpose to form conjointly a nucleus of experienced personnel.'[21] In the meantime, the spies would await the outcome of the negotiations of Cripps and his cohorts.

On 10 April the Cabinet Delegation had decided privately, on the basis of their consultations, that there were only two feasible options for Britain's Indian Empire.

Scheme A would be a loose federation of Hindu-majority, Muslim-majority and Princely States, with communications, defence and foreign affairs being conducted by a central government. At the centre, Hindus and Muslims would have, importantly for the League, equal representation. There would be a three-tier system of administration. At the top would be the small central 'union government', and at the bottom individual provinces. In the middle there would be groupings of provinces with a large degree of autonomy, and even the possibility of future secession.

Scheme B (which was treated as an emergency fall-back position) was for the creation of 'Hindustan' and a truncated 'Pakistan', with treaties of alliance between the two countries but no mutual centre. Attlee's reaction to this was that the demand for Pakistan should be accepted only if the alternative was 'complete failure to reach agreement and consequent chaos. But India will be confronted by grave dangers as a result of this partition.'[22] He ordered an urgent report from the Chiefs of Staff, who pointed out that 'Pakistan' would be vulnerable from all sides and might be forced to link up with neighbouring Muslim states in Central Asia. The Chiefs believed that: 'To operate effectively the communications of Hindustan and Pakistan must supplement each other as they were designed to do. Again, central control is essential.' Perhaps their greatest unspoken worry was that the established system of Commonwealth Defence, which depended crucially on the Indian army, would be destroyed. They asserted that India's defensive position would be weakened by the creation of Pakistan, and its 'strong and well-equipped' army destroyed.[23]

It is clear that Attlee was anxious to maintain India as a loose, united federation, since he had an instinctive antipathy towards Jinnah and the Pakistan demand. The problem he faced was whether Jinnah would accept such a compromise, with its inherent risks of Hindu domination of Muslim-majority areas. On 11 April Attlee held a meeting of the Cabinet, and for the first time the British government gave a formal authorization of Pakistan, if only in principle and as a final resort. It was agreed that the Cabinet Delegation should strive to preserve unity, but could accept a Muslim homeland 'if they were satisfied that there was no other basis on which an agreed settlement could be reached'.[24]

In early May the Cabinet Delegation decided that everybody should decamp up to the cool of Simla and begin discussion on the basis of the positions that had been outlined in New Delhi. It was time for face-to-face meetings between the Cabinet ministers, Congress and the Muslim League. Throughout the month of May they sat and talked: Wavell, Cripps, Alexander and Pethick-Lawrence on one side, and opposite them four representatives of each party. There was manifest mutual hostility, Jinnah refusing to shake hands with Azad at the opening session, and calling him a 'stooge' of the Hindus. Maulana Azad by now had to put up with extremely offensive vilification from many Muslims, who referred to him not only as a 'stooge' and 'show-boy', but as 'the dog of the Hindus'.

The League's quartet included two placemen, while the well-tailored Jinnah made the running in consultation with his genial colleague Liaquat Ali Khan. Congress sent a pair of Muslims as a matter of principle: the worried, cooperative but increasingly uninfluential Azad, and the giant frontiersman Khan Abdul Ghaffar Khan, who sat with his head wrapped in a *khadi* shawl saying little, and was deemed by Wavell to be 'stupid but obstinate'. Jinnah compared the Khan to 'a bearer who comes with a chit saying he speaks perfect English but when you talk to him he doesn't understand a word'.[25] The serious negotiating was done for Congress by Nehru, who was 'able and clear in statement', and the omnipotent Sardar

Patel, a man described by Wavell as having 'a Roman face, powerful, clever, uncompromising'.[26]

Sardar Vallabhbhai Patel was now seventy-one. He had shaved off his moustache and become almost bald, which gave a smooth setting to his penetrating eyes. His many years of political experience, from *satyagraha* campaigns in Gujarat in the 1920s to control over the 1937–39 Congress provincial ministries, had given him an unchallenged status at the heart of the Congress machine. When a visiting sycophant said to him, 'Sardar Saheb, you must write India's history,' he responded with a sardonic growl, 'We do not write history. We make history.'[27] He rarely wrote anything down, preferring to give verbal orders, which he expected to be fulfilled without demur. His office and household were under the control of his stone-faced widowed daughter Manibehn, who wore a large bunch of keys round her waist, and was renowned for issuing peremptory commands. It was assumed that her word was that of the Sardar, so it was never challenged.

From time to time Gandhi would intervene, although never at the main negotiations. He had been brought to Simla in a special train, accompanied by a fifteen-strong entourage of whey-faced disciples. On appropriate evenings he would materialize, listen, and break his silence at ten minutes to eight precisely. He would generally try to resurrect the subject of the salt tax ('As a means of harassing the masses, it is a measure of which the mischief is indescribable'), demand the dismissal of his enemy the scheduled caste leader Dr Ambedkar, and oppose any concessions that his side looked like making.[28] Wavell was surprised when the Mahatma 'seemed quite unmoved at the prospect of civil war', and reached the conclusion that Cripps's secret dealings with Gandhi were leading nowhere.

Throughout his time in India, Sir Stafford had acted as if he were on the verge of a breakthrough, scuttling about hither and thither at ever greater speed. He worked exceptionally hard, and was knocked sideways once or twice by intestinal ailments despite his carrot and orange-juice diet, and the daily delivery of a pot of goat's curd by one of Gandhi's assistants. The tangible results of his scuttling and his obsession with textual detail were hard to find. 'I am not at all persuaded that C[ripps] had led G[andhi] up to the altar,' wrote the jaundiced Viceroy. 'I believe it is more likely that G. has led C. down the garden path.'[29]

On 12 May 1946 this second Simla Conference was closed down by

Lord Pethick-Lawrence, as there seemed no prospect of agreement. The Cabinet Delegation's next step was to issue a statement of their position, in the hope that it could be used as a structure around which a solution might be built. In this May Statement they said their aim was to create a 'constituent assembly' of elected representatives from the eleven provinces, who would frame a new constitution. They outlined 'Scheme A', promoting a unitary state with a weak centre controlling foreign affairs, communications and defence, the provinces being free to form autonomous regional groups. The document was fairly even-handed, despite explicitly opposing the creation of Pakistan. On 6 June the Muslim League accepted the May Statement, while saying it represented 'the first step on the road to Pakistan', which shows that Jinnah was willing to compromise in his search for a better deal.

Although the aims of Congress and the Muslim League were radically different, and Cripps thought Jinnah 'quite immovable in regard to the policy of Pakistan', it was apparent that he could be persuaded to accept something less than the full Pakistan demand.[30] The Delegation had made it clear early on that Jinnah could not expect the whole of Bengal and Punjab to be incorporated into Pakistan, but would probably have to be content with the removal of those districts where Hindus were in a clear majority. After Simla, 'Mr Jinnah said he would like to make it clear that the Muslim League had gone a long way in accepting the idea of a Union confined to three subjects.'[31]

Despite initial favourable noises, the leaders of Congress did not accept the May Statement. The Cabinet Delegation then concentrated on creating an interim government (a politicized version of the old Viceroy's Executive Council) as a way of breaking the stalemate, with Wavell as its only non-Indian member. Jinnah still maintained he should have the right to nominate all Muslim members, an idea which Azad denounced as 'an evil step'. Internal disputes in Congress followed over whether to insist on including a nationalist Muslim in their list of nominees. Wavell tried to get round this by making his own list of ministers, drawn from all parties. Although Patel and Nehru were willing to let the matter pass, Gandhi intervened and blocked agreement by insisting that the interim government would have to contain at least one Congress Muslim. His view was that any new administration needed not communal parity, but rather the 'best and incorruptible men or women'.[32]

Various compromises were then put forward by Wavell and the Delegation, both Congress and the League being nervous that any solution would set a precedent. A 5:5:2 Cabinet was proposed (the two extra members being a Sikh and an Indian Christian), then a 5:5:3 Cabinet (with a Scheduled Caste Congress nominee), then a 5:5:4 Cabinet (the spare one being a Parsi). Just when it looked as if Wavell had found a credible balance, Congress decided to launch strong opposition to the nomination of a Bombay Parsi, Sir Noshirwan Engineer, on the grounds that he had served as Advocate General and was therefore tainted by officialdom.

Unmoved by the deferential attitude of the visiting British dignitaries, Gandhi told Cripps that although Congress Working Committee members such as Azad, Asaf Ali, Khan Abdul Ghaffar Khan, Sarojini Naidu, Pant, Nehru and Patel wished to join a constituent assembly, he 'would not be able to advise the leap in the dark'.[33] When Pethick-Lawrence sent him a 'Dear Gandhiji' letter outlining various points, Gandhi replied (beginning with the salutation 'Dear Lord') with an account of an earlier meeting he had held with the Delegation. The Secretary of State responded that Gandhi's version did not 'accord with my recollection or that of Sir Stafford', prompting the Mahatma to stick in the stiletto. 'Dear Friend,' he began (always a fatal preliminary with Gandhi), 'Your letter is in the best imperialistic style which I thought had gone for ever.'[34] To a figure such as Pethick-Lawrence, this was a grave and calculated insult.

By now the optimism of Cripps and the idealism of Pethick-Lawrence had been severely dampened. Wavell, who had been thinking of the future throughout the talks, took the chance to formulate a fallback strategy. On 2 June, in his capacity as Governor General, he quietly took personal charge of the Home Department. This gave him direct control over India's internal security apparatus, including the IB and hence IPI.

The next day, at his prompting, the Delegation sent a collective letter to Attlee saying they were concerned that there might soon be 'open opposition from Congress which may develop into a mass struggle on 1942 lines but more widespread and better organized . . . We understand that it would be difficult to supply reinforcements of British troops on any substantial scale.'[35] They stressed that the army, police and civilian services were 'tired and discouraged', and that while a renewed 'repressive policy' would be unlikely to succeed, a rapid British withdrawal in the event of hostile Congress action would be likely to lead to 'famine and civil war'.

An alternative plan, 'designed to mitigate the consequences of with-drawal would be to announce our intention of withdrawing from India by a certain date, say, 1st January 1947'.[36] This was the closest that Wavell had come to securing government support for a fixed time-limit. However, Attlee's reply stated that, 'Cabinet did not like alternative . . . of announcing our intention to withdraw from India by a specific date,' although 'I am taking up with Minister of Transport possibility of speeding up removal of European women and children waiting for passages home.'[37] After some confusion as to numbers, it was deduced that there were ninety-six thou-sand of these women and children, including 'some six thousand Poles', and contingency plans were laid down for their evacuation.

On 16 June, with their May Statement languishing, the Delegation issued a new document. It was a short paper relating principally to the interim government, but it now became the crux of the whole negoti-ations. Point 8 of this June Statement asserted that if any party did not join a coalition government, the Viceroy would still assemble one, 'which will be as representative as possible of those willing to accept the Statement of May 16th'.[38]

When Congress rejected the June proposal, Jinnah therefore took it as a clear indication that he would be brought into an interim government. However, Congress decided on 24 June to have their cake and eat it by issuing a retrospective and heavily qualified acceptance of the May Statement, which allowed them to be brought back into the proceedings. Wavell acknowledged in a secret memorandum that the move was a 'dishonest one', and questioned whether it should be accepted.[39] To his amazement it then transpired that this action had been suggested not by some sharp-eyed Gujarati lawyer, but by Cripps, who had pointed out to Congress that acceptance would place them in a better tactical position.[40]

Although bad faith and hostility was produced by the Cabinet Del-egation's duplicity, the most enduring complication was over the question of 'grouping'. Under the May Statement, a united India would be 'free to form groups'. There would be three groups: the first was Sind, Punjab, Baluchistan and the North-West Frontier Province; the second was Bengal and Assam; and the third was the rest of India. In other words, the boundaries would be along the lines of the two regions in the Muslim League's claim for 'Pakistan'. It would then be up to each group to vote on whether it wished to be an autonomous unit.

This scheme was intended to provide a lure to the Muslim League, since 'Pakistan' territory would not be partitioned: the Muslims would be exchanging power for land. In addition they would have the advantage of Hindu–Muslim parity in the central government. Although Pakistan would not be a sovereign nation, it would be large, undivided and autonomous. For this proposal to appeal to Jinnah, he had to be certain that the 'groups' (or autonomous Pakistans) would have the power to hold themselves together by voting as a unit. But Congress chose to interpret the May Statement as meaning that initial membership of each group would be optional, enabling an area such as the North-West Frontier Province to opt out of its designated area. This would, in effect, have enabled Congress to break up the two nascent autonomous 'Pakistans' before they were even created.

Although this interpretation was at odds with the original intention of the Cabinet Delegation, Cripps chose not to clarify the matter for fear of alienating Congress. Despite Wavell's insistence that the matter should be set straight, there was no definitive ruling on the matter. Gandhi for one was adamant over 'the honourableness of opposition to grouping', which made the Delegation believe that coaxing might be more effective than a firm stand. Wavell opposed these unilateral concessions to Congress, as he knew it was only likely to make Jinnah more uncooperative.

As the Delegation prepared to go home, Jinnah felt he had been betrayed, both over grouping and over membership of the interim government. He was adamant that he was the only person to have emerged from the negotiations with 'clean hands', and insisted he would not begin 'higgling and haggling like a *bania*' over the question of Muslim representation. Although he was a naturally intransigent and legalistic man, Jinnah had been more flexible than in previous negotiations, despite knowing full well that Cripps was biased against him.

Jinnah made a public statement on 27 June that the leaders of Congress spoke only for the higher castes: 'They certainly do not represent the Muslims and the mere fact that they have a handful of Muslim henchmen for the purpose of window-dressing cannot give the national character which they claim, nor the right to represent India.'[41] This was followed soon afterwards by an ominous assertion that the Muslim League thought 'constitutional' methods had failed.

FIFTEEN

Leave Her to Her Fate

The Cabinet Delegation flew back to London on the last day of June 1946, with Cripps not having bothered to say goodbye to Wavell. He would soon become Chancellor of the Exchequer, gaining the nickname 'Austerity Cripps'. His lack of success in New Delhi compounded his flop of 1942, broke his reputation as a diplomatic fixer and left him as a footnote to Indian history. He died five years later.

His failure, and the failings of his two ministerial fellow-travellers, should not obscure the sincerity of their mission, or how close they came to success. There is certainly truth in Woodrow Wyatt's assertion that the Cabinet Delegation 'tried to give away an Empire' but 'found their every suggestion for doing it frustrated by the intended recipients'.[1] The delay in reaching a solution was based not on British intransigence over decolonization, but on the inability of different Indian leaders to agree on what terms the handover of power should take place. In the end the Cabinet Delegation created more problems than they solved, and the last chance to retain a united India disappeared. Had matters gone a little differently, federation might have been accepted, although whether this would ultimately have prevented bloodshed and secession in the Punjab and Bengal is arguable.

As the Delegation reached London, the Viceroy escaped to Simla for a rest, and penned a Wavellian pastiche of Lewis Carroll's poem 'Jabberwocky':

> He took his crippsian pen in hand
> Long time in draftish mode he wrote
> . . . And as he mused with pointed phrase,
> The Gandhiji, on wrecking bent,
> Came trippling down the bhangi ways,
> And woffled as he went.[2]

Throughout the four exhausting months, Wavell had been obliged to keep up with his administrative duties as well as taking part in the negotiations. Now he was left to deal with the fall-out, and to try and find a solution. The DIB was giving him a 'most gloomy forecast of the law and order situation', saying 'he considered the country ripe for serious trouble'.[3] Shortly afterwards Norman Smith ordered the disposal of 'certain dangerous CID records', the more important documents being returned to London.

Some months later Wavell concluded that it had been the most gruelling summer of his life, and that the failure of the mission had stemmed from the 'duplicity' of Cripps, the 'abject attitude' of the Delegation as a whole, the 'unyielding' approach of Jinnah, and the fact that Congress had known that if it sat tight it could not be dislodged. 'The Mission gave away the weakness of our position, and our bluff has been called,' the Viceroy wrote in desperation. 'Our time in India is limited and our power to control events almost gone.'[4] An acquaintance had written during the war that Archie Wavell 'exudes serenity – as if he knew trouble well and had often stared it in the face and now was not afraid of it any more. I thought, to myself, that if I ever saw him ruffled I would be terrified.'[5] It was a perceptive view of Wavell's personality. Now, in July 1946, he was ruffled. He had been left with no clear instructions, and a duty to try to control a country which was beginning to fall apart.

The Viceroy sent a frank letter to George VI, telling the King's right-hand man 'Tommy' Lascelles in a covering note that 'Gandhi was the wrecker', while admitting that his own outlook was 'jaundiced' after four months of deadlock. He praised the Delegation for their dedication and patience, but thought they had failed to realize that when making a retreat you should 'show as bold a front as possible'.

His impression of India's major politicians ran as follows: Gandhi 'never makes a pronouncement that is not so qualified and so vaguely worded that it cannot be interpreted in whatever sense best suits him at a later stage'; Jinnah was 'a lonely, unhappy, arbitrary, self-centred man, fighting with much resolution what I fear is a losing battle'; Azad was 'a gentleman and stood for good sense and moderation . . . But up against Gandhi he was as a rabbit faced with a stoat'; Khan Abdul Ghaffar Khan, 'whose intelligence and grasp of English are both limited, was regarded by Jinnah as a gratuitous and deliberate provocation'; Nehru he found 'sincere, intelligent and personally courageous. But he is unbalanced – witness his ploy in Kashmir.' This referred to an episode during the negotiations when Nehru had decamped to the Princely State of Kashmir to defend Sheikh Abdullah, the leader of the pro-Congress National Conference, who had been arrested for agitating against the Maharajah.

The rest of the Congress Working Committee were dismissed as 'poor stuff', with the exception of Sardar Patel who was 'by far the most forcible character amongst them'.[6] Patel was the only politician, British or Indian, for whom Wavell seems to have had undimmed respect, despite believing that 'his nature is fascist and he is always likely to be on the side of direct action and if necessary violence . . . He is entirely communal and has no sense of compromise or generosity towards Moslems, but he is more of a man than most of these Hindu politicians.'[7] Later he wrote that although Patel believed 'the Muslim League should be fought and suppressed . . . we respect one another'.[8]

Wavell's letter to the King Emperor ended with an entertaining if slightly tactless attack on hereditary rulers. Of India's five 'twenty-one-gun salute' princes, Hyderabad was 'an eccentric miser with a bad record of misrule'; Kashmir 'little better'; Mysore 'a religious recluse'; Gwalior 'a nice lad and means well, but cares more for his horses and racing than anything else'; while Baroda 'does little for his State or people'. As for the 'nineteen-gun' incumbents, Kalat of Baluchistan was 'stupid but pleasant enough', although he 'hardly belongs to India'; Kolhapur 'a minor, with a mad mother'; Travancore 'a non-entity'; Udaipur 'a cripple' with a 'medieval' administration; Bhopal not worth mentioning; and Indore 'a poor creature, physically and morally'.

Meanwhile the Sikh minority, who were 'threatening to make trouble', were deemed to have 'more conceit than political sense', while the military and civil services were 'tired and discouraged'. Wavell concluded: 'We may be able to secure an orderly withdrawal from our rule over India without a rebellion or civil war; but it is likely to be a close-run thing.'[9] He was now seriously worried about the potential for a total breakdown of law and order. Matters were not helped by a public statement from Nehru that Congress was 'not bound by a single thing except that we have decided for the moment to go into the Constituent Assembly', and that 'the big probability is that there will be no grouping'.[10]

Attlee continued to be casual in his approach, despite the risk of civil war. At a Defence Committee meeting a few days after the return of the Cabinet Delegation, the Chiefs of Staff made a request to discontinue plans for reinforcing India with five British divisions. A.V. Alexander, attending in his capacity as First Lord of the Admiralty, intervened to say that there could still be 'serious internal disturbances in India', and that contingency plans should not be abandoned. Attlee chose to override him, saying the situation had 'improved considerably', and told the Chiefs to 'discontinue the preparation of plans for the reinforcement of India'.[11]

Attlee's growing dislike of Wavell had been reinforced by the views of Cripps, who thought the Viceroy's bluntness was damaging his ability to draw the parties together. The Prime Minister suggested to Wavell that he might like a political 'adviser' to assist him, only to receive a sharp reply that the Viceroy believed in 'dealing direct', and thought that the Delegation had suffered from 'too many unofficial advisers and indirect contacts'. Frank and humble as ever, he added that if the Prime Minister 'would rather have a politician than a soldier at the head of India at present', he would be perfectly happy: 'I have no personal ambition.'[12]

Wavell's pessimism was confirmed at his regular meetings with the governors of the eleven provinces, most of whom had reports of administrative subversion of various kinds. His gloom was only lightened when he learned from an intelligence source that Patel was apparently willing to let an interim government operate, since Congress had little to gain from open unrest. During this period the Congress leadership showed considerable forbearance in not ordering a mass uprising against British rule, believing they had more to gain from keeping the country quiet.

Around this time the Viceroy had a number of 'rather trying and very painful' interviews with anglophilic sycophants, who had suddenly realized that their masters really meant to depart. Wavell took an unsentimental line: 'Some of these so-called "friends" of the British have done nothing more really than support us because we kept order and enabled them to draw their rents from the land in ease and safety; few of them have been good landlords or looked after their tenants . . . I have not a great deal of sympathy for them.'[13]

The Viceroy knew that he needed to create a politicized interim government if he were to keep demonstrators off the streets, and told the members of his Executive Council that 'for reasons they would understand, I must try to get rid of them as soon as possible'.[14] In mid-July he wrote privately to Jinnah and Nehru, the presidents of the two main parties, asking them to join a new government. As Governor General he would nominate three ministers from the minorities, Congress would choose six (one of whom should be from the scheduled castes), and the

Muslim League would choose five. Congress finally agreed to this, but the League refused, so it was decided that the five posts should be filled in the meantime by Congress Muslims. On 23 July Jinnah sent a letter to Attlee saying the conduct of the Cabinet Delegation had 'impaired the honour of the British Government' and 'shaken the confidence of Muslim India and shattered their hopes for an honourable and peaceful settlement'.[15]

A week later the Muslim League passed a crucial resolution which stated that following the actions of Congress and the breach of faith by the Delegation, they would now reject the May Statement. Since 'Congress is bent upon setting-up Caste–Hindu Raj in India with the connivance of the British', and Muslims wanted nothing less than a 'fully Sovereign State of Pakistan', they were 'convinced that now the time has come for the Muslim Nation to resort to Direct Action to achieve Pakistan'. To symbolize this, Muslims should 'renounce forthwith the titles conferred upon them by the alien Government'.[16] The following day Wavell met Nehru, and told him his 'intemperate' speeches had been largely responsible for provoking Jinnah.

The great advantage the British had during this crucial time was their secret intelligence. They had spies and police informers all over the Indian Empire, as well as intercepts of letters, telegrams and telephone calls, which often enabled them to stay one step ahead. Congress had been aware of these underhand activities for many years, and generally used couriers to carry important communications of any kind. The historian Z.H. Zaidi has written that a study of Intelligence Bureau material soon 'reinforced my conviction that one of the factors which had sustained British rule in India was the competence of its Intelligence Service which had been able to penetrate the most difficult and sensitive areas'.[17]

On 30 July Wavell sent a letter to all the provincial governors containing an intercept of a letter from Nehru to the Congress leader Dr Khan Sahib (brother of Khan Abdul Ghaffar Khan) in Peshawar. In it Nehru made the reasonable suggestion that instead of demanding a full-scale inquiry into the savage repression in 1942, as many in Congress circles wanted but which the British were unlikely to permit, individual Congress chief ministers should make representations to their governors. In cases where an official was known to have been guilty of 'extreme misconduct or corruption' it was assumed he would retire. Wavell's covering letter implied an endorsement of this solution.

At first Wavell had assumed that the repeated Congress demands for the dismissal of officials involved in Linlithgow's clampdown on the Quit India movement were political propaganda. However, after talks with Congress leaders, he realized there was substance to their claims, and that brutality had been used. This was confirmed when he spoke to Sir Francis Wylie, the Governor of the United Provinces, who told him that 'the suppression really was drastic and that some indefensible things were done'.[18] Wavell responded to this news with soldierly caution, and tried to ignore it. He was aware of the wrong the British had done in 1942, but felt he had to 'protect our officials', since he knew the catastrophic effect on service morale any genuine public inquiry would provoke.

He had somehow to support the administrators of British India, knowing that stability depended on them, yet without antagonizing or provoking Congress in the process. Frank Wylie wrote in early August that there was 'a marked deterioration in the tone and spirit of the services'. Most Indian officials were 'wobblers', unsure which way to jump, while 'European officers simply do not know where they are', and were uncertain what to do about their wives and children. 'They do not know whether they will be expected to suppress any disturbances which may be forthcoming over the months ahead of them or not,' although they did know that in outlying areas 'their own chances of survival are very small' if there was an uprising.[19]

While the structures of imperial rule crumbled, Mohandas Gandhi continued in his ash-smeared *sadhu* mode. His attention had now shifted from the nefarious provisions of the salt tax to the perils of gambling, and in early August he made a pronouncement in his Gujarati-language newspaper *Harijanbandhu*. His concern was over 'the ruination of men and money through horse racing'. Although he believed it was 'not as great an evil as drinking of alcohol', racecourse betting had to be stamped out at once. 'I do not know the intricacies of horse racing. All I can say is that if it is within the competence of the present Government to put an end to the evil; it should certainly do so.'[20] With other worries on his mind, the Viceroy took no immediate action on this matter.

For Wavell had just been told by both his Private Secretary George Abell and Abell's deputy Ian Scott that they believed 'our only course is to get out of India as soon as possible and leave her to her fate, which will be civil war'.[21] On 13 August the Chiefs of Staff met in Downing Street, and were joined by Auchinleck, the Commander-in-Chief in India.

They considered a report from the Joint Intelligence Staff, which suggested that 'in the event of civil war ... the Indian Armed Forces as a whole cannot be relied on.'[22] Auchinleck's reaction to this was that the situation was a little better than it had been a few weeks before, and that provided the Indian army remained loyal, 'he had ample forces to deal with any situation that might arise'.[23] This optimistic statement was to be undermined three days later, when the Great Calcutta Killings began.

The violence in Calcutta in August 1946 represented the final breaking-point in Hindu–Muslim relations. Any pretence that a time of communal peace and harmony might have been lurking round the corner now evaporated. It was the moment at which moderates on both sides were pushed into the background, and even the secularists found they came to be defined by their name, their dress, their food and their religion. As Wavell wrote to Pethick-Lawrence a few months later: 'The small fry seem to have taken charge on both sides and they are rabid, ignorant, and irresponsible.'[24]

The primary cause of the outbreak was Jinnah's call for a 'universal Muslim *hartal*' as part of his plans for 'direct action'. It was to take place after Friday Prayers on 16 August, and would be a show of strength by the Muslim *qaum* against the putative tyranny of Congress. In Indian history books this is presented as the day when perfidious Muslim Leaguers showed themselves in their true colours, and began genocidal pogroms against defenceless Hindus. As one writer recently put it, no Indian could ever forget 'the dastardly role of these communalists and the depths to which they descended to curry flavour [sic] with their British masters ... The Muslim League perpetrated the atrocity of the "Direct Action Day" of 16 August 1946 in which their sectarian communalism caused the deaths of tens of thousands of innocent Hindus.'[25] In fact, about 75 per cent of the victims were Muslim.

The exact course of the three days of the Great Calcutta Killings, and the precise communal identity and motivation of the killers, has never been properly documented. It is certain that both sides suffered terrible violence and loss. The initial provocation in Calcutta came from processions of Muslim Leaguers, 'well armed with *lathis*, iron rods and missiles', marching to the Ochterlony Monument to listen to their corpulent Chief Minister, H.S. Suhrawardy. On the way they were greeted by Hindus throwing stones and bricks. At the Monument Suhrawardy is alleged to have made a speech which incited violence, and told his supporters that the police would 'hold back' while Muslims did whatever they chose. As the Special Branch had failed to send a shorthand writer to the gathering, no transcript of the speech was taken. When the public meeting ended, a crowd of around a hundred thousand people set off and began to attack isolated groups of Hindus across the city.

Although Suhrawardy may well have encouraged violence against Hindus, the last thing he needed was mass communal unrest, which might unseat his ministry. As the violence became serious, he went to the control room of the Commissioner of Police in Lall Bazar, and attempted to interfere in operations in his capacity as the province's Home Minister. One British official noted that the 'Chief Minister showed an exasperating preoccupation with the sufferings undergone by members of his own community'. Communal violence now spread throughout the poorer districts of Calcutta, and to the docks, with the minority community in each place coming off the worst. The poor and the defenceless took the brunt, as so often in communal riots, as they were easier to locate and drive out of their flimsy homes.

That night small gangs set out with knives and short swords, and the next morning hundreds of corpses were found lying in the gutters. Troops were called out, but the killers seemed to melt away wherever they appeared, only for the violence to recommence the moment they had left. The Governor of Bengal, Sir Frederick Burrows, noted in a secret report: 'I can honestly say that parts of the city on Saturday morning were as bad as anything I saw when I was with the Guards on the Somme . . . I actually saw . . . a crowd clubbing three unfortunate individuals to death . . . Many corpses were stripped and mutilated.'[26] It was not until Monday 19 August that the situation was properly under control, with members of Jat, Gurkha and Green Howard regiments patrolling the streets.

The Governor had made a serious mistake in acquiescing to his Chief Minister's demand that 16 August should be a public holiday. Burrows was said to be 'steady, sensible, straight, with a slow West Country speech', but he had only been in the job for a few months.[27] The result was that the army had been confined to barracks, and there were minimal preparations for the possibility of rioting. Congress subsequently blamed

Burrows for permitting the violence, and claimed he was incompetent. When the Viceroy arrived in Calcutta the following week he doubted whether Burrows could have predicted what was coming, although his already low opinion of Suhrawardy was exacerbated by his strong 'communal bias'.

In other Muslim-majority provinces, Direct Action Day passed off peacefully. In Assam the religious exclusivity of a League procession was marred only 'by the fact that it was accompanied by a band comprised mainly of Hindus led by a Chinaman and giving an indifferent rendering of "The British Grenadiers"'.[28]

At the end of the three days of killing, the official reports stated that four thousand people had been murdered and ten thousand wounded. Wavell himself thought the numbers were closer to five thousand killed and sixteen thousand injured, and today it is usually accepted that six thousand people lost their lives in the Great Calcutta Killings. Over a hundred thousand people were left homeless, some through eviction, some through fire and some through fear of remaining in their homes. India's mass migration was beginning, with terrified groups of people departing in search of the security of areas where their co-religionists were in the majority.

Although Fred Burrows blamed the League for the initial rioting, he thought little would be gained from declaring governor's rule under Section 93. He found it 'almost uncanny' that no British or even Anglo-Indian shops had been attacked, unlike riots during the previous year over the INA trials. Burrows was convinced that the outbreak was as much about gangland warfare as it was about politics: 'It was a pogrom between two rival armies of the Calcutta underworld. The fact that over two thousand persons of the "*goonda*" type who had been confined under the Defence of India Rules during the war were released between July and December 1945 is of great significance.'

This view is supported by various reports which claim that known criminals were responsible for leading many of the gangs. Nirad Chaudhuri has observed that most of the killing was done not by mobs but by *goondas*, and that all sides suffered mutilation and death. Sikhs were seen driving around in armoured jeeps in search of victims, and in one Hindu neighbourhood a Muslim boy was stripped, thrown into a pond and poked with bamboo poles until he drowned, while an England-returned engineer timed the operation on his Rolex watch.

The events in Calcutta were a human and political disaster for the Muslim League. Mohammad Ali Jinnah had made requests to his people to act peacefully, hoping the *hartal* would strengthen the negotiating position of the League through a show of mass power on the streets. In the event it did the opposite, and fatally damaged his reputation among Hindus throughout India. The Congress leaders believed that he had blood on his hands. Aware that his followers were restless, British power was fading and the chances of Congress control of India were growing, Jinnah had decided to act in a deliberately communal way. But unlike Patel, who manipulated communal antagonism as part of a strategic agenda, Jinnah was trying to play a game that he did not fully understand, and could never hope to control.

The Muslim leader cannot escape indirect responsibility for unleashing the forces of destruction, although there is no evidence that he personally foresaw or encouraged the massacres. Sitting in his ivory tower dressed in his London suit, he had not realized how the criminal underworld of Calcutta might behave. The Muslim League was too ramshackle an organization to have genuine control over its supporters. H.S. Suhrawardy ran the Bengal League, and his organization had entrusted direct action to Calcutta's *pirs* and *mullahs*, who were told to mobilize the Muslim community at Friday Prayers.

The language of the publicity for 16 August was explicitly religious, for all the secularism of Mr Jinnah. 'Let Muslims brave the rains and all difficulties and make the Direct Action Day meeting a historic mass mobilization of the *Millat*,' ran one handbill. 'Muslims must remember that it was in *Ramazan* that the Quran was revealed. It was in *Ramazan* that the permission for *jihad* was granted by Allah.'[29]

After his visit to Calcutta, Wavell became increasingly certain that rioting was likely to spread across India. The following month there were outbreaks in Bombay and Karachi. The Viceroy was worried that the violence had hardened Congress leaders against Jinnah, and at a meeting on 27 August he found Gandhi 'malevolent' and Nehru 'full of hate against the League'. This made him more determined than ever to bring the Muslim League into the interim government, believing it was the only way to prevent a further breakdown in communal relations. His hope was that by tasting power, the League might be encouraged to cooperate with their opponents.

After this meeting, Gandhi sent an angry letter to Wavell accusing him of bias towards the League, and threatening Congress withdrawal from an interim administration unless 'you can wholly trust the Congress Government which you have announced . . . The Congress cannot afford to impose its will on warring elements in India through the use of British arms.'[30] The threat to leave the Viceroy in the lurch was a dangerous one, and after the events in Calcutta, Wavell knew that the probable consequences of any further deterioration in political relations was more public slaughter. Congress were now dictating terms which the British had little choice but to accept.

Gandhi came to the conclusion that Lord Wavell should be dismissed, and a more amenable Viceroy and Governor General installed in his place. He sent a cable to a member of his own entourage who had just reached London, where he was to act as a multi-purpose, roving Congress emissary. This was Sudhir Ghosh, a Bengali political activist who had established links with Quakers and Labour politicians while he was study-ing at Cambridge. He was a friend of Stafford Cripps, although Lady Cripps thought him insincere and untrustworthy, and Wavell considered him a 'snake in the grass' with 'a very swollen head'.

Gandhi instructed Ghosh to tell 'friends' – meaning Labour ministers – that the Viceroy was not up to the job. Cripps was away in Switzerland, so Ghosh saw Pethick-Lawrence, who was unreceptive to his suppli-cations. Attlee, though, was in Ghosh's words 'a great deal more under-standing', telling him at a meeting in early September that 'there was a good case for a new Viceroy but there was no sense in making a change unless he was in a position to find someone who was obviously better than the present occupant of the post'.[31] The Viceroy's position was now shaky.

Ironically, the day after his hostile encounter with Gandhi, Wavell had written a strong letter to Attlee complaining about the conduct of the British government. He enclosed an intercept of a telephone conversation between Ghosh in London and Sardar Patel at the Congress stronghold of Birla House in New Delhi. Patel had said: 'Cripps had promised if there was any disturbance in Calcutta, he will order for section 93. What is he doing?' to which Ghosh replied that Cripps was out of the country, but he would take up the matter with another minister. Patel then told him to remain in London and await further orders, adding ominously: 'We are taking charge on the second of September.'

Understandably enough, Wavell objected to this secret diplomacy, which seriously undermined his own authority. Although he did not know that Attlee was himself encouraging Ghosh, he wrote: 'I think it is essential that I should know your mind more fully as regards India; and also that I should have a definite policy from HMG . . . I cannot continue to be responsible for affairs in India if some members of your Government are keeping in touch with the Congress through an independent agent behind my back.'[32]

Attlee drafted three different handwritten answers to Wavell, but sent none of them. Instead he procrastinated before eventually replying two months later, beating even Winston Churchill's poor response time. Wavell had to be content with a bland assurance 'that we are very conscious of your anxieties and of the potential dangers of the situation'.[33]

SIXTEEN

A Secret Coup

On 2 September 1946, the members of the new interim Government of India were sworn into office. For the first time ever, the significant departments of state were to be run by nationalist politicians rather than by toadies or bureaucrats. Although at the time nobody was entirely certain what this would achieve, in retrospect it is the most important moment in the demission of British authority – more significant, in many ways, than the handover of power in August 1947.

The reforms of the 1930s had not anticipated a move of this kind, so there was no way of predicting what would happen when a genuine politician ran a government department. In the past, the distinction between the various powers embodied in the person of the Viceroy had been of interest primarily to constitutional lawyers. Now they became a matter of crucial importance, as the power of the Viceroy over his ministers was put to the test.

Ever since the reforms following the great revolt of 1857, the Viceroy of India had held four different jobs. The first and most important was as Governor General, running the Government of India; the second was as Viceroy, representing the British monarch in the Indian Empire; the third was as Crown Representative, dealing with relations between the British Government and the autonomous Princely States; and the fourth was as Governor General in Council, whereby he followed the decisions of the departmental ministers or 'members' of his Executive Council. In theory, the Viceroy had legal powers which superseded the decisions of his Council, but Wavell only dared to exercise them once, and that was over a fairly insignificant matter.

Patel's assertion that Congress were 'taking charge on the second of September' proved to be correct. In exchange for keeping its followers in check, the party was given responsibility for a huge tranche of the Government of India. It was now in office in New Delhi for the first time, and it employed the clever strategy of acting as if it had even greater power as a means of consolidating its position. This undermined British confidence further. Before each Executive Council meeting, chaired by Wavell in his capacity as Governor General, the Congress ministers met for tea to decide policy. Wavell was not invited to attend what he called the 'tea-party Cabinets'.

The League had refused to join the interim government because of the dispute over Muslim nominees, so Congress were obliged to include five 'show-boys', who knew they would be ousted as soon as the League deigned to join the coalition. One was Sir Shafaat Ahmed Khan, a League defector who exuded 'the cheap butter of insincere compliments' and who was soon stabbed to death, the killers having links to a branch of the Muslim League.[1] Nehru took the Foreign Affairs portfolio and was Vice-President of the Executive Council, so J.B. Kripalani assumed his place as Congress President. Patel wisely secured the Home Department, knowing that real influence in an autocracy depends on getting your hands on its internal security mechanisms. He was now in charge of the Intelligence Bureau, and joked to Wavell that the DIB had destroyed all the most interesting files; in fact they had been sent to IPI in London.

Sardar Patel was India's consummate machine politician. His decades of experience had taught him the importance of having an iron grip on the levers and mechanisms of authority. Nehru talked lyrically about the community of nations; Patel was more interested in securing maximum power for Congress as the British faded from the scene. Two days after being sworn in, he summoned Norman Smith, the Director of the Intelligence Bureau, to his office.

It had been decided in Whitehall that the DIB should come clean and tell the truth to Patel about IPI. A proposal from Vickery that this could be avoided by hiding IPI's operational budget under a different heading in the Home Department's account books had been rejected as too risky. Smith sent a report back to London on the night of the meeting, which reveals a mixture of relief and trepidation. Aware that he was likely to be winkled out of his job before long, he had suggested to his new boss that it might be easier for both sides if he were to retire as DIB at some point during the following year, and an Indian director appointed in his place.

'I mentioned to HHM [Honourable Home Member] the existence of an organization paid for by this Bureau but working in England under the name of IPI,' wrote Smith. This implies that Patel had not heard of IPI before, which, if correct, does not say much for Congress's own intelligence networks. Smith added that IPI had already been informed that the DIB 'must henceforth be regarded solely as a servant of an Indian Government and that I should not be sent any intelligence which I was not permitted to disclose to the Government of India . . . I explained that [IPI's] position had now become more than a little anomalous in that it had become an organization paid for by India but occupying the completely exceptional position of operating on British soil. This was a privilege not enjoyed by any Empire intelligence organization, and it was doubtful whether the British security authorities would permit it to continue.'

Vickery takes up the story in an internal document he wrote the following month for the recently knighted India Office stalwart Sir Paul Patrick. The good news was that Patel was in favour of continuing surveillance of all kinds, both internal and external. Although he wanted the spies to be called off the Congress Working Committee, he was happy for them to continue watching members of the Congress Socialists and the Forward Bloc: 'Mr Patel, who is rabidly anti-Communist, is fully aware of the importance of keeping a very close eye on Communist activities and the potentially subversive tendencies of extreme left wingers in general.'[2]

Although the immediate risk of Congress abolishing IPI or the IB had disappeared, a far more serious problem now arose. Patel made a crucial decision around this time, which was to have a critical impact on the capacity of the British authorities to make coherent day-to-day policy decisions, and was to be an important determinant in the closing months of their rule. Rather than closing down India's intelligence agencies, Patel turned the tables on Whitehall by keeping them going, but altering the outlet for the information they gathered.

'Since we know that Mr Smith has had no access to Viceroy since Interim Govt took office,' wrote the Permanent Under-Secretary at the India Office Sir David Monteath in a 'top secret' note, 'we can not assume that Viceroy is aware of developments.' Quite simply, Patel blocked the 'personal access' of the DIB to the Viceroy.[3] Not only was the regular monthly private briefing curtailed, but the Viceroy was no longer permitted to request covertly obtained material from the Intelligence Bureau, or to seek risk and threat assessments from them. All the King Emperor's representative now received was the widely circulated weekly IB reports, which were often little more than a rehash of information that was already in the public domain.

Patel's action, which (like Lord Linlithgow's declaration of war in 1939) was legally and constitutionally permissible, meant the DIB's intelligence was now available to Congress alone. Monteath's note on the subject, which can be found in the recently declassified IPI files, appears to have been written as late as April or May 1947, showing that the British authorities must have been unable to overturn Patel's cunning decision of September 1946.

In addition, the nature of the information that was now fed to the Intelligence Bureau altered. Since the introduction of provincial autonomy in 1937, the powers of local governments had been bypassed through the appointment of a Central Intelligence Officer in each province, who reported directly to the DIB in Delhi.[4] These Central Intelligence Officers, who had in the past been highly influential, now had to be very cautious about what they reported to the DIB, knowing it would be passed to Patel and then back to provincial Congress officials. The Viceroy began to depend on the reports of the eleven provincial governors, the quality of which varied according to circumstance. Thus, on all fronts, the intelligence machine on which the British authorities depended was crippled.

With his life's work unravelling before his eyes, Philip Vickery made an attempt to salvage what advantage he could from the debacle. He suggested that London should act quickly by sending out intelligence operatives to India, who would re-recruit local agents and informers, and report to him via MI5, thereby circumventing the Government of India. His plan was that existing arrangements should now be supplemented by 'sending out a Defence Security Officer to Delhi to receive intelligence locally; this intelligence would be passed by him to the Security Service in London and there distributed by IPI'.[5] Since the paragraphs that follow Vickery's proposal have been blanked out by MI5's declassification department, this is presumably what did happen.

Having joined the Viceroy's Council, the Congress ministers took to dining with Lord and Lady Wavell. Since the days of the 'Simon, Go Home!' campaign in 1928, there had been a Congress policy of not accepting official hospitality from their British rulers, but this was now quietly dropped. Vallabhbhai Patel was the first to come to dinner, telling Wavell he had 'broken all rules in doing so'. During the course of Sep-

tember, Chakravarti Rajagopalachari, the Sikh leader Baldev Singh, Sarojini Naidu, Jawaharlal Nehru, his sister Vijaya Lakshmi Pandit and the
'embarrassingly deferential' Rajendra Prasad all dined in the glorious
splendour of Lutyens and Baker's Viceroy's House. Naidu kept everybody
entertained, and amused Wavell with her usual quip about Gandhi: 'If
only that old man knew how much it costs us to keep him in poverty.'[6]

Within days of installing the new government, Lord Wavell sent a top
secret document to London. It was marked 'Breakdown Plan', although
privately he gave it the nickname 'Operation Madhouse'. It had been
compiled by himself, George Abell, Auchinleck and three other British
officials. Circulation was restricted to Attlee and Pethick-Lawrence,
although whether Sudhir Ghosh got a peep is anyone's guess. It was a
frank and deliberately provocative tract, in which Wavell presented the
options in the event of Congress non-cooperation, with a view to stimulat-
ing the Prime Minister into defining and clarifying his drifting India
policy. For two years now he had been attempting to impress upon
successive occupants of 10 Downing Street the gravity of the crisis in
India, and this was his starkest warning yet.

In the document, Wavell declared that unless the government wished
to extend British rule for another couple of decades through a massive
military reinforcement, the options were seriously limited. In his view,
Britain would not be able to exercise control for much longer, and 'on
administrative grounds we could not govern the whole of India for more
than a year and a half from now'. In most of the provinces of British
India, the legal powers of the Governor could now 'only be enforced to
a limited degree by persuasion and bluff'. Given this situation, 'we must
have at once a definite plan, worked out in considerable detail, for withdrawal of our control from India [to be] completed not later than the
spring of 1948'. Wavell favoured gradual withdrawal northwards, and the
announcement of a set date for departure.

Wavell's most dangerous scenario dealt with a 'general deterioration'
leading to a breakdown within the next three months. In such a case, it
should be announced that 'HMG do not intend that the handing over
of control to Indian hands should be delayed by the failure of the Indian
parties to agree among themselves.' The new interim government would
be disbanded and all British troops and officials withdrawn from Madras,
Bombay, Orissa and the Central Provinces, leaving only Indian regiments
which would remain under the control of the Commander-in-Chief.

With the last Britishers tucked up in the north-eastern and north-western wings of the country, it would be announced that 'political power in India would be demitted entirely' within three months, and there would then be an evacuation of personnel through the ports at Karachi and Calcutta. Auchinleck made a footnote to these proposals stating that a 'wholesale defection or disintegration of the Indian army' was possible, so any reduction of British forces in India could not be accepted.[7] Wavell and Auchinleck were experienced military commanders. They were not running scared; rather they were convinced that the situation in India had reached breaking point.

Attlee's private jottings on the Breakdown Plan are revealing. Although he attempted no serious rebuttal of Wavell's arguments, his own stand is summed up in the sentence: 'While it is reasonable for the Viceroy to want to have a break down plan, it is unreasonable of him to expect us to envisage failure.'[8] Given the fact that Attlee's India policy had been in a continual state of failure since the moment he inherited it from Churchill, this statement was absurd. The official response from London was that any fixed plan of this type, or even the setting of a time limit, would provoke 'a scramble for power and an attempt to set up Pakistan by force either at once or in the wake of our withdrawal ... our view is that what you propose in the event of a breakdown involves risks which far exceed any possible advantages'.[9]

The Cabinet thought evacuation through Calcutta and Karachi would be extremely risky, which was true, especially given the news that Subhas Bose's brother Sarat was planning to call a general strike in Bengal. Stafford Cripps took the view that Wavell was being alarmist, and was concerned that any such withdrawal would have to be sanctioned in advance by Parliament. Pethick-Lawrence made the typically hopeful claim that the League and Congress might shortly start cooperating, and suggested the administration might be strengthened by recruiting some new British ICS officers.

Wavell replied in late October that they had missed the point: 'As a military commander, I have naturally some knowledge of the conduct of retreats, and also, unfortunately, some experience of conducting them. I submit that our present position in India is analogous to that of a military force compelled to withdraw in the face of greatly superior numbers.' He finished his letter with the observation that 'once we have lost all power of control', there would be little the British could contribute to a settlement. 'If HMG is unable to accept my plan, on what plan am I to base our withdrawal?'[10]

Clement Attlee, busily building the New Jerusalem at home in Britain, had no answer to give this troublesome plenipotentiary. As Prime Minister, he had to contend with explosions in Palestine, widespread flooding in the south of England, transport strikes, depleted coal stocks, a severe shortage of housing and continued bread rationing. The easiest solution to the India problem was to find a new Viceroy.

When the Congress leadership was released from Ahmednagar Fort for the first Simla Conference in 1945, Abul Kalam Azad had still been the party's President, owing to the break in democratic political developments and the imprisonments during the Quit India campaign. His had been a cynical appointment, intended as a rather feeble sop to India's Muslims. During the elections of 1945–46 Azad declined to let Patel play an active role, since he disliked him and believed he was a communalist. In his dealings with the Cabinet Delegation, Azad went beyond the brief given to him by the Congress Working Committee, and 1946 marked the end of his career as a serious politician; from then on he was little more than the token Congress Muslim that Jinnah had always claimed he was.

The election of his successor as Congress President was one of the most important decisions in the movement's history, since the nominee was almost certain to be the first Prime Minister of free India. The vote had been held during April 1946, in the midst of the Cabinet Delegation's deliberations, and was a significant distraction for the Congress leaders. Azad wished to stay on, but the idea was soon vetoed by Gandhi, who had grown to distrust him. Twelve of the party's fifteen provincial committees chose Patel, who was the clear choice of most rank-and-file Congress activists. But Gandhi proposed his protégé Jawaharlal Nehru, who had not even been nominated, since he was younger, more conciliatory and more palatable to the outside world than Patel. As one ICS officer put it, Nehru was 'Gandhi's Western face'.[11]

Ironically, half a century later, Patel's origins, authenticity and prejudices might have made him a far more acceptable choice for the job than Nehru. Although he abided by Gandhi's decision, Patel from then on declined to follow the Mahatma's political guidance, and 1946 marked a break between them despite their many years of comradeship. The Sardar was wise enough to know that real power did not depend on your official title, and consolidated his own role within Congress. He admired Nehru and accepted his leadership, although at times he grew irritated by what he saw as his 'emotional outbursts' and 'childish innocence'.

Gandhi was quite explicit in his choice, saying that the chosen one, 'who was educated at Harrow and Cambridge and became a barrister is greatly needed to carry on the negotiations with the Englishmen'.[12] Nehru's international outlook made him an acceptable public face for Congress, and the appointment enabled him to perhaps inadvertently sow the seeds of a quasi-royal dynasty when he allowed his underqualified daughter Indira to become Congress President in 1958. As one fictional character said, 'What is so comforting is that the man at the helm of affairs is so much like a British gentleman.'[13] Yet, as another novelist asked, would people have taken so much notice of Motilal, Jawaharlal, Indira, Sanjay and Rajiv 'if the family came from south of the Vindhyas, if it had a dark skin and spoke Tamil or Telugu, if its name was Venkataraman or Balasubramaniam?'[14]

By the time Pandit (an honorific generally given to learned Brahmins, although in this case referring to the fact that the family were Kashmiri Hindus) Nehru was released from prison in 1945, he had spent a total of nine years of his life incarcerated, often in harsh conditions. He had been hit by *lathis* while demonstrating on the streets of his home town, and had experienced his own mother being beaten by policemen till she bled. He was now fifty-six years old, a widower, and his friend and brother-in-law Ranjit Pandit had died behind bars during the war. Somehow, Nehru remained optimistic and free from bitterness. There was however an unstable edge to him, and a determination to win power as quickly as possible.

Jawaharlal Nehru's reputation as a world statesman at the time of his death in 1964 masks the inadequacies of his political achievement before 1947. Despite misjudgements in old age during his final years as Prime Minister of free India, his premiership was by any standards a triumph. Under his leadership, India was to turn from a country on the brink of chaos and civil war to one with substantial internal coherence and a functioning system of government. The Princely States were integrated into the Indian Union, secular parliamentary democracy was entrenched, education was expanded, a specific if ultimately misguided foreign policy was devised, and laws on inheritance, caste and civil liberties were introduced. Any one of these accomplishments can be criticized for its failings, but the potential for a complete administrative collapse in India in the late 1940s should not be forgotten.

Nehru was charismatic, spontaneous, idealistic, moody, artistic, passionate, arrogant, mercurial, thoughtful, short-tempered, patrician and self-righteous, yet he had an essential goodness of heart that is not easily identifiable in either Gandhi or Jinnah. He embodied paradox, combining an Anglo-Brahminical imperiousness with an almost spiritual empathy with the Indian masses, and autocratic tendencies with a profound belief in democracy. He once wrote an aggressive anonymous attack on himself, and arranged for his friend Padmaja 'Bibi' Naidu to get it published in Calcutta's *Modern Review*. His initial meteoric rise in Congress depended not on his own merits, but on the fact that he was the son of Motilal Nehru, and the 'adopted son' of Mohandas Gandhi. Yet he disagreed with Gandhi in many areas of politics, and complained openly of his 'psychic coercion . . . which reduces many of his intimate followers and colleagues to a state of mental pulp'.[15]

Even in crucial periods between 1945 and 1947, Nehru dissipated his energy in agitation against India's princely rulers and vague work to promote the brotherhood of nations. Many of his colleagues doubted whether he would have the strength of character or the realism to be a successful Prime Minister. As the Fabian campaigner Beatrice Webb put it after meeting him, Nehru was 'the last word of aristocratic refinement and culture dedicated to the salvation of the underdog whether in race or class; but I doubt whether he has the hard stuff of a revolutionary leader'.[16] Although he never hardened, he did turn into a good leader.

He retained a strong sense of playfulness. His niece Nayantara Sahgal remembers him persuading her to stand on her head in their drawing-room, to her mother's disapproval. There was always a boyish element to him. 'One rainy night after dinner at Anand Bhawan,' wrote Sahgal, 'Mamu [Uncle, in the sense of mother's brother] took us up to the library with him and we got out an enormous, dusty book of his Harrow school songs. Together we sang the fag song, "Jerry, You Duffer and Dunce", and "When Grandpapa's Grandpapa was in the Lower Lower First". The library held reminders of his school days, for there were two large pictures of him there, taken while he was at Harrow, one of them showing a solemn-faced fourteen-year-old dressed in the smart uniform of the Harrow Rifle Corps.'[17]

Although he became a born-again Indian under Gandhi's guidance, Nehru's public-school and Oxbridge education remained deeply embedded. Nirad Chaudhuri noted that he always needed privacy, and 'disliked anyone fawning on him as well in the usual Hindu reverent manner . . . His unaffected English gentleman's manner was adopted only when one spoke to him in an English which approached his in accent. Towards anyone who had the Hindi or Bengali accent he would almost behave like an Englishman to a "native" . . . I wondered how he endured the English of normal Congressmen.'[18]

He was an agile man with a strong physical presence. Each day he did a headstand and ran backwards at speed. He was said to have numerous lovers, including the social activist Mridula Sarabhai, the actress Devika Rani, and Sarojini Naidu's voluptuous elder daughter Padmaja, who allegedly had 'a perpetual bedroom look'.[19] Nehru's biographer Sarvepalli Gopal dismissed his sexual attraction with the line that women 'sought to thrust themselves into his life; and he did not always resist their gross ardours', which is a considerable over-simplification.[20] The daughter of another of his supposed paramours made the point that it was 'impossible to be a woman and not be attracted to Pandit-ji'.[21]

Nehru was a genuine secularist, and did not harbour the anti-Muslim prejudice of colleagues such as Rajendra Prasad and Vallabhbhai Patel. As he once complained, 'Many a Congressman was a communalist under his national cloak.'[22] The newspaper editor Ian Stephens thought his 'passionate animosity' towards Jinnah and the Muslim League stemmed not only from his 'high-caste Hinduism', but also from 'that strange, special distaste for Islam – as compared with other religions – shown by the British secularist intelligentsia'.[23] There may have been some truth in this, but Nehru's support of Indian Muslims after independence was both heartfelt and deeply impressive. His mistake was to dismiss strong religious affiliations and communal animosity as foolish and reactionary, without realizing that for many of his fellow humans, their religion was an essential part of their sense of self-worth and identity. This led him to miscalculate in his dealings with the Muslim League.

Wavell's efforts to persuade the Muslim League to join the Executive Council finally bore fruit, although he believed many in Congress were anxious to exclude the Leaguers. Finally, at the end of October 1946, he secured a coalition, although doing so gave him a feeling of depression at the difficulties that lay ahead. He doubted whether he could 'induce them to work together'. Light relief was provided only by the arrival of Chips Channon and Peter Coats, who had come to stay for a few weeks.

By late 1946, Jinnah was in a potentially disastrous position. Wavell noted that he had become 'much more tractable than before' since the violence in Calcutta. The League's hold over the Muslim-majority provinces was tenuous, and it was apparent that Congress would be able to dominate any interim administration or constitution-making assembly. Jinnah's only chance was to play for time, in the hope that the British might impose a settlement. Out of desperation, his party joined the interim government, without having won either parity or the right to veto legislation concerning Muslims.

This decision was preceded by considerable conflict, Wavell suggesting that a Muslim League nominee should take the Home Department. He had rather foolishly underestimated Patel's clout, and Congress threatened to collapse the government if this happened. Knowing that power would slip through his hands unless the League entered central government, Jinnah compromised, taking Finance and a handful of insignificant portfolios. As he had no wish to be in a subordinate position to Nehru, who was now known as the 'uncrowned prime minister' of India, Jinnah himself stayed out of the Executive Council and installed the fifty-one-year-old Liaquat Ali Khan in his place. Liaquat was a rotund lawyer and great popular orator who had been educated at Aligarh and Oxford, and was perhaps the most publicly impressive Muslim League politician. Although he always deferred to Jinnah, they made a strong double act.

Under the guidance of his adviser Chaudri Mohamed Ali, Liaquat put together a budget which squeezed the rich Hindu commercial and industrial businesses that supplied Congress with their funds, and exposed the gap between Nehruvian socialism and the ambitions of business families such as the Birlas and the Tatas. Although Wavell thought this was as much a matter of luck as design, he was to develop a high regard for his new Finance Minister, writing to the King, 'I have formed a very good opinion of Liaquat, who has a great fund of imperturbable commonsense and a gift of clear statement. I wish I had to deal with him instead of Jinnah as the League leader.'[24]

Wavell had secured a substantial triumph in coaxing both Congress and the League into New Delhi's first genuinely political Viceroy's Executive Council, but he felt the degree of antagonism generated by the killings in Calcutta and subsequent riots in the United Provinces and east Bengal had destroyed all chance of longer-term success. The first meeting of the new Legislative Assembly was held at the end of October, with Nehru and Liaquat sitting grimly beside each other on the government front bench, not speaking.

On 30 October, Smith of the IB reported to London that Sardar Patel had given more guidance about the gathering of covert intelligence. Realizing its usefulness, he had ordered a continuation of surveillance of 'particularly dangerous individuals' in the Congress Socialist Party and the Forward Bloc, although not of the organizations themselves. Smith observed that 'it is not going to be easy to draw this fine distinction', and asked that, 'to avoid embarrassment', information on 'anti British activities of professed supporters of the Interim Government' should no longer be passed to him by London.

A report from the India Office admitted that although the 'target set for IPI' was altering, it was clearly 'essential to be aware of the activities of such persons as Krishna Menon and of other persons of even more dubious record' in case the interim government resigned. The British would therefore need to find 'other means . . . of obtaining information about such persons'. The India Office noted that 'Mr Patel is understood to have already approved the proposals of the Director of the Intelligence Bureau, Mr N.P. Smith, to discontinue the collection of intelligence on orthodox Congress and Muslim League activity while continuing to observe that of extremist organizations.'[25] Patel's ban on surveillance of the League did not last long; the following summer he was obtaining confidential reports of their meetings 'through a source of the Intelligence Bureau'.[26]

Philip Vickery wrote that when IPI was handed over to the direct control of the British government at some point in the future, the obvious course of action would be to divide it up and transfer 'the part which deals with UK and the Commonwealth to the Security Service and the part which deals with foreign countries to the Intelligence Service [SIS]'. However, since IPI not only 'receives valuable facilities in kind from the

Security Service', but also 'maintains organizations of its own in the UK (London and the Provinces), the USA and certain European countries', he believed 'strong arguments can be adduced in favour of the retention of IPI as a self-contained unit for some time to come. Admittedly if it is so retained by the Security Service it will be performing some functions which are outside the Security Service charter – but this would seem to be justifiable until the situation is clarified.' Quite what he meant by 'some functions' is not made clear.[27]

In early November there were savage killings of Muslims in Bihar, in revenge for the equally horrendous slaughter of Hindus at Noakhali in east Bengal, which had in turn been provoked by the Great Calcutta Killings. Historians have tended to present these conflicts as if they were purely communal, yet they often also extended to matters of social conflict – debtors against creditors, the landless against the landlords, the bosses against the workers – and most significantly of all, India's *goondas, badmashes* and ruffians against the rest. The violence in Noakhali, for instance, was controlled by a local leader, Golam Sarwar, who had been defeated by a Muslim League candidate in the recent elections.

Wavell travelled to Bihar in the aftermath, and had interviews with officials whose families had been killed and their property destroyed. This experience strengthened his belief that much of northern India was now heading towards anarchy. Nehru's secular line came under strong pressure from Congress politicians in Bihar, who wanted him to take a much stronger anti-Muslim stand. Many activists believed that Congress should launch another mass campaign, and drive out the British altogether.

As the crisis deepened, the new Viceroy's Executive Council was scarcely functioning. Nehru was angry that League members refused to attend his 'tea-party Cabinets'. The Muslim League's entry into the interim government had been dependent on their reacceptance of the Cabinet delegation's May Statement, but the League made this assurance conditional in turn upon the British government and Congress accepting their interpretation of 'grouping' – meaning the shape of any new regional borders. Until this matter was settled, they would not attend the Constituent Assembly, which was supposed to be framing a new constitution. Nehru wanted the assembly to be summoned immediately, but Jinnah said that to do so would be the 'greatest possible mistake', and would provoke violence.

Wavell personally took the view that the whole dispute about the terms under which regional blocs or groups would be formed stemmed from the failure of the Cabinet Delegation to give a definitive ruling on the subject back in June. He suggested to George Abell that if 'those weak-kneed people in Whitehall . . . could only be persuaded to issue a clear and authoritative statement, I think that might satisfy Jinnah'.[28] Although in theory a coalition government now existed, in practice it was continually on the verge of collapse.

Jinnah upped the stakes in mid-November by publicly denigrating Congress for referring to Nehru as the 'Prime Minister', and declared that 'the only solution' to India's problems was 'absolute Pakistan – anything else would be artificial and unnatural'. He claimed that when this had happened, tension would cease and 'minorities will then settle down as minorities', and added that following the violence in Bihar, 'exchange of populations will have to be considered seriously'.[29] Nehru thought this statement had created 'a very grave situation', and the Punjab's Chief Minister Sir Khizar Hyat Khan Tiwana told Wavell that he thought talk of mass population shifts was impractical nonsense.

There were now continual riots and violence in east Bengal, Bombay, the United Provinces and Bihar. In Noakhali local thugs and visiting Hindu 'volunteers' were creating havoc, while in Tippera there were forced conversions to Islam, with Hindus being made to parade wearing caps inscribed 'Pakistan' and Muslim-style *lungis*. They had their caste marks removed, the conch bracelets of married women were smashed, and women were forced to marry Muslim men. At Meerut a police officer's wife and eight children were murdered, and the provincial Home Minister responded by recruiting sixty former INA soldiers as 'special constables' to protect local Congress officials.

As Hindu refugees poured into Bihar with tales of pogroms and looting in Noakhali, revenge was taken on local Muslims. Village after village was purged, the survivors streaming out towards areas where they hoped to find their co-religionists in a majority. The killings centred around Patna, and seem to have been committed by gangs organized by local Hindu landlords, while Marwari businessmen in Calcutta provided the funds for the purchase of weapons. The carnage spread through Patna, Monghyr, Saran and down towards Bodh Gaya.

The Muslim League claimed at the time that officials of the Congress administration in Bihar had allowed preparations for slaughter to be made, and Wavell believed that much of the trouble stemmed from the decision by the Chief Minister, Pandit Pant, to release a large number of supposedly political prisoners, who were in fact *goondas*. By the middle of 1947, an estimated twenty thousand Bihari Muslims were dead, and tens of thousands more were living in makeshift relief camps.

The reaction of the Muslim League was to run black-bordered epitaphs in its newspaper *Dawn* exhorting the survivors to remain united and invincible in the face of Hindu aggression, as the 'martyrs for Islam clustering around the throne of God' would have wished. Activists and 'helpers' from the League travelled through the refugee camps with political manifestos, and Jinnah again raised the possibility of population shifts as a means of dealing with communal antagonism. His belief that India was 'two nations' – Muslim and Hindu – was starting to be physically realized.

By 20 November 1946, Wavell was writing to Pethick-Lawrence: 'We are very near what will amount almost to open civil war between the communities ... Bitterness between the leaders and the communities generally could hardly be worse than at present.' A week later he wrote again in desperation to press London for some sort of guidance: 'The absence of a definite policy on the part of His Majesty's Government is a very serious matter indeed at a critical time like this.'[30] Unless there was a political breakthrough of some kind in New Delhi, the Indian Empire would continue its slide into anarchy. The dispute over the structure of the regional groups in a united India had to be clarified, or the League would not cooperate in a constitution-making body. Several senior British ministers thought Wavell's insistence on this point was itself a cause of conflict, and that it was more important to keep Congress sweet so as to facilitate an orderly British retreat.

Realizing at last the severity of the crisis, Attlee agreed to summon Indian leaders to London for urgent talks. After a good deal of horse-trading over who should go, Nehru, Jinnah, Liaquat and Wavell flew out of Karachi on 1 December, accompanied by Baldev Singh, who had been chosen as a Sikh representative. India's chief political opponents were now confined in closer physical proximity than ever before, but their personal relations remained frosty. Jinnah irritated his fellow passengers by arriving late for take-off, and ordering a glass of beer from the cabin crew straight after breakfast.

The delegates met in Downing Street for four days, and although there was a degree of détente there was no agreement. Both Congress and the League now believed that Wavell was biased against them. Although the Prime Minister went out of his way to pacify Nehru, the League were able to claim a partial victory when British constitutional experts backed their interpretation of the May Statement over grouping. This was in accordance with the original meaning of the Cabinet Delegation's document, and much bad feeling would have been avoided had the question been clarified six months earlier. Congress may have considered themselves hard done by, but Attlee's underlying bias against the Muslim League was still pronounced. As he remarked to his confidant Arthur Moyle some years later, Jinnah was 'the only Indian fascist I ever met'.[31]

On 7 December, Singh and Nehru flew back to India to attend the first session of the new Constituent Assembly, which was supposed to be agreeing a constitutional answer to India's problems. The seventy-nine seats that the Muslim League had won remained empty. Sardar Patel was reported to be extremely angry at the British decision over grouping of the provinces, but despite various prophecies of doom the Governor of Bombay Sir John Colville, who was acting as Viceroy, was able to report that the occasion had passed off peacefully without 'black-flag' demonstrations. Photographs of this historic meeting show a sea of Gandhi caps.

Jinnah remained in England for a few days, haggard and ill, with his usual tin of Craven A cigarettes by his side. He met up with his late wife's old friend Kanji Dwarkadas, who had acted from time to time as an informal link between Congress and the League and was now staying in London. Dwarkadas thought Jinnah looked 'sick and depressed', but noted he had lost none of his shrewdness: 'His self-esteem, his pride and his feeling of being personally hurt had embittered him and he had created ghosts of suspicion and distrust all round him.' He felt that much of Jinnah's intransigence and bitterness stemmed from the way he had been treated on a personal level by members of Congress. The leaders of the two main parties would not even speak to each other outside formal negotiations.

Dwarkadas was one of a number of people who claimed that Jinnah used the Pakistan demand as a negotiating position of last resort, rather than a desired policy. He wrote in his book *Ten Years to Freedom*: 'I do not think Jinnah wanted Pakistan. Right till 1946 he was prepared to work for one united India. So all the time he was talking in terms of Pakistan, this was, I always believed, a bargaining point for him.' Under this interpretation, Jinnah only accepted the creation of an independent Muslim state because he 'had rightly come to the opinion that the Congress leaders did not want any settlement with him'.[32]

This question has been debated in all directions by historians, without any side establishing a watertight case. Jinnah's own statements on the subject do not provide a definitive answer. It does seem clear from his preliminary acceptance of the Cabinet Delegation's plan that he was not irrevocably set on an independent Pakistan. He may simply have been out for the best deal he could manage, whatever that might be. One of the cleverest responses to the quandary of his genuine intentions can be found in Mukul Kesavan's novel *Looking Through Glass*. When the protagonist, who is working as a waiter at the Cecil Hotel, asks, 'Mr Jinnah, sir, do you really want the country partitioned?' the Quaid-i-Azam responds with a scribbled reply at the bottom of his bill: 'Leading question. Barristers do not have opinions – they have briefs.'[33]

When Nehru and Singh returned to India, the Viceroy remained in London to wrestle with his masters, engage in futile discussions with Pethick-Lawrence, and attend several meetings of the Cabinet and the India and Burma Committee. He felt he was being treated like a 'poor relation', and tried to impress upon them the need for fast decisions. In his opinion, withdrawal from India should be treated like a 'military plan made in time of war'. Still the politicians went round in circles. Wavell decided his friend A.V. Alexander and the Foreign Secretary Ernest Bevin were 'in reality imperialists', and was stunned by the degree of ignorance about India exhibited by the Cabinet. The irritable Field Marshal noted that one minister was surprised to hear that Sikhs lived in the Punjab.

Ernest Bevin disliked Wavell's tone, and wrote to Attlee to express 'strong views' about his 'defeatist attitude'. Like a fair number of Labour ministers, Bevin was a romantic imperialist who wished he could turn the clock back. He wanted a viceroy, he declared to a blast of trumpets, 'who, even if he were the last man left there would come out with dignity and uphold the British Empire'. Britannia should not 'knuckle under at the first blow'. The Empire was going to the dogs. 'In fact you cannot read the telegrams from Egypt and the Middle East nowadays without realizing that not only is India going, but Malaya, Ceylon, and the Middle East is going with it, with a tremendous repercussion on the African territories. I do beg of you to take a stronger line and not give way to this awful pessimism.'[34]

Wavell had numerous discussions about the future of members of the 'Secretary of State's Services' – namely the Indian Civil Service, the Indian Political Service (which included those British officials who served in the Princely States) and certain members of the military and police forces. He felt very strongly that their loyalty and morale during the present crisis would be secured only if they were assured of adequate compensation when British rule ended. The issue was complicated by the fact that, under existing legislation, they would have to be paid from Indian revenues, which a government of free India would clearly be unwilling to spend on their former oppressors. It was finally agreed that if necessary the Services would be compensated out of the disputed sterling balances, which was a small but important step forward.

By 20 December Wavell was telling Attlee that he 'had been very discourteously treated' by being kept waiting so long, and he made preparations to fly back to New Delhi, leaving his Private Secretary George Abell to represent him. He felt he 'could not go back without some definite policy', and asked for an assurance that the British government would 'make arrangements with a view to the transfer of power in India not later than March 31, 1948'. When Abell returned to India a few weeks later he told Wavell that the Cabinet had been unwilling to take decisions of any kind, and that 'he was really horrified by their lack of realism and honesty'.[35]

Back at Viceroy's House in the closing days of 1946, Archie Wavell sank into a morass of gloom. He knew that he had less ability to control events in India than any viceroy had ever had. His powers had been further eroded by the appointment in November of Sir Terence Shone as British High Commissioner in India, responsible for direct liaison on government-to-government matters, thereby bypassing the Viceroy.

The country was cracking up before his eyes, yet nobody in London appeared to have any clear idea how to handle the situation. They were not willing to take decisions, nor were they willing to give him the discretion to make decisions on their behalf. His diary was accorded a sad summing-up of events: 1946 had been 'the most gruelling year I have ever had ... The Cabinet Mission was really our last chance to bring about a settlement in India, a temporary one which would have enabled us to leave India with peace and dignity.'

Wavell felt that 'while the British are still legally and morally responsible for what happens in India ... we are simply running on the momentum of our previous prestige . . . I have now committed myself, and very nearly committed HMG to a plan of announcing a definite date of termination of our control of India and of withdrawing on a definite plan . . . It has been my fate for the last 5 or 6 years to have to conduct withdrawals and to mitigate defeats, and I have had no real opportunity of success. This is inevitably depressing . . . No rest, no success.'[36]

SEVENTEEN

Our Previous Prestige

The breakdown in law and order spread across many parts of northern India during the early months of 1947. There was increased communal disturbance in Bihar, spurred on by the propaganda of the Congress Socialist Party, which proposed the immediate abolition of *zamindari*. The group's leader, Jai Prakash Narayan, gave a press conference at which he said the interim government would break down within six months, adding that the Muslim League was a 'British front', and that what was needed was further 'revolutionary struggle'.

On 4 February, while the Conservative MP Harold Macmillan was staying at Viceroy's House and the Wavells were busily preparing for their daughter Felicity's forthcoming wedding, a King's Messenger arrived from London carrying a fatal letter. 'I think you may agree,' wrote Attlee to Wavell, 'that the time has come to make a change in the Viceroyalty.' As a consolation prize, would he care to have his name submitted for 'the dignity of an Earldom'?[1] Wavell's response, blunt as ever, was that this was an undignified way to sack him, especially since he had in the past made several offers to retire, only for the Prime Minister to say he should remain. 'The divergence, as I see it,' wrote the Field Marshal, 'is between my wanting a definite policy for the Interim period and HMG refusing to give me one.'[2]

When he learned that his replacement was to be Lord Mountbatten, Wavell wrote privately: 'An unexpected appointment but a clever one from their point of view, and Dickie's personality may perhaps accomplish what I have failed to do.' Although he was insulted by the manner of his own dismissal, Wavell took a positive view of his successor's capabilities. He knew him well from Mountbatten's period as Supreme Allied Commander in South-East Asia, admired his boldness, and had received support from him when tackling the Bengal famine. In character and style the two men were radically different, yet their ideological outlook regarding decolonization was broadly similar. It was only several months after India's independence that Wavell concluded his successor had 'very much gone over to the Congress side'.[3]

Attlee's tactless sacking of the Viceroy was preceded by many months of duplicity. He had first considered Mountbatten as a replacement for Wavell in January 1946, following a recommendation from the former Vicereine Lady Willingdon.[4] In December, while Wavell was still in England holding talks about India's future, Mountbatten was summoned to Downing Street and offered his job. This was followed by a protracted period of horse-trading, with Mountbatten laying down the terms on which he would accept the post. These ranged from an assurance that his naval career would not be jeopardized, to a promise of the continued use of the old York MW102 aeroplane that he had used at SEAC.

While these negotiations took place in Whitehall, the Prime Minister continued to dither in his treatment of Wavell, assuring him of support while arranging his dismissal. In mid-January 1947, Attlee told Wavell it would 'not be advisable to fix a day' for the British to quit India, yet only five days previously Mountbatten had written to Attlee: 'It makes all the difference to me to know that you propose to make a statement in the House, terminating the British "Raj" on a definite and specified date.' His only concern, he continued, was that 'I am not really sure, however, what H.M. Government wish me to try and achieve in India.'[5]

This was the crux of the matter: Wavell had been facing a similar problem for some years. Mountbatten's refusal to go to India without a precise set of instructions from London forced the British government to define its position, or at least to specify its ambitions. The truth was that Attlee's policy was in a state of continual flux, being buffeted by events, and he was willing to change his mind when encouraged by somebody he respected. He disliked Wavell, mistrusted his judgement, and so ignored his advice, but ironically when Mountbatten made almost identical demands he took notice and accepted them. By this stage Freddie Pethick-Lawrence had such a shaky grip on his portfolio that plans were made to replace him as India Secretary. As Attlee's biographer states, the Prime Minister 'was in fact his own Secretary of State for India'.[6]

Mountbatten was given, at his own request, a precise if hopeful remit by Attlee, which bore little relation to actualities in India. He was told to reach a fair accommodation with the Princely States, to retain the unity of the Indian army, and to demit British authority by the end of

June 1948. This date was later than Wavell had originally suggested. In his view, as expressed to Attlee throughout the previous year, March 1948 was the latest point by which power should be transferred if serious civil disorder was to be avoided. In June 1946 Wavell had even suggested 1 January 1947 as a suitable date for British departure, a fact which is often forgotten by denigrators of Mountbatten's speedy withdrawal from India.

The Prime Minister's most important instruction, announced on 18 March, was 'to obtain a unitary Government for British India and the Indian [Princely] States, if possible within the British Commonwealth'.[7] In reality Attlee had abandoned any serious hope of keeping India united. As he admitted in retrospect: 'You might have got a united settlement at the beginning of the thirties' – implying that it was unlikely at a much later date.[8] The insistence on India retaining its link to the Crown was to be an overriding factor in Mountbatten's negotiations. At the time it was seen as a matter of great importance, yet within a matter of years it had become irrelevant.

Any hopeful dreams of a united India were killed off for good by a Congress resolution agreed in New Delhi on 8 March. Following the public British announcement in February that power would be handed over come what may, even if necessary 'to the existing provincial governments' of British India, the ever-watchful Patel had realized that coherence at the centre was the only way of retaining Congress control. He took the view that the best cure for a 'diseased limb' was amputation. The last thing he wanted was a transfer of authority to a variety of different regional administrations. He had discussed the matter in some detail with his ally the Reforms Commissioner V.P. Menon at the end of the previous year, and Menon had even sent proposals to London which were secretly based on Patel's opinions.[9]

With Nehru's backing, Vallabhbhai Patel bounced the Congress Working Committee into an acceptance of Pakistan, on the condition that the Punjab would be divided. With Gandhi tucked up out of the way on a peace mission to Bihar, the Working Committee passed a resolution which stated that there should be 'a division of Punjab into two provinces, so that the predominantly Muslim part may be separated from the predominantly non-Muslim part'.[10] Jinnah could have his Pakistan, but it would be a moth-eaten, truncated version.

This decision put Nehru and Patel in a much stronger position. The stalemate with the Muslim League was broken, as was Gandhi's decades-old hold over Congress. 'No one listens to me any more,' the Mahatma told one of his afternoon prayer meetings soon afterwards. 'I am crying in the wilderness.'[11] Jinnah was confronted with the logical consequences of his own theory – if he wanted partition of territory, he could have it, even at district level. Attlee's decision to depart from India come what may had dealt a serious blow to Jinnah's strategy, which depended on the British maintaining some sort of role in India in the medium term. As civil unrest grew, the British government's priorities came to tally with the aims of the Congress leadership.

It would appear that many figures in the higher echelons of Congress believed a Pakistan consisting of Bengal's 'rural slum' in the east and a portion of Punjab together with Sind and Baluchistan in the west would be too weak to survive, and would eventually be bound to merge with the central authority. By the time Mountbatten arrived in New Delhi a fortnight after the Congress resolution, the chances of retaining India as a united country had evaporated. The power of the Mahatma's 'inner voice' had been superseded by the harsh *realpolitik* of the Sardar.

Mountbatten was given far greater discretion than Wavell had ever had to make decisions without reference to the India Office. Unlike previous Viceroys, he was allowed to meet and speak to anybody he wished without prior permission from London. In later life, when his reminiscences had come to owe more to fantasy than to fact, Mountbatten maintained that this discretion amounted to something greater. A conversation with Attlee supposedly went as follows: 'You are asking for plenipotentiary powers above His Majesty's Government. No one has been given such powers in this century.' After a short silence and a nod from Cripps, Attlee apparently continued: 'All right, you've got the powers and the job.'[12] There is no documentation to support Mountbatten's claim. The need for plenipotentiary powers in India had disappeared seventy years earlier, when the first telegrams were sent from London to Calcutta; by 1947 communication was almost instantaneous.

During the weeks before his departure for New Delhi, Mountbatten was sent a number of letters by Wavell outlining remaining issues that needed to be clarified by the British government. The result was that Mountbatten left London with far clearer instructions than his predecessor had ever been given, even if the policy that Wavell had initiated remained essentially unchanged. This helped to mitigate his ignorance of Indian politics. As one of his inner circle wrote at the time, 'Mountbatten,

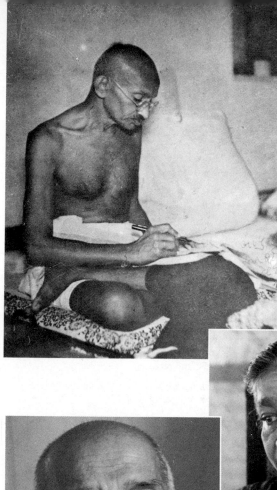

Left Mohandas Gandhi.

Below left A rare photograph showing Chakravarti Rajagopalachari's eyes.

Below The Congress politician Sarojini Naidu.

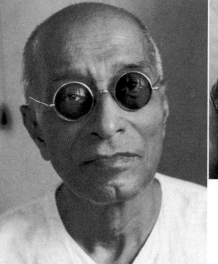

Organizers of political rallies such as this one in Bengal were required to provide a table and chair for the ubiquitous Special Branch shorthand reporter.

Below left The dapper Muslim League leaders Liaquat Ali Khan and Mohammad Ali Jinnah during emergency talks at Downing Street in December 1946.

Below right The end-game: Archie Wavell and Freddie Pethick-Lawrence on their way to see the Prime Minister in December 1946.

Street painting of Netaji Subhas Chandra Bose dressed as the Supreme Commander of the Indian National Army.

Above Calcutta, 1946. A temporary moment of Hindu-Muslim unity.

Right Vallabhbhai Patel.

Left 'The momentum of our previous prestige': Mountbatten takes over the remains of British power from Wavell in March 1947.

Below Dickie Mountbatten and Mohandas Gandhi at their first meeting, 1 April 1947.

Above The founder of Pakistan, the Quaid-i-Azam Mohammad Ali Jinnah, portrayed as an Islamic hero by a street artist.

Right Street painting of Pakistan's first Prime Minister, Liaquat Ali Khan.

Above The back-seat driver: Sardar Patel and Pandit Nehru.

Right V. P. Menon, the civil servant who formulated the plan under which British rule in India came to an end.

Below 'A date with destiny'? The Prime Minister Pandit Jawaharlal Nehru with Lord and Lady Mountbatten on the day of India's independence.

Muslim families from east Punjab in a refugee camp in Lahore.

Hindu families from east Bengal fleeing their village by boat.

'The light has gone out': a man shields himself from the Calcutta sun on the morning after Mahatma Gandhi's murder.

Looking 'inexpressibly sad and careworn', and surrounded by a crowd of nearly a million people, Nehru accompanies his mentor's corpse to its cremation.

in briefing himself for the political task that lies ahead of him, is starting from scratch.'[13]

Vallabhbhai Patel's reported reaction to the new appointment is both characteristic and revealing. On learning from Congress sources in London that Mountbatten was a politically radical aristocrat, the Sardar murmured: 'Ah, he will be a toy for Jawaharlalji to play with – while we arrange the revolution.'[14]

The Congress grip on power tightened during the early months of 1947, aided by news of the change at the top. Ministers began to fail to turn up to meetings with Wavell, although their social and political relations with him remained fairly good. The only time he overruled them was in his refusal to release all INA prisoners immediately. Nehru strengthened the Congress position overseas by sending Asaf Ali to the United States as Ambassador. Wavell held a low opinion of his new man in Washington, describing him as 'a little cock-sparrow who would like to be a peacock . . . without much ability or character but a very exaggerated idea of his own talents'.[15]

As the pace quickened, further steps were taken to maintain the security of intelligence communications between India and London. Philip Vickery at IPI made a note that the DIB 'holds certain Security Service ciphers and I am dealing with these in consultation with the Security Service'. The 'India three figure cipher' and 'A.(B).T. special liaison code' would all have to be destroyed. In the meantime, 'the S codebook used with one-time pads between the Intelligence Bureau and IPI, Kabul, Kabul with repeat IPI . . . should be retained by the DIB for communication with me at any rate so long as my office is a part of the DIB's.'[16] Soon afterwards, George Abell wrote to the secretaries of the eleven provincial governors telling them to destroy any compromising documents.

As Wavell's viceroyalty came to an end, the last link between Whitehall and India's security apparatus was severed by Patel. He decided to dismiss Norman Smith and replace him with his own nominee as Director of the Intelligence Bureau. This fact was kept secret at the time, and the editors of the *Transfer of Power* documents refer to Smith as having remained in his post until the end of British rule. There was a half-hearted attempt in London to prevent Patel from sacking him, but on 15 March Monteath drafted a cable to George Abell on the subject. Ostensibly the communication was between Pethick-Lawrence and

Wavell, although by now the bureaucrats were making much of the running. It said:

> Top Secret and Personal. From SoS to Viceroy: You should know (a) that appointment of Indian DIB is accepted as probably inevitable by security authorities here (b) that in these circumstances IPI would not be able to continue in privileged position he [i.e. Vickery] enjoys here and that his organization will have to be close[d] down, being replaced by some kind of Liaison Office on reciprocal basis if that is acceptable to Patel, (c) that Liddell, Deputy Director of MI5 now in Far East will be reaching Delhi on return journey about March 24th (d) that Shone [the British High Commissioner in India] has just been instructed to approach Patel and suggest that opportunity of Liddell's visit should be taken for discussion of future liaison arrangements.[17]

A fortnight later, a telegram arrived in London which read: 'To Vickery from Smith. Shall hand over 11th [April] afternoon to Raobahadur T.G. Sanjavi Pillai who arrives Delhi 7th. Am sailing for UK on 15th.'[18] Pillai was a forty-nine-year-old District Superintendent of Police from Madras – the police equivalent of an ICS Deputy Commissioner, and so one of the more senior indigenous policemen within the service. It can be presumed that Patel deemed him loyal to the aims of the Indian National Congress. This meant that by the time Mountbatten arrived in New Delhi, Indian Political Intelligence had virtually stopped functioning, and there was an Indian DIB. On Patel's orders, Mountbatten was not permitted to see him.

On 22 March, Lord Wavell went out on his usual early-morning horseback ride from Hauz Khas, accompanied by members of his staff, and that afternoon his successor arrived. Like Gandhi, Mountbatten travelled with an entourage, although in his case it consisted of smooth young thrusters and high-profile fixers rather than goat-milkers and *bhajan*-chanters. They were named the 'Dickie Birds' by the staff at Viceroy's House, who did not look kindly on interlopers from London.

Many of them were Mountbatten's old colleagues from SEAC days and before, including Captain 'Ronnie' Brockman as 'Personal Secretary', Colonel Vernon Erskine-Crum as 'Conference Secretary' and Alan Campbell-Johnson as 'Press Attaché'. Sir Eric Miéville, a senior but outdated former ICS officer, came as 'Principal Secretary'. Peter Murphy, a man considered by his detractors to have been Mountbatten's Svengali (Douglas Fairbanks Jr. once described him as 'a large, devout Irish homosexual

and Communist sympathizer'), joined the retinue as an all-purpose confidant. Sir Stafford Cripps had offered to come along for the ride, but
Mountbatten ducked out speedily on the grounds that he would feel
overshadowed by Cripps's prestige. 'I should never relish the idea of
having him either on my staff or staying in my house,' observed Mountbatten's cousin King George VI.[19]

The most impressive member of the new team was General Lord
Ismay, who became 'Chief of the Viceroy's Staff'. He had been born in
India, and worked as Military Secretary to the Viceroy Lord Willingdon
after a stint in the Somaliland Camel Corps. Hastings 'Pug' Ismay was a
big, squat-faced man, who had been Churchill's Chief of Staff and 'right
arm' during the war. His high standing within the British Establishment
was to be invaluable to Mountbatten, especially in his dealings with
Auchinleck, with whom Ismay acted as a mediator.

The Viceroy and the Viceroy-designate had a short and intense discussion, at which Wavell said (according to the highly dubious recollections of Mountbatten in old age): 'I am sorry for you ... I have only
one solution, which I call Operation Madhouse – withdrawal of the
British, province by province, beginning with women and children, then
civilians, then the army. I can see no other way out.'[20] Afterwards Lord
and Lady Mountbatten escorted Lord and Lady Wavell to Palam airport.
'The baton has mounted,' remarked the Field Marshal cryptically to his
ADC David Walker as he said farewell. Walker was given exclusive permission to record the departure for posterity on his cine-camera, but
unfortunately he had already used the same reel to film his baby son,
which gives the finished product a surreal quality.

Wavell was seriously worried about the situation in the Punjab as he
flew back to Britain. The province had degenerated into communal
slaughter in the struggle for political ascendancy, with Sikhs as the principal target. He was concerned that ministers in London were still more
worried about 'coal, electricity and Palestine' than events in India.

Back in London, he discovered that an Indian clerk belonging to his
staff had been leaking papers and information to Congress politicians.
These documents were then shown to Stafford Cripps, probably by Sudhir
Ghosh, as evidence of Wavell's perceived anti-Congress bias. Cripps had
not bothered to inform the Viceroy of this leak, although he did advise
Mountbatten to employ only British stenographers. He also attempted
to have the Viceroy's Private Secretary George Abell sacked on the grounds

that Nehru considered him an 'English mullah', but Mountbatten refused on account of Abell's experience. Wavell, learning for the first time that the government had been planning to get rid of him since the previous year, arrived at Downing Street for a frosty final meeting. After a short discussion, he was bowed out of the room by the 'singularly ungracious' and inclement Attlee without a word of thanks.

Archie Wavell died three years later, lauded as a war hero, but never having been given fair recognition for his achievements in India. He was bored in his final years, receiving honours and awards, although he was glad to be told by the Secretary of State for India that it had been his intransigence at the end of 1946 that had finally driven Attlee into a definite policy. As his friend Chips Channon wrote, Wavell was 'vague, yet shrewd, and when he is attending to the subject, he darts rapier-like to the point'.[21] Although he was hopeless when confronted with the legalistic repartee of politicians like Cripps, Wavell always returned ruthlessly to the heart of each problem that needed to be faced. This was his greatest strength as Viceroy. The constitutional settlement that emerged in India was to be based on his work over the previous three years.

On a summer's day in 1910, a bearded man lay writhing in bed in a house in central London. He stank of old cigar smoke and eau-de-Portugal, and feebly waved a hand of ruby rings at the roomful of servants. They knew he enjoyed sex in the afternoons, that he held firmly right-wing political opinions (disapproving in particular of a concept called democracy), and they could not have failed to notice that he was irascible and very fat, renowned as a keen consumer of plovers' eggs, salmon steaks, asparagus, Parisian whores, claret, *foie gras*, iced puddings and other delicacies. A week earlier he had been in Biarritz, cavorting with the last of his mistresses, a ripe, chestnut-haired woman thirty years his junior, but today he was suffering from fainting fits and bronchial attacks.[22]

Across the room sat another plump, bald, bearded man of German origin, holding a bulging wad of banknotes. They amounted to £10,000, or around half a million pounds in today's terms. Helped by mutual back-scratching, both men had accumulated vast fortunes, largely through share trading, wire-pulling and fast deals. The money, which was apparently intended for the sick man's mistress, was passed from one to the other, and placed on a bedside table. The visitor, disturbed by his friend's coughing and spluttering, decided it was time to leave. Doors opened, servants and doctors scurried, and the recipient of the cash sank back on his pillows. A few minutes before midnight, after a rapid succession of heart attacks, he died.

The man who brought the banknotes was Sir Ernest Cassel, financier, speculator and grandfather to Lady Mountbatten. The dead man was the King Emperor Edward VII, great-uncle to Lord Mountbatten.

The symbiotic friendship between Cassel and the King was mirrored in the relationship between Lord and Lady Mountbatten. Their alliance was based not on passion, but on pragmatism. It was an extremely effective working partnership: like the Chiang Kai-sheks, they were a storming double act who knew exactly how to operate, socially and politically. This is not to suggest that their marriage was simply a business arrangement; it had begun in a blaze of puppy love, and although they irritated each other, there was strong mutual emotional dependence.

His Serene Highness Prince Louis Francis Albert Victor Nicholas of Battenberg was born in 1900, and christened in the presence of his great-grandmother Queen Victoria. 'Dickie', as he was known to his intimates, was related to most of the royal families of Europe, and had the usual English upper-class schooling before joining the Royal Navy. In 1917 his father succumbed to the prevailing anti-German hysteria and was transformed into the Marquess of Milford Haven, the son mutating into Lord Louis Mountbatten.

During the early 1920s Dickie travelled to India in the retinue of his cousin the Prince of Wales. While he was there he consorted with the visiting Edwina Ashley, who had been brought up with wealth, connections, but little love. Their relationship blossomed under the disapproving eye of the Vicereine Lady Reading, who doubted Dickie's motives and hoped Edwina would find 'someone older, with more of a career before him'.[23] The newspapers were delighted when the couple became engaged. Both were beautiful, she was an heiress, and he was almost royalty.

The Mountbattens were young and immature when they married in 1922. They kept pets, to which they were devoted, such as Rastas the honey bear and Gandhi the chameleon. In time a pair of daughters appeared, named Patricia and Pamela, but Edwina soon grew tired of Dickie. He fussed over her and issued endless trivial orders, even specifying the appropriate colour of the buttons on her chauffeur's coat. In response she became a rather brittle vamp, and took to her bed with a string of polo players and lounge lizards. Dickie saw his failings as a husband, yet felt powerless to change himself, writing to her in 1927 in a sad, honest and pathetic letter: 'I wish I could drive a car like Bobby Casa Maury, play the piano and talk culture like Peter, make enthusiastic remarks like Ralph, play golf like Ronnie, shoot like Daddy, play polo like Jack. I wish I knew how to flirt with other women and especially with my wife . . . and could excite you more than I fear I do.'[24]

As a couple, 'Lord and Lady Louis' led the flamboyant life of the very rich, which alienated many of Dickie's contemporaries and superiors in the navy. He had a special 'cabin' bedroom constructed in his house, featuring naval charts, brass handrails and electric fans which blew 'sea air' into the room. In a corner stood a full-size model of an admiral wearing his father's uniform and medals.

Mountbatten was intriguing in that he rejoiced in the superficial fripperies of wealth and glamour, yet was devoted to hard work and practical matters. As one of his colleagues put it: 'The frivolous public image was very far from the truth. If anything he was an under-sexed workaholic rather than a playboy.'[25] In his everyday and his professional life he was fascinated by gadgets and scientific inventions. According to his lifelong valet Charles Smith, his technical ingenuity 'knew no bounds . . . he devised a "Simplex" shirt with built-in Y-fronts that he could slide into like a stretch suit . . . Then, while he dried his chest, I took another towel to dry his back.'[26]

Mountbatten was always happy to turn his thoughts to anything new and unconventional. The Duchess of Windsor wrote in her memoirs, with a sharp edge to her pen: 'Dickie bubbled with ideas on every conceivable subject – housing, relieving unemployment, new strategies of attack in polo, or how to cure the chronic maladies of the British Exchequer. The more baffling these problems were to the experts, the more convinced Dickie was that he had a fundamental contribution to make and was determined to make it.'[27] The same applied to the 'India Question'.

Mountbatten's serious career was launched when Winston Churchill made him Chief of Combined Operations in March 1942, to the irritation of the three established Chiefs of Staff. Around the same time Edwina took up nursing and St John's Ambulance work, becoming an extremely effective and diligent organizer. Churchill liked Mountbatten's impetuosity and charisma, and in late 1943 he sent him to South-East Asia as Supreme Commander. In the aftermath of the war, Mountbatten played an important part in the decolonization of Burma, Indo-China and Indonesia. Although he was not a political theorist, and did not share Edwina's socialism, he took a firmly pragmatic approach towards colonial rule. Where it was apparent, as in most of Asia in 1945, that nationalist forces were in the ascendant, he saw little point in pretending there could be a return to the *status quo ante*. This was particularly true in Burma, where his treatment of the 'father of the nation' Aung San secured temporary stability at a time when the country was close to revolution. He took a similar approach when Nehru visited Singapore on behalf of Congress in 1946. By treating him courteously, he reduced the scope for tension and unrest locally, and wooed Nehru for the future.

Mountbatten was not distressed by the post-war Labour victory, and in a four-day trip to London after the Potsdam Conference managed to have conversations with Alexander, Attlee, Bevin and Cripps, to mention only the first three letters of the alphabet. It came as no great surprise to him when he was offered the Viceroyalty of India at the end of 1946. Although he knew he was being handed a poisoned chalice, the offer was irresistible.

Even today, the subject of Lord Mountbatten generates remarkably strong opinions. Although he is admired by some people, he still attracts an extraordinary degree of fascinated and largely unfounded loathing. While I was writing this book, one man said to me, 'I hope you're going to give Mountbottom a good thrashing.' 'Why?' I asked. 'Because he lost India, of course,' was the answer. While left-wingers despise him for his privilege and arrogance, for traditional British patriots of all ages Mountbatten is the man who gave away 'the jewel in the crown'; the fact that Britain's Indian Empire had been in a state of nascent chaos from the early 1940s is forgotten. There is a vague assumption that had it not been for the shenanigans of this far too charming, far too handsome and far too braided sailor (and his pinko wife), New Delhi might still be controlled from London today.

Everyone seemed to have a story – usually apocryphal – about Dickie Mountbatten: he cheated at polo; he had a controlling interest in a male brothel in Knightsbridge; he always pretended he had just been speaking to the Queen on the telephone; he believed in flying saucers; he was caught in bed with Noël Coward, and so on. While photocopying some notes about him at Salisbury Public Library one winter's afternoon, I was offered a variety of spontaneous character assessments. One woman told me he was 'horribly Machiavellian', a second that he was 'definitely the greatest hero of the war years', while a third made allegations about Edwina's supposed lust for what she termed 'dark-skinned men'.

Much of the problem stems from Mountbatten's own efforts to rewrite history during the last years of his life. His public-relations adviser Alan Campbell-Johnson makes the point that 'during his last eighteen years, without Edwina there to cut him down to size, his surface vanity flourished. He did a lot of damage to his own reputation in those years.'[28]

By attempting to create his own myth with such assiduous care, Mountbatten sowed the seeds of its posthumous collapse. In the late 1960s he took to denigrating the role of Lord Wavell, whose policy he had inherited and carried through, and whose achievements he had always previously acknowledged. Then came a multi-episode television documentary, *The Life and Times of Lord Mountbatten*, detailing the great man's role in the major events of the twentieth century. It was followed in 1975 by *Freedom at Midnight*, an inaccurate though readable book on his viceroyalty by Larry Collins and Dominique Lapierre which, as his biographer Philip Ziegler elegantly puts it, 'is remarkable chiefly for the faithfulness with which it portrays the history of the period as Lord Mountbatten would have wished it to be seen'.[29]

Grateful at being granted more than thirty hours of ill-judged interviews by the aged Mountbatten, the authors appear to have assumed that whatever he told them was the historical truth. Mountbatten retrospectively adjusted the facts, glorifying British rule: 'The people of India – I haven't got the statistics but it must be over 99 per cent – were absolutely satisfied with the way they were ruled. That's the point. They *loved* it.' The role of Jinnah was traduced, so that he emerged as 'this clot', 'that clot', a 'lunatic' and an 'evil genius'.[30] Mountbatten may have caught his prejudice from Gandhi, who remarked in an interview with his hagiographer Louis Fischer in July 1946: 'Jinnah is an evil genius. He believes he is a prophet [but] he has cast a spell over the Muslim, who is a simpleminded man . . . he is a maniac.'[31]

Mountbatten exalted his own position to a ludicrous degree, retrospectively conflating the outward trappings of viceregal pomp with a genuine ability to exercise political control. Describing his swearing-in ceremony as Viceroy and Governor General to Collins and Lapierre, he recalled his pleasure at being able to wear so many decorations ('And I wore the aiguillettes as personal ADC to the King Emperor'), and said that once he had taken the oath of office, 'I realized I had been made into the most powerful man on earth. One-fifth of humanity I held in my hand. A power of life and death.'[32] This might be contrasted with Lord Wavell's diary entry for his own investiture, which ran, in full: 'Sworn in as Viceroy. Ceremony went off all right.'[33]

Mountbatten was sentimental, unreflective, and a doer rather than a thinker. He suffered from an odd combination of conceit and lack of self-assurance, which grew worse as he grew older. In the last years of his life he was never content with his very considerable achievements: they had to be exaggerated, and the role of others had to be denigrated. As one of the Queen's Ladies-in-Waiting recalled: 'I told the Master of the Household, who arranged the seating plan [at meals, that] if I had to sit through one more account of how Dickie won the war, I'd scream.'[34] Ian Stephens, the former editor of the English-language Calcutta newspaper the *Statesman*, described this in 1969 as 'a peculiar kind of perfectionism, or vanity in his character ... the sort of thing you might find in quite a young man, but which is bewildering, and extraordinary, in someone so "fulfilled" ... This perfectionism apparently causes him to want public approbation which is total; to yearn to be thought a complete success, almost incapable of misjudgement or error.'[35]

Although the likes of Stephens and Leonard Mosley made dents in his reputation, Mountbatten was usually treated with a degree of reverence during his lifetime. The first encomium to come out after his assassination by the IRA in 1979 was called *Mountbatten: Hero of our Time*, and is full of remarks about 'slow, patient negotiations with the Oriental mind', while Edwina is written up as a 'beautiful forty-five-year-old Englishwoman of such notable wealth and aristocracy, with a good stiffening of Jewish blood in her veins', whatever that might mean.[36]

Philip Ziegler's official biography, published in 1985, proved less complimentary than expected, as if its author had been shocked by the discovery of his subject's weaknesses. More recently Mountbatten has been attacked by countless Pakistani historians, and by the anthropologist Akbar Ahmed, who came out with the fine line that 'if Jinnah is the first Pakistani, Mountbatten is the first Paki-basher.'[37] The most vicious and effective ambush has been 'Lord Mountbatten and the Perils of Adrenalin' by Andrew Roberts, in his book about a selection of mid-century figures, some of whom were eminent and none of whom were Churchillians. Here Mountbatten is blamed for a wide variety of disasters, including his own murder. Roberts's work has caused considerable pleasure in Pakistan, where it has even been pirated under the engaging title *Lord Mountbatten's Deceit*.

The essay is an entertaining, take-no-prisoners assault on the man and his reputation, which falls for the line that the settlement of 1947 was entirely the work of the last Viceroy. Mountbatten is presented as 'a mendacious, intellectually limited hustler' who was 'promoted wildly above his abilities, with consistently disastrous consequences', and whose 'negligence and incompetence resulted in many unnecessary deaths'.[38] He even gets the blame when a sailor falls overboard from his ship: 'When suddenly without warning and for no particular reason,' writes Roberts, 'Mountbatten swung HMS *Kelly* sharply to starboard while going at full speed ahead in the North Sea, it was a stoker who fell to his death rather than a brother officer.'[39] 'I think Mr Roberts must be under the impression,' observed Mountbatten's daughter Lady Pamela Hicks, 'that the *Kelly* was a speedboat.'[40]

Mountbatten emerges from this portrait as little more than a dim and callous popinjay. The trouble with such a portrayal is that it ignores a variety of practicalities in the cause of a good polemic. Certainly he had flaws in his character, which developed into gaping fissures in old age, but even so, it is unlikely that a wide range of Britain's major politicians, from Winston Churchill to Clement Attlee, and Denis Healey to Douglas Hurd, should have been seriously deluded over Mountbatten's abilities. As Alan Campbell-Johnson asked rhetorically: 'Do you honestly think that a chap like Pug Ismay would have worked for a complete idiot?'[41]

Healey, who had to cope with Mountbatten as Chief of the Defence Staff while he was Secretary of State for Defence in the 1960s, maintained that he 'showed a unique energy and vision in his defence roles, with a sense of the wider political context, rare in service chiefs . . . Without the ruthless clarity of Mountbatten's vision, I doubt whether Attlee would have found the strength to take the difficult decisions demanded of him during those traumatic months.'[42] Ian Stephens, one of Mountbatten's harshest (and best-qualified) early detractors, could write from personal experience of his 'sheer intellectual range' and praise his 'first-class brain: quick, wide-ranging, practical, and intuitive'.[43]

Mountbatten's strength lay in making and implementing tough decisions. He was not a deep thinker, but he was extremely good at analysing a problem and formulating an immediate strategy with which to tackle it. The role given to him by Attlee's government was to be the lubricant of imperial withdrawal; nothing more. His task was to give Britain – a harassed, war-torn, penniless little island – freedom from its Indian Empire, which had turned from a valuable asset into a frightening burden. As David Cannadine has written: 'Most members of the royal family are employed to open things . . . But Mountbatten was quite brilliant at the much more difficult and important job of *closing things down* . . . As such he was the pioneering and pre-eminent *de*-imperialist, who was followed, in the next quarter century, by many other morticians of empire.'[44] Mountbatten wore his medals with pride in the process, and made the most of the thin hand he inherited.

Lord Mountbatten was Viceroy of India for fewer than five months. The most crucial decisions relating to the transfer of power were taken before he even left London; indeed a good deal of what remained of British authority had already been handed over in September 1946. Far from being the cause of the bloodshed and political crisis in 1947, he was never much more than a spectator, sent out by a desperate Attlee to oversee and attempt to manage the imperial collapse. As Ismay wrote within days of arriving in Delhi: 'The situation is everywhere electric, and I get the feeling that the mine may go up at any moment . . . If we do not make up our minds on what we are going to do within the next two months or so, there will be pandemonium.'[45]

To imagine that Mountbatten had the option of sitting tight for another few years is to misunderstand the extent to which British control had already been demitted by default during the period 1944–1946, to ignore the disastrous legacy of Churchill's wartime policy vacuum, and to misconstrue the complexities of India's internal politics. Demobilization was almost complete, and there was simply no political will, on either side of the House of Commons, for stopping this process and reinforcing India with the necessary five divisions. Indeed, it would not have been possible without US funding, which would never have been forthcoming.

During his time in New Delhi, Mountbatten's scope for manoeuvre was severely limited by the control exercised through the Congress-dominated interim government. He faced an exceptionally difficult task, and he did his job fairly well, despite his prejudice against the Muslim League. The truth is that far from being the man with a fifth of humanity in the palm of his hand, Lord Mountbatten was a bit-part player in the story of Indian independence.

EIGHTEEN

Liberty

Two days after their arrival in New Delhi, Mountbatten and the Dickie Birds began to hold meetings with India's leading politicians. These took place at Viceroy's House in a whirl of publicity: the words 'directed Press Adviser to arrange for photographers to be present to photograph the meeting' occur frequently in the minutes of the new Viceroy's staff meetings. Notes were dictated after each interview, and circulated among Mountbatten's team. He was determined that he should establish a personal rapport with the politicians with whom he would be negotiating, and hoped to make it clear through the media that he would not be operating in the style of an old-fashioned imperialist.

The political encounters were matched by a simultaneous social offensive on all fronts. 'You will be doing the young people,' the Hon. Pamela Mountbatten, fresh out of finishing school, was told by her father.[1] Edwina was ordered to 'establish early contact with the women who matter in India', since Patel's daughter Manibehn and Jinnah's sister Fatima were believed to be very influential.[2] Her Excellency performed this task with the greatest of skill, even managing to lure the radical leftist Aruna Asaf Ali into her drawing-room. Aruna Asaf Ali realized earlier than most of her fellow freedom fighters that what was taking place was not the grassroots liberation of which they had dreamed. 'It's a transfer of power,' she asserted. 'It's not revolutionary transformation at all.'[3]

There were garden parties and dinners and luncheons, to which all manner of people came, by invitation rather than 'by command', as in the past. Guests included an elderly Congressman who began his meal by unwrapping a pair of dentures from his handkerchief and inserting them into his mouth, with some deliberation. Herbivores, omnivores, carnivores, vegans, fruitarians and Gandhian nut-crunchers were all accommodated, their dietary preferences being indicated by an appropriately coloured ribbon pinned to the back of their chair. It can be presumed that a more tactful song than Lord Linlithgow's 'The Roast Beef of Old England' was played as they walked through to dinner.

The 'good-will campaign', as the Mountbattens called it, had an important impact on Delhi's new elite. Nehru's niece Nayantara Sahgal remembers a letter from her mother which told her that 'the new Viceroy and his wife had dropped in informally to my uncle's house in York Road, and sat in the garden eating strawberry ice-cream. I just couldn't believe it, and thought she must be joking . . . I had left the country to go to America during the Quit India movement, when all my family were in prison and such an idea would have been totally unheard of. It may seem unimportant now, but at the time it really did make people believe that Dickie was genuine in what he was trying to do for India.'[4]

The Viceroy began to exhibit anti-Muslim League tendencies almost at once. He was happy for the 'most sincere' and 'extremely frank and fair' Jawaharlal Nehru to brief him against Jinnah at their first meeting. Nehru's rival was described as a 'financially successful though mediocre lawyer' who had 'found success late in life. He had not been politically successful until after the age of sixty.' 'The secret of his success . . . was in his capacity to take up a permanently negative attitude.'[5] For Nehru to describe the League leader as a mediocre lawyer and unsuccessful politician demonstrates his own bias by this time, and forgets the fact that Jinnah was a major nationalist politician at a time when Nehru was still a Harrow schoolboy in short trousers.

Vallabhbhai Patel was deemed by Mountbatten to be 'most charming' and 'apparently very fond of Sir Stafford Cripps', which was hardly surprising, given that Congress had Cripps in their pocket. He said his opposition to Jinnah was based partially on the supposition that 80 per cent of India's Muslims were simply 'forcible converts' from Hinduism. When asked about the purpose of forced religious conversions, Patel said he could not discuss the matter 'because he had no idea of the Muslim mentality'.[6] The press attaché Alan Campbell-Johnson thought the Home Minister was at least straightforward in his opinions: 'His approach to the whole problem was clear and decisive. India must get rid of the Moslem League.'[7]

Mohandas Gandhi arrived to meet the Viceroy on 1 April, trailed as ever by a retinue of three dozen loyal disciples. The most famous person in the Indian subcontinent was 'recognizable only because of the loin cloth that he wore', according to Mountbatten's valet Charles Smith. 'He stayed on for afternoon tea, which was arranged on the lawn ... The Indian leader did not touch either the cakes or sandwiches, but chose to eat a bowl of goat's curd which he had brought with him. He even persuaded Lord Louis to sample a mouthful!'[8]

Conversation proceeded along expected lines, Gandhi telling the story of his life at some length before diversifying to political matters. Mountbatten was delighted to record that the importance of his own position had been recognized: 'During the course of the discussion Mr Gandhi gave it as his considered opinion as a student of history and of world politics that never before, in any case of history he had read about in recent or past times, had so difficult or responsible a task been imposed on any one man as that which now faced me. I thanked him sincerely for realizing the position in which I was placed.'[9]

The Mahatma attempted to reactivate the Bose Protocol of 1939, by which he offered the Muslim League the opportunity to self-destruct. He made 'an astonishing proposal ... to solve the whole problem. It was nothing less than to dismiss the present Cabinet and call on Jinnah to appoint an all-Moslem administration.'[10] Congress would cooperate, Gandhi promised, 'so long as all the measures that Mr Jinnah's Cabinet bring forward are in the interests of the Indian people as a whole ... If Mr Jinnah rejects this offer, the same offer to be made *mutatis mutandis* to Congress.'[11]

Mountbatten was rather taken by this idea, until he realized its true implications. George Abell pointed out that it would probably provoke open civil war, since a Jinnah Cabinet would be wholly subordinate to the Congress majority in the Central Legislature. Even V.P. Menon, who usually veered towards Congress, could write that such a move 'would certainly place Jinnah in the position of having to adjust his views to those of the Congress. This is perhaps not unintended by Gandhi ... It is no solution to suggest that power should be transferred to the Congress to the exclusion of the Muslim League. If the proposition were as simple as that, it would have been solved long ago.'[12]

The Viceroy's first meeting with Jinnah was not a success. Mountbatten complained that his guest alternated between 'a most frigid, haughty and disdainful frame of mind' and 'a gracious tea-party hostess manner'. Liberal doses of the famous Mountbatten charm had some effect, although Jinnah maintained a rigid stance over what the Muslim League would and would not be prepared to accept. The meeting ended with Mountbatten saying he was still unsure what recommendations to make to the British government, although 'at the present I was utterly impartial'.[13]

When they met again a few days later, Mountbatten pointed out that under the principle of partition, Bengal and the Punjab would also have to be divided, since their populations were communally mixed. Jinnah 'expressed himself most upset at my trying to give him a "moth-eaten" Pakistan. He said that this demand for partitioning the Punjab and Bengal was a bluff on the part of Congress to try and frighten him off Pakistan.'[14] Jinnah was resolute that Bengalis and Punjabis were indivisible, and had too much in common to be split into two. By now the Viceroy was losing his patience with Jinnah, perceiving him not as the chosen spokesman of a substantial minority of the Indian people, but as a troublemaker.

He wrote in a report to London soon afterwards that the Quaid-i-Azam was 'a psychopathic case; in fact until I had met him I would not have thought it possible that a man with such a complete lack of administrative knowledge or sense of responsibility could achieve or hold down so powerful a position'.[15] Mountbatten felt Jinnah 'had not thought out one single piece of the mechanics of his own great scheme, and he will have the shock of his life when he really has to come down to earth and try and make his vague idealistic proposals work on a concrete basis'.[16]

The social element in all this cannot be discounted. Both of the Mountbattens liked and identified with Nehru, but found Jinnah difficult to handle. The Muslim leader was rich and elitist, but not in the British mould, despite his spats, pince-nez and Hanover Square suits. For all the propaganda of Congress, he was never an insider in British governing circles, and was considered a spiv by many ICS officers. In terms of a comprehension of the nuances of Viceroy's House, he was no more anglicized than somebody like Patel. For instance, he breached protocol by walking out of a function in front of Their Excellencies, something that Jawaharlal Nehru would never have done. Even after independence, Nehru was happy to stand and toast King George VI at dinner, despite having once made a famous speech declaring himself 'no believer in kings and princes'.[17]

Like Wavell, Mountbatten preferred the company of Liaquat Ali Khan to that of Jinnah, and would have found him easier and more amenable to negotiate with as a Muslim League leader. On hearing that Mountbatten wished to return to the Royal Navy when he had finished his work in India (the Admiralty Fleet Orders referred to him as 'seconded temporary duty Viceroy'), Liaquat said that if he agreed to the creation of Pakistan, the first thing they would do would be to build him a battleship. Pandit Nehru would serve as the pilot to keep him out of the way, Maulana Azad as the *dhobi wallah*, while Mahatma Gandhi would provide 'hot air to breathe into the boilers'.

Jinnah attempted to undermine the Congress plan of partitioning the two main provinces of his new nation by suggesting there should be an eight-hundred-mile corridor between the two wings of Pakistan, and that Calcutta could become a 'free port'. Congress reaction to this was extremely hostile, and the idea soon foundered. The powerful determination of Bengali politicians to keep their province united was also destroyed, since neither Jinnah nor Nehru could risk weakening their own position in New Delhi. On 23 May, Patel wrote to a political associate in Calcutta: 'Talk of the idea of a sovereign republic of independent Bengal is a trap to induce the unwary and unwise to enter into the parlour of the Muslim League . . . Bengal has got to be partitioned, if the non-Muslim population is to survive.'[18] When Suhrawardy later proposed that Calcutta might remain a free port for six months after the British had left, the Sardar said he would not permit such a thing for even six hours.

Various other political leaders and claimants visited the Viceroy in his freshly painted office to make representations, including an embassy on behalf of the Princely States and a delegation from the North-West Frontier Province led by Abdul Ghaffar Khan. Dr Ambedkar was still maintaining that Congress could not speak for sixty million members of the Scheduled Castes, or for three million Christians. A contingent of Sikh luminaries arrived, headed by Master Tara Singh and the pro-Congress Defence Minister Baldev Singh. By the end of their interview, Mountbatten's head was so riddled with confusing and contradictory information that he 'arranged for them to meet Sir Eric Miéville, and to put their case to him, since it was difficult for me to remember everything they had told me'.[19]

Having seen the principal Indian leaders, the Viceroy called a conference of the eleven provincial governors in mid-April. He told them he was worried about the various 'private armies' of the different political groupings, totalling around half a million people, that had sprung up across India. The governors responded that the breakdown in civil control was accelerating. In Bihar, communal killing and migration continued, while it had been reported that there was 'increasing lawlessness in Noakhali. Attempts at roasting people alive have been traced twice, and loot, etc., is going on.'[20] The Punjab was approaching civil war following the massacres in Sikh villages during March.

Apart from the Governor of Assam, who was slightly more optimistic than he had been a few months before, all the governors urged 'the greatest possible speed in making a decision and an announcement; for even the quieter provinces feel that we are sitting on the edge of a volcano and that an eruption might take place . . . at any moment'.[21]

The Viceroy's difficulty was that he had to try to find a solution to the present crisis, yet had little choice but to follow the dictates of India's most powerful political party, the Indian National Congress. The British were no longer in a strong enough position to impose a settlement on India, in the way that they would have been at, say, the time of the 1942 Cripps Mission. As Mountbatten admitted to a 'top secret' meeting of his staff on the morning of 1 May – although he made sure the words were deleted from the minutes – 'If he fell foul of Congress it would be impossible to continue to run the country . . . it was evident . . . that anything but a clean partition would produce enmity on the part of Congress.'[22] As the pace quickened, Clement Attlee decided that Freddie Pethick-Lawrence should be put out to grass, and replaced by the Earl of Listowel, a shy and unassuming young hereditary peer who had sat on the India Committee for some time. Although he was to prove a more effective Secretary of State for India than either Pethick-Lawrence or Amery, Listowel only remained in office for four months, and his work was largely confined to pushing legislation through the Houses of Parliament.

With his options narrowing by the day, the Viceroy set about formulating a plan for rapid departure, which would enable His Majesty's Government to cut loose from India under the guise of delivering liberty.

Mountbatten's first solution, known as 'Plan Balkan', was an extraordinary kedgeree of opposing ideas. Drawn up by a small team consisting of Miéville, Ismay, Abell and Mountbatten, it was the constitutional embodiment of Attlee's instructions to his Viceroy, which were so broad and optimistic as to be mutually contradictory when united in one document. It was supposedly based on the Cripps offer of the previous summer, but as one insider wrote, 'everyone in Delhi knew that the Cabinet Mission's proposals were as dead as mutton.'[23] Constructed out of a variety of conflicting ambitions and intentions, Plan Balkan was intended to satisfy everyone, but succeeded only in doing the opposite. It went through 'innumerable different drafts', and was flashed impetuously at various people in New Delhi before being rushed to London by Lord Ismay and presented to the Cabinet on 3 May for swift approval.

In essence the Plan broke down the subcontinent into its constituent parts and then thought about putting them back together again. Each of the eleven provinces of British India would decide its own fate, Bengal and the Punjab could divide down the middle if they chose to, and the Princely States would have the choice of standing alone or forming alliances with anybody they chose 'in the best interests of their people'. Once this had occurred, all the parties could reunite, according to taste. The result of this plan would have been the destruction of the status of the Constituent Assembly, and the creation of a collection of miniature autonomous warring states across India.

Attlee's Cabinet, most of whose members were almost wholly ignorant of India and its politics, set about adjusting and reworking Plan Balkan. An option was introduced enabling the North-West Frontier Province to become independent if it chose, while the future of Baluchistan was to be settled by a handful of nominated landlords. Whitehall's Parliamentary draftsmen made some further amendments and clarifications, and the textual changes were transmitted back to India. Mountbatten announced that he would call a meeting of the Indian leaders in the middle of May, with a view to securing their rapid agreement to the proposals.

On 9 May Patel tightened the ratchet one more notch. He announced that the current British policy of 'remaining neutral, but holding power is a way of propagating civil war', and that control should be transferred immediately to 'the Central Government as it now stands with the Viceroy standing out . . . If there were conflicts in the Cabinet on any question, the majority would rule.'[24] As if this was not enough, on the same day the most senior indigenous officer in the Indian Army, Brigadier Cariappa, suggested at a private meeting that once the British had left there should be a military dictatorship. The forces, 'with either Nehru or Jinnah as Commander-in-Chief should take over power'. Mountbatten replied that such a course of action would be 'not only wholly impracticable but highly dangerous'.[25]

Meanwhile the Viceroy and his retinue had travelled to Simla to escape the heat. He was joined at the hill-station by Jawaharlal Nehru, with his daughter Indira, his confidant Krishna Menon, and his South Indian secretary M.O. 'Mac' Mathai. They stayed at Viceregal Lodge, and spent much of their time at 'The Retreat', a resting place at Mashobra. There was a side of Nehru that sought the approbation of the British Establishment, and the reverence of Dickie and Edwina came as more than a political boon: it was an affirmation of his own identity. Two years earlier he had been languishing in prison, and now here he was as the personal house-guest of the King's cousin. As Mathai wrote: 'One thing that I could not fail to notice was that whenever Nehru stood by the side of Lady Mountbatten, he had a sense of triumph.'[26]

The visit was a definite social success. 'Jawa', as the Mountbattens called him owing to the congenital British inability to pronounce Indian names, consolidated his instinctive bond with Edwina, and impressed the rest of the house party by exhibiting an ability to walk fast backwards uphill. 'We have made real friends with him,' the Viceroy reported, 'and whatever else happens I feel this friendship is sincere and will last.'[27]

This favouritism towards the head of one political grouping was consolidated on the night of 10 May, when Nehru was invited into the Viceroy's study for a drink. That day the final amended text of Plan Balkan had been telegraphed to Simla. Mountbatten was determined to bludgeon the Indian leaders into swift acceptance, and even made plans with the India Office for an announcement of its terms 'at 1930 Indian Standard Time Tuesday 20th May', with a simultaneous statement in the House of Commons. Now, feeling suddenly nervous about its viability, he broke with both protocol and even-handedness by allowing the Congress leader to see a copy of the document 'as an act of friendship', and even to 'take the draft to bed'.

Nehru's response came the next morning in the form of a 'Personal & Secret' note to his new benefactor: 'I need hardly tell you how much I appreciate your confidence in me or that I am convinced of your earnest desire to help India to achieve her freedom as early as possible. It has been a privilege to get to know you better.' However, the Plan presented 'a picture of fragmentation and conflict and disorder'. Blame must surely lie with London, since 'HMG seems to function in an ivory tower of their own isolated from realities in India. They proceed apparently on certain assumptions which have little relevance and ignore the basic factors of the situation in India.' In fact the document was not significantly different to the version that Ismay had taken to London, and so was the work of Mountbatten rather than the British government. 'If my reactions were so powerful,' Nehru concluded. 'you can well imagine what my colleagues and others will think and feel.'[28]

'Nehru bombshell' ran the heading in Mountbatten's diary that day. 'Nehru, having read it, has vehemently turned it down,' noted Campbell-Johnson, and 'is convinced that it involves a major departure in principle from the original draft prepared by Mountbatten and his staff'. The Viceroy told his press attaché that he had only given the Plan to Nehru on 'a hunch ... Without that hunch, "Dickie Mountbatten," he said, "would have been finished and could have packed his bag" ... He said that most of his staff, with natural caution, had been against his running over his Plan with Nehru, but by following his advice rather than their advice he had probably saved the day.'[29]

The Viceroy had certainly saved himself, as his credibility would have been destroyed if he had tried to press ahead with the farcical Plan Balkan. What is extraordinary, and indicative of his naivety about Indian politics, is the fact that he can ever have seriously imagined it would be accepted by Congress. Various historians have sought to read a conspiracy into this, and suggested that the Plan was drawn up with a view to rejection, so that a rival proposal could be imposed in the resulting confusion. There is no evidence of this. As Mountbatten's biographer has written, such an interpretation 'argues a cunning in the Viceroy which was wholly lacking'. Mountbatten could be duplicitous in pursuit of his ambitions, but his was a straightforward and often transparent duplicity. That day he was dealt 'one of the worst blows he had suffered in his life. Not only did it seem that British policy was once more in ruins, but he had endured a personal and most humiliating rebuff.'[30]

A crisis meeting of officials was called at Viceregal Lodge that afternoon. Mountbatten tried to wriggle out of his blunder by claiming the draft Plan he had sent to London 'represented in his ... considered opinion what the leaders had implied that they would accept'.[31] This was not quite true, since none of the Indian leaders had been given the chance to study the draft, and their only knowledge of it stemmed from vague briefings from Miéville and Mountbatten during April. They had been told that the proposals were based on the Cabinet Mission Plan, under which provinces could opt out of groups within the union of India, when in fact Plan Balkan offered numerous successor states, which could then join groups if they wished. As Nehru told one official, it would create 'Ulsters' all over the subcontinent. The Viceroy had assured Attlee that the Plan would win support in India, yet it had fallen before reaching the first fence.

Casting around for a way out, Mountbatten turned in desperation to his Reforms Commissioner, V.P. Menon. A cheerful, engaging man with snaggled teeth, Menon's career had been one of the more exceptional in Indian public life. While he was a young man his family had declined into poverty, and he had worked in a goldmine in Mysore and as a clerk in a tobacco firm in Bangalore before gaining a clerical post in the Government of India's Reforms Office in 1914. His obvious talents had led to rapid promotion, and during the Quit India movement he had fallen into the position of Reforms Commissioner. He was the first Indian to occupy the post, but as the British were concentrating on repression rather than reform at the time, nobody took much notice. It was only in 1945 that his importance was realized, and by then nobody was keen to sack a man of such experience and ability.

Rao Bahadur Vapal Pangunni Menon was by temperament a conservative, with no time for the social radicalism of Nehru or Gandhi. His natural ally was the Congress puppet-master, Sardar Patel, with whom he had formed close links since the creation of the interim government in September of the previous year. Although he exhibited the trained neutrality of the ICS bureaucrat, Menon's instincts were those of the traditionalist Hindu. For example, in his writings he praised the Udaipur royal family for their 'prolonged resistance against the Muslims' during the Mughal period, and noted that it was 'the boast of the family that it never gave a daughter in marriage to any of the Muslim emperors'.[32]

The closeness of his links with Patel had begun to worry the Viceroy's Private Secretary, George Abell, some months earlier. He had written a confidential minute on the subject for Mountbatten in March, in which he stated that Menon had enjoyed a remarkable career, but had lately come 'under pressure from Congress ... Mr Menon now is genuinely convinced of the rightness of the Congress view on the general political position. Thus, although he is an old friend of mine, and one of the people I like best in Delhi, I am convinced that it is not possible to take him into confidence as fully as has been done in the past.'[33]

This advice was acted upon, and during the first six weeks of Mountbatten's viceroyalty Menon was kept in the background. With the collapse of Plan Balkan, his faults suddenly became advantages. Here was a draftsman who was unlikely to produce a document which would be rejected by Congress.

With Nehru storming around Viceregal Lodge in a state of high emotion, Menon was summoned by Mountbatten and asked to revive a proposal he had been floating for some time. It proposed that power should be transferred to two central governments, one in India and one in Pakistan. The handover would take place on the basis of dominion status, giving the two countries independence within the framework of the British Empire, or rather the Commonwealth, as it was now called for reasons of public relations. There would be voting in the provincial assemblies of Bengal and the Punjab to see whether they wished to be divided. Rather than waiting for a Constituent Assembly to draw up a working constitution, authority would be handed over at once to the two new governments, and they would operate for as long as they chose under the terms of the 1935 Government of India Act.

Nehru was leaving Simla that very night, so Menon was given three hours in which to prepare an acceptable document. Rushing back to his hotel, since he was too lowly an official to have been given a bedroom at Viceregal Lodge, he dashed off a few pages on his typewriter. Nehru examined them, and returned to New Delhi contented with the general theme. The Menon Plan, as it became known, was to form the body of the settlement under which the British left India three months later; within three hours, he had achieved the solution that had eluded so many eminent politicians for so many years. 'I was keeping Vallabhbhai Patel informed of the developments in Simla,' Menon wrote later, 'and he was delighted by the turn of events.'[34]

Mountbatten was equally pleased, buoyed up by the Commonwealth link implied in the term dominion status, and knowing that V.P. Menon had saved his skin. He later referred to him as 'my brilliant Indian Staff Officer', and admitted: 'I was very greatly influenced in my own negotiation development by his ideas.'[35] Telegrams were sent to Delhi and London cancelling all the carefully laid arrangements relating to Plan Balkan. With Attlee and the Cabinet in a state of dismay over these bizarre developments, the Viceroy was ordered back to Britain to offer an explanation. He flew out from Delhi on 18 May, taking Edwina and Menon with him. The Reforms Commissioner now entered the inner circle of the

Viceroy's staff, and sat at the right hand of Abell and Ismay, who had remained in London throughout this curious and baffling debacle.

Mountbatten glided around London, meeting ministers, reassuring Clem Attlee, briefing the India and Burma Committee, and taking a 'trembling' Rao Bahadur Menon to meet the King Emperor. By the end of the month the Viceroy and his staff were back in Delhi, with the new draft plan having been approved in principle by the Cabinet. The Mountbattens stepped up their 'good-will campaign', fearful that the Muslim League would reject a plan which offered them only a truncated Pakistan. Her Excellency sent a letter to 'My dear Miss Jinnah' saying: 'We got back from London last night, and I brought you this little old box which I send with my very best wishes. I hope to see you very soon.'[36]

On the morning of 2 June, the Indian leaders assembled for a meeting at Viceroy's House. Mountbatten began by stating that he 'could remember no meeting at which decisions had been taken which would have such a profound influence on world history'.[37] It was already apparent that Congress would in principle accept the Menon Plan, and the Defence Minister Baldev Singh, who had been chosen for no obvious reason to represent six million Sikhs, had little choice but to acquiesce. Mountbatten was at his best, using his substantial powers of persuasion to secure an acceptance from all the parties. 'Never was Mountbatten's genius for informal chairmanship and exposition more signally displayed,' wrote Campbell-Johnson afterwards.[38]

Immediately after this session, Mountbatten saw the Mahatma, who scribbled some thoughts on the back of five old envelopes, revealing that 'when I took the decision about the Monday silence I did reserve two exceptions, i.e. about speaking to high functionaries on urgent matters or attending upon sick people'. The Viceroy noted laconically that 'he apparently did not consider the occasion of sufficient importance for him to break this rule'. Gandhi made no direct comment on the Menon Plan, but suggested instead that they might reconsider the Cabinet Delegation's proposals he had so busily opposed the previous year. He also asked Mountbatten to sack the Governor of the North-West Frontier Province, on the grounds of his supposed pro-Muslim League bias.[39]

By now the Congress Working Committee had realized that temporary dominion status within the British Empire under the Menon Plan would be to their advantage, since it would deliver most remaining British control to the existing interim government in New Delhi, as well as cutting off the 'diseased limbs' of east Bengal and west Punjab. Mountbatten's obsession with the Commonwealth link made him oblivious to the reasons why Congress politicians might be accepting it. Any ideological opposition they felt towards swearing allegiance to the King Emperor could be swallowed for a few months while they secured control over a unified India. Chunks of territory would be removed in the east and in the west, but it was always possible the land would revert to a central authority at a later date.

The only remaining obstacle was the Quaid-i-Azam, Mohammad Ali Jinnah. Ismay wrote that he and Mountbatten had to leave dinner early that evening 'to go and wrestle with Jinnah. He was in one of his difficult moods. After a good deal of "horse trading", the most the Viceroy could squeeze out of him was an admission that Mr Attlee might safely be advised that he could go ahead with his announcement about the plan to the House of Commons on the following day.'[40]

Jinnah was in a desperate bind, knowing he had no chance of breaking the Congress hold on power at the centre, and that he had been left with a 'moth-eaten' Pakistan as his only alternative. His strategy had always depended on the British remaining in some capacity to implement an agreement, but now it was apparent that they were about to depart. His dream of a greater Pakistan had been destroyed by the decisions of both Congress and the British government, and the unified India with strong regional autonomy that Cripps had proposed the previous summer was no longer on offer.

At a provincial level, the Muslim League was in poor shape, with local leaders in the Punjab being more interested in securing their own status in any future administration than in finding a way of keeping their province united. Meanwhile, in Punjabi villages League supporters were killing and being killed by Hindus and Sikhs. In Bengal the local League wanted an independent and united Bengal, and were losing sympathy with Jinnah's conduct at the centre. The Viceroy's original wish 'to frighten Jinnah into cooperation on the basis of the short length of time available' had been realized, and he gave a provisional acceptance at a meeting the following morning.[41]

As the press photographers were hustled out of the Viceroy's pale green study on 3 June by Alan Campbell-Johnson, Dickie Mountbatten confronted the Indian leaders with the corollary of their agreement to the Menon Plan. It came in the form of a document which had been prepared by George Abell and Evan Jenkins in April, and had now been dusted down and relabelled 'The Administrative Consequences of Partition'. It covered questions of boundaries and diplomatic representation, and the division of the armed forces, civil departments, assets, railways, courts and so forth. The introductory paragraph stated that once legislation for partition had passed through Parliament, dominion status would be 'brought into operation at the earliest possible date after its enactment, in any case not later than 15th August, 1947'.[42]

That evening Mountbatten, Nehru, Jinnah and Baldev Singh arrived at the studios of All India Radio to broadcast to the nation. They had to run the gauntlet of a demonstration of *sadhus* in orange caps, who were protesting angrily against the possible vivisection of Mother India. The broadcast coincided with an announcement by Attlee in the House of Commons and Listowel in the House of Lords. Mountbatten spoke first, outlining the decisions that had been reached, and using the phrase 'if there is partition' to indicate that it depended on a vote in the Punjabi and Bengali legislative assemblies. He was followed by Nehru and Jinnah, who ended his speech with the slogan 'Pakistan *Zindabad!*' (Long Live Pakistan), which some listeners apparently mistook for the words 'Pakistan's in the bag!' Singh was permitted to say a few words, in consolation for the fact that the Sikhs were suffering the trauma of partition without receiving a homeland as a reward.

Vallabhbhai Patel got off to a swift start on the morning of 4 June by firing a salvo at Jinnah, telling the Viceroy that the Muslim leader had 'committed a sacrilege by making a political, partisan and propagandist speech' over the wireless.[43] Later that day Patel chaired a giant press conference in the Legislative Assembly, since he had managed to slip responsibility for Information and Broadcasting into his Home Minister's portfolio. The Viceroy expounded the 3 June Plan to the world's media. Campbell-Johnson, who is an essential source on Mountbatten's viceroyalty despite his sycophancy, wrote that his master gave 'the most brilliant performance I have ever witnessed at a major Press conference'.[44]

Defusing the tension with humour, and sidestepping tricky hypothetical questions, the Viceroy communicated his intentions with great panache. He mentioned almost in passing that 'the transfer of power is going to be much earlier ... I think the transfer could be about the 15th of August.' Significantly, few people at this stage saw his decision to bring forward the date of departure by ten months as crucial, and a week later the Viceroy was still having to emphasize to the press that 'the date of June 1948 now had no significance whatsoever'. Many of the journalists seemed unable to grasp the fact that the British genuinely meant to quit India, and enquired as to the precise meaning of dominion status, and whether India would be able to move towards full independence without British consent. 'I am simply amazed at these questions,' exclaimed Mountbatten. 'There is no question of imposing any decision on you.'[45]

The plan to advance the date of the transfer of power to August 1947 was accepted at the time by all parties as inevitable, and only subsequently attacked as a blunder, owing to the mistaken perception that a premature British departure was the primary cause of the massacres that followed. It was accepted by all that the transfer of power should occur the moment legislation had been rushed through Parliament; and Whitehall had decided that early August was the soonest by which that could possibly occur. The change of date was based partially on an assumption that there was no need for the British to remain once an agreement had been reached, but more importantly on the fact that the instability that would result from any interim alternative was so terrifying, given that legislators in the Punjab and Bengal were bound to vote for division.

At the next meeting of the Indian leaders there was an aggressive dispute over who had legal responsibility for dividing India, Jinnah claiming it was the British government and Congress that it was the Indian government. The Viceroy ruled in favour of Congress, asserting that 'it would be for the Governor-General-in-Council to issue whatever orders were necessary', meaning himself in his capacity as the voice of his ministers. The matter was referred to India's Chief Justice for clarification, who pronounced that the implementation of partition 'clearly involves the exercise of the executive authority of the Central Government and that executive authority is required by sub-sections (1) and (3) of Section 313 of the Constitution Act to be exercised by the Governor-General-in-Council'.[46]

This meant that in the period before the handover, the Congress-controlled interim government would in effect hold power. With Pakistan in the process of creation, this would give the nascent government of free India a quite unjustifiable advantage over its rival, and even the possibility of aborting the new nation before birth. Since it was clear that a reconstitution of the central administration on the basis of communal parity would never be accepted by either Patel or Nehru, Jinnah knew he had to take control of Pakistani territory as fast as possible. With precisely ten weeks left until the arrival of liberty, death was stalking through the towns and villages of the Indian subcontinent.

In the weeks immediately following the announcement of the 3 June Plan, the politicians and bureaucrats of New Delhi operated in a daze, as the implications of what had been agreed struck home. There was a sense of relief that a decision had at last been taken, despite their foreboding. Many ICS officials at the Secretariat took a similar line to Rajagopalachari, who told Mountbatten in retrospect: 'If you had not transferred power when you did, there would have been no power to transfer.'[47]

George Abell, who 'obviously didn't instinctively like or trust Mountbatten', wrote privately that it had been 'a triumph for the Viceroy . . . The fact that the more sane elements of the Congress, and especially Vallabhbhai Patel, were at this stage prepared to do business enabled the Viceroy to use V.P. [Menon] and his influence with Patel to a remarkable effect. The second point, of course, was that the moment the Muslim League definitely realized what was the maximum they could get out of HMG they began for the first time to be sensible.'[48]

During June there were innumerable petty political disputes and legal wrangles between Congress and the League, as if they had failed to grasp the fact that history was now overtaking them. The pent-up dam of years of frustration, suppression and stagnation burst, and the river swept past the political leaders in New Delhi. The All-India Congress Committee gave its assent to the 3 June Plan, despite vocal opposition from hard-line Hindu nationalists and anti-Jinnah Muslims. The resolution was seconded by Maulana Azad, who claimed: 'The division is only of the map of the country and not in the hearts of the people, and I am sure it is going to be a short-lived partition.'[49] This was a commonly held view among many Indians.

The Council of the All-India Muslim League met in the ballroom of the Imperial Hotel in Delhi to make their decision, but were disrupted by a gang of Khaksars, a militant Punjabi Muslim group who wanted Delhi to be included in Pakistan. They rushed into the room wielding knives and overturning tables, intent on stabbing Jinnah. 'The Muslim League Guards took position,' reported one witness. 'As soon as the Khaksars rushed in, some were bodily dubled [sic] and thrown out. It was indeed pathetic to see some of them bleeding or dealt with severely by the police.'[50] Although Bengali merchants and the Pakistan National Movement back in Cambridge had denounced the Plan as 'the greatest betrayal' in the history of the *millat*, it was accepted by the delegates. After the meeting Patel and Nehru complained to Mountbatten about the wording of the Muslim League's resolution, and objected to the content of some of the Leaguers' speeches. Their source, it should be noted, was an Intelligence Bureau agent who had been sent by Patel to infiltrate the meeting.[51]

All that remained was for the legislative assemblies of the Muslim-majority provinces to cast their vote. In both Bengal and the Punjab members generally divided along communal lines, Muslims voting against the division of their province but in favour of joining Pakistan, and Hindus and Sikhs favouring partition as a means of remaining in India. In Sind there was no question of partition, since there were comparatively few Hindus in the province, and they voted by a clear majority in favour of joining Pakistan. Baluchistan did the same, although using a more arcane method of democracy involving local tribal leaders and municipal appointees from Quetta.

In the almost entirely Muslim North-West Frontier Province, where Congress had a special interest owing to the power of Abdul Ghaffar Khan's 'Red Shirts', it was decided that there should be a popular refer-endum. For some years there had been serious conflict between the Governor Sir Olaf Caroe and the Congress leadership, owing to Caroe's supposed bias in favour of the League. In the end Mountbatten felt he had no option but to acquiesce to the province's Chief Minister Dr Khan Sahib, who told him on 5 June that it was 'absolutely necessary' to send Caroe on 'extended leave' before any voting took place. Despite this happening, Dr Khan Sahib's brother Abdul Ghaffar Khan ordered a boy-cott on the grounds that an independent NWFP or 'Pakhtunistan' had not been put forward to the voters as an option. Even so, more than half the electorate voted to join Jinnah, and the power of the anomalous Khan brothers was temporarily broken.

With the creation of Pakistan officially sanctioned, Whitehall's constitutional lawyers got moving. Operating in liaison with V.P. Menon and the Law Secretary Sir George Spence in Delhi, they had to amend the 1935 Act, create two new nations, and undo three and a half centuries of British involvement in India in a matter of days. By an odd coincidence of history, the principal Parliamentary draftsman responsible for the Indian Independence Bill was Sir John Rowlatt, whose father had achieved fame thirty years earlier in unhappier circumstances as the author of the 'Rowlatt Act'. Against precedent, the text of the legislation was agreed in advance by both Congress and the League. On 3 July the British government's India Committee sat until midnight, and gave the final draft of the Bill to the Clerk of the House of Commons at 1 a.m. It was printed overnight, and presented to the House by Attlee the following morning.

The Parliamentary response to India's looming freedom is instructive. When Mountbatten was first appointed as Viceroy, Winston Churchill, as Leader of the Opposition, had told the House of Commons that 'the whole thing wears the aspect of an attempt by the Government to make use of brilliant war figures in order to cover up a melancholy and disastrous transaction ... In handing over the Government of India to these so-called political classes, we are handing over to men of straw of whom in a few years no trace will remain' – a richly ironic statement, given that Congress was to retain power in India for forty-six of the fifty years following independence. Alan Campbell-Johnson sensed while listening to the debate that 'the gulf between Government and Opposition was far narrower than some of Mr Churchill's more sombre polemics might suggest'.[52]

The true nature of most Tory opinion was conveyed by the former Viceroy Lord Halifax, who said that although he had grave doubts about what was being decided, 'I am not prepared to condemn what His Majesty's Government are doing unless I can honestly and confidently recommend a better solution.'[53] The Bill sailed through Parliament, unamended, its passage eased by 'understanding and sympathy' from Rab Butler. With the former Foreign Secretary Anthony Eden deputed to keep Churchill quiet, the bulldog confined himself to growling and grumbling at the legislation, heartened only by the thought that the new nations would remain in the Commonwealth under dominion status. As the Bill passed into law in the middle of July, the Prime Minister despatched a tangled metaphor to 'My dear Dickie': 'I am very conscious that I put you in to bat on a very sticky wicket to pull the game out of the fire. Few people would have taken it on and few, if any, could have pulled the game round as you have.'[54]

While British politicians debated and voted, V.P. Menon held a press conference about the legislation, chaired by the omnipotent Sardar Patel. Most of the questions related to the hundreds of Princely States, which covered more than a third of the land mass of the British Indian Empire and contained two-fifths of its inhabitants. These autonomous dictatorships were the forgotten crux of Indian independence, since the 3 June Plan related only to the freedom of the eleven provinces of British India. As the numerous rulers each had an individual treaty with the British Crown, it was decided that there was no legal basis on which responsibility for their territory could be handed over to a successor government. The subject was a constitutional Pandora's Box: some lived in Princely States, some in Unions of States, some in Petty States, some in Agencies, a few in Protectorates, while others owed theoretical fealty to a more prestigious neighbouring ruler. They exercised varying degrees of territorial control, and each one had to be dealt with individually.

Like non-white slave traders, indigenous princely oppressors complicate the picture of straightforward exploitation by European colonialists, and so their role has tended to fade from history. As Ian Copland points out in his paper 'The Black Hole in the Historiography of Colonial India', the importance of India's princely rulers has been largely ignored by historians. Yet during the 1920s and thirties, 'the princely order was able to exercise real leverage both over Whitehall and the provincial politicians', owing to its power as an ally of the British. Copland points out that the Nizam of Hyderabad 'ruled over a kingdom whose income and expenditure in 1947–48 rivalled Belgium's and exceeded that of twenty founder-member states of the United Nations'.[55]

There was an assumption by many of the princes that their rule would continue unhindered after independence, probably in some kind of treaty alliance with the British government. However, the collapse of the princely order was to be rapid, and in many ways more remarkable than the liberation of the eleven provinces, which were already under substantial democratic control.

Although nationalist politicians claimed that paramountcy – meaning overall control and responsibility for the Princely States – should devolve to whoever inherited power in New Delhi, this stance had been explicitly rejected by Cripps during his 1942 Mission. Sir Conrad Corfield, a senior official in the Political Department who was responsible for liaison with the princes as 'Political Adviser to the Crown Representative', made it plain in November 1946 that if the new Constituent Assembly started to challenge the power of the princes, 'or if the effectiveness of [current British] paramountcy is frustrated, the only equitable alternative is for Crown to begin at once restoration of States' rights (e.g. retrocession of jurisdiction over railway lands and administered areas, etc)'.[56]

Corfield was not simply indulging in power politics. Although Gandhi denounced the situation as 'wicked', it was clear that from a legal or constitutional perspective the states had the right to declare independence once the British had gone. In reality this looked impractical, since with the exception of Kashmir and Hyderabad, each of which covered around eighty thousand square miles of land, individual states were too small to be viable as independent units.

When Mountbatten arrived in India in March he had concentrated on doing a deal with Congress and the Muslim League over the provinces of British India. He postponed action regarding the Princely States and took little notice of representations from the notoriously stiff Corfield, preferring to listen to Nehru, who told him he would 'encourage rebellion' in any states that tried to stand alone. Jinnah's views were unimportant, as with the exception of Bahawalpur, Kalat and Kashmir, there were no serious states within putative Pakistani territory. Once again V.P. Menon offered the Viceroy a solution, which was that the princes might be encouraged to sign treaties of accession to the new governments, handing over responsibility for foreign affairs and defence in return for total autonomy and the retention of their 'privy purses' – meaning the chunk of local taxation that accrued to them personally.

Lord Mountbatten, who was always a realist despite his royalist tendencies, saw this as the perfect answer. He could see that the smaller states stood little chance of survival after independence without the goodwill of the new government, and so 'took the calculated risk' of 'personally sponsoring the Instrument of Accession and undertaking to get all the Princes into this particular bag, while V.P. sold the project to Congress'.[57] Corfield took a more legalistic approach. In his opinion, the princes should not sign anything before 15 August, when paramountcy would lapse. At this point they would be free as independent countries to band together and dictate the terms of any merger with India.

Sir Conrad Corfield felt duty-bound to protect the position of the princes against any inroads a new administration in Delhi might seek to make. He responded to Mountbatten's indifference by seeking direct support from the India Office, and flew to London with Ismay in May, before slipping back to Delhi with new instructions from Listowel just as Mountbatten was flying out to London. Corfield's return took place without Mountbatten's permission, which led to the Viceroy describing his Political Adviser as a 'son-of-a-bitch'.

Once the 3 June Plan was sewn up, Corfield's position was rapidly undermined. Although the right of the Princely States to decide their own future had previously been announced in Parliament, the Viceroy overturned it by supporting the Congress plan to pressure them into accession before 15 August. This contradicted earlier promises, but Attlee and Listowel chose to reverse government policy rather than challenge their subordinate in New Delhi.

Once the decision had been made, Mountbatten gave his full support to the snaring of the royals. On 25 July he addressed a meeting of the Chamber of Princes. Their Highnesses were in a state of disarray, the Chancellor of the Chamber, the Nawab of Bhopal, having recently resigned over his dislike of the terms of the 3 June Plan. The unfortunate princes and their ministers were looking 'divided and uncertain, baffled by the pace of events', togged up in elaborate frock-coats and turbans in the heat of the Delhi summer. His Highness the Jam Saheb stood beneath the sole fan, complaining that it was going too slowly.

Ever the showman, the Viceroy turned up 'in full uniform, with an array of orders and decorations calculated to astonish even these practitioners of Princely pomp', and spoke fluently without notes, pointing out that the Instrument of Accession was a generous offer which might not be repeated. Afterwards he told Alan Campbell-Johnson that 'very few of the Princes or their representatives seemed to have any idea of what was going on around them. Unless they accepted the Instrument they would be finished.'[58]

Mountbatten's approach was ruthlessly pragmatic. Although his treatment of the princes was plainly unjust, it was based on the belief that it was the only way of avoiding the creation of a plethora of conflicting principalities across the subcontinent. Given that many of the princes had their own state armies, a showdown between a Congress government in New Delhi and an alliance of princely rulers could easily have led to a civil war similar to that in China during the 1920s and thirties. Although several of the leading princes were his personal friends, Mountbatten took the view that almost any manipulation was permissible in the pursuit of what he saw as a greater good.

India's nawabs and maharajahs were written personal letters, invited to dinner, and called in for private chats by the Viceroy. Dickie's favourite line was that his cousin King George VI would be personally affronted if His Highness did not accede, since India and Pakistan were about to become imperial dominions. He even told them that if India later decided to become a republic, they would be free to 'reclaim full sovereign independence', which was clearly untrue. One princely minister told Corfield after receiving the full Mountbatten treatment that 'he now knew what Dollfuss felt like when he was sent for to see Hitler: he had not expected to be spoken to like that by a British officer', adding after a few seconds that he 'withdrew the word "British"' – a statement that is in itself indicative of the reason why the princely order was despised by so many Indian nationalists.[59]

Iqbal Mohammed Khan, formerly the Nawab of Palanpur, remembered the arrival of the instrument of accession to the Indian Union. His family ruled a large Muslim state on the borders of Rajputana with 'a thirteen-gun salute and so forth. My father was one of George VI's honorary ADCs. Dickie's form simply came in the post one day and I signed it and sent it back. What else could we have done? We had no access to the sea and could never have operated alone; it was a case of accept the change or die.'[60]

One of the most remarkable features of this project of princely accession to the 'Indian Union' was that the Indian Union did not legally exist. All that Congress was inheriting under the terms of the 3 June Plan was a proportion of British India, which amounted to less than half of the total land mass of the subcontinent. It consisted of six complete provinces (Bihar, Bombay, Madras, Orissa, the United Provinces and the Central Provinces), and truncated portions of three others (Assam, the

Punjab and Bengal). However, Congress control of the interim government, and the fact that they were acting as if they were the single successor state to the British administration, made their actions appear credible. It was a self-fulfilling prophecy: by the end of 1947, the Indian Union was a more cohesive unit than the British Indian Empire had ever been.

With the backing of both the Viceroy and Jinnah, who was under the misguided impression that the Minister for Posts and Air, Abdur Rab Nishtar, would have some say in the conduct of the new ministry, the Congress-dominated interim government set up a 'States Department'. Sir Conrad Corfield gave in his notice at this point, packed his bags, and flew back to England 'with a feeling of nausea'. The States Department took over almost all of the Political Department's powers, and had a remit to woo as many of the 561 princely rulers as it could in as short a time as possible, either with 'standstill' treaties or with full documents of accession.

The newly appointed States Minister – a *khadi*-clad Congressman renowned for being 'harder than steel' – issued a statement proclaiming sweetly that 'it is not the desire of the Congress to interfere in any manner whatever with the domestic affairs of the States', and wishing the princes 'and their people, under this aegis, all prosperity, contentment and happiness'.[61] This strange assertion was entirely at odds with the virulent propaganda that Congress had been running against the Princely States since the early 1920s, and represented as abrupt a reversal in policy as the British government's betrayal of their former allies. As the States Minister had himself warned some years earlier: 'For the princes to claim the Empire's friendship is sheer nonsense, like friendship between a lion and a jackal!'

The Minister's statement had been drafted by the new Secretary to his Department, who took the view that a successful turkey-shoot depended on first lulling your victims into docility. It was notably successful in its effect, provoking a letter from the influential Maharajah of Bikaner saying: 'It is most gratifying to recall that you have always shown a realistic and cordial attitude towards the States. The friendly hand you have so spontaneously extended to the Princes and States, as evidenced by your statement, is, I need hardly assure you, greatly appreciated by us.' His Highness, being a speaker of the King's English, would not have understood an earlier speech in Gujarati by the States Minister describing the princes as 'rotten fruit ... incompetent, worthless human beings, deprived of the power of independent thinking and whose manners and morals are those of the depraved'.[62]

The Minister was Sardar Patel, his Secretary was V.P. Menon, and by the end of November they would between them have added more territory to India than was lost to Pakistan through partition.

India's politicians entered a state of frenzy as they attempted to divide the nation's assets in two. In June a 'Partition Council' had been formed, with the impossible task of implementing the division of the assets of the Government of India, which consisted of everything from railway lines, food stocks, ships and bulldozers to printing presses, chairs and typewriters. The Council consisted of Liaquat Ali Khan and Abdur Rab Nishtar for the League, and Vallabhbhai Patel and Rajendra Prasad for Congress. As the importance of its task became apparent, Jinnah himself took over from Nishtar. From the start it was beset by disputes, which Mountbatten tried to smooth over as best he could.

Although Lord Listowel had admitted it would be 'unfair to Pakistan' to accept 'Hindustan' as 'the successor of the former India', exactly such a move was agreed by Attlee's India and Burma Committee, on the assumption that 'there will be a financial adjustment of the assets involved'.[63] This was a doubtful constitutional decision, however, since legally no 'Indian Union' existed at this point, and so it was unclear from what precisely Pakistan was seceding. This matter was never entirely resolved, and was overtaken by the rush of events. Once Congress had decided to call their new nation 'India' rather than 'Hindustan', the impression of continuity was complete. As Alan Campbell-Johnson remembered, 'Pakistan was cutting itself off from India. I can't pretend we thought of it any differently.'[64]

This meant that the shaky interim government Lord Wavell had set up in September 1946 lost any ability to function, and had to be reconstituted and split in two. Now there were a pair of parallel administrations, one for the new India and one for Pakistan. This move came into effect on 19 July, which meant that for just under a month, Pakistan's only influence in New Delhi was through the Partition Council. As the split in the administration was implemented, every employee of the old

Government of India, from provincial governors to peons in the Works, Mines and Power Department, had to choose between India and Pakistan. For Hindus whose families came from a part of the new Pakistan, or for Muslims working in New Delhi but with strong Muslim League affinities, this was a desperate and hopeless choice to have to make.

The 'optees', as those who chose Pakistan came to be known, were drummed out of their offices within days. Patel told Mountbatten that 'Muslim officials in the Government of India should be got rid of as soon as possible,' and in early August he ordered the Transport Minister to ban optees from working on the railways, supposedly for fear of sabotage. Even senior civil servants who had opted for Pakistan were turfed out of their buildings, and 'in some cases they have had to move tables and chairs out and are working under the shade of trees'. Soon Liaquat Ali Khan was telling the Viceroy: 'I now wish to God you could get partition through by the 1st August.'[65]

Anwar Ahmed Hanafi, who worked in the Finance Department under Liaquat, remembered being ejected from his office: 'We were not allowed to take files, typewriters or anything. We used to work in tents, and I remember using thorns instead of paperclips. Only one goods train of our office equipment ever reached Pakistan.'[66] The process of dividing India's assets was hopeless and impractical. As one writer said of the neem trees along the border at Wagah, 'Why not divide the leaves and branches equally between India and Pakistan? Why not tell the tree which of its branches and its leaves are Hindu or Muslim?'[67]

The bias of Attlee and Mountbatten in favour of Congress was pronounced. Nehru's friend Krishna Menon, who had been designated as India's future High Commissioner in London despite still being under surveillance by IPI, was given access to the highest levels of the British government.[68] Mountbatten had known him socially and received briefing papers from him before becoming Viceroy, and was now content to receive letters from him referring to Jinnah by a blatantly offensive nickname. After a meeting with Attlee in mid-July, Menon wrote that there was 'no lack of desire on the part of the P.M. to be of assistance. I found there and everywhere else that the "Fuhrer" had overplayed his hand.'[69]

There was an aggressive dispute between Mountbatten and Jinnah over who should be chosen by the nascent governments of India and Pakistan as Governor General. Mountbatten assumed he would hold both posts himself, which he hoped would provide vital continuity after independence, as well as ensuring that relations between the two new dominions did not degenerate. Congress agreed to his appointment early on, but Jinnah avoided giving an answer, before finally announcing that he would take the post of Pakistan's Governor General himself. This put Mountbatten into a rage and a quandary, since he now had to choose between going home in the middle of August, or destroying any reputation he still had for impartiality. Pug Ismay was sent to London to discuss the matter with the Cabinet, who decided that if Mountbatten wished to he should serve as Governor General of India alone.

Only Cripps demurred, as had Edwina and George Abell, believing this would be harmful to Mountbatten's position as an umpire. Although he had previously stated he would only remain if it was as Governor General of both dominions, Mountbatten decided to stay with India. It was a grave mistake, and one that was to damage his reputation and cause great harm to Pakistan in the months that followed.

While Jinnah's decision to become Governor General was perceived by Mountbatten as sheer vanity, it was an understandable move. Jinnah knew it was essential to consolidate power as fast as possible if Pakistan was not to be swept back into the powerful new Indian Union, and that with Mountbatten as Governor General his own control would be reduced. As soon as the new Pakistan Legislative Assembly met in Karachi in early August, he was handed a range of emergency powers, which gave him dictatorial powers greater than those any Viceroy had ever exercised. As Alan Campbell-Johnson put it: 'Here indeed is Pakistan's King Emperor, Archbishop of Canterbury, Speaker and Prime Minister concentrated into one formidable Quaid-e-Azam.'[70]

While these serious political and constitutional disputes took place, Mountbatten had to give his attention to hundreds of minor matters, any one of which had the capacity to blow up into a serious crisis. It was little wonder that before long he was in what one member of his staff called a 'tired flap'. For instance, there was a vicious running dispute over the Andaman Islands, the crops of rock in the Bay of Bengal that had previously been used as a penal colony for revolutionaries like Savarkar, and had been briefly put under the control of Subhas Bose during the war. Congress was convinced they were an inalienable part of India, the Muslim League thought they were an essential refuelling point between East and West Pakistan, and the British service chiefs were determined they should be kept as a Commonwealth naval base. Similar disputes took place over other pieces of land on and off the coast of India, and about overseas assets such as India House in London, and the valuable treasures in the library of the India Office in King Charles Street.

Many matters of pressing concern had to be faced. What should be done about the Governor of Bombay, Sir John Colville, who threatened resignation if he was not allowed to fly the Union Jack after 15 August? Would the armlets worn by Mountbatten's ADCs need to be altered after that date? Would the nascent Pakistani Navy agree to fly the white ensign on its ships? What was to happen to the magnificent crown that had been worn by George V at the Delhi *durbar* of 1911? It had been made especially for the occasion, with the Indian masses picking up the tab of £60,000, and Attlee was worried whether it should go to India, or Pakistan, or remain in London in the charge of Lord Listowel.

Then there were questions of protocol. Would George VI be able to go on signing himself 'George R.I.' once he was no longer an Imperator but merely a Rex, given all the costly implications for the Empire's pillarboxes and coins? Congress said yes, but Jinnah the stickler stipulated that Pakistanis would never countenance 'a legally incorrect signature'. The unfortunate monarch had to drop the 'I' and call himself 'George R.'. According to Attlee's recollection, Bertie dealt with the loss of his Indian Empire quite calmly, taking it 'without a murmur. You can't imagine old Queen Victoria sacrificing the Imperial Crown without a struggle, not a bit of it. But George VI didn't mind at all.'[71] Luckily Buckingham Palace was content not to proceed with a droll plan of Lord Halifax's that the King and his spouse should pay a visit to their Indian subjects in the middle of August, 'for the purpose of formally saying goodbye, and wishing them good luck'.[72]

On the morning of 13 August the Viceroy and his entourage flew to Karachi. That evening there was a banquet at Government House, at the end of which Jinnah adjusted his monocle and read a long speech. It was followed by an alcohol-free reception 'attended by some 1,500 of the leading citizens of Pakistan, which included some very queer looking "jungly" men', accompanied by 'sweet music played by a band of bearded warriors in kilts'. Campbell-Johnson thought Jinnah 'an aloof, almost lonely figure . . . Here, indeed, was the apotheosis of leadership by remote control. I had never dreamt that the creator of a nation at the moment of reaching the promised land, could, when surrounded by his devoted followers, be at such a distance from them.'[73]

The next day, 14 August, Mountbatten addressed the new Pakistan Legislative Assembly, then flew across the emptying Punjab to New Delhi. India's Constituent Assembly met at midnight, owing to some astrological doubts about a daytime assumption of power. As clock-hands joined palms in respectful greeting, Nehru made a speech which had gone through a number of drafts. He had started with the phrase 'a date with destiny', but his secretary M.O. Mathai suggested this might be construed to have romantic connotations. They had tried 'a rendezvous with destiny' instead, but Nehru finally settled for: 'Long years ago we made a tryst with destiny, and now the time comes when we shall redeem our pledge ... At the stroke of the midnight hour, when the world sleeps, India will awake to life and freedom. A moment comes, which comes but rarely in history, when we step out from the old to the new, when an age ends, and when the soul of a nation long suppressed finds utterance.'[74]

A little after midnight he and Rajendra Prasad arrived at Rashtrapati Bhavan, as Viceroy's House would now be called, and formally asked Mountbatten to become independent India's first Governor General. The atmosphere was informal, with Pandit Nehru sitting on Mountbatten's desk. The next morning there were parades and bands and rainbows and firecrackers, and Lady Mountbatten distributed sweets in the Roshanara Gardens at the instigation of the ubiquitous Campbell-Johnson. A quarter of a million people attended a ceremony to raise India's new tricolour, Mountbatten having ensured it would not be accompanied by an untoward lowering of the Union Jack.

During the subsequent crush, the Mountbattens' daughter Pamela got a little squashed by the crowds, and was only saved by India's new Prime Minister 'striking people right and left and eventually taking the topee off a man who had annoyed him particularly and smashing it over his head'. The squeeze became so intense that several fainting women, a press photographer and some stray children had to be pulled up onto the Mountbattens' horse-drawn landau as it edged forward. Even Pandit Nehru climbed aboard and proceeded through the crowds of cheering people, 'sitting like a schoolboy on the front hood'.[75] India was free, if in pieces.

PART III

The Beginning of History

'To be an Indian is to be a Hindu – Hindus are Hindus,
Sikhs are Hindus, Muslims are Hindus'

Shiv Sena activist, Mumbai, 1996

NINETEEN

A Communal War of Succession

Sir Cyril Radcliffe K.C. was a wealthy, reserved, stocky, fastidious man with a protuberant forehead, poor eyesight and a slight twist at the corners of his thin lips. He has gone down in history not for his precisely argued constitutional objections to deposited covenants, freedom of information or race relations legislation, but as the man who drew the border line between India and Pakistan. Like Clement Attlee he was educated at Haileybury, where he was known as Squit. After leaving Oxford he enjoyed immediate success as a barrister, combining an incisive legal mind with a capacious memory.

The commonly held perception of Radcliffe among writers on Indian independence is that he was a dutiful, brilliant, neutral umpire, summoned from the Inner Temple by the forces of history to divide a nation on strictly impartial grounds. In fact he was far from being an apolitical lawyer, having spent the war as Director-General of the Ministry of Information under Brendan Bracken, running government censorship and propaganda. He was responsible for organizing the campaign against Nehru's sister Vijaya Lakshmi Pandit when she travelled to the United States, and for harassing P.G. Wodehouse when he made ill-judged broadcasts while in German captivity.

Squit Radcliffe was the insider's insider – the ultimate Establishment figure who could be trusted to put the interests of the state before any other consideration. His philosophy is perhaps encapsulated in a quotation he once copied into his commonplace book: 'Free speech is all right as long as it does not interfere with the policy of the government.'[1] His loyalty was to the nation rather than to any one political party, and after the war he was quickly absorbed into the ruling Labour Party power nexus. By 1947 he was forty-eight, and according to Lord Ismay in line for 'a high judicial appointment' as 'probably one of the first three at the English Bar'.[2] He was a natural choice for the job of cutting up the British

Empire's rough diamond. As one admiring senior civil servant said later, 'Cyril Radcliffe was in the super league. He had everything, intellectual ability, balance, the lot.'[3]

Another myth to complement the image of the disinterested barrister is that during Radcliffe's six weeks in India from 8 July 1947 he was closeted in hot purdah, isolated entirely from any social contact and far removed from the political machinations of the closing days of British rule. This is untrue: during his brief stay he dined with Auchinleck, Mountbatten, the Chief Justice Sir Patrick Spens, his old friend Sir Walter Monckton, the Governor of the Punjab Sir Evan Jenkins, and several other figures of influence within British Indian society. While in Lahore he even attempted to stay with Jenkins at Government House, and had to be dissuaded on the grounds that such a move might be 'misinterpreted'.[4]

The image of total impartiality was propagated by Radcliffe and Mountbatten in the aftermath of independence, both maintaining that they were 'mutually most careful never to have any discussions about the boundaries'.[5] However, according to Mountbatten's Deputy Private Secretary Ian Scott, the Viceroy attended a meeting of the Boundary Commission in Lahore on 22 July, and 'there is thus no question, as people like [Mountbatten's personal secretary] Ronnie Brockman and Campbell-Johnson maintain, that he kept aloof'.[6] This is not to suggest that Radcliffe was corrupt or incompetent, but rather that he took advice, as might be expected, from his client. As the historian Alastair Lamb put it: 'There is simply no way that the Government of India would have allowed somebody with so little experience of India to make the key decisions. Radcliffe was a barrister following a brief.'[7]

The need for a precise border line between Pakistan and India had only been realized late in the day. Despite representations from Wavell in his crucial telegram of 7 February 1946, in which he had laid down a 'detailed demarcation' of projected Pakistani territory, at no point had these proposals been definitely confirmed or rejected by Attlee's government.[8] The result was that throughout the negotiations of 1946 and 1947, nobody was entirely certain what 'Pakistan' would mean.

This lack of precision was used to great effect by the Muslim League during the elections at the beginning of 1946, since voters were encouraged to support a greater Pakistan which stood no realistic chance of ever being created. Muslims cast their votes for the League in the belief that the best way to safeguard their position was through a strong Muslim bloc vote; at no point was there any kind of popular referendum over the creation of the truncated Pakistan to which Jinnah finally agreed in June 1947. The India Office's failure to provide a precise definition in 1946 – despite the best efforts of Wavell, Glancy and Jenkins – meant that Pakistan ultimately came into being as the result of the votes of a few dozen provincial legislators.

At the start of Mountbatten's viceroyalty there were plans to refer any boundary disputes between India and Pakistan to the United Nations, but this was rejected in favour of a pair of Boundary Commissions, one for Punjab and one for Bengal, which would each consist of two Muslim and two non-Muslim High Court judges. Sir Cyril Radcliffe was initially chosen as the Chairman of an Arbitral Tribunal, which was to adjudicate over the division of assets between India and Pakistan, but he soon moved into chairing the Boundary Commissions instead. Since they were communally split, it was agreed in the Indian Independence Act that the 'award' of the Commissions would mean the decision of the Chairman. In practice, Radcliffe took no notice of his eminent warring legal colleagues, and made all the decisions on the awards himself.

What is astounding in retrospect is that the significance of the forthcoming 'Radcliffe Line' only became apparent in late July 1947. In May, Nehru had told Mountbatten that 'when Congress referred to the partition of the Punjab, they had not gone into the question in any great detail'.[9] Even in June, it had been assumed on all sides that relations between India and Pakistan would be fairly amicable, and that the precise borders between them would be settled by negotiation at a later date. Nehru said in June that at some point in the future, India and Pakistan would 'mutually consider modifications and variations of their frontiers so that a satisfactory arrangement might be arrived at. That is likely to be a fairly lengthy process involving the ascertainment of the wishes of the people concerned in any particular area affected.'[10]

Most Muslims saw Pakistan as a homeland from which they would come and go at leisure; even Jinnah himself did not sell his house on Malabar Hill in Bombay, apparently on the assumption that he would flit cheerfully between India and Pakistan. Yet as relations worsened with the growth in communal violence, it became clear that give-and-take between the two new nations was unlikely, and by the end of August the scale of the communal slaughter had destroyed any prospect of friendly co-existence.

Cyril Radcliffe was initially recommended for the job by his friend the Lord Chancellor, Viscount Jowitt, who told Listowel on 13 June that Radcliffe was 'so impressed with the importance of the task' that he would accept, on various conditions. Since he was making 'at least £60,000 a year' at the Bar, Radcliffe was anxious that his plans for exemption from income tax and surtax should not be affected by the appointment. Apart from his salary (which he waived in the end, in disgust) he wanted 'living allowances', suitable accommodation and free travel for his wife and stepchildren, to enable them to 'live in comfortable style without expense to him'.[11] Having done his work as Sir Cyril's tax adviser, the Lord Chancellor confirmed the appointment, following the agreement of Congress and the Muslim League.

Radcliffe began work in New Delhi on 8 July, assisted by a secretary, Christopher Beaumont. He was given thirty-six days in which to dissect the subcontinent. It was only now that his crucial importance became apparent to Indian politicians, and they attempted to make representations to him both privately and at public hearings of the Boundary Commissions. Like the Pandava brothers in the *Mahabharata*, Nehru and Jinnah were to have the future of their kingdoms decided on a roll of the dice.

Radcliffe was put under the care of a hulking Punjabi bodyguard, who escorted him wherever he went toting a pair of pistols and wearing bandoliers over a long white *kurta*. It had been agreed by Congress and the League that Radcliffe should draw his boundaries on the basis of 'contiguous majority areas of Muslims and non-Muslims', while taking into account 'other factors'.[12] This was a loose definition, since 'areas' could be taken to mean either districts (which are around the same size as English counties) or *tehsils* (revenue-collecting units covering around a sixth of that area). Matters were complicated further by the knowledge that the census statistics on communal composition were six years out of date, and supposedly biased against the Sikhs, many of whom had been away at war when the information was collected.

Although Radcliffe was to destroy all his papers relating to India later that year, it is apparent that the basis for his border line was the 'detailed demarcation' produced by Wavell in February 1946. It might be noted that the civil servant who was originally responsible for drafting Wavell's document was none other than the astute Reforms Commissioner V.P. Menon, assisted by another Hindu constitutionalist, Sir Benegal Rau. There were no other maps of possible demarcations for Radcliffe to consult, since the India Office had been so dilatory in defining the borders of the proposed Pakistan. The notional boundary that was laid down in the Second Schedule of the Indian Independence Act corresponds exactly to Wavell's line, except that it places the district of Gurdaspur in Pakistan.

Radcliffe had never before been further east than Gibraltar, and so had no choice but to rely on whatever information was made available to him from the Government of India's archives. Probably acting on the advice of the Viceroy's Private Secretary George Abell, who knew the importance of the Punjabi canal systems, he made a particular effort to ensure adequate irrigation and water supply in all parts of central Punjab. His final boundaries corresponded closely to Wavell's original plan, although in Bengal he gave the predominantly tribal Chittagong Hill Tracts in the far east to Pakistan (presumably in order to safeguard the security of the crucial port of Chittagong), while allocating a small amount of Muslim territory to the north of Calcutta to India. In the Punjab he followed Wavell's original instructions almost to the letter, and even included Gurdaspur and a small portion of Lahore district in Indian territory so as to give protection to the Sikhs' holy city of Amritsar.

Although it had originally been intended that the Radcliffe Awards would be announced a few days before the transfer of power, Mountbatten decided to postpone disclosure until 16 August, so as not to interfere with the independence celebrations. He subsequently made vigorous if unconvincing efforts to assert that he had no knowledge of the boundaries until that date. Mountbatten's Press Attaché Alan Campbell-Johnson described the publication of the boundaries as 'a Public Relations problem of some magnitude which had a direct bearing on the maintenance of morale and order'.[13] Mountbatten's decision to defer a public announcement has been blamed by some historians for encouraging massacres and migration. It is however hard to see how a delay of three days made much difference, although one hapless consequence was that power was transferred to a pair of new dominions that did not even know their own frontiers.

More important than the timing of the announcement is the fact that the route of the Punjab border was changed at the last moment. Elaborate conspiracy theories have been built up around this, and the compressed

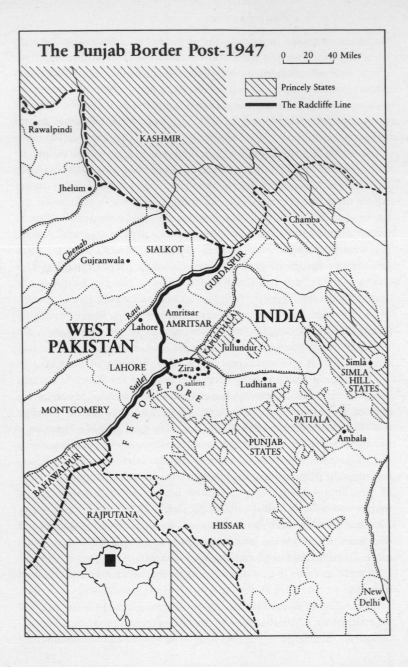

The Punjab Border Post-1947

0   20   40 Miles

Princely States

The Radcliffe Line

Rawalpindi

KASHMIR

Jhelum

Chamba

Chenab

SIALKOT

Gujranwala

Ravi

Amritsar
AMRITSAR

GURDASPUR

INDIA

WEST
PAKISTAN

Lahore

KAPURTHALA

Jullundur

Simla
SIMLA
HILL
STATES

LAHORE

Zira
salient

Sutlej

Ludhiana

F E R O Z E P O R E

MONTGOMERY

PATIALA

Ambala

BAHAWALPUR

PUNJAB
STATES

RAJPUTANA

HISSAR

New
Delhi

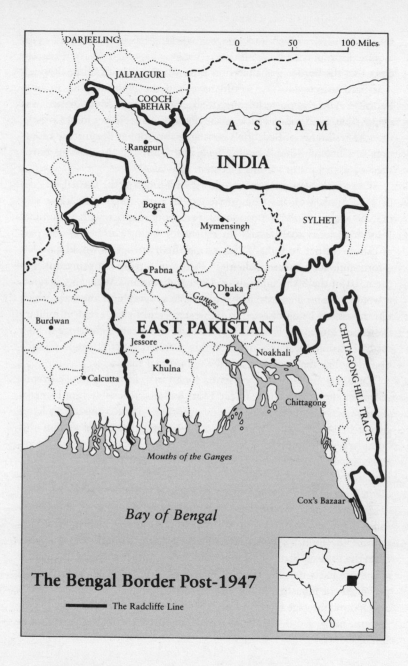

DARJEELING

JALPAIGURI

COOCH
BEHAR

A S S A M

INDIA

Rangpur

Bogra

Mymensingh

SYLHET

Pabna

Dhaka

Ganges

Burdwan

EAST PAKISTAN

Jessore

Noakhali

CHITTAGONG HILL TRACTS

Khulna

Calcutta

Chittagong

Mouths of the Ganges

Cox's Bazaar

Bay of Bengal

0   50   100 Miles

The Bengal Border Post-1947

—————— The Radcliffe Line

time-scale within which Radcliffe was working has given his draft maps a quite disproportionate significance. Viceregal apologists have tended to deny that the border was altered at Mountbatten's instigation, although it is hard to see who else would have had the political clout to sway Radcliffe. There is powerful anecdotal evidence that Mountbatten was responsible, from sources such as the diary of his secretary John Christie, the 1992 testimony of Radcliffe's assistant Christopher Beaumont, a footnote in Penderel Moon's book *Divide and Quit*, and the dubious retrospective assertions of various Pakistani officials.[14]

The course of events was as follows. At a lunch at the United Services Club in Simla with his Commissioners in early August, Radcliffe said that he would award a portion of Ferozepur district with a nominal Muslim majority to Pakistan, 'in return for giving Gurdaspur and part of Lahore district' to India.[15] This extraordinary proposal would have left a forty-mile-long spur or salient of Pakistani territory sticking out into the heart of the Sikh community. Like Afghanistan's Wakhan Corridor, it would have been an extremely vulnerable geographical anomaly, which ran the risk of being bisected at its western end in the event of military hostilities. Moreover, it was an obvious and provocative challenge to Sikh security. Ironically it was news of this planned but ultimately rejected boundary line that was to spark the communal massacres.

On 8 August, George Abell sent a rough map featuring the Ferozepur salient to the private office of Sir Evan Jenkins, to enable him to make security arrangements along the new border. An accompanying letter signed by Abell said: 'There will not be any great changes from this boundary.'[16] Mountbatten later claimed this was done without his knowledge, which is improbable given that 'at two separate staff conferences' he had told Abell that 'Jenkins should have the earliest possible notice of the line, so that he could make police and military dispositions.'[17]

Over the next two or three days the border was altered, supposedly following representations from V.P. Menon, Jawaharlal Nehru, the Chairman of the Punjab's Waterways and Irrigation Commission, ministers from the Princely State of Bikaner, and various other suspects. In practice it is more likely that the views of experienced ICS officials such as Abell provoked the adjustment. On either 10 or 11 August, Jenkins received a Secraphone message from Viceroy's House telling him to 'eliminate salient', meaning that the whole of Ferozepur district would now remain in India.[18]

The fact that Radcliffe adjusted the border at this late stage in an apparently furtive manner lends weight to the notion that his earlier version was somehow the 'true' border between India and Pakistan. It is however worth considering how realistic it would have been as an international frontier.

Neither the Wavell line of February 1946 nor the notional boundary attached to the Second Schedule of the Indian Independence Act placed any of Ferozepur district in Pakistan.[19] As the Maharajah of Bikaner told Mountbatten, an attempt to put the salient under Pakistani control would 'gravely prejudice' the water supply into northern Rajputana.[20] Even an apolitical cotton farmer a hundred miles south at Khanewal could refer in late June to a Bahawalpur canal-head as being 'in Ferozepur district i.e. in Hindustan'.[21] It never occurred to anybody – except Radcliffe and some local Muslim League activists – that the nominally Muslim-majority revenue divisions of an essentially Sikh district might be transferred to Pakistani control.

There is no way of knowing the precise reasoning behind Radcliffe's original decision. It appears from anecdotal evidence that he was particularly anxious to avoid disputes over water, given that the fertility of the Punjab depended on irrigation channels. He made various attempts during early August to have all common canal systems put under joint control, but this proved politically impossible. Placing Ferozepur in Muslim hands may have been an attempt to give Pakistan some degree of control over one of its water sources, since the main headworks of the Sutlej Valley canal system were in Ferozepur. It is also likely that Radcliffe wished to compensate for having given a small portion of Lahore district and most of Gurdaspur district to India, which had been done to prevent the Sikhs of Amritsar from being isolated.

It is certainly true that in general the Radcliffe Line favoured India. In the eyes of Jinnah and Liaquat Ali Khan, not only was their homeland being partitioned, but even the fringes were being gobbled up by Congress. Yet in practice it is hard to see how this could have been avoided, given the need to placate the justifiable anger of the Sikh minority. If the Sikhs' holy city of Amritsar was to be located in India, it was essential that it was not cut off in a hostile Pakistani sea. This inevitably meant that surrounding pieces of territory had to be allocated to India, to the detriment of Pakistan. The Ferozepur salient may have been an attempt to redress the balance, but it was a dangerously misguided one, and Radcliffe was right to alter it. Pakistan would in the long term have gained little benefit from having to defend a strip of land that was in such a strategically vulnerable position.

'Down comes the Union Jack,' wrote Sir Cyril with amiable condescension in a letter to his stepson as India attained independence, 'and up goes – for the moment I rather forget what, but it has a spinning wheel or a spider's web in the middle.'[22] He returned to London on 17 August, as the decisions of the Boundary Commissions were published to the fury of all sides, Congress objecting to the inclusion of the predominantly tribal Chittagong Hill Tracts in Pakistan, and the League to the loss of Ferozepur and most of Gurdaspur to India. For the rest of his life Radcliffe refused to disclose any details about his work, although a newspaper reporter who interviewed him a few months before his death was struck by his 'genuine anguish' over what had happened in the Punjab in 1947.[23] When asked whether he would ever like to return to India, he answered: 'God forbid. Not even if they asked me. I suspect they'd shoot me out of hand – both sides.'[24]

Back in England, Radcliffe was soon appointed a Law Lord in recognition of his services to the state, becoming the first lawyer for more than half a century to be elevated direct from the Bar. He went on to chair innumerable committees on matters such as taxation and 'D' notices, and acted as a discreet adviser on recruitment into SIS. He died a Viscount in 1977, apparently somewhat disenchanted by 'the marked lowering of public tone' in British society.

When the last-minute change to the boundary line was raised in the United Nations by Pakistan in 1948, a question was asked in Parliament about the propriety of the alteration. Radcliffe personally drafted the government's reply, which stated: 'I understand from Sir Cyril that he found the treatment of this area a question of considerable difficulty and on this point he reached a final conclusion differing from that which he was disposed to adopt at the time when Sir George Abell asked him for advance information.' In an accompanying private note, Radcliffe pointed out quite reasonably that the concept of 'provisional' versus 'final' boundaries was meaningless, since his decision was an 'award' which had no status until it was formally presented to the Viceroy. 'Earlier drafts,' he wrote, 'and there were quite a few, were drafts and no more.'[25]

It would be easy but probably unjust to blame Radcliffe for the consequences that stemmed from his decisions. He was given an impossible job, and his attempt to resolve the Punjab's water problems was well-intentioned, if unwise. The real responsibility lies not with Radcliffe, but with the politicians who gave a man from London six weeks in which to divide three hundred million people. Had the boundaries of any proposed 'Pakistan' been specified in 1945 or 1946, his task would not have been necessary.

The battle to the death between Congress and the Muslim League during the course of the 1940s had left India's six million Sikhs in a state of isolation. Their proclaimed political leaders lacked both knowledge and influence, and floundered on the margins of New Delhi's power politics. Sikhs were split between several parties. Some were in Congress, but from the 1920s onwards most activists belonged either to the Punjab's Unionist Party, the pro-Unionist Khalsas, the Central Akali Dal or to an offshoot known as the Official Akali Party. The original Akalis were radical Sikhs who had started a movement after the First World War to wrest control of Sikh temples or *gurdwara* from Hindu priests.

The Official Akalis were led by Master Tara Singh, a seventy-two-year-old former Hindu known to be well-versed in the Sikh holy book the *Granth Saheb*, but regarded by Lord Wavell as 'stupid and emotional'. He was renowned for his fierce demeanour, and for his repeated threats to travel to London to 'put the Sikh case to the British public', apparently in the belief that he would attract great support. His fiery speeches had led to his becoming a dominant figure in Sikh politics, and he was given the title 'Master'. This honorific referred, rather feebly, not to his martial vigour but to the fact that he had at one time been a schoolmaster in Lyallpur. Unfortunately his abilities as a passionate orator were not matched by political skills, but for want of an alternative he attained an influential position. As Sir Evan Jenkins noted in May 1947, it was 'lamentable that at this juncture the affairs of the Punjab should be so largely in the hands of this eccentric old man'.[26]

Despite the large number of Sikhs involved in revolutionary activity against British rule from the First World War onwards, many became soldiers in the Indian Army. Sikhs were classified by the British as a 'martial race', and during the Second World War they formed a crucial part of Allied forces in the Middle East; ironically they also made up almost half of Bose's INA. Yet politically they lacked power, and with the death of Sir Sikander Hayat Khan in late 1942 and the consequent rise of the Muslim League, they inevitably became more radical. At the same time the British sidelined their cause, with ultimately fatal consequences. For London's politicians, Sikhs were a troublesome irritant who had the misfortune to be caught between the demands of antagonistic Hindus and Muslims.

Although Sikhs were spread over northern India, often working as bus drivers and mechanics in the big cities, the large majority were concentrated in east Punjab. There were however substantial Sikh pockets in west Punjab, up through Rawalpindi to the North-West Frontier Province, and it was clear that any demarcation of Pakistan would leave hundreds of thousands of them stuck in a Muslim homeland. While a line of division through the Punjab might satisfy some Hindus and Muslims, it could not fail to be anything other than brutally unfair to the Sikhs.

Throughout the 1920s and thirties Sikh–Muslim relations had deteriorated, provoked by a conflict over a site in Shahidganj which Muslims claimed was a mosque and Sikhs said was a *gurdwara*. Although relations between Hindus and Sikhs were fractious, there was a degree of affinity between them, and some even regarded Sikhism and Hinduism as branches of the same faith. The position is perhaps best summed up by a 'joke' I was told by an elderly man in Amritsar: 'If a Sikh has one bullet left in his gun, and he sees a Muslim, a Hindu and a Britisher coming towards him, which should he shoot? The Muslim – you only shoot Hindus and Britishers for pleasure.'

The idea of a Muslim homeland provoked a strong Sikh reaction. In August 1944 a leading campaigner, Giani Kartar Singh, proclaimed in Amritsar that 'if Pakistan is foisted upon the Sikhs with the help of British bayonets, we will tear it into shreds as Guru Gobind Singh tore up the Mughal Empire.'[27] Others suggested that Sikhs should campaign for a sovereign state, but Kartar Singh acknowledged this would be an 'impossible demand'. The only person who took it seriously seems to have been Leo Amery, whose suggestion in 1942 of a 'Sikhdom' was met by Lord Linlithgow with the marginal note, 'My hat, what an idea!'[28]

In the provincial elections of 1945–46, Sikhs united into a 'Panthic Pratinidhi', and won twenty-two seats in the Punjab legislative assembly. Tara Singh then put forward a demand to the Cabinet Delegation that there should be a 'province' in which Sikhs would be in a 'dominant, or almost dominant position', and able to federate with either India or Pakistan. This was however not a clear or unanimous demand, and with other things to worry about, the Delegation ignored it. Cripps's assistant Major 'Billy' Short was left to ponder the Master's demands, on the grounds that as a former officer of the 5/11th Sikhs he was an expert on such matters.

Around this time there was an attempt to cut a deal between the Muslim League and the Sikh leadership. A meeting was held in Delhi between Jinnah, Tara Singh, Kartar Singh, the Sikh Maharajah of Patiala and his most senior minister. Jinnah asked for support in return for total Sikh autonomy within Pakistan, but the response was a statement to the press that Sikhs would 'under no circumstances accept Pakistan'.[29]

During 1947 Billy Short continued to keep in touch with Cripps, Attlee and the India Office. Although his prophecies of doom regarding the Sikh minority were listened to, little notice was taken of them, since he had no obvious solution to offer. The Sikh leaders were clear that they did not want Pakistan or a Congress-dominated India, yet they realized there was no real chance of winning an independent Sikh state. The result was that they resorted to internal squabbling, which provoked more radical elements within the community to suggest a military struggle to safeguard their position.

As the potential for violence grew, Mohammad Ali Jinnah did nothing to dissipate the fears of Sikhs in west Punjab. Caught up in the rapid and confusing power struggle at the centre, he was almost oblivious to what was happening at a local level, and made no attempt to offer any conciliatory statements. According to the Chief Minister of Bahawalpur, Mushtaq Ahmad Gurmani, the cursory structures of the local Muslim League meant that its leadership in New Delhi had little idea how serious the situation had become. After a private conversation with Jinnah, Jenkins came to the conclusion that his view of the Sikh question was 'perilously unsound'.

Throughout February there were riots all over the Punjab, encouraged by the decision of the Unionist-led coalition government to ban the paramilitary Muslim League Guards. Tara Singh threatened a Sikh uprising, and ordered an 'Anti-Pakistan Day' on 11 March. Soon afterwards the administration led by the Chief Minister Sir Khizar Hyat Khan Tiwana fell apart, and Jenkins took control under Section 93 of the 1935 Government of India Act. The powerful, cohesive Unionist Party that had been flourishing under Sir Sikander Hayat Khan's leadership only five years earlier was now in pieces, and communalism had become the primary form of political motivation in the Punjab.

The most savage outbreak of violence came just before the wheat harvest in March, when several thousand Sikhs were murdered by armed Muslim gangs in villages in the district of Rawalpindi, including Thamali, Doberan and Choa Khalsa. This was supposedly provoked by a speech by Tara Singh from the steps of the legislature in Lahore, in which he said: 'Our motherland is calling for blood and we shall satiate the thirst of our motherland with blood . . . I have sounded the bugle. Finish the Muslim League.'[30] Another of the Master's provocative lines was the slogan of the Tenth Sikh Guru, '*Raj karega Khalsa, aki rahe na koi,*' or 'The pure Sikhs will rule, and no resister will survive.'[31]

Whatever the immediate cause of the massacres, it was the Sikhs around Rawalpindi who suffered, and the killings provoked an exodus of around eighty thousand refugees into east Punjab. By this stage there were gangs of paramilitary Muslim League Guards parading in Lahore, although whether they were directly linked to the Rawalpindi massacres has never been established. The Sikh survivors were however certain that the killers were not local. In November 1946, a League activist had attempted to persuade Jinnah of the need to create an army of 'militarized Musalmans' in case of an increase in communal violence, but the plan was rejected. The role of guerrilla leader was one for which the ailing Jinnah was clearly ill-equipped, so supporters of the local League in the Punjab appear to have taken matters into their own hands. Survivors of the Rawalpindi massacres believed the British authorities had connived with the killers: 'the Muslims had been given a week . . . the *angrezis* [English] had told them that they could do anything till 12 March, and then the military would move in . . . It was in the time of the *angrez*, it was under their rule, who else could have done it?'[32]

By April 1947, Tara Singh was declaring publicly that his people were bitter and angry, and would fight for their cause. Sikh men had their beards set on fire by Muslims, and were taunted for having degenerated and grown rich and fat on British patronage, given their prominent role in the Indian Army. Punjabi Hindus were also fearful of their future, and began to plan retaliatory measures against the Muslim League Guards. As a Lahore activist of the Hindu group the RSS says in Ved Mehta's memoir *The Ledge Between the Streams*: 'We Hindus have to change if we are to survive and rule India – the only language a Muslim understands is that of a knife and a grenade.'[33]

The Sikh response was to raise a defence fund and form preliminary squads, or *jathas*, using the military expertise of former INA soldiers. When Evan Jenkins reprimanded Master Tara Singh for 'the violence of some of his statements', he replied that 'he did not intend to take revenge for Rawalpindi now, but he could never be friendly with the Muslims again, and after the British went he would, if necessary, see that the Muslims were dealt with'.[34] In April, Billy Short wrote in a letter to Cripps that 'the Sikh is beginning to feel neglected', and added, 'I don't doubt he is due to go off with the worst bang we've yet had.'[35]

The rapidly formulated 3 June Plan ignored the position of the Sikhs. Jenkins thought it was likely to provoke 'large scale disturbances ... particularly in Jullundur, Amritsar, Lahore, Sheikhupara, Lyallpur and Montgomery', which were the principal districts of central Punjab.[36] By now, the Defence Minister Baldev Singh had been appropriated as a Sikh spokesman at the centre, and he was invited to Mountbatten's crucial meetings as a token gesture. In practice he could do nothing, and acquiesced to whatever was proposed. The wording of Mountbatten's radio broadcast was indicative of the fact that 'this valiant community' was being abandoned. 'We have given careful consideration to the position of the Sikhs,' he began, and from that moment on his listeners must have known there was nothing he could offer them.[37]

In July a 'Sikh Memorandum to the Boundary Commission' was put forward, suggesting that a frontier running along the Chenab River would keep the important shrine of Nankana Saheb out of Muslim hands, and leave around 90 per cent of Sikhs inside India. This was true, but any such line would have left only a fraction of the Punjab under Muslim control, which was clearly politically impossible, given that P for Punjab was the first letter of Pakistan. Any boundary that satisfied the Sikhs would clearly be unacceptable to the rulers of an already diminished Pakistan. This was the crux of the problem: Sikhs were so inextricably intertwined in Pakistani territory that nothing short of a giant population transfer would keep them in India. Such a course of action was suggested by the Akali leader Giani Kartar Singh, but rejected at the time as both impractical and alarmist.

Sikhs were now in a state of fear and apprehension, and Baldev Singh's acceptance of the 3 June Plan was widely condemned by the rest of his community. As Kartar Singh told Sir Evan Jenkins, Mountbatten had simply wanted to 'get his thumb impression'. Jenkins considered declaring martial law throughout the Punjab, but decided there was little point in doing so given that the police force was 'physically tired and services generally are disintegrating'. Jenkins was renowned as one of the most experienced administrators in the ICS, yet the situation had spun so far out of control that he could see no solution other than 'active intervention by political leaders' to bring 'genuine private pressure to bear on their own *goonda* supporters'.[38] This did not occur.

In a report to the Viceroy, Jenkins wrote that Kartar Singh had told him the British had always promised to protect India's minorities, but were now abandoning the community that had so loyally provided them with troops for decades. Sikhs were inclined to 'fight on revolutionary lines – by murdering officials, cutting railway lines and telegraph lines, destroying canal headworks and so on'. When Jenkins said this was would be 'a very foolish policy . . . the Giani retorted that if Britain were invaded, he had no doubt that my feelings would be much the same as his'. Jenkins ended his report by noting that the Sikh leader 'wept when he made his final appeal. This is the nearest thing to an ultimatum yet given on behalf of the Sikhs.'[39]

As Sikh grievances were articulated with growing vigour during the last weeks of British rule, Jenkins had to make a decision whether to arrest the likes of Kartar Singh and Tara Singh. With popular feeling running so high, he decided that the consequences of incarcerating them were likely to be more dangerous than leaving them free to 'blow off steam'. Political meetings were held at *gurdwaras*, at which plans were made for *hartals* and civil disobedience, and in the districts of Lahore and Gurdaspur Muslim villages were raided and burnt.

Jenkins wrote to Mountbatten on 4 August that he was witnessing nothing less than a 'communal war of succession' in the Punjab as rival groups struggled 'for the power we are shortly to abandon . . . Moreover, there is very little doubt that the disturbances have in some degree been organized and paid for by persons or bodies directly or indirectly under the control of the Muslim League, the Congress, and the Akali Party.'[40]

The next day Jenkins sent a police officer called Gerald Savage on an urgent mission to Delhi. Savage of the CID told the Viceroy that he had reports of Sikh plans to derail trains and detonate bombs. There was even a plan to assassinate Jinnah in Karachi during the independence day celebrations. Ex-INA soldiers were operating in conjunction with the RSS, and Master Tara Singh was believed to be personally implicated in the conspiracy. Jenkins was consequently informed by Mountbatten that Tara Singh and other activists could be arrested at a time of his choosing. In the event, the Governor made preparations for their arrest but decided not to act, on account of the practical implications of operating 'in places like the Golden Temple where Police action causes much excitement'.[41]

On 8 August the sketch map of the Radcliffe Line, showing the provocative but erroneous Ferozepur salient, was sent to Jenkins. He made immediate moves to communicate the information to local civil, military and police officials so they could make advance police and troop deployments. According to a handwritten note by Jenkins dated 8 August, he planned to hold a conference at '0845 hrs' the following day with the Punjab's Inspector General of Police, after which the Inspector General would 'get out information to Deputy Commissioners, Sialkot, Gurdaspur, Amritsar, Lahore and Ferozepur' and 'make our dispositions'. The next morning Jenkins's secretary telegraphed Abell in New Delhi to tell him that Jenkins was 'taking law and order action on preliminary information given'.[42] Simultaneously, it appears that news of the proposed boundary was leaking through other sources, including clerical staff attached to Viceroy's House.

By 9 August widespread rumours about the creation of the Ferozepore salient were circulating not only among the political elite of New Delhi, but in towns and villages throughout central Punjab. It was devastating news for the Sikh community, who were losing not only as expected countless farms and properties in Sialkot, Gujranwala, Sheikhupura, Lahore, Lyallpur and Montgomery districts (and the birthplace of the founder of their faith Guru Nanak at Nankana Saheb), but now apparently a long tranche of land below Amritsar which cut through the heart of their territory, and snatched the two sacred Sikh battlefields of Sobroan and Ferozeshah into Pakistan. It is apparent that advance news of Radcliffe's draft plan provoked an upsurge of violence.

That night came the opening move in the war of attrition. The 'Pakistan Special No. 1' train carrying senior civil servants of the new Muslim homeland from Delhi to Lahore was derailed by a Sikh *jatha* using electronic detonators, with several people being killed. Over the following days, Muslim policemen in Amritsar were forcibly disarmed, and many began to desert. By 12 August, Jenkins was telegraphing to the Viceroy: 'Feeling in Lahore city is now unbelievably bad and Inspector General tells me that Muslim League National Guard appearing in uniform and that Police are most unsteady.' The following day he reported that almost four hundred people had been murdered in the province, and Amritsar was burning. His telegram concluded: 'General situation deteriorating.'[43] The communal holocaust was now underway.

In his final retrospective report on his viceroyalty to the British government, Mountbatten tacitly accepted that he had made a mistake not to order the pre-emptive arrest of communalist activists. He also made the perfectly valid point that Savage's report was the only 'direct evidence' of Sikh intentions, 'due to the rundown of the British Intelligence Organization, which was functioning far below its previous well-known competence'.[44]

The fact that the Viceroy of India did not even know the name of the Intelligence Bureau is indicative of how far removed he was from the vital information on which his predecessors had depended. Although he received some scraps of local intelligence via provincial governors, he had no access to the DIB, thanks to Patel's ruling of the previous year. As H.V. Hodson has written: 'Lack of intelligence, such as had always reached district officers, magistrates, policemen and Criminal Investigation Departments, cost many Indian lives ... in the disorders of 1946 and 1947.'[45] What Hodson did not know at the time of writing was just how profound the breakdown of communication had become.

In New Delhi the Intelligence Bureau continued to function under the sharp eye of the Home Minister, Vallabhbhai Patel. Alan Campbell-Johnson noted that Patel's 'powers and responsibilities are as wide as they well can be', since he was supervising not only the capture of the Princely States, but also had 'control over all Government Information, Internal Security, the Police ...'[46] Patel was presumably being kept informed by his new appointee as DIB of all information that was received from the Central Intelligence Officers of the eleven provinces, although how much he personally knew of the murderous plans of rival communal groups remains a matter for speculation.

'Patel's private conversation is reported to be menacing,' Jenkins had told Mountbatten in June. 'A Minister in the Coalition Government told me he had heard him say that Hindustan could quickly make an end of its Muslim inhabitants if Pakistan did not behave.'[47] Jinnah believed that

Patel 'would welcome trouble from the Sikhs in the Central Punjab'.[48] The Sardar was certainly adamantly opposed to the planned arrest of the unstable Master Tara Singh, despite the fact that Congress were to imprison the Sikh leader five times during the years following independence.

Back in London little useful intelligence was being received, and IPI had in effect ceased to function. Plans by the Director General of the Security Service to send out a Defence Security Officer to re-recruit Indian agents and then pass information back to Whitehall had not been successful, presumably owing to the breakdown of old ties and loyalties in the chaos of 1947, and nervousness among Indians of being implicated in the old order after independence.

As the date of the transfer of power approached, Sir Paul Patrick at the India Office thanked the spymasters for going 'out of their way to take special interest in Indian problems'. In reply came letters from Sir Stewart Menzies of SIS (on paper headed 'C/1143') and Sir Percy Sillitoe (of 'Box No. 500'). Sillitoe was a burly autocrat who had recently been appointed to run MI5, and he told Patrick he was glad that 'you and the other officers who have done so much to foster the happy relations that have existed between us will be moving into the Commonwealth Relations Office where further opportunities for friendly cooperation may recur'.[49]

Patrick also received a letter on 31 July signed, astoundingly, 'P. Vickery'. This is the only document in the archives of Indian Political Intelligence that bears the chief's signature rather than his usual acronym 'IPI'. Philip Vickery was taking the battered remnants of his operation into the Commonwealth Security Intelligence System, which was a part of MI5, and he must have been painfully aware that the organization he had spent so much of his life constructing was now fatally compromised.

'In taking leave as from 1st August of the India Office qua India Office,' he wrote, 'I should like to express my most grateful thanks to you and the many other members of the staff . . . who have helped me since I have been in IPI. I was first associated with IPI from 1915 [and] have been in charge of IPI since 1926. I may say that I have an exceedingly great affection for the India Office and I am as pained to witness its passing as I am to see the partition of the Punjab.' He looked forward, however, to what 'may include a continuance of our relations in a somewhat altered form'.[50] Vickery was knighted the following year, and remained a significant player within the security and intelligence services. He died in 1987, a few weeks short of his ninety-seventh birthday, having perhaps done as much as any single person to prolong British rule in India.

On the other side of Whitehall, things were little better. No serious attempt was made by Attlee or his Cabinet to analyse what was happening in India, or to provide anything more than cursory assistance, which had the effect of leaving many of the final decisions to Mountbatten and his advisers; or to fate. The inadequacy of the British government's response can largely be explained, but not excused, by the grave crisis in which it found itself in the summer of 1947, the true seriousness of which has only become apparent in recent years.

After VJ-Day, President Truman had written off a huge British war debt to the United States, but also cancelled lend-lease, the arrangement that had enabled Churchill to finance the economy until 1945. Britain's debts in sterling to other countries amounted to over £3 billion, of which £1.16 billion was owed to India. Attempts had been made to negotiate this sum into thin air, but Vallabhbhai Patel made it clear to Attlee that the 'sterling debt forms the most important asset for the future development of this country', and that he regarded its eventual payment as 'Britain's sacred obligation'.[51] This left the new Labour government in a desperate economic position, having to borrow $3.5 billion from the Americans at the harsh terms of 2 per cent interest per year.

Maynard Keynes having died in 1946, a former financial journalist called Richard 'Otto' Clarke was summoned to the Treasury to give advice. In the summer of 1947 he produced a document which the historian Peter Hennessy has described as 'the most alarming economic policy file I've encountered in the entire postwar period'.[52] It outlined contingency plans in the event of America not coming up with any more cash. Clarke believed that Britain faced an unbridgeable trade deficit, and raised the spectre of total economic collapse. To get by, Attlee might have to introduce a famine regime with rations reduced to 1,700 calories per person per day, which was below the subsistence level. Schoolchildren would have to be conscripted to bring in the harvest.

One of the USA's conditions for its 1945 loan had been that sterling should be fully convertible into dollars by 15 July 1947. This date developed great importance as it loomed nearer, and the Chancellor of the Exchequer Hugh Dalton ringed it in his diary in red ink. When it arrived, holders of sterling took the chance to convert their money into dollars, and Britain's currency reserves were depleted at a ferocious rate. Dalton, an Old Etonian socialist, tried fruitlessly to hold the line. On 13 August, as Mountbatten flew to Karachi for the formal creation of Pakistan, Dalton retreated to his Wiltshire home, covered in boils and dosing himself with benzedrine. On 15 August, as India and Pakistan attained their freedom, a pair of civil servants arrived and told him he had to take immediate action. Over the five previous days, $176 million had been milked out of Britain's minimal dollar reserves.

On Sunday 17 August there was an emergency Cabinet meeting. Ministers were brought in from all over Britain by plane and car, and entered 10 Downing Street by different doors in an attempt to avoid an obvious display of panic. Cripps threatened resignation if the economic crisis was not resolved. Convertibility was suspended, foreign holidays were banned, demobilization was accelerated, the meat ration was reduced, and deep government spending cuts were introduced. Britain's finances took a lurch back from the abyss.

The dollar-sterling crisis of August 1947 represented a fateful moment for Attlee's government. Few things were further from ministers' minds than events in Asia, so during the closing days of Britain's Indian Empire, London's politicians followed tradition by relegating the subcontinent's affairs to the margins. As the historian John Gallagher wrote, was it not 'notorious that debates on India would find members of parliament rushing away for refreshment, leaving the chamber to those few who could pronounce these sesquipedalian Indian names'?[53]

TWENTY

Death

India's Commander-in-Chief Field Marshal Sir Claude Auchinleck's father had quelled the mutiny of 1857 before dying young of pernicious anaemia. His son 'the Auck' abhorred Mountbatten and had a reputation for being bluff and undiplomatic, although like Wavell he provoked great loyalty among those who worked under him. His tendency towards biding his time and seeing if the situation improved had made him unpopular with Churchill during the war, and led to his being outfoxed in North Africa by Rommel, and replaced by Montgomery in August 1942.

Auchinleck did not relish his appointment as Commander-in-Chief, and he had a fervent objection to the notion of dividing the Indian Army in two. He believed it amounted to the destruction of one of the most impressive achievements of British rule in the Indian subcontinent. As his friend Lord Ismay said, such a move would be 'the biggest crime and the biggest headache'. As a result he responded to the 3 June Plan like a rabbit caught in the headlights, and hoped that through procrastination its effects might be dissipated. His mood during this period was not helped by the recent scandalous elopement of his wife Jessie with India's Air C-in-C.

In late April 1947 there was a meeting of the Defence Committee at which Liaquat Ali Khan proposed that a contingency plan should be drawn up for the division of the Indian Army. Baldev Singh, as Defence Minister, spoke out against this, since the creation of a state of Pakistan had not yet been agreed. Auchinleck backed him, pointing out that it would be hard to make plans for division, since he had 'been given no clear terms of reference as to the relations between the two States'. He also thought that even the whisper of such a plan would damage military morale, and that the army, navy and air force 'as they now stand, cannot be split up into two parts each of which will form a self-contained Armed Force', since 'the Army and Air Forces required to defend "PAKISTAN" from external aggression would be virtually the same as those now required to defend India as a whole'.[1]

A few days later Auchinleck flew to London for discussions and then, amazingly, went on leave to Switzerland. By the time he returned, the V.P. Menon Plan was about to be authorized by Attlee, and it was apparent that the Indian Army would have to be cut in half, fast. More plans were drawn up and considered, but the Jang-i-Lat Saheb's temperamental aversion to the idea of a break-up caused him to avoid taking decisions. Mountbatten shared his views on the inadvisability of creating two new armies, but accepted that if Pakistan insisted on having its own armed forces, the request could not be refused.

It was not until July that Auchinleck presented his terms of reference to the euphemistically named Armed Forces Reconstitution Committee. The dismemberment of the military took place in a desperate rush, with soldiers being given a matter of days to decide whether to opt for India or Pakistan. Absorbed by political events, the Viceroy left the practicalities of reinventing regiments, dividing ordinance and distributing motor-minesweepers to the Committee. According to Auchinleck's biographer, India's politicians treated the armed forces as 'one more insignificant item of office equipment, as easily disposed of as the telephones, the type-writers and the filing cabinets, over which there was to be such fierce haggling in the next few weeks'.[2]

The practicalities of the division were hampered by Auchinleck's relations with the Congress leadership, which had degenerated badly owing to his supposed pro-Jinnah bias. The Commander-in-Chief's determination to ensure a just allocation of equipment and stores to Pakistan provoked further conflict, since India's forthcoming rulers were able to use their power at the centre to limit Pakistan's future military capability. In Mountbatten's view, their dealings were hampered by a 'complete lack of knowledge ... of anything to do with the Armed Forces'.[3] Auchinleck's attempts at a fair division were not successful: India retained the bulk of the country's military hardware, including much that had been legally allocated to the new Muslim state.

It was agreed, with some reluctance on the part of Nehru and Patel, that after 15 August Auchinleck would remain in Delhi, and would become a joint Supreme Commander of both sets of armed forces. Beneath him would be a pair of senior British officers as Commanders-in-Chief of the new dominions, General Sir Frank Messervy in Pakistan and General Sir Rob Lockhart in India. In practice this arrangement proved unworkable, since within a matter of weeks the two countries were on the verge of war. Auchinleck's efforts at impartiality were perceived as pro-Pakistani bias, and in late September Nehru's government sacked him.

In his parting letter, Auchinleck told Attlee and the British service chiefs that he had 'no hesitation whatever in affirming that the present Indian Cabinet are implacably determined to do all in their power to prevent the establishment of the Dominion of Pakistan on a firm basis', adding that 'there is not one of the officers of Supreme Commander's HQ, senior or junior, who is not imbued with the greatest disgust for and dislike of the creators of this state of affairs'.[4]

The most damaging political and military misjudgement of 1947 was the failure to anticipate the degree of communal violence and migration that would accompany the division of the Indian Empire, or to make appropriate preparations for it. In 1946 Nehru had naively told a journalist: 'When the British go, there will be no more communal trouble in India.' As his biographer points out: 'He was wrong, but so was everyone else in a position of responsibility at this time.'[5] There was a stunning incapacity among politicians of all kinds to realize what was likely to occur. Even Jinnah, who might have been expected to foresee the impact of the creation of Pakistan, did not request a neutral military force either before or after 15 August. The only early proponents of a peacekeeping force were a few senior army officers such as General Sir Francis Tuker of Eastern Command, but they were ignored.

In his autobiography, which he wrote in prison in 1934, Nehru had stated that when independence came, it would be 'a humiliating thought for any Indian of spirit to ask for an outsider's protection'.[6] In January 1947 his views were unchanged, and he told a Cabinet meeting that it was 'contrary to all ideas of independence to have British troops on Indian soil', adding that 'opinion among responsible leaders in England was strongly against their being used for internal security'.[7] By responsible leaders he presumably meant senior Labour ministers.

The degree of chaos in India by mid-1947 meant there was a continual, serious risk of mass civil disorder, but the Congress leadership still assumed that decolonization would be accompanied by a resultant wave of national tranquillity. Nehru's stand was based on a credulous idealism about the nature of the human race, and an assumption that communal hatred would simply evaporate. Congress bears a large share of the responsibility for creating the climate in which the violent events of 1947 were able to take place, although it must be doubted whether they would ever have wrested control from British hands without a substantial destabilization of the Government of India.

The task of ensuring adequate support for the transfer of power was theoretically the responsibility of the Secretary of State for India Lord Listowel, acting on the advice of the Viceroy and the Commander-in-Chief. Ultimately, it was the decision of the British Prime Minister. However, Attlee was busy with the sterling crisis, while the forty-year-old Billy Listowel was inexperienced and in awe of the man on the spot. They both preferred to defer to the Viceroy, who took the view that 'it is not possible to hedge a political transfer of power with military reservations'.[8] Although this now looks like a tragic and fatal misjudgement, it was an opinion that was backed fully by India's nationalist leaders and the British government. Indeed, it is extremely doubtful whether the use of troops in an active peacemaking role would have been possible in practice without Congress and Muslim League support.

Even before the creation of the 3 June Plan, Mountbatten proposed 'withdrawing British Forces as soon as possible after enactment of legislation providing for the transfer of power'. Auchinleck disagreed, and supported the indefinite retention of British troops, but only to protect European civilians from revenge attacks. In fact, to universal surprise, the level of inter-communal rioting was such that anti-British violence did not occur. At no point did Auchinleck or Mountbatten promote the use of British troops as peacekeepers between antagonistic Sikhs, Muslims and Hindus, apart from the use of a handful of officers in the Punjab Boundary Force.

Attlee decreed that from 15 August, all British regiments would be withdrawn, depending on the availability of shipping. With fatal consequences, the instinctive dislike of India's nationalist leaders for imperial weaponry dovetailed with the British desire to get out of India as fast as possible. At the instigation of Auchinleck and Mountbatten, Lord Listowel authorized an announcement that 'since responsibility for maintaining law and order from that date will rest with the Governments of India and Pakistan, British Forces will not be used operationally and will not be able to intervene in internal disorder.'[9]

General Gerald Scarlett formed the 4th Indian Division at the outbreak of the Second World War. It fought under the symbol of the red eagle in campaigns at Benghazi, Eritrea, El Alamein and Monte Cassino. By the end of hostilities it was a battered and battle-scarred force, having suffered more than twenty-five thousand casualties. In 1947 the division had been partially demobilized, and the depleted remnants were stationed in the Punjab under the command of a wiry, intense, Welsh-speaking veteran, Major General Thomas 'Pete' Rees. It consisted of Rajputs, Baluchis, Gurkhas and Dogras, many of whom had no wish to remain in uniform. By the time the 4th Indian Division metamorphosed into the Punjab Boundary Force on 1 August, it was around fifteen thousand strong, although this figure rose to twenty-three thousand when the Force was strengthened later that month with a paratroop brigade and other units.

The Punjab Boundary Force was a haphazard, improvised body, concocted late in the day by Auchinleck. It was formed without consultation within the army, and amid political disagreement. Several senior ICS officials shared the Governor of Sind's opinion that it would be 'constitutionally and politically wrong' to create such a force. It was made responsible for thirty-eight thousand square miles of territory, which included seventeen thousand villages, many of them not linked by road. Given the scale of the organized communal slaughter that took place in late 1947, it was hopelessly underequipped and undermanned for the task that lay before it. According to the historian Robin Jeffrey, 'Even Mountbatten does not appear to have been aware of the precise strength and constitution of the Force.'[10]

Facing it was not the expected handful of *goondas*, *badmashes* and RSS backstreet stabbers. Instead there were well-organized Sikh *jathas*, usually consisting of twenty to thirty men, assisted by messengers and mounted scouts – a 'sound and enterprising' military tactic, noted Major General Rees. These squads appear to have been commanded by former soldiers from the Indian Army or the INA, and 'possessed hard cores of skilled fighters armed with rifles, grenades, tommy guns and machine guns'. The rival Muslim bands were initially less well organized, and looked more like 'a rabble of medieval peasants, armed only with flails, scythes and other crude weapons shaped from the instruments of the field'.[11] Other Muslims had arms, ammunition, military uniforms and 'iron jackets' which had been purchased from the North-West Frontier Province by the Khan of Mamdot.

Crucially, the Punjab Boundary Force was legally unable to operate within the territory of bordering Princely States such as Faridkot, Patiala and Nabha. In some cases, such as Kapurthala, the state sat like an island in the midst of otherwise accessible territory. In many instances, especially after attacks on refugee trains, gangs of killers were able to escape unharmed into Princely territory. There is some evidence that Sikh *jathas* were assisted and supplied with hardware by the state armies of Patiala and Faridkot, although the precise constitution of the different communal killing squads has never been established. It is however apparent that by late August, the likes of Master Tara Singh had little control over the slaughter that was taking place.

The accounts of the Boundary Force's attempts to maintain order make depressing reading. On 14 August they found the bodies of thirty-five Sikhs who had been knifed at Lahore railway station. That night, while Muslim police officers looked on, they tried unsuccessfully to stop a mob from burning down the principal *gurdwara* in Lahore, which contained hundreds of sheltering Sikhs. The next day, as India awoke to Nehru's 'life and freedom', Rees and his troops rushed to Amritsar to try to prevent retaliatory action. Most of the city's police force had already deserted. By the time the Boundary Force arrived, many Muslim women had been dragged from their homes and paraded naked through the streets outside the Golden Temple. Afterwards they were raped, then hacked to death.

As the boundaries fell, an estimated fourteen to seventeen million people were uprooted from their homes in what was to be the largest migration in human history. The reciprocal killing became ever more extravagant. Across northern India, through Bengal, Bihar, the United Provinces and in Delhi, each rival community murdered and was murdered. Gone were the days when a person could choose to be defined by birthplace, occupation, province or personality. Now even secularists were identified as Muslims, Hindus or Sikhs, circumcised or uncircumcised. Christians took to wearing little red crosses sewn onto their clothing, so as not to be mistakenly murdered. The need for retribution came to exceed any communal, political or territorial logic, and bloodlust and revenge gained a momentum of their own. As the Urdu writer Saadat Hasan Manto wrote in a chilling short story, death became random: 'The knife slid down his groin. The pyjama cord was cut into two. His genitals were exposed. "Chi, chi, chi, I've made a *mishtake*," the assassin said, with a sense of remorse.'[12]

On 20 August the Punjab Boundary Force fired on a Muslim mob near Gurdaspur, killing eighty-four people. Four days later, Muslim soldiers who had shot Hindu looters were challenged by Sikhs and Hindus from within their own unit, and the force began to break down along communal lines. By now bombs were being detonated along canal banks, destroying villages in central Punjab through flooding. By the end of the month, the army and what remained of the police had lost control. On 1 September the Punjab Boundary Force was dissolved and its units dispersed to their respective countries. It had been created with soldiers of the British Indian Empire, but in the end the urge for self-preservation had shifted their allegiance. Now, they were either Indians or Pakistanis.

By the end of August, any sense of law and order in the Punjab had collapsed. The authorities had little idea what was happening in the innumerable remote, isolated villages. Thousands of people were being massacred daily, and whole districts of refugees were making their way by foot and bullock-cart towards places where their co-religionists might be in a majority, in long, desolate *kafilas* or human caravans. Soldiers were supposed to be acting in aid to the civil power, yet the civil power no longer existed. Instead there were newly-formed, chaotic rival administrations in the new provinces of Indian Punjab and Pakistani Punjab, each convinced that the other side was responsible for instigating the worst atrocities. Both new governments had to cope with refugees arriving literally in their millions, with tales of slaughter and rape, looting and abduction.

The number of people killed during the creation of independent India and Pakistan has never been established. It was in the interests of the governments of Attlee, Jinnah and Nehru to play down the scale of the massacres, since they all bore a degree of responsibility for what had happened. Mutual genocide never attracts attention in the way that a one-way genocide does, so the terrible, squalid deaths in countless streets and fields were sidelined. In October the visiting Earl of Listowel con-

demned 'exaggerated reports' about the carnage, which led Nirad Chaudhuri to describe him as 'the weak man with the sponge following the
footsteps of the strong man with the dagger'.[13]

At the time, the figure of two hundred thousand deaths was widely
quoted, based on the numbers that were reported to the civil authorities
by the police and the army. Indian and Pakistani newspapers today tend
to put the figure at anything from seven hundred thousand to an arbitrary
two million. The truth is that the number of people who died across the
subcontinent in late 1947 and early 1948 will never be known. It is however
noticeable that independent eyewitnesses to the communal genocide
thought the politicians were underestimating the numbers. The BBC radio
reporter Wynford Vaughan Thomas, who travelled through the Punjab
by jeep with the poet Louis MacNeice, said subsequently, 'I think I would
go on record, stick my neck out and say nearly a million killed,' while
Louis Heren of *The Times* thought 'after talking to many of the senior
military officers involved, including Major General T.W. Rees ... that
about 1 million had been killed or had died from wounds.'[14]

My own opinion, based both on written records and on conversations
with officials and survivors in India, Pakistan and Bangladesh, is that the
number of people killed is unlikely to have been much lower than one
million. Anecdotally, it would appear that Muslims suffered the highest
casualties. The former ICS officer Penderel Moon, who was working in
Bahawalpur at the time, wrote that in Indian Punjab, 'Sikhs and Hindus
were there guilty of excesses against Muslims which equalled and, in my
judgement, exceeded in scale and atrocity the outrages perpetrated by
Muslims in West Pakistan.'[15]

The liberation of the Indian subcontinent was accompanied by a
holocaust of unconscionable horror that bit deeply into the memories of
its inhabitants. 'The psychological legacy of partition,' wrote Ayesha Jalal,
'has left a much deeper impact on people's minds than the social, economic and political dynamics that led to the division.'[16] That was the irony
of Jinnah's dream of a Muslim homeland: its consequences were far
worse than its causes. As the historian Mushirul Hasan has suggested,
the carve-up of India was not inevitable, but was 'a man-made catastrophe
brought about by cynical and hot-headed politicians who lacked the
imagination to resolve their disputes and the foresight to grasp the implications of dividing their country along religious lines'.[17]

Charles Still spent the war as a Major in Egypt and Italy, but nothing he witnessed there prepared him for the carnage of the Punjab in 1947. A tall, dark-haired man of forty-one, he had taken a job running eleven cotton-ginning factories mainly in the Punjab and the Princely State of Bahawalpur. The senior staff at his office at Khanewal, about 150 miles south-west of Lahore, were primarily Hindu, but the farm-workers and the local population were Muslim. In late May riots broke out, and Still made arrangements to stockpile petrol and revolvers. He wrote a letter to his head office back in Manchester saying he felt as if he was 'sitting on a volcano, the rumblings and minor disturbances of which seem to indicate a major eruption in the near future'.

During June and July there were a number of violent incidents. The Bahawalpur police found a hand-grenade workshop being run by one of Still's Hindu carpenters, and richer Sikhs and Hindus started to move across the border into east Punjab. But it was not until 13 August that Still became seriously frightened, when he heard that 'bands of armed Sikhs, even up to 700 strong in one party, have been attacking Moslem villages in the districts around the boundary areas'. A week later the violence had switched direction, with gangs of local Muslims taking revenge on Hindus in Multan and Bahawalpur town, cutting their sacred tufts of hair, forcing them to eat beef, and then hacking them to death.

By the end of August local schools and farm buildings were full of Muslim refugees, and cholera was spreading. Nearly all Still's Hindu and Sikh employees had either been evicted, killed or converted, such as a junior farm manager called Ram Kishen who had become Ghulam Rasul. By 4 September Still was writing that Jinnah's version of a Muslim home-land had been abandoned: 'The masses' idea of Pakistan is that everything in the country will become the property of Moslems – including Hindu women – and the leaders are quite unable to stop them behaving accordingly. It is Civil War ... Sikhs in Pakistan are finished. None can ever remain here in the future.' In less than a month the communal composition of the region had been altered for good, and in late October the 129 surviving Hindu workers were secretly evacuated to India by truck.[18]

Still's account is representative of what happened across the Punjab and much of northern India at this time. Nobody was able to remain free from religious attachment, not even the agnostic protagonist of Khushwant Singh's novel *Train to Pakistan*, who has the cross-denominational name of Iqbal. In the book he is repeatedly mistaken for an infiltrator from 'the other' religious group: 'He could be a Muslim, Iqbal Mohammed. He could be a Hindu, Iqbal Chand, or a Sikh, Iqbal Singh.'[19]

Many people experienced a sense of overwhelming bewilderment at what was happening, having shared Nehru's optimistic hope that the coming of freedom would bring communal peace. It was hard to believe that the old India could be torn apart so casually. The minutiae of the Indian Independence Act meant little to non-politicians. They made assumptions. Many Muslims had thought that Delhi, with its domes and turrets, its centuries of Mughal rule, and its specifically localized Islamic culture, would have to be included in a Muslim homeland. As one woman said, 'a Pakistan without Delhi was a body without a heart.'[20]

At first, few took much notice of the new boundaries, assuming that they would be permeable and fluid. They thought the relationship between India and Pakistan would be similar to that between Canada and the United States. Families would come and go at leisure: Muslims from the United Provinces would do business in Karachi but keep their homes in Lucknow; Hindus from Lahore would flit to Amritsar and back in a day. As the old soldier in Bhisham Sahni's short story 'The Train has Reached Amritsar' asks, would Mr Jinnah move from his house in Bombay now that Pakistan was being created? The narrator answers: 'What would be the point? He can always go to Pakistan and come back.'[21]

Once the reciprocal genocide had attained a certain critical momentum, it continued until a previously communally diverse province had been purged. By 1950, the Muslim population of Indian Punjab was just above 1 per cent, and the Hindu and Sikh population of Pakistani Punjab just below 1 per cent. As Marn Singh, an eye specialist whose father was a Sikh preacher in Rawalpindi, remembered: 'Integration between the communities was no longer possible. One man came to me at the hospital and said, "Doctor Saheb, once the Sikhs were spread all over the Punjab like salt in a *daal*, but now we are either dead or living as refugees in Amritsar." Personally I believe it was the fault of the politicians, who were so keen for power, especially that Mr Jinnah, who hoped to gain a nation without damaging the crease of his trousers, like some lord of England.'[22]

Although the initial outbreaks of violence had complex political and historical origins, and each killer had a personal motivation – whether it was anger, hatred, peer pressure, greed, drunkenness, cowardice, blood lust or mob fury – the escalation of the slaughter had two principal causes: fear and revenge. As news of the violence spread, the narrow streets of towns and villages would be fortified with gates and barricades, and guns and knives collected. These strongholds themselves then became a source of fear and provocation, and antagonists took to shooting into them from nearby rooftops. When refugees arrived by train or on foot with tales of killing and looting, violent action was taken against the relevant community.

In many cases the butchery would be provoked by a methodical pogrom by one of the roaming armed gangs – Sikh *jathas*, renegade Muslim soldiers or RSS killing squads – often armed with lists of names provided by local ration dealers, which in most cases indicated a person's religion. Death was often preceded and accompanied by humiliation, torture and genital mutilation. One of the effects of the level of killing was that any normal ideas of law, order and justice evaporated. It was politically impossible for the authorities in either Pakistan or India to bring suspects to trial. As one historian of the period said, it is unlikely that the full story of 1947 will ever be known, since 'it cut across every boundary. Nobody will admit what happened, as most of the killers were simply reabsorbed into society.'[23]

Weaponry ranged from improvised 'country guns' made by the local blacksmith, to sophisticated hardware left over from the war in Burma and the Middle East. Khushdeva Singh, a Sikh doctor who became famous for evacuating Muslims to safety from a small town near Simla, wrote that cheap guns were easily available: 'These fire-arms were primarily those which belonged to the British military officers in the cantonments near Dharampore. They had collected these at different fronts during World War II and had kept them as souvenirs. Since these officers were to leave India for good in the near future, they thought it best to sell the arms and make some money.'[24]

Old friendships and relationships evaporated. Narinder Singh Soch, a journalist and writer in Amritsar, found that his Muslim colleagues became afraid of him. 'What is so strange,' he recalled, 'is that we started to see everything in terms of the community to which somebody belonged. Very few of us could avoid that, even though before the partition I remember the Sikh–Muslim relationship as being rather good. Some people tried to pretend it was not happening, like my friend the *maulvi* [Quranic scholar] and poet Gulam Mohammed Tarranum, who would walk to my house through the riots, and say: "I am risking my life purely to make a social call. I will not succumb to the hatred." But I have to say I do not think there are any Muslims left in Amritsar today.' Jinnah's hope that 'the Muslims in the Indian state will be treated just as we propose to treat non-Muslim minorities' was coming true in a way that he had never intended.[25]

Nirmal Mangat Rai, who was Director General of Food and Civil Supplies in the Punjab, remembered the abrupt disappearance of a Sikh who worked as an inspector in his department. 'We all thought he must have been killed or had migrated. Out of the blue he came back and told us that he had been away doing "important work". "What was the work?" we asked. He replied: "I have been killing *Musalas* [a derogatory term for Muslims]. I have killed seventy-two of them in thirty-five days." That was how people thought at that time . . . It worked both ways. I watched a truckload of Muslim soldiers leaving Amritsar for Pakistan, and as if for sport they were bayoneting Sikhs on bicycles as they drove down the road, one after the other. I picked up one Sikh man who was having terrible convulsions and took him to the hospital. I don't know whether he lived.'[26]

Even when a terrified, misplaced community wanted to migrate to either India or Pakistan, the process of escape was fraught with problems. It was extremely dangerous to travel without military protection, but most people had little choice but to go by foot in the *kafilas* and risk death on the journey. Although the railway massacres in the Punjab are one of the most famous images of the communal holocaust of 1947, only a minority of victims met their end in this way, since trains soon stopped running unless they were accompanied by a substantial armed guard. But when trains were derailed and attacked, the occupants faced a terrible, squalid, claustrophobic death. The *Times* reporter Louis Heren watched carriages being shunted into a siding so that around four thousand Muslims could be massacred by a mixed Sikh and Hindu mob.[27]

In Bengal the process of migration was slightly less hazardous, and fewer people were murdered or turned out of their homes. Still, in the south-east of the province, Hindus were persecuted, while in Calcutta many Muslims decided to go to what was now East Pakistan. A Bengali journalist who was a child in Jalpaiguri at the time recalled his intense fear at the sight of Hindu gangs in the street. 'Our house was protected by some Afghans, *Kabuli-wallah*s we called them, who carried long knives and terrified everybody. On the afternoon of 14 August we boarded a train to Rajshahi. I remember as we crossed the border, everybody on the train started shouting in unison, "Pakistan Zindabad! Long live Pakistan!" I can still feel my mother's reassuring grip on my arm as we came to Pakistan.'[28]

In one village near Hoshiarpur in east Punjab an extended family of prosperous Muslim landlords spent over a week in a fortified building being besieged by Sikhs from a nearby village. Several of them were killed, and six Muslim women drowned themselves rather than face rape or abduction. They were saved when one member of the family, a trainee journalist in Lahore, persuaded an army convoy to make a detour to the village. When the soldiers appeared the mob fled and the besieged family emerged and lay on the ground shouting '*Allah-ho-Akbar.*'

'The commander told them they could each take one box and one bedroll, and that they would be able to return when things had settled down. There were around forty people including servants who set off as soon as it was light the next morning, leaving all our assets – our horses, buffaloes and goats – in the care of local Hindus. We drove out past our citrus gardens and reached Lahore the same night, reciting the holy Quran. On the way there were villagers shouting that we were "unclean Turks", escaping to Pakistan. There was a woman's body there. She had been chopped up into several pieces. She was being eaten by kites.'[29]

For those who did manage to get through to their promised land, conditions were pitiable. Delhi in particular faced an influx of hundreds of thousands of Punjabi Hindus, often wounded and starving, who had been driven from their homes by Muslim mobs, members of their families often being murdered in the process. A giant camp grew up at Panipat to the north of the city, while Muslims huddled together at Purana Qila and Humayun's Tomb, having been chased out of their homes in Old Delhi. In Karachi, which was to be the capital of Jinnah's new nation, the refugees became the responsibility of the city's Deputy Commissioner, Hashim Raza, an Oxford-educated ICS officer who had previously been Secretary to the Governor of Sind. 'Pakistan was bankrupt, for a start,' he noted. 'I'd been told to expect a few thousand, but by the end of the year I had around half a million people on my hands. It was really impossible to know what to do with them. I turned thirty-two empty Hindu schools into shelters.'[30]

Even the refugee camps were not safe. One woman who worked as a nurse at Walton Camp near Lahore remembered the 'total chaos, total squalor and endless, endless people. In one hut there were about two dozen young men, who did not have a hand between them. The ground was so hard that we had trouble burying the dead. The vultures were so fat they could hardly get off the ground.'[31] At this camp and at others, women and girls were traded 'in much the same manner as people who buy cattle at a fair assess the age of a cow or a buffalo by pushing aside its snout and testing the teeth'. The vendors made 'an exhibition of their beauty and their youth, of their most precious and most intimate secrets, of their dimples and tattoo-marks, to the gaze of the buyers'.[32] In some cases, women were sold from man to man for months on end before being put to work in brothels.

As in so many genocidal conflicts, from the Trojan Wars to the former Yugoslavia during the early 1990s, 'women were targeted for rape and impregnation so as to change the religious or racial identity of a particular area'.[33] While men and boys would be killed, women and girls were in many cases raped, abducted, converted and forced into marriage. By 1952 about thirty thousand women from both sides had been recovered and repatriated under an inter-governmental agreement, but in a society where marriage was usually based on status rather than romance, this could create problems of its own. Many women did not wish to return to their original families, which would involve not only social humiliation but the abandonment of the babies they had had with their abductors.

The Sikh and Hindu emphasis on ritual purity meant that a substantial number of women chose suicide or 'sacrifice' rather than dishonour. During attacks on Sikh villages near Rawalpindi, one patriarch, Sant Raja Singh, killed several of his own family retainers and twenty-five female relatives. His daughter remembered 'clutching on to his *kurta* as children do, I was clinging to him . . . my sister, with her own hands moved her *dupatta* [scarf] aside and then he swung the *kirpan* [knife] and her head and neck rolled off and fell'. In the same village around eighty women jumped into a well in order to preserve themselves from probable rape and conversion to Islam, and were afterwards acclaimed as martyrs by their community.[34]

The horror of India and Pakistan's holocaust imprinted itself on the minds of all those who survived. The writer Nirmal Verma was an ideal-istic young student in Delhi in 1947, and he volunteered to help clear the dead from buildings in the old city. Although he has tried to blank those days from his mind, there is one image that is always present: 'We were at the top of some steps trying to lift the body of a woman who had been killed three or four days earlier. It was a very hot month. It was August. There were bangles on her thin wrist, all slimy, and her corpse started to fall apart. We just couldn't keep it in one piece.'[35]

TWENTY-ONE

Midnight's Parents

On the morning of 15 August the old badges of protest – a *khadi* and *dhoti-kurta* topped by a Gandhi cap – became the uniform of a new elite. In the provinces, Congress stalwarts such as Naidu and Rajagopalachari were made governors, and in New Delhi the existing administration continued largely unchanged with Nehru becoming Prime Minister and Patel Deputy Prime Minister, while retaining responsibility for home affairs, information, broadcasting and the princes.

Mountbatten had to adjust to a ceremonial role as India's constitutional Governor General, but on 4 September he was summoned from Simla to assist in dealing with the mounting chaos in New Delhi. Although he liked to claim that this happened because a floundering Nehru and Patel thought that 'the situation was now so serious that his presence alone could save it', it was in fact done on the spontaneous initiative of V.P. Menon.[1] When Nehru, Patel and the Cabinet discovered what had taken place, they were furious. Mountbatten did however play an important subsequent role in chairing an emergency committee to limit the communal violence and coordinate humanitarian relief. His bias against Pakistan now became pronounced, and his enthusiasm for the Indian cause proved to be extremely useful to the new Congress government, especially during the coming conflict over Kashmir.

Edwina Mountbatten became a prominent organizer of aid for refugees, launching appeals and visiting camps. Her efforts moved and impressed Jawaharlal Nehru. Some historians have concocted elaborate theories about the significance of their mutual admiration in the political machinations leading to the transfer of power, but it is apparent that the relationship did not flourish until after August 1947, and in particular during subsequent years when Edwina took to visiting 'Jawa' in New Delhi each February. Their love affair has nevertheless acquired a huge symbolic significance, and is one of the best-known aspects of the story of India's independence, as if the British people had offered the last Vicereine to India's new ruler as a vestal (or at least vestigial) virgin in a final gesture of sacrificial atonement for three and a half centuries of enforced intimacy.[2]

By early 1947, Mohandas Gandhi's political influence had diminished significantly. Although Mountbatten consulted him throughout the negotiations, Gandhi knew that the Congress leadership would no longer obey his commands. When it became clear that Pakistan was to be created, he described independence accompanied by partition as a 'wooden loaf', and made half-hearted efforts to find an alternative solution before finally giving way. As he had written in his magazine *Harijan* in 1942: 'If the vast majority of Moslems regard themselves as a separate nation, no power on earth can compel them to think otherwise. If they want to partition India they must, unless Hindus want to fight against such division.'[3]

When the violence began to spin out of control, Gandhi used all his remaining moral authority to promote an end to the mayhem. It had some effect, although the seventy-seven-year-old Mahatma was perplexed by what he was witnessing, and convinced he was personally responsible in some way. He travelled from Noakhali to Bihar, preaching peace and imploring all communities to end the killing. To his distress he encountered hostility from Muslims, who saw him as the embodiment of *Ram Rajya*, and from Hindus, who claimed he was appeasing their persecutors. On the night of independence he stayed in a poor Muslim *mohalla* in Calcutta, fasting and praying for peace, which had a significant if temporary impact on the communal violence. Mountbatten referred to him as a 'one man boundary force'.

In September Gandhi returned to New Delhi and installed himself at Birla House, the residence of his financiers and a long-time headquarters of Congress activity. He felt pessimistic and isolated, and his determination to defend Old Delhi's Muslims against pogroms angered many Hindus, as did his practice of reading sections of the Quran at prayer meetings. One colleague who saw him at this time was 'shocked by the change in him. He looked physically weaker and mentally disturbed.'[4] His grandson Rajmohan believes it was one of the hardest times of his life, and remembers a look of 'total anguish' coming across his face when he heard about the massacres in the Punjab.[5]

It was not only the killing that distressed Gandhi. For him, real freedom meant not only an Indian Government of India, but a change of heart among the people in accordance with his particular vision of society. Until Indians gave up 'the vain imitation of the tinsel of the West', they would not be truly liberated. During the course of 1947 he had made plans to transform Congress into a Lok Sewak Sangh, or People's Servants Society, meaning a *khadi*-clad army of social activists. The first president of free India would be 'a chaste and brave *bhangi* [low-caste] girl', and Nehruvian socialist economics would be replaced by a system of village bartering.

Although the new Congress government took little notice of most of these ideas, Nehru agreed to abolish price controls on basic food supplies, which had the effect of promoting speculative buying and hoarding. By the end of the year salt, that most symbolic of commodities, had risen in price by 500 per cent in five months. 'We now have the spectacle,' noted one observer, 'of a government trying to create a modern state and depriving itself of the power to tackle food-hoarders and price-ring profiteers save through appeals to their social conscience, the one commodity in which they are totally lacking.'[6] After Gandhi's death Nehru quietly reimposed price controls.

During the chaotic violence of August and September, the hard-line Hindu organization the Rashtriya Swayamsewak Sangh (Society for Service to the Nation) asserted its authority. Although it was and is notoriously secretive, most estimates suggest the RSS had around half a million activists and many more tacit supporters. Its role in anti-Muslim violence led to a bitter dispute between Prime Minister Nehru and his deputy Sardar Patel. Nehru pointed out that while they 'have had a great deal to do with the present disturbances not only in Delhi but elsewhere ... noted members of the RSS were appointed as special magistrates and special police officers'.[7] Patel, in his capacity as Home Minister, was responsible for this, and refused to have the RSS activists dismissed from their official posts.

Nehru believed he was witnessing 'an upheaval of the lower middle classes – the classes that first supported Hitler'.[8] By 6 January 1948 he was telling Gandhi that he had 'temperamental differences' with Patel over 'economic and communal matters', and that if they were not resolved, 'the only alternative left is for either me or Sardar Patel to leave the Cabinet'.[9] The Mahatma's attempts to encourage a rapprochement were not helped when Patel publicly described the RSS two days later as 'patriots who love their country ... You cannot crush an organization by using the *danda* [stick]. The *danda* is meant for thieves and *dacoits*.' In his view, reports of their activities were 'somewhat exaggerated'.[10]

The precise role of senior figures in the RSS and the Hindu Mahasabha in Gandhi's murder has never been established, although it is known that his killers were RSS activists and fanatical believers in a Hindu India. The conspirators operated in a small group, the actual murderer being a Maharashtrian Brahmin and Agatha Christie addict named Nathuram Godse, who was funded and advised by the former India House revolutionary Vinayak Savarkar. Like the bomb-throwers before the First World War, the killers were 'rank amateurs, shockingly incompetent in almost everything they did', and made several bungled attempts at assassination before succeeding.[11]

Perhaps their saddest mistake was to have believed that Gandhi was personally responsible for the creation of Pakistan, simply because he spoke out so passionately against the persecution of India's Muslim minority. It was the final irony that a man who said his 'heart owed allegiance to only one religion – the Hindu *Dharma*', should have been murdered by a deluded extremist of his own faith.

A little after 5 p.m. on 30 January 1948, Gandhi walked out of Birla House to his evening prayer meeting, his hands resting on the shoulders of a pair of female disciples. He looked frail, since earlier that month he had undertaken a hunger-strike in an attempt to quell the communal violence, and to encourage the new Indian government to pay money it owed to Pakistan. As he reached the crowd of devotees, he was detained by a bowing figure. It was Nathuram Godse, who fired three bullets into his chest using a primitive pistol. Gandhi was dead within minutes. A Sikh businessman called Gurbachan Singh who witnessed the assassination later claimed that he died with an invocation to Lord Ram on his lips, a myth that is now generally accepted. His actual last words were the equally characteristic: 'It irks me if I am late for prayers even by a minute.'[12]

As the news spread throughout the city, surging swarms of people converged on Birla House, where Mountbatten and Campbell-Johnson arrived to find a desolate Patel and an 'inexpressibly sad and careworn' Nehru.[13] The Prime Minister's niece Nayantara remembered her uncle looking 'absolutely broken' by the death of his mentor: 'It was as if it had destroyed something within him.'[14] That night Nehru broadcast a spontaneous message to the nation over All India Radio. 'The light has gone out of our lives,' he said. 'Our beloved leader, *Bapu* [father], as we called him, the father of the nation, is no more.' At eleven o'clock the next morning, Gandhi's body was placed, inappropriately enough, on a gun carriage, and draped in the saffron (for Hindus), green (for Muslims) and white (for the rest) flag of independent India. Escorted by most of the Cabinet and surrounded by a crowd estimated at a little under a million, the funeral cortège processed along a six-mile route to Raj Ghat on the banks of the Jumna for Gandhi's cremation. Patel sat beside the body, staring straight ahead, looking pale and weary. Nehru walked beside the gun carriage.

Gandhi's ashes were scattered at the confluence of the Ganges and the Saraswati (with the exception of a small handful which were mysteriously deposited in the State Bank of India in Orissa, and eventually released in 1997). A memorial service was held at which the Mahatma's favourite hymns were sung, namely 'Abide with Me' and 'When I Survey the Wondrous Cross'. Despite Gandhi's objections to capital punishment, his killer and an accomplice named Narayan Apte were hanged from a prison gibbet. They died clutching saffron flags, reciting the *Gita* and shouting the slogan '*Akhand Bharat Amar Rahe*', 'Long Live Undivided India'.

The people of divided India experienced a profound sense of loss. Even Gandhi's opponents such as Jinnah recognized the passion behind his belief in non-violence. His murder seemed to be the ultimate manifestation of the slaughter that had overtaken the subcontinent, and there was a certain sacrificial symmetry in it occurring at this point. As Sarojini Naidu asked a group of mourners, would they rather that the father of the nation had died of indigestion? In the aftermath, Bengali Communists claimed that 'the Hindu Mahasabha, RSS and Sardar Patel planned to kill the Mahatma with a view to perpetuating fascist rule in India.'[15] It is inconceivable that Patel could have been involved in a plot to take Gandhi's life, but his reputation was seriously damaged by his failure to have taken pre-emptive action against Hindu extremists. Now Nehru outlawed the RSS.

In his last months, Gandhi had continued to try to promote his idealistic vision of moral *swaraj* and communal harmony, even though the odds were stacked against him. For all his failings and contradictions, he remains the central figure in India's journey to independence and division, and an iconic leader in twentieth-century world history. Without his success in turning Congress into a mass movement in the 1920s, it is unlikely that the British would have been dislodged by 1947.

As his biographer Judith Brown has written, Gandhi may not have found 'lasting and real solutions to many of the problems he encountered. Possibly he did not even see the implications of some of them.' Yet he 'asked many of the profoundest questions that face humankind as it struggles to live in community', and it is this 'which marks his true stature and which makes his struggles and glimpses of truth of enduring significance. As a man of his time who asked the deepest questions, even though he could not answer them, he became a man for all times and all places.'[16]

The Mountbattens remained in India until June 1948, when the widely respected southern Brahmin and Congress traditionalist Chakravarti Rajagopalachari took over as Governor General. During his last days in Delhi, Mountbatten was honoured with a farewell address by the city's municipality. To receive it he had to drive through tightly packed cheering crowds along Chandni Chowk, a thoroughfare that had been out of bounds to viceroys since the attack on Lord Hardinge and his elephant in 1912. Now that V.P. Menon's 'dominion status' ploy had outlived its usefulness, Congress made moves to abandon the remaining British link. Aware that the Commonwealth was in danger of losing over half of its citizens, Attlee arranged an urgent reform to enable a crownless India to remain a member. On 26 January 1950, on the anniversary of the *purna swaraj* day of 1930, a new constitution was promulgated and the Republic of India was born.

Pakistan started life with two hundred million rupees in its treasury, and outstanding debts of almost four hundred million. Paying for the armed forces alone cost fifty million rupees a month. Governor General Jinnah had to use all his considerable financial skills in dealing with the crisis, and a loan to Pakistan of two hundred million rupees from the Nawab of Hyderabad did something to alleviate it. However, Jinnah and his Prime Minister Liaquat Ali Khan were still in a desperate plight, having to build a nation from scratch with no administrative infrastructure. Jinnah even had to draw up a statistical and accounting system for his government. Pakistan's first budget was put together in February 1948: three-quarters of all projected expenditure was to go on the military, setting a lasting precedent for the country.

The Quaid-i-Azam's methods remained autocratic, and he quickly became irritated by any of his colleagues who failed to come up to standard. A British journalist who accompanied him on a visit to the north-west frontier described him treating local politicians 'like a medieval monarch receiving tribute from feudal barons', and thought Jinnah saw himself as 'the heir to the British Raj and the Moghul emperors'.[17]

Pakistan had a quarter of the land mass of the old British Indian Empire, just under a fifth of the population, and less than a tenth of the industrial base. It contained several fundamentally inimical groups with no single language, heritage or culture. Pathans and Baluchis from the frontier had little in common with Punjabis, who in turn were often antagonistic towards Sindhis, many of whom soon began to call for an autonomous 'Sindhudesh'. Although the size and diversity of old India had always created problems, none was comparable to the difficulty of having thirty-five million citizens located on the other side of a thousand miles of hostile Indian territory. From the beginning, Pakistan's Bengalis felt abandoned, since the government was run primarily by Punjabis and *mohajirs* or migrants, such as Jinnah and Liaquat. There was nothing but Allah to bind together sixty million Pakistanis, as Rahmat Ali's 'Pakistanites' were now known.

In an extraordinary speech in August 1947, Jinnah seemed to question the basis on which his new kingdom had been established: 'I know there are people who do not quite agree with the division of India ... but in my judgement there was no other solution and I am sure future history will record its verdict in favour of it ... Maybe that view is correct; maybe it is not; that remains to be seen.' He went on to say that his ambition was that Pakistan should become a nation in which there were no distinctions of 'colour, caste or creed':

You are free, you are free to go to your temples. You are free to go to your mosques or to any other places of worship in this State of Pakistan. You may belong to any religion or caste or creed – that has nothing to do with the business of the State ... We are starting in the days when there is no discrimination, no distinction between one community and another, no discrimination between one caste or creed or another. We are starting with this fundamental principle that we are all citizens and equal citizens of one State . . . Now, I think we should keep that in front of us as our ideal and you will find that in course of time Hindus would cease to be Hindus and Muslims would cease to be Muslims, not in the religious sense, because that is the personal faith of each individual, but in the political sense as citizens of the State.[18]

It was a magnificent vision for the new nation, but one that was to be destroyed by the end of the month. Jinnah did his best to cope with the effects of the massacres and migrations. He based himself in Karachi, supported by his sister Fatima, who wrote that her brother 'worked in a frenzy to consolidate Pakistan . . . He had little or no appetite and had even lost his ability to will himself to sleep . . . he began his day discussing these mass killings with me at breakfast and his handkerchief furtively often went to his moist eyes.'[19] His daughter Dina had decided to remain behind in Bombay, where he had retained his house on Malabar Hill. It is widely claimed that Jinnah became estranged from Dina because she married a Parsi Christian, but her letters to her father during this time do not give this impression, being full of affectionate messages such as 'lots of love and kisses and a big hug'.[20]

By 1948 Jinnah was very weak, suffering from bronchiectasis but still consuming endless packets of Craven A cigarettes. The idea that the fate of the subcontinent would have altered had anyone known that he was ill is one that has gained wide currency. According to *Freedom at Midnight*, Jinnah collapsed during the Cabinet Delegation's meetings in May 1946, and was rushed to Bombay by train. There he saw his physician, Dr J.A.L. Patel, who X-rayed his lungs, revealing that he was in the advanced stages of tuberculosis and 'living under a sentence of death'. The diagnosis was placed in a safe in an 'unmarked envelope', and became the 'most closely guarded secret in India'. According to Collins and Lapierre's version of events, had Mountbatten, Nehru or Gandhi been aware of it, 'the division threatening India might have been avoided', and it 'would almost certainly have changed the course of Asian history'.[21]

The idea that Jinnah's poor state of health was a closely guarded secret is absurd; it was referred to in the press at the time, and it is obvious from photographs taken in the mid-1940s that Jinnah was unwell. Moreover, the reduction of the Muslim League's wide popular backing to the whim of one 'rigid and inflexible' man is indicative of the way that Pakistan's history has been traduced. A second problem with Collins and Lapierre's story is that it is not accurate. Jinnah did not go to Bombay in May or June 1946, since he was busy negotiating with Cripps in Simla and New Delhi. Nor did he have a doctor by the name of J.A.L. Patel, although he did have one called Commander Jal Patel, who had treated him some years earlier. During this time he was diagnosed as having 'remnants of old healed lesions', but 'no active lung disease'. Although it is possible that Jinnah had tuberculosis in 1946, there is no evidence among his archive papers to support the theory.[22]

In the autumn of 1948, while resting in Baluchistan, Jinnah's bronchial condition worsened. On 11 September, Fatima decided her brother should be flown back to Karachi. They were accompanied by several oxygen cylinders and a terrified entourage, and after a long flight followed by a journey in a stalling army ambulance, they reached the city the same night. The seventy-one-year-old Mohammad Ali Jinnah died a few hours later. His political achievement had been colossal, and more remarkable in several respects than that of his opponents in Congress. Although in retrospect the creation of Pakistan may in many ways seem to have been a pyrrhic victory, its impact has been enormous. As Jalal has written: 'Few political decisions in the twentieth century have altered the course of history in more dramatic fashion than the partition of India in 1947.'[23]

After Jinnah's death, Liaquat took control and did his best to establish a secular democracy. In October 1951 he was assassinated in Rawalpindi, for reasons that have never been properly established, and since then Pakistan has lurched from disaster to disaster under successive governments, giving Indians the precarious pleasure of knowing that however badly their country was being run, it was probably not as bad as the situation across the border.

Liaquat was followed by a succession of ineffectual administrators, until in 1958 the Commander-in-Chief, General Ayub Khan, led a coup. Martial law was intended to be a temporary solution while, in the words of President Iskander Mirza, some 'bright young chaps' drew up a new constitution. The tough and ruthless Field Marshal Ayub Khan took a different line, sending Mirza into exile in London and establishing a US-backed military dictatorship. Despite a vigorous campaign against him by East Pakistani politicians and 'the mother of the nation' Fatima Jinnah, Ayub retained power for a decade.

In 1969 he handed over control of an unhappy and divided country to a protégé, General Yahya Khan, who agreed after prompting by his American masters to hold Pakistan's first full general election in both its eastern and western wings. In December 1970 the Awami League led by the Bengali Sheikh Mujibur Rahman won almost every seat in East Pakistan on a ticket of increased autonomy for the province. In West Pakistan a majority was won by the Pakistan People's Party, led by an Oxford-educated Sindhi landowner named Zulfiqar Ali Bhutto. Although legally Sheikh Mujib should have assumed power, this was resolutely resisted by the Punjabis, Sindhis and *mohajirs* who had controlled Pakistan almost since its foundation. Sheikh Mujib was arrested on charges of subversion, and shortly afterwards a 'government-in-exile' was proclaimed in Calcutta.

This marked the start of the crisis that created Bangladesh ('Bengaliland'). It developed into two distinct wars: a civil war, which deprived West Pakistan of its political legitimacy over its eastern wing, and a subsequent war between Pakistan and India. In March 1971 there was an abortive crackdown on rioting Bengali nationalists, and Yahya Khan flew to Dhaka for talks. His senior military officers thought it would be 'an act of madness' to try to suppress the Bengalis militarily, but as the riots spread and no solution was found, Yahya summoned a pair of senior generals and ordered them to disarm all of East Pakistan's military units, and to treat the Awami League as rebels. The popular uprising was suppressed in six weeks, with astounding ferocity, while millions of refugees fled over the border into India. They consisted mainly of Hindus, Awami Leaguers, political activists, students, and renegade soldiers, many of whom now joined a new rebel army called the Mukti Bahini. They were given covert backing by India, including weapons, ammunition and training in sabotage.

By July the number of refugees in west Bengal had swelled to a stupendous seven million, and was still rising rapidly. Nervous of provoking demands for a new, united Bengal, India's Prime Minister Indira Gandhi bided her time, while the West Pakistanis attempted to recruit an 'East Pakistan Civil Affairs Force' to administer internal security. The province was however in a state of administrative paralysis, with Yahya Khan's brutal government hated by all except a handful of loyal Urdu-speakers who had migrated there in 1947. In August, Indian soldiers covertly joined the Mukti Bahini, blowing up bridges, disrupting communications and destroying some ships in the port of Chittagong. In late November, with nearly eleven million refugees now in west Bengal, the Indian Army invaded East Pakistan.

Pakistan reacted by launching air strikes on north-west India, which curtailed the possibility of a United Nations-imposed ceasefire and gave Indira Gandhi's troops a good excuse to march on Dhaka. President Nixon despatched 'Task Force 74' of the US Navy to the region, provoking countless subsequent theories that America intended to fight for the integrity of a united Pakistan. On 17 December 1971 Yahya Khan's forces capitulated. The surrender took place at the symbolic location of Ramna Racecourse in Dhaka, where the soon-to-be-murdered Sheikh Mujib had first made his call for Bengali freedom. On behalf of the remaining portion of Mohammad Ali Jinnah's Muslim homeland, General 'Tiger' Niazi signed the instrument of defeat. It was accepted by three victorious Indian generals: a Parsi, a Jew, and a Sikh.[24] Muslim power in the subcontinent was broken for good.

In the aftermath of India's independence, Sardar Patel had moved rapidly to integrate the remaining Princely States. Aided by the invaluable V.P. Menon, he cajoled, browbeat and manipulated several hundred princely rulers, old and young, sane and mad, Hindu and Muslim, Sikh and Buddhist, to give up control of their ancient hereditary kingdoms. It was a conspicuous achievement, which Nehru described as 'one of the dominant phases of Indian history'.[25] By 1950 New Delhi had a degree of direct control over the 'Indian Union' that would have been unimaginable to the British three years earlier.

Menon and Patel flew around the country for two years, persuading the rulers to move from earlier standstill agreements to full integration. Their tactic in the case of a powerful ruler was to offer him the symbolic title of *rajpramukh* [chief ruler] and a privy purse or pension to compensate for the assets and political power he was losing. Attempts by leading nawabs and maharajahs to unite and dictate the terms of their own accession failed because of internal arguments and indecision. In most cases, gentle flattery was enough to make the prince sign. 'It is high statesmanship,' wrote Alan Campbell-Johnson with reference to Menon's achievement in making Rajputana's rulers merge their kingdoms, 'that can cover a revolutionary act in the mantle of traditional form.'[26] In 1971,

Indira Gandhi was to abolish the special rights and privy purses of India's princes.

The Maharajah of Cochin signed on the dotted line only after Menon promised him he would still receive free copies of the *Panjangam* – the annual state almanac. Many of the smaller rulers conceded without a murmur. In the four-thousand-square-mile state of Tripura in Assam, which was ruled by an ancient royal family that could be found in the Bengali epic the *Rajmala*, the monarch was a child, and his politically inexperienced mother signed away his kingdom on his behalf. In Bhopal, the largest Muslim state in central India, the once-powerful Nawab's determination to have a referendum before acceding was overruled by Patel.

The British had left a host of territorial anomalies for their successors to confront, such as the mountain kingdom of Sikkim on India's northern border. Its ruler, the Chogyal, had never been obliged to swear loyalty to the British Crown. However, in February 1948 Menon persuaded him to sign an agreement linking Sikkim to the Foreign Affairs Ministry in New Delhi, and two years later it became a protectorate of India while remaining sovereign. Relations were often strained, and in 1975 Sikkim was invaded and annexed on the orders of Indira Gandhi. The neighbouring kingdom of Bhutan also had unusual status. The Bhutanese monarch received a subsidy from India, yet he paid an annual tribute to the Tibetan government. In August 1949 he agreed that he would be 'guided by the advice of the Government of India' in matters of defence and external relations, and received some disputed land in Bengal in return. The treaty has held to this day, with the King of Bhutan's control over his territory almost intact.

Tibet was not so lucky. Under Nehru's 'Hindi–Chini bhai-bhai' or 'Sino–Indian brotherhood' policy, India did all it could to appease China, and became one of the first countries to recognize Mao Zedong's new regime in 1949. Five years later Nehru signed an agreement with Mao describing Tibet as part of China, following the Chinese invasion of 1950. This was despite the British government's acceptance of Tibet's *de facto* independent status in 1943, and Nehru's government having kept a representative in Lhasa from 1947 to 1950. When the Chinese army built a road through large sections of supposedly Indian territory in the late 1950s, Nehru's placatory policy collapsed. In 1962, at the instigation of his unstable Defence Minister (the former London-based Congress activist

Krishna Menon), he ordered the Indian Army to reconquer the lost land. They failed dismally, and Nehru had to abandon his much-vaunted policy of 'non-alignment' and turn to the United States and Britain for military hardware.[27]

A number of Princely States were initially unwilling to cooperate with Sardar Patel and V.P. Menon, the most significant being the giant kingdoms of Hyderabad in the south and Kashmir in the north, together with the smaller but symbolic state of Junagadh on the west coast. Ultimately, all three states were absorbed into India: Hyderabad on the grounds of administrative necessity and internal unrest, although its Muslim ruler wished to be independent; Kashmir because its Hindu maharajah chose to join India, despite the majority of his three million subjects being Muslim; and Junagadh on account of the state being culturally Hindu, even though its Muslim ruler had already acceded to Pakistan.

The Junagadh crisis was dealt with swiftly. Although none of its territory was contiguous with Pakistan, the fact that it was a substantial coastal state only three hundred miles south-east of Karachi persuaded the Nawab of Junagadh that he need not join India. On 15 August 1947 he signed an instrument of accession to Pakistan, and this move was accepted by Mountbatten. The Nawab was heavily influenced in his decision by his sharp *diwan* or chief minister, Sir Shah Nawaz Bhutto, a Sindhi landowner and the father of Pakistan's future ruler Zulfiqar Ali Bhutto. Patel's fury was instant. In his role as constitutional Governor General, Mountbatten attempted to defuse the situation by suggesting a referendum be held in Junagadh after the matter had been referred to the United Nations. Although Nehru favoured a conciliatory response of this type, Patel would not accept such a solution, believing it might set a precedent for the separation of other bits of disputed territory.

The Indian Army was sent into the area surrounding Junagadh to enforce a total blockade. Within a couple of months, with mass starvation looming and minimal supplies coming in by sea from Pakistan, the Nawab fled to Karachi and ordered Bhutto to reopen negotiations with India. An agreement was cobbled together under Mountbatten's guidance, whereby a UN-administered referendum would be held in the state, and the resolution of Junagadh's precise international status postponed until other more pressing concerns had been resolved. Although it appeared that this solution had been accepted, Patel in his role as States Minister quietly arranged for troops to invade and capture Junagadh, assisted by an internal 'liberation army'. On 13 November Patel arrived in triumph at Junagadh's main Bahauddin College, hailed as a hero by the swirling crowds. A subsequent plebiscite, held under Indian auspices and without international intervention, resulted in a decisive endorsement of the annexation. Only 0.07 per cent of the voters favoured joining Pakistan.

The Princely State of Hyderabad was more complicated, in that it covered tens of thousands of square miles and had its own well-equipped army. The ruler, His Exalted Highness the Nizam, was inordinately rich and notoriously eccentric, and was determined to maintain his state's independence from both India and Pakistan. He was a small but vehement man, with a stoop, bad teeth and knocking knees. Despite his immense wealth (much of which was said to be kept in the form of gold bars and hidden under his bed) he always dressed shabbily, and refused ever to wear socks. As a committed supporter of the British Empire, he was distressed by what was happening to the subcontinent, and did his best not to let it affect the fate of his own kingdom.

In June 1947, acting on the advice of several high-powered British advisers, the Nizam issued an edict or *firman-e-mubarak*, saying that he was not inclined to join either India or Pakistan, since he did not believe in the construction of nations on a communal basis. The *firman* revealed that he had 'always regarded the Muslims and the Hindus as two eyes of the State', and so was 'satisfied that the course of political wisdom lies in not taking sides'.[28]

After 15 August, the Nizam showed immediate signs of leaning towards Pakistan, by giving Jinnah's new government two hundred million rupees to enable it to escape from its initial financial crisis. At the same time, he claimed he was still willing to agree a 'treaty of association' with India. Although at Nehru's instigation Lord Mountbatten tried to play a conciliatory role by entering into protracted negotiations with the Nizam and his representatives on behalf of the Indian government, Patel was adamant that India could never accept 'a snake in its belly'. During the last months of 1947 there were sporadic communal riots within Hyderabad, with the predominantly Muslim police force being accused of brutality towards the Hindu community. Some Hindus began to flee into neighbouring territory.

Matters were resolved temporarily in late November when the Nizam signed a 'standstill' agreement with India, preserving his kingdom's tenuous neutrality for one year while he considered its future. During subsequent months, however, he made several moves to assert his independence, for instance attempting to appoint representatives in foreign countries. Under Mountbatten's influence, Nehru was anxious to conclude a compromise agreement, but the Nizam's refusal to integrate with India made this impossible. In March 1948, Patel suffered a heart attack and was confined to his bed, and so could only look on in irritation while Hyderabad continued to strengthen its position. After Mountbatten's departure as Governor General in June, Nehru hardened his approach. Under strong pressure from Patel, who was by now back in the driving seat, he agreed in September to authorize the military annexation of Hyderabad.

Despite pressure from the Chiefs of Staff, who thought it militarily risky, Sardar Patel ordered two divisions of the Indian Army's Southern Command into action on 13 September. In a remarkably successful manoeuvre against Hyderabad's state forces (codenamed 'Operation Polo', and referred to euphemistically as 'police action'), Indian troops destroyed their rivals within four days. A week later, His Exalted Highness the Nizam capitulated, and withdrew his case of protest from the United Nations. Soon afterwards the state of Hyderabad was incorporated into India for good.

Although, fifty years on, Pakistan still lays claim to Junagadh on its maps, and a handful of people in Hyderabad complain of the injustice of annexation, Kashmir is the only Princely State that remains a serious source of friction between India and Pakistan. Indeed, a territorial dispute between two new nations has expanded into the central focus of Indo–Pakistan relations, and is the source of continued fighting and bloodshed. Kashmir has become a diplomatic pawn, used internally by both sides for political purposes, while the actual wishes of the Kashmiri people are generally ignored.

Despite the fact that over 80 per cent of his subjects were Muslim, the Maharajah of Kashmir Sir Hari Singh was Hindu, and his administration was communally exclusive. His son Karan Singh remembered: 'As for the Kashmiri Muslims, our contacts were mostly limited to the gardeners and the shooting and fishing guards.'[29] With the possible exception of Jammu in the south and Ladakh in the east, it seemed logical that the beautiful, mountainous kingdom would join Jinnah's Muslim homeland; after all, K for Kashmir was the third letter of Pakistan.

The Nehrus were, however, one of India's most prominent Kashmiri Hindu families, and it is apparent that Jawaharlal Nehru's personal feelings were an important determinant in the state's future. Mountbatten regarded Kashmir as 'the one subject on which he could not get Nehru to see sense'. Yet if Kashmir did not remain part of India, would the Prime Minister still be able to consider himself an Indian? The retiring Commander-in-Chief of Pakistan, General Sir Frank Messervy, commented after a private conversation with Nehru in February 1948: 'He said that he quite appreciated my arguments [in favour of Kashmir joining Pakistan] but "As Calais was written on Queen Mary's heart, so Kashmir is written on mine." In other words, sentiment overcame reason on this particular issue. What a tragedy.'[30] Although his role in the military takeover of Kashmir was, as might be expected, more propitiatory than that of Patel, the fact that Nehru remained as India's Prime Minister into the 1960s made the chance of any subsequent concession unlikely.

The future of Kashmir after the end of British rule had been a matter of concern and speculation throughout 1947. It has been argued by some historians that the accession to India rather than Pakistan was planned all along by Mountbatten, based on the fact that jurisdiction over British-run Kashmiri territory around Gilgit was returned to the Maharajah before independence, thereby enabling India to gain strategic access to the subcontinent's northern frontier. In addition, at a meeting held on 17 July, Mountbatten is known to have said that although the future of Kashmir 'presents some difficulty . . . it can claim an exit to India, especially if a portion of the Gurdaspur district goes to East Punjab'.[31] A portion of Gurdaspur did go to India, but Sir Cyril Radcliffe subsequently denied that this had been done in order to facilitate Indian access to the Kashmiri capital Srinagar.

The theory that there was a British conspiracy to ensure an Indian takeover of Kashmir rests on tenuous ground, and in practice road access to Srinagar from Gurdaspur was unimportant, since India's takeover depended on an airlift and not on any road link.[32] Like many of the important events of 1947, it would appear that India's successful capture of Kashmir was in fact as much a matter of luck and swift action as of design.

The Maharajah of Kashmir was a pompous, proud and rather tragic character. He had inherited the throne from his uncle in awkward circumstances, and as a young man had been caught in an embarrassing scandal when an English woman had tried to blackmail him about his unusual sexual practices. Although he liked to be considered a progressive ruler, since he had introduced a nominal state assembly, his political reforms were in general limited to matters such as a law against soliciting in Srinagar, and a ban on smoking by teenagers. Much of his time was spent killing bears, panthers, stags, partridges and ducks, the last being a feat which would be achieved with the help of no fewer than three double-barrelled Webley & Scott shotguns, a loader standing on either side of him.

During the weeks leading up to independence, Mountbatten had made several attempts to persuade the Maharajah to make a definite decision about Kashmir's future. His Highness, however, refused to discuss the matter seriously, and was more interested in worrying about the protocol of entertaining the Viceroy in his palace at Srinagar. An elaborate electric bell system was rigged up to enable him to order the state band to play 'God Save the King' at the appropriate moment during dinner; unfortunately, Mountbatten's long legs hit the switch at the wrong moment, and all the guests had to rise awkwardly to their feet during the soup course.

The Maharajah's refusal to decide what to do after the British had left stemmed from his firm conviction that they were planning to remain in the subcontinent, despite their talk of political settlements. As he told his son as late as July 1947, 'You know, Tiger, the British are never really going to leave India.'[33]

After 15 August, the surprised and nervous Maharajah was placed in an awkward position. The imprisoned leader of the popular pro-democracy and pro-Congress All-Jammu and Kashmir National Confer-ence, Sheikh Abdullah, had close links with Nehru. Moreover, a rumbling revolt soon began in the south-west of the state in the province of Poonch, which had always historically been antagonistic towards the Maharajah's rule. Muslim farm-workers in Poonch began an uprising against their Rajput landlords, killing some of the local Hindu population and driving others from their homes. Although he still had vague hopes of turning Kashmir into a neutral 'Switzerland of Asia', the Maharajah began to incline towards India, believing that his own power would be destroyed if he allied himself with Pakistan.

By mid-October, the problems across Kashmir had grown into a serious crisis. For several weeks India had been secretly supplying weapons and ammunition to the state's armed forces, and making preparations for a military advance. At the same time, the uprising in Poonch was joined by Pakistani irregulars, apparently with official encouragement.

The turning-point came with the arrival in Poonch and surrounding areas of several thousand Pathan tribesmen. On 22 October, accompanied by a few hundred Poonchis, a rag-tag army began to proceed towards Srinagar. They advanced in a long convoy of spluttering civilian buses and trucks, many of which broke down on the journey. The haphazard nature of their invasion belies the theory that the 'raiders' (as the Pathans have become known in Indian folklore) were acting on Jinnah's direct orders. They also managed to inflict considerable damage in and around the Pakistani city of Lahore, and it is apparent that their ambitions were principally covetous, rather than political. On reaching Baramula, Uri, Pattan and Muzaffarabad, they proceeded to murder, rape and loot any-body and anything they could lay their hands on, including the inmates and contents of a Franciscan convent at Baramula.

The Maharajah called in the Chief of Staff of the Kashmir State Forces, Brigadier Rajinder Singh Jamwal, and told him to 'fight to the last man and the last bullet'. The Brigadier delayed the Pathans for two days, but his Muslim troops then mutinied and he was left wounded on the roadside with nothing but a gun and a pocketful of bullets, saying that the enemy would advance only over his dead body. On 24 October, while the rebels back in Poonch declared a government of Azad (Free) Kashmir, the slovenly invaders stopped for a rest at the Mahura electricity station thirty miles from Srinagar, and cut off supplies into the capital. Late the following night, the terrified Maharajah abandoned his palace and headed south in a large car, with his jeweller Victor Rosenthal by his side and a pair of staff officers perched on the back seat, revolvers at the ready. His Highness was silent throughout the long drive, but when he reached Jammu the next evening, he let out a single sentence: 'We have lost Kashmir.'[34]

Sir Hari Singh's royal dynasty may have lost Kashmir, but India certainly had not. Making skilful public relations use of the violence perpetrated by the marauding Pathans, the Indian government set about recovering the kingdom for themselves. Mountbatten provided useful assistance, since he was convinced of the righteousness of the Indian case, telling Patel that he had heard from a British officer, who had heard from another British officer, that the Pathans were 'very definitely organized'. A fortnight later he wrote to King George VI: 'It was unquestionable that, if Srinagar was to be saved from pillage by the invading tribesmen, and if the couple of hundred British residents in Kashmir were not to be massacred, Indian troops would have to do the job . . . I therefore made it my business to over-ride all the difficulties which the Commanders-in-Chief, in the course of their duty, raised to the proposal.'[35]

It was only some time later that Mountbatten realized how far the whole procedure must have been planned in advance by Patel, who had apparently kept Nehru in the dark about procedural details. On 26 October, V.P. Menon supposedly flew to Jammu and persuaded the Maharajah to sign an instrument of accession to the Indian Union, enabling the Indian Army to formally intervene and oust the 'raiders'. According to one Indian Army officer who was present at a meeting of the Defence Committee in New Delhi later that day, Nehru still had doubts about intervention, and 'talked about the United Nations, Russia, Africa, Godalmighty, everybody, until Sardar Patel lost his temper. He said, "Jawaharlal, do you want Kashmir, or do you want to give it away." Nehru said, "*Of course I want Kashmir*" . . . and before he could say anything Sardar Patel turned to me and said, "You have got your orders." '[36]

Patel issued a command over All India Radio requisitioning all planes owned by private airlines, and the next morning there was a substantial airlift of Indian troops and weapons into the little airport at Srinagar, involving the deployment of over a hundred Dakota transport aircraft.

It was a stunning operation, and given the inaccessibility of Srinagar by road, was almost certainly critical in enabling India to gain possession of Kashmir. Considering the practicalities of airborne operations, there is no way that this exercise could have been spontaneous or improvised, and Mountbatten told Alan Campbell-Johnson that 'as a military operation the speed of the fly-in on 27th October left our SEAC efforts standing.'[37] Even the confirmed pacifist Mohandas Gandhi endorsed what was taking place, pronouncing at his daily prayer meeting: 'The job of armed soldiers is to march ahead and repel the attacking army. The soldiers will have really done their duty when all of them lay down their lives in saving Srinagar, and with Srinagar the whole of Kashmir would be saved.'[38]

It is apparent, given the physical location of V.P. Menon at the relevant times, that the instrument of accession could not have been signed at Jammu on 26 October, and that India's military intervention almost certainly took place without written legal authorization. Complex arguments and counter-arguments have been built up around this fact, with Pakistan claiming that it invalidates the entire Indian position, and India producing tortuous possible explanations of the signing procedure. The essential point, however, is that the traumatized Maharajah of Kashmir agreed to join India, and never later sought to deny the validity of his state's accession.[39]

Baffled by the speed of events, Jinnah tried to counter-attack by ordering the Pakistan Army into action. Nervous of launching an inter-dominion war, Pakistan's acting Commander-in-Chief General Douglas Gracey postponed action while Auchinleck flew urgently to Lahore in his role as Supreme Commander. The Auck informed Jinnah that since Kashmir had in Mountbatten's view legally joined India, 'no British Officer could be committed to the fighting'. This 'of course prevented the Regular Pakistan Army from taking any part'.[40] The result was that Jinnah cancelled his orders for Pakistani troops to move into Kashmir.

Sporadic fighting and communal violence however continued through November and subsequent months, resulting in slaughter and displacement on all sides. Although, as Governor General, Mountbatten was useful in providing international respectability to India, there was always a risk that he might try to soften its policy over the capture of the recalcitrant Princely States such as Kashmir, Hyderabad and Junagadh. Perhaps with this in mind, Patel wrote a letter to Nehru suggesting that the Governor General should be asked to represent the Indian government at the forthcoming wedding of George VI's elder daughter Princess Elizabeth to Mountbatten's nephew Philip in London on 20 November. 'At the present juncture,' noted the Sardar, 'such a move would be both tactically and politically wise.'[41] Mountbatten accepted, and was out of the country for a few days at a critical stage of the Kashmir and Junagadh operations.

India had installed Sheikh Abdullah in place of the Maharajah, retaining control over all of the state except the northern areas around Gilgit, and the territory around Poonch which has become known as either 'Azad Kashmir' or 'Pakistan-occupied Kashmir'. A ceasefire brokered by the United Nations came into force on 1 January 1949, one of its conditions being that a plebiscite should be held in the whole of Kashmir. India refused to do so unless Pakistan made the first move by withdrawing from Azad Kashmir, and Jinnah responded that he would only accept a simultaneous retreat by both sides. As a result there has never been a popular referendum over Kashmir's status, although India claims that subsequent state elections have vindicated its position. This unsatisfactory settlement persists to the present day, with neither India nor Pakistan recognizing the other's jurisdiction over any of Maharajah Sir Hari Singh's territory.

Jawaharlal Nehru's government was under the impression that its military success in Kashmir had settled the matter for good, but Lord Ismay, for one, thought it was mistaken to assume the matter was resolved. After a conversation with Nehru in November 1947, he wrote in his diary that he had failed 'to impress on him the folly of turning Kashmir into a running sore and a permanent military commitment. They have won a small battle and they think that they have won a war! Such is the intoxication of a slight military success.'[42] The Pakistani government was deeply shaken by its failure to secure Kashmir, and by its many other strategic reverses. After a meeting with Jinnah at Government House in Karachi, Ismay wrote that the Pakistani leader looked 'very dignified and very sad', and thought that India was 'determined to strangle Pakistan at birth'.[43]

Kashmir was to remain the central source of continued conflict between the two nations through the 1950s, with Pakistani aircraft not being permitted to fly through Indian airspace when travelling between East and West Pakistan, but being forced to divert via Ceylon. In 1965 there were repeated violations of the United Nations ceasefire line through Kashmir by Pakistan, with India claiming that secret agents were being sent across the border to encourage a revolt. On 30 August, Indian troops crossed the border 'to clear up the Pakistani raiders', and the next day Pakistani tanks responded by advancing towards Jammu. A brief but bitter war developed, resulting in a Pakistani defeat. The Indian Army pulled back when only three miles from Lahore, but would clearly have been able to capture the city had they wished. A Soviet-brokered settlement was agreed at Tashkent in February 1966, with Pakistan's chastened leader Ayub Khan taking a moderate position.

The issue flared again in 1984, when the Prime Minister Indira Gandhi dismissed Indian-controlled Kashmir's comparatively popular Chief Minister Farooq Abdullah, son of the Sheikh. From 1989 the situation there became worse than it had ever been, with most neutral sources estimating that between fifteen and eighteen thousand people were killed between 1990 and 1996. Indian security forces behaved in a shockingly brutal way, especially during the early 1990s, when it seemed that they had been sanctioned to use any methods they chose to reassert New Delhi's authority. Pakistan's response to the unrest was to train irregulars and supply weapons, in the hope that this might make the revolt against Indian rule succeed. The strategy failed, and only hardened the resolve of the Indian government to remain in control.

During this time, a serious risk developed of a third Indo–Pakistan war over Kashmir, although now with the possibility that either side might have a nuclear capability. The combination of a pair of weak prime ministers – V.P. Singh in India and Benazir Bhutto in Pakistan – allowed the situation in Kashmir to escalate dangerously, and the refusal of either side to engage in informal *détente* meant the capacity for an accidental drift to war was always present. According to the intelligence specialist Christopher Andrew, the stand-off over Kashmir during 1990 was seen by the CIA as being so dangerous that 'for a brief period, the intelligence reaching [President] Bush had suggested perhaps the most serious threat of nuclear conflict since the Cuban missile crisis.'[44]

In the view of the last Maharajah of Kashmir's son, Dr Karan Singh, who is regarded by some as the present Maharajah, the best solution in 1947 would have been a partition of his father's territory: 'The north-western areas would have gone to Pakistan, and Jammu and Ladakh would have gone to India.' When I asked him the crucial question –

where the Kashmir Valley would have gone – Karan Singh refused to give an answer. He maintained, however, that Pakistan's covert activities in the state of Jammu and Kashmir were only making the problem worse. 'I sometimes think,' he said, 'that Pakistan would be willing to sacrifice every last Kashmiri in its battle with India.'[45]

TWENTY-TWO

No Bitterness

At the traffic lights in central Bombay, beneath a giant poster advertising a sparkling Motorola mobile telephone, a man stuck a stump of sealed scar tissue through the taxi window and chanted, 'Uncle, Uncle, handicap, Holy Mary, blood cancer, lunch money, bless you please, Uncle,' at me. It was hard not to stare at him. His face was so burnt, and his moving lips looked like slabs of meat in his waxy face.

I was heading for the offices of Shiv Sena, the political party that controls the city, from the pinnacle of the state government, through the contracts of the big construction companies, down to the suburban slumlands where they organize religious events such as the Ganesh festival. On their orders Bombay is now officially called by its Marathi name, Mumbai. With Bangalore, the city is the symbol of the financial resurgence of India under the mildly deregulated capitalism introduced through the reforms of the early 1990s. Most of Mumbai's citizens are very poor, but property prices on Malabar Hill, where Jinnah's house remains under armed guard, its ownership disputed between the governments of India and Pakistan, are higher than in Mayfair or Manhattan.

Although it runs a modern city of fifteen million people, as well as much of the state of Maharashtra, Shiv Sena is a reactionary, bigoted political party which harks back to the golden age of 'Chatrapati' ('Lord of the Universe') Shivaji, the bandit chieftain who welded together the Marathas against the Mughals in the seventeenth century and was famed for ripping out the stomach of a rival warlord, Afzal Khan, with a set of steel 'tiger claws'. The Sena has been built up over thirty years by its omnipotent leader Bal Thackeray, a shadowy, effete former newspaper cartoonist who has expressed admiration for Adolf Hitler's treatment of the Jews. It is an organic, regional party, but one which is perhaps more representative of the hard-line trend in Hindu triumphalism than its coalition ally in Mumbai, the larger and more diffuse Bharatiya Janata Party (BJP).

Fifty years after independence, religious nationalism has all but evaporated in Pakistan and Bangladesh, where specifically Islamic parties such as the Jamaat-e-Islami make no appreciable mark at the polls. Ironically it is flourishing in India, where the BJP has raised its share of the popular vote from 11.4 per cent in 1989 to 34.2 per cent in 1996, when it was able to form a short-lived minority government in New Delhi. The rise of Hindu nationalism appears to validate the old fears of Jinnah and the Muslim League, and is a source of embarrassment and shame to many Westernized Indians, who generally dismiss it as either ignorance (the bigotry of the uneducated masses) or opportunism (politicians cashing in on social and economic fears). There is an optimistic assumption among most political commentators that Hindu extremism has reached its peak, and will now decline into oblivion.

The stirrings of the present revival can be traced to the writings of figures such as Bal Thackeray's hero Veer Savarkar, and to the foundation of the RSS, which was itself in part a response to the threatening nature of Muslim organization in the 1920s. Although Hindu nationalists like to trace their lineage to the prehistory of India, they are in fact involved in a spurious reconstruction of a mythical past. Attempts to give Hinduism a monolithic identity similar to Islam or Christianity are at variance with the lavish diversity of its manifestations.

During 1947–48 all the ingredients were present for the creation of the 'Hindu Raj' that Jinnah had prophesied. Hundreds of thousands of Hindus had been massacred by Muslims during the shift of populations, there was a continuing dispute over territories such as Hyderabad and Kashmir, and more than four-fifths of the population of the new India was Hindu. But it never happened, largely owing to the determined secularism of Pandit Nehru. For three years after independence there was a continuous battle between Nehru and his theoretical deputy Sardar Patel over the treatment of the Muslim minority, with Patel believing that Nehru was far too conciliatory.

In March 1950 Patel held a tea party for around sixty fellow MPs at which he praised the 'cultural and social' role of the RSS. He also came out with the *aperçu* that there was only one true nationalist Muslim in India – Maulana Nehru. When the Prime Minister heard about this, he wrote a bitter letter to his deputy asking whether their 'joint working' was worth going on with, to which Patel replied that in his view India's Muslims still had 'a responsibility to remove the doubts and misgivings entertained by a large section of the people about their loyalty'.

Nehru wrote back that such a stand amounted to a betrayal of the principles of the freedom movement:

> The position is that while Pakistan has followed and is following an intensely communal policy, we are tending to do the same and thus completely playing into the hands of Pakistan . . . There is hardly a Muslim in west Bengal or even in Delhi and many other places in India who has a sense of safety . . . due to our own wavering policy and to the thought in the minds of many of us that Muslims are aliens in India, not to be trusted, and to be got rid of as soon and as tactfully as possible.

A few days later Nehru followed this letter with the tragic sentence: 'I see every ideal that I have held fading away and conditions emerging in India which not only distress me but indicate to me that my life's work has been a failure.'[1]

The degree of violence against Hindus in East Pakistan during 1950 prevented Nehru and Patel's quarrel from being resolved. Matters came to a head that August when the explicitly Hindu nationalist politician Purushottamdas Tandon did what Subhas Bose had done in 1939, and stood for the Congress Presidency against the leader's official candidate. This took place with the backing of Sardar Patel, whose huge clout within the party organization assured victory for Tandon. The result was applauded by the RSS, and was a weighty blow to Nehru's authority and his secular vision for India. It created what looked like a fatal degree of internal tension, which was only dissipated by the sudden death of Patel that December.

During the 1950s, Nehru reversed the plight in which he found himself, and built up a power over Congress similar to that which Gandhi had exercised in the 1930s, the *Times of India* noting that 'while the rank and file do not see eye to eye with the Prime Minister . . . they idolize him and applaud his speeches even when he gets tough with them.'[2] In the ten years preceding Nehru's death in 1964, a total of 344 people were killed in Hindu–Muslim riots – an astonishingly low figure for a country of India's size and religious composition.[3] There were good reasons for thinking that communal hatred had been an aberration caused by the divisive policies of the British colonialists, and that it had disappeared for good.

After a brief interregnum under Lal Bahadur Shastri, Nehru's daughter Indira took over as India's Prime Minister in early 1966, having gained a felicitous surname from her late husband Feroze Gandhi. Operating in a more fragmented political landscape than her father had ever faced, Indira Gandhi proved a skilful and ruthless fighter. In 1971 she won a massive electoral victory with the Orwellian campaign slogan 'Garibi Hatao!' or 'Abolish Poverty!' When she was opposed by the veteran Congress Socialist leader Jai Prakash Narayan (who had once been described by Lord Wavell as an 'intelligent blackguard'), she accused him of being in league with the CIA, and in June 1975 declared a state of 'Emergency'. She unleashed the most savage repression of civil liberties in India since Lord Linlithgow's crackdown of 1942, assisted by her delinquent son Sanjay. In 1977 'Madam' called elections and was swept from office, returning to power three years later only because of the grave incapacities of her opponents. Back in office, she engaged in what one political analyst has called 'a cynical manipulation of religious symbolism', which involved making public appearances at Hindu temples, and espousing the concept of Hindu victimhood. Thus, while claiming Congress was still the party that gave succour to the Muslim minority, Indira Gandhi 'tried to deploy the language of minority rights *simultaneously* within the idiom of Hindu politics'.[4]

Since 1947 Hindu revivalism had been quietly flourishing in the RSS, and in political vehicles such as the Jana Sangh and the Vishwa Hindu Parishad. It burst through from peripheral status during the 1980s, when the Jana Sangh transmuted into the BJP and widened its base to include many politicians who were Hindu nationalist in their inclination, but did not endorse anti-Muslim and anti-Christian extremism. By the mid-1980s India's truce on the communal manipulation of votes had broken down, with even the Congress Party under the premiership of Indira Gandhi's ineffectual son Rajiv becoming willing to use religious affiliation as a political weapon. During the course of the decade, the number of *swayamsevaks* or RSS volunteers in India almost doubled to 1.8 million, and a new militancy was exhibited by Hindu extremists as they talked of reconquering India's 'lost' territories of Pakistan and Bangladesh.[5]

The most potent symbol of the campaign to reassert Hindu identity was a plan to build a temple on the site of the supposed birthplace of the Hindu deity Lord Ram at Ayodhya, where a mosque was presently situated. This had first become a serious issue in the 1940s, when a group of *sadhus* had engaged in a nine-day recitation of the epic the *Ramayana* outside the mosque, and images of Lord Ram had been 'miraculously' installed inside it. The issue bubbled during the 1980s, with mass rallies and processions of volunteers setting off to 'liberate' Ayodhya. Finally in 1992 (while a Congress administration abandoned Nehruvian secularism for ever by turning a blind eye) fanatics in saffron headbands burst through the gates, smashed the huge domes of the mosque with mallets and crowbars, and reduced the place to rubble under the eyes of passive policemen and eminent national politicians including the BJP's L.K. Advani and Murli Manohar Joshi. It was a defining moment in the history of independent India.

When the mythical birthplace of Ram had been 'reclaimed', the Shiv Sena leader Bal Thackeray declared himself 'the happiest man in the world'. In the clashes that followed all over the country between outraged Muslims and victorious Hindu extremists, Muslims in Mumbai were given the 'trouser test' by mobs of Sena activists, a euphemism which refers to the ripping off of a man's trousers in search of a foreskin. If he lacks one, he is drenched in kerosene and lit. The Sena also revived the murderous slogan of 1947: 'Pakistan or *qabristan*' – 'Pakistan or the graveyard'. In revenge several bombs were detonated across the city, supposedly by irate Muslims working for an Arab country. Between 660 and four thousand people were killed in Mumbai during the riots of 1992–93, depending on whose figures you believe.

Outside the Shiv Sena offices there were numerous armed policemen. The taxi driver, a man with oiled hair and a mouthful of gold named Prahlad, said proudly and unprompted that he was a supporter of Bal Thackeray. When I asked him why, he said that it was because Shiv Sena kept Shivaji Park clean. 'No dirty people. Only good people. A precious metal will always rise to the surface.'

The offices were air-conditioned and very cold. I sat and talked to 'the boys', the new generation of young professionals who run the party's political campaigns. They were mainly in their early thirties, with Marathi rather than English as their first language, looking sporty with gold chains, big watches, pagers and little mobile phones. The group included Bal's cousin Jitu Thackeray, plump, friendly and plausible in blue jeans and loafers, and Bal's nephew and probable heir Raj Thackeray in a white polyester shirt, black slacks and droopy dark glasses. Raj sat in a separate part of the room, unsmiling and silent, guarded by a very big man in clean white *kurta* pajama with a stubby sub-machine gun. A few weeks after my visit, Jitu and Raj would be implicated in the murder of a recalcitrant local tenant, Ramesh Kini.

'Congress is finished,' said a stocky man called Jai. 'Shiv Sena is the future. We want to be powerful but we don't want foreigners and outsiders taking our resources. That is why Balasaheb gives praise to Hitler – because he worked hard and united the German people. Hitler may have done some bad things, but he did a lot of good ones also. You need one dictator at the head of each party rather than changing your ideology all the time. You need one king, and that is what we have in Shiv Sena.'

'We are ready to do anything,' said another, called Prasad. 'Anything. We are ready to die for Mr Balasaheb Thackeray. He is our rising sun. He is strong, like the Japanese and your Mrs Margaret Thatcher. He says to us get up, stand up, you are not a carrot, you can make your own future. That is what I believe.'

I asked them what future there was for the Muslims of India if their policies were implemented nationally.

'A very happy future, if they are loyal to their country, a very happy future,' answered Prasad. 'But many of them are secretly helping terrorists from Pakistan. Muslims cannot be trusted.'

'What are the Muslims?' asked one of his colleagues. 'They are Turks and Arabs who invaded our country, and the rest are converted Hindus. Now they want to take three wives and have multiple issue. Why should we allow this? To be an Indian is to be a Hindu – Hindus are Hindus, Sikhs are Hindus, Muslims are Hindus.'

'Have they ever apologized or tried to make amends for what they have done to Mother India over the centuries,' asked Jai, 'thinking they can sit on our heads?'

'Pakistan was born out of treachery and bred on butchery,' added Prasad. 'The Muslims are fanatics and blood-spillers, causing trouble here in Mumbai, and we say they cannot be changed any more than a spoonful of sugar can sweeten the flavour of a bitter gourd.'

It was a simplified, Maharashtrian version of the anti-Islamic prejudice that is now prevalent throughout much of the world. When 'the boys' disappeared to go and inspect one of their building projects, I spoke to an older man with yellow eyes called Vasant, who worked as a journalist on the Shiv Sena newspaper *Saamana*.

'I have been an Indian nationalist all my life,' he told me, 'and when I was young I heard Gandhi-ji speak. I admired him. But he made mistakes. He was too favourable towards the Muslim, and destroyed our country by allowing the Muslim to steal Pakistan from the breast of Bharat. It is fashionable to say we in Shiv Sena are anti-Muslim, but Islam is an intolerant religion. They have a ghetto mentality. If anything it is we Hindus who are persecuted. Our people are killed by Sikh terrorists in Punjab and by Pakistani agents in Kashmir. It is not the Hindu who is making trouble. The Muslim has an easy time, a happy time, here in India, with special privileges under the civil code.'

I had spent the previous day first in the Muslim district of Girgaum, where much of the killing had taken place and nobody would talk, and later in the poor, crowded area of Mahim. As night fell I had sat sipping a beverage called 'spatial masala milk' and discussing politics with a vendor of pumpkin *halwa*. In the middle of our conversation a tall, expectorating man with a tight jersey and a vermilion smear between his eyes had come and sat beside us. After that the talking had stopped.

'When I spoke to people in Mahim yesterday they told me things weren't easy,' I said to Vasant. 'They say the police come and arrest them for no reason, and that when people go to prison to get their friends released, they get arrested themselves.'

'*Chota* [little] Pakistan,' answered Vasant, with a look of disgust. 'They're just troublemakers down that side. Illegals and infiltrators from Bangladesh; that's why the police have to be firm with them. All the problems the Muslim has in Mumbai, he brings upon himself.'

'Do you support what happened at Ayodhya?' I asked.

'Why do you complain? The Babri Masjid is only one *masjid*. Mosques are often being broken, and our leader could have three mosques destroyed in Mumbai tomorrow if he wished.' He smiled boastfully.

'Do you feel sorry for the victims of the riots?'

'I certainly feel sorry for the policemen who were injured by Muslims at that time. The rioters came from outside Mumbai. It was planned.'

I asked him what he thought of Salman Rushdie's portrayal of Bal Thackeray in his novel *The Moor's Last Sigh*, in which the Shiv Sena leader is lampooned as the extremist head of 'Mumbai's Axis', Raman 'Mainduck' Fielding.

Vasant replied that they had a policy of never mentioning the name of Salman Rushdie in *Saamana*. 'Nobody can hurt Balasaheb. He is the nicest man. You must understand that the Muslim Rushdie has a secret pact with the Iranian *mullahs*. He pays them money in return for not lifting the death sentence on him, so he is able to continue to gain publicity for his books in Europe and America.'

'How do you know that?' I said.

'I have information,' he replied. 'I know it.'

Mohammed Yunus was very old with a grey and black beard, and a strong, slightly bulbous nose. He wore a long, thick, grey *kurta* made of finely woven wool. Sitting in a high-backed chair in his Lutyens bungalow in New Delhi, surrounded by signed photographs of Jawaharlal Nehru, Indira Gandhi and Rajiv Gandhi, he spoke in a slow, quiet voice.

'I first became involved in politics when I was a student in Peshawar. My father belonged to that place. He had forty-two children, although today I only have one sister alive, and she lives in Pakistan. I was a Congress-wallah all the way, like my kinsman Khan Abdul Ghaffar Khan. I am a Pathan and a Congressman. In 1942 I was taken to jail in Peshawar where I remained for three years, much of the time in fetters. Then I travelled all over India with Pandit Nehru, helping him in his work.

'When independence came I flew to Delhi from the North-West Frontier. I did not wish to stay in a Pakistan ruled by Mr Jinnah, a traitor to the freedom movement. How could the division of our country on the basis of religion bring solace or benefit to our people? That is why Bangladesh broke free: the Pakistanis destroyed themselves by dint of their own actions. Even today the Muslims who went to Pakistan have not settled down. They are repenting their crimes now.

'There was great violence in Delhi at that time. One day I drove with Pandit Nehru to the scene of a riot at Jamia Millia Islamia University and he went right into the middle of the crowd and shouted at them: "I want to be the Prime Minister of a country where Hindus, Muslims, Sikhs and Christians can live in harmony. Did we get our freedom so that you could kill each other?" He was a man who had no fear.

'There was no discrimination against us on account of being Muslims.

Of course there wasn't. We were respected people. Nehru said to me, "Yunus, you go to Indonesia on your first posting." So I went there, and later became ambassador to Turkey and Algeria. Today there are some problems in Congress, some people who have anti-Muslim prejudice, but they are in a minority. What happened at Ayodhya was a mistake and will never happen again. I still believe in a secular India. We have the second largest Muslim population in the world after Indonesia – more than in Pakistan, you should know.'

He insisted on escorting me to the front door, a process that took about ten minutes as he hobbled, tall but bent, on sticks. When he had opened the latch, Mohammed Yunus peered out into the distance for some time, then whispered, 'Sometimes I feel lonely, but that is the way when you are old.' Then he said, twice, 'I have no bitterness.'

Madhab Chandra Kanzsa Banik was a man with soft brown eyes, shaggy hair and a dark moustache. He was in his mid-thirties and worked as a counsellor at the Centre for the Rehabilitation of the Paralysed, two hours of traffic jam outside Dhaka. When he was twelve he had fallen out of a tree and broken his neck, and he had used a wheelchair ever since.

As a Hindu in Bangladesh, he was a member of a small and shrinking minority.

'The real problem came not in 1947 but in 1950, when there was great communal killing and migration. It began because many of the Hindus were wealthy and that made people jealous. The Muslims just killed us, in our thousands. People say that before the British came, Hindus and Muslims were united, they preached together the language of the spirit, justice and brotherhood. Some of my family were killed at that time and many fled to Calcutta. Over two million Hindus went west. Now there are very few of us left in Bangladesh. Still Hindus are going to Calcutta and other parts of India like a stream, like a stream.'

'Are things no better now?' I asked.

'The worst thing that ever happened to us was in 1992 following the smashing of the *masjid* in Ayodhya. That was when problems became really serious in Bangladesh. The Hindus in India don't think about what their actions can do to Hindus outside India. Muslims came and broke our temples, looted our houses, captured our paddy land and gave threats. They also took women away. It was mental torture, you could say.'

'Did they attack your family?'

'People came to Shongrambid, my village, in the night-time and my uncles were beaten. Five times thieves came and took all the goods from our house, as much as they could take. It became a normal practice. We had five acres and nice facilities in our house at that time. They even came and took away our furniture and electricity. Can you believe it – they took away our electricity wires? The last time our house was looted, my younger brother Babu informed the police, but all they said was, "We will see." They asked who was doing this but he was afraid to say the names. When I was young my village was around 80 per cent Hindu, but now there are only a few of us left.'

Madhab was twisting his head in pain as he spoke. 'How many are left?' I asked.

'Around four families. We Hindus are spread all over Bangladesh. We are not in a majority in any area and we are not well organized. Most of the rich ones have gone away to west Bengal or to Assam. After our house was ransacked my parents tried to live with a relative but the situation did not improve, so finally they got some papers and went to Calcutta with nearly no money. You could say we have lost everything.

'If there is a dispute and people know you are a Hindu, they will say insulting words. They use bad comments. I heard one story of a Hindu family of seven who were killed just recently. They were taken from their village and drowned by a Muslim who wanted their property. All this, for land. Can you believe it? Who was helped by what happened in 1947? I think it is funny, crazy that it happened. It makes me laugh.'

Parveen Ahmed believed she had been helped by the partition. Over tea one afternoon in her house in a rich suburb of Dhaka, she told me she had been born in 1921 in Calcutta into a prosperous Muslim family ('My people have good blood'), and sent to a convent school. The family lived near Park Circus, where her father was a barrister. After the Great Calcutta Killings of 1946, they had decided they needed a safe homeland of their own, and had moved east to Dhaka. Although she disliked the boundaries of Bangladesh ('It was that Radcliffe – he was tossed money by the Congress Marwaris'), Parveen Ahmed was certain that without a Muslim homeland, she and her people would have been wiped out by Hindus.

Her views were similar to those of Tazeen Faridi, who had also been born into a wealthy Indian Muslim family, which migrated west rather than east in 1947. I had met her fifteen hundred miles from Dhaka, in Karachi.

When the Simon Commission visited India in 1928, with Major Clem Attlee as one of its marginally more progressive members, it was met with boycotts and crowds of freedom fighters shouting, 'Simon, Go Home!' In Lahore, the veteran nationalist leader Lala Lajpat Rai was struck with a *lathi* during a demonstration, and died soon afterwards. A young protester in Lucknow called Jawaharlal Nehru was beaten up and carted off to prison with his colleague Pandit Pant. Tazeen Faridi was eight years old at the time, the daughter of a *taluqdar* and deputy collector in the United Provinces.

Lucknow had once been the capital of the huge flank of north India known as the Kingdom of Oudh, the rich Gangetic plain where the focus of Muslim rule had shifted in the twilight days of the Mughal Emperors. It was the ousting of the 'debauched and capricious' old Nawab of Oudh and his courtiers by the British, and the annexation of his lands, that had been one of the sparks of the revolt of 1857. Tazeen Faridi and her brothers were brought up in the 1920s at the elegiac centre of traditional north Indian Islamic culture, surrounded by the relics of the Mughal period: lace-workers, *nautch* dancers, Islamic scholars, embroiderers, musicians and miniaturists. It was the heartland of the Pakistan movement.

Her parents, being notably progressive, sent their sons to school in England and engaged a governess for their daughter. She had ended up as Secretary General of the All-Pakistan Women's Association. Now she was a widow, living in a good suburb of Karachi, wearing a silvery-blue *salwar kameez* and big pearl earrings and sitting on a sofa eating cake. She had moles on her face and a saggy neck and the lively, dogmatic, opinionated air of a Muslim matriarch. I liked her nerve.

'I had to go up together with a Hindu girl and present a bouquet to Lady Simon. She spoke to me afterwards and I said to her, "I don't want to give you any flowers, because last night your soldiers were beating our people outside my house." Lady Simon was so surprised and the next day I was asked to go to Government House in Lucknow to tell my story again. I was a freedom fighter and I had no qualms about doing so, I can tell you.'

'Did your parents mind what you had done?' I asked.

'Well, they had mixed feelings,' she answered, laughing. 'My father didn't do badly under the British, but he still felt nationalist pride. I was always interested in politics. I persuaded my parents to let me go to Lucknow University, where I became the first Muslim girl in the whole of India to be the president of a Students' Union. The male students were really terrible, persecuting me, but I would certainly not give in.'

'Were you ever a Congress supporter?'

'Oh, at first we were all pro-Congress, it was the only thing to be. All the disputes at that time were between Sunnis and Shias, not with the Hindus. But by the mid or late thirties when the [Congress] ministries came in we just got sick of the terrible discrimination against Muslims. Our opinions changed when we understood the hypocrisy of the Congress. We saw that our people needed protection, and after the Lahore Resolution in 1940 the split was complete. I had Hindu friends in Lucknow but I was not even allowed into their kitchens. I told them, "Why do you treat people like this?"'

'And what did they say?'

'You know, there was no reason, it's just the way the Hindus think, that everybody else is impure. Every railway station used to have "Hindu pani [water]" and "Mussulman pani". We would give our water to everyone since our religion teaches equality, but the Hindus would not. That is the people we had to deal with. Like Gandhi-ji – he was a very mixed-up person, always slipping in and out of situations. Muslims have the same psyche as Christians and Jews and are people of the book. We have only one God and that makes us see questions of right and wrong more clearly. That is why Mr Jinnah attained Pakistan. He knew what he wanted, and he got it. We were terribly impressed by him when he came to speak to us. He was never glib and would always listen to the opinion of the younger generation. He had massive support from us.'

Tazeen Faridi poured a third cup of green tea. She said she had been back to Lucknow, but it felt very different now because people mixed Hindi words into the language. This made them hard to understand.

'It was very difficult when Pakistan started,' she said forcefully. 'We had nothing really, not even the most basic things, no infrastructure and no government assets. There was a lot of violence with the Sikhs and the place was filled with refugees.'

'Wouldn't it have been better if India had stayed as one country?'

'Oh, no – look at these Hindu *fundos* in India now and what they have done to the *masjid* at Ayodhya. I still believe in the idea of Pakistan. As Mr Jinnah said, it would be the land of the pure. If we had no Pakistan, we would be in the same situation today as the people of Kashmir.'

The former editor of the *Pakistan Times* I.A. Rahman took a more acerbic view of his country.

'I come originally from Hassampur village to the south of Delhi, which at that time was part of east Punjab. We were attacked on 10 December 1947 by a gang of around eight thousand well-organized Hindus. Many people in our village were killed, including my father's brother, my cousins, my aunt's husband and many others. I was sixteen and away at Aligarh University at the time. Finally the army arrived and the surviving Muslims were taken to Pakistan. I myself went by train through Rajasthan, which was the safest route.

'At that time although I had Communist leanings I thought in a hazy way that Jinnah's idea of a Muslim state was the way to salvation, but my father, who was a lawyer, did not believe in this two-nation theory, or in national division on a religious basis. As I grew older it began to dawn on me that by separating us out on the basis of religion, Jinnah sowed the seeds for a lasting hatred and division for the people of both India and Pakistan. The effect of what he was doing was never thought out in advance.'

I.A. had lank grey hair, sharp eyes, dirty fingernails, large features and a face that was deeply imprinted with experience. He was one of the few Leftists I had met in Asia who did not have a servant to make his tea, which made me feel he must have a degree of integrity.

'Jinnah was a good lawyer, and an incorruptible man, but he was not a statesman. He looked at things from a legal rather than a social point of view. Both sides, Congress and the League, were steeped in late-nineteenth-century theories of state, and their thinking about human politics lacked maturity. It was the Muslim League's initial disregard for democracy that first led to the periods of military rule in our country. Of course, in Pakistan there is no tradition of critical assessment of our history – it is a penal offence here to suggest that the original basis on which Pakistan was created was mistaken – so people still praise Jinnah for saving us. But what did Pakistan achieve? It created Muslim government in places where there was originally Muslim government.'

Muslim government, of a communally harmonious variety, was run in the Punjab during the late 1930s and early forties by the Unionist Party leader Sir Sikander Hayat Khan. His daughter Tahira went to school at Queen Mary's in Lahore, and later became a Communist and women's movement activist, and, incidentally, the mother of the well-modulated street-fighter Tariq Ali. She was imprisoned three times during the dictatorship of General Zia ul-Haq, and lived in an opulent house in Lahore. We sat on wooden chairs beneath a flowing bougainvillaea bush by her swimming-pool, surrounded by chirping birds.

Tahira Mazhar Ali, a charismatic woman, had known Jinnah when she was a child.

'I met him several times when he came see my father. He was a cold man, but he was honest. We had political arguments, as I was already a Communist when I was young. I told him we had not been brought up to have religious prejudice, and that I did not agree with the idea of Pakistan. I had quite a nerve. He said he believed in religious harmony and freedom. That was true, I think, but it is so different from what came about.'

A servant brought us glasses of fresh fruit juice. 'It is painful for me even thinking about 1947. My family had friends from every community, so it was a great loss to me when many of them, the Hindus and Sikhs, had to leave here and go east. Lahore was just a sea of dead bodies at that time. I can remember the only people who dared to venture out onto the streets were our former colonizers, the British, who were safe from the gangs of murderers. It was a terrible thing, a humiliating thing. People were not themselves full of hatred, but politicians encouraged the hatred for their own ends.

'Pakistan has been a betrayal, and I believe it all began at partition with the corruption over evacuee properties. That was when the rot set in. All the best houses, instead of going to refugees from India, were taken by Punjabi bureaucrats. I remember going around an empty parachute factory where hundreds of women refugees were housed – their husbands and fathers had been killed – and they kept saying to me: "Bibi [girl], where is the paradise that we were promised? Where is it?" and I could only say to them, "The rich have got paradise, they have taken all the empty houses." I knew from that moment that political corruption had entered the soul of the Quaid-i-Azam's paradise. They got something for nothing.

'Everybody forgets now the closeness between the two sides of the Punjab. My father used to say that we were the land of five rivers, which could never be divided. Now all these years later we are left with a pointless arms race between Pakistan and India. I just hope that in time people realize we cannot afford this Cold War.'

New Delhi is full of people who still feel they are Lahoris. One man, Raj Khanna, told me his family had assumed that the city would never become part of Pakistan, since so many Hindus lived there. But in late 1947 it became too dangerous to remain, so they locked up their house and travelled to Delhi, assuming they would soon return. When, with some difficulty, they went back to Lahore the following year, their house in Jail Road was being lived in by a senior civil servant of the new Pakistan. The furniture and paintings were intact, but they had lost it for ever. Raj Khanna's father had gone to his library and taken down one book, his favourite and most treasured book, as a memory of the world that was being taken from him. The civil servant had refused to part with it, since it was classed as 'evacuee property' and he did not wish to transgress regulations.

Manorma Dewan was nine years old when she left Lahore. Her parents had been involved in politics and the freedom movement all their lives, and were imprisoned during the Quit India movement.

'We never thought, not for one moment, that we would ever leave the Punjab. Lahore was where we belonged. My mother had won a seat in the Punjab Legislative Assembly at the elections in 1946, so she knew it was her duty to stay and represent her constituents. Besides, she had never made distinctions between people on the basis of religion. She thought the communal riots would soon settle down, with everything getting back to normal, but it just got worse and worse.'

Manorma had lived in Delhi for nearly fifty years, where she worked for a features agency and sat on the Press Council of India. I asked her whether she still remembered life in Lahore.

'Every bit of it. Our house was a large property in Lajpat Rai Bhavan. It became a virtual refugee camp in the early summer of 1947, with people coming from all over the city for protection. Each day my mother and father would go out to help at the hospital, where there would be about five truckloads of bodies. I remember my mother saying she became immune to death. I saw, with my own eyes, when I was a little girl, corpses being unloaded off the lorries one after another and stacked in the morgue.'

'Was it mainly Hindus who were killed?'

'All communities were killed and were killing. You lose your religion when you are all together in a heap of flesh. That's what you should learn, that religion means nothing when you are a corpse. It was on 23 September that we left. Our Muslim friends had said to my parents, "We are helpless to help you, it is better if at least the children go." We left in a caravan of refugee buses at 3 o'clock in the morning, my father, my younger brother and my two elder sisters. My mother stayed behind, thinking we were being evacuated just for a short time. It was three months before we saw her again. For three months we had no idea if our mother was alive or dead.

'Each family was only permitted to bring one box, so we took two changes of *khadi* each and a little bedding but no pillows. We were just crying and crying because we had to leave our mango trees and our guava trees and our dogs. The convoy moved slowly and there was rioting all along the route. I could hear the sound of screaming as we went along, but my father said it was too dangerous to stop. We were escorted by the army as far as the border at Wagah. Some people cheered when we reached India but I and my sisters were crying, crying bitter tears.'

Manorma began to break down as she described the events of her childhood. 'It was the biggest migration. For the younger generation now it is just history, like something you read of in a book, but for us it was our lives. It was all very different from what my parents had dreamed about. People don't talk about 1947 very much today, but it is etched into their lives. The tragedy of the partition is the tragedy of the Indian subcontinent.'

'Did you ever go back to Lahore?'

'Yes. Lajpat Rai Bhavan was full of Muslim families from Meerut. They were very kind to me and gave me cold drinks. I was crying and crying. They let me go upstairs in our house and I kept thinking that when I went into my bedroom I would find a clapping monkey, a toy monkey I had left there when we fled to India all those years before.' She smiled. 'It was gone, of course.'

In Lahore, *kurtas* have rounded hems and folded collars and are longer than in Delhi, and the auto-rickshaws have flapping doors on the sides to hide passengers who keep *purdah*. Otherwise there are the same streets and shops and dishes and hotels, the same Star and Zee TV channels, the same moustachioed men on motorbikes and brisk women working behind the bank counters, the same juxtapositions of colonial and modern architecture, the same squalid streets with boys carrying planks on their heads, and the same wealthy babes schooled on satellited repeats of *The Bold and the Beautiful* who hang around outside pasta restaurants saying: 'It's so boring here, Tina. Let's go to Maxi's, yaaah?'

One difference is the omnipresence of pictures of Mohammad Ali Jinnah, invariably in Muslim dress. In India, Jinnah does not exist, except as a villain who popped up in the mid-1940s with the aim of destroying the freedom movement. In Pakistan he is ubiquitous, although little notice is taken of his actual opinions or ideals. In a bookshop on the Mall in Lahore I came across a biography titled *Jinnah the Conqueror* by one Ibadur Rahman Khan. The blurb on the back cover said: 'Humanity has never been plagued with more lethal specimens of despots than the colonial British and the *banya* Hindu. The unique credit goes to Quaid-e-Azam Muhammad Ali Jinnah that he waged a single-handed battle against both of these menaces. He came out victorious simply because of his straightforwardness, integrity and faith.'

Lahore is outwardly a little more prosperous than Delhi, although only in places. When I walked to Shah Alam Market it was raining and the city seemed poor and sad, with the road severely potholed. A *tonga*-load of fat Punjabi men, one of them carrying a shrouded, wriggling chicken, locked wheels with another *tonga* which was driven by a very old man with a long beard. His horse was so thin and weak and frightened that it was unable to get up again when it fell, and the men had to jump out and shout in an effort to improve the situation. The street stank of chemicals. At the edge of the market I passed a food stall with a big aluminium cooking pot holding cows' brain fritters, each one topped with a chilli.

I ended up drinking tea with a man called Khurshid, who had a soft mouth, pale skin and a very long, rather elegant face. When he laughed he showed red, betel-stained teeth. He was in his late sixties, and had been a student in Lahore at the time of independence. I asked him whether he had been involved in politics, and he said he had gone on marches, and that once somebody had thrown a brick and killed the man next to him. In 1947 there had been very serious riots in Shah Alam Market, where many Hindu and some Sikh businesses had been based. I asked him if he had been involved, and he said no, but I did not believe him.

'There were many Hindu businesses there, and also some Sikhs, and some of the Muslims I knew wanted to act against them. The Hindus had stockpiled a large number of weapons, guns and ammunition. They were armed up to their teeth so in the end all we could do was set fire to the place. I was living in a Hindu area, and so I used to be afraid.

'The time when we felt really angry was when people came from Amritsar and said that Muslims were being killed, and asked us why we were doing nothing about it. I used to work in the migrants' camp, and people would arrive with wounds from lances, swords and guns – women, children, everybody. The corpses were taken out and buried near the cantonment on the edge of the city. The grief was so big that we could not help ourselves. We were actually baffled.

'One day a child, a young boy, was stabbed to death near Shah Alam Market by some Hindus. How could we not feel anger, how could we not take revenge? Who would want to kill a child? The Hindus are the biggest liars and cheats. They are intolerant, treacherous people. That is their nature.'

'But didn't Hindus and Muslims live fairly happily together in Lahore before 1947?'

Khurshid scraped his teeth with a pen-knife. 'If you look at the sea,' he answered, 'you will see a placid surface, but beneath the water there are hot and cold currents, going in different directions.'

I walked up the road, and asked some of the stallholders whether any Hindus still lived in the area. 'I know one Sikh,' said Tariq, a forty-two-year-old pot and pan salesman. 'He comes here to trade.' When I said I was interested in what had happened in 1947, he shook his head, puffed out his cheeks and said: 'You should read a history book.' A little further on was Mohamed Usman, a wholesaler and dry goods merchant with a wild beard and a traditional white lace *topi*. Over the noise of the local mosque's loudspeakers I asked him whether there were any Hindus left in this part of Lahore. He did not understand my question, and I had to repeat it. He leant forward over the brushes and the scouring powder and laughed. 'Hindus? No Hindus are here. Sikhs? No Sikhs are here. We are Mussulmans only at Shah Alam Market,' he answered, adding for good measure that there was no God but Allah.

Later I bumped into Khurshid, who inveigled me into another conversation. I was anxious to leave but I listened to him for a few minutes, since he said he had a joke he wanted to tell me.

'Around the time of the partition, a Sikh was walking on a track in the countryside near Lahore when some Muslims saw him there. He ran away but one of the Muslims said, "Haaaah, Lion, come back here." They caught him and brought him back. The Muslims said, "Now, Sardarji, if you do not chop off your long hair and follow Islam, we will chop off your head with these knives." The Sikh said yes and there was a ceremony. They shaved his head, clipped his beard and cut his skin.'

Khurshid moved his fingers as if he was twanging an elastic band, and continued.

'The fellow recited the *kalma*, he made *namaz* and then he said, "Now please kill me." "Why do you wish us to kill you, crazy man?" said the Muslims. The Sikh replied, "Because when you kill me one more Muslim will be gone from this earth."'

Khurshid slapped his hands together. 'The Sikhs are very funny people.'

TWENTY-THREE

Wrestling with Crocodiles

Begum Saida Isa and Begum Piari Rashid were sisters, both in their seventies. They were small, wrapped in shawls, with grey-white hair tied up in buns, and had the warmest smiles I had seen for months. Their home had once been in the United Provinces in India. I met them in Lahore, although Saida Isa lives for most of the year in the wilds of Baluchistan. After we had eaten lunch, she tripped on a rug and fell, but seemed to recover and was keen to talk about the past. Out on the streets of Lahore, bombs were going off, although nobody seemed entirely sure who was planting them, or what their detonation was intended to achieve.

'I was born in Lucknow in 1919,' began Begum Piari Rashid. 'I did well in college. I remember as a student thinking that the most important thing was freedom, although later I came to think that maybe it was more important to protect the future of the Muslims. My family owned a village outside Lucknow called Raghopur where we used to go for [the religious festival of] *Eid* and feast the whole village. I suppose you could say that we were *taluqdars*, feudal landowners, although we didn't see it in those terms at the time. My father was a civil engineer and he travelled a good deal. He was very progressive.'

'Were you sent to school?'

'To a girls' boarding school in Nainital, and then to Isabella Thoburn College in Lucknow. My grandmother had a great fear that we would be turned into Christians, so during the holidays we had a special Quranic master to give us daily lessons. It was quite an ordeal, I can tell you. My mother refused resolutely to learn the language of the British invaders, since her family had fought against them in the Mutiny. I suppose I was a bridge between the two generations – I was even taught how to play tennis.

'I was not especially interested in politics, but I was swept into it, as one was in those days. In 1940 I was appointed to the Women's Committee of the Muslim League. I remember going to lots of meetings and talking policy and collecting money for the Calcutta famine victims. It was in 1939 that I first met Mr Jinnah. He was an immaculate man and a terrible disciplinarian, and was most dogmatic. We considered him as a symbol of the freedom of Islam. The Hindus hated him at that time, although we greatly admired him and called him "Quaid-i-Azam". There was a story that my sister's husband Qazi Mohammed Isa christened him by that name.'

'Well, that's what people say,' said Saida Isa. 'My husband gave him a *Baluch* hat, and that is certainly the origin of what is usually called the Jinnah Cap. You can see him wearing it in photographs. Isa first met Mr Jinnah in 1939 when they were introduced to each other by Palanpur, at the races. He was devoted to the Quaid from that day forward.'

'Palanpur?' I asked.

'The Nawab, dear old chap. I wonder what's happened to him now.'

'Tell him about Miss Jinnah's costume, sweetheart,' said Begum Rashid. 'The outfit of Miss Jinnah!'

'Oh, yes, the *gharara*,' laughed Saida Isa. The sisters began reminiscing about the quality of the clothes that people had worn in Lucknow. Begum Rashid turned to me: 'Coming from the United Provinces we sometimes wore saris but usually wore *gharara*, which is a sort of baggy skirt-like pajama. I'll show you some later. Now, Mr Jinnah's sister Fatima came from Bombay, and so she had only ever worn a sari. We had *gharara* made for her in Lucknow in around 1943, which was much more in keeping with her new position within the League. Most of the Muslims in Lucknow were artisans, you see. We had the finest laceworkers in the whole of India.'

Saida Isa continued: 'Now let me tell you about what happened at the races. Hearing that Isa came from Baluchistan, Mr Jinnah said to him, "Why don't you go to Baluchistan and start the Muslim League there?" Isa had just come back from doing his Bar exams in London and was about to start in practice as a barrister. He was so inspired by Mr Jinnah that he abandoned his legal plans and went into politics in Quetta. My husband's people are predominantly Pathans, religion-ridden types. He soon established a full party, and by 1940 was able to go to Lahore for the historic session when they made the Pakistan demand. He was so taken over by Jinnah's approach that he backed him entirely. Before that date my husband had been more interested in opera and music than in politics. He had been to see Nehru at the Oxford Union, but found him arrogant.'

The sisters looked at each other, lost in the past. 'We don't often talk about all this,' said Begum Rashid. 'I think I had better tell you about the time when the British left our country.

'In August of 1947 I was with my mother in Lucknow, living there together with my grandmother and aunt. They were all widows by that time. My two younger sisters were also there, both unmarried. My mother decided that as we had property and servants and good connections she would not move to Pakistan. "I am too old," she said. We had Hindu friends, you understand, friends we called "Uncle". There was a local doctor who was a Kashmiri Pundit, and we thought we would be safe under his care. We believed in Pakistan, the idea of Pakistan, but at that time we thought we would be able to travel backwards and forwards between the two countries.

'It was when Gandhi was assassinated that we felt really petrified. In March or April of 1948 the army came and encircled the house. They sent all the women into one room – all our men had gone, and there were only servants to protect us. I was the oldest English-speaker present, so I gave the soldiers the keys to our property. We were searched for several hours on account of my brother, Shahid, being in Pakistan and being in the army. That put us under suspicion. Luckily all our guns had been thrown down into the well by the cook. Most of them were antiques, but I think if they had been found we would have been put into prison and that would have been the end of it. After this my mother was absolutely shattered and unnerved.'

While she spoke, Begum Rashid covered and uncovered her head with her *chunni*.

'In May we moved, leaving everything behind – carpets, furniture, even the fridges. We could only take suitcases. The family travelled with some of our older servants from Bombay to Karachi on a boat. My brother had arranged for me and the younger children to travel to Karachi by plane. Then in June my son Ahmed was born in the military hospital in Rawalpindi. We had to try to build everything up again almost from the beginning. All the best houses and evacuated properties went to Punjabi bureaucrats who put in false claims, and not to the genuine refugees.

'My husband was an engineer, and we went to London to set up an engineering company. I founded the All-Pakistan Women's Association branch in Ladbroke Grove. We had a lovely time and people were very interested in Pakistan, and I gave talks to women's associations around the country. But in the early 1960s this "Paki-bashing" started because we were all building up our businesses and being successful. People became very snooty towards us. By 1964 we decided to go back to Pakistan.'

Her sister joined in. 'You're quite right, darling. I never understood all this "Paki-bashing" in England, taking a name we had worn with pride and turning it into an insult. Things were much easier for us in London when I went there in the 1950s. I really enjoyed it then. I remember once on an underground train at Leicester Square we were caught in the rush hour. My husband said to me in Pashtu, which was his language: "We are all packed in here like a flock of goats." An old gentleman in a good suit agreed with him – in Pashtu! It turned out that he had served up on the frontier at Quetta when he was in the army, and he still knew a few words of the language.'

We all laughed and then there was silence. 'Did you ever return to India?' I asked Begum Rashid.

'I went back to Lucknow in 1952 to fetch some papers concerning our land and village. In our house – it was called Ferozekothi – I found there were thirty families. I only looked in from the outside. I just could not bear to go in, it was so dirty, full of Hindus from a lower strata of life, and they had caused total devastation. I went back once more in 1964, and the house was totally falling apart and the orchard had all been cut down.'

There was a look of loss in her eyes. I asked her whether she thought Jinnah's vision of Pakistan had been right, in retrospect. She rang for the maid to bring her a woollen cardigan.

'I just don't know,' came the answer, finally. 'I do think that Pakistan has helped Muslims, but at the same time if we had remained as a federated country like the USA we might have been a stronger power. The Muslims in India still have a difficult time, but . . .' She broke off. 'My personal bearer said the other day that he preferred a disciplined way of living like we had under the British. He came to me and said: "Madam, *Angreez kabhi na jatay, insaf bahut tha*" – "The English should never have left, there was more justice in their time." He was an army man, though, and I have to say there are not many around who think as he does.'

I left them reminiscing and took a bus to Islamabad.

The sisters' late brother, Shahid Hamid, was also a military man. He opted for Pakistan at independence, becoming a General and later the country's Minister of Information and Minister of Culture during successive military dictatorships. The General's widow, Begum Tahirah Hamid, lived in a well-appointed house in the military cantonment in Rawalpindi, with barefoot servants padding about the corridors. She has the embarrassing distinction in Pakistan's ruling circles of being Salman Rushdie's auntie; indeed the late General bears a decided resemblance to Saleem Sinai's cruet-shifting Uncle Zulfi in Rushdie's novel *Midnight's Children*. Tahirah had pink-painted nails, scraped-back brown hennaed hair and golden earrings, and was enveloped in a cloud of endearing, youthful sensitivity, which I sensed was combined with a definite operational toughness.

Major General Shahid Hamid wrote a book called *Disastrous Twilight: A Personal Record of the Partition of India*, a rabidly anti-Mountbatten 'diary' of the events surrounding the end of British rule. It purports to be a day-by-day account written while he was serving as Private Secretary to Field Marshal Auchinleck between 1946 and 1947. *Disastrous Twilight* was first published in Britain in 1986 to some acclaim, with a rather awkward foreword by Philip Ziegler. Although the book is viewed with benign amusement by most Pakistani historians, Andrew Roberts relies on it as an important source in his essay 'Lord Mountbatten and the Perils of Adrenalin'.

A close reading of *Disastrous Twilight* shows clearly that much of it is not contemporaneous, and that it must have been rewritten, or at least heavily revised, at a later date. This is especially true of the entries relating to the controversy over the Radcliffe Line and the accession of Kashmir to India. Certain phrases in the introduction imply this, such as: 'This book has been written incorporating the diary I kept diligently during those days,' and 'After the Auck's death I gave the final touches to my diary and procured copies of some of the documents which were incomplete.'

Thus on the day of the Cabinet Delegation's arrival in India, Hamid writes that A.V. Alexander was 'the only member capable of considering things in their correct [i.e. anti-Congress] perspective', although Alexander had no known views on Indian politics at that time. On 13 August 1947, Hamid knows that the historic flag from Lucknow Residency will end up in the museum at Windsor Castle, although its destination had yet to be decided. His diary entry for the following day reads: 'Nehru made his famous speech: "Long years ago we made a tryst with destiny"', as if the phrase had become famous that very night. By 16 August this Pepys of partition knows the details not only of supposed secret meetings between Mountbatten and a delegation from Bikaner regarding the Punjab boundary, but even the precise sequence of events relating to bits of paper hundreds of miles away in Lahore. This is despite that fact that he asserts that Mountbatten 'closely guarded many decisions he had taken' from Auchinleck.

Although Shahid Hamid was apparently taken into Auchinleck's confidence to a degree that was unusual even for a Private Secretary, *Disastrous Twilight* contains plenty of information that he simply could not have known at the time it is supposed to have been written. Much of his 'diary' seems to derive from the plethora of books, memoirs and documents that have been published over the decades since the creation of Pakistan. There are even lines in the book which are quite clearly extracted from the interviews Mountbatten gave to Collins and Lapierre for *Freedom at Midnight*, but which are quoted as if Mountbatten was saying them in 1947.[1]

When I brought up the question of *Disastrous Twilight*'s veracity, or lack of it, with the General's widow, she refused to countenance even the possibility of a flaw in his legacy. I was hustled downstairs on a pilgrimage to his study, which was stacked with all the expected books, the twelve thick volumes of *The Transfer of Power* ranged on a shelf.

'We should not discuss such things,' she said as we walked up the steps and into the drawing-room. Tea and cakes were summoned by pressing a button on the end of a length of wire, like the sort you might find in a hospital.

'Well, let's talk about your early life.'

'I was born in Aligarh in 1920. My father's family came originally from Kashmir. He was an eye specialist who had qualified at the King

Edward Medical College in Lahore and then studied in Berlin.' The opening of *Midnight's Children* hit me on the end of the nose. 'We moved in Muslim circles, but we did have some Hindu friends and also some British friends. I had a very happy childhood and went to Aligarh Muslim Girls' School, and to please my father I later studied medicine at the Lady Hardinge Medical College in Delhi.

'In 1940 while I was a third-year medical student I met Shahid, who was then a young army officer fresh from Sandhurst. My family were very happy for me to marry him. We were in 'Pindi to start with, which was a Sikh town really at that time. We had some other postings and Shahid was sent to Burma, and then in February 1947 he went to Delhi to be Private Secretary to the Commander-in-Chief, Field Marshal Auchinleck. It was a great honour.

'The Auck was a strong, cussed man who was hard of hearing, and his wife had just walked off with the Air C-in-C and so he was very lonesome. He was being looked after by his sister, Mrs Jackson, who was a difficult woman. The Auck was like a father to both of us, and really adopted us as his second family and used to play with our children in the garden. We lived in a house in the grounds near to the C-in-C's house, and we both spent a lot of time with him and went for strolls. A few times we saw Mountbatten at social events. There was no rapport between him and the Auck, which left the Auck very frustrated. I could sense this – my instinct as a woman was that Mountbatten was much too full of himself and very vain for a man.

'When the time of the partition came we opted for Pakistan. I was packing up the house in Delhi in the middle of August 1947, and Shahid said we should go up to Simla as the weather was so hot. I saw him off at Safdarjang Airport on the sixteenth and he flew to 'Pindi. When I came back to the house the Auck was pacing up and down like a caged lion and said: "Tahirah, I would like to talk to you. These are difficult times, and I don't think my Private Secretary appreciates just how serious the situation is. You will leave for Simla and this young ADC from Jaipur will accompany you up there." I was scared, so we went up to Simla in the Auck's car.

'Three days later I got a call saying that we ought to move to Snowden, the C-in-C's house in Simla. After a couple of nights there, the Auck's ADC said we must leave Simla by 6 a.m. the next morning. He told me, "You must be ready, Begum Saheb." So the children, our relations and servants all got ready and the trucks arrived in the early morning and drove us out.'

The Begum looked desolate, and spoke very softly.

'All along the route were Sikhs. There were three of them in a jeep. Their eyes were red and they'd been drinking alcohol. They had guns and one was carrying a knife with blood all over it. They knew that some Muslim families were being evacuated in the convoy, but luckily they did not dare to attack. As our convoy set off the ADC said to the children, "Just give your pet names if anybody asks what you are called." That way they would not know if we were Hindu or Muslim. It took us several hours until finally we reached Ambala, where the Auck's plane was waiting to carry us out. The place was seething with Sikhs and riff-raffs who were all carrying spears and swords. It was very frightening. Luckily there were enough troops to protect us. Then we flew into Delhi, and as we circled over the city fires were burning, burning everywhere.

'Each evening at the C-in-C's house,' said Tahirah, 'there were Generals and other senior officers sitting around wondering how on earth to proceed. Even the Area Commanders were admitting to me that they had no control over their troops. It was truly terrible. The Auck made plans to fly us out to 'Pindi in his own plane. We were so lucky. Mass fury is irrational. The British had wanted to get out of the situation before the handover of power had occurred, and that was a big mistake. They just wanted to get out. It was not them who were harmed; it was the rival communities.'

Some miles down the road in Islamabad was another army man, General Ejaz Azim. He wore a golfing sweater, and his sitting-room was replete with brass, glass, soft furnishings and signed photographs of 'Ron and Nancy' Reagan. The General had served as Pakistan's Ambassador to the United States for most of the 1980s.

'I was almost twenty, doing a Masters in Economics at the university in Lahore when the rioting began. I can remember some of my Sikh friends advising me to get out, as they knew that some other Sikhs were forming *jathas* – sort of organized gangs – with a view to attacking and killing Muslims. The killings were being planned. I think that the burden for the snowballing of the violence lies with the Sikhs of east Punjab. They were organized state armies which were used for what is now called ethnic cleansing.

'Luckily, in the first week of July my father was posted to Rawalpindi, so we were able to move lock, stock and barrel while things were still safe. I came from a military background, and as Pakistan was being created and we heard stories of the massacres, I felt I ought to join the graduate fast stream into the army. I can remember trains washed clean of blood arriving in Rawalpindi and the wounded and the desolate getting down from the trains. They had nothing, nothing at all. The administration had totally broken down by this point. I really thought that maybe the world was coming to an end, and that we had got into a cauldron that was going to continue to bubble and that sanity would never return.

'The important thing to remember now is that people like me have a connection with old schoolfriends in India, while the younger generation simply believe all the propaganda. They have no links at all with India, and their attitude to India – say over Kashmir – is very negative and very dangerous. I was a Major in the 15th Lancers during the 1965 war with India, as second-in-command to 'Bachu' Karim. We knew quite a few of the fellows on the other side; the senior officers had been together at Sandhurst. In 1981 I left the army when my old friend Zia ul-Haq said he wanted me to head for Washington.'

'So you organized the supply of American weapons to fight the Soviets in Afghanistan?'

The General did not miss a beat.

'Well, not directly – at that time the CIA dealt directly with the leadership of Inter-Services Intelligence, who did all the liaison.'

'When Pakistan was created, did you ever imagine it would be placed under military rule?'

'No, we never did. When Ayub Khan and Zia ul-Haq imposed martial law I thought it was the right decision. Now I wonder whether it might not have been better to have left it to the politicians. Today we rather take the view that they should fight it out amongst themselves.'

A thousand miles to the east, in Bangladesh, stood General Iskander Karim, otherwise known as 'Bachu' or 'Boy' on account of his youthful face. He was born in Chittagong when his mother was fourteen, and his father was an official of the Bengal Civil Service. It was late in the evening, and Ejaz Azim's former commanding officer had been unwilling to see me any earlier, as he had been engaged in prayer. General Karim had small teeth, and wore striped trousers, a purple waistcoat, little black slippers and a beautiful turquoise and gold ring. He had impeccable manners, and he inspired reverence.

We sat down on straight-backed chairs. 'I've had a long innings,' he said, 'and I've served three flags. I was commissioned into the Central India Horse in 1944 and sent to Basra after the war to deal with POWs under General Loftus Tottenham, and I became the first Indian Adjutant in my regiment. We were completely isolated from political events in the army; to be honest I preferred going out on a *shikar* after some duck with the other chaps to discussing politics.

'We were all great admirers of Lord Wavell; his son-in-law Francis Humphrys was my Squadron Commander. Wavell was a rational man. I remember him saying to us once, after a parade: "Humility, patience, and understanding of your fellow human beings are the essentials of a leader. If you add to that professional competence, you will be a good commander." That has always stuck in my mind.

'We were stationed at Ahmednagar near Poona in 1947. Things became difficult as the Hindu soldiers in the regiment became hostile, although there was certainly no active insubordination. So I said to Colonel Ridley, my commanding officer, "I think I had better be going." I took a boat from Bombay to Karachi and then a train to Rawalpindi. At that time I felt the break-up of Bengal was wrong. We should never have allowed the Indians into Assam. Bengal should certainly have remained as one unit – after all, the Muslim League was born here in Dhaka.'

Despite being a Bengali, Bachu Karim did well in the Pakistan Army during the 1950s and 1960s, serving as Assistant Military Attaché in Washington and Military Secretary to the Governor of East Pakistan. By 1971 he was commanding the 6th Armoured Division, and he was one of only two generals in the Pakistan Army who originated from East Pakistan.

'During the civil war of 1970 and 1971 I felt I had no alternative but to back the government, although I was kept away from the front. After the ceasefire I opted for what was to become Bangladesh, since my family came from Chittagong. It was a perfectly reasonable thing to do, but Bhutto put me under house arrest. He used Bengali soldiers who were trapped in West Pakistan as bargaining pawns, so as to retrieve his own troops from Bangladesh, including soldiers who were guilty of war crimes.'

'How long were you kept under arrest?'

'For two years. I stayed in our house with my three daughters and my wife, reading books very slowly and painting from time to time. I was being guarded by my own troops, who said to me, "Sir, I feel very bad about this." I just told them, "Don't worry. Do your duty." One day my house electrician came to me in a worried state and said, "I have taken your salt, Saheb, so I must tell you what is to happen. They are coming to raid your house." So I burnt all my documents and the memoirs I had been writing, and many years of history went up the chimney.

'Finally in December 1973 I was flown back to Dhaka with my family in an East German aeroplane. The liberators gave us a mixed reception. You see, in theory I was now the most senior officer in the Bangladesh Army, but in the eyes of many I was associated with the Punjabis. I had worked in military intelligence, and I was offered an important ceremonial position on the understanding that I betrayed the operational secrets of the Pakistan Army. I said, "If I were to tell you all the secrets you wish to know, how would you ever be able to trust me? I swore an oath to King George VI in 1944, and I would no more have broken my oath to him than I would break the oath I took to the Government of Pakistan in 1947." So it was mutually agreed that I should retire.

'Then certain people asked me to become a politician. I said to our leader Zia Rahman, "I am a military man. If I have got to wrestle with a crocodile, I would like to do it on land and not in the water." I have to tell you I think politics is a dirty, changeable, corrupt affair throughout the subcontinent. In the past, politics was done by people with means, who had an objective of serving their country, but now it is simply a game of exploitation. As soon as they get into power, these politicians have no choice but to settle scores and pay off their debts.'

General Karim had sat bolt upright throughout our conversation. He continued: 'There is a very sad level of corruption today. There are very few dedicated, sincere lovers of their country left in politics. What have our young people left to look forward to? I do not have an optimistic view of the future of my country.'

'Can the corruption be stopped?' I asked.

'I think the only answer is to follow the Chinese model and hang a few hundred people to make an example. That stops corruption.' He stood up smartly, this British Army officer who had been born an Indian, become a Pakistani and was now a Bangladeshi. He shook my hand briskly, and then he was gone.

'In India some were Muslims, and some were Hindus. That you must remember. Sir Radcliffe drew his line with the motive of making as many problems as he could. It curved backwards and forwards over either side of riverbanks. You know what I say?' At this point a pen was waved in the air. 'I say that the British COULD NEVER DRAW A STRAIGHT LINE!' Two dozen people laughed, vigorously.

General Mir Shawkat Ali had once been an army man, but now he was in the water, wrestling with crocodiles. I rather suspected that he might be a crocodile himself. He was dressed in an expensive *kurta* with gold trimmings, and displayed a luxuriant moustache which twirled up at the ends in the fashion of Terry-Thomas. Local journalists had told me he was renowned for being arrogant, and an opportunist. As Minister for Labour and Manpower in a country which exported many workers, he was certainly occupying a position which afforded opportunities.

'Enough of Sir Radcliffe. Now you must wait while I talk to my people,' he said. 'The problem is that Bangladesh is a small country, so we need to expand eastwards to gain more living space for our people. Things will settle down in our politics – things are already settling down.'

I had arrived at his office long after dark, by cycle-rickshaw. The room was grey-blue, with a toilet-tiled floor and a curved desk on which sat three large brown telephones. Behind the desk sat the General, looking down at rows of supplicants. To his side was a group of thin, feckless-looking young men, who were introduced as his 'secretaries'.

Behind him hung a white plastic board marked 'Work Schedule'. It detailed the places he intended to visit during the campaign for the forthcoming, uncontested general election. The main opposition party, which seemed marginally more appealing than the existing government, had called for nationwide demonstrations and a boycott of the poll. They were using an array of industrial and political instruments that would make Arthur Scargill blush: strikes, sit-ins and stoppages, *bandhs* and *hartals*, blockades and self-imposed curfews. There was chaos in Dhaka.

An old woman with flashing eyes, no teeth and a white shawl on her head shuffled forward. She carried a cloth-wrapped bundle, and looked as if she had come in from the countryside. There was an exchange of words and she handed over a piece of paper. The General glanced down and put it to one side, so the woman began to talk, in a rising and falling voice. The General winked at me and the secretaries laughed, but the old woman kept on talking, determined to tell her story. The General wiggled his eyebrows and began to pull faces, and everybody giggled at his wit. When he had tired of her, he pulled out a couple of 100-taka notes from a large bag, and flicked them across the desk. She picked them up and shuffled off to one side. The General turned to me and murmured in a benign tone: 'One day we will be old like her, and helpless.'

Then all the lights went out, and there was silence. One of the secretaries lit a match. 'I have lived in several European countries,' said the General in an apparently calm voice. 'There is no need to be afraid.' The match went out. It occurred to me that I was in a fourth-floor office in central Dhaka surrounded by very frightened people, and that I was sitting between the General and the door, should anybody choose to burst through it and do to him what they had done to Sheikh Mujib fifteen years before. A few seconds later there was a flash and a very loud explosion which made the desk and the windows rattle, followed immediately by a second explosion. Oh, I thought, a coup.

There was screaming and scrambling, then more silence. Some rustling followed, and the General turned on a torch – the kind you might find in the glove compartment of a small car – and pointed it at his own face. He had the bulging eyes of a deranged frog. 'They only do this to try and scare me,' he announced with a tremulous lack of concern. 'It is no problem.' There was a sound of running and shouting in the street outside.

'You had better leave at once,' the General said to me.

'Right,' I answered.

'Wait!' He scribbled on a piece of paper and handed it over. Was it his last will and testament? It said: 'LIEUTENANT GENERAL (RETIRED) MIR SHAWKAT ALI, BIR UTTAM'. 'That is my full designation,' he barked. 'You have heard of the Victoria Cross and the George Cross?'

'Yes,' I answered, as another bomb exploded in a nearby building. There was a smell of smoke.

'Well, Bir Uttam, that is like your Military Cross. From our war of liberation, you understand?'

I shook his plump hand and pushed my way out of the room, following one of the feckless secretaries, who held a match. We felt our way down some stone steps until we reached the street. There were men and soldiers everywhere. It took three hours to get back to the house where I was staying.

That night I lay awake for hours. What would you do if you were a politician in Bangladesh? Fight your political opponents, or try to cooperate with them? Invite in the World Bank and the transnational corporations to exploit the economy? Try taxing the elite, then watch them shift their cash and their children abroad? Decide that 120 million people in a tiny area of watery land above the fingers of the Ganges did not make a nation, and give up? Stay optimistic and idealistic, although the average annual wage of a Bangladeshi only buys a hundred bottles of mineral water in the Dhaka Sheraton? Or make your money and run?

The next day a local Ward Commissioner, Haji Mohammed Alim, was hacked with knives and shot through the chest at close range. The Haji was a known opponent of General Shawkat's party, and the newspapers claimed that the 'muscle men' who carried out the killing were acting on the orders of a powerful government minister. Later that day an attempt was made to set fire to General Shawkat's residence, although he told the press the murder was not carried out at his instigation. 'I am very shocked,' he was reported as saying.

Senior army men in India are less likely to hold subsequent political appointments than their counterparts in Bangladesh and Pakistan. Apart from Indira Gandhi's brief aberration in the late 1970s, India has remained a roughly democratic country since independence. General Mehta thought this was a good thing, although he held politicians in the very lowest esteem.

'They are the biggest bugs, really, the biggest creeps. They were the same in 1947. What I want for India now is a civilian tyrant who can keep the economy in shape and have regard for the rule of law. Now look here – this is not a time for sloganizing, let's look at it rationally. Let's keep the country on the right tracks like it was before the British left.'

I met the General at the Gymkhana Club in Delhi, a cream building filled with anglophilic accents. Sweeping up from the pinched lawns were innumerable tennis courts, a 'Rummy Room' and a 'Lady Willingdon Swimming Bath'. As we were talking, the Club Secretary appeared, shaking hands heartily with men he recognized, and doing a quick bow and *namaste* to the women.

'Well, old boy,' he said to the General, patting him on the back, 'have you had lunch yet?'

'Of course, Ronnie,' was the answer. 'We have had an excellent tucking-in.'

The General's family had come from Quetta, and he had never expected it to become part of a Muslim homeland.

'I went to school in Murree and then did a short stint at Gordonstoun. I've got nothing against the Muslims around Quetta – the Pathans were loyal, honest, friendly, reliable types. The problem came with the bugs down in Delhi and the Muslims of the Punjab, who were rabid communalists.'

He took another swig of his drink.

'All the normal bonhomie between Hindus and Muslims began to disappear during the mid-1940s. The common folk demanded freedom, with no idea what freedom might mean. The decision to have a partition of the Indian Empire was a very destructive thing – both sides were equally to blame. It produced a kind of carnage you hope you won't see in your lifetime, and if you do see it, you wish to forget it.'

His mood was changing as he spoke.

'I reached Delhi on 1 September 1947, and went to the railway station to look for some relations who were coming from Pakistan. There was a train there, filled with massacred people. Some of them . . . some of them were still living.'

The General put down his drink, rubbed his hands across his face, and stopped talking.

TWENTY-FOUR

Awaiting Full Integration

In north London's suburbs, somewhere between Cricklewood and the Scratchwood Service Area of the M1, sits the International Secretariat of the Mohajir Qaumi Movement. After much faxing, I had come there to meet the leader of the MQM, Altaf Hussain. He controls Karachi, by telephone. If he orders a strike tomorrow afternoon, there will be one.

I waited for some time in a fortified reception area, surrounded by mounted colour photographs of mutilated bodies, and was then asked to return in two hours. After being buzzed through security doors I walked down the stairs, past a Benefits Agency Job Club and a car showroom and into an 'American Burger with Egg a Speciality' café. There were pinched women with pushchairs and scraped-up hair eating doughnuts. I drank cups of tea and watched the condensation wriggling down the windows, noticing that while in Asia poverty makes you thin, in Europe it makes you fat.

Altaf Hussain was in his mid-forties, with a slug moustache, large spectacles and a strangely wavering voice. His office was filled with sticky, scented air. He told me that when he was in prison before coming to England, he was tortured 'mentally and physically, but they could not surrender me'. His appearance is that of a respectable Asian businessman – the kind you see at airports – grey suit, white shirt, patterned tie and bouffant hair. While we talked, his plump fingers fiddled with recording equipment and he murmured intermittently into a mobile phone. It was hard to get anything more than a platform speech out of him; there was something disturbed and blank about his version of communication. Bodyguards stood by the door, alert.

Altaf was wanted by the Pakistani government for alleged involvement in over a hundred murders. They are trying to extradite him – although not very vigorously according to undiplomatic sources, who thought the authorities in Islamabad preferred to leave him skulking in north London, out of the way.

For all his unprepossessing appearance, Altaf is a hero to many Pakistanis, the unassailed leader of the Mohajir *qaum* or nation. The Mohajirs are the Urdu-speaking people who migrated west from the United Provinces, Maharashtra, Rajputana, the Central Provinces and Hyderabad at the time of independence, to build the new Pakistan. There were six to eight million Muslim migrants, who generally arrived in the promised land with bits of their family missing; either massacred, or abandoned back in India. Today, according to the MQM, there are nearly thirty million Mohajir descendants in Pakistan, around a quarter of the total population, of whom the large majority live in the southern province of Sind.

At first they did well, taking jobs in the judiciary and the civil service. They had substantial power – or disproportionate power, according to the indigenous Sindhis. Many of the Mohajirs were after all the ones who had wanted Pakistan to be created in the first place. As Jinnah himself said in a speech three days after the creation of the new state: 'I recognize that it is the Muslim minority provinces in this subcontinent who were the pioneers and carried the banner aloft for the achievement of our cherished goal of Pakistan . . . they were the pioneers in the vanguard of our historic struggle for the achievement of Pakistan.'[1]

Their downfall began in 1951 with the assassination of the country's first Prime Minister, Liaquat Ali Khan, who came from the United Provinces. When the self-promoted Field Marshal Ayub Khan took over and introduced 'basic democracy' – so basic that only 0.1 per cent of the population was allowed to vote – Mohajirs were quietly drummed out of government service. Zulfiqar Ali Bhutto accelerated the process in the 1970s. As a big landowner in rural northern Sind, Bhutto supported the claims of resentful Sindhi 'sons of soil' over those of the immigrants.

In 1984 the MQM was founded by Altaf Hussain. It was ridiculed at first, for it had grown out of minor political groupings at Karachi University, where Altaf was a pharmacy student. (One fellow undergraduate remembered him as a ludicrous figure, driving about with an air of great importance on a small moped.) The movement and its leader soon went through a phenomenal rise to fame, gaining support among many different types of Mohajir.

By the early 1990s, through the use of carefully controlled extortion and violence, the MQM was in effective control of Karachi. The end of the war in Afghanistan had flooded the city with an estimated fifteen thousand automatic weapons, leftovers from the countless AK47s that the CIA had purchased for the Mujahadin during their proxy war with the Soviet Union. The government of Zulfi's daughter Benazir Bhutto, which had yet to be ousted, responded to the new power of the Mohajirs with 'Operation Clean-Up', using paramilitary 'Rangers' and an officially sponsored splinter group known as 'MQM (Haqiqi)' to regain control.

Altaf Hussain's brother and nephew had been picked up in Karachi a few weeks before I met him. He pushed a clump of pictures across the desk.

'This is my young nephew Arif. He was an engineer, and not even a member of the MQM. The Rangers took him and tortured him for three days before they killed him.'

Arif's face had a look of total surprise. There were red gashes and purple bruises and his body was full of holes. It reminded me of a photograph I had seen of some victims of the MQM, whose corpses had been dumped in gunny bags on wasteland in Korangi.

'This is what they are doing to the Mohajir nation. I request you to please understand that ever since Quaid-i-Azam Jinnah's death, our people have been persecuted by the feudal power-barons of Sind and Punjab. My parents came from Agra where my father was a station master under the British Raj, but they never expected such treatment in the new Pakistan at the hands of their Muslim brothers.

'There is discrimination at all levels against us,' he continued, producing a table of statistics which showed how few Mohajirs held senior positions within the government and police force of Sind. 'They invent cruel and insulting words for the masses to use against us, names like *bhayya* or *tilyar*. They misguide the innocent Pakhtuns and Baluchis, telling them we are outsiders in our own homeland.'

'What do these names mean?' I asked.

'These are words like "nigger", to insult my people,' he replied, then spoke into a microphone very quietly. Within moments a bowing assistant came in with a word-processed piece of paper. It said:

DEROGATORY TERMS USED FOR MOHAJIRS
Tilyar – a migratory bird

Makkar – a locust pest
Panah Guzeen – a destitute refugee
Bhayya – a weak, coward person

'The Urdu-speakers of Pakistan are being pushed to the wall by these feudals,' grunted Altaf. 'What the feudal rule of Benazir Bhutto is doing is pushing the Mohajir nation to the wall. When her father was in power he subjugated us economically and now she is doing it with the military. This Benazir talks about humanity and was educated at Oxford University, but you should just go to her feudal fiefdom at Naudero and Larkana and see how people are treated. They would be surprised to see that people are living there like slaves.'

He seemed to have a pain of some kind in his chest. A Pakistani woman I had spoken to before seeing the MQM leader had said that unspeakable things had been done to him in prison, and that he was now in bad health. 'They say I am autocratic, but just look at the barbaric law enforcement agencies. I am only following the needs of my people.' He spread his arms towards some hangers-on, who were standing in front of a spangly, wine-red curtain. 'Am I not following the needs of my people?'

'Yes, you are, bhai saheb,' answered the entourage.

'I have twenty-two million supporters,' said Altaf. 'When I return to Karachi, I will be showered with rose petals in the street.'

Karachi was hot and dusty, and in its prosperous centre there was a buzz at night around the international 'export standard' hotels. In the suburbs you passed through mile upon mile of low, discoloured, ugly concrete blocks which housed the city's vast population. In order to hinder the communications of the MQM, all public telephones had been removed, and mobile telephones jammed. The whole place had a grim, tense, hard air. As soon as the evening newspaper, the *Star*, appeared, people rushed out to buy a copy and read details of that day's 'shoot-out'.

Quite early one morning, I was standing on Raja Ghazanfar Ali Road in the centre of Karachi talking to a trim man with a beard and a long smock. He was called Haasan, and he pressed sugarcane for a living. His family had migrated from Hyderabad in southern India some years before.

Two thousand people had been murdered in Karachi in a matter of months, many in internecine war between the MQM (Altaf) and the splinter group MQM (Haqiqi). Some victims were policemen, who had been taken to 'torture cells' before being executed. About 250 of the dead were MQM activists, killed in 'encounters' with the paramilitary Rangers. In most cases, the suspected terrorist was kidnapped and taken for interrogation, the prospect of 'head money' being an added enticement for the arresters. The tip-off generally came from Field Security, a shadowy intelligence offshoot of the Rangers. The suspect was then released a day or two later, dead.

The police, who were afraid of the Rangers, and effectively subordinate to them thanks to Naseerullah Babar, the retired General-turned Interior Minister who was running 'Operation Clean-Up', would organize an autopsy, and usually concluded that the victim had died from gunshot wounds during a shoot-out. There was no mention of evidence that hot metal rods had been inserted into the ears, or that flesh had been gouged with pincers. Faheem Commando, for instance, a hardcore MQM activist, was taken into police custody in August 1995 with his brother and two colleagues. Four days later the four were dead, killed by crossfire, although the timing and location and bullet trajectories did not tie together.

Haasan the sugarcane presser, like most people I had spoken to in Karachi, was a passive admirer of Altaf Hussain. Supplying cash on demand to local MQM leaders did not bother him: 'No problem,' he said. 'They are with the people. The Mohajirs are the ones who gave up everything to come to Pakistan, and somebody must give us a voice.' I asked him what he thought about the then Prime Minister Benazir Bhutto, and he answered: 'No good.' When I asked him about Benazir's husband, the plump Sindhi playboy Asif Zardari formerly known as 'Mr Ten Per Cent' but now referred to as 'Mr Forty Per Cent', Haasan kicked the ground and said: 'He is a very corrupted man. He will destroy Benazir in time. If he comes to this city it will be bad for him.' A few months later Benazir was dismissed from office on charges of maladministration, and subsequently humiliated at the polls, to be replaced by her rival Nawaz Sharif.

On the opposite side of the road a group of Tajiks were doing a deal, and a pair of mechanics were dragging a disembowelled engine into their workshop. All of a sudden there was a popping noise, and Haasan ran inside a shopfront for cover. I was too amazed to move, laughing almost, as a 'mobile' – a converted police pick-up with metal mesh up the sides – sped towards us, chasing a swerving white car. The mobile contained a mob of policemen, all firing their rifles wildly as they raced along. The car tried to turn when it reached the junction at the end of our street, but curled left into a concrete pole a few metres from where I was standing.

The police jumped down and dragged the driver onto the road. He was middle-aged, with the usual moustache and long brown *salwar*, and he was squealing like an animal or a child. The head policeman forced him into a kneeling position and pushed his face into the road several times while a younger colleague kicked him in the bottom casually, as if he were joking. Then the head policeman pulled him up by the hair and rammed his face into the edge of the car door, the bit where the lock is, until he stopped screaming. The other passengers from the car were beaten randomly with rifle butts, and herded into the mobile to be taken to Artillery Maidan Police Station for interrogation.

That evening I spoke to some people on Ghazanfar Ali Road who said the men in the car had been MQM, or connected to it, or were carjackers, or bandits, or had shot a red light. Another version had them trying to extort a wad of dollars from an African national, or a Russian businessman, and being spotted in action by the policemen. Everybody was agreed that such things happen, this being Karachi. Some days later I walked to the spot and could see a light sprinkling of glass and two patches of dry, brown blood.

Dhaka was full of hustlers in chequered *lunghis*, and helpless traffic directors wearing gaiters and globular white helmets. There was a take-over going on, as usual, the daughter of the dead leader busily ousting the widow of another dead leader.

When I mentioned that I was visiting Geneva Camp, a Bangladeshi friend called Uday said I was crazy. 'You can't go there. Nobody goes there. Not even my driver, and he's a Bihari.'

When Muslim refugees from Bihar came to east Bengal in 1946 and

1947, traumatized and destitute, they found they were aliens in the land of the pure. They had been promised paradise, a country in which their Quaid-i-Azam had said there would be 'a removal of want and fear of all types', and 'liberty, fraternity and equality for all'. At first some of them got jobs in factories and on the railways, and all the people in Dhaka and Rajshahi shouted 'Pakistan Zindabad!' in unity.

It was seven months before Governor General Jinnah found time to make a brief visit to the east wing of his new country, and seven months after that he was dead. When he arrived in Dhaka in March 1948 he told his listeners that he had wanted to come sooner, 'But unfortunately, other matters of greater importance had so far prevented me from doing so.' In the same speech he ordered the citizens of East Pakistan to 'for God's sake give up this provincialism', and, memorably, made it clear that the Bengali language, which was spoken by 56 per cent of the population of Pakistan, would have to be subordinated to Urdu, which was spoken by fewer Pakistanis than spoke Punjabi. 'But let me make it very clear to you,' declaimed the Quaid-i-Azam, 'that the state language of Pakistan is going to be Urdu and no other language.'[2]

To his audience, steeped in centuries of Bengali literature and culture, it was a provocation. In the years that followed there were language riots, and alienation grew between the successive military regimes in Karachi and Islamabad and their Bengali subjects a thousand miles away to the east. A common religion was the only thing that bound them together, the mutton-chewers and the fish-eaters, but this was hardly enough to create fraternal bonds, let alone a genuine feeling of national coherence and identity.

The Biharis became the stooges and the cannon-fodder of the Generals who ran Pakistan, while the indigenous Bengali Muslims turned against them. In the civil war of 1971 these Urdu-speaking outsiders backed the wrong side, and in some cases committed atrocities against Bengalis, so when Bangladesh was established as an independent state they were chased out of their homes in revenge.

In their own minds, the Biharis felt they were Pakistanis, for it was to the state of united Pakistan that they had sworn their allegiance a quarter of a century earlier. Requests to be repatriated to West Pakistan were acknowledged, accepted, and then ignored. With Zulfikar Ali Bhutto busily ousting the Mohajirs from his own administration, the last thing he needed was another dollop of newcomers in his country. Some of the Biharis were allowed to go to Pakistan, but around a quarter of a million people were shoved into squalid refugee camps, where they remain to this day.

It is probably fair to say that there were no winners in the break-up of the Indian Empire, unless you count the dubious recipients of evacuee property. However, the greatest losers were the displaced or 'stranded' Pakistanis. They are the living legacy of the historical decisions of Indian and British politicians in 1947, and a daily reminder, if anyone cared to think about them, that the division of India is a matter of more than academic interest.

When I was in Pakistan, nobody had been very concerned about Bangladesh. The war of 1971 was a forgotten embarrassment, although most people were vaguely agreed that it had been a mistake to have one country in two separate halves. There was little guilt, or even knowledge, about the atrocities that had been carried out against their fellow Pakistanis in the east. In the words of one retired official in Lahore, the Bengalis were 'just black fellows with monkey beards' – colonial subjects who had been a liability to the Exchequer, and could now be forgotten.

Tahira Mazhar Ali, the political activist and daughter of the Punjabi leader Sir Sikander Hayat Khan, was the only person who had become noticeably angry when talking about the treatment of the East Pakistanis. She told me a story about a demonstration by a women's group against the military action at the time.

'We were all spat upon and then arrested by the police. As we were being taken away one woman, just a woman from the *bustis* [slums], shouted, "When the flower falls from the hair of the Bengali girl, it is the Punjabi girl who weeps." That was an incredible moment, but most people weren't thinking along those lines at all. I can remember at one official function where there was a group of women, wives of members of the elite, and I overheard one laughing to the others, "What does it matter if women in Bengal are being raped by our soldiers? At least the next generation of Bengalis will be better looking." That was the kind of attitude that you found here in 1971, and it is still around today.'

Geneva Camp was home to eighteen thousand Biharis, crammed into rows of wooden shacks on a tiny piece of land, wedged into a hole in the pitted cityscape of Dhaka. Uday's driver had told me to be on my guard. 'There are musclemen and *goondas*, followers of Ali,' he warned, grimacing. It seemed that there had been an incident during the religious festival of Muharram when a group of frenzied, self-lacerating Bihari Shias had clashed with local Bengali Sunnis. Now retaliatory land-grabbing was going on, and relations were tense.

As soon as I went through the gates of the camp I was surrounded by a swarm of children, shouting and dragging at me as I made my way in search of the Stranded Pakistanis General Repatriation Committee. There was some confusion, as there is a splinter group of the SPGRC in the camp which uses the same name. It was dusk, and I pressed through doors and alleyways, past piles of oozing, stinking rubbish, walking fast, afraid. There were families living in rooms about the size of a double bed, which had been partitioned onto two levels. Downstairs, as it were, boys were folding sweet-boxes fast for cash. These were the worst living conditions I had ever seen in Asia. When I reached the SPGRC office I was pulled inside by a young man with teeth and a beard, who cuffed the escorting mob and presented me to his leader, Mohammad Nasim Khan.

We were in a narrow, bottle-green room containing books, a bed, some chairs and a table, dotted with ceremonial portraits of Muslim luminaries. A very shiny, brightly painted auto-rickshaw was stabled incongruously at the far end. 'This is my only transport,' said Nasim Khan, pointing at it. 'My diplomatic vehicle, you could say. At the end of our meeting my driver will return you to the gate of our camp, or Paris as I call it.'

'Paris?'

'I call it that because it is the finest of our camps. Once it was only a ditch, but now it is Paris. The Red Cross say it is Geneva Camp, but I was thinking we should choose our own name.' There was a look in his eye. It made me feel he was testing me in some way. Dhaka was full of aid workers in Land Cruisers, peering down at the masses from on high, and one rather eminent local journalist had told me he would like to take all the jeeps in Bangladesh and shove them up the arse of the Secretary General of the United Nations.

Nasim Khan said that Geneva Camp had been rebuilt in 1986 after a great fire, and that in the aftermath some of the stranded Pakistanis had considered deliberate self-immolation as a means of promoting their cause.

'They said they would sooner burn themselves to death than continue suffering in a foreign land. I understood why they wanted to do this, but I did not think it was wise. Still, the government in Pakistan came under pressure and they allowed some of us to go to Karachi.'

'How many people went?' I asked.

'Three hundred and twenty-five people – one planeload only. There are still 2.38 *laks* [238,000] remaining in Bangladesh. There were also promises by General Zia ul-Haq to take us all to Pakistan, but he died just at the moment when his promises were to come true. You see, what can we do?' asked Nasim Khan, clacking his tongue around his mouth as if he were goading a young bullock. 'We are poor refugees in a poor country, and everybody ignores our problem: Clinton of America, Rafsanjani of Iran, and even our sister in Pakistan. When Falklands were in danger on the high seas, troops went. When Kuwait was in danger, troops went. History is all there. Are they helping us? My people were travelling through rivers and jungles, fighting and dying for Pakistan when these politicians Lady Benazir Bhutto and Nawaz Sharif were not even in the mother's womb.

'We have suffered state carnage and state torture,' he went on, 'although I do not blame the *Banglas* for what happened in 1971. History is all there. At first we had a little integration. We worked in the jute and paper mills and on the railways. Some of our people were ingenious mechanics and technicians. Then the Generals in West Pakistan said to us, "We need your help and our borders are under threat." They said to us, "You are Pakistanis, the people of the land of the pure. You must defend your country." So we went to help them, and even young boys of twelve or thirteen years took up weapons to defend our nation.'

'Did you think you would defeat the Bengalis?'

'We did not know. We just fought for our country, the country we had helped to found. Bengali nationalism was too strong, so the Generals were defeated.'

'What happened to you then?'

'After the Bengali victory my people were killed mercilessly and we were driven from our homes. Personally I spent six months in prison. All our property and land was taken. They herded us into these concentration camps where we live like animals to this day. The tears were drying in our hollow eyes, and our bodies were hovering with infirmity.'

Nasim Khan coughed and turned away from me to attend to some papers. Then he began to speak again, very sadly.

'As I said to you, I do not blame the *Banglas*. They wanted their own nation. We were betrayed by the Generals and the people of Pakistan. In 1973 they agreed that anybody who was once a Pakistani had the right to come to Pakistan, but the promise has never been fulfilled. Always they are fiddling and presenting obstacles.'

'What can you do now?'

'Now all we can do is hope that we shall be saved with the help of my God and the help of the Prophet, Peace be upon His Name. What else can we do? I have no loyalty to Bangladesh, but I am a peace-loving man and I will not break the rule of law.'

He handed me a bundle of papers, one of which was a photocopy of his own, self-created, international identity document. Besides showing that he was sixty-six years old, five feet five inches with a 'mixed (black and white)' beard, it revealed that M. Nasim Khan was born in India, lived in Bangladesh but claimed he was a Pakistani.

A pamphlet outlined the plight of one Abdur Rauf, an elderly railway worker who had been evicted from his hut, apparently by 'miscreants moving freely under the protective umbrella of the police and vested interests'. Although Mr Rauf was 'a recipient of the Gallantry Award of Tangh-e-Shujat' and had 'outstanding performance with railway', he was now suffering 'a tragedy of betrayal and disrespect and is threatened with total destruction'. The appeal in support of Abdur Rauf ended with a general plea for the SPGRC, since 'just like the Kashmiri Muslims, the Bosonian [sic] Muslims and all other humen [sic] beings who are the victims of suppression, Stranded Pakistanis are socially rejected, they politically stand no where and they are economically crippled'.

When I made a reference to his fellow Biharis, Nasim Khan snapped at me.

'Biharis! Do not use insulting words! What do we have to do with Bihar? None of us have been in Bihar for fifty years. Some of my people are Urdu-speakers whose families had been living in west Bengal for generations. What we are is true supporters of the two-nation theory embodied in the Pakistan demand of Quaid-i-Azam Mohammad Ali

Jinnah, who have now been left in lurch by the people we helped. We are stranded Pakistanis. We are sincere.'

'Have you ever thought of returning to Bihar?' I asked. Today Bihar is the most notorious state in India, the acknowledged show-home of corruption, poverty and degradation.

'There is nothing for us in Bihar. What would the Hindus say to us if we returned? They would laugh at us and say, "Brother, what has happened to your Pakistan? Where is your paradise now?" We could never go back to Bihar.'

The fate of the occupants of Geneva Camp is complicated by the conduct of their *doppelgängers* in the west, the Urdu-speaking Mohajirs who fled to West Pakistan at the time of independence. When I mentioned the activities of Altaf Hussain and the MQM to Nasim Khan, he became angry.

'Who are these chaps, these fused lightbulbs, saying they are a Mohajir nation? How can there be a "nation" of people who migrated to join their Muslim brothers and build a new country? It is a snare and a delusion to think such things, and it creates many problems. These gun-shooters are destroying the Pakistan we believe in.'

'But they say the local Sindhis exclude them, and that makes them feel like a separate nation,' I said.

'No, no, no. They are betraying the vision and the dream of our Quaid-i-Azam Mohammad Ali Jinnah. Like us, they are Pakistanis who are simply awaiting full integration. Many of the Mohajirs living in Karachi are well established, you know, with houses set nicely with tele-vision and freeze.'

Nasim Khan's young secretary interrupted, and said he wanted to take me to see the rest of the camp. As we went out into the cramped lane I asked Nasim Khan, obliquely, whether he still believed Jinnah had made the right decisions during the 1940s.

'Of course,' he answered, waving a pair of large spectacles at me. 'History is all there. We shall continue our struggle, *inshallah*, until such time as we succeed or are bodily lifted up and thrown into the Bay of Bengal.'

The mob of yelping children surrounded us as soon as we got out of the door. Some of them were carrying sticks. On top of one building was a Pakistani flag, with a blood-red stripe painted through the middle of it. A young woman with a heavy nose-stud and a badly patched lime-green sari dashed into her shack, looking nervous. As we walked past I could see a man lolling on a *charpoy* inside. He looked deranged and his tongue was hanging out, dribbling saliva onto the ground. One of the boys banged the side of the building and shouted at him. Further along, two men were standing in a passageway, screaming at each other.

'This is how things are. People are very cramped together,' declared Nasim Khan's secretary, briskly. 'There is not even the room,' he said, pointing at a six-inch gap between two buildings, 'to remove the bodies of people when they die.' We marched on into the depths of the camp through a flurry of filthy, scrabbling chickens. A minute or two later he turned to me and spoke angrily, out of the blue: 'We are not beggars. We are working hard. It is not our choice to live in this way. All I wish to do is to return to Pakistan, my homeland.'

He was in his thirties, and I knew he had never been to Pakistan, and would probably never get there, so I said nothing.

By a makeshift mosque, near a fetid water-pump, sat Zarina. A group of women were washing themselves, fully clothed, under a trickle of dark water. 'My name is just Zarina,' she whispered, frightened to be asked. She was about seventy, with bare feet, brown teeth and a thin pink sari. Gradually she told me that her husband and her son Anwar 'and my youngest boy' had been murdered 'by the other community' in the Great Calcutta Killings of 1946. After that she had left her home in Manikali Bazaar to walk with a group of people to east Bengal. They had lived in disused railway wagons for a while, and she had cleaned houses to get money for food, but when the civil war came in 1971 they had fled to the camp.

'Who do you blame for what happened?' I asked.

She looked puzzled.

'I don't blame anybody. I don't understand about politics. I was in *purdah* until I came across the border. All I know is that I've been a refugee for fifty years, and have still not found a home.'

EPILOGUE

I got on the train at Amritsar. In my pocket were two tiny cardboard tickets: one read 'Indo-Pak Traffic – Amritsar to Atari Border', and the other simply 'Lahore'. Their price was 42 rupees, or a little over 60 pence. The brick-red, banana-striped railway carriages lumbered out of the city and through the fields of the Punjab at a walking pace, past wet green fields, chained buffaloes and half-built houses. When I asked a guard if the carriages were the same ones that had been in use in 1947, he replied, 'New bodies, same bogies.'

It was stark, dirty and dark inside the second-class carriage as we rattled along through the fields. There were gouged wooden benches, and puddles of water on the floor. By a window with sliding metal shutters stood two jaded soldiers from India's Border Security Force, holding thin-barrelled rifles. There were four passengers on the train. On the seat opposite me was a silent, worried woman in a stained green and white *salwar kameez*, clutching a carpet bag which said 'USA Los Angeles', and beside her sat a scrawny, persistent Canadian who looked as if he had been in Asia for too long, and who spoke at length on the benefits of European integration. Next to me was a tall, serious, upright Sikh called Mr Sandhu, with a blue suit and a briefcase.

I had spent the previous day at the Golden Temple in Amritsar, the sacred heart of Sikhism which was stormed by Indira Gandhi's troops in 1984 during the militant campaign for an independent Sikh state, or Khalistan. It was a stunning building, aflame with white marble, full of women and garlanded children sitting by the pool that surrounds the inner sanctum in which the *Granth Saheb* was recited unceasingly. I had always felt a little afraid of Sikh men, with their martial bearing and their obligatory beards and knives, but here they were at home and surprisingly welcoming. The atmosphere was unlike that in any other place of worship I could remember, with everybody keen to explain the meaning of particular aspects of their religion. Standing together in bare feet with our heads covered by handkerchiefs, an exhaust-fitter from south London told me

427

about the special holiness of the place, and how he came there each year on a pilgrimage.

The train stopped by a water tower while the gun-carrying soldiers talked to some farmers. It was mid-afternoon now. I had arrived at Amritsar railway station early that morning to take the twice-weekly train to Pakistan, and waited for hours while preparations were made for our departure. Sitting on a long bench I had watched while dozy men loaded clusters of fresh ginger, baskets of betel leaves, and jute bags of green tea and bindi seeds onto the train. When this task was eventually completed, the packages had all been removed on the orders of a Customs Officer who said that 'Plantquarantine' rules were being infringed. By some cast-iron steps a dog was rolling in a heap of smouldering ashes, trying to get warm. Its front left leg stuck out from its body at a peculiar angle.

I wandered along the platform in the rain to a man with a handcart, and bought a packet of wafers and a glass of *chai*, ordering the same again for an importunist who stood beside me. At the *Bookstall – Good Literature for Purification*, there was nothing I had not already read that morning, with the exception of the Bollywood magazine *Stardust*. A group of beggars sat nearby. One of them, a youngish man with matted hair and a broad grin, had a scabby stump for an arm, which was wrapped up in cloth and string, like a parcel. Every so often he would flick a scoop of puffed rice to the limping dog, and flies would rise from his blanket for an instant before dropping back. The dog was nervously grateful, hopping backwards and forwards as it ate the food, suspicious at the unexpected generosity.

Back at the train, eight hundred sewing-machines in cardboard boxes were being loaded up, very slowly. A protracted and baffling procedure ensued, involving innumerable pieces of paper and a slow, officious Platform Manager. Then there was a security check, and a customs inspection. Eventually a more senior official arrived and attached a lead seal to the door of the wagon, with string looped through it. Another man dropped lumps of sealing wax onto the string, which were promptly stamped 'Parcels and Luggage' by a colleague, with the aid of a small brass club.

I looked out of the window. The train was still stationary. The distance from Amritsar to Lahore was only forty miles, but it had already taken most of the day to get this far. The soldiers were still chatting to the farmers when the train jumped forward, and began to advance at speed.

Five minutes later we were in Atari, the only rail-crossing between the two nations. It was a small station, overlooked by a concrete watchtower and high walls. Running across it was an endless metal fence, the floodlit electric curtain that divides India and Pakistan. There was a hostile, uncertain, exciting, frightening atmosphere: the feeling of a border. It reminded me of a journey I had made to Warsaw in 1985, passing slowly on a train from West to East Berlin.

At a small table an Indian official with epaulettes sat squarely on a moulded plastic chair. We all lined up in front of him. The Canadian was first. His passport was inspected, and he was told he would have to go to the road-crossing at Wagah, since he had the wrong kind of visa. He went off quite cheerfully. The woman with the 'USA Los Angeles' carpet bag came next. With great certainty, she pulled out a small, grubby piece of paper and handed it across the table.

'Here,' she said, abruptly, 'I have this chit.'

The official looked at it stolidly, and said nothing.

'I have this chit,' she repeated in a firm voice. She had a striking appearance, with a white streak running through her hennaed hair, but her clothes were very dirty. 'Look. It has the number and departure time of my train. Look.'

The official looked. Then he stared at her, and muttered, 'Madam, this is not good.'

'It is a chit,' she replied forcefully, and pulled her carpet bag up to her chest. A group of policemen in khaki trousers and berets came forward, and she was escorted to the Upper Class Gents Waiting Hall.

It was my turn. I gave the official my passport, which he inspected with great care before passing it to a colleague. While the inspection was repeated he filled in a form, and when he had finished he told me, 'You will have to go back to Amritsar.'

'Why?'

'It is too late. You did not reach Atari before 11.30 a.m. That is our latest time for migration.'

'What time does the train usually reach Atari?'

'1.30, 2 o'clock, 2.30,' he answered, as if it was the most normal thing in the world.

'Does it ever arrive before 11.30?'

'Oh no, sir.'

'So nobody can ever get through passport control here?'

He smiled at me as if I were being funny, and said, 'Not on a usual day, not from Amritsar.'

After a long discussion, I was taken to see the Assistant Commissioner of Customs, who relented and gave me the relevant authorization. After being searched, I was allowed through a big metal gate onto the adjacent platform, from which the train to Lahore would depart. I sat down to wait, and watched the Indian Police walking up and down, prodding people with their *lathis*. After some time Mr Sandhu walked through the metal gate. He said that he had spent the previous day at the road-crossing at Wagah, where he had been told he could only cross to Pakistan by rail. Today he had been told the opposite, but had refused to back down, so they had allowed him through.

At 4 o'clock a new train arrived, occupied by about a hundred people. They were mainly Pakistanis who had been in New Delhi for a cricket match. We climbed aboard, and were soon in the strip of no-man's-land which runs between the two frontiers. Beside us galloped an Indian horseman from the Border Security Force, holding a revolver. Everybody in the carriage was silent. In the middle of some wheat fields the train stopped, and I wondered which nation was permitted to harvest the crop. After a while the train started again, and then stopped. Soon we were surrounded by figures in blue, wearing a different style of uniform. We were in the middle of nowhere, but we were in Pakistan.

As we were ordered out of our carriage, a fleshy, moustachioed police officer told us to line up in front of three tables, with the women in a different queue. I stood in the 'Foreigners' Registration Line' with five old Yemeni pilgrims, an Algerian, and a gentle medical student from Kenya called Ignatius. He was studying in Karachi, and said that life in Pakistan was 'more difficult than you could ever imagine', on account of the colour of his skin. While we stood there, I noticed a placid, smiling man with torn clothing and spiked black hair weaving along by the train. He looked as if he was mentally disturbed. I lost sight of him, but a few minutes later saw him being pushed into what looked like a cowshed by a customs official. When he tried to resist he was kicked hard, and collapsed forlornly in some filthy, wet straw, muttering to himself. He stood up, crying and laughing, and the process was repeated a few times.

Back on the train I stopped the fleshy policeman and asked what had happened to the man. At first he could not work out who I was talking about, but when he did he erupted into a rumble of laughter. He was just a fool, he said, an idiot. He travelled backwards and forwards from Amritsar with no papers. Who was he? He was nobody, he was just an idiot, a Bangladeshi Hindu who had found his way to the Punjab, and was now shunted regularly between the two borders. 'We put him on a train to India. The Indians send him back. That is how it is.' The policeman walked off with a swagger, enjoying himself.

There is a well-known short story by Saadat Hasan Manto called 'Toba Tek Singh', about the inmates of a lunatic asylum in Lahore. Under an inter-governmental agreement after independence, the Hindu and Sikh patients are to be sent to India. This causes some confusion, since the spiritual affiliation of several of the asylum's inmates is unclear. One man is so distressed that he climbs into a tree and lectures his comrades 'extensively and non-stop on the matter of Pakistan versus Hindustan. When ordered by the guards to come down, he climbed higher up; when threatened with force, he said, "I want to live neither in Pakistan nor in Hindustan – I will live in the tree." ' Another man becomes so confused that he decides he is the Quaid-i-Azam. This leads a fellow inmate into thinking that he must be Master Tara Singh.

When they are taken by truck to the border at Wagah to be handed over to the Indian authorities, some of the men shout 'Pakistan Zindabad! Pakistan Murdabad!' (Long Live Pakistan! Death to Pakistan!), 'which infuriated both the Muslims and the Sikhs, and altercations between them were avoided with great difficulty'. One man, known only by the name of his home town, Toba Tek Singh, becomes so confused about whether he is meant to be Indian or Pakistani that he begins to spout gibberish, and refuses to move out of the no-man's-land between the two border posts. The guards allow him to remain there, and as morning comes he lets out a piercing cry, and falls to the ground. 'Beyond a wire fence on one side of him was Hindustan, and beyond a wire fence on the other side was Pakistan. In the middle, on a stretch of land which had no name, lay Toba Tek Singh.'[1]

The train started to move again, gathering speed as we advanced further into Pakistan. I could not stop thinking about the man in the cowshed, but it was getting late and I was impatient to reach Lahore.

NOTES

ABBREVIATIONS

OIOC – Oriental and India Office Collections of the British Library

PRO – Public Record Office, Kew

TOP – *Constitutional Relations Between Britain and India: The Transfer of Power 1942–7* (12 volumes), editor-in-chief Nicholas Mansergh, HMSO London 1970–83

In order to reduce the surfeit of hovering numbers in the body of the text, a few successive quotations have been amalgamated into a single note. All references to the P&J and POL(S) documents of IPI (Indian Political Intelligence) are based on the original running file numbers used when they were created. The IPI papers are currently being recatalogued, before being put on general public release at the Oriental and India Office Collections of the British Library. Any unsourced personal recollections come from interviews by the author in Bangladesh, India or Pakistan between January and April 1996. The notes below should be used in conjuction with the Select Bibliography.

INTRODUCTION

1 TOP XII, jacket quotations.
2 See Chatwin, Bruce, *What Am I Doing Here*, London 1989, p. 123.
3 Nehru p. 70.
4 Naipaul, V.S., *An Area of Darkness*, London 1964, p. 201.
5 Chopra *passim*; Sahgal, p. 94; Bose, S.C., *Selected Speeches of Subhas Chandra Bose*, New Delhi 1962, p. 156.
6 Quoted Singh, Anita Inder p. 153.

ONE: Spies and Bomb-Throwers

1 Hardinge pp. 47–51.
2 OIOC Mss. Eur. D1004.
3 Rushdie, Salman, *Imaginary Homelands*, New Delhi 1991, p. 27.
4 Quoted Wolpert, Stanley, *A New History of India*, New York 1993, p. 140.
5 In the last analysis, the Gurkhas of Nepal were the only 'martial race'

that maintained unflinching loyalty to the British authorities.
6 Hardinge pp. 34, 80.
7 It is believed that the Bengali revolutionary Rash Behari Bose, who later backed the Ghadr movement, was responsible for the attack on Lord Hardinge.
8 Popplewell p. 5.
9 Quoted ibid p. 129.
10 OIOC POL(S) 1521/1946. Shortly before the assassination of Sir William Curzon Wyllie, the Department of Criminal Intelligence in India had sent a secret agent of Indian origin, code-named 'C', to infiltrate India House. This took place without the knowledge of the authorities in London.
11 Quoted Popplewell p. 45.
12 Popplewell p. 331; and see Popplewell Chapter 9. See also Hopkirk; and Andrew, Christopher, *Secret Service:*

The Making of the British Intelligence Community, London 1985, pp. 148–53.

13 Quoted Gordon p. 196.
14 Quoted Masani p. 115.
15 See Griffiths, Masani p. 115 and OIOC Mss. Eur. F161/247.
16 Nehru p. 31.
17 See Hopkirk, Sarkar and Chandra.
18 OIOC POL(S) 643/1947; and see Popplewell. See also Hopkirk pp. 386–99, on the fate of Reginald Teague-Jones, alias Ronald Sinclair, who seems to have worked for IPI.

TWO: Two Men from Gujarat

1 This chapter draws on Brown (2), Copley, Mehta, Nanda, Sayid and Wolpert.
2 Moon (2) p. 424.
3 Rushdie, Salman, *Imaginary Homelands*, New Delhi 1991, pp. 102, 105.
4 Brown (2) p. 336.
5 Mehta p. 40.
6 Gandhi, M.K. (2) vol.LXXXVI p. 420.
7 Desai vol.I p.i.
8 Ibid vol.II p. 262.
9 Quoted Mehta p. 13.
10 Author's interview with Ashok Row Kavi, February 1996.
11 Mehta pp. 191–2.
12 Gandhi, M.K. (1) p. 233.
13 Ibid p. 26.
14 Quoted Nanda p. 97.
15 Desai vol.I p. 169.
16 Collins (2) p. 40.
17 Gandhi, M.K. (2) vol.LXXXV p. 514. (In an interview with Louis Fischer, July 1946.)
18 Wolpert p.vii.
19 Quoted ibid p. 33.
20 Quoted ibid p. 42.
21 Ibid pp. 37–8.

THREE: The Force of Truth

1 Tharoor, Shashi, *The Great Indian Novel*, New Delhi 1989, p. 116.
2 Quoted Wolpert pp. 61–2.

3 Popplewell pp. 299–304. Charles Tegart spent time in Britain after the First World War 'undertaking special duties', one of which was to advise the Rowlatt Committee on methods of tackling unrest. In 1918 the Department of Criminal Intelligence was renamed the Department of Central Intelligence, although this was subsequently changed to the Intelligence Bureau.
4 OIOC P&J(S) 991/1937. During his imprisonment before his trial, Udham Singh attempted to escape. He wrote a letter in Urdu to a friend in Streatham saying: 'Get hold of a thick book and in its binding place a saw suitable for cutting iron about ten inches in length, half an inch in breadth can be bought in Woolworth's for 3d. or 6d. . . . Do not fail in this.' As he was under close surveillance by 'a very secret source' (meaning an Indian nationalist who was working as an IPI agent), his plan was foiled, although to be on the safe side the prison authorities sent him to have a bath so that they could search his cell. See OIOC P&J(S) 737/1940, 838/1940, 874/1940.
5 Quoted Menon p. 16. Three months later came an equally significant statement by the British government, namely the Balfour Declaration, in support of 'the establishment of a national home for the Jewish people'.
6 Gallagher p. 102.
7 See Chandra pp. 61–81, OIOC Mss. Eur. F130/-.
8 Desai vol.II p. 236.
9 Quoted Gandhi, Rajmohan, p. 97.
10 Pirzada vol.I pp. 51–2.
11 Desai vol.III p. 154.
12 Chaudhuri p. 19.
13 Quoted Reading, Marquess of, *Rufus Isaacs: First Marquess of Reading* (vol.2), London 1945, p. 152.
14 Quoted ibid, p. 306.

15 Pirzada vol.I pp. 4–5.
16 See Robinson, Francis, *Separatism Among Indian Muslims: The Politics of the United Provinces' Muslims, 1860–1923*, London 1974, Chapter 5.
17 Johal, Sarbjit, *India Fights Colonialism*, London 1995, p. 13.
18 See ibid; and TOP IX pp. 542–3.
19 Sahni pp. 209, 106.
20 Barnes p. 676.
21 Menon p. 1.
22 Quoted Wolpert p. 47.
23 Pirzada vol.III p. 185.
24 Ibid p. 181.
25 Desai vol.II p. 141.
26 Wolpert p. 72.

FOUR: Routes to Freedom
1 Birkenhead pp. 506–7.
2 Campbell-Johnson p. 150.
3 Quoted Krishna p. 124.
4 Nehru p. 27.
5 Krishna pp. 57–8.
6 Birkenhead pp. 515–19. See also Roberts, Andrew, 'The Holy Fox': A Biography of Lord Halifax, London 1991.
7 Quoted Nanda p. 161
8 Quoted Gopal Sarvepalli, *Jawaharlal Nehru: A Biography*, New Delhi 1989, p. 73.
9 On exhibition at Teen Murti, New Delhi.
10 Nehru p. 49.
11 Ibid pp. 73–6. See also Wolpert, Stanley, *Nehru: A Tryst with Destiny*, New York 1996.
12 Quoted Brown (2) p. 234.
13 Chaudhuri p. 47.
14 See Gandhi, Rajmohan, Chapter 1. See also Mehta, C.C., *The Harijan Ashram on Sabarmati*, Ahmedabad 1970.
15 Gandhi M.K., (2) vol.XLIII pp. 3–6.
16 Quoted Krishna p. 139.
17 Pirzada vol.I p. 577.
18 Ibid vol.II p. 127.
19 Chagla p. 53.
20 Ibid pp. 26, 79.
21 Ibid pp. 117–18.

FIVE: The March to the Sea
1 See Gopal, Sarvepalli, *Jawaharlal Nehru: A Biography*, New Delhi 1989, p. 76.
2 See Brown (1) p. 104.
3 See Naidu, Dr Ch.M., *Salt Satyagraha in the Coastal Andhra*, New Delhi 1986.
4 Sarkar p. 287.
5 Quoted Brown (1) p. 108.
6 Bose, Sisir K. (ed.), *Subhas Chandra Bose: Fundamental Questions of Indian Revolution*, Calcutta 1970, p. 6.
7 Nehru p. 293.

SIX: A Half Nude Gent
1 Nehru p. 443.
2 OIOC Mss. Eur. F237/11.
3 Ibid.
4 Brown (2) p. 255.
5 Nehru p. 399.
6 OIOC Mss. Eur. E220/34.
7 Wolpert p. 150.
8 Quoted Aziz p. 92.
9 Ibid p. 20.
10 Robinson, Francis, *Separatism Among Indian Muslims: The Politics of the United Provinces' Muslims, 1860–1923*, London 1974, p. 345.
11 Pimlott, Ben (ed.), *The Second World War Diary of Hugh Dalton 1940-1945*, London 1986, p. 126.
12 Gilbert, Martin, *Winston S. Churchill: Prophet of Truth, 1922–1939*, London 1976, p.xviii.
13 Ibid p. 473.
14 Ibid p. 354.
15 Ibid p. 390.
16 Charmley p. 272.
17 See Gerald Studdert-Kennedy, 'The Christian Imperialism of the Die-Hard Defenders of the Raj, 1926–35', *Journal of Imperial and Commonwealth History*, London October 1990.
18 Nanda p. 243. See also Rhodes James, Robert, *Churchill: A Study in Failure 1900–1939*, London 1970.

19 OIOC Misc. POL(S) files.
20 Nehru p. 154.
21 Popplewell p. 6.
22 Hodson p. 185.
23 OIOC P&J(S) 2061/1940.
24 Andrew, Christopher, *Secret Service: The Making of the British Intelligence Community*, London 1985, p. 277.
25 OIOC P&J(S) 1521/1946. See also OIOC POL(S) 296/46. Communist activists, despite Soviet financial backing, had little success in establishing effective structures within India.
26 OIOC Mss. Eur. F125/22, no. 19.
27 Barnes p. 691.
28 Glendevon p. 22.
29 Ibid pp. 72, 77.
30 Quoted Rizvi p. 36.
31 Brown (2) p. 302.
32 Ibid p. 284.
33 Quoted Gandhi, Rajmohan p. 179.
34 Naipaul, V.S., *India: A Wounded Civilisation*, London 1977, p. 153.
35 Hasan (2) p. 67.
36 Mathai, M.O., *Reminiscences of the Nehru Age*, New Delhi 1978, p. 152.
37 Gandhi, Rajmohan, *India Wins Errors: A Scrutiny of Maulana Azad's* India Wins Freedom, New Delhi 1989, p. 92. *India Wins Errors* has been studiously ignored by most historians, although H.M. Seervai makes a fierce but unsuccessful attempt to refute it in *Partition of India: Legend and Reality* (revised edn) Bombay 1990. See also the chapter on Azad in Ahmad, Aijaz, *Lineages of the Present: Political Essays*, New Delhi 1996.

SEVEN: The Limits of Government

1 OIOC P&J(S) 553/1937.
2 Chandra p. 324.
3 Quoted Krishna p. 179.
4 Quoted Chandra p. 339.
5 OIOC P&J(S) 1120/1938.
6 Shahid p. 174.
7 Hasan (2) p. 422.
8 Kesavan pp. 188–9.
9 Pirzada vol.II p. 274.
10 Jalal p. 38.
11 Quoted Wolpert pp. 147–8.
12 Hardy p. 227. See Chapter 9 for the disparate response of India's Muslims to the League's demands.
13 Rizvi p. 104.
14 Quoted Gordon p. 46.
15 Quoted ibid p. 57. Indians were banned by the War Office from taking part in military service in Britain for fear that they would disrupt the structures of the Indian Army, with its elaborate hierarchies and theories of the 'martial races', when they returned home.
16 Chaudhuri p. 476.
17 See OIOC POL(S) 1521/1946, and five unnumbered files on Subhas Chandra Bose in the OIOC IPI collection.
18 Quoted Gordon p. 375.
19 Moon (2) p. 244.
20 Quoted Krishna p. 194.
21 Pirzada vol.II pp. 305–6.
22 Hutchins p. 179.
23 OIOC Mss. Eur. F125/8, enc. 1–10.
24 Ibid, enc. 2–10.
25 OIOC POL(S) 1256/1944.
26 Ibid 921/1942.
27 OIOC P&J(S) 1220/1941.
28 OIOC POL(S) 2651/1942.
29 Particular targets were Harry Pollitt and Michael Carritt, who were known to be supplying information to Krishna Menon. Pollitt was the General Secretary of the Communist Party of Great Britain, and Carritt was a former ICS officer in Bengal who had become disillusioned with imperialism, and switched sides. In the summer of 1941 a special squad was sent to raid his father's house at Boars Hill in Oxford, as it was believed he was in receipt of material from India relating to the overthrow of British rule. A search found nothing, until a sharp-eyed officer spotted signs of disturbed

earth in the garden. A black tin uniform case was exhumed, and confiscated as evidence. It contained numerous communications with Communist activists in India. See OIOC POL(S) 230/1943.

30 OIOC P&J(S) 471(T)/1937.
31 TOP III pp. 1052–3.
32 TOP IV p. 669.
33 Quoted Rizvi p. 116.
34 Quoted Wolpert p. 181.
35 Pirzada vol.II p. 335.
36 Quotations from both of these resolutions were transcribed from an engraving on a pillar at the Minar-i-Pakistan in Minto Park, Lahore.
37 Jalal pp. 5, 52.
38 Author's interview with Nayantara Sahgal, March 1996.
39 OIOC Mss. Eur. F125/19, no. 94, 4 April 1940.
40 Ibid, no. 127, 8 April 1940.

EIGHT: Outside India

1 Webb, Beatrice, Our Partnership, Cambridge 1975 (first published 1948), p. 269.
2 Storr p. 213.
3 Ibid p. 241.
4 Charmley p. 493.
5 Barnes p. 635.
6 Ibid p. 834.
7 OIOC Mss. Eur. F125/19, no. 271, 30 June 1940.
8 Barnes p. 637.
9 Quoted Jalal p. 62.
10 Rizvi p. 174. It would appear, in retrospect, that plans of this kind were never seriously developed by the Germans and the Japanese. See Thorne.
11 Quoted Glendevon p. 187.
12 Quoted Wolpert p. 193.
13 Enclosure to OIOC POL(S)2295/1941.
14 TOP I p. 14.
15 Ibid p. 75.
16 Ibid pp. 149, 234.
17 Ibid p. 195.
18 Ibid p. 186.

19 Ogden, Christopher, Life of the Party, London 1994, pp. 122–3.
20 Quoted Thorne p. 60.
21 Harriman p. 130.
22 Ibid pp. 126–7.
23 Ibid p. 266.
24 PRO PREMIER 4/42/9/1008.
25 Kimball vol.I p. 374.
26 Ibid p. 395.
27 TOP I p. 403.
28 Ibid p. 420.
29 Rhodes James p. 446.

NINE: Do or Die

1 TOP I p. 173.
2 Ibid p. 295.
3 Ibid p. 601. Linlithgow was not alone in his mangling of Sir Stafford Cripps's name. When I was visiting the Nehru Museum in New Delhi in March 1996, I met an ancient Congress activist called Prabubhai Patel who was up in the capital on a visit from Gujarat using his Freedom Fighter's Rail Pass – which entitled him to free 'Second Class AC' travel. He had met the leader of the Cripps Mission in 1942, and approved of him because he attended one of Gandhi's pujas. Mr Patel referred to the Lord Privy Seal first as Sir Scuppered Creeps, then as Sir Scattered Spliffs, and finally as Sir Craphead Stiffs.
4 Ibid p. 634.
5 Kimball vol.I pp. 400–3.
6 TOP I p. 407.
7 TOP II p. 854.
8 On exhibition at Teen Murti, New Delhi.
9 Gopal (vol.1) p. 286.
10 TOP I p. 641.
11 Barnes p. 786.
12 TOP I p. 704.
13 Kimball vol.I pp. 445–7.
14 Ibid pp. 548–50.
15 Thorne p. 358.
16 Barnes p. 786.
17 Ibid pp. 785–95.
18 Moore, R.J., Churchill, Cripps and

India: 1939–1945, Oxford 1979, p. 122.
19 TOP I pp. 539–40.
20 Jalal p. 79.
21 TOP II p. 50.
22 TOP I pp. 633–4.
23 TOP II p. 226.
24 Ibid p. 43.
25 Ibid p. 141.
26 TOP III p. 236.
27 Sahgal p. 94.
28 OIOC POL(S) 525/1945. See Griffiths for the changing structure of India's police force.
29 TOP II p. 63.
30 Ibid p. 196.
31 Chopra pp. 64–5.
32 TOP II pp. 66–7.
33 Ibid p. 132.
34 Ibid p. 115.
35 Ibid p. 616.
36 Chopra pp. 9–10.
37 TOP II p. 624.
38 Campbell-Johnson p. 57.
39 Quoted Chandra pp. 459–60.

TEN: Blackmail and Terror
1 TOP II p. 807.
2 Akbar p. 349.
3 Quoted Hutchins p. 268.
4 Sahgal p. 37.
5 Mirabehn, *The Spirit's Pilgrimage*, London 1960, p. 242.
6 Chopra p. 16.
7 Ibid p. 115.
8 Ibid pp. 138–9.
9 TOP II p. 865.
10 Chopra p. 185.
11 Ibid p. 193.
12 Ibid p. 102.
13 Ibid p. 188.
14 Ibid p. 277.
15 Quoted Masani p. 119.
16 OIOC Mss. Eur. F161/220.
17 Author's interview with Manorma Dewan, March 1996.
18 Hutchins p. 216.
19 TOP II p. 700.
20 Ibid pp. 869–70.
21 Ibid p. 853.
22 Chopra p. 171.

23 Gopal (vol.1) p. 252.
24 TOP II pp. 629–30.
25 TOP III P.313.
26 Quoted Charmley p. 514.
27 Kimball vol.I p. 563.
28 TOP III p. 690.
29 Ibid p. 749.
30 OIOC POL(S)1977/1943.
31 TOP III p. 3.
32 TOP II p. 920.
33 TOP III p. 143.
34 Ibid p. 209.
35 TOP II p. 833.
36 Ibid p. 683.
37 TOP III p. 684.
38 Ibid p. 737.
39 Quoted Gilbert, Martin, *Winston S. Churchill: Road to Victory 1941–45*, London 1986, p. 343.
40 TOP III p. 738.
41 Quoted Gilbert, *Winston S. Churchill: Road to Victory 1941–45* pp. 350–1.
42 TOP II p. 489.
43 TOP III p. 692.
44 Ibid p. 751.
45 TOP IV p. 26.
46 Ibid p. 148.
47 Ibid p. 187. The stork died of exhaustion the following day.
48 TOP III p. 918.
49 Quoted Moon (1) p. 20.
50 TOP IV p. 756.
51 Ibid p. 324.
52 Barnes p. 832.
53 Ibid p. 836.
54 Pimlott, Ben (ed.), *The Second World War Diary of Hugh Dalton 1940–1945*, London 1986, p. 538.
55 Grigg, John (ed.), *Nehru Memorial Lectures: 1966–1991*, New Delhi 1992, p. 139.
56 TOP I p. 111.
57 Barnes p. 840.
58 Ibid p. 848.
59 Ibid pp. 892–3.

ELEVEN: Living in a Golden Age
1 Author's interview with Willa Walker, October 1996.
2 Rhodes James p. 291.

3 Ibid p. 366.
4 Robert Rhodes James in a letter to the author, 30 July 1996.
5 Rhodes James p. 368.
6 World Congress of Faiths Younghusband Memorial Lecture, 1976.
7 Hodson p. 184.
8 Moon (2) pp. 12, 18.
9 Ibid p. 23.
10 Ibid p. 22.
11 TOP IV p. 376.
12 Barnes p. 946
13 PRO PREMIER 4/46/12/955.
14 Moon (2) p. 33.
15 Barnes p. 690.
16 TOP I p. 111.
17 OIOC POL(S) 2181/1943.
18 Quoted Ziegler p. 220.
19 Quoted ibid p. 247.
20 Moon (2) p. 68.
21 Wolpert p. 226; Moon (2) p. 81.
22 Barnes p. 976.
23 Kimball vol.III p. 117.
24 TOP V p. 35.
25 TOP IV pp. 706–7.
26 Ibid p. 1157.
27 Ibid p. 1194.
28 Moon (2) p. 88.
29 Ibid p. 79.
30 TOP V p. 1.
31 PRO PREMIER 4/46/12/811.
32 TOP V p. 4.
33 Ibid p. 43.
34 Ibid p. 168.
35 Ibid pp. 81–2.
36 Moon (2) p. 111.
37 TOP IV p. 1123.
38 Sarkar p. 357.
39 Quoted Wolpert pp. 232–3.
40 Quoted Ibid p. 236.
41 TOP V p. 91.
42 Moon (2) p. 91.
43 TOP V pp. 111–12.
44 Moon (2) p. 89.
45 Barnes pp. 750, 779.
46 Ibid p. 993.
47 TOP V p. 127-132.
48 Younghusband, Francis, Dawn in India, London 1930, p.ix.
49 TOP V p. 131.
50 Moon (2) p. 93 & TOP V pp. 235, 260.
51 TOP V p. 261.
52 Ibid pp. 296–7.
53 Moon (2) p. 235.
54 TOP V p. 696.

TWELVE: *Dilli Chalo*

1 TOP V p. 733.
2 Moon (2) p. 123.
3 Ibid p. 119.
4 Ibid p. 129.
5 TOP V pp. 340, 342.
6 No file number, but see OIOC POL(S) for January 1945.
7 OIOC POL(S) 525/1945.
8 Ibid 829/1945.
9 Ibid 1369/1945.
10 Ibid 2181/1945.
11 Ibid 1369/1945.
12 PRO CAB 66/65/247–57.
13 Barnett p.xi.
14 Rhodes James pp. 403–4.
15 TOP V p. 1258.
16 Moon (2) pp. 146–7.
17 TOP V p. 1125.
18 Barnes p. 1045.
19 TOP V p. 1262–3.
20 Moon (2) p. 151.
21 Chaudhuri p. 646.
22 Ibid p. 781; and see Asian Age, London, 27 January 1997.
23 Times of India, 24 January 1996.
24 Quoted Gordon p. 441.
25 With the help of Military Intelligence, IPI collected detailed information on the wartime activities of Indians in Germany during 1939–1945. See OIOC IPI files.
26 Quoted Gordon p. 476.
27 Bose, Sisir K. (ed.), Subhas Chandra Bose: Fundamental Questions of Indian Revolution, Calcutta 1970, p. 87.
28 Tape-recording of the speeches of Subhas Bose, sold at the Mumbai Netaji Bose Exhibition, February 1996.

29 See Sahgal, Dr Lakshmi and Col, P.K., *Netaji Subhas Chandra Bose*, New Delhi 1993.
30 TOP IV pp. 1032–3.
31 Toye, Hugh, *The Springing Tiger: A Study of a Revolutionary*, London 1959 (Appendix II), pp. 215–17.
32 See OIOC POL(S) 127/1945.
33 TOP V pp. 1284–5
34 TOP VI p. 1.
35 OIOC POL(S) 68/1947. This account corresponds closely to the version of events pieced together by Bose's biographer, Leonard Gordon. See Gordon pp. 539–43.
36 TOP VI pp. 279–80.
37 Ibid pp. 512–13.
38 TOP VII p. 1092.
39 TOP VI p. 587.
40 Author's interview with K.G. Mustafa, February 1996.

THIRTEEN: A Mass Battle for Freedom
1 TOP VI p. 57.
2 Wyatt p. 139.
3 TOP VI p. 57.
4 Ibid p. 41.
5 Charmley p. 649.
6 TOP VI p. 71-72.
7 Moon (2) pp. 169–70.
8 Rhodes James pp. 412–13.
9 Author's interview with Roger Ellis, August 1996.
10 Moon (2) p. 180.
11 TOP VI pp. 451–3.
12 Ibid p. 484.
13 See ibid p. 486.
14 Ibid p. 577.
15 Moon (2) p. 201.
16 TOP VI p. 313.
17 Ibid p. 739.
18 Wyatt p. 124.
19 TOP VI p. 589.
20 Ibid p. 950.
21 Ibid p. 699.
22 Ibid p. 701. See the introduction to Zaidi, Z.H. (ed.) vol.2 for an analysis of the genesis of these demarcations of Pakistan.

23 TOP VI p. 913.
24 Ibid p. 912.
25 Ibid annex to no.428, OIOC L/PO/6/114:f166.
26 Ibid p. 965.
27 Moon (2) p. 206.
28 Quoted Masani p. 126.
29 Hasan (1) vol.1 p. 44.
30 Jalal p. 135.
31 Talbot, Ian A., 'The Growth of the Muslim League in the Punjab, 1937–46', in Hasan (2) p. 256. See also Gilmartin, David, 'Religious Leadership and the Pakistan Movement in the Punjab', ibid.
32 Singh, Anita Inder, p. 135.
33 Moon (2) p. 225.

FOURTEEN: A Large Piece of Green Baize
1 TOP VI p. 592.
2 Ibid p. 833.
3 TOP VII p. 3.
4 Quoted Gopal (vol.1) p. 286.
5 Wyatt p. 136.
6 Moon (2) p. 235.
7 Ibid p. 247.
8 Quoted Mosley p. 21.
9 Pirzada, vol.II, p. 520.
10 Moon (2) pp. 235–6.
11 Ibid pp. 278–9.
12 Ibid p. 301.
13 Ibid pp. 249–50.
14 TOP I p. 541.
15 TOP VII p. 527.
16 Moon (2) pp. 239, 249.
17 OIOC POL(S) 97/46.
18 Ibid 296/46.
19 Ibid 680/1946.
20 Ibid 1521/1946.
21 Ibid 1521/1846 (JIC(46) 50th meeting (C) Item I).
22 TOP VII p. 261.
23 Ibid p. 260.
24 PRO CAB 128/5, 11 April 1946.
25 Wyatt p. 149.
26 Moon (2) p. 259.
27 Krishna p.xv.
28 TOP VII p. 82.

29 Moon (2) pp. 26–7.
30 TOP VII p. 310.
31 Ibid p. 525.
32 Ibid pp. 622, 637.
33 Ibid p. 1029.
34 Ibid pp. 642, 660.
35 Ibid p. 790.
36 Ibid p. 791.
37 Ibid pp. 830–1.
38 Ibid p. 955.
39 Ibid p. 1039.
40 See Moon (2) p. 313.
41 TOP VII p. 1072.

FIFTEEN: Leave Her to Her Fate
1 Wyatt p. 135.
2 Moon (2) p. 316.
3 Ibid p. 321.
4 Ibid p. 368.
5 Ranfurly, Countess of, To War With Whitaker, London 1994, p. 90.
6 TOP VII pp. 1090–3.
7 Moon (2) pp. 261, 429.
8 TOP VIII p. 772.
9 TOP VII pp. 1094–5.
10 TOP VIII p. 517.
11 Ibid p. 15.
12 Ibid p. 167.
13 Moon (2) p. 333.
14 TOP VIII p. 18.
15 Ibid p. 106.
16 Ibid pp. 138–9.
17 Zaidi, Z.H. (ed.) vol.1 p.xiii.
18 Moon (2) p. 212.
19 TOP VIII p. 201.
20 Gandhi, M.K. (2), vol.LXXXV p. 130.
21 Moon (2) p. 336.
22 TOP VIII p. 225.
23 Ibid p. 227.
24 TOP IX p. 197.
25 Asian Age, London, 17 July 1996.
26 TOP VIII, enclosure to document 197.
27 Moon (2) p. 210.
28 Quoted Singh, Anita Inder, p. 187.
29 TOP VIII, enclosure to document 197.
30 Gandhi, M.K. (2) vol.LXXXV pp. 215–16.

31 Ibid p. 518.
32 TOP VIII pp. 328-329.
33 See TOP IX p. 19.

SIXTEEN: A Secret Coup
1 TOP VIII p. 772.
2 OIOC POL(S) 1521/1946.
3 Ibid 263/1947.
4 See Griffiths.
5 OIOC POL(S) 1521/1946.
6 Moon (2) p. 383.
7 TOP VIII, document 286.
8 TOP IX p. 69.
9 TOP VIII pp. 621–3.
10 Ibid pp. 796–8.
11 Campbell-Johnson pp. 54–5.
12 Quoted Gandhi, Rajmohan, p. 379.
13 Hosain, Attia, Sunlight on a Broken Column, New Delhi 1992 (1st edn 1961) p. 308.
14 Sahgal, Nayantara, Rich Like Us, London 1985, p. 58.
15 Nehru p. 539.
16 Quoted Gopal (vol.1) p. 235.
17 Sahgal p. 129.
18 Chaudhuri p. 452.
19 Mathai, M.O., Reminiscences of the Nehru Age, New Delhi 1978, p. 203.
20 Gopal p. 105.
21 Author's interview with Pamela Hicks, August 1996.
22 Nehru p. 136.
23 'The 1947 Partition'; lecture to the Centre for South Asian Studies, Cambridge, February 1969.
24 TOP IX p. 803.
25 OIOC POL(S) 1521/1846.
26 TOP XI p. 244.
27 OIOC POL(S) 1521/1946.
28 TOP IX p. 2.
29 Ibid pp. 74–5.
30 Ibid pp. 119, 197.
31 Quoted Harris, Kenneth, Attlee, London 1995 (revised edn), p. 552.
32 Dwarkadas pp. 190–1, 224.
33 Kesavan p. 176.
34 TOP IX pp. 431–2.
35 Moon (2) pp. 397–409.
36 Ibid pp. 402–3.

SEVENTEEN: Our Previous Prestige

1 TOP IX p. 583.
2 Ibid p. 624.
3 Moon (2) pp. 419, 437.
4 See TOP VI p. 872.
5 TOP IX pp. 510, 451. Mountbatten was responsible for propagating the term 'the British Raj', or 'the Raj', as a way of referring to Britain's Indian Empire. It rarely appears before 1947, and is not generally used in India today, since 'Raj' simply means 'rule', and could apply equally well to Ram Raj, Permit Raj or Congress Raj. 'Angrezi Sarkar' was the term used at the time by Indians, while the British usually referred to the 'Indian Empire'.
6 Harris, Kenneth, *Attlee*, London 1995 (revised edn), p. 362.
7 TOP IX p. 972.
8 Pitts, Denis (ed.), *Clem Attlee: The Granada Historical Records Interview*, London 1967, p. 42.
9 See Menon pp. 358–9. In late 1946 Wavell had become worried that V.P. Menon was turning into the 'mouthpiece' of Patel.
10 Quoted Krishna p. 277.
11 Quoted Brown (2) p. 369.
12 Grigg, John (ed.), *Nehru Memorial Lectures: 1966–1991*, New Delhi 1992, p. 22.
13 Campbell-Johnson p. 29.
14 Quoted Mosley p. 81.
15 TOP IX p. 804; Moon (2) p. 212.
16 OIOC POL(S) 1681/1947.
17 Ibid 263/47.
18 Ibid 327/1947.
19 Quoted Ziegler p. 356.
20 Quoted Hodson p. 204.
21 Rhodes James p. 360.
22 The mistress was Alice Keppel, later described by Virginia Woolf as 'a swarthy thick set raddled direct old grasper'. See Souhami, Diana, *Mrs Keppel and her Daughter*, London 1996.
23 Quoted Ziegler p. 69.
24 Quoted Morgan pp. 198–9.
25 Author's interview with Alan Campbell-Johnson, August 1996.
26 Smith, Charles, *Fifty Years with Mountbatten*, London 1980, p. 46.
27 Windsor, Duchess of, *The Heart has its Reasons*, London 1956, pp. 206–7.
28 Author's interview with Alan Campbell-Johnson, August 1996.
29 Ziegler pp. 666–7.
30 Collins (2) pp. 37, 64, 44.
31 Gandhi, M.K. (2) vol.LXXXV p. 514.
32 Collins (2) pp. 24–5.
33 Moon (2) p. 34.
34 Quoted Hoey, Brian, *Mountbatten: The Private Story*, London 1994, p. 145.
35 'The 1947 Partition'; lecture to the Centre for South Asian Studies, Cambridge, February 1969.
36 Hough, Richard, *Mountbatten: Hero of our Time*, London 1980, pp. 230, 217.
37 1997 Longman/*History Today* Awards Lecture.
38 Roberts p. 55.
39 Ibid p. 61.
40 Author's interview with Pamela Hicks, August 1996.
41 Author's interview with Alan Campbell-Johnson, August 1996.
42 Healey, Denis, *The Time of my Life*, London 1989, p. 258.
43 'The 1947 Partition'; lecture to the Centre for South Asian Studies, Cambridge, February 1969.
44 Cannadine, David, *The Pleasures of the Past*, London 1989, p. 65.
45 Quoted Wingate, Ronald, *Lord Ismay: A Biography*, London 1970, p. 145.

EIGHTEEN: Liberty

1 Author's interview with Pamela Hicks, August 1996. Hour-by-hour accounts of Mountbatten's negotiations thoughout his viceroyalty can be found in TOP X–XII.

2 Campbell-Johnson p. 34.
3 Quoted Masani p. 127.
4 Author's interview with Nayantara Sahgal, March 1996.
5 TOP X pp. 11–12; Campbell-Johnson p. 44.
6 TOP X p. 425.
7 Campbell-Johnson p. 46.
8 Smith, Charles, *Fifty Years with Mountbatten*, London 1980, p. 79.
9 TOP X pp. 69–70.
10 Campbell-Johnson p. 52.
11 TOP X p. 141.
12 Ibid pp. 124–5.
13 Ibid p. 138.
14 Ibid pp. 159–60.
15 Ibid p. 300.
16 Ibid p. 164.
17 See p. 55; and see Sahgal.
18 Das vol.4 p. 43. See Rashid for a detailed account of the claim for Bengali autonomy or independence.
19 TOP X p. 324.
20 Gandhi, M.K. (2) vol.LXXXVII p. 223.
21 TOP X p. 302.
22 Ibid p. 511.
23 Moon (1) p. 63.
24 TOP X p. 716.
25 Ibid p. 755.
26 Mathai, M.O., *Reminiscences of the Nehru Age*, New Delhi 1978, p. 209.
27 TOP X p. 836.
28 Ibid p. 756.
29 Campbell-Johnson p. 89.
30 Ziegler p. 380.
31 TOP X p. 763.
32 Menon, V.P., *The Story of the Integration of the Indian States*, London 1956, p. 258.
33 TOP X p. 27.
34 Menon p. 365.
35 Collins (2) p. 31.
36 Zaidi, Z.H. (ed.) vol.1 p. 973.
37 TOP XI p. 39.
38 Campbell-Johnson p. 101.
39 TOP XI p. 48.
40 Ismay, Hastings, *The Memoirs of Lord Ismay*, London 1960, p. 424.

Mountbatten's own description of this meeting was more colourful. See Campbell-Johnson p. 103, and Collins (1) pp. 158–60.
41 TOP X pp. 11–12.
42 TOP XI p. 53.
43 Das vol.4 p. 125.
44 Campbell-Johnson p. 108.
45 Mountbatten pp. 43–5; TOP XI p. 238. In later life, Mountbatten pretended that the early date for the transfer of power was chosen on the spur of the moment at the press conference, when in fact it had already been decided some time earlier by the India Office.
46 TOP XI p. 192.
47 Campbell-Johnson p.xii.
48 Author's interview with Roger Ellis, August 1996; TOP XI p. 279.
49 Quoted Menon p. 385.
50 Pirzada vol.III p. 429.
51 See TOP XI docs 129, 130, 153.
52 Campbell-Johnson pp. 28–9.
53 Quoted Ziegler p. 358.
54 TOP XII p. 215.
55 *Asian Studies Review* (Monash), vol.19, no.3, April 1996, p. 60.
56 TOP IX p. 231.
57 Campbell-Johnson p. 139.
58 Ibid p. 142.
59 Quoted Ziegler p. 409.
60 Author's interview with the Nawab of Palanpur, March 1996.
61 TOP XI p. 930. The States Department did not technically become a ministry until later in 1947.
62 Quoted Krishna pp. 296–323.
63 TOP XI pp. 347, 481.
64 Author's interview with Alan Campbell-Johnson, August 1996.
65 TOP XII p. 339.
66 Author's interview with Anwar Ahmed Hanafi, March 1996.
67 Hasan (1) vol.1 p. 244.
68 See OIOC POL(S) 1521/1846.
69 TOP XII p. 255.
70 Campbell-Johnson p. 156.
71 Pitts, Denis (ed.), *Clem Attlee: The*

Granada Historical Records Interview, London 1967, pp. 42–3.
72 TOP XI p. 435.
73 TOP XII p. 770; Campbell-Johnson p. 155.
74 See Mathai, M.O., *Reminiscences of the Nehru Age*, New Delhi 1978. Nehru's speech is quoted in Gopal (1) p. 362.
75 TOP XII p. 773.

NINETEEN: A Communal War of Succession

1 Quoted Heward, Edmund, *The Great and the Good: A Life of Lord Radcliffe*, Chichester 1994, p. 240.
2 Zaidi, Z.H. (ed.) vol.2 p. 296.
3 Quoted Hennessy, Peter, *The Great and the Good*, London 1986, p. 30.
4 See TOP XI p. 931.
5 Grigg, John (ed.), *Nehru Memorial Lectures: 1966–1991*, New Delhi 1992, p. 37.
6 Abell Papers, private collection. Note by Ian Scott, 29 February 1992. See also TOP XII pp. 290–1.
7 Author's interview with Alastair Lamb, August 1996.
8 See TOP VI p. 912 and TOP VI annex to no.428, which depicts Gurdaspur as part of 'Pakistan'.
9 TOP X p. 759.
10 TOP XI p. 292.
11 Ibid p. 342.
12 See ibid pp. 293, 580.
13 Campbell-Johnson p. 151.
14 See TOP XII p. 611; Jha pp. 141–3; Moon (1) p. 91; Hamid p. 222; Ali, Chaudhri Muhammad, *The Emergence of Pakistan*, Lahore 1973, pp. 217–19. Theorists about the change in the border include Lamb pp. 101–20; Lamb, Alastair, *Birth of a Tragedy: Kashmir 1947*, Karachi 1994, pp. 24–41; Roberts pp. 91–101; Pirzada, S.S., *Radcliffe Award: A Note*, Islamabad c.1984, pp. 40–57; and Shah, Nasim Hasan, *Frontier of Pakistan: Trust Betrayed*, Lahore 1995, pp. 1–19. Christopher Beaumont's account of Radcliffe being instigated to change the Punjab boundary at a lunch on 12 August is undermined by the fact that George Abell's 'eliminate salient' secraphone message had already been sent on either 10 or 11 August. See TOP XII p. 579.
15 TOP XII p. 619.
16 Sadullah, Mian Muhammad, *The Partition of the Punjab 1947: A Compilation of Official Documents*, vol.1, Lahore 1983, p. 245.
17 Abell Papers, private collection. Note by Ian Scott, 29 February 1992.
18 TOP XII p. 579.
19 See ibid p. 249.
20 Ibid p. 638.
21 Private collection, 29 June 1947.
22 Quoted Heward, Edmund, *The Great and the Good: A Life of Lord Radcliffe*, p. 42.
23 Author's conversation with Peter Hennessy, July 1996.
24 Quoted Mosley p. 200.
25 OIOC L/P&J/10/119.
26 TOP X p. 894.
27 Quoted Singh, Khushwant, *A History of the Sikhs* (vol.2), New Delhi 1991 (revised edn), p. 252.
28 TOP II p. 770. The idea of a Sikh homeland or 'Khalistan' was revived with a vengeance in the early 1980s.
29 See Singh, Patwant, *The Sikhs and the Challenge of the Eighties*, in O'Connell, Joseph (ed.), *Sikh History and Religion in the Twentieth Century*, Toronto 1988.
30 See Jeffrey, Robin, 'The Punjab Boundary Force and the Problem of Order, August 1947', *Modern Asian Studies* (Cambridge), vol.8, 1974, p. 494.
31 Quoted Moon (1) p. 77.
32 Quoted Hasan (1) vol.2 p. 147.
33 Mehta, Ved, *The Ledge Between the Streams*, London 1984, p. 313.
34 TOP X p. 894.
35 Ibid p. 694.

36 Ibid p. 1009.
37 TOP XI p. 87.
38 Ibid p. 606.
39 TOP XII pp. 73–4. See also ibid p. 429.
40 Ibid p. 512.
41 Ibid p. 637. Indira Gandhi would doubtless have concurred with Sir Evan's statement.
42 Sadullah, *The Partition of the Punjab 1947*, vol.1, p. 245.
43 TOP XII, pp. 675, 709. At a meeting of the Joint Defence Council on 16 August, Mountbatten admitted that 'the present series of disturbances had started on the 9th August'. See *Disturbances in the Punjab, 1947*, National Documentation Centre, Islamabad, 1995, p. 351.
44 Quoted Hodson, Appendix II, p. 550.
45 Ibid p. 186.
46 Campbell-Johnson p. 150.
47 Das vol.4 p. 141.
48 TOP XII p. 559.
49 OIOC POL(S) 1681/44.
50 Ibid 643/1947.
51 Das vol.3 p. 226.
52 Hennessy p. 299. See also Barnett, Correlli, *The Lost Victory: British Dreams, British Realities 1945–1950*, London 1995.
53 Gallagher p. 79.

TWENTY: Death

1 Quoted Connell, John, *Auchinleck*, London 1959, p. 878; TOP X p. 423.
2 Connell, *Auchinleck*, p. 887.
3 TOP XII p. 95.
4 Quoted Connell, *Auchinleck*, pp. 920–1.
5 Quoted Gopal (vol.2) p. 14; Gopal, Sarvepalli, *Jawaharlal Nehru: A Biography*, New Delhi 1989, p. 175.
6 Nehru p. 242.
7 TOP IX p. 534.
8 Campbell-Johnson p. 123.
9 TOP XII p. 257. See also ibid note 3, p. 61.
10 Jeffrey, Robin, 'The Punjab Boundary Force and the Problem of Order, August 1947', *Modern Asian Studies* (Cambridge), vol.8, 1974, p. 499.
11 Stevens, G.R., *Fourth Indian Division*, London n.d. (c.1948), pp. 406–7.
12 Hasan (1) vol.1 p. 99.
13 Chaudhuri p. 856.
14 Quoted Lapping, Brian, *End of Empire*, London 1985, p. 95; Heren, Louis, *Memories of Times Past*, London 1988, p. 82. See also Moon (1); Mosley; Roberts and Stephens, Ian, *Pakistan*, London 1964. The semi-official Indian publication *Stern Reckoning: A Survey of the Events leading up to and Following the Partition of India*, New Delhi 1989 (1st edn 1949), by the Punjab's former High Court Chief Justice, Gopal Das Khosla, has a detailed analysis of the massacres and migrations, but is diminished by its anti-Muslim prejudice.
15 Moon (1) p. 9.
16 Jalal, Ayesha, 'Secularists, Subalterns and the Stigma of "Communalism": Partition Historiography Revisited', *Modern Asian Studies* (Cambridge), vol.30, part 3, July 1996, p. 681
17 Hasan (1) vol.2 p. 10.
18 Private collection.
19 Singh, Khushwant, p. 48.
20 Quoted Hasan (1) vol.1 p. 33.
21 Bhalla vol.1 p. 147.
22 Author's interview with Marn Singh, March 1996.
23 Author's interview with Mushirul Hasan, March 1996.
24 Hasan (1) vol.2 p. 102.
25 Author's interview with Narinder Singh Soch, March 1996; Shahid p. 87.
26 Author's interview with Nirmal Mangat Rai, March 1996.
27 See Heren, Louis, *Memories of Times Past*, London 1988.
28 Author's interview with Ataus Samad, February 1996.

29 Author's interview with Mumtaz Ahmed Khan, March 1996.

30 Author's interview with Hashim Raza, April 1996.

31 Author's interview with Aileen Fisher Rowe, July 1996.

32 Hasan (1) vol.1 p. 185.

33 Author's interview with Urvashi Butalia, February 1996.

34 See Butalia, Urvashi, 'Community, State and Gender: Some Reflections on the Partition of India', *Oxford Literary Review*, c.1993; and see Menon, Ritu and Bhasin, Kamla, 'Recovery, Rupture, Resistance: Indian State and Abduction of Women During Partition', *Economic and Political Weekly* (Bombay), vol.28, no. 17, 24 April 1993.

35 Author's interview with Nirmal Verma, March 1996.

TWENTY-ONE: Midnight's Parents

1 Campbell-Johnson p. 177; and see Mathai, M.O., *Reminiscences of the Nehru Age*, New Delhi 1978, who claims that Mountbatten cajoled Nehru into recommending the last Viceroy to King George VI for a marquessate, the request being turned down by Tommy Lascelles.

2 Author's interviews with Pamela Hicks, August 1996, and Nayantara Sahgal, March 1996; and see Mathai, Morgan and Ziegler.

3 TOP I p. 807.

4 Hasan (1) vol.2 p. 221.

5 Author's interview with Rajmohan Gandhi, March 1996.

6 Campbell-Johnson p. 257.

7 Das vol.4 pp. 297–8.

8 Campbell-Johnson p. 197.

9 Choudhary, Valmiki (ed.), *Dr Rajendra Prasad: Correspondence and Select Documents*, vol.8, New Delhi 1987, pp. 180–2.

10 Quoted Jaffrelot p. 86; Das vol.6 p. 179.

11 Malgonkar, Manohar, *The Men Who Killed Gandhi*, New Delhi 1978, p. 85.

12 Gandhi, M.K. (2) vol.XC p. 436.

13 Campbell-Johnson p. 276.

14 Author's interview with Nayantara Sahgal, March 1996.

15 Das vol.6 p. 28.

16 Brown (2) p. 394.

17 Heren, Louis, *Growing up on* The Times, London 1978, p. 56.

18 Jinnah pp. 16–18.

19 Quoted Wolpert p. 343.

20 See Zaidi vols 1 and 2. One aspiring member of the Jinnah entourage was Mohammad Anwar Khan, a Staff Captain at GHQ in Delhi whose interests were 'rugger, riding and swimming', and who had been educated at Stowe before joining the Oxfordshire and Buckinghamshire Light Infantry. Although he told Jinnah it would be 'the greatest honour' to serve under him, his offer appears to have been declined. Despite his conversion to Islam, Mohammad Anwar Khan's friends in the regiment still knew him by his given name, Captain Godfrey Hoare.

21 Collins (1) pp. 109–10.

22 See Zaidi, Z.H., 'Jinnah's Health and his Doctors: Myth and Reality', published in *Dawn*, Karachi, 25 December 1994. I am indebted to Dr Zaidi for supplying me with an original copy of his paper.

23 Jalal, Ayesha, *Democracy and Authoritarianism in South Asia*, Cambridge 1995, p. 9.

24 See Sisson.

25 Quoted Menon, V.P., *The Story of the Integration of the Indian States*, London 1956, p. 489.

26 Campbell-Johnson p. 322.

27 See Singh, Amir Kaur Jasbir, *Himalayan Triangle: A Historical Survey of British India's Relations with Tibet, Sikkim and Bhutan, 1765-1950*, London 1988

28 TOP XI p. 309.

29 Singh, Karan, *Autobiography* (revised edn), New Delhi 1994, p. 20.
30 Letter from Frank Messervy to Roy Bucher, 4 March 1969, in a private collection.
31 TOP XII pp. 213–14.
32 See Hodson p. 354.
33 Author's interview with Karan Singh, March 1996.
34 Singh, Karan, *Autobiography* p. 59.
35 Quoted Hodson p. 452.
36 Interview with Sam Manekshaw, in Jha p. 135.
37 Campbell-Johnson p. 230.
38 Quoted Gandhi, Rajmohan, pp. 24–5.
39 See Das vol.I; Jha; Krishna; Lamb; Lamb, Alastair, *Birth of a Tragedy: Karshmir 1947*, Karachi 1994; and Menon, V.P., *The Story of the Integration of the Indian States*, London 1956. The question of the Maharajah of Kashmir's accession to India is complicated by the apparent disappearance of the relevant document from the archives.
40 Letter from Frank Messervy to Roy Bucher, 25 February 1969, in a private collection.
41 Das vol.4 p. 502
42 Quoted Wingate, Ronald, *Lord Ismay: A Biography*, London 1970, p. 173.
43 Ismay p. 439.
44 Andrew, Christopher, *For the President's Eyes Only: Secret Intelligence and the American Presidency from Washington to Bush*, London 1995, p. 517.
45 Author's interview with Karan Singh, March 1996. See also Singh, Tavleen, *Kashmir: A Tragedy of Errors*, New Delhi 1995.

TWENTY-TWO: No Bitterness

1 Das vol.10 pp. 19–23.
2 Quoted Jaffrelot, p. 101.
3 See ibid, Appendix B. These are official figures, and probably underestimate the real numbers of people killed.
4 Hewitt, Vernon, *Reclaiming the Past*, London 1995, p. 134. See also Hasan, Mushirul, *Legacy of a Divided Nation: India's Muslims from Independence to Ayodhya*, London 1997; and Khilnani, Sunil, *The Idea of India*, London 1997.
5 See Jaffrelot p. 383.

TWENTY-THREE: Wrestling with Crocodiles

1 Hamid pp. xxix–xxx, 44, 224, 230, 235, 292, 197–201.

TWENTY-FOUR: Awaiting Full Integration

1 Jinnah p. 26.
2 Ibid pp. 97–106.

EPILOGUE

1 Bhalla vol.III pp. 1–7.

SELECT BIBLIOGRAPHY

Akbar, M.J., *Nehru: The Making of India*, London 1988

Azad, Maulana Abul Kalam, *India Wins Freedom* (revised edn), New Delhi 1988

Aziz, K.K., *Rahmat Ali: A Biography*, Lahore 1987

Barnes, John and Nicholson, David (eds), *The Empire at Bay: The Leo Amery Diaries, 1929–1945*, London 1988

Bhalla, Alok, *Stories About the Partition of India* (3 vols), New Delhi 1994

Birkenhead, Earl of, *F.E.: The Life of F.E. Smith*, London 1959

Brown, Judith (1), *Gandhi and Civil Disobedience: The Mahatma in Indian politics 1928–1934*, Cambridge 1977

Brown, Judith (2), *Gandhi: Prisoner of Hope*, New Haven 1989

Campbell-Johnson, Alan, *Mission with Mountbatten*, London 1972 (1st edn 1951)

Campbell Ker, James, *Political Trouble in India 1907–1917*, New Delhi 1973 (1st edn 1917)

Chagla, M.C., *Roses in December: An Autobiography*, Bombay 1974

Chandra, Bipan, *India's Struggle for Independence*, New Delhi 1988

Charmley, John, *Churchill: The End of Glory*, London 1993

Chaudhuri, Nirad, *Thy Hand, Great Anarch!*, London 1987

Chopra, P.N. (ed.), *Quit India Movement: British Secret Documents*, New Delhi 1986

Collins, Larry and Lapierre, Dominique (1), *Freedom at Midnight*, London 1975

Collins, Larry and Lapierre, Dominique (2), *Mountbatten and the Partition of India* (vol. 1), New Delhi 1982

Copley, Antony, *Gandhi: Against the Tide*, Calcutta 1993 (1st edn 1987)

Coupland, Reginald, *The Cripps Mission*, London 1942

Das, Durga (ed.), *Sardar Patel's Correspondence 1945–50* (10 vols), Ahmedabad 1971–74

Desai, Mahadev, *Day-to-Day with Gandhi*, Varanasi 1968

Dwarkadas, Kanji, *Ten Years to Freedom*, Bombay 1968

Gallagher, John, *The Decline, Revival and Fall of the British Empire*, London 1982

Gandhi, M.K. (1), *An Autobiography*, Ahmedabad 1927

Gandhi, M.K. (2), *The Collected Works of Mahatma Gandhi* (90 vols), New Delhi 1969–1984

Gandhi, Rajmohan, *The Good Boatman*, New Delhi 1995

Glendevon, John, *The Viceroy at Bay: Lord Linlithgow in India 1936–1943*, London 1971

Gopal, Sarvepalli, *Jawaharlal Nehru: A Biography* (3 vols), London 1975–84

Gordon, Leonard, *Brothers Against the Raj: A Biography of Sarat and Subhas Chandra Bose*, New Delhi 1990

Griffiths, Percival, *To Guard My People: The History of the Indian Police*, London 1971

Hamid, Shahid, *Disastrous Twilight: A Personal Record of the Partition of India* (revised edn), Barnsley 1993

Hardinge, Lord, *My Indian Years: 1910–1916*, London 1948

Hardy, Peter, *The Muslims of British India*, London 1972

Harriman, W. Averell and Abel, Elie, *Special Envoy to Churchill and Stalin*, New York 1975

Hasan, Mushirul (ed.) (1), *India Partitioned: The Other Face of Freedom* (2 vols), New Delhi 1995

Hasan, Mushirul (ed.) (2), *India's Partition: Process, Strategy and Mobilization*, New Delhi 1993

Hennessy, Peter, *Never Again*, London 1992

Hodson, H.V., *The Great Divide: Britain – India – Pakistan* (revised edn), Karachi 1985

Hopkirk, Peter, *On Secret Service East of Constantinople*, London 1994

Hutchins, Francis, *Spontaneous Revolution: The Quit India Movement*, New Delhi 1971

Ismay, Hastings, *The Memoirs of Lord Ismay*, London 1960

Jaffrelot, Christophe, *The Hindu Nationalist Movement and Indian Politics, 1925 to the 1990s*, London 1996

Jalal, Ayesha, *The Sole Spokesman: Jinnah, the Muslim League and the Demand for Pakistan*, Lahore 1995 (1st edn 1985)

Jha, Prem Shankar, *Kashmir, 1947: Rival Versions of History*, New Delhi 1996

Jinnah, Mohammad Ali, *Speeches*, Lahore 1989

Judd, Denis, *Empire: The British Imperial Experience, from 1765 to the Present*, London 1996

Kesavan, Mukul, *Looking Through Glass*, London 1995

Khan, Abdul Wali, *Facts are Sacred*, Peshawar n.d. (c.1986)

Kimball, Warren F. (ed.), *Churchill and Roosevelt: The Complete Correspondence* (3 vols), Princeton 1984

Korejo, M.S., *The Frontier Gandhi: His Place in History*, Karachi 1994

Krishna, B., *Sardar Vallabhbhai Patel: India's Iron Man*, New Delhi 1995

Lamb, Alastair, *Kashmir: A Disputed Legacy*, Hertingfordbury 1991

Masani, Zareer, *Indian Tales of the Raj*, London 1987

Mehta, Ved, *Mahatma Gandhi and his Apostles*, New Haven 1993 (1st edn 1977)

Menon, V.P., *The Transfer of Power in India*, Madras 1957

Moon, Penderel (1), *Divide and Quit*, London 1961

Moon, Penderel (ed.) (2), *Wavell: The Viceroy's Journal*, London 1973

Morgan, Janet, *Edwina Mountbatten: A Life of her Own*, London 1991

Mosley, Leonard, *The Last Days of the British Raj*, London 1961

Mountbatten of Burma, Earl, *Time Only to Look Forward*, London 1949

Nanda, B.R., *Mahatma Gandhi* (revised edn), New Delhi 1989

Nehru, Jawaharlal, *An Autobiography*, London 1936

Pirzada, Syed Sharifuddin (ed.), *Foundations of Pakistan: All-India Muslim League Documents: 1906–1947* (3 vols), Karachi 1969–1990

Popplewell, Richard, *Intelligence and Imperial Defence: British Intelligence and the Defence of the Indian Empire, 1904–1924*, London 1995

Rashid, Harun-or, *The Foreshadowing of Bangladesh: Bengal Muslim League and Muslim Politics, 1936–1947*, Dhaka 1987

Rhodes James, Robert (ed.), *Chips: The Diaries of Sir Henry Channon*, London 1967

Rizvi, Gowher, *Linlithgow and India: A Study of British Policy and the Political Impasse, 1936–43*, London 1978

Roberts, Andrew, *Eminent Churchillians*, London 1994

Royle, Trevor, *The Last Days of the Raj*, London 1989

Rushdie, Salman, *Midnight's Children*, London 1981

Sahgal, Nayantara, *Prison and Chocolate Cake*, London 1954

Sahni, Bhisham, *Tamas*, New Delhi 1988 (1st edn in Hindi, 1974)

Saiyid, Matlubul Hasan, *Mohammad Ali Jinnah: A Political Study*, Lahore 1945

Sarkar, Sumit, *Modern India: 1885–1947*, New Delhi 1983

Shahid, Mohammad Haneef (ed.), *The Quaid-i-Azam on Important Issues*, Lahore 1989

Singh, Anita Inder, *The Origins of the Partition of India, 1936–1947*, New Delhi 1987

Singh, Khushwant, *Train to Pakistan*, New Delhi 1988 (1st edn 1956)

Sisson, Richard and Rose, Leo, *War and Secession: Pakistan, India, and the Creation of Bangladesh*, Berkeley 1990

Stephens, Ian, *Horned Moon: An Account of a Journey Through Pakistan, Kashmir and Afghanistan*, London 1966 (1st edn 1953)

Storr, Anthony, *Churchill: Four Faces and the Man*, London 1969

Talreja, Kanayalal M., *Secessionism in India*, Mumbai 1996

Thorne, Christopher, *Allies of a Kind: The United States, Britain and the War Against Japan, 1941–1945*, London 1978

Wolpert, Stanley, *Jinnah of Pakistan*, New Delhi 1985 (1st edn 1984)

Wyatt, Woodrow, *Confessions of an Optimist*, London 1985

Zaidi, Z.H. (ed.), *Quaid-i-Azam Mohammad Ali Jinnah Papers* (2 vols to date: *Prelude to Pakistan* and *Pakistan in the Making*), Islamabad 1993–1994

Ziegler, Philip, *Mountbatten: The Official Biography*, London 1985

INDEX

PENGUIN HISTORY

TIBET, TIBET
PATRICK FRENCH

The book that showed the real Tibet for the first time.

Tibet has long fascinated the West, but what really lies beyond our romantic image of a mystical mountain kingdom of peace and spirituality? Patrick French set out to discover the truth, and his extraordinary account has been widely acclaimed.

Travelling through the country, French meets exiled monks, nomads and a nun secretly fighting Chinese rule, but also young Tibetans with a more pragmatic attitude to their situation. Interweaving these encounters with little-known stories of war and turmoil from Tibet's past, he reveals a more nuanced, fascinating and surprising picture of this complex place than any other book has done.

'Mixes a compelling subject, magnificent prose and deep understanding' *The Times*

'A gripping mix of history, travel writing and personal memoir ... vividly told'
Observer

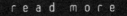
PENGUIN HISTORY

YOUNGHUSBAND
PATRICK FRENCH

Soldier, explorer, mystic, guru and spy, Francis Younghusband began his colonial
career as a military adventurer and became a radical visionary who preached free
love to his followers.

Patrick French's award-winning biography traces the unpredictable life of the
maverick with the 'damned rum name', who singlehandedly led the 1904 British
invasion of Tibet, discovered a new route from China to India, organized the
first expeditions up Mount Everest and attempted to start a new world religion.
Following in Younghusband's footsteps, from Calcutta to the snows of the
Himalayas, French pieces together the story of a man who embodies all the
romance and folly of Britain's lost imperial dream.

'Beautifully written, wise, balanced, fair, funny and above all extremely original'
William Dalrymple

'Dazzling' Niall Ferguson